A Guide to the Major Trusts

2001/2002 Edition

Volume 2

700 further trusts

Louise Walker
and
Alan French

DIRECTORY OF SOCIAL CHANGE

Published by
Directory of Social Change
24 Stephenson Way
London NW1 2DP
Tel. 020 7209 5151; Fax 020 7209 5049
e-mail info@dsc.org.uk
www.dsc.org.uk
from whom further copies and a full publications list are available.

Directory of Social Change is a Registered Charity no. 800517

First published 1993
Second edition 1995
Third edition 1997
Fourth edition 1999
Fifth edition 2001
Reprinted 2001

ISBN 1 900360 81 0

British Library Cataloguing in Publication Data
A catalogue record for this book is available from the British Library

Text designed by Lenn Darroux and Linda Parker
Cover design by Keith Shaw
Typeset by the Directory of Social Change
Printed and bound by Page Bros., Norwich

Other Directory of Social Change departments in London:
Courses and conferences tel. 020 7209 4949
Charity Centre tel. 020 7209 1015
Charityfair tel. 020 7209 1015
Publicity and research tel. 020 7209 4422

Directory of Social Change Northern Office:
3rd Floor, Federation House, Hope Street, Livepool L1 9BW
Courses and conferences tel. 0151 708 0117
Research tel. 0151 708 0136

Contents

Introduction

Welcome to *A Guide to the Major Trusts Volume 2*. This guide contains 700 major UK trusts, following the 300 largest detailed in Volume 1. The trusts in this book collectively give about £127 million a year. (Trusts in Volume 1 gave a total of £1,400 million.)

The guide's main aim is to help people raise money from trusts. We provide as much information as we can to enable fundraisers to locate relevant trusts and produce suitable applications.

There is also a secondary aim: to be a survey of the work of grant-making trusts, to show where trust money is going and for what purposes.

What trusts do we include?

Our criteria are as follows: trusts must have the potential to give at least £60,000 a year in grants, and these grants should go to organisations in the UK. Most give far more than this, with over 450 giving at least £100,000. There are actually about 20 trusts giving £500,000 or more, which appear large enough to be included in Volume 1. However, in most cases the income of the trust was lower than the total given in grants for the latest financial year and the level of giving by such trusts may well decrease in future. For a full list of the trusts in size order see page 11.

What is excluded?

Trusts which appear large enough to warrant inclusion in this guide may be excluded for the following reasons:

- Some or all of their money is given to individuals, so that £60,000 a year is not available for organisations. The following two guides, also available from the Directory of Social Change, provide information on trusts which support individuals: *A Guide to Grants for Individuals in Need* and *The Educational Grants Directory*.

- They give exclusively, or predominantly, to local causes in a particular geographical area of England. There are many very large trusts which restrict their grant-making in this way. So if a trust restricts its giving to a single county or city (or smaller geographical area) it is generally excluded. In this way we hope that Volume 2 remains a national directory and therefore is relevant for more people. For information on such local trusts, see our four local guides: *A Guide to Local Trusts in Greater London*, *A Guide to Local Trusts in the Midlands*, *A Guide to Local Trusts in the North of England* and *A Guide to Local Trusts in the South of England*.

- They only, or predominantly, support causes in Northern Ireland, Scotland or Wales. Information on these trusts is detailed in *A Guide to the Major Trusts Volume 3*.

- They only, or predominantly, support international charities. Such trusts were previously included in this guide, but information on them can now be found in *The International Directory*, available from May 2001.

- They are company trusts, established as a vehicle for a company's charitable giving. These are detailed in our *Guide to UK Company Giving*.

The layout of this book

The layout of the entries is similar to that established in the previous editions of Volumes 1 and 2, illustrated on page 9. Please also see page 8 for other information on how to use this guide.

Please note, in this guide, we have used the term Chair in preference to Chairman, unless specifically requested to do otherwise by the Chair of the trust.

Indexes

The trusts are listed alphabetically in this guide. To help you locate the most relevant trusts there are two indexes, which are a useful starting point.

- **Subject index** (page 289). This can be useful for identifying trusts with a particular preference for your cause. However, there are many trusts which have general charitable purposes (either exclusively or as well as other specific criteria) but there is no general category in the indexes. It would include so many trusts as to be useless. The index therefore should not be used as the definitive guide to finding the right trusts to apply to.

- **Geographical index** (page 301). Although trusts limiting their support to one particular area have been excluded, there are many which have some preference for one or more areas. These are listed in this index. Again, in a similar way to the subject index, care is needed. Many trusts state their beneficial area is the UK, so are not included in this index.

It is important to note that a trust which appears under a particular index heading may have other criteria which exclude you. Please always read the relevant entry carefully so you can be sure you fit in with all the trust's criteria. Don't just use the index as a mailing list.

It may also be a good idea to start in the middle of the alphabet. Most people when applying to trusts naturally start with the letter A and apparently trusts with names beginning with L – Z get fewer applications!

How we compiled the guide

The following are the practical guidelines we followed to produce this guide:

* concentrate on what the trust does in practice rather than the wider objects permitted by its formal trust deed

* provide extensive information which will be of the most use to readers i.e. publish the trust's criteria and guidelines for applicants in full, where available

* include, where possible, details of the organisations which have received grants, to give the reader an idea of what the trust supports and the amounts it usually gives

* provide the most up-to-date information available at the time of the research

* include all trusts which meet our criteria for inclusion.

Availability of information

We believe that charities are public bodies, not private ones, and that they should be publicly accountable. This view is backed up by Charity Commission regulations and the SORP (Statement of Recommended Practice).

Many trusts recognise the importance of providing good, clear information about the work they do. However, there are some that wish to believe they are private bodies and ignore their statutory obligation to provide information to the public. Information held at the Charity Commission is sometimes many years out of date. For further details about trusts' legal obligations please refer to the introduction to Volume 1.

Failure to supply accounts on request

Charities are required to send their annual reports and accounts to the Charity Commission and also to any member of the public who requests them in writing. They are obliged to send the information within two months of the request, although they can make a 'reasonable charge' for this (i.e. the costs of photocopying and postage). Unfortunately when we requested copies of the accounts from about 800 trusts only a fifth took the trouble to fulfil their obligation.

Failure to disclose grants

The SORP requires trusts to detail at least their 50 largest grants (if these are for £1,000 or more). This should be accompanied by a proper analysis and explanation of their grant-making in the narrative report (see below). Without this information the work of the trust remains a secret. Among those not providing this information were: The R J Harris Charitable Settlement, The Pennycress Trust, The Tikva Trust and Truedene Co. Ltd.

Failure to provide a narrative report

All trusts should provide a narrative report describing the work of the trust. It is here that the trust should give an account of its work during the year with an explanation and analysis of the grants it has made. Many trusts' reports are extremely brief, giving very little away about their activities. The following trusts are some of those guilty of this: The Fox Memorial Trust, Good Deed Foundation and Joshua and Michelle Rowe Charitable Trust.

Good trust reports

On a positive note, there are some trusts which provide excellent reports. When these have been particularly interesting or informative for applicants we have reproduced them in the entries. The following trusts have a history of providing good reports: The ADAPT Trust, Newby Trust Limited, Idlewild Trust and Morris Charitable Trust.

What's new?

There are 142 trusts which are new to this edition. Some of these have come from Volume 1 as they are no longer large enough to qualify for the top 300 (while some from the last edition of this guide have grown so they now warrant an entry in Volume 1). Others are newly established, or newly discovered trusts. Prominent new trusts include The Earl & Countess of Wessex Charitable Trust, Mercury Phoenix Trust and The Simpson Education and Conservation Trust.

Applying to trusts

There is a lot of competition for grants. Many trusts in this guide receive many more applications than they can support. For instance, The Charles Sykes Trust received 1,079 applications in 1999 of which only 136 (about 13%) were successful. However it is important to note that of these 1,079 many were not appropriate. The trust writes 'the trustees welcome the availability to the public of information about charities and the mode of application to them but nevertheless regret the receipt of so many unsuitable applications which cause wasted time to all parties'.

The point therefore is to **do the research**: read the trust's criteria carefully and target the right trusts. This can only lead to a higher success rate and save you from spending a lot of time writing applications which are destined only for the bin. Applying to inappropriate trusts is bad practice and, as well as annoying trusts, can potentially cause problems for future applicants.

Unsolicited applications

A number of trusts state that they do not want to receive applications (and usually therefore do not want to appear in this guide). There can be good reasons for this. For example, the trust may do its own research, or support the same list of charities each year. There are some trusts, however, which believe they are a 'private' trust. No registered charity is a private body. We believe trusts should not resent applications but be committed to finding those charities most eligible for assistance.

We include these trusts for two reasons. Firstly it may be that they state 'no unsolicited applications' simply as a deterrent, in an effort to reduce the number of applications they receive, but will still consider the applications they receive. The second reason relates to the secondary purpose of this guide: to act as a comprehensive survey of grant-making trusts.

If you choose to write to one of these trusts, do so with caution, and only write to those where your organisation very clearly fits the trust's criteria. We would advise you not to include a stamped addressed envelope and to state that you do not expect a response unless you are eligible. If they do not reply, do not chase them.

Further information

Please see the introduction to Volume 1 for further discussion on issues affecting the world of grant-making, the role of trusts, how they are run, the influence of the National Lottery, etc.

Finally ...

The research has been done as fully and carefully as possible. Many thanks to those who have made this easier: trust officers, trustees and others who have helped us. We send draft entries to all the relevant trusts and their comments are noted, although the text and any mistakes within it remain ours and not theirs.

We are also extremely grateful to Dave Bishop, Michael Ekundayo and Rachel Thompson at the Charity Commission who have ordered an endless number of files for us.

We are aware that some of this information is incomplete or will become out of date. We are equally sure we will have missed some relevant charities. We apologise for these imperfections. If a reader comes across any omissions or mistakes please let us know so they can be rectified in the future. We can be contacted at the Research Department of the Liverpool office of the Directory of Social Change either by phone on 0151 708 0136 or by e-mail: north@dsc.org.uk

The most up-to-date information will be available on our CD-ROM, which is updated annually. Also, our journal, *Trust Monitor*, available three times a year, contains information on new trusts and updates on the work of the large grant-making trusts.

To end on a positive note, there are more potential funders out there than you think, and some do not receive enough relevant applications. Several trusts in this guide even had unspent surpluses – many complain that they don't receive enough really good interesting applications. We hope this gives you extra encouragement and wish you success in your fundraising.

How to use this guide

The contents

The entries are in alphabetical order, describing the work of 700 trusts. Most give over £60,000 a year, almost all have the potential to give over £60,000 a year from ordinary income.

The entries are preceded by a listing of the trusts in order of size and are followed by a subject index and geographical index. There is also an alphabetical index at the back of the guide.

Finding the trusts you need

There are three basic ways of using this guide:

(a) You can simply read the entries through from A – Z (a rather time-consuming activity).

(b) You can look through the trust ranking table which starts on page 11 and use the box provided to tick trusts which might be relevant to you (starting with the biggest).

(c) You can use the subject or geographical indexes starting on pages 289 and 301 respectively. Each has an introduction explaining how to use it.

If you use approaches (b) or (c), once you have identified enough trusts to be going on with, read each entry very carefully before deciding whether to apply. Very often a trust's interest in your field will be limited and specific, and may require an application specifically tailored to its needs – or, indeed, no application at all.

Sending off applications which show that the available information has not been read antagonises trusts and brings charities into disrepute within the trust world. Carefully targeted applications, on the other hand, are welcomed by most trusts and usually have a reasonably high rate of success.

A typical trust entry

The Fictitious Trust

Welfare

£180,000 (1999/2000)

Beneficial area UK

The Old Barn, Main Street,
New Town ZC48 2QQ

Correspondent Ms A Grant,
Appeals Secretary

Trustees *Lord Great; Lady Good;
A T Home; T Rust; D Prest.*

Information available Full accounts
were on file at the Charity Commission.

General The trust supports welfare
charities in general, with emphasis on
disability, homelessness and ethnic
minorities. The trustees will support both
capital and revenue projects. 'Specific
projects are preferred to general running
costs.'

In 1999/2000 the trust had assets of
£2.3 million and an income of £187,000.
Over 200 grants were given totalling
£180,000. Grants ranged from £100 to
£20,000, with about half given in New
Town. The largest grants were to: New
Town Disability Group (£20,000),
Homelessness UK (£18,000) and Asian
Family Support (£15,000). There were 10
grants of £2,000 to £10,000 including
those to the Charity Workers Benevolent
Society, Children without Families, New
Town CAB and Refugee Support Group.

Smaller grants were given to a variety of
local charities, local branches of national
charities and a few UK welfare charities.

Exclusions No grants to non-registered
charities, individuals or religious
organisations.

Applications In writing to the
correspondent. Trustees meet in March
and September each year. Applications
should be received by the end of January
and the end of July respectively.

Applications should include a brief
description of the project and audited
accounts. Unsuccessful applicants will not
be informed unless an sae is provided.

Name of the trust

Summary of main activities
What the trust will do in practice rather
than what its trust deed allows it to do.

Grant total (not income) for the
most recent year available.

Geographical area of grant-giving
including where the trust can legally
give and where it gives in practice.

Contact address plus telephone and fax
numbers; e-mail and website addresses
if available.

Contact person

Trustees

Sources of information we used and
which are available to the applicant.

Background/summary of activities
A quick indicator of the policy to show
whether it is worth reading the rest
of the entry.

Financial information We try to
note the assets, ordinary income and
grant total, and comment on unusual
figures.

Typical grants range to indicate
what a successful applicant can expect to receive.

Large grants to indicate where the
main money is going, often the clearest
indication of trust priorities.

Other examples of grants – listing
typical beneficiaries, and where possible
the purpose of the grant. We also indicate
whether the trust gives one-off or
recurrent grants.

Exclusions – listing any area, subjects
or types of grant the trust will not
consider.

Applications including how to apply
and when to submit an application.

Trusts ranked by grant total

☐	£2,700,000	**The Rhodes Trust Public Purposes Fund**	Oxford University, overseas, general	Page 226
☐	£2,200,000	**The Vardy Foundation**	Christian, education in the North East, general	Page 269
☐	£1,600,000	**The Jack & Pat Mallabar Charitable Foundation**	Medical, education	Page 179
☐	£1,500,000	**Nemoral Ltd**	Jewish	Page 198
☐	£952000	**Blatchington Court Trust**	Education of people under 30 who are blind and partially sighted	Page 58
☐	£805,000	**The Freshfield Foundation**	Not known	Page 116
☐	£773,000	**Mike Gooley Trailfinders Charity**	Mainly cancer research	Page 123
☐	£762,000	**British Record Industry Trust**	Musical education	Page 63
☐	£741,000	**Marshall's Charity**	Parsonage and church improvements	Page 183
☐	£668,000	**The Alliance Family Foundation**	Jewish, general	Page 41
☐	£663,000	**The Football Association National Sports Centre Trust**	Play areas, football	Page 111
☐	£650,000	**Altamont Ltd**	Jewish	Page 41
☐	£610,000	**Beis Aharon Trust Fund**	Jewish, general	Page 38
☐	£601,000	**Mercury Phoenix Trust**	AIDS, HIV	Page 186
☐	£548,000	**The Austin & Hope Pilkington Trust**	General	Page 213
☐	£528,000	**Help the Hospices**	Hospices	Page 137
☐	£522,000	**The Cadogan Charity**	General	Page 71
☐	£522,000	**The M A Hawe Settlement**	General	Page 134
☐	£518,000	**The Stoller Charitable Trust**	Medical, children, general	Page 253
☐	£503,000	**United Trusts**	General	Page 268
☐	£492,000	**The Chase Charity**	Social welfare, heritage, the arts	Page 77
☐	£481,000	**Clover Trust**	Older people, young people	Page 80
☐	£475,000	**Ridgesave Limited**	General, education	Page 227
☐	£470,000	**Wessex Cancer Trust**	Cancer prevention, early detection, care and research in Dorset, Hampshire, Wiltshire, the Isle of Wight and the Channel Islands	Page 274
☐	£469,000	**The 1989 Willan Charitable Trust**	General	Page 33
☐	£469,000	**The Amberstone Trust**	Civil rights, arts, Jewish, general	Page 42
☐	£469,000	**The Radcliffe Trust**	Music, crafts, conservation	Page 220
☐	£465,000	**The Leigh Trust**	Drug and alcohol rehabilitation, criminal justice, asylum seekers/racial equality	Page 170
☐	£444,000	**The Mendel Kaufman Charitable Trust**	Jewish charities	Page 160
☐	£442,000	**Viscount Amory's Charitable Trust**	Welfare, older people, education	Page 42

☐	£439,000	The Francis Winham Foundation	Welfare of older people	Page 280
☐	£436,000	The British Council for Prevention of Blindness	Prevention and treatment of blindness	Page 62
☐	£435,000	The Golden Bottle Trust	General	Page 121
☐	£434,000	The Rudolph Palumbo Charitable Foundation	Education, relief of poverty, conservation, general	Page 208
☐	£428,000	Rowanville Ltd	Orthodox Jewish	Page 231
☐	£428,000	The Douglas Turner Trust	General	Page 266
☐	£426,000	The Barnabas Trust	Evangelical Christianity	Page 51
☐	£426,000	The Sheepdrove Trust	Environment, educational	Page 243
☐	£425,000	Lloyd's Charities Trust	General	Page 173
☐	£420,000	The Orpheus Trust	Music, especially for people with disabilities, Orpheus Centre	Page 206
☐	£416,000	The Holly Hill Charitable Trust	Environmental education and conservation	Page 140
☐	£415,000	The Martin Harris Charitable Trust	Education, general	Page 133
☐	£408,000	Jewish Child's Day	Jewish children in need or with special needs	Page 156
☐	£407,000	The National Hospital Trust	Hospitals	Page 198
☐	£406,000	The Luck-Hille Foundation	Jewish, disability, children	Page 175
☐	£406,000	The Charles and Elsie Sykes Trust	General	Page 255
☐	£405,000	The Joseph Strong Frazer Trust	General	Page 115
☐	£405,000	The Polden-Puckham Charitable Foundation	Peace and security, ecological issues, social change	Page 215
☐	£394,000	Hurdale Charity Limited	Jewish	Page 148
☐	£388,000	The South Square Trust	General	Page 249
☐	£387,000	The Prince of Wales's Charitable Foundation	General	Page 217
☐	£383,000	The Mulberry Trust	General	Page 194
☐	£379,000	The Arnopa Trust	Children	Page 45
☐	£378,000	The Swire Charitable Trust	General	Page 255
☐	£376,000	The Ofenheim & Cinderford Charitable Trusts	Health and welfare, arts, environment	Page 204
☐	£372,000	The Avenue Charitable Trust	General	Page 50
☐	£368,000	Maranatha Christian Trust	Christian	Page 180
☐	£364,000	Gordon Cook Foundation	Education and training	Page 85
☐	£364,000	The Englefield Charitable Trust	General, in Berkshire	Page 103
☐	£359,000	Michael Marks Charitable Trust	Arts, environment	Page 181
☐	£356,000	The Kohn Charitable Trust	Scientific and medical projects, the arts – particularly music, education, Jewish charities	Page 161
☐	£354,000	The Adint Charitable Trust	Children, medical and health	Page 37
☐	£351,000	Fordeve Ltd	Jewish, general	Page 112
☐	£350,000	The Lennox Hannay Charitable Trust	Health, welfare, general	Page 130
☐	£348,000	Simon Gibson Charitable Trust	General	Page 120
☐	£347,000	The Almond Trust	Christian	Page 41

☐	£345,000	The Normanby Charitable Trust	Social welfare, disability, general	Page 202
☐	£344,000	The Colt Foundation	Occupational and environmental health research	Page 84
☐	£340,000	The Equity Trust Fund	Welfare of professional performers and stage managers	Page 104
☐	£340,000	St James's Place Foundation	Children	Page 235
☐	£333,000	The Kobler Trust	Arts, Jewish, medical	Page 161
☐	£324,000	The Sylvia Adams Charitable Trust	General	Page 35
☐	£321,000	The Clara E Burgess Charity	Children	Page 68
☐	£321,000	The Yapp Charitable Trust	Social welfare	Page 285
☐	£320,000	Rees Jeffreys Road Fund	Road and transport research and education	Page 154
☐	£319,000	The Towry Law Charitable Trust	Education, medical research	Page 264
☐	£318,000	P H Holt Charitable Trust	General	Page 143
☐	£317,000	Vyoel Moshe Charitable Trust	Not known	Page 193
☐	£316,000	The Alice Ellen Cooper-Dean Charitable Foundation	General	Page 86
☐	£315,000	The Ajahma Charitable Trust	General	Page 38
☐	£315,000	Haberdashers' Eleemosynary Charity	People who are unemployed, homeless, disabled, terminally sick; excluded young people	Page 128
☐	£315,000	Melow Charitable Trust	Jewish	Page 185
☐	£313,000	Solev Co Ltd	Jewish charities	Page 248
☐	£312,000	The R M Burton Charitable Trust	Jewish charities, social welfare, education, the arts, especially in Yorkshire	Page 69
☐	£305,000	Sir Harold Hood's Charitable Trust	Roman Catholic	Page 144
☐	£304,000	The Anton Jurgens Charitable Trust	Welfare, general	Page 158
☐	£302,000	The Paget Charitable Trust	General	Page 207
☐	£302,000	The Schreib Trust	Jewish, general	Page 239
☐	£301,000	The Teresa Rosenbaum Golden Charitable Trust	Medical research	Page 230
☐	£301,000	The Sandra Charitable Trust	Health, social welfare, animal welfare	Page 238
☐	£301,000	The Vincent Wildlife Trust	Wildlife, environmental conservation	Page 269
☐	£300,000	Elman Charitable Trust	Jewish charities	Page 101
☐	£300,000	Garrick Club Charitable Trust	Probably arts, children in London	Page 118
☐	£300,000	The Woo Charitable Foundation	Education in the arts	Page 281
☐	£298,000	The Neil Kreitman Foundation	Jewish charities, arts	Page 162
☐	£296,000	St Gabriel's Trust	Higher and further religious education	Page 234
☐	£296,000	The J E Posnansky Charitable Trust	Jewish charities, health, welfare	Page 216
☐	£295,000	The Childs Charitable Trust	Christian	Page 78
☐	£295,000	The Saddlers' Company Charitable Fund	General	Page 233
☐	£294,000	Mrs Waterhouse Charitable Trust	Medical, health, welfare, environment, wildlife, churches, heritage	Page 271

☐	£292,000	Lady Hind Trust	General	Page	140
☐	£291,000	The Stanley Kalms Foundation	Jewish charities, general	Page	158
☐	£290,000	The A M McGreevy No 5 Charitable Settlement	General	Page	179
☐	£289,000	The Mary Webb Trust	General	Page	272
☐	£287,000	The Andrew Anderson Trust	Christian, social welfare	Page	43
☐	£287,000	Clydpride Ltd	Jewish charities, general	Page	80
☐	£286,000	John Coates Charitable Trust	Arts, children, environment, medical, general	Page	81
☐	£286,000	George A Moore Foundation	General, mostly in Yorkshire and Isle of Man	Page	190
☐	£284,000	The Balcombe Charitable Trust	Education, environment, health and welfare	Page	50
☐	£284,000	The Haramead Trust	Welfare, childen's welfare, health education	Page	131
☐	£284,000	The Hudson Foundation	General	Page	146
☐	£284,000	The Iliffe Family Charitable Trust	General	Page	148
☐	£283,000	Bear Mordechai Ltd	Jewish	Page	53
☐	£282,000	The Tajtelbaum Charitable Trust	Jewish, welfare	Page	257
☐	£281,000	The Maurice Wohl Charitable Foundation	Jewish, health and welfare	Page	281
☐	£280,000	The Daiwa Anglo-Japanese Foundation	Anglo-Japanese relations	Page	91
☐	£278,000	Kleinwort Benson Charitable Trust	Arts, conservation, inner cities, medical, young people, welfare	Page	160
☐	£278,000	World in Need	Christian objects	Page	282
☐	£274,000	The Laura Ashley Foundation	Art and design, higher education, local projects in mid-rural Wales	Page	47
☐	£271,000	The W F Southall Trust	Quaker, general	Page	250
☐	£269,000	The Märit and Hans Rausing Charitable Foundation	Architecture and other arts, children, medical and agricultural research, science, nature preservation	Page	224
☐	£265,000	The Handicapped Children's Aid Committee	Equipment for children with disabilities	Page	130
☐	£265,000	The George Cadbury Trust	General	Page	70
☐	£265,000	The Irish Youth Foundation (UK) Ltd	Irish young people	Page	151
☐	£265,000	The Forbes Charitable Trust	Learning disabilities	Page	111
☐	£264,000	The Norman Family Charitable Trust	General	Page	201
☐	£259,000	The Comino Foundation	Education	Page	84
☐	£258,000	The Charities Fund	Health, disability	Page	76
☐	£258,000	The Grocers' Charity	General	Page	126
☐	£257,000	The Emmandjay Charitable Trust	Social welfare, medicine, young people	Page	102
☐	£257,000	Robert Luff Foundation Ltd	Medical research	Page	176
☐	£254,000	Four Acre Trust	Respite care and holidays, vocational guidance, health, disability, social housing	Page	112
☐	£254,000	Miss Agnes H Hunter's Trust	Social welfare	Page	147
☐	£252,000	The Britten-Pears Foundation	Promotion of the work of Benjamin Britten and Peter Pears, the arts particularly music by living composers	Page	64

14

☐	£252,000	The Arnold James Burton 1956 Charitable Settlement	General	Page	69
☐	£252,000	The Grace Charitable Trust	Christian	Page	123
☐	£252,000	The John Swire (1989) Charitable Trust	General	Page	255
☐	£251,000	The Dellal Foundation	General, Jewish	Page	93
☐	£250,000	The Toy Trust	Children	Page	264
☐	£249,000	Achiezer Association Ltd	Jewish	Page	35
☐	£249,000	The Privy Purse Charitable Trust	General	Page	219
☐	£247,000	The Beaverbrook Foundation	General	Page	53
☐	£247,000	The Edith Murphy Foundation	General	Page	195
☐	£247,000	The River Trust	Christian	Page	228
☐	£246,000	The Whitley Animal Protection Trust	Animal care and protection, conservation	Page	278
☐	£244,000	The Russell Trust	General	Page	232
☐	£243,000	All Saints Educational Trust	Education, Anglican religious work, home economics	Page	39
☐	£242,000	The Harold Hyam Wingate Foundation	Jewish, medical, research, education, the arts, general	Page	280
☐	£241,000	The Inman Charity	Social welfare, disability, older people, hospices	Page	149
☐	£238,000	The Dorus Trust	Health and welfare, disability, homelessness, addiction, underprivileged children, environment	Page	95
☐	£238,000	The Hilda & Samuel Marks Foundation	Jewish, general	Page	180
☐	£237,000	The Joseph & Annie Cattle Trust	General	Page	74
☐	£236,000	The Helen Hamlyn 1989 Foundation	Older people, health	Page	130
☐	£236,000	The Bernard Kahn Charitable Trust	Jewish	Page	158
☐	£236,000	Premierquote Ltd	Jewish, general	Page	217
☐	£235,000	The Sidney & Elizabeth Corob Charitable Trust	Jewish charities, arts, general	Page	88
☐	£234,000	Garvan Limited	Jewish	Page	118
☐	£234,000	Norwood & Newton Settlement	Christian	Page	203
☐	£233,000	The Eleanor Rathbone Charitable Trust	Merseyside, women, unpopular causes	Page	223
☐	£233,000	The Cecil Rosen Foundation	Welfare, especially older people, infirm, people who are mentally or physically disabled	Page	230
☐	£230,000	The Williams Family Charitable Trust	Jewish, medical	Page	279
☐	£229,000	The Neville & Elaine Blond Charitable Trust	Jewish, education, general	Page	59
☐	£229,000	The Doris Field Charitable Trust	General	Page	107
☐	£229,000	Edith and Ferdinand Porjes Charitable Trust	Jewish, general	Page	216
☐	£228,000	The Cleopatra Trust	Health and welfare, disability, homelessness, addiction, underprivileged children, environment	Page	79
☐	£228,000	The Epigoni Trust	Health and welfare, disability, homelessness, addiction, underprivileged children, environment	Page	103
☐	£226,000	The Bowland Charitable Trust	Young people, education, general	Page	61

☐	£226,000	The Simon Heller Charitable Settlement	Medical research, science and educational research	Page	136
☐	£226,000	The Sir Sigmund Sternberg Charitable Foundation	Jewish, inter-faith causes, general	Page	252
☐	£225,000	The Bromley Trust	Human rights, conservation	Page	65
☐	£224,000	The Elani Nakou Foundation	Education, international understanding	Page	196
☐	£223,000	The Rowlands Trust	General	Page	231
☐	£220,000	The Ellinson Foundation Ltd	Jewish	Page	100
☐	£219,000	The Richard Desmond Charitable Trust	General	Page	94
☐	£219,000	The R V W Trust (Ralph Vaughan Williams)	British music, both contemporary and neglected music of the past	Page	220
☐	£217,000	Brushmill Ltd	Jewish	Page	66
☐	£217,000	The Homelands Charitable Trust	The New Church, health, social welfare	Page	144
☐	£217,000	The Van Neste Foundation	Third world, disability, older people, religion, community and Christian family life, respect for the sanctity and dignity of life	Page	268
☐	£217,000	The Whitaker Charitable Trust	Music education, prisons, farming and woodland education, countryside conservation and alternative spirituality	Page	276
☐	£216,000	The Children's Research Fund	Child health research	Page	78
☐	£214,000	The Ove Arup Foundation	Construction – education and research	Page	46
☐	£214,000	The Coates Charitable Settlement	Medical, health, welfare, education	Page	81
☐	£213,000	The Kennel Club Charitable Trust	Dogs	Page	160
☐	£213,000	The Fidelity UK Foundation	General	Page	107
☐	£212,000	Trumros Limited	Jewish	Page	265
☐	£210,000	The Broadfield Trust	Education	Page	64
☐	£210,000	Carlee Ltd	Jewish	Page	72
☐	£210,000	The William & Katherine Longman Trust	General	Page	175
☐	£209,000	The Huggard Charitable Trust	General	Page	147
☐	£209,000	The Bassil Shippam & Alsford Charitable Trust	Older people, health, education, Christian	Page	244
☐	£209,000	Stervon Ltd	Jewish	Page	253
☐	£209,000	The Woodroffe Benton Foundation	General	Page	282
☐	£208,000	The Sheldon Trust	General	Page	243
☐	£207,000	The John Jarrold Trust	Arts, third world, social welfare, medical research	Page	154
☐	£207,000	The Colonel W H Whitbread Charitable Trust	Health, welfare, general	Page	277
☐	£206,000	Grimmitt Trust	General	Page	125
☐	£206,000	The Kathleen Hannay Memorial Charity	Health, welfare, Christian, general	Page	130
☐	£205,000	The Batchworth Trust	Medical, social welfare, general	Page	52
☐	£205,000	The Inverforth Charitable Trust	General	Page	150
☐	£205,000	Newby Trust Limited	Medical welfare, education and training, relief of poverty	Page	199

☐	£204,000	Beauland Ltd	Jewish	Page	53
☐	£204,000	Saint Sarkis Charity Trust	Armenian churches and welfare, disability, general	Page	236
☐	£204,000	The Ward Blenkinsop Trust	Medicine, social welfare, general	Page	271
☐	£203,000	Woodlands Green Ltd	Jewish	Page	282
☐	£201,000	The Chapman Charitable Trust	General	Page	76
☐	£201,000	The Jean Sainsbury Animal Welfare Trust	Animal welfare	Page	234
☐	£200,000	The Thomas Sivewright Catto Charitable Settlement	General	Page	74
☐	£200,000	The D W T Cargill Fund	Religious, medical, older people, general	Page	71
☐	£200,000	The Madeline Mabey Trust	Medical research, children's welfare	Page	178
☐	£200,000	The Robert McAlpine Foundation	Children, social welfare, medical research	Page	178
☐	£200,000	The Spear Charitable Trust	General	Page	250
☐	£200,000	Spar Charitable Fund	Children	Page	250
☐	£199,000	Lord Barnby's Foundation	General	Page	52
☐	£199,000	The C A Redfern Charitable Foundation	General	Page	225
☐	£198,000	The Carole & Geoffrey Lawson Foundation	Jewish, general	Page	168
☐	£198,000	The Priory Foundation	Health and social welfare, especially children	Page	218
☐	£198,000	Coral Samuel Charitable Trust	General, health, the arts	Page	238
☐	£197,000	The Misses Barrie Charitable Trust	Medical, general	Page	52
☐	£197,000	The Holst Foundation	Arts	Page	143
☐	£197,000	Marbeh Torah Trust	Jewish	Page	180
☐	£197,000	The National Catholic Fund	Catholic welfare	Page	197
☐	£195,000	The Bowerman Charitable Trust	General	Page	61
☐	£194,000	The Debmar Benevolent Trust	Jewish	Page	93
☐	£193,000	Riverside Charitable Trust Limited	Health, welfare, older people, education, general	Page	228
☐	£192,000	The A B Charitable Trust	Promotion and defence of human dignity	Page	33
☐	£191,000	The Burden Trust	Christian, welfare, medical research, general	Page	67
☐	£191,000	The Cotton Trust	Relief of suffering, elimination and control of disease, people who are disabled and disadvantaged	Page	88
☐	£191,000	The Odin Charitable Trust	General	Page	204
☐	£189,000	Access 4 Trust	Children, welfare	Page	34
☐	£189,000	The Lillie C Johnson Charitable Trust	Children, young people who are blind or deaf, medical	Page	156
☐	£188,000	The Delves Charitable Trust	Environment, conservation, medical, general	Page	93
☐	£188,000	The Dyers' Company Charitable Trust	General	Page	97
☐	£188,000	The Gertner Charitable Trust	Jewish	Page	118
☐	£188,000	The Truemark Trust	General	Page	265
☐	£187,000	The Albert & Florence Smith Memorial Trust	Social welfare	Page	247

☐	£186,000	The Millichope Foundation	General	Page	187
☐	£186,000	St James' Trust Settlement	General	Page	235
☐	£186,000	Ruth and Conrad Morris Charitable Trust	Jewish, general	Page	192
☐	£186,000	The Three Oaks Trust	Welfare	Page	261
☐	£184,000	Joshua and Michelle Rowe Charitable Trust	Not known	Page	231
☐	£184,000	Truedene Co. Ltd	Jewish	Page	264
☐	£184,000	The Weavers' Company Benevolent Fund	Young people at risk from criminal involvement, young offenders and prisoners' organisations	Page	272
☐	£183,000	The Archbishop of Canterbury's Charitable Trust	Christianity, welfare	Page	44
☐	£183,000	The Hockerill Educational Foundation	Education, especially Christian education	Page	142
☐	£181,000	The Sylvia Aitken Charitable Trust	Medical research, general	Page	38
☐	£180,000	The Norman Trust	General, young people	Page	202
☐	£179,000	The GRP Charitable Trust	Jewish, general	Page	127
☐	£178,000	The Ralph Levy Charitable Company Ltd	Educational, medical, general	Page	171
☐	£178,000	The Tanner Trust	General	Page	258
☐	£178,000	The Ulverscroft Foundation	People who are sick and visually impaired, ophthalmic research	Page	267
☐	£177,000	Hobson Charity Ltd	Social welfare, education	Page	141
☐	£176,000	The Lauffer Family Charitable Foundation	Jewish, general	Page	166
☐	£175,000	The Martin Laing Foundation	General	Page	163
☐	£175,000	The Lyndhurst Settlement	Social problems, civil liberties, environment, conservation	Page	176
☐	£175,000	The Chevras Ezras Nitzrochim	Jewish	Page	200
☐	£175,000	The Hugh & Ruby Sykes Charitable Trust	General, medical, education, employment	Page	256
☐	£174,000	The Schreiber Charitable Trust	Jewish	Page	240
☐	£173,000	The Lord Austin Trust	Social welfare	Page	50
☐	£173,000	The Ecological Foundation	Environment/conservation	Page	98
☐	£173,000	London Law Trust	Children and young people	Page	174
☐	£172,000	The Hon. Dorothy Rose Burns Will Trust	Education, medicine, general	Page	68
☐	£172,000	The M & C Trust	Jewish, social welfare	Page	177
☐	£172,000	A H and B C Whiteley Charitable Trust	Art, environment, general	Page	277
☐	£171,000	The George W Cadbury Charitable Trust	Population control, conservation, general	Page	71
☐	£171,000	National Committee of The Women's World Day of Prayer for England, Wales, and Northern Ireland	Christian education and literature	Page	197
☐	£171,000	The Norman Whiteley Trust	Evangelical Christianity, welfare, education	Page	278
☐	£171,000	The Lindale Educational Foundation	Roman Catholic	Page	172
☐	£169,000	J A Clark Charitable Trust	Health, education, peace, preservation of the earth, the arts	Page	79
☐	£169,000	The Sir John Fisher Foundation	General	Page	108

☐	£169,000	Servite Sisters' Charitable Trust Fund	General	Page	242
☐	£167,000	Macdonald-Buchanan Charitable Trust	General	Page	179
☐	£167,000	Morris Family Israel Trust	Jewish	Page	191
☐	£167,000	Princess Anne's Charities	Children, medical, welfare, general	Page	218
☐	£166,000	The Grahame Charitable Foundation	Jewish	Page	124
☐	£166,000	The Leche Trust	Georgian art, music and architecture	Page	169
☐	£166,000	The Moss Charitable Trust	Christian, education, poverty, health	Page	193
☐	£165,000	The R J Harris Charitable Settlement	General	Page	133
☐	£165,000	The Mizpah Trust	General	Page	189
☐	£165,000	The Scurrah Wainwright Charity	Social reform, root causes of poverty and injustice	Page	270
☐	£164,000	The Black Charitable Trusts	Evangelical Christianity, social welfare, young people	Page	57
☐	£163,000	The Benham Charitable Settlement	Young people, general	Page	54
☐	£162,000	The Charles S French Charitable Trust	Community projects, disability, children and youth	Page	116
☐	£162,000	The James Weir Foundation	Health, social welfare, heritage, research	Page	273
☐	£161,000	The Miller Foundation	General, animal welfare	Page	186
☐	£161,000	The Scouloudi Foundation	Medicine and health, humanities and disabilities	Page	240
☐	£160,000	The Edgar E Lawley Foundation	Older people, disability, children, medical research	Page	167
☐	£159,000	The Joseph & Lena Randall Charitable Trust	Jewish, general	Page	222
☐	£158,000	The John Slater Foundation	Medical, animal welfare, general	Page	246
☐	£158,000	Wychdale Ltd	Jewish	Page	284
☐	£158,000	The Cyril & Betty Stein Charitable Trust	Jewish causes	Page	252
☐	£156,000	The Miriam K Dean Refugee Trust Fund	Third world development	Page	93
☐	£156,000	The Alfred Haines Charitable Trust	Christian, health, welfare	Page	128
☐	£156,000	The David Laing Foundation	Children, families, disability, environment	Page	163
☐	£155,000	The Harbour Charitable Trust	General	Page	131
☐	£155,000	The Stone Foundation	Research into addiction, medical research, welfare	Page	253
☐	£154,000	The Charles Littlewood Hill Trust	Health, disability, service, children (including schools)	Page	139
☐	£154,000	Largsmount Ltd	Jewish	Page	165
☐	£154,000	Rachel & Jack Lass Charities Ltd	Jewish, children, education, medical research	Page	165
☐	£154,000	The Patrick Charitable Trust	Children, disability	Page	210
☐	£153,000	The Football Association Youth Trust	Sports	Page	111
☐	£153,000	The Ratcliff Foundation	General	Page	220
☐	£152,000	The Carpenters' Company Charitable Trust	Education, general	Page	72
☐	£152,000	The Dennis Curry Charitable Trust	Conservation, general	Page	90
☐	£152,000	The Ouseley Trust	Choral services of the Church of England, Church in Wales and Church of Ireland	Page	207

☐	£152,000	The Rainford Trust	Social welfare, general	Page	221
☐	£151,000	The Inlight Trust	Religion	Page	149
☐	£151,000	The George & Esme Pollitzer Charitable Settlement	Jewish, health, social welfare	Page	215
☐	£151,000	The Peter Samuel Charitable Trust	Health, welfare, conservation, Jewish care	Page	238
☐	£150,000	The Raymond & Blanche Lawson Charitable Trust	General	Page	168
☐	£149,000	Melodor Ltd	Jewish, general	Page	185
☐	£148,000	The M J C Stone Charitable Trust	General	Page	254
☐	£148,000	The Sylvanus Charitable Trust	Animal welfare, Roman Catholic	Page	256
☐	£147,000	The Charlotte Marshall Charitable Trust	Roman Catholic, general	Page	183
☐	£147,000	The Primrose Trust	General	Page	217
☐	£147,000	The I A Ziff Charitable Foundation	General, education, Jewish, arts, young people, older people, medicine	Page	287
☐	£146,000	The Hawthorne Charitable Trust	General	Page	134
☐	£146,000	The Cecil Pilkington Charitable Trust	Conservation, medical research, general on Merseyside	Page	213
☐	£145,000	The George Elias Charitable Trust	Jewish, general	Page	100
☐	£145,000	The Mark Radiven Charitable Trust	Jewish, general	Page	221
☐	£145,000	The Florence Turner Trust	General	Page	266
☐	£144,000	The Kasner Charitable Trust	Jewish	Page	159
☐	£143,000	The Acacia Charitable Trust	Jewish, education, general	Page	34
☐	£143,000	The Ireland Fund of Great Britain	Welfare, community, education, peace and reconciliation, the arts	Page	150
☐	£143,000	The Stella and Alexander Margulies Charitable Trust	Jewish	Page	180
☐	£143,000	The Maxwell Family Foundation	Disability/medical, welfare, conservation, education and animals	Page	184
☐	£143,000	The Roger Raymond Charitable Trust	General	Page	224
☐	£143,000	The Sinclair Charitable Trust	Jewish learning, welfare	Page	246
☐	£142,000	The Mark Leonard Trust	Environmental education, youth, general	Page	170
☐	£142,000	Harry Livingstone Charitable Trust	Jewish, general	Page	172
☐	£142,000	Old Possum's Practical Trust	Literary history	Page	205
☐	£142,000	The Michael Sacher Charitable Trust	Jewish, general	Page	232
☐	£142,000	The Elizabeth and Prince Zaiger Trust	Welfare, health, general	Page	287
☐	£141,000	Panahpur Charitable Trust	Missionaries, general	Page	209
☐	£141,000	Salters' Charities	General	Page	237
☐	£140,000	The Richard Attenborough Charitable Trust	Acting, human rights, overseas, general	Page	49
☐	£140,000	The Wilfrid & Constance Cave Foundation	Conservation, animal welfare, health, welfare	Page	75
☐	£139,000	The Astor Foundation	General	Page	48

☐	£139,000	Marston Charitable Trust	General	Page 183
☐	£138,000	The Lord Faringdon First & Second Charitable Trusts	Medical, general	Page 106
☐	£137,000	The Jephcott Charitable Trust	Alleviation of poverty in developing countries, general	Page 155
☐	£137,000	The Audrey Sacher Charitable Trust	Arts, medical, care	Page 232
☐	£136,000	The Blair Foundation	General	Page 58
☐	£136,000	Criffel Charitable Trust	Welfare, health, Christianity	Page 90
☐	£136,000	The Loftus Charitable Trust	Jewish	Page 174
☐	£136,000	The Reginald M Phillips Charitable Foundation	Medical research, general	Page 212
☐	£136,000	C B & H H Taylor 1984 Trust	Quaker, general	Page 258
☐	£136,000	Dame Violet Wills Charitable Trust	Evangelical Christianity	Page 279
☐	£135,000	The Naggar Charitable Trust	Jewish, general	Page 196
☐	£135,000	The Ogle Christian Trust	Evangelical Christianity	Page 205
☐	£135,000	The Sir James Roll Charitable Trust	General	Page 229
☐	£134,000	The Cattanach Charitable Trust	Homelessness, disability	Page 73
☐	£134,000	The Huntly & Margery Sinclair Charitable Trust	Medical, general	Page 246
☐	£134,000	Warbeck Fund Ltd	Jewish, the arts, general	Page 271
☐	£133,000	The W G Edwards Charitable Foundation	Care of older people	Page 100
☐	£133,000	The Barry Green Memorial Fund	Animal welfare	Page 125
☐	£132,000	Buckingham Trust	Christian, general	Page 67
☐	£132,000	The Mrs F B Laurence 1976 Charitable Settlement	Social welfare, medical, disability, environment	Page 166
☐	£131,000	The SMB Trust	Christian, general	Page 246
☐	£130,000	Ashe Park Charitable Trust	Possible preference for hospitals	Page 47
☐	£130,000	The Bulldog Trust	Arts, medical, young people, general	Page 67
☐	£130,000	The Gordon Fraser Charitable Trust	Children, young people, environment, arts	Page 115
☐	£130,000	The Gerald Palmer Trust	Education, medical, religion, general	Page 208
☐	£130,000	The Samuel & Freda Parkinson Charitable Trust	General	Page 209
☐	£130,000	The Tay Charitable Trust	General	Page 258
☐	£129,000	The Finnart House School Trust	Jewish children and young people in need of care	Page 108
☐	£129,000	Newpier Charity Ltd	Jewish, general	Page 200
☐	£129,000	The Oakdale Trust	Social work, medical support, medical research, general	Page 203
☐	£129,000	The Rayne Trust	Jewish, general	Page 224
☐	£128,000	The Billmeir Charitable Trust	General, health and medical	Page 55
☐	£128,000	The Erich Markus Charitable Foundation	Medical, welfare, general	Page 181

☐	£127,000	ATP Charitable Trust	Jewish, education, medical	Page 49
☐	£127,000	The Duke of Cornwall's Benevolent Fund	General	Page 87
☐	£126,000	The Timothy Franey Charitable Foundation	Children, health, education, arts	Page 113
☐	£125,000	Quercus Trust	Arts, general	Page 219
☐	£125,000	Daisy Rich Trust	General	Page 227
☐	£125,000	The Simon Whitbread Charitable Trust	Education, family welfare, medicine, preservation	Page 277
☐	£124,000	The Vivienne & Samuel Cohen Charitable Trust	Jewish, education, health and welfare	Page 82
☐	£124,000	The Green Foundation	General, social welfare, Jewish	Page 124
☐	£124,000	The Ulting Overseas Trust	Training of Christian workers	Page 267
☐	£123,000	The Coppings Trust	General	Page 87
☐	£123,000	The Rose Flatau Charitable Trust	Jewish, social welfare	Page 109
☐	£123,000	The Ruzin Sadagora Trust	Jewish	Page 233
☐	£122,000	The Ashworth Charitable Trust	Welfare	Page 48
☐	£122,000	The Walter Guinness Charitable Trust	General	Page 127
☐	£121,000	The Morris Charitable Trust	Welfare, health, older people, education	Page 191
☐	£121,000	Dr Mortimer and Theresa Sackler Foundation	Arts, hospitals	Page 232
☐	£121,000	The Schapira Charitable Trust	Jewish	Page 239
☐	£120,000	The ADAPT Trust	Access for disabled and older people to arts and heritage venues	Page 36
☐	£120,000	The G M Morrison Charitable Trust	Medical, education, welfare	Page 192
☐	£119,000	Farthing Trust	Christian, general	Page 107
☐	£119,000	Florence's Charitable Trust	Education, welfare, health	Page 110
☐	£119,000	M N R Charitable Trust	Christian, general	Page 177
☐	£119,000	The Annie Schiff Charitable Trust	Orthodox Jewish education	Page 239
☐	£118,000	The Charles Shorto Charitable Trust	General	Page 244
☐	£117,000	The Atlantic Foundation	Education, medical, general	Page 48
☐	£117,000	The Mayfield Valley Arts Trust	Arts, especially chamber music	Page 184
☐	£117,000	Onaway Trust	General	Page 206
☐	£117,000	The Fred & Della Worms Charitable Trust	Jewish, education, arts	Page 283
☐	£116,000	The Dinam Charity	International understanding, general	Page 94
☐	£116,000	The Lawlor Foundation	Social welfare, education, general	Page 167
☐	£115,000	Adenfirst Ltd	Jewish	Page 37
☐	£115,000	The Animal Defence Trust	Animal welfare	Page 43
☐	£115,000	The J G Hogg Charitable Trust	Welfare, animal welfare, general	Page 142
☐	£115,000	The Kulika Charitable Trust	Sustainable agriculture, poverty alleviation and development, environment and conservation	Page 162
☐	£115,000	Menuchar Ltd	Jewish	Page 185
☐	£115,000	The N Smith Charitable Trust	General	Page 247

☐	£114,000	The Lambert Charitable Trust	Health, welfare, Jewish, arts	Page 164
☐	£114,000	The M D & S Charitable Trust	Jewish	Page 177
☐	£114,000	The Marsh Christian Trust	General	Page 182
☐	£113,000	The Eventhall Family Charitable Trust	General	Page 105
☐	£113,000	The Old Broad Street Charity Trust	General	Page 205
☐	£112,000	Ashburnham Thanksgiving Trust	Christian	Page 46
☐	£112,000	The Bluston Charitable Settlement	Jewish, general	Page 59
☐	£112,000	The Craps Charitable Trust	Jewish, general	Page 89
☐	£112,000	The Harbour Foundation	Jewish, general	Page 131
☐	£111,000	The A H & E Boulton Trust	Evangelical Christian	Page 61
☐	£111,000	The Ruth & Lionel Jacobson Trust (Second Fund) No 2	Jewish, medical, children, disability	Page 153
☐	£111,000	The Christopher H R Reeves Charitable Trust	Food allergies, disability	Page 225
☐	£111,000	Midhurst Pensions Trust	General	Page 186
☐	£110,000	The Idlewild Trust	Performing arts, culture, restoration & conservation, occasional arts education	Page 148
☐	£110,000	The Michael & Ilse Katz Foundation	Jewish, general	Page 159
☐	£110,000	A M Pilkington's Charitable Trust	General	Page 213
☐	£110,000	Leslie Sell Charitable Trust	Scout and guide groups	Page 242
☐	£110,000	The Stanley Foundation Ltd	Older people, medical, education, social welfare	Page 251
☐	£109,000	The Bertie Black Foundation	Jewish, general	Page 57
☐	£109,000	The Mason Porter Charitable Trust	Christian	Page 183
☐	£109,000	The Muriel Edith Rickman Trust	Medical research, education	Page 227
☐	£109,000	Talteg Ltd	Jewish, welfare	Page 258
☐	£108,000	The Francis Coales Charitable Foundation	Historical	Page 80
☐	£108,000	Morgan Williams Charitable Trust	Christian, welfare	Page 191
☐	£108,000	The T.U.U.T. Charitable Trust	General, but with a bias towards trade union favoured causes	Page 257
☐	£107,000	The A Bornstein Charitable Settlement	Jewish	Page 60
☐	£107,000	The Dumbreck Charity	General	Page 96
☐	£107,000	The J E Joseph Charitable Fund	Jewish	Page 157
☐	£107,000	The Oliver Morland Charitable Trust	Quakers, general	Page 191
☐	£107,000	REMEDI	Research into disability	Page 226
☐	£107,000	Cliff Richard Charitable Trust	Spiritual and social welfare	Page 227
☐	£106,000	The Sir Jack Lyons Charitable Trust	Jewish, arts, education	Page 177
☐	£106,000	The Noel Buxton Trust	Child and family welfare, penal matters, Africa	Page 200
☐	£106,000	The Philanthropic Trust	Homelessness, developing world, welfare (human and animal), environment, human rights	Page 212

☐	£105,000	The Harry Bottom Charitable Trust	Religion, education, medical	Page 60
☐	£105,000	Marc Fitch Fund	General	Page 109
☐	£105,000	The Jenour Foundation	General	Page 155
☐	£104,000	The Oliver Ford Charitable Trust	Mental disability, housing	Page 112
☐	£104,000	The Peter Harris Charitable Trust	Education, general	Page 133
☐	£104,000	The Christopher Laing Foundation	General	Page 163
☐	£103,000	The J P Jacobs Charitable Trust	Art, community, health, religion, research, youth	Page 153
☐	£103,000	The Puebla Charitable Trust	Community development work, relief of poverty	Page 219
☐	£103,000	Rokach Family Charitable Trust	Jewish, general	Page 229
☐	£102,000	The Marjorie Coote Animal Charity Fund	Wildlife and animal welfare	Page 87
☐	£102,000	Marr-Munning Trust	Overseas aid	Page 181
☐	£102,000	The Mount 'A' & Mount 'B' Charitable Trusts	General	Page 193
☐	£102,000	The Seedfield Trust	Christian, relief of poverty	Page 241
☐	£102,000	The Thompson Family Charitable Trust	Medical, veterinary, educational, general	Page 260
☐	£101,000	The Jill Franklin Trust	Overseas, welfare, prisons, church restoration	Page 114
☐	£101,000	The Stuart Hine Trust	Evangelical Christianity	Page 141
☐	£100,000	The Edward & Dorothy Cadbury Trust (1928)	Health, education, arts	Page 70
☐	£100,000	Hospital Saturday Fund Charitable Trust	Medical, health	Page 146
☐	£100,000	The Cooks Charity	Catering, general	Page 86
☐	£100,000	The Jungels–Winkler Charitable Foundation	Visually impaired – generally and in the arts	Page 157
☐	£100,000	The R J Larg Family Charitable Trust	Education, health, medical research, arts particularly music	Page 165
☐	£100,000	The Millfield Trust	Christian	Page 186
☐	£99,000	Belljoe Tzedoko Ltd	Jewish	Page 54
☐	£99,000	The Earth Love Fund	Community-based rainforest conservation projects, Artists for the Environment (AFTE) Festival	Page 98
☐	£98,000	The Chamberlain Foundation	General	Page 75
☐	£98,000	The Chownes Foundation	General	Page 78
☐	£98,000	The Eighty–Eight Charitable Trust	General	Page 100
☐	£98,000	The Michael & Morven Heller Charitable Foundation	University and medical research projects	Page 136
☐	£98,000	The Penny in the Pound Fund Charitable Trust	Hospitals, health-related charities	Page 211
☐	£98,000	The Helen Roll Charitable Trust	General	Page 229
☐	£98,000	L H Silver Charitable Trust	Jewish, general	Page 245
☐	£98,000	The Thornton Foundation	General	Page 261
☐	£97,000	The Gunter Charitable Trust	General	Page 127
☐	£97,000	The Peggy Ramsay Foundation	Writers and writing for the stage	Page 222
☐	£96,000	The Simpson Education and Conservation Trust	Environmental conservation, with a preference for the neotropics (South America)	Page 245

☐	£96,000	The Janet Nash Charitable Trust	Medical, general	Page	196
☐	£95,000	The Thomas Arno Bequest	Young British men in business, education, personal development of young people	Page	45
☐	£95,000	The Birmingham Hospital Saturday Fund Medical Charity & Welfare Trust	Medical	Page	55
☐	£95,000	The Britland Charitable Trust	Christian	Page	63
☐	£95,000	The Edwina Mountbatten Trust	Medical	Page	194
☐	£95,000	The Schmidt-Bodner Charitable Trust	Jewish, general	Page	239
☐	£94,000	The Mansfield Cooke Trust	Evangelical Christian work	Page	85
☐	£94,000	The Dent Charitable Trust	Jewish, general	Page	94
☐	£94,000	The Willie Nagel Charitable Trust	Jewish, general	Page	195
☐	£94,000	The Stella & Ernest Weinstein Charitable Trust	Jewish	Page	273
☐	£94,000	The Constance Travis Charitable Trust	General	Page	264
☐	£94,000	The Westcroft Trust	International understanding, overseas aid, Quaker, Shropshire	Page	275
☐	£94,000	The Wyseliot Charitable Trust	Medical, welfare, general	Page	284
☐	£94,000	The William Allen Young Charitable Trust	General	Page	286
☐	£93,000	The Charlotte Bonham-Carter Charitable Trust	General	Page	59
☐	£93,000	Charles Boot Trust	General	Page	60
☐	£93,000	The Harold and Alice Bridges' Charitable Foundation	General	Page	62
☐	£93,000	The Golden Charitable Trust	Catholic, Jewish, preservation, conservation	Page	121
☐	£92,000	The Alan Evans Memorial Trust	Preservation, conservation	Page	104
☐	£92,000	The Sir Harry Pilkington Trust	General	Page	214
☐	£92,000	The Thornton Trust	Evangelical Christianity, education, relief of sickness and poverty	Page	261
☐	£91,000	The Dorothy Gertrude Allen Memorial Fund	General	Page	40
☐	£91,000	The Sir Jeremiah Colman Gift Trust	General	Page	83
☐	£91,000	Localtrent Ltd	Jewish, educational, poverty	Page	173
☐	£91,000	The Ruth & Michael Phillips Charitable Trust	General, Jewish	Page	212
☐	£91,000	Songdale Ltd	Jewish	Page	249
☐	£90,000	The Cross Trust	Christian work	Page	90
☐	£90,000	The Kurt and Olga Koerner Charitable Trust	Conservation, environment, education	Page	161
☐	£90,000	The Langdale Trust	Social welfare, Christian, medical, general	Page	164
☐	£90,000	The Willie & Mabel Morris Charitable Trust	Medical, general	Page	192
☐	£90,000	The Jessie Spencer Trust	General	Page	251
☐	£90,000	The Yamanouchi European Foundation	Medical	Page	285
☐	£88,000	The Denise Cohen Charitable Trust	Health, welfare, arts, humanities, education, culture, Jewish	Page	82
☐	£88,000	The Hope Trust	Temperance, reformed protestant churches	Page	145

☐	£88,000	The C L Loyd Charitable Trust	General	Page 175
☐	£88,000	The Saintbury Trust	General	Page 236
☐	£87,000	The Kathleen Laurence Trust	General	Page 166
☐	£87,000	The Roughley Charitable Trust	General, with a preference for the West Midlands	Page 230
☐	£87,000	Tudor Rose Ltd	Jewish	Page 265
☐	£87,000	The Matthews Wrightson Charity Trust	Caring and Christian charities	Page 284
☐	£86,000	The GNC Trust	General	Page 120
☐	£86,000	The Charles Harris Charitable Trust	Education, general	Page 132
☐	£86,000	The Arnold Lee Charitable Trust	Jewish, educational, health	Page 170
☐	£86,000	The Platinum Trust	Disability	Page 214
☐	£85,000	Good Deed Foundation	Health, children	Page 122
☐	£85,000	The Leslie Smith Foundation	General	Page 247
☐	£85,000	The Weinstein Foundation	Jewish, medical, welfare	Page 273
☐	£84,000	The Peter Birse Charitable Trust	Health and welfare	Page 56
☐	£84,000	The Bill Butlin Charity Trust	General	Page 69
☐	£84,000	Gableholt Limited	Jewish	Page 117
☐	£84,000	The Laurence Misener Charitable Trust	General, Jewish	Page 188
☐	£84,000	The Mitchell Charitable Trust	Jewish, general	Page 188
☐	£84,000	The Nigel Moores Family Charitable Trust	Arts	Page 190
☐	£84,000	The Stanley Smith UK Horticultural Trust	Horticulture	Page 248
☐	£84,000	Humphrey Whitbread's First Charitable Trust	Churches, the arts, elderly, disability, AIDS, general	Page 276
☐	£83,000	The Fitton Trust	Social welfare, medical	Page 109
☐	£83,000	The National Manuscripts Conservation Trust	Conserving manuscripts	Page 198
☐	£82,000	The Augustine Courtauld Trust	General	Page 89
☐	£82,000	Harnish Trust	Christian	Page 132
☐	£82,000	The Bellinger Donnay Trust	General, medical, disability, youth	Page 54
☐	£82,000	The Earl & Countess of Wessex Charitable Trust	General	Page 275
☐	£81,000	The B G S Cayzer Charitable Trust	General	Page 75
☐	£81,000	Andrew Cohen Charitable Trust	Jewish	Page 81
☐	£81,000	The Vernon N Ely Charitable Trust	Christian, welfare, disability, children and young people, overseas	Page 102
☐	£81,000	The Christina Mary Hendrie Trust for Scottish & Canadian Charities	Youth, older people, general	Page 138
☐	£80,000	The Brian & Eric Abrams Charitable Trusts	Jewish charities	Page 34
☐	£80,000	The Leach Fourteenth Trust	Disability, general	Page 169
☐	£80,000	The Saints & Sinners Trust	Welfare, medical	Page 236
☐	£80,000	The Tory Family Foundation	Education, Christian and medical	Page 263

☐	£80,000	The Felicity Wilde Charitable Trust	Children, medical research	Page	278
☐	£79,000	The Leopold De Rothschild Charitable Trust	Arts, Jewish, general	Page	92
☐	£79,000	The Good Neighbours Trust	People who have mental or physical disabilities	Page	122
☐	£79,000	MYA Charitable Trust	Jewish	Page	195
☐	£78,000	Elshore Ltd	Jewish	Page	101
☐	£78,000	The Fox Memorial Trust	General	Page	113
☐	£78,000	The Jack Goldhill Charitable Trust	Health, arts, welfare	Page	121
☐	£78,000	The Gresham Charitable Trust	General	Page	125
☐	£78,000	The Haymills Charitable Trust	Education, medicine, welfare, young people	Page	135
☐	£78,000	The Ironmongers' Quincentenary Charitable Fund	General	Page	152
☐	£78,000	The Millhouses Charitable Trust	Christian, overseas aid, general	Page	187
☐	£78,000	The Mole Charitable Trust	Jewish, general	Page	189
☐	£77,000	May Hearnshaw's Charity	General	Page	135
☐	£77,000	The Boris Karloff Charitable Foundation	General	Page	158
☐	£77,000	The John Oldacre Foundation	Research and education in agricultural sciences	Page	205
☐	£76,000	Sir Felix Brunner's Sons' Charitable Trust	General	Page	66
☐	£76,000	The Grand Order of Water Rats Charities Fund	Theatrical, medical equipment	Page	124
☐	£76,000	The Locker Foundation	Jewish	Page	174
☐	£76,000	Mountbatten Festival of Music	Royal Marines and Royal Navy charities	Page	194
☐	£76,000	The Shipwrights Charitable Fund	Maritime or waterborne connected charities	Page	244
☐	£76,000	The William and Ellen Vinten Trust	Industrial education, training and welfare	Page	269
☐	£75,000	The Miss Jeanne Bisgood's Charitable Trust	Roman Catholic purposes, older people	Page	56
☐	£75,000	The Mutual Trust Group	Religion, education	Page	195
☐	£75,000	The Salamander Charitable Trust	Christian, general	Page	237
☐	£74,000	The Palgrave Brown Foundation	Education, medical, service/ex-service	Page	66
☐	£74,000	Bill Brown's Charitable Settlement	Health, social welfare	Page	66
☐	£74,000	The Haydan Charitable Trust	Jewish, general	Page	134
☐	£74,000	The Hinrichsen Foundation	Music	Page	141
☐	£74,000	The Late Barbara May Paul Charitable Trust	Older people, young people, medical care and research, preservation of buildings	Page	210
☐	£73,000	The David Brooke Charity	Young people, medical	Page	65
☐	£72,000	The Beacon Trust	Christian	Page	53
☐	£72,000	The George Drexler Foundation	Medical research, education, older people	Page	96
☐	£72,000	The Harebell Centenary Fund	General, education, medical research, animal welfare	Page	132
☐	£72,000	The Alabaster Trust	Christian Church and related activities	Page	39
☐	£72,000	The Minos Trust	Christian, general	Page	187
☐	£71,000	The Violet and Milo Cripps Charitable Trust	General	Page	90

☐	£71,000	The Gilbert & Eileen Edgar Foundation	General	Page	98
☐	£71,000	The Emerton-Christie Charity	Health, welfare, disability, arts	Page	102
☐	£71,000	The Gibbs Charitable Trusts	Methodist	Page	119
☐	£71,000	The Hamamelis Trust	Ecological conservation, medical research	Page	129
☐	£71,000	The Heinz & Anna Kroch Foundation	Medical research and severe poverty or hardship	Page	142
☐	£71,000	The Solo Charitable Settlement	Jewish, general	Page	249
☐	£71,000	The Thriplow Charitable Trust	Higher education and research	Page	262
☐	£70,000	The Horace & Marjorie Gale Charitable Trust	General	Page	117
☐	£70,000	The Bernhard Heuberger Charitable Trust	Jewish	Page	139
☐	£70,000	Jack Livingstone Charitable Trust	Jewish, general	Page	172
☐	£70,000	The Raymond Oppenheimer Foundation	General	Page	206
☐	£70,000	Robson Charitable Trust	General	Page	228
☐	£70,000	The Searchlight Electric Charitable Trust	General	Page	241
☐	£70,000	Tomchei Torah Charitable Trust	Jewish educational institutions	Page	263
☐	£69,000	The Earl Fitzwilliam Charitable Trust	General	Page	109
☐	£69,000	Help the Homeless Ltd	Homelessness	Page	136
☐	£69,000	The Edward Sydney Hogg Charitable Settlement	General	Page	142
☐	£69,000	The Sir Edward Lewis Foundation	General	Page	171
☐	£69,000	The Albert Reckitt Charitable Trust	General	Page	225
☐	£69,000	The Yorkshire & General Trust	Christian, welfare	Page	286
☐	£68,000	Salo Bordon Charitable Trust	Jewish, some health-related	Page	60
☐	£68,000	The Roger & Sarah Bancroft Clark Charitable Trust	Quaker, general	Page	79
☐	£68,000	The Gibbins Trust	General	Page	119
☐	£68,000	The Ebenezer Trust	Evangelical Christianity, welfare	Page	98
☐	£68,000	The H F Johnson Trust	Christian education world-wide but mainly in the UK	Page	156
☐	£68,000	The Richard Newitt Fund	Education	Page	200
☐	£68,000	The Worshipful Company of Chartered Accountants General Charitable Trust	General, education	Page	283
☐	£67,000	The Leslie Mary Carter Charitable Trust	Conservation/environment, welfare	Page	73
☐	£67,000	Rosanna Taylor's 1987 Charity Trust	General	Page	259
☐	£66,000	The Euroclydon Trust	Christian	Page	104
☐	£66,000	Famos Foundation Trust	Jewish	Page	106
☐	£66,000	The Graff Foundation	General	Page	123
☐	£66,000	The Lawson-Beckman Charitable Trust	Jewish, welfare, education, arts	Page	168
☐	£66,000	The Susanna Peake Charitable Trust	Disability, general	Page	210
☐	£66,000	The Ten Charitable Trust	Jewish	Page	259

28

☐	£65,000	The Pat Allsop Charitable Trust	Education, medical research, children, relief of poverty	Page	41
☐	£65,000	The Cooper Charitable Trust	Medical, disability, Jewish	Page	86
☐	£65,000	The Follett Trust	Welfare, education, arts	Page	110
☐	£65,000	The C S Kaufman Charitable Trust	Jewish	Page	159
☐	£65,000	The Lady Eileen Joseph Foundation	General	Page	157
☐	£65,000	The Janatha Stubbs Foundation	General	Page	254
☐	£65,000	The Tisbury Telegraph Trust	Christian, overseas aid, general	Page	262
☐	£65,000	The Wilkinson Charitable Foundation	Scientific research, education	Page	279
☐	£64,000	The Lord Cozens-Hardy Trust	Medicine, health, welfare, general	Page	89
☐	£63,000	The P G & N J Boulton Trust	Christian	Page	61
☐	£63,000	The Elmgrant Trust	Education, arts, social sciences, ecology and environment	Page	101
☐	£63,000	The Dorothy Jacobs Charity	Jewish care, medical	Page	153
☐	£63,000	The Beryl Evetts & Robert Luff Animal Welfare Trust	Animal welfare	Page	176
☐	£63,000	The John Porter Charitable Trust	Jewish, education, general	Page	216
☐	£63,000	The R D Turner Charitable Trust	General	Page	266
☐	£62,000	The Henry & Grete Abrahams Second Charitable Foundation	Jewish, medical welfare, general	Page	33
☐	£62,000	Mrs M H Allen Trust	Service/ex-service	Page	40
☐	£62,000	The Reginald Graham Charitable Trust	Children, medical, education	Page	123
☐	£62,000	The Victor Mishcon Charitable Trust	Jewish, social welfare	Page	188
☐	£62,000	The Tufton Charitable Trust	Christian	Page	266
☐	£61,000	The Country Landowners Charitable Trust	Disabled facilities and training	Page	88
☐	£61,000	John Coldman Charitable Trust	General, Christian	Page	83
☐	£61,000	The Edinburgh Trust, No 2 Account	Education, service, scientific expeditions	Page	99
☐	£61,000	The Pennycress Trust	General	Page	211
☐	£61,000	W W Spooner Charitable Trust	General	Page	251
☐	£60,000	The Barber Charitable Trust	Evangelical Christian causes, churches	Page	51
☐	£60,000	The D C Moncrieff Charitable Trust	Social welfare, environment	Page	189
☐	£60,000	The Searle Charitable Trust	Sailing	Page	241
☐	£60,000	The Linley Shaw Foundation	Conservation	Page	242
☐	£60,000	The Tolkien Trust	Christian – especially Catholic, welfare and general	Page	262
☐	£60,000	The F J Wallis Charitable Settlement	General	Page	270
☐	£59,000	AM Charitable Trust	Jewish, general	Page	42
☐	£59,000	Mrs E G Hornby's Charitable Settlement	General	Page	145
☐	£59,000	The Stella Symons Charitable Trust	General	Page	257

☐	£58,000	**The Victor Adda Foundation**	Fan Museum	Page	37
☐	£58,000	**The Michael Bishop Foundation**	General	Page	57
☐	£58,000	**The Catholic Charitable Trust**	Catholic organisations	Page	73
☐	£58,000	**The Fairway Trust**	General	Page	105
☐	£58,000	**The Pilkington General Charity Fund**	Welfare in north west England	Page	214
☐	£58,000	**The Sutasoma Trust**	Education, general	Page	254
☐	£57,000	**The Daily Prayer Union Charitable Trust Ltd**	Evangelical Christian	Page	91
☐	£57,000	**The Gerald Fogel Charitable Trust**	Jewish, general	Page	110
☐	£57,000	**The Frognal Trust**	People who are elderly, blind or disabled, ophthalmological research, environmental heritage	Page	116
☐	£57,000	**The Sydney & Phyllis Goldberg Memorial Charitable Trust**	Medical research, welfare, disability	Page	120
☐	£57,000	**Philip Henman Trust**	General	Page	138
☐	£57,000	**The Frank Parkinson Agricultural Trust**	British agriculture	Page	209
☐	£57,000	**West London Synagogue Charitable Fund**	Jewish, general	Page	275
☐	£56,000	**Michael Davies Charitable Settlement**	General	Page	92
☐	£56,000	**Alan and Sheila Diamond Charitable Trust**	Jewish, general	Page	94
☐	£56,000	**The Dinwoodie (1968) Settlement**	Postgraduate medical education and research	Page	95
☐	£56,000	**Samuel William Farmer's Trust**	General, education	Page	106
☐	£56,000	**The Duncan Norman Trust Fund**	General	Page	202
☐	£55,000	**The Christopher Cadbury Charitable Trust**	Nature conservation, general	Page	70
☐	£55,000	**The Carmichael-Montgomery Charitable Trust**	United Reformed Church, general	Page	72
☐	£55,000	**The Dwek Family Charitable Trust**	General, Jewish	Page	97
☐	£55,000	**The Higgs Charitable Trust**	General	Page	139
☐	£55,000	**The Mrs C S Heber Percy Charitable Trust**	General	Page	211
☐	£55,000	**The Sammermar Trust**	General	Page	237
☐	£54,000	**The Loke Wan Tho Memorial Foundation**	Environment, medical	Page	260
☐	£54,000	**The Thompson Fund**	Medical, welfare, education, general	Page	260
☐	£54,000	**The Weldon UK Charitable Trust**	Major arts-related projects	Page	274
☐	£53,000	**The John & Freda Coleman Charitable Trust**	People with disabilities, technical education for young people	Page	83
☐	£53,000	**J A R Charitable Trust**	Roman Catholic, education, welfare	Page	152
☐	£53,000	**The Leonard Matchan Fund Ltd**	Social and medical welfare	Page	184
☐	£52,000	**The Friarsgate Trust**	Health and welfare of young and older people	Page	116

☐	£51,000	**Col-Reno Ltd**	Jewish	Page	82
☐	£51,000	**The Manny Cussins Foundation**	Older people, children, health, Jewish, general	Page	91
☐	£50,000	**The Richard Langhorn Trust**	Sport for children	Page	164
☐	£49,000	**Hesed Trust**	Christian	Page	139
☐	£49,000	**The Cuthbert Horn Trust**	Environment, older people	Page	145
☐	£48,000	**The Lyons Charitable Trust**	Health, medical research, children	Page	177
☐	£47,000	**The Armourers and Brasiers' Gauntlet Trust**	Materials science education, general	Page	44
☐	£47,000	**Premishlaner Charitable Trust**	Jewish	Page	217
☐	£45,000	**The J R S S T Charitable Trust**	Development of democracy and social justice	Page	152
☐	£44,000	**The Humanitarian Trust**	Education, health, social welfare, Jewish	Page	147
☐	£40,000	**The Maurice Wohl Charitable Trust**	Jewish, general	Page	281
☐	£30,000	**The Northmoor Trust**	General	Page	203
☐	£24,000	**The AS Charitable Trust**	Christian and social concern	Page	46
☐	£15,000	**The Lister Charitable Trust**	Watersports	Page	172
☐	£14,000	**The Starfish Trust**	Health, medical	Page	252
☐	£14,000	**The Viznitz Foundation**	Not known	Page	270
☐	£13,000	**The Louis Freedman Charitable Settlement**	General	Page	115
☐	£11,000	**The Langley Charitable Trust**	Christian, general	Page	164

The 1989 Willan Charitable Trust

General

£469,000 (1998/99)

Beneficial area Worldwide, but mainly the north east of England

8 Kelso Drive, The Priorys, Tynemouth, Tyne & Wear NE29 9NS

Tel. 0191 258 2533

Correspondent A Fettes, Trustee

Trustees Miss E Willan; P R M Harbottle; A Fettes.

Information available Full accounts were on file at the Charity Commission.

General The trust has general charitable purposes with a preference for the north east of England. In 1998/99 the trust had assets of £12 million which generated an income of £500,000. The trust also received donations of £1.2 million from the settlor (£1.7 million in the previous year) which were transferred to the capital funds. A total of £469,000 was given in grants to a variety of causes. Information on the beneficiaries was not available for this year.

In 1997/98 the trust gave 128 grants totalling £414,000. The largest were £10,000 each to Brinkburn Summer Music, Greggs Trust, Oxfam and Tyne & Wear Foundation. Other larger grants included Calvert Trust Kielder (£7,500) and £5,000 each to Barnardos, Northumbria Hospice and World Wildlife Fund.

Grants of £3,000 each went to 100 organisations; they included East Newcastle Victim Support, Hartlepool Dyslexia Support Group, North Pennines Heritage Trust, Parent and Toddler Care at Home, South Shields Volunteer Life Brigade, Sunderland Counselling Services and Trimdon Grange Community Centre. Smaller grants included those to Disability North, Raleigh International and Youth for Christ.

Exclusions Grants are not given directly to individuals. Grants for gap years may be considered if the individual will be working for a charity (in this case the grant would be paid to the charity).

Applications In writing to the correspondent. Grants appear to be given four times a year. In 1997/98 they were distributed in February, June, September and November.

The A B Charitable Trust

Promotion and defence of human dignity

£192,000 (1999/2000)

Beneficial area UK and third world

12 Addison Avenue, London W11 4QR

Correspondent T M Denham, Secretary

Trustees Y J M Bonavero; D Boehm; Mrs A G M-L Bonavero; Miss C Bonavero; Miss S Bonavero; O Bonavero.

Information available Full accounts were provided by the trust.

General The trust gives grants for the promotion and defence of human dignity. Grants are only given to UK-registered charities with an income of between £100,000 and £1.5 million.

In 1999/2000 the trust had assets of £138,000 and an income of £131,000 including £129,000 from donations received. Grants totalled £192,000. Only 64 of the 623 applications received were succesful.

The 14 organisations to receive £5,000 each were Africa Now, Bethany project, Catholic Housing Aid Association, ChildHope, Cotswold Care Hospice, Howard League for Penal Reform, New Horizon Youth Centre, POPAN, Prison Reform Trust, Prisoners Abroad, Prisoners of Conscience, Respond, Searchlight Workshops, Willen Hospice, The Women's Therapy Centre and Youth at Risk, three of this groups received the same amount in the previous year.

Other grants ranged from £500 to £420, although over most of them were between £2,000 and £3,000. Examples included £420 to Family Matters, £3,000 each to Asian Research Centre and Oxfordshire Association for the Blind, £2,500 each to Cambridge Female Education Centre, Eastern European Development Association, Phoenix Sheltered Workshop and Wintercomfort, £2,000 each to BIA Quaker Social Action with £1,000 each to Aconcagua 2000, Association of Wheelchair Children and The Family Nurturing Network and £500 to Parochial Church Council of Icomb.

Exclusions Grants are given to medium sized UK-registered charities only.

No support for education, medical research, animal or plant welfare, expeditions, scholarships, conservation, environment or areas which should reasonably be funded by the govenment.

`The trust does not normally support local charities with links to large national bodies.`

Applications In writing to the secretary, up to a maximum of four A4 pages if appropriate, plus the most recent detailed audited accounts. The trustees meet on a quarterly basis in March, June, September and December.

The Henry & Grete Abrahams Second Charitable Foundation

Jewish, medical welfare, general

£62,000 (1998/99)

Beneficial area UK

D. Maislish & Edwin Coe, 2 Stone Buildings, Lincoln's Inn, London WC2A 3TH

Tel. 020 7691 4000
e-mail david.maislish@edwincoe.com

Correspondent D Maislish, Trustee

Trustees Mrs G Abrahams; D M Maislish; M H Gluckstein.

Information available Full accounts were on file at the Charity Commission.

General Established in 1987 by Henry and Grete Abrahams, the foundation supports a variety of medical and health organisations. In the past there has also been a preference for Jewish and London-based organisations.

In 1998/99 it had an income of £58,000 and gave grants totalling £62,000 to 18 organisations, 4 of which were supported in the previous year.

Grants ranging from £250 to £20,000 were awarded. The largest went to Royal Star & Garter Home (£20,000), Wizo Charitable Foundation (£13,000), with £10,000 each to St John's Hospice and Wingate Youth Trust. Other larger grants went to Gurkha Welfare Trust (£3,000), Nightingale House (£2,000) and Evelina Children's Hospital Appeal (£1,000).

Grants of £250 were given to 10 organisations including British Epilespy

Association, Mudchute Park & Farm and Pavilion Opera Educational Trust.

Applications The trust states: 'We are fully committed to a number of charities for the next few years, therefore cannot undertake any more appeals.' The trustees meet in May and October.

The Brian & Eric Abrams Charitable Trusts

Jewish charities

£80,000 in total (1998/99)

Beneficial area UK, Israel

Alexander Layton Chartered Accountants, 130–132 Nantwich Road, Crewe, Cheshire CW2 6AZ

Tel. 01270 213475

Correspondent R A Taylor

Trustees *Both trusts: Eric Abrams; Brian Abrams.*

Brian Abrams Charitable Trust only: Betty Abrams; Gail Gabbie.

Eric Abrams Charitable Trust only: S M Abrams.

Information available Recent accounts were on file at the Charity Commission, but without details of donations.

General Two trusts are administered from the address above, Eric Abrams Charitable Trust and Brian Abrams Charitable Trust. The trusts operate so closely together that their accounts are practically identical. The trusts support UK-registered charities in the areas of education, welfare and the relief of poverty, especially amongst people of Jewish faith.

Brian Abrams Trust
In 1998/99 this trust had assets of £993,000 and an income of £45,000. A total of £40,000 was given in 30 grants. No information was given on the beneficiaries.

Eric Abrams Trust
In 1998/99 the trust had assets of £980,000 and an income of £45,000. It also gave £40,000 in nine grants, ranging from £1,000 to £8,000. The larger grants went to ITRI Foundation (£8,000), The Friends of the Centre for Torah Education (£7,500) and Halacha Le Moshe Trust and Rabbi Nachman of Breslov Charitable Foundation (£5,000

each). Other grants went to Joint Jewish Charitable Trust (£3,800), Friends of Ohr Akiva Institution (£2,500), Heathlands and King David School (£1,300 each) and Manchester Jewish Federation (£1,000).

Exclusions No grants to individuals.

Applications The trusts stated that their funds are fully committed and applications are not invited.

The Acacia Charitable Trust

Jewish, education, general

£143,000 (1998/99)

Beneficial area UK

5 Clarke's Mews, London W1G 6QN

Tel. 020 7486 1884   **Fax** 020 7487 4171

Correspondent Mrs Nora Howland, Secretary

Trustees *K D Rubens; Mrs A G Rubens; S A Rubens.*

Information available Information was provided by the trust.

General In 1998/99 the trust had assets of £1.6 million and an income of £88,000. From a total expenditure of £178,000, grants totalled £143,000, which were broken down as follows:

Education	51%
Overseas aid	21%
UK charities	20%
Jewish charities (other than education)	8%

The largest single donation continued to be £31,000 to University of Reading to provide a lectureship in Land Management. The other main beneficiary was again CBF World Jewish Relief which received £28,000. Other large grants went to World ORT Union (£25,000), British ORT (£10,000), Jewish Museum (£16,000) and £5,000 each to Community Security Trust and Royal Engineers Museum Foundation. Seven further grants of £1,000 or over including those to British Museum, Institute for Jewish Policy Research and Royal National Theatre. There were 20 smaller grants of up to £500, mostly to organisations which received a grant in the previous year.

Applications In writing to the correspondent.

Access 4 Trust

Children, welfare

£189,000 to organisations (1998/99)

Beneficial area Worldwide

Slater Chapman & Cooke, 7 St James' Square, London SW1Y 7JU

Tel. 020 7930 7621

Correspondent C Sadlow

Trustees *Miss S M Wates; J R F Lulham.*

Information available Full accounts were on file at the Charity Commission.

General The trustees' report for 1998/99 states: 'The trust has directed a major part of its resources towards women and children to assist in the relief of poverty and to overcome disadvantages; it is intended that this policy will continue.' Most grants, as in previous years, were to assist families in need and their children with funds going overseas to developing countries, mainly to Bangladesh, Uganda and Ghana.

The assets in 1998/99 stood at £658,000. The income was £223,000, of which £152,000 was from donations (compared to only £400 in the previous year when the income totalled £54,000). Grants totalled £202,000. The trust listed 30 grants of £850 and above in the accounts, of which 4 were to individuals.

The largest grants were £50,000 to Womankind Worldwide, £35,000 to Post Adoption Centre, £12,000 to Anglican Diocese of Tamale-Ghana and £10,000 to ActionAid. Other larger grants included those to Friends of the Centre for Rehabilitation of the Paralysed (£8,000), MIND – Tower Hamlets (£6,000) and Rains Appeal Ghana (£5,400). Grants of £5,000 each went to Comonwork Land Trust, London Lighthouse, Wates Foundation and Wulugu Project – Ghana.

Grants ranging from £1,000 to £3,000 went to 14 organisations, including Entebbe All Christian Womens Association, Parent to Parent Information on Adoption and Welfare Centre for Disabled – Bangladesh. A grant of £850 was given for the full attendance of a social worker at a child welfare course. Smaller grants totalled £12,000, no information was given on the beneficiaries. Of those listed, 10 grants were recurrent from the previous year. Grants to individuals totalled about £13,000.

Applications In writing to the correspondent.

Achiezer Association Ltd

Jewish

£249,000 (1996/97)

Beneficial area Worldwide

132 Clapton Common, London E5 9AG

Tel. 020 8800 5465

Correspondent David Chontow, Trustee

Trustees *Mrs J A Chontow; D Chontow; S S Chontow; M M Chontow.*

Information available Accounts were on file at the Charity Commission, but without a list of grants.

General Unfortunately we have been unable to update the following information since the last edition of this guide.

In 1996/97 the trust had an income of £241,000, most of which was from donations received, with £20,000 being profits covenanted from a wholly owned subsidiary company, Gedebee Ltd. This company is involved in property and investment dealing and the leasing of motor cars.

Grants totalled £249,000. Although the accounts stated that 'grants are detailed in a separate publication', this was not available from the file at the Charity Commission.

Previously, Jewish organisations have been the main beneficiaries. A few small grants have also been given to medical and welfare charities.

Applications The trust states that funds are already committed to existing beneficiaries for the next two years. Unsolicited applications are therefore very unlikely to be successful.

The Sylvia Adams Charitable Trust

See below

£324,000 (1998/99)

Beneficial area Eastern region of England, the London borough of Barnet, Africa, the Indian sub continent and South America

Sylvia Adams House, 24 The Common, Hatfield, Hertfordshire AL10 0NB

Tel. 01707 259259 **Fax** 01707 259268

Correspondent Kate Baldwin, Director

Trustees *A D Morris, Chair; R J Golland.*

Information available Information was supplied by the trust. Guidelines for applicants are available from the trust.

General This trust was set up using the income from the sale of works of art at Bonhams, following Sylvia Adams' death. In 1998/99 the trust had assets of £9 million and an income of £5.4 million. Grants totalled £324,000.

The trust's aim is to improve the quality of life of those who are disadvantaged, through alleviation of disease, sickness and poverty. Both UK causes and causes in the developing world are supported, grants are divided about equally between the two. The trust divides its giving into three main areas: children and young people, people with disabilities and people living in poverty. It is particularly interested in helping to enable people to become self-supporting and supporting self-help projects. In the UK the trust aims to focus on enabling people to participate fully in society. The focus worldwide is on primary healthcare and health education, access to education, appropriate technology and community enterprise schemes.

2000 Priority Areas for Grantmaking in the UK

'The trustees target their grantmaking in the Eastern Region (the counties of Bedfordshire, Cambridgeshire, Essex, Hertfordshire, Norfolk and Suffolk) and the London Borough of Barnet. The trustees will also consider projects which are of national benefit or those which could be considered beacon projects.

'Children and young people

The trust's main priority is to provide equipment and facilities for children with severe disabilities. Projects that expand the opportunities available to young people who are disadvantaged will also be considered.

'People with disabilities

The trust has a particular interest in disability and will consider a wide range of applications from organisations working with people with physical or leaning difficulties.

'People living in poverty

Projects that enable homeless people towards independence will be considered. The trust will consider applications which meet the practical needs of people living in poverty.'

2000 Priority Areas for Grantmaking Overseas

Overseas grants are given in 'the Indian sub continent, Africa and South America but not Eastern Europe, the former Soviet Union or the Middle East. The trust targets children and young people, people with disabilities and people living in poverty. The trustees are interested in schemes which enable people with disabilities or other marginalised groups to participate fully in the societies of which they are a part. This may include projects which promote access to education, training or employment'.

Grants are not made to projects in war zones or to emergency relief appeals. The trust makes all its grants through UK-registered charities and not directly to the country concerned.

In 1998/99 grants were given to 29 organisations; 16 to charities working in the UK and 13 to those working overseas.

Grants in the UK

The largest grant was £66,000 to Hertfordshire Community Foundation. Other grants ranged from £3,900 to £16,000. Larger ones were given to: National Autistic Society towards the playground for Radlett Lodge School and £10,000 each to Emmaus UK for a workshop for people who are homeless and to The PACE Centre in Aylesbury for a school for children who have cerebral palsy. Other grants included those to Ormiston Children & Families Trust for basic literacy skills for users of family centre (second instalment of £6,000); Chicken Shed Theatre Company to support fully inclusive workshops (first instalment of £5,000); and Deafblind UK for volunteering for people to work with deafblind adults (£3,900).

Grants to organisations working overseas

These ranged from £1,800 to £25,000. The largest went to The Graham Layton Trust for the building of a new eye hospital in Pakistan. Other large grants went to Uganda Society for Disabled People for a vehicle for community rehabilitation (£19,000) and Sense International for a full service for deafblind children and adults in India (£18,000). Other recipients included Womankind Worldwide for training and income generation in Peru (£11,000) and Nepal Leprosy Trust to establish a self-care training unit for people cured of leprosy learning to live with their disabilities (£8,700). Smaller grants went to supporting a literacy course in South America and to a Bradford Study Group for research in Bangladesh.

Exclusions The trust restricts its support to the three key areas shown above. Grants are not given to charities only benefiting older people, UK charities benefiting those with AIDS or people who are HIV, medical research or animal charities. No grants to individuals.

Applications In writing to the correspondent. Guidelines for applicants are available from the trust, and are quoted below. Applicants are encouraged to contact the correspondent for an informal discussion (please see telephone number above).

'All applicants are asked to state their case for funding in their own words. Applications should be presented in the following form:

- a half-page summary, on headed notepaper, signed by the trustee or officer who is the contact person
- a description of your charity, your project and your request on not more than four sides of A4
- a budget
- your latest annual report.

'Your application should cover all the following:

- what your organisation does, who it helps and how it is doing so
- the purpose for which the grant is being sought. What is the need for your project? What practical benefits will result? How many people will benefit and in what ways? How will you measure whether your project is meeting its objectives?
- a breakdown of costs with an explanation of how any significant figures have been calculated
- what funds you have already raised, what other sources of funding you have approached or expect to obtain and the specific amount you are applying for from SACT.'

Deadlines for UK applications are 31 May and 30 November, and successful applicants will be advised in August and February. Deadlines for overseas grants are 28 February and 31 August, and successful applicants will be advised in May and November.

Short-listed applicants are visited by a representative from the trust and successful projects are monitored.

The ADAPT Trust

Access for people who are disabled and older people to arts and heritage venues

£120,000 (1999)

Beneficial area UK

8 Hampton Terrace,
Edinburgh EH12 5JD

Tel. 0131 346 1999 **Fax** 0131 346 1991
e-mail adapt.trust@virgin.net
website www.adapttrust.co.uk

Correspondent Stewart Coulter, Director

Trustees *Dr Gillian A Burrington, Chair; Michael Cassidy; Elizabeth Fairbairn; Gary Flather; John C Griffiths; Alison Heath; Trevan Hingston; Robin Hyman; C Wycliffe Noble; Maurice Paterson.*

Information available A detailed annual report was provided by the trust including full accounts.

General The ADAPT (Access for Disabled People to Arts Premises Today) Trust aims to improve accessibility for people who are disabled and older people to arts and heritage venues. It does this in several ways. It encourages broader consideration of access at the planning stage of buildings by providing a consultancy service and carrying out disability awareness training. It gives grants to adapt existing facilities through a number of schemes, and awards for excellence, described below. It also seeks to influence government policies and regulations by contributing to relevant committees and commenting on new strategies.

During the year the trust piloted a student award competition at the Glasgow School of Art. The students were given training in disability issues and they then produced innovative designs which were fully inclusive. The trust plans to expand this area by providing further training and awards for students throughout the UK.

In 1999 the trust had assets of £440,000 and an income of £323,000. It gave grants totalling £120,000.

	1999	(1998)
ADAPT – General	£2,500	(£1,300)
Scottish Grants Scheme	£9,800	(£1,000)
British Gas Awards	–	(£7,500)
Capital Access	£6,625	(£56,000)
Sightline Millennial Grants	£38,598	(£36,000)
Railtrack Museum Grants	£38,970	(£26,000)
Millennial Awards	£21,000	(£21,000)
Hugh Fraser Foundation	£2,500	(–)
Total	**£120,000**	**(£149,000)**

Sightline Millennial Grants

These are funded by Guide Dogs for the Blind Association (GDBA) and administered by ADAPT Trust. Grants are given to performing arts venues to help improve access for people who are visually impaired. Applicants must operate an 'open doors' policy for accompanying guide dogs. The maximum grant is £4,500 and can cover 75% of costs. During the year 12 grants were given, of £1,000 to £4,500. Beneficiaries included Blue Coat Arts Centre, Liverpool; Norwich Arts Centre; Theatre Royal, Windsor; Traverse Theatre, Edinburgh; and Yorkshire Dance Centre, Leeds. Closing dates for these applications are 31 March and 30 September.

ADAPT Millennial Awards

These awards are made to recognise good practice venues where access has been designed for the benefit of all users. The awards were made in seven categories:

Cinéma sponsored by Richard Attenborough Charitable Trust
Concert Halls sponsored by John S Cohen Foundation
Galleries Heritage Venues Museums all sponsored by Railtrack PLC
Libraries sponsored by Carnegie United Kingdom Trust
Theatres sponsored in memory of Teddy and Freda Mautner.

Seven awards were made, they went to: Film and Television, Bradford; Kidderminster Library; National Museum of Photography; National Railway Museum, York; Paxton House, Berwick upon Tweed; Potteries Museum and Art Gallery, Stoke-on-Trent; and Snape Maltings Concert Hall, Aldeburgh.

Applications are invited from venues (in these categories) which have facilities for people who are disabled which can be looked upon as role models. Main awards of £33,000 are made in each category, with additional certificates for Highly Commended entries. The closing date for entries is the end of June.

Adapt General
A grant of £2,500 was made to Walk the Plank, Salford.

Other
Information on the funding given by The Hugh Fraser Foundation was not given in the trust's annual report.

The trust also gave grants in three categories which have been discontinued. Railtrack Grants for Museums gave grants ranging between £1,000 and £3,500 to 31 museums to tackle physical, sensory and intellectual barriers and put in place a programme to make their buildings and displays widely accessible. The Scottish Grants Scheme gave three grants to Scottish organisations. Two capital access grants totalling £6,700 were also given.

During the year the trust organised another one-day conference on the theme Access v Aesthetics in Glasgow. At this conference it launched its new guide Open Sesame – The Magic of Access. The guide is a CD-ROM aimed at everyone involved in the design process and is intended to ensure that inclusive design becomes the norm. The guide was funded as part of a Railtrack plc sponsorship.

Exclusions No grants to stately homes, heritage centres, crafts centres; halls designed and used for other purposes such as church halls, hospitals or educational establishments even though they sometimes house the arts; or festivals, unless at a permanent arts venue.

Applications Guidelines and application details are available from the ADAPT office. Applicants for grants have to demonstrate that all aspects of access have been considered, including parking, publicity and staff training.

The Victor Adda Foundation

Fan Museum
£58,000 (1998/99)
Beneficial area UK, but in practice Greenwich

c/o Kleinwort Benson Trustees Limited, PO Box 191, 10 Fenchurch Street, London EC3M 3LB
Tel. 020 7956 6600 **Fax** 020 7626 6319
Correspondent The Clerk

Trustees Mrs H E Alexander; R J Gluckstein; Mrs B E Hodgkinson.
Information available Full accounts were on file at the Charity Commission.

General Virtually since it was set up in 1984, the foundation has been a stalwart supporter of the Fan Museum in Greenwich. It owns the property in which the museum is sited and has granted the Fan Museum Trust a 999 year lease. In addition, the foundation has made a loan of £573,000 to the trust. Previously the trust has stated that 'the success of the Fan Museum Trust justifies the continuation of this policy for the time being'. The 1998/99 annual report states that it supports new charities as well as its regular beneficiaries. In practice, the Fan Museum Trust receives the bulk of the income, with very little funds available for other organisations: The Fan Museum has received nearly all of the grant total for the last three years.

In 1998/99 the foundation had assets of £1.9 million (£1.6 million in 1997/98). The income totalled £360,000, of which £323,000 came from donations and only £36,000 from investments. The Fan Museum received £58,000 and only one other grant of £25 was given to the Catford & Bromley Combined Charities Appeal (which had received £50 in the previous year).

Applications In writing to the correspondent. Only successful applications are notified of a decision.

Adenfirst Ltd

Jewish
£115,000 (1998)
Beneficial area Worldwide

479 Holloway Road, London N7 6LE
Tel. 020 7272 2255
Correspondent I M Cymerman, Governor
Trustees Mrs H F Bondi; I M Cymerman; Mrs R Cymerman.
Information available Brief accounts were on file at the Charity Commission, including a grants list.

General The trust supports mostly Jewish organisations, with a preference for education and social welfare.

Grants totalled £115,000 in 1998. Six organisations received £10,000 each, Beis Yaakov Institutions, Friends of Harim

Establishments, Gur Trust, Reshet Ganei Yeladim, Torah Vechessed L'Ezra Vesaad and Yeshiva Le'Zeirim. There were a further 12 grants of £1,000 or more. Smaller grants totalled £2,400 but were not listed.

Applications In writing to the correspondent.

The Adint Charitable Trust

Children, medical and health
£354,000 (1997/98)
Beneficial area UK

BDO Stoy Hayward, 8 Baker Street, London W1M 1DA
Correspondent D R Oram, Trustee
Trustees Anthony J Edwards; Mrs Margaret Edwards; D R Oram; Brian Pate.
Information available Full accounts were provided by the trust.

General The trust gives mainly to UK organisations concerned with children, medicine and health. Grants range in size from a few hundred pounds to tens of thousands. Several organisations have received payments for a number of years.

In 1997/98 income of £450,000 (up from £271,000 in the previous year) was generated from assets of £7.5 million. The assets include shares in Friendly Hotels plc worth over £4 million and producing dividends to the trust of £175,000. The trust had very low management and administration costs of £7,100. A total of £354,000 was awarded in 50 grants.

The largest grants were £50,000 to St Mary's Hospital and £45,000 to HCBA which regularly receives large grants from the trust. Other large grants went to Clyde Action (£18,000) and Milton Keynes Community Trust (£14,000). Nine grants of £10,000 each included those to BACUP, ChildLine Charitable Trust, CRISIS, Sight Savers International and Voluntary Service Overseas. Children's Liver Disease Foundation received £7,500.

Nearly half the grants were of £5,000. Beneficiaries included Action Research, Alone in London Service, Child Growth Foundation, National Star Centre for

Disabled Youth and Sargent Cancer Care for Children.

Examples of smaller grants are Wessex Healthy Living Centre (£2,500), Peanut Club (£1,600) and Alzheimer's Research Trust (£250).

Exclusions Grants can be made to registered charities only and in no circumstances to individuals.

Applications To the correspondent, in writing only. There is no particular form in which applications are required; each applicant should make its own case in the way it considers best. The trust notes that they cannot enter into correspondence.

Beis Aharon Trust Fund

Jewish, general

£610,000 (1997/98)

Beneficial area UK

7 Darenth Road, London N16 6EP

Tel. 020 8806 6248

Correspondent J Lipschitz, Company Secretary

Trustees *D Frand; J Lipschitz; A Spitzer.*

Information available Accounts were on file at the Charity Commission but with no grants list and with very little information in the report.

General Originally named Edenheights Limited, the trust's interests are primarily the advancement of religion, in accordance with the Jewish faith.

In 1997/98 the trust had an income of £629,000, all from donations, almost double that of the previous year when it was £382,000. Grants were made totalling £610,000 (£380,000 in 1996/97). The assets at the year end totalled £56,000. Its management and administration costs were very low totalling only £2,300.

Unfortunately the amount of information available on the trust is very small, it has so far kept its activities a secret and no information has ever been available on what it does. This is a great shame given its considerable size. It would seem that the trust is choosing to ignore its legal obligation to detail its activities, and provide an analysis and explanation of its grant-making.

Applications In writing to the correspondent.

The Sylvia Aitken Charitable Trust

Medical research, general

£181,000 paid (1998/99)

Beneficial area UK, with a preference for Scotland

24 Woodside, Houston, Renfrewshire PA6 7DD

Tel. 01505 610412 **Fax** 01505 614944
e-mail jim@webprofessional.co.uk
website www.webprofessional.co.uk

Correspondent Jim Ferguson, Trust Administrator

Trustees *Mrs S M Aitken; Mrs M Harkis; J Ferguson.*

Information available Full accounts were provided by the trust.

General The trust only makes grants to registered charities with the primary areas to have benefited in the past being charities:

* specialising in medical research projects particularly in cancer
* benefiting children and older people
* providing care to animals.

The assets of the trust in 1998/99 stood at £4.1 million which generated an income of £152,000. Grants paid during the year totalled £181,000 and were given to 80 beneficiaries.

Grants paid ranged from £200 to £15,000. The largest grants went to British Lung Foundation (£15,000) and Association for International Cancer Research (£10,000). The 28 beneficiaries given between £1,000 and £9,000 included Animal Care, Blue Cross, Border Woman's Aid, Carrifan Wildwood Initiative and YMCA Scotland.

Smaller grants included those to Capability Scotland, Dumfries and Galloway Council Action on Alcohol Scotland, Fairbridge in Scotland, Hebridean Whale and Dolphin Trust, Scottish Dyslexia Association, Scottish Mask and Puppet Centre and Who Cares? Scotland.

A further six grants were approved. These ranged from £5,000 to £35,000, and totalled £133,000 and were all to medical research organisations or projects, for example, GRI Myeloma Project Year 2 (£33,000), Association of International Cancer Research (£30,000) and Renal Project GRI (£20,000).

Applications In writing to the correspondent. The trustees meet at least twice a year, usually in March/April and October/November.

The Ajahma Charitable Trust

See below

£315,000 (1998/99)

Beneficial area Worldwide

4 Jephtha Road, London SW18 1QH

Correspondent Suzanne Hunt, Administrator

Trustees *Jennifer Sheridan; Elizabeth Simpson; James Sinclair Taylor; Michael Horsman.*

Information available Full accounts and funding guidelines were provided by the trust.

General The trust generally supports established charities. They aim to balance their donations between international and UK charities. The trust considers grants in the following areas:

* development
* health
* disability
* poverty
* women's issues
* family planning
* human rights
* social need.

It has also favoured applications from new groups and those which may have difficulty finding funds from traditional sources are particularly encouraged.

In 1998/99 the trust had assets of £6.2 million and an income of £235,000. Grants totalled £315,000, of which 32% went to charities benefiting overseas work and 68% for charitable work in the UK. A total of 47 grants were given ranging from £1,000 to £25,000. Local Headway groups have continued to receive substantial support from the trust, with grants totalling £36,000.

The largest grants went to Oxfam (£25,000), UNIAS (£20,000), Health Unlimited (£15,000) and International Agency on Tobacco and Health (£11,000). Five grants of £10,000 were given to City Dysphasic Group, New Bridge, One World Action, Redress and Who Cares? Trust.

Other beneficiaries included Civil Liberties Trust (£8,000), Prisoners

Abroad (£7,500), Action on Disability & Development (£6,800), Education for Choice (£5,400), Kids Company (£5,000), Maternity Alliance and Village Aid (each £3,000) and Gingerbread (£2,000).

Exclusions Large organisations with a turnover above £4 million will not normally be considered nor will applications with any sort of religious bias or those which support animal rights/welfare, arts, medical research, buildings, equipment, local groups, overseas projects where the charity income is less than £350,000 a year. Applications for grants or sponsorship for individuals will not be supported.

Applications The trustees meet in May and November, the closing dates for applications are mid-February and mid-March. Information about applying should be sought first from the administrator.

The Alabaster Trust

Christian Church and related activities

£72,000 (1998/99)

Beneficial area UK and overseas

1 The Avenue, Eastbourne, East Sussex BN21 3YA

Tel. 01323 644579 **Fax** 01323 417643

Correspondent J R Caladine, Accountant

Trustees G A Kendrick; Mrs F Forster; M Buchanan; Mrs J Kendrick.

Information available Accounts were provided by the trust, but with a brief report and without a grants list.

General This trust was set up to make grants to evangelical Christian organisations in the UK and abroad. In 1998/99 it had an income of £52,000, mostly derived from Gift Aid donations. Grants totalled £72,000 (up from £52,000 in the previous year). More details about grants were not available, and the annual report did not include a grants list.

Applications In writing to the correspondent. The trustees meet to consider grants quarterly, in March, June, September and December.

All Saints Educational Trust

Education, Anglican religious work, home economics

£243,000 to organisations (1998/99)

Beneficial area UK

St Katherine Cree Church, 86 Leadenhall Street, London EC3A 3DH

Tel. 020 7283 4485 **Fax** 020 7283 2920

Correspondent R Poulton, Clerk

Trustees Rt Hon. Richard Chartres, Bishop of London, Chair; Revd Prebendary Swan; Mrs M R Behenna; P Chandler; D Clark; T L Guiver; Revd Hartley; D W Lankshear; Ms D McCrea; Miss A Philpott; Revd K G Riglin; Mrs A Rose; Revd T Thornton; D Trillo; John K Hoskin.

Information available Guidance notes were available from the trust. Full accounts were on file at the Charity Commission, including a detailed narrative report.

General Grants are given to both organisations and individuals for the promotion of research and development in education, particularly in religious education, home economics and kindred subjects, and multi-cultural and inter-faith education. The trust also has a programme of awards for beneficiaries to attend establishments of higher or further education to enable them to become qualified, or better qualified, as teachers. (For grants to individuals please see *The Educational Grants Directory*.)

The trust was formed following the closure and sale of the College of All Saints in 1978. The college itself had been formed in 1964 from an amalgamation of St Katherine's College, Tottenham and Berridge House, Hampstead. Following a decline in the birth rate and a reduction in the number of teachers required for training, the Secretary of State for Education and Science directed in 1978 that the college be amalgamated with Middlesex Polytechnic (now University).

The object of the trust is based broadly on the objects of the former college which had been to train teachers within a Christian foundation. Whilst St Katherine's had been concerned mainly with general teaching, Berridge House

had been established primarily to train teachers in domestic science (later known as home economics and now partly within the subject area of technology).

The trustees will give priority to the support of imaginative new projects which will enhance the church's contribution to higher and further education. Most particularly the trust is interested in:

- religious education – an emphasis on Christian education
- the multi-faith/inter-faith/multi-cultural dimension
- worship in educational establishments
- home economics/dietetics/nutrition
- development education
- awareness of third world issues
- provision of suitable materials for schools
- access courses as a preliminary to formal teaching training
- further education (as distinct from higher education)
- special educational needs including moral and ethical aspects
- ethical issues from a Christian standpoint.

They will also give priority to projects whereby teachers, particularly of religious education or home economics, are helped either directly or indirectly. Preference will be given to the support of projects on a 'pump-priming' basis and grants will not normally be made for a period in excess of five years. The trustees will wish to make suitable arrangements for monitoring research or the progress of a project.

In 1998/99 the trust had assets of £11.6 million and an income of £641,000. Grants totalled £400,000, of which £243,000 was given to organisations and £157,000 to 88 individuals.

The trust broke down its expenditure and grant-making as follows:

EXPENDITURE CATEGORY

	1998/99	(1997/98)
Grants to organisations	49%	(42%)
Grants to individuals	32%	(40%)
Administration cost	19%	(18%)

GRANTS TO ORGANISATIONS IN 1998/99

Size of grants	No. of grants	%
£1 – £4,999	4	5
£5,000 – £9,999	5	12
£10,000 – £19,999	3	21
£20,000 – £40,000	6	62

The following organisations supported during the year are regular beneficiaries. The largest grants were £30,000 each to National Association of Teachers of Home Economics & Technology for a project to produce 'a comprehensive learning resource for use in schools with young people (15 - 18)' (the last instalment of a three year grant) and to Religious Education Recruitment and Research Initiative (second year of three). Other grants included: £23,000 to Middlesex University towards the Ecumenical Chaplaincy Trust (twentieth year of support) and to National Society for a project to work alongside teachers and pupils to promote a clearer understanding of 'spiritual development' (final grant of three); £19,000 to University of North London, School for Life Sciences to review work-based learning in Home Economics and consumer studies at degree and higher education level (final year of three); £6,000 to Middlesex University for seminars on 'Values and Morals and the Role of the Modern University' (second grant of three); and £5,000 to London Diocesan Lay Ministry to support further development of adult Christian education through step-by-step courses in Hackney, Islington and Tower Hamlets by funding a part-time Lay Training Officer (twelfth year of support). Several smaller grants were given.

New projects supported by the trust included £21,000 to Chester College for Stage Two of a long distance learning programme focussing on church schools, leading to an MA in Church Schools Education/Religious Education and £5,000 to British Nutrition Foundation towards the Nutrition in Initial Teacher Training Guidance Document. Prospective beneficiaries for future grants are Christian Action Research and Education, London Diocesan Board for Schools, The National Society, The Society for Promoting Christian Knowledge and UK Home Economic Federation. In addition, Guildhall School of Music and Drama Foundation will receive support for two students to pursue a course in Music Therapy.

Exclusions The trust cannot support:

- schools by providing grants for buildings, equipment, supplies
- the general funds of any organisation
- public appeals
- the establishment of courses or departments in universities and colleges, which is a prime responsibility of the institutions themselves
- chaplaincies other than Middlesex University Ecumenical Chaplaincy.

Grants are not made retrospectively.

Applications Applications must be submitted on forms available from the correspondent. The closing date for all

applications is 31 January preceding the academic year to which the application relates. Final decisions will normally be made by June.

Please note that the trust defines beneficiaries as 'persons who are, or intend to become, engaged as teachers or in other capacities connected with education, in particular education in home economics and kindred subjects and in religious subjects'.

The trust normally responds to all written enquiries received, but in order to reduce administration costs, the trust will not be able to reply to letters seeking assistance in respect of projects detailed in Exclusions above.

The Dorothy Gertrude Allen Memorial Fund

General
£91,000 (1998)
Beneficial area UK

Teigncombe Barn, Chagford, Devon TQ13 8ET
Tel. 01647 433235
e-mail dgallen.memorialfund@btinternet.com
website www.members.nbci.com/dgallenmemfund
Correspondent P B Shone, Trustee
Trustees *H B Allen; P B Shone.*
Information available Full accounts were on file at the Charity Commission up to 1997/98.

General This trust has been included in this guide, giving grants of £91,000 in 1998. However, the core income is £30,000–35,000 a year. Its grant total has been considerably larger than this because of Gift Aid payments made to it – these are not guaranteed to continue. The total income in 1998 was £92,000 including a £46,000 Gift Aid payment.

The trust states that there is no typical grant size, though the trustees make a large number at £2,000 to £3,000. Grants can be recurring or one-off, and for revenue or capital purposes. The trust also states that they have no restrictions as to the kinds of project or the areas supported, and are generally prepared to consider any field. Intending applicants should note that organisations that have

received grants in the past should not be taken as indicative of a geographical or other bias.

In 1998, four charities received £5,000: Windmill Hill City Farm, Childhope – street children, Radio Lollipop and Medic Alert Foundation. There were 10 grants of £3,000, 11 of £2,000 and the remaining 19 were for £1,000. The wide range of causes supported included Scottish Wildlife Trust, International Otter Survival Fund, Rural Youth Trust, National Eye Research Centre, Hunter Trust for Education in Malawi, Understanding Industry, Prisoners Abroad and Wee Stories Theatre for Children.

Exclusions No grants to individuals or to organisations which are not UK-registered charities.

Applications In writing to the correspondent. Applications should be received by October for consideration in November/December. Due to an increasing number of appeals (the amount has doubled in the last few years) the trustees do not acknowledge appeals, applicants are contacted usually only when they are successful or where further information is required.

Mrs M H Allen Trust

Service/ex-service
£62,000 (2000)
Beneficial area UK

West Field, Gelt Road, Brampton, Cumbria CA8 1QH
Correspondent Col. A F Niekirk, Trustee
Trustees *Col. A F Niekirk; Capt. A P C Niekirk; Maj.W D Niekirk.*
Information available Accounts were on file at the Charity Commission.

General The trust can only support naval or military charities or institutions. The trustees prefer to support service charities that assist people rather than support buildings or property. In 2000 the trust had assets of £1.2 million and an income of £49,000. Grants totalled £62,000.

Grants ranged from £1,000 to £5,000. The largest of £5,000 each went to King Edward VII Hospital for Officers and

Dunstans. Grants ranging from £2,500 to £3,000 went to British Limbless Ex-Servicemen's Association, Ex-Services Mental Welfare Society, Princess Louise's Scottish Hospital, St David's Home and Scottish National Institute for the War-Blinded.

Applications In writing to the correspondent.

The Alliance Family Foundation

Jewish, general

£668,000 (1997/98)

Beneficial area UK, with some preference for charities in the Manchester area

12th Floor, Bank House, Charlotte Street, Manchester M1 4ET

Tel. 0161 236 3456

Correspondent G N Alliance, Trustee

Trustees *Sir David Alliance; G N Alliance; Mrs S D Esterkin.*

Information available Full accounts were on file at the Charity Commission.

General In 1996/97 the foundation had assets of £8.7 million, an income of £230,000 and gave grants totalling £576,000. This rose again to £668,000 in 1997/98.

A total of 111 grants were given. Although the trust generally supports Jewish charities, the three largest grants in 1996/97 were to other organisations. Grants of £1,000 or more were given to 21 organisations. An exceptional grant of £250,000 was given to the Lord Mayor of Manchester Emergency Fund following the Manchester bombing. Other large grants included £100,000 to UMIST Millennium Project (the first of five annual payments), £50,000 to the Museum of Science and Industry, in Manchester and £41,000 to Jerusalem Foundation.

Other grants of £1,000 or more do not show an obvious Manchester connection and were mostly to Jewish causes.

Exclusions No grants to individuals.

Applications In writing to the correspondent.

The Pat Allsop Charitable Trust

Education, medical research, children, relief of poverty

£65,000 (1998/99)

Beneficial area UK

c/o Monier Williams & Boxalls, 71 Lincoln's Inn Fields, London WC2A 3JF

Tel. 020 7405 6195   **Fax** 020 7405 1453

Correspondent J P G Randel, Trustee

Trustees *J P G Randel; A Collett; A G Butler; B C Fowler.*

Information available Full accounts were on file at the Charity Commission, with a detailed narrative report.

General A number of educational grants are made each year, e.g. towards research and organising educational events. The founder of the trust was a partner in Allsop & Co. Chartered Surveyors, Auctioneers and Property Managers, therefore the trust favours supporting those educational projects and charities which have connections with surveying and property management professions.

In 1998/99 the trust had assets of £750,000 and an income of £56,000 from both rent and investments. It gave 73 grants totalling £65,000.

The largest grant was £10,000 to Annigton Trust. Grants of £1,000 or more were made to 17 organisations, including Jewish Care, The Story of Christmas, Centrepoint, Cottage Homes Charity, Sparks, NSPCC, Norwood Ravenswood, National Schizophrenia Fellowship and Babes in Arms.

The remaining grants were mostly for less than £500 and the range of organisations was similar to those listed above.

Exclusions No grants to individuals.

Applications In writing to the correspondent, but please note, the trust does not accept unsolicited applications.

The Almond Trust

Christian

£347,000 (1998/99)

Beneficial area UK and worldwide

111 Dulwich Village, London SE21 7BJ

Tel. 020 7583 0404

Correspondent J L Cooke, Trustee

Trustees *J L Cooke; Barbara H Cooke; E E Cooke.*

Information available Full accounts were on file at the Charity Commission.

General The trust's aims are the support of evangelistic Christian projects, Christian evangelism and the translation, reading, study and teaching of the Bible.

In 1998/99 the trust had an income of £364,000, virtually all of which was comprised of Gift Aid donations. After making grants totalling £347,000, the trust had a balance at the year end of £227,000.

The trust made 15 grants of which 12 were recurrent. The largest were £100,000 to All Saints Crawborough, £95,000 to Oasis Trust, £50,000 to Summer Institute of Linguistics, £18,000 to Wycliffe Bible Translators (the latter three organisations also received large grants the year before) and £17,000 to Christian Youth and Schools Charitable Company. Smaller grants ranged from £4,000 to £7,500, including those to Canadian Baptist Ministries, International Films Limited and Overseas Missionary Fellowship.

Applications In writing to the correspondent, but please note that the trust states it rarely responds to uninvited applications.

Altamont Ltd

Jewish

£650,000 (1994/95)

Beneficial area Worldwide

Gerald Kreditor & Co, Tudor House, Llan Vanor Road, Finchley Road, London NW2 2AQ

Tel. 020 8209 1535

Correspondent The Clerk

Trustees *D Last; H Last; Mrs H Kon; Mrs S Adler; Mrs G Wiesenfeld.*

Information available Full accounts were on file at the Charity Commission, but only up to 1994/95.

General Unfortunately we have not been able to update this entry from the previous edition of this guide. Then we stated: 1994/95 appears to have been an exceptional year for this trust, with grants totalling £650,000, up from £114,000 the previous year. The income totalled only £109,000 with the result that the balance carried forward decreased substantially during the year to £683,000.

The larger grants were given to Jewish organisations that are themselves grant-making trusts, including Premierquote Ltd (£270,000), Natlas Trust (£150,000) and Fordeve Ltd (£147,000). In all, nine grants were made with all except one (the smallest) going to Jewish organisations. Smaller grants included £10,000 to Friends of Wiznitz and £5,000 to Friends of Bobov. BBC Children in Need received £500.

Applications In writing to the correspondent.

A M Charitable Trust

Jewish, general

£59,000 (1997/98)

Beneficial area UK and overseas

PO Box 191, 10 Fenchurch Street, London EC3M 3LB

Tel. 020 7956 6600   **Fax** 020 7626 6319

Correspondent The Secretary

Trustees *Kleinwort Benson Trustees Ltd.*

Information available Full accounts were on file at the Charity Commission.

General This trust supports a range of causes, particularly Jewish organisations but also medical, welfare, arts and conservation charities. Certain charities are supported for more than one year, although no commitment is usually given to the recipient.

In 1998/99 the trust had an income of £70,000 and an expenditure of £58,000. Further information for this year was not available at the time of going to print.

In 1997/98 it had assets of £2.2 million and an income of £76,000. The 46 grants

made totalled £59,000. Larger donations were £10,000 to Joint Jewish Charitable Trust, £8,000 to Jewish Care, £7,000 to World Jewish Relief and £5,000 each to British Ort, British Technion Society and Friends of the Hebrew University of Jerusalem.

Other grants ranged between £100 and £3,000, but were mainly for less than £500. At least half of these grants also went to Jewish organisations, with the remainder to a variety of organisations including: Artists General Benevolent Institution, British Heart Foundation, Children and Lone Parents Ltd, John Grooms Association for Disabled People, Kent Stress Centre, League of Friends of Alder Hey Children's Hospital and Sports Aid Foundation.

Exclusions No grants to individuals.

Applications Unsolicited applications are not welcomed. The trust stated that its funds are fully committed and only a small percentage of its income is allocated to new beneficiaries. Only successful applications are notified of the trustees' decision. Trustees meet in March and applications need to be received by January.

The Amberstone Trust

Civil rights, arts, Jewish, general

£469,000 (1998)

Beneficial area Worldwide

c/o Buss Murton (ref 46), The Priory, Tunbridge Wells, Kent TN1 1JJ

Tel. 01892 510222

Correspondent The Trustees

Trustees *Hon. D S Bernstein; Hon. P S Zuckerman.*

Information available Full accounts were on file at the Charity Commission.

General This trust was established in 1978 by the late Rt Hon. Sidney Lewis, Baron Bernstein of Leigh. In 1995/96 it received the residue of the estate of the settlor, with £2.8 million transferred to the capital fund and £403,000 to the income fund. The assets of the trust have risen from just under £1 million to over £7.7 million.

In 1998 the trust had an income of £171,000 and gave grants totalling £469,000. (The deficit of income for the year was covered partly from undistributed income brought forward of £198,000 and from the expendable endowment.)

A wide range of causes were supported, especially civil rights, the arts and Jewish causes. The trust gave 32 grants ranging from £1,000 to £100,000. The largest went to the Intermediate Technology Group. Other large grants went to One World Broadcasting Trust (£58,000), Vetiver Network (£42,000), Soho Theatre Company (£25,000), National Centre for Volunteering (£24,000) and Jerusalem Foundation (£18,000). The latter organisation received the largest grant of £182,000 in the previous year.

Grants ranging from £10,000 to £15,000 included those to African Medical Research, Contact a Family, Free and Democratic Bulgaria Foundation, Poetry Society, Prisoners Abroad and World Jewish Relief.

Smaller grants included those to Israel Palestine Human Rights Committee (£7,200), St John's College Cambridge and START (£5,000 each), Prisoners of Conscience (£4,000), English Chamber Orchestra (£3,000) and Rugby School Science Appeal (£1,000).

Applications The trustees are not accepting applications from the public as all the trust's funds are fully committed.

Viscount Amory's Charitable Trust

Welfare, older people, education

£442,000 to organisations (1999/2000)

Beneficial area UK, primarily Devon

The Island, Lowman Green, Tiverton, Devon EX16 4LA

Tel. 01884 254899   **Fax** 01884 255155

Correspondent The Trust Secretary

Trustees *Sir Ian Heathcoat Amory; Sir John Palmer.*

Information available Accounts, with a schedule of grants but only a brief narrative report, were provided by the trust.

General This trust has a strong preference for organisations in Devon, many of which are recurrent. Local organisations in the south west of England are also supported and a variety of UK charities.

In 1999/2000 the trust had assets of £8.8 million and an income of £376,000. Grants totalled £442,000 to organisations with £13,000 given to 29 individuals. The grants were divided as follows:

	Individuals	Institutions
Educational	£11,600	£172,900
Religious	nil	£37,800
General	£1,300	£231,300
Total	£12,900	£441,900

Grants of £1,000 or more were listed in the accounts. Altogether 93 were listed. The largest were £67,000 to London Sailing Project and £64,000 to Blundells School. Other larger grants went to Tiverton & Mid Devon Museum (£25,000), Eton College (£15,000), Marlborough College (£12,000). Maynard School (£11,000) and St Peter's Church – Tiverton (£10,000). Grants ranging from over £1,000 to £8,000 went to 39 organisations including Mencap (£8,000), National Trust (£6,000), Sedbergh School (£5,300), Mid Devon Enterprise Agency (£4,000), RoRo Sailing Project (£3,000), St Thomas' Church – Chevithorne (£2,000) and World Challenge (£1,400).

The remaining 45 grants were of £1,000 each. Examples of local grants in Devon and the south west of England included Christ Church Exmouth, Devon Youth Clubs, St John Ambulance – Barnstaple, St Mawgan Church – Nr Newquay, SSAFA Forces Help Devon, Tiverton Sub Aqua Diving Club, Torquay Museum and YMCA Cornwall. Examples of UK charities supported included Disability Aid Fund, Discovery Dockland Trust, Hope and Homes for Children, Mental Health Foundation, NSPCC, Royal Academy of Music, SeeAbility and Sight Savers International.

Applications In writing to the correspondent.

The Andrew Anderson Trust

Christian, social welfare

£287,000 to organisations (1998/99)

Beneficial area UK and overseas

84 Uphill Road, Mill Hill, London NW7 4QE

Correspondent The Trustees

Trustees *Miss A A Anderson; Miss M S Anderson; Revd A R Anderson; Mrs M L Anderson.*

Information available Accounts were on file at the Charity Commission but without a list of grants.

General The trust gives most of its money to evangelical organisations and churches, but also makes a large number of small grants to health, disability and social welfare charities.

In 1998/99 the trust had assets of £8.5 million (£8.8 million in 1997/98) which generated an income of £290,000. Grants totalled £328,000, of which £287,000 was given to UK and overseas charitable organisations. No grants list was available. Also supported are individuals who are involved in charitable activities and the dependants of individuals who were formerly involved in charitable activities, receiving a total of £37,000. Grants totalling £3,500 were given to individuals studying theology. Other grants totalled £250. In the 1996/97 accounts the trust provided a grants list.

Over 450 grants were given totalling £223,000, most of them recurrent. A total of 47 grants were between £1,000 and £10,000. Most of the donations (280) were small amounts of under £1,000 and the great majority of these were for under £280. There were 80 donations, mostly for up to £250, given to missionaries, ministers of religion and their widows, theological students, and evangelists. Larger grants were given to Fellowship of Independent Evangelical Churches (£12,000), Garston Bridge Chapel (£10,000), London Bible College (£7,300), Latin Link (£6,500), The Evangelical Alliance Relief Fund (£5,700) and Blythswood (£5,500).

Grants of £5,000 were made to Cornhill Training Course, Evangelical Theological College of Wales, Great St Helen's Trust and Wetherden Baptist Church. Whilst the trust gives predominantly to Christian, particularly evangelical, work

and to individual churches, a large number of the small grants are given to a very wide range of organisations dealing with health, disability and social welfare including ACET (AIDS Care Education and Training), Avon Riding Centre for the Disabled, Barnet Mencap, Brain Research Trust, Credit Action, Disablement Income Group Charitable Trust, Drug and Alcohol Foundation, Family Welfare Association, KIDS, London Connection, Institute of Child Health, Mental Health Foundation, NACRO, National Back Pain Association and Save the Children Fund.

Exclusions Individuals should not apply for travel or education.

Applications In writing to the correspondent. The trust states 'we prefer to honour existing commitments and initiate new ones through our own contacts rather than respond to applications'.

The Animal Defence Trust

Animal welfare

£115,000 (1999)

Beneficial area UK

Halsey Meyer Higgins, 56 Buckingham Gate, London SW1E 6AE

Tel. 020 7828 8772 **Fax** 020 7828 8774

Correspondent A A Meyer, Trustee

Trustees *Marion Saunders; Alan A Meyer; Vivien McIrvine; Celia Haddon.*

Information available Information was provided by the trust.

General The trust makes grants for capital projects purely to animal welfare charities. In 1999 its assets totalled £1.4 million and its income was £151,000, including £96,000 from legacies. Donations totalled £115,000 and were made to 25 organisations.

Grants of £7,500 each were made to The Brook Hospital for Animals, Celia Hammond Animal Trust, Greatwood Caring for Horses, Lagos Animal Protection Trust, Thoroughbred Rehabilitation Society and Woodside Animal Welfare. There were 9 grants of £5,000 each and 10 grants of £2,500 also made.

Applications In writing to the correspondent.

The Archbishop of Canterbury's Charitable Trust

Christianity, welfare

£183,000 to organisations and individuals (1998)

Beneficial area Worldwide

1 The Sanctuary, Westminster, London SW1P 3JT

Tel. 020 7222 5381

Correspondent P F Beesley, Secretary

Trustees *Archbishop of Canterbury; Sir John Owen; Rt Revd Richard Llewellin; Jeremy Harris.*

Information available Accounts were on file at the Charity Commission, but without a list of grants.

General The former Archbishop of Canterbury, Lord Runcie, set up this charitable trust in 1983. The main objects are to advance the Christian religion and Christian education, in particular the objects and principles of the Church of England. It also aims to relieve poverty and sickness both within the UK and overseas.

In 1998 the assets of the trust stood at £2.2 million and the income to the unrestricted fund was £277,000. Grants made from unrestricted funds totalled £183,000 to both organisations and also individuals working for the Church. Under £10,000 was given in restricted grants. There was no further information on the grants given.

The trust has stated previously that unfortunately its grant-making abilities can in no way match the need it is being asked to meet. Income is earmarked for several years in advance.

Applications Unsolicited applications will not be supported.

The Armourers and Brasiers' Gauntlet Trust

Materials science education, general

£47,000 (1999/2000)

Beneficial area UK, with some preference for London

Armourers and Brasiers' Company, Armourers' Hall, 81 Coleman Street, London EC2R 5BJ

Tel. 020 7606 1199 **Fax** 020 7606 7481

Correspondent Cmdr T J K Sloane, Secretary

Trustees *R M Moody, Chair; G A Garnett; Ven. C J H Wagstaff; Rear Adm. J P W Middleton; Revd P E de D Warburton; B R Pontifex.*

Information available Full accounts were provided by the trust.

General The trust, which provides the charitable outlet for the Worshipful Company of Armourers and Brasiers, was set up in 1979. Three-quarters of charitable giving is directed towards materials science education, supporting students and also teachers. The remaining funds are therefore quite limited and are directed towards 'people' rather than 'things', with the emphasis on youth and community projects. Grants are given in single payments, not on an ongoing basis. However, organisations can still apply for grants each year.

In 1999/2000 the trust had assets of £5.9 million and an income of £350,000, including donations of £114,000, nearly half of which was given by The Worshipful Company of Armourers & Brasiers. Grants to charities, individuals, schools and for scholarships – particularly to students of material sciences, totalled £181,000. The trust had a surplus for the year of £142,000.

Grants to 76 organisations totalled £47,000 and were broken down as follows:

Armed service
Five prizes and two grants totalled £3,300. Grants of £300 each were given to Inns of Court & City Yeomanry and VC & GC Association. £2,000 was given towards Royal Armoured Corps for Silver Statuettes, with other prizes ranging from £100 to £200.

Youth
STA received a grant towards cruises of £2,900 and a donation of £500.

City of London
Grants to seven organisations totalled £4,100. Guildhall School of Music received three grants totalling £2,400. Lord Mayor's Charity received £1,000 and other grants ranged from £30 (Inter Livery Swimathon) to £250 (St Margaret Lothbury).

Others
A grant of £100 was given to Alexander Forsyth Award and £410 towards the cost of medals.

Hospices
Three grants totalled £2,600. Greenwich & Bexley Cottage Hospice and Willen Hospice received £1,000 each and £620 was given to Phoenix Lodge.

Community and social care
16 grants totalled £6,900. Grants included £950 to The Passage, £500 each to Aidis Trust and Tower Hamlets Mission, £300 each to Crossroads Christian Counselling Centre and Women's Link and £200 each to Addiction Recovery Foundation and Neighbours in Poplar.

Children/youth
18 grants totalled £10,000. Beneficiaries included Operation New World and Princes Youth Business Trust (£1,500 each), Association for Research into Stammering in Childhood and React (£500 each), Happy Days Children's Charity (£390), 1st City of London Scout Group (£80) and Handicapped Children's Outing (£50).

The arts
Grants of £500 each went to Millennium Bridge Trust and St Mary the Less Church.

Medical/health
Grants to 12 organisations totalled £6,700, including Milex Training Centre and Regain (each £1,000), Dyslexia Institute (£600), Defeating Deafness and National Endometriosis Society (£500 each) and Headway National Head Injuries Association and St Luke's Hospital for the Clergy (each £200).

Arms & armour
Grants were given to Fitzwilliam Museum (£1,500), The Wallace Collection (£1,000) and an individual for research (£350).

Armed forces
Grants of £250 each to St Clement Danes, Submarine Centennial Fund and Ulysses Trust.

Spiritual renewal
Grants of £1,500 to Wycliffe Hall, £440 to Mission Aviation Fellowship, £300 to JC 2000 and £200 to a vicar.

The trust also gave: £55,000 in their Armourers' Alcan Scheme in educational grants at school, undergraduate and research level; £20,000 in their Armourers' Corus Scheme in educational grants to students in further/higher education and industrial experience awards; and £59,000 in scholarships for students of materials sciences.

Exclusions In general grants are not made to:

- organisations or groups which are not registered charities
- individuals
- organisations or groups whose main object is to fund or support other charitable bodies which are in direct relief of any reduction of financial support from public funds
- charities with a turnover of over £4 million
- charities which spend over 10% of their income on fundraising activities
- to organisations whose accounts disclose substantial financial reserves.

Nor towards general maintenance, repair or restoration of buildings, including ecclesiastical buildings, unless there is a long standing connection with the Armourers and Brasiers' Company or unless of outstanding importance to the national heritage.

Applications In writing to the correspondent, with a copy of the latest annual report and audited accounts. Applications are considered quarterly.

The Thomas Arno Bequest

Business start-up, education, personal development of young people

£95,000 to organisations (1998/99)

Beneficial area UK and Greater London

Haberdashers' Company,
39–40 Bartholomew Close,
London EC1A 7JN

Tel. 020 7606 0967 **Fax** 020 7606 5738
e-mail charities@haberdashers.co.uk
Correspondent B J Blair, Assistant Clerk for Charities

Trustees *Haberdashers' Company.*

Information available Accounts were on file at the Charity Commission, included in the consolidated accounts of the Haberdashers' Company's charities, but without a list of grants.

General The following information is taken from the consolidated accounts of the Haberdashers' Company charities which lists 46 different funds, including the Thomas Arno Bequest and Haberdashers' Eleemosynary Charity (*see separate entry*).

The bequest supports pupils and ex-pupils of Haberdashers' schools and charities which are:

- helping young UK people start their own businesses or helping those who have started
- aimed at the personal development of young people and encouraging ideas of good citizenship amongst them.

In 1998/99 the bequest had assets of £2.9 million and an income £110,000. Grants totalled £137,000 and were broken down as follows:

	1998/99	(1997/98)
Arts & sport	£500	(£11,900)
Christianity and the Church	£10,500	(£22,500)
Disadvantaged people	£10,800	(£12,600)
Education & training	£65,000	(£53,700)
Healthcare	£700	(-)
Young people	£49,000	(£47,800)
Miscellaneous	-	(£3,700)

During the year the main focus was on the education, training and personal development of young people. Charities received £95,000, including £30,000 from Unrestricted General Reserves and £42,000 was distributed in grants to individuals, mainly to pupils of Haberdashers' schools. The 11 grants of £1,000 or more were listed in the accounts. The largest grants were £15,000 each given to Prince's Youth Business Trust and The Sail Training Association, £12,000 to Adam's Grammar School and £10,000 to The Grubb Institute of Behavioural Studies. The other grants went to The Arkwright Scholarship Trust and St John the Baptist C of E Primary School – Hoxton (£5,000 each), Aldersey C of E Primary School Bunbury and Hackney Business Venture (£3,000 each), Charterhouse in Southwark and The Royal College of Art (£2,500 each), and UC Trust – UK (£1,500).

Exclusions No grants to individuals, except those mentioned above.

Applications In writing to the correspondent. Charities should submit a copy of their latest annual report and accounts, up-to-date financial information, and other information illustrating their aims and activities.

The Arnopa Trust

Children

£379,000 (1999)

Beneficial area UK

1 Connaught Place, London W2 2DY
Tel. 020 7402 5500 **Fax** 020 7298 0003
Correspondent Jane Leek
Trustees *Charport Ltd.*

Information available Full accounts were provided by the trust.

General The trust was established in 1977 principally for the care and protection of children in need. It provided financial support towards the cost of running a residential home for up to eight children from disturbed backgrounds until the home was closed in 1990. Since then it has been making grants to charities working with deprived children and young adults.

In 1999 it had assets of £344,000, an income of £24,000 but a grant total of £379,000. Over the last few years the trust has been using both its capital funds and income to make grants; the assets have halved since the previous year. A total of 18 grants were given ranging from £4,000 to £55,000.

The main beneficiary was Barnardos which received three grants for different projects: £55,000 for Dundee City Council, £38,000 for Supporting Parents Supporting Children and £30,000 for St Andrew's College. Other large grants went to Community Service Volunteers (£45,000), Constable Educational Trust Ltd (£30,000), Swansea & Brecon Diocesan Council for Social Responsibility (£28,000), Plymouth Hospitals NHS Trust General Charity (£25,000), Cornerstone Church (£20,000) and St Margaret's Roman Catholic Parish (£20,000). Five grants were given ranging from £10,000 to £16,000, including those to East London Schools Fund, Kids Company and PACT Community Projects. Four smaller grants included those to Brighton Oasis and Fair Play Training.

In previous years the trust derived its main income from lettings. Following the disposal of the property in 1997, the income received in that year, together with the balance of the proceeds (£350,000), have funded the trust's grant-making. It is not known whether the trust will continue to spend its capital. If it does so at the current rate it will be winding up in the next few years.

Applications Applicants should write a brief letter outlining the project; on the basis of this an application form will be sent. Trustees meet most months.

The Ove Arup Foundation

Construction – education and research

£214,000 (1999/2000)

Beneficial area Unrestricted

13 Fitzroy Street, London W1P 4BQ

Tel. 020 7465 3752

e-mail keith.dawson@arup.com
website www.theovearupfoundation.com

Correspondent K D Dawson, Secretary

Trustees *P Ahm; P Dowson; B Perry; J Martin; D Michael; R F Emmerson; R B Haryott.*

Information available Full accounts were on file at the Charity Commission.

General The trust was established in 1989 with the principal objective of supporting education in matters associated with the built environment. It also supports construction-related academic research. The trustees are appointed by the board of the Ove Arup Partnership. It gives grants for research and projects, including start-up and feasibility costs. Grants are generally for around £5,000.

In 1999/2000 the trust had assets of £2.6 million. It gave £214,000 in grants. The largest were £80,000 to London School of Economics for course development and £55,000 to Imperial College, London, for a visiting design professorship.

Other larger grants included those to Cambridge University for bursaries on IDBE course (£18,000), University of Sussex for research in education and built environment (£17,000) and Royal Society of Arts for design awards (£10,000).

Grants of £5,000 each went to Equinox 2000 for sponsorship of a seminar and to both Hackney Building Exploratory and Learning Through Landscapes for schemes to inform young people. Other grants included Arkright Scholarships to encourage young people into engineering (£4,000) and The Edge for core running costs (£3,500).

Exclusions No grants to individuals, including students.

Applications In writing to the correspondent, with brief supporting financial information. Trustees meet quarterly to consider applications (March, June, September and December).

The AS Charitable Trust

See below

£24,000 (1998/99)

Beneficial area UK and the third world

Bix Bottom Farm,
Henley-on-Thames RG9 6BH

Tel. 01491 577745

Correspondent The Administrator

Trustees *Roy Calvocoressi; Charles Brocklebank.*

Information available Full accounts were on file at the Charity Commission.

General This trust makes grants in particular to projects which combine the advancement of the Christian religion, with Christian lay leadership, with third world development, with peacemaking and reconciliation or with other areas of social concern.

In 1998/99 the trust's assets increased to £6.2 million, it had an income of £167,000 and total expenditure was £50,000, including property expenses of £20,000. A total of £24,000 was given in nine grants. The largest grant was of £12,000 to Christian International Peace Service. A grant of £1,100 went to Langley House Trust. The remaining seven grants were of £1,000 each including those to Dean Close School (Mityana Hope Project), Healing and Family Tree, International Films and Penhurst Retreat Centre.

Applications In writing to the correspondent.

Ashburnham Thanksgiving Trust

Christian

£112,000 to organisations
(1997/98)

Beneficial area UK and worldwide

Agmerhurst House, Ashburnham, Battle, East Sussex TN33 9NB

Correspondent Mrs M Bickersteth, Trustee

Trustees *Mrs M Bickersteth; Mrs E M Habershon; E R Bickersteth; R D Bickersteth.*

Information available Full accounts were on file at the Charity Commission.

General The trust supports a wide range of Christian mission organisations and other Christian organisations in the UK and worldwide. Individuals are also supported.

In 1997/98 the trust's assets totalled £3.2 million and it had an income of £195,000, including £67,000 in donations received. A total of £121,000 was distributed in 112 grants to organisations and some to individuals.

The largest grant of £15,000 went to Penhurst Retreat Centre Charitable Trust, a further 17 grants of £1,000 or more were also made. Larger grants included those to Lawrence Barham Memorial Trust (£9,800), St Stephen's Society – Hong Kong (£5,200) and Genesis Arts Trust (£4,400). Grants between £1,000 and £2,000 included those to Greenbelt, International Films, St Paul's Church Northfields and Youth with a Mission. Smaller grants (ranging from £80 to under £1,000) included Food for Thought, Latin Link, Oak Centre Group, St Michael's Hospice, Scripture Union and World Vision.

Grants were given to 28 individuals and totalled £9,500.

Applications The trust has stated that its funds are fully committed and it only supports Christian work which is already known to the trustees. Unfortunately it receives far more applications than it is able to deal with.

Ashe Park Charitable Trust

Possible preference for hospitals

£130,000 committed (1998/99)

Beneficial area UK

Ashe Park, Steventon,
Hampshire RG25 3AZ

Tel. 01256 771689

Correspondent Mrs Jan Scott, Trustee

Trustees P J Scott; Mrs J M T Scott.

Information available Accounts were on file at the Charity Commission, but without a detailed description of its grant-making policy.

General Registered with the Charity Commission in 1987, the first accounts for this trust on file were for 1998/99.

In 1998/99 the trust's assets totalled £37,000 and it had an income of £179,000, mainly derived from fundraising events. The main fundraising event was The Ashe Park Polo Challenge which raised £115,000.

After fundraising costs of £62,000, a grant of £80,000 was made to Wallace and Gromit's Children's Hospital Grand Appeal. A further £50,000 was pledged to NHS London Hospital Trust and was to be matched by the NHS.

Applications In writing to the correspondent.

The Laura Ashley Foundation

Art and design, higher education, local projects in mid-rural Wales

£274,000 to organisations and individuals (1997/98)

Beneficial area England and Wales

3 Cromwell Place, London SW7 2JE

Tel. 020 7581 4662 **Fax** 020 7584 3617
e-mail info@laf.uk.net
website www.laf.uk.net

Correspondent The Administrator

Trustees *Jane Ashley, Chair; Prof. Susan Solombok; Martyn C Gowar;*
Martin Jones; Emma Shuckburgh; Marquis of Queensberry.

Information available Full accounts were on file at the Charity Commission; detailed guidelines are available on the foundation's website.

General The foundation was set up in 1986 in memory of Laura Ashley by her family. It has a strong commitment to art and design and also to Wales, particularly Powys, where the Laura Ashley business was first established. In the last few years the foundation has undergone change, new policies were expected to be finalised by the end of the year 2000. It states that 'we will be moving away from seeking applications, towards finding projects to fund and in some cases setting up tailor-made projects ourselves. As a result, we will be seeking applications in narrower, more focused areas'. Potential applicants are advised to check the website for the latest details.

At July 2000, the trust's main activities, already reflecting changes in the trust's policy, were as follows:

Projects in mid-rural Wales
- to enhance the lives of families
- rural regeneration e.g. Farmer's Markets
- adult education
- music or art & design projects

Education
Special bursaries have been set up through institutions of the trustees' choice

- music conservatoires – bursaries for talented musicians
- LSE – scholarship for a mature anthropology MA student
- City Literacy Institute - learning opportunities for mature students
- Royal College of Art - scholarship for mature textile students, preferably from Wales.

Fellowship Awards
These are aimed at encouraging individuals with truly innovative and workable ideas in fields as diverse as music and design, engineering and physics to bring those ideas to fruition. The Awards are made either under the heading of Science or the Arts. The trustees are looking for ideas which 'not only promise benefit to others and a practical outcome, but will also ideally be aesthetically and intellectually appealing'. An example of a successful project was a bicycle for use by people who are disabled. Awards will be made for up to three years and will range from £10,000 to £30,000 a year. The website states that next year they are looking to support Art

and Design; however, it is not clear which year this is.

The Arts in London
- a six month pilot project set up by Jane Ashley called SLATE – a network of documentary film makers to encourage wider use of their talents
- music at the Tabernacle in Notting Hill – showing the music of unsigned bands.

In 1998/99 the trust had an income of £370,000 and an expenditure of £465,000. Unfortunately we were unable to see these accounts at the Charity Commission.

In 1997/98 the trust had assets of £10.2 million and an income of £520,000. Grants totalled £274,000. Grants usually range from £500 to £15,000 and can be one-off or recurrent.

Details of a sample selection of grants 1998/99 were available. The largest grant was £15,000 awarded each year for three years to Soil Association Wales to support a field worker. Other larger grants listed were £10,000 to Welsh College of Music and Drama in Cardiff to help 10 music students, £5,000 to Mid-Wales Opera in Newtown for student singer costs for the Festival of the Opera, £3,200 to Powys Young Carers for workers to help young carers with activities and £2,800 to Carad in Powys towards a multi-purpose use of an arts centre for local families.

Smaller grants went to Barnardos – Merthyr Tydfil for a young carers scheme and The Opera School – Wales for master classes (each £1,500), Bonymaen Family Centre – Wales for equipment (£930) and St Michael's School in Newtown for adults to accompany children with special needs on a trip to London (£100).

Exclusions The foundation does not fund the following:

- individuals
- further education
- new buildings
- medical research
- overseas travel/exchange visits
- private education
- purchase cost of property/land
- restoration of historic buildings or churches
- university or similar research
- vehicle purchase or upkeep
- alcohol or drug programmes
- projects concerned with domestic violence
- penal affairs
- sport
- youth clubs/projects concerned with 'youth at risk'

- general funds
- taking projects into schools
- outward bound courses
- newspapers/journals/publications/information packs
- video projects
- safety devices
- theatre, dances, shows/touring
- internet related projects.

Applications Potential applicants are encouraged to telephone the trust to discuss eligibility before submitting an application. An initial application should be made in writing to the correspondent, enclosing an sae. It should include a summary of your activities and work, outline the actual project and for what specific purpose the grant is required and what funds have already been raised. It should be typed on one side of headed notepaper.

The Ashworth Charitable Trust

Welfare

£122,000 to organisations (1998/99)

Beneficial area UK and worldwide, with some preference for certain specific needs in Ottery St Mary, Honiton and Sidmouth in Devon

Foot Anstey Sargent, 4–6 Barnfield Crescent, Exeter, Devon EX1 1RF

Tel. 01392 411221 **Fax** 01392 218554 **e-mail** alexander.elphinston@foot-ansteys.co.uk

Correspondent A Elphinston, Secretary

Trustees *C F Bennett, Chair; Miss S E Crabtree; A Elphinston; Mrs K A Gray; G D R Cockram.*

Information available Full accounts were on file at the Charity Commission.

General The trust currently supports:

- Ironbridge Gorge Museum Trust
- people living in the areas covered by the medical practices in Ottery St Mary, Honiton and Sidmouth. Such grants are to be paid only for particularly acute needs.
- humanitarian projects.

In 1998/99 the trust's assets were £3.6 million, it had an income of £153,000. Grants to 49 organisations totalled £126,000 and ranged from £500

to £10,000 and were made to 49 organisations.

The largest grants of £10,000 each went to Iron Bridge Gorge Museum Trust and Hospiscare. Other larger grants included £6,000 to Starlight Foundation and £5,000 each to Child Hope, Fiveways School and Médecins sans Frontiéres. Three-quarters of the grants were between £1,000 and £3,000. Examples of these include ADD Action on Disability, Anti-Slavery Trust, Children's Head Injury Fund, Christian Aid, Deaf Blind Association, Fairbridge and Pembrokeshire Single Action for the Homeless. Four grants of £500 each were given. Generally, grants appear to be one-off.

There were 13 grants to individuals, totalling £3,600, given from the designated fund to help those in the areas of Ottery St Mary, Honiton and Sidmouth in Devon.

Applications In writing to the correspondent.

The Astor Foundation

General

£139,000 (1998/99)

Beneficial area UK

2 Kew Gardens, Shalbourne, Wiltshire SN8 3QW

Correspondent Mrs Pam Garraway, Secretary

Trustees *Sir William Slack; J R Astor, Chair; Lord Astor of Hever; Dr H Swanton; R H Astor; Hon. C Money-Coutts.*

Information available Full accounts were on file at the Charity Commission.

General The trust supports a variety of causes, particularly disability and health and medical research. The grants list also shows some preference for conservation projects. In the past the trust has not favoured giving large grants for building projects although they are not excluded.

In 1998/99 the trust had an income of £139,000, all of which was given in 82 grants. The assets at the year end stood at £3.6 million. Grants ranged from £250 to £18,000.

The larger grants went to Astor Fellowship for Post Graduates (£18,000) and University College London Medical

School for the purchase of equipment (£7,500). Grants ranging between £1,000 and £3,500 went to 65 organisations including Bryson House, Discovery Docklands Trust, Epilepsy Research Foundation, Help the Hospices, Horticultural Therapy, Mobility Trust, Rochester 2000 Trust Music Appeal, RNLI, Tower Hamlets Mission, Woodland Trust and Youth at Risk.

Smaller grants included those to Borders Forest Trust, Disabled Living Foundation, Thames Valley Partnership and Women Caring Trust.

The trust has made commitments to 11 organisations to give future grants mostly up to three years.

Exclusions No grants to individuals and no salaries. Grants are given to registered charities only.

Applications There are no deadline dates, applications should be *in writing only* to the correspondent. If the appeal arrives too late for one meeting it will automatically be carried over for consideration at the following meeting. The trustees meet twice yearly in October and March. A reply will always be sent irrespective of whether an appeal is successful or not.

The Atlantic Foundation

Education, medical, general

£117,000 (1998/99)

Beneficial area Worldwide, though with some preference for Wales

7–8 Raleigh Walk, Atlantic Wharf, Cardiff CF10 4LN

Tel. 029 2046 1651

Correspondent Mrs B L Thomas, Trustee

Trustees *P Thomas; Mrs B L Thomas.*

Information available Full accounts were on file at the Charity Commission.

General This trust relies on covenanted donations each year for its income, which totalled £149,000 in 1998/99. It supports a range of causes, with a strong interest in Wales. Grants totalled £117,000 and were categorised by the trust as follows:

	1998/99	1997/98
Independent schools and colleges	£55,000	£89,000
Registered charities	£33,000	£45,600
Community aid	£15,900	£15,400
Medical appeals and support	£6,900	£6,500
Local authority support	£4,800	£6,200
Trust funds	£240	£3,000
International appeals	£200	£1,600
Religious foundations	£1,050	£1,200

Independent schools and colleges

Grants were given to 33 organisations. The largest went to Clifton College (£11,000), Royal Academy of Dramatic Art (£5,900) and Bristol Old Vic (£4,100); all three beneficiaries received large grants in the previous year. The smaller grants went to schools, colleges and universities throughout England and Wales, with a few given overseas.

Registered charities

Under this category 56 grants were given ranging from £30 to £4,400. The largest grants went to Cities in the Schools (£4,400), PHAB Wales (£2,000), Motor Neurone Disease Association and Wales Council for the Deaf (£1,500 each), Twice Limited (£1,300) and South Wales Federation of Town Women's Guilds (£1,100).

Five grants of £1,000 each including those to Barnardos, Deafblind UK and Y-Bont. Smaller grants included those to Action Research, Hope House, Monmouth Youth Project, Plantlife, Council for Music in Hospitals and Sherman Theatre. Mostly health and welfare charities were supported.

Community aid

A total of 47 grants were given ranging from £100 to £1,000. Grants of £1,000 each were given to Abercynon FC and Flashback Film Company. Smaller grants went to Blackwood Users & Drop-in, Festiniog Village Hall, Llanishen Mother & Toddler Group, Pendyrus Male Choir, Ragland Terrace Beaufort Pensioners, Welsh under 16's Cadet Basketball Team and Parc Bryn Bach Angling Club.

Medical appeals & support

Grants were given to 13 organisations ranging from £100 to £1,000. Grants of £1,000 each went to Alzheimer's Research, Cystic Fibrosis and Whizz-Kids.

Local authority

11 grants were given ranging from £50 to £1,400. About four Welsh councils received grants. Other grants were given to Education Services, three schools,

Welsh Heritage School Initiative and Ski Council for Wales.

The remaining categories gave the following grants: under Trust funds the Lewis Martin Trust received help; under Religious foundations two churches were supported and St David's Cathedral Appeal received £350.

Applications In writing to the correspondent. Applications are considered throughout the year.

ATP Charitable Trust

Jewish, education, medical

£127,000 (1999/2000)

Beneficial area Worldwide

31 Millharbour, Isle of Dogs, London E14 9TX

Tel. 020 7510 0623

Correspondent M R Bentata, Trustee

Trustees *M R Bentata; J A Bentata; A G A Macfadyen.*

Information available Full accounts were on file at the Charity Commission.

General In 1999/2000 the trust had assets of £134,000 generating an income of £8,500. (In the previous year the trust had an income of £115,000, of which £100,000 was from Gift Aid donations.) Grants totalled £127,000 using the income from this year plus undistributed income from previous years. There was no indication as to levels of future income. There were 62 grants given ranging from £150 to £15,000.

The largest grants were £15,000 each to Jewish Care and West London Synagogue, £12,000 to Leo Baeck College, £10,000 each to Community Security Trust (in two grants), Givat Haviva, Kibbutz Shoval, Reform Synagogues of GB and West London Synagogue. Other grants included United Jewish Israel Appeal (£6,000) and Newham College (£2,500) and £1,000 each to Brighton Jewish Film Festival, Joint Jewish Charitable Trust, Atlantic College and University of Southampton.

The remaining 47 grants ranged from £150 to £750, about half of these went to colleges and universities mostly in the UK, some receiving more than one grant.

Other beneficiaries included Get Kids Going and Teenage Cancer Trust.

Applications In writing to the correspondent. Individuals who apply must include two personal references and a current cv. Applications are considered throughout the year.

The Richard Attenborough Charitable Trust

Acting, human rights, overseas, general

£140,000 (1998/99)

Beneficial area UK and overseas

Beaver Lodge, Richmond Green, Surrey TW9 1NQ

Tel. 020 8940 7234

Correspondent Lady Attenborough, Trustee

Trustees *Lady Attenborough; Lord Attenborough.*

Information available Full accounts were on file at the Charity Commission.

General This trust not surprisingly focuses much of its grant-making towards acting-related organisations. It also makes a number of grants to overseas and human rights organisations.

In 1998/99 the trust's assets totalled £418,000, mostly held in Attenborough Securities Ltd (£173,000) and Henry Moore Bronze (£100,000). The trust's income was £232,000 and it made 42 grants totalling £140,000, 13 of which were recurrent. Grants ranged from £100 to £21,000. The largest went to Royal Academy of Dramatic Art (£21,000), Breton Hall (£20,000), Waterford School Trust (£16,000), Prison Charity Shops (£13,000) and One World Action (£11,000), with £10,000 each to Centre for German Jewish Studies and Tate Gallery and £8,000 to Mandela Sponsorship Fund.

Grants of £5,000 each went to The Gandhi Foundation, Royal Academy of Arts and Toynbee Hall. Nine grants ranged from £1,000 to £1,500, including British Appeal for the Preservation of Venice, Chicken Shed Theatre Co. and National Film and Television School.

Smaller grants included those to Amnesty International, Human Rights Watch,

Battle of Britain Historical Society and Vineyards Project.

Applications The funds of this trust are donated principally to charities with which the trustees are associated. They greatly regret, therefore, that they are unable to reply to any external applications.

The Lord Austin Trust

Social welfare

£173,000 (1998/99)

Beneficial area England, with a special interest in the West Midlands

c/o Martineau Johnson, St Phillip's House, St Phillip's Place, Birmingham B3 2PP

Tel. 0121 200 3300

Correspondent D L Turfrey, Secretary

Trustees *Baring Trust Co Ltd; J M G Fea; R S Kettel.*

Information available Accounts were on file at the Charity Commission but without a list of grants.

General The trust was established by the will of Lord Austin of Longbridge, the creator of the motor car company of that name, and came into effect following his death in 1941. Although the trustees were given absolute discretion, in his will Lord Austin expressed preferences as to the types of organisations to be supported. These were:

- hospitals and clinics
- medical and/or surgical research establishments and similar bodies
- organsiations concerned with the 'care, maintenance, education and upbringing of poor children'
- organisations concerned with the welfare of older people.

In 1998/99 the assets of the trust stood at £4 million generating an income of £154,000. Grants totalled £173,000 and were categorised as follows:

Young people	£59,000
Older people	£33,000
Miscellaneous	£81,000

No further information on the size of grants or number of beneficiaries was available.

Applications In writing to the correspondent. Trustees meet twice a year to consider grants.

The Avenue Charitable Trust

General

£394,000 (1997/98)

Beneficial area Worldwide

c/o Sayers Butterworth, 18 Bentinck Street, London W1M 5RL

Tel. 020 7935 8504 **Fax** 020 7487 5621

Correspondent Sue Brotherhood

Trustees *Hon. F D L Astor; Hon. Mrs B A Astor; S G Kemp.*

Information available Full accounts were provided by the trust.

General In 1997/98 the assets of the trust decreased from £960,000 to £526,000 (the assets had been over £1.1 million in 1995/96). The income was £30,000 and 85 grants ranging from £17 to £100,000 totalled £394,000. A wide variety of charitable purposes were supported, with the grants list showing a preference for human rights organisations.

The largest grant of £100,000 went to Primrose Hill Trust. Other large grants included those to Replay Trust (£39,000), Prison Charity Shops Trust (£33,000), Progressive Farming Trust (£27,000), Legal Assistance Trust (£20,000), Prison Video Trust (£13,000), Richmond Fellowship International and Sutton Courtenay Pre-school (£11,000 each) and New Renaissance Group (£10,000).

Eight grants were given ranging from £3,500 to £10,000, including Koestler Award Trust (£10,000), Young Minds (£6,000), Park School (£5,000) and Asylum Aid (£4,600). Grants ranging from £1,000 to £3,500 went to 33 groups including Anna Freud Centre, Anti-Slavery Society, Friends of the Elderly & Gentlefolks Help, Kurdish Human Rights Project, Medical Aid for Palestinians, Northern Ireland Voluntary Trust, Royal National Theatre and St Katherine's House.

Smaller grants included those to The Child Psychotherapy, Council for the Protection of Rural England and Polish Institute & Sikorski Museum. Nine individuals received grants ranging from £400 to £7,600 which totalled £21,000.

Applications The trust has previously stated that all available income is now committed to existing beneficiaries.

The Balcombe Charitable Trust

Education, environment, health and welfare

£284,000 (1999/2000)

Beneficial area UK

c/o Citroen Wells, Devonshire House, 1 Devonshire Street, London W1N 2DR

Tel. 020 7304 2000

Correspondent Henry Charles, Trustee

Trustees *H Charles; R A Kreitman; Mrs P M Kreitman; H Kreitman; Mrs S I Kreitman.*

Information available Full accounts were on file at the Charity Commission.

General This trust generally makes grants in the fields of education, the environment and health and welfare. It only supports registered charities.

In 1999/2000 the trust had assets of £8.4 million and an income of £325,000. A total of 33 grants totalled £284,000. They ranged from £500 to £25,000. The largest grants were £25,000 each to British Red Cross, Princes Trust and Save the Children Fund, £22,000 to Young Minds Trust, £20,000 to Brook Advisory Centre, £15,000 to ChildLine, £12,000 to Jersey Wildlife Preservation Trust while six grants of £10,000 each included those to ActionAid, Friends of the Earth and MIND.

Nine grants ranging from £5,000 to £8,000 included those to Ammesty International, The Disabilities Trust and Womankind. Grants ranging from £1,000 to £4,000 went to 10 organisations including Cancer Research Campaign, Headway, ParentLine and Youth at Risk. One grant of £500 was given to The Children's Society.

Exclusions No grants to individuals or non-registered charities.

Applications In writing to the correspondent.

The Barber Charitable Trust

Evangelical Christian causes, churches

£60,000 (1998/99)

Beneficial area UK with some preference for West Sussex, and overseas

Tortington Cottage, Tortington, Arundel, West Sussex BN18 0BG

Tel. 01903 882337

Correspondent E E Barber, Trustee

Trustees *E E Barber; Mrs D H Barber.*

Information available Full accounts were on file at the Charity Commission.

General The trust makes grants to churches and Christian charities for evangelical Christian causes and also makes a few grants to individual missionaries and Christian workers personally known to the trustees.

In 1998/99 the trust's assets totalled £44,000 and it had an income of £73,000, mostly from donations. Grants totalled £60,000, with nearly 50 organisations supported.

Grants over £1,000 were made to 16 organisations, all of which received grants the year before although of different amounts.

Projects supported included:

- ongoing outreach events through churches in Arundel, West Sussex
- evangelism and care support in Ukraine and South Africa
- Bible distribution in the British Isles and overseas
- missionaries in Africa and Madagascar (personally known to the trustees)
- training of Christian leaders in developing countries
- Christian radio
- training of students in Bible colleges (personally known to the trustees)
- mission hospitals
- hospices in UK.

Exclusions Requests from individuals are not considered unless personally known by the trustees. Requests from non-registered charities are not considered. Requests for building construction or renovation are not considered.

Applications In writing to the correspondent. Funds tend to be committed several years in advance and therefore unsolicited appeals are unlikely to be considered.

The Barnabas Trust

Evangelical Christianity

£426,000 to organisations (1998/99)

Beneficial area UK and overseas

63 Wosley Drive, Walton-on-Thames, Surrey KT12 3BB

Tel. 01932 220622

Correspondent Mrs Doris Edwards, Secretary

Trustees *N Brown; K C Griffiths; D Helden.*

Information available Full accounts were on file at the Charity Commission.

General In 1998/99 the trust had assets of £4.7 million generating an income of £208,000. Grants to 108 organisations totalled £426,000 and to 8 individuals – £11,000. Grants were split into the following categories:

Community welfare
Grants totalling £83,000 were given to 27 organisations. Local, UK and international medical institutions were supported and charities concerned with the welfare of children, the elderly, prisoners, the poor and the general community. Beneficiaries included Shaftesbury Society (£12,000), Princess Alice Hospice (£10,000), Prison Fellowship and Torch Trust for the Blind (£5,000 each), Birmingham City Mission (£2,500) and £1,000 each to Aids Care, Education and Training (ACET), Mathare Community Outreach – Kenya, Victims Outreach UK and Worldshare – Guatemala.

Educational
There were 30 grants given to organisations totalling £61,000.

Grants were given to establishments in the UK and overseas, and general educational charities, including religious education. Beneficiaries included Schools Outreach (£6,500), Haggai Institute (£6,000), Institut Biblique European – France and Book Aid (£3,000 each),

Overseas College – Kenya (£2,000), Bishop Allison Theological College – Uganda (£1,500) and £1,000 each to Church Army, Danoka Training College – Kenya, National Bible Study Club – Eire and Westminster College.

Christian mission overseas
A total of £244,000 was given in 28 grants. The largest grants were £100,000 to SGM International and £75,000 to Bulgarian Church Support Fund. Other grants ranged from £1,000 to £6,000 (although one grant of £75 was also given) and beneficiaries included Medical Missionary News and Wycliffe Bible Translators (£6,000 each); Active Service Support, Operation Mobility and United Mission to Nepal (£5,000 each); Latin Link (£2,500); Emmaus Bible Society and Love Russia (£2,000 each); and LifeLine Network International (£1,000).

Christian mission in the UK
Grants totalling £38,000 were given to 23 organisations. They included £5,000 to Counties Evan Trust, £2,000 to Scripture Union, £1,500 to Manchester City Mission and £1,000 to Christians in Sport. Smaller grants were also given.

The accounts state grants were given to applications from family members of the trustees; S M Lennard's daughter received a grant of £2,000, his son's organisation, Ichtmus Fellowship, received £2,000, and his son-in-law, a vicar, was given £75,000 in grants and £54,000 in loans to buy land in Bulgaria to build a church; and £2,000 was also given to Africa Inland Mission in an application sent by the daughter of N Brown.

Exclusions 'The trust is no longer able to help with building, refurbishment or equipment for any church, since to be of any value grants need to be large.'

Applications In writing to the correspondent, giving as much detail as possible, and enclosing a copy of the latest audited accounts, if applicable. The trust states: 'Much of the available funds generated by this trust are allocated to existing donees. The trustees are willing to consider new applications, providing they refer to a project which is overtly evangelical in nature.' If in doubt about whether to submit an application, please telephone the secretary to the trust for guidance.

The trustees meet four times a year, or more often as required, and applications will be put before the next available meeting.

Lord Barnby's Foundation

General

£199,000 (1998/99)

Beneficial area Unrestricted

PO Box 71, Plymstock,
Plymouth PL8 2YP

Correspondent Mrs J A Lethbridge,
Secretary

Trustees *Sir John Lowther; Lord Newall;
Sir Michael Farquhar; Hon. George Lopes;
Countess Peel.*

Information available Accounts were
available at the Charity Commission,
with only a brief narrative report.

General The foundation has established
a permanent list of charities which it
supports each year, with the remaining
funds then distributed to other charities.
The grants list does not indicate which
charities are on the permanent list. It is
likely that the five charities for the benefit
of the Polish community in the UK are
part of that list, as they receive regular
grants from the trust. The other
beneficiaries are very diverse.

In 1998/99 the trust had assets of
£5.2 million and an income of £190,000.
Grants totalled £199,000 and 75
organisations were supported.

The Countryside Foundation was
allocated two grants totalling £40,000.
Other large grants were £25,000 to
Sherwood Forester War Memorial Trust
and £13,000 to Atlantic College. Nine
grants of £5,000 each included those to
Animal Health Trust, Fairbridge, Prince
Rock Youth Club, Victim Support and
Volunteer Reading Help.

Two-thirds of the grants were for £1,000
to £2,000. Examples include Council for
Music in Hospitals, Disability Challenge,
English Performing Arts Education Trust,
Families Matter, Gordon Foundation,
King Edward VII Hospital for Officers,
Voluntary Services Overseas and Yehudi
Menuhin School. Smaller grants of £200
to £500 included those to Ashtead PCC,
County Air Ambulance Trust and Marine
Conservation Society.

Management and administration costs
were high at £40,000 or 21% of the
income. This works out at a cost of £533
per grant given. When most of the grants
are not more than £2,000 this is not
economic. Unusually, some or all of the
trustees are paid; in 1998/99 they received
a total of £3,800. These editors would like

to note that it is possible to find trustees
of the highest quality that do not require
payment for the interesting and
charitable job of giving someone else's
money away. They also believe that any
professional services provided by a
trustee should ideally be donated to the
trust.

Exclusions No grants to individuals.

Applications Applications will only be
considered if received in writing
accompanied with a set of the latest
accounts.

The Misses Barrie Charitable Trust

Medical, general

£197,000 allocated (1997/98)

Beneficial area UK

Messrs Raymond Carter & Co, 1b Haling
Road, South Croydon CR2 6HS

Tel. 020 8686 1686

Correspondent Raymond Carter,
Trustee

Trustees *R G Carter; R S Waddell;
R S Ogg.*

Information available Full accounts
were on file at the Charity Commission.

General In 1998/99 the trust had an
income of £224,000 and an expenditure
of £197,000. This information was
available on the Charity Commission
database but the accounts were not yet in
the public file. The following information
is repeated from the last edition.

In 1997/98 the income of the trust was
£215,000 and grants totalled £157,000. In
addition, the trustees' report notes that
an amount of £40,000 has been set aside
towards an ultimate grant of a much
larger sum to the RNLI. The assets had
increased to over £5 million by the year
end.

The largest grant was £15,000 to
University of Dundee Biomedical
Research Centre – Influence of Diet. A
further grant of £10,000 went to the same
university for biochemical and genetic
analysis on HIV-1. University of Oxford
– Molecular Immunology Group also
received £10,000.

Other larger grants went to Across Trust
(£7,500), Princess Royal Trust for Carers

(£5,000), Fountain Centre – Cancer Care
(£4,000), and £3,000 each to British
Wireless for the Blind, Children's
Transplant Foundation, Fairplay
Training – Dundee and Winged
Fellowship.

The other grants ranged from £500
upwards, with many of the causes
supported being medical-related,
although a wide range of charities
received grants, both UK charities and
local organisations. Examples included
British Wheelchair Sports Foundation,
Carlisle Cathedral Development Trust,
Croydon HomeStart, Elimination of
Leukaemia Fund, Meridian Trust
Association – Portsmouth, South Cave
Scout Group – East Yorkshire and Wirral
Inroads.

Applications In writing to the
correspondent. Trustees meet quarterly
in March, June, September and
December. Applications need to be
received the month prior to the trustees
meeting.

The Batchworth Trust

Medical, social welfare, general – see below

£205,000 (1998/99)

Beneficial area Worldwide

33–35 Bell Street, Reigate,
Surrey RH2 7AW

Tel. 01737 221311

Correspondent M R Neve,
Administrative Executive

Trustees *Lockwell Trustees Ltd.*

Information available Full accounts
were on file at the Charity Commission.

General The trust mainly supports
large, well-known charities, in the
categories shown below.

In 1998/99 it had assets of £6.3 million
and an income of £257,000. It made 32
grants totalling £205,000, broken down
as follows:

Category	1998/99 %	(1997/98) (%)
Social welfare	44	(38)
Foreign aid	22	(22)
Medical	20	(24)
Youth & education	13	(13)
Environment	1	(2)
The arts	–	(1)

Grants ranged from £1,000 to £15,000. The largest went to International Red Cross (£15,000), Newham Community Health Trust (£13,000) with eight grants of £10,000 each included those to African Medical Mission, Amnesty International, Brick by Brick, Cornerstone Community Care and Nairobi Hospice Charitable Trust.

Smaller grants included those to Action for Kids, Dumfries & Galloway Befriending Project, National Meningitis Trust, Oxford Community Mediation and Village Retail Association. Some of the grants may be recurrent.

Exclusions No applications from individuals can be considered.

Applications In writing to the correspondent. An sae should be included if a reply is required.

The Beacon Trust

Christian

£72,000 (1998/99)

Beneficial area Worldwide

2 Tongdean Avenue, Hove, East Sussex BN3 6TL

Tel. 01273 552036

Correspondent G A Stacey, Trustee

Trustees *Mrs D J Spink; G A Stacey; Miss J M Spink.*

Information available Accounts were on file at the Charity Commission, but with a very brief report and without a list of grants.

General The trust's objects are 'to advance the Christian faith, relieve poverty and advance education'. In 1998/99 the trust had assets of £673,000 generating an income of £55,000. Grants totalled £72,000.

The emphasis of the trust's support is on Christian work overseas, particularly amongst students, although the trust does not support individuals. It gave 28 grants in the year, only the largest was stated. This was £22,000 to Cascadas, a Spanish charity which also received a large grant in the previous year, the trust intends to continue its support of this charity. None of the other grants were listed in the accounts on file at the Charity Commission. The trust has previously stated that it has a list of charities that it supports in most years.

This leaves very little funds available for unsolicited applications.

Exclusions Applications from individuals are not considered.

Applications In writing to the correspondent. The trustees normally meet once a year in December and all applications are generally dealt with at that meeting.

Bear Mordechai Ltd

Jewish

£283,000 (1998/99)

Beneficial area Worldwide

136 Holmleigh Road, London N16 5PY

Correspondent Mrs Leah Benedikt, Secretary

Trustees *Y Benedikt; C Benedikt; E S Benedikt.*

Information available Accounts were on file at the Charity Commission with only a brief report and no grants list.

General Grants are made to Jewish organisations. The trust states that religious, educational and other charitable institutions are supported. In 1998/99 the assets stood at £971,000 and the income was £149,000. Grants totalled £283,000, but no list of beneficiaries was included or any explanation or analysis of grants was available.

Applications In writing to the correspondent.

Beauland Ltd

Jewish

£204,000 (1996/97)

Beneficial area Worldwide, possibly with a preference for the Manchester area

4 Cheltenham Crescent, Salford M7 4FP

Correspondent W Neuman, Trustee

Trustees *W Neuman; F Neuman; H Neuman; M Friedlander; H Roseman; J Bleir; R Delange; M Neuman; P Neuman; E Neuman; E Henry.*

Information available Accounts were on file at the Charity Commission.

General In 1998/99 the trust had an income of £292,000 and an expenditure of £254,000. Unfortunately, no further information for this year was available and this information is repeated from the last edition of this guide.

The trust's objects are the advancement of the Jewish religion in accordance with the Orthodox Jewish faith and the relief of poverty. It gives grants to 'religious, educational and similar bodies'.

In 1996/97 it had assets of £1.4 million and an income of £286,000. Grants totalling £204,000 were mostly given to Jewish organisations, with a possible preference for the Manchester area. No information was available on the recipients of grants in this year.

Previous beneficiaries include Shaarei Zion, MH Communities and Jewish High School. Grants in the Manchester area have included those to Charity Association Manchester, Manchester Junior School, North Salford Synagogue, Manchester Seminary and Manchester Yeshiva.

Applications In writing to the correspondent.

This entry was not confirmed by the trust but was correct according to information on file at the Charity Commission.

The Beaverbrook Foundation

General

£247,000 (1997/98)

Beneficial area UK and Canada

11 Old Queen Street, London SW1H 9JA

Tel. 020 7222 7474

Correspondent Jane Ford, General Secretary

Trustees *Lord Beaverbrook, Chair; Lady Beaverbrook; Lady Aitken, Deputy Chair; T M Aitken; Laura Levi; J E A Kidd; M F Aitken.*

Information available Accounts were on file at the Charity Commission with an inadequate report and without a list of grants.

General In 1997/98 the trust had assets of £15.9 million and an income of £798,000. Grants totalled £247,000. Other

53

expenditure included £180,000 on management and administration, presumably related to managing the trust's properties and £326,000 on renovations to Cherkley Court owned by the trust.

Very little is known about the work of this trust. It has not provided any information on its activities since 1993 when, from an income of £477,000, donations of £332,000 were made in 49 grants. Examples of the largest included: Beaverbrook Canadian Foundation (£100,000); National Association of Boys Clubs (£32,000); Reading University (£14,000); with six awards of £10,000 each to the National Association for the League of Hospital Friends, Raleigh International, Cartoon Art Trust, Isle of Wight Youth Trust, St Thomas Hospital – Tommy Campaign and ReSolve.

Exclusions Only registered charities are supported.

Applications In writing to the correspondent with an sae. Trustees meet in May and November.

The Bellinger Donnay Trust

General, medical, disability, youth

£82,000 (1998/99)

Beneficial area UK, with a preference for Buckinghamshire

30 Burlington Road, Fulmer, London SW6 4NS

Correspondent L A Bellinger

Trustees Sir R I Bellinger; Lady C M L Bellinger; Ms L E Spackman; I A Bellinger.

Information available Accounts were on file at the Charity Commission but without a narrative report.

General In 1998/99 the trust had assets of £1.6 million and an income of £114,000. It gave 53 grants totalling £82,000 and ranging from £50 to £25,000.

The largest grants of £25,000 went to The Broderers Charity Trust and The S A Charitable Trust. Other large grants went to WellBeing (£5,100), Stoke Mandeville Hospital (£5,000), Greater London Fund for the Blind (£1,500) with £1,000 each going to British Red Cross, Dermatrust,

National Society for Epilepsy and Riding for the Disabled South Buckinghamshire.

Smaller grants ranged from £50 to £500 and included those to Blonde McIndoe Centre, Friends of the Earth, Mark Davies Injured Riders' Fund, St Christopher's Fellowship and Westminster Children's Society.

A few grants were recurrent from the previous year.

Exclusions No grants to individuals for education or organised visits abroad.

Applications In writing to the correspondent.

Belljoe Tzedoko Ltd

Jewish

£99,000 (1997)

Beneficial area UK

27 Fairholt Road, London N16 5EW

Tel. 020 8800 4384

Correspondent H J Lobenstein, Trustee

Trustees H J Lobenstein; Mrs B Lobenstein; D Lobenstein; M Lobenstein.

Information available Accounts were on file at the Charity Commission.

General The trust's objects are 'the advancement of religion in accordance with the orthodox Jewish faith and the relief of poverty'.

In 1998/99 the trust had an income of £107,000 and an expenditure of £104,000, this information was available on the Charity Commission database. Unfortunately the accounts for this year were not yet available on file. Only very brief financial statements were available for 1998, giving only the trust's assets at £3,300.

The following information is repeated from the last edition. In 1997 this trust's assets totalled only £5,500, it had an income mainly from donations of £108,000. No grants list was included with the accounts for this year, although they totalled £99,000.

The most recent grants list available in the Charity Commission file was for 1995 when grants totalled £76,000. Donations ranged from £10 to £8,600 and were made to 87 Jewish organisations. The three largest grants were £8,600 to

Marbeh Torah Trust, £7,500 to Society of Friends of the Torah and £5,500 to Yesodey Hatorah School.

Applications In writing to the correspondent.

The Benham Charitable Settlement

Youth, general

£163,000 (1999/2000)

Beneficial area UK, with a special emphasis on Northamptonshire

Hurstbourne, Portnall Drive, Virginia Water, Surrey GU25 4NR

Correspondent Mrs M M Tittle, Managing Trustee

Trustees Mrs M M Tittle; Mrs R A Nickols; E N Langley.

Information available Full accounts were on file at the Charity Commission, together with a narrative report.

General The settlement was founded in 1964 by the late Cedric Benham and his wife Hilda, then resident in Northamptonshire, 'to benefit charities and for divers' good causes and considerations'.

'The trust's policy is to make a substantial number of relatively small grants to registered charities working in many different fields – including charities involved in medical research, disability, elderly people, children and young people, the disadvantaged, overseas aid, missions to seamen, the welfare of ex-servicemen, wildlife, the environment, and the arts. The trust also supports the Church of England, and the work of Christian mission throughout the world. Special emphasis is placed upon those churches and charitable organisations within the county of Northamptonshire.'

In 1999/2000 the trust had assets of £5.9 million which generated an income of £158,000. A total of £163,000 was given in 247 grants. Grants ranged from £100 to £20,000. Northamptonshire Association of Youth Clubs received two grants of £20,000 and £10,000. Other larger grants included £12,000 to The Lambeth Partnership and £10,000 to Coworth Park School, £5,000 to Ridley Hall Development Campaign, £2,000 each to Northampton CCC Appeal,

Northampton High School Appeal and Northampton Symphony Orchestra, with £1,500 to Holy Trinity Church, Sunningdale.

Most other grants ranged from £100 to £500 including those to Anglo Peruvian Child Care Mission, British Lung Foundation, British Wheelchair Sports Association, Church Housing Trust, Defeating Deafness, Friends of the Elderly, Irish School of Ecumenics, MIND, Northampton Festival of Dance, RSPB, Scripture Union, St Andrew's Church Spratton, Disabilities Trust and Mental Health Foundation. A small number of grants ranging from £600 to £900 were also given.

Exclusions No grants to individuals.

Applications In writing to the correspondent. The trust regrets that it cannot send replies to all applicants, nor will they accept telephone calls.

'Applications will be dealt with promptly at any time of year (no application forms necessary), but no charity will be considered more than once each year (repeated applications are automatically ignored for twelve months).'

The Billmeir Charitable Trust

General, health and medical

£128,000 (1998/99)

Beneficial area UK, with a preference for the Surrey area, specifically Elstead, Tilford, Farnham and Frensham

Moore Stephens, 1 Snow Hill, London EC1A 2EN

Tel. 020 7334 9191

Correspondent T T Cripps, Accountant

Trustees B C Whitaker; F C E Telfer; M R Macfadyen.

Information available Full accounts were provided by the trust.

General The trust states it supports a wide variety of causes. About a quarter of the grants are given to health and medical charities and about a third of the grants are given to local organisations in Surrey, especially the Farnham, Frensham, Elstead and Tilford areas.

In 1998/99 the trust had assets of £3.9 million and an income of £109,000. It gave 39 grants totalling £128,000. Of the grants, 23 were to organisations supported in the previous year and were of similar amounts.

The largest grant of £10,000 went to Elstead United Reform Church and Reed School Cobham. Other large grants included those to Elstead Village Halls (£9,000) and £6,000 each to Lord Mayor Treloar School, The Meath Home and RNLI. Grants ranging between £1,000 and £5,000 comprised half of the grants given and included: £5,000 each to Arundel Castle Cricket Foundation, Lodsworth Village Hall, Marlborough College and Youth Sport Trust; £4,000 to Frensham PCC; £3,000 to Royal Star and Garter Home; £2,000 each to Cancer Research Centre Oxford, National Star Centre for Disabled Youth, Pembroke College Oxford and Volunteer Reading Help; and £1,000 to Alzheimer's Research Trust.

Smaller grants included those to Milford & Village Day Centre (£500) and Camelsdale Scout Group (£300).

Applications The trust states that it does not request applications and that its funds are fully committed. Of the grants that were not recurrent, most of the recipients have personal contact with the trustees.

The Birmingham Hospital Saturday Fund Medical Charity & Welfare Trust

Medical

£95,000 (1999)

Beneficial area Birmingham and elsewhere

Gamgee House, 2 Darnley Road, Birmingham B16 8TE

Tel. 0121 454 3601

Correspondent P V Ashbourne, Secretary

Trustees Dr R P Kanas; S G Hall; E S Hickman; M Malone; D J Read; J Salmons.

Information available Full accounts were on file at the Charity Commission.

General The trust was set up to 'maintain an efficient convalescence service, provide comforts and amenities for patients or staff in hospitals and medical charities, assist medical research, education and science, and support of charitable organisations concerned with the sick or disadvantaged'.

In 1999 grants totalled £95,000. The accumulated fund stood at £946,000. The trust's income was £1.9 million of which £1.2 million came from the convalescence centres' accommodation charges. Most of the income was expended with £1.2 million spent on the running costs of the convalescence centres. Other charitable expenditure totalled £115,000.

Grants were given to 35 organisations with the largest being £15,000 to University of Birmingham Centre of Applied Gerontology for specialist research equipment. Seven grants ranging from £3,500 to £5,100 included those to Abbeyfield Stafford Society for a stair-lift for a home for older people, City of Birmingham Special Olympics for a one-day special event, Cruse Bereavement Care for the training of volunteers for bereavement counsellors and Kaleidoscope – Shropshire for an alarm and emergency system for a day care building.

Grants ranging from £1,000 to £3,000 went to 22 organisations and included those to Action on Pre-Eclampsia – Harrow in London for a study day for midwives at City Hospital Birmingham, Albert Bradford School for new seats and seatbelts for a minibus for children with learning disabilities, Brook Advisory Centre for a two-year medical pilot screening programme, Foundation for Conductive Education for a disabled access ramp to a new converted centre, South and West NHS Executive Bristol for a nurse travel scholarship and book prize (1999/2000) and Trinity House Venture for three, three-piece-suites for a refuge for women and children.

Four smaller grants were given ranging from £300 to £875, including those to Kinmos Volunteer Group Ltd for an education programme involving outings and resources for a centre for people who are mentally disadvantaged and to Midlands Art Centre for a sign language interpreter for a show for children who are deaf.

Most grants appear to be one-off.

Exclusions The trust will not generally fund: administration expenditure including salaries; bank loans/deficits/mortgages; items or services which should normally be publicly funded; large general appeals; vehicle operating costs; and motor vehicles for infrequent use and where subsidised vehicle share schemes are available to charitable organisations.

Applications On a form available from the correspondent.

The Peter Birse Charitable Trust

Health and welfare

£84,000 (1998/99)

Beneficial area Worldwide, some preference for the East Riding of Yorkshire and North Lincolnshire

c/o Birse Group plc, Humber Road, Barton-on-Humber DN18 5BW

Tel. 01652 633222

Correspondent Linda Clark, Secretary to the Trust

Trustees *Peter Birse; Helen Birse.*

Information available Full accounts were on file at the Charity Commission.

General The trust's objects are to support the following:

- Local charities in East Yorkshire and North Lincolnshire, particularly those associated with people who are severely disabled or chronically ill.

- To support charities concerned with people who are severly physically disabled, particularly children with cerebral palsy where early treatment can dramatically transform their future.

In 1998/99 the trust had assets of £641,000 (including shares held in the Birse Group plc with a market value of £86,000). The income was £46,000 and £84,000 was given in 19 grants ranging from £100 to £40,000. The largest grants went to Iran Aid (£40,000), Youth at Risk (£20,000) and Médicins Sans Frontiéres (£10,000). Grants ranging from £1,000 to £3,500 went to Christian Orphanage, Hull Women's Aid, Red Cross Sudan Appeal, Save the Children Fund and Welsh Centre for Conductive Education.

Seven grants of £500 were awarded, amongst those to benefit were Disability

Aid Fund, Faith in Leeds and Starlight Children's Foundation. Three grants of £250 each included those to Andrew Marvell Youth Centre and Discovery Camps Trust. One grant of £100 went to Riding for the Disabled.

Exclusions No grants to animal welfare charities or organisations associated with sport or the arts.

Applications In writing to the correspondent. Applications can be considered at any time.

The Miss Jeanne Bisgood's Charitable Trust
(*also known as* The Bisgood Charitable Trust)

Roman Catholic purposes, older people

£75,000 (1998/99)

Beneficial area UK, overseas and locally in Bournemouth and Dorset, especially Poole

12 Waters Edge, Brudenell Road, Canford Cliffs, Poole, Dorset BH13 7NN

Tel. 01202 708460

Correspondent Miss J M Bisgood, Trustee

Trustees *Miss J M Bisgood; Miss P Schulte; P J K Bisgood.*

Information available The information for this entry was provided by the trust. Full accounts were on file at the Charity Commission.

General This trust has emerged following a recent amalgamation of The Bisgood Trust with The Miss Jeanne Bisgood's Charitable Trust. Both trusts had the same objects. It now operates a sub-fund, Bertram Fund (see below). The General Fund has the following priorities:

1. Roman Catholic charities.

2. Charities benefiting people in Poole, Bournemouth and the county of Dorset.

3. National charities for the benefit of older people.

No grants are made to local charities which do not fall under categories 1 or 2. Many health and welfare charities are supported as well as charities working in relief and development overseas.

The trust was given 12 paintings to be held as part of the trust funds. Most of the paintings were sold and the proceeds of the fund were placed in a new fund, The Bertram Fund, established in 1998, the income of which is purely for Roman Catholic causes. It is intended that it will primarily support major capital projects. In 1998/99 the general fund had assets of £850,000 and an income of £70,000. Over 180 grants were given totalling £75,000, ranging from £25 to £2,500. Three grants of £2,500 were made to CAFOD. Grants of £2,500 were also made to St Joseph's Missionary Society, Society of the Holy Child Jesus and The White Fathers.

Grants of £1,000 to £2,000 went to 24 organisations. Beneficiaries were for Aid to the Church in Need, Cardinal Hume Centre, De Paul Trust, Drug and Alcohol Foundation, Help the Hospices, Medical Foundation for the Victims of Torture, The Passage, Research into Ageing, St Barnabas Society and St Francis Leprosy Guild.

Grants ranging from £200 to £500 included those to ADD (Action on Disability & Development), Alzheimer's Research Trust, Bournemouth & Poole College Foundation, Dorset Victim Support, One Plus One Research, Relate and Wessex Cancer Trust.

The majority of the grants (115) were for £100 or less. They included those to Bournemouth Churches Housing Association, Catholic Marriage Guidance, Catholic Scout Chaplaincy, Not Forgotten Association and Sudan Relief and Rehabilitation Association.

The Bertram Fund, in 1998/99, had assets totalling £3.8 million and its income was £126,000. No grants were made during the year.

Exclusions Local charities are excluded unless they fit into categories 1 or 2, see above. Individuals and non-registered charities are also not supported.

Applications In writing to the correspondent, quoting the UK registration number and registered title of the charity. Applications should **not** be made directly to the Bertram Fund. Applications for capital projects 'should provide brief details of the main purposes, the total target and the current state of the appeal'. The trust regrets that they are unable to acknowledge appeals.

The Michael Bishop Foundation

General

£58,000 (1996/97)

Beneficial area Worldwide, preference for the Midlands

BDO Stoy Hayward, Peter House, St Peter's Square, Manchester M1 5BH

Tel. 0161 203 2700

Correspondent Kevin Rourke

Trustees *Sir Michael Bishop, Chair; Grahame N Elliott; John T Wolfe; Peter H T Mimpriss; John S Coulson.*

Information available Accounts were on file at the Charity Commission, but without a list of grants.

General In 1998/99 the trust had an income of £70,000 and an expenditure of £23,000. Unfortunately we were unable to see the accounts for this year as they had not yet been placed in the files at the Charity Commission. The information below is repeated from the last edition.

Sir Michael Bishop of British Midland set up the foundation in 1987 by giving almost £1 million of shares in Airlines of Britain (Holdings) plc, the parent company of British Midland. A further sum was given in 1992. Apparently, it is 'his personal foundation' and he gives to 'charities he's particularly interested in'.

In 1996/97 the foundation had assets of £982,000 and an income of £79,000. Grants totalled £58,000. No further information was given other than the following statement from the trustees' report.

'The D'Oyly Carte Opera Trust has continued to receive the largest share of the foundation's income. Following an unsuccessful application by the D'Oyly Carte Opera trust to receive regular funding from the Arts Council of England ... the trustees have considered it prudent to provide for the withstanding loans due from that trust'. The amount owed to the trust was £760,000.

'Additionally, the foundation has been able to distribute grants to charitable associations or groups supporting activities devoted to health, child welfare, educational and religious aims.'

Support is given primarily in Birmingham and the Midlands.

Exclusions Due to the long-term commitment to the D'Oyly Carte Opera Trust, the foundation is unable to support new applicants at the present time.

Applications To the correspondent in writing, but note the above comments.

The Black Charitable Trusts

Evangelical Christianity, social welfare, young people
See below

Beneficial area UK

6 Leopold Road, London SW19 7BD

Tel. 020 8947 1041

Correspondent M B Pilcher, Secretary

Trustees *K R Crabtree; Mrs J D Crabtree.*

Information available Accounts were filed at the Charity Commission but since 1983/84 without schedules of donations.

General This entry covers three trusts which have the same trustees and share the same administration. In the past a brief report preceding the annual accounts stated that Cyril Black Charitable Trust provides assistance to religious bodies and charities, Edna Black Charitable Trust provides support for evangelism and Sydney Black Charitable Trust provides assistance to youth organisations. The report for all trusts in the latest year stated that support is given to religious, medical and other institutions, such as those helping people who are disadvantaged or disabled.

The Cyril W Black Charitable Trust (CC No. 219857)
In 1998/99 the trust had assets of £1.3 million and an income of £123,000. It gave grants totalling £45,000. Further information was not available.

The Edna Black Charitable Trust (CC No. 253578)
In 1997/98 the trust had assets of £804,000 and an income of £58,000. Grants totalled £46,000. Unfortunately, there is no grants list filed so it is again impossible to see who has benefited from these donations.

The Sydney Black Charitable Trust Limited (CC No. 219855)
In 1998/99 the trust had assets of £741,000 and an income of £73,000. Grants totalled £40,000.

Applications The three trusts effectively operate as one. Applications, made in writing to the correspondent, will be considered by the appropriate trust.

The Bertie Black Foundation

Jewish, general
£109,000 (1998/99)

Beneficial area UK, Israel

Abbots House, 198 Lower High Street, Watford WD1 2EH

Correspondent Mrs I R Broido, Trustee

Trustees *I B Black; Mrs D Black; H S Black; Mrs I R Broido.*

Information available Full accounts were on file at the Charity Commission.

General The trust tends to support organisations which are known to the trustees or where long-term commitments have been entered into. In the trust's 1998/99 annual report they stated that they had reviewed their grant-making policy and had agreed to give some grants over a three-year period 'allowing the beneficiaries a sum for major expenditure'.

In 1999/2000 the trust had assets of £1.7 million and an income of £141,000. Grants totalled £109,000. The largest grants were £25,000 to Exeter University and £22,000 to Jewish Music Heritage Trust, both of which received similar amounts in the previous year. Other larger grants included those to Assaf Harofeh Hospital (£8,200), Norwood Ravenswood (£6,000) and LST (£5,000). Grants ranging from £2,000 to £2,500 included those to Bournemouth & Christ Church Fund, Child Resettlement Fund, Jewish Marriage Council, Kish Aron Day School and Royal Bournemouth Hospital. Many of these grants were recurrent.

Applications In writing to the correspondent, but please note, the trust states it 'supports causes known to the trustees'.

The Blair Foundation

General

£136,000 (1997/98)

Beneficial area UK and overseas

Smith & Williamson, Onslow Bridge Chambers, Bridge Street, Guildford, Surrey GU1 4RA

Tel. 01483 407100

Correspondent Graham Healy, Trustee

Trustees *Robert Thornton; Jennifer Thornton; Graham Healy; Alan Thornton; Philippa Thornton.*

Information available Full accounts were available from the trust, with a detailed narrative report

General Unfortuately we were unable to update this information since the last edition. Figures for 1998/99 were available on the Charity Commission database: the trust had an income of £219,000 and an expenditure of £173,000, but the accounts were not on file.

The foundation was set up by Robert Thornton, of Blair House, Ayrshire, in 1989. It is particularly concerned with creating environmental conditions in which wildlife can prosper, and also with improving access to such areas for people who are disabled. It is currently carrying out work on the Blair estate and other sites it owns in Scotland, Wales and England. In addition, grants are made to other causes.

For the first four years of operation the trust received income from a covenant, this ended in 1993. Since 1993/94 the trust's assets have more than quadrupled, from £181,000 (of which £153,000 was in the form of Bradford & Bingley shares) to £840,000 by 1997/98. The income for the year was £170,000 (£53,000 from investment income and £117,000 from donations and gifts). During 1997/98 the trust gave 28 grants totalling almost £132,000 and smaller donations of less than £1,000 totalled almost £5,000.

During 1997/98, 16 of the beneficiaries listed in the annual report received a grant in the previous year, indeed many have received a number of grants over recent years. The largest grant made up half of the grant total and was given to Ayrshire Wildlife Services (£67,000). The next largest grants were £10,000 to Jewish Care, £5,000 each to Queen Elizabeth Foundation, Home Farm Trust and Macmillan Cancer Relief and £4,000 each to Sense and MNCT. The remaining grants were for £1,000 to £2,500 and were given to organisations such as Live Music Now!, National Trust for Scotland, English National Opera, Daily Football Club and Society for Mucopolysaccharide Diseases.

Applications To the correspondent in writing, for consideration at trustees' meetings held twice a year. A receipt for donations is requested from all donees. The correspondent stated 'I have been inundated with appeals for help, which far exceed the resources available ... the costs of administration are now becoming disproportionate to the funds available'.

Blatchington Court Trust

Education of people under 30 who are blind or partially sighted

£950,000 to organisations (1998/99)

Beneficial area UK, preference for Sussex

Ridgeland House, 165 Dyke Road, Hove, East Sussex BN3 1TL

Tel. 01273 727222 **Fax** 01273 722244

website www.blatchington-court.co.uk
e-mail blatchington.court@virgin.net

Correspondent Derek Arnold, Hon. Treasurer

Trustees *Mrs Margaret Hollinshead; Roger Jones; Dr Geoffrey Lockwood; Richard Martin; Dr Gill R S MacDonagh; Lady Helen Trafford; Mrs Lesley Clarke; Bruce McCleod; Colin Finnerty.*

Information available Full accounts were on file at the Charity Commission.

General This trust's initial income arose from the sale of the former Blatchington Court School for people who are partially sighted at Seaford. Its aim is 'the promotion of education and employment (including social and physical training) of blind and partially sighted persons under the age of 30 years'. There is a preference for Sussex.

In fulfilling its objects, the trust's aims are to:

- develop as a distinct trust with a primary role of an independent facilitator
- focus its resources on clearly defined needs and to avoid any duplication of provision
- listen to, and further the interests of, people who are visually impaired relevant to its objects
- initiate and develop working partnerships with statutory and voluntary organisations concerned with the care of the young people who are visually impaired
- provide professional specialist service to people up to 30 years who are visually impaired
- make grants in pursuance of its objectives.

In 1998/99 the trust has assets of £11.5 million and an income mainly from investments of £494,000. Grants were exceptionally high totalling £1.1 million (in 1997/98 grants totalled £308,000). In addition, expenditure on counselling was about £225,000.

The two largest grants went to SeeAbility for different projects: £525,000 towards the residential unit and day centre for children and young adults who are visually impaired at Barclay House (the trust, which owns the building, has leased it to the organisation for 99 years); and £300,000 towards the construction of a centre for children with Battnes Disease in Hampshire. Other grants included £40,000 to Dorton House School Distance Learning Project, £17,000 to LOOK for the provision of advocacy services and the costs of producing a newsletter, £6,200 to Eastnet Project, £6,000 to Scope and £5,500 to West Sussex Association for the Blind. Smaller grants included those to Berkshire County Blind Association, Bibles for Children, Brighton Society for the Blind, Peter Pan Nursery at Selby and Understanding Industry. Grants to individuals of £1,000 or under totalled £148,000.

Applications In writing to the correspondent from whom individual or corporate/charity grant application forms can be obtained. Applications can be considered at any time. An application on behalf of a registered charity should include audited accounts and up-to-date information on the charity and its commitments.

The Neville & Elaine Blond Charitable Trust

Jewish, education, general

£229,000 (1998/99)

Beneficial area Worldwide

c/o H W Fisher & Co, Chartered Accountants, Acre House, 11–15 William Road, London NW1 3ER

Tel. 020 7388 7000

Correspondent The Trustees

Trustees *Dame S R Prendergast; Peter Blond; Mrs A E Susman; S N Susman; Mrs Jennifer Skidmore.*

Information available Full accounts were on file at the Charity Commission.

General In 1998/99 the trust had assets of £2 million and an income of £111,000. Management and administration costs were low at £4,500. Grants totalling £229,000 were made to 23 organisations, 20 of which were recurrent from the previous year. The main beneficiary was Royal College of Surgeons of England which received £73,000 for The Blond Surgical Training Unit, this is the first part of three grants which will total £197,000.

Other large grants went to East Grinstead Medical Research Trust (£66,000) and JPAIME (£30,000), with £10,000 each to CBF World Jewish Relief, Federation of Women Zionists and WIZO. Other beneficiaries included GRET (£5,000), Halle Orchestra (£4,000) and Jewish Lads and Girls Brigade (£2,500). Grants ranging from £1,000 to £2,000 went to 12 organisations, including Anglo Israel Association, British Friends of Neve Shalom, British Heart Foundation, Chicken Shed Theatre, Institute of Child Health and Westminster School Council for Development.

Exclusions Only registered charities are supported.

Applications In writing to the correspondent. Applications should arrive by 31 January for consideration in late spring.

The Bluston Charitable Settlement

Jewish, general

£112,000 (1998/99)

Beneficial area Mostly UK

BDO Stoy Hayward, 8 Baker Street, London W1U 3LL

Tel. 020 7486 5888

Correspondent Edward Langton, Trustee

Trustees *Edward Langton; Mrs L E Bluston; Martin D Paisner.*

Information available Full accounts were on file at the Charity Commission.

General The trust has general charitable purposes, although in practice most grants are given to Jewish organisations.

The trust had assets of £229,000 in 1998/99, which included 505,000 ordinary shares in Bluston Securities Ltd. The income for the year was £135,000 and grants totalled £112,000.

There were 10 beneficiaries, 9 of which had also received grants in the previous year. Grants ranged from £1,000 to £32,000. The beneficiaries included Nightingale House (£36,000), Jewish Care (£30,000), Norwood Ravenswood (£25,000), Children's Trust (£10,000), Family Welfare Association (£7,000), CHAI Lifeline (£3,000), Centrepoint (£2,000) and St John and Elizabeth Hospice (£1,000).

Exclusions No grants to individuals.

Applications In writing to the correspondent. The trustees meet annually in March.

The Charlotte Bonham-Carter Charitable Trust

General

£93,000 (1998/99)

Beneficial area UK, with some emphasis on Hampshire

66 Lincoln's Inn Fields, London WC2A 3LH

Tel. 020 7242 2022 **Fax** 020 7831 9748

Correspondent Sir Matthew Farrer, Trustee

Trustees *Sir Matthew Farrer; Norman Bonham-Carter; Nicholas Wickham-Irving.*

Information available Full accounts were on file at the Charity Commission.

General The trust is principally concerned with supporting charitable bodies and purposes which were of particular concern to Lady Bonham-Carter during her lifetime or are within the county of Hampshire.

In 1998/99 the trust had assets of £3.8 million and an income of £113,000. It gave £93,000 in 59 grants, ranging from £250 to £15,000. The largest grants went to The National Trust (£15,000), Abbot Hall Art Gallery and Museum (£10,000), Binsted Church (£5,000), Ashmolean Museum (£4,500) and The British Museum (£4,000).

Grants ranging from £1,000 to £2,500 were given to 33 beneficiaries. They included those to British Institute of Archaeology at Ankara, Helen Arkell Dyslexia Centre, Quaker Social Action, Ryedale Folk Museum, St Matthew's C of E Primary School – Blackmoor and York Minster Fund.

Smaller grants, mostly of £500, included those to 2nd Bentley Scout Group, The Barn Owl Trust, Marriage Care, Morland Choristers, Notting Hill Housing Trust, Paintings in Hospitals, St Peter's Church Carnalway and Volunteer Reading Help.

Of the grants, 12 were recurrent from the previous year.

Exclusions No grants to individuals or non-registered charities.

Applications In writing to the correspondent, although the trust states that 'unsolicited general applications are unlikely to be successful and only increase the cost of administration'.

There are no application forms. Trustees meet in January and July; applications need to be received by May or November.

Charles Boot Trust

General

£93,000 (1998/99)

Beneficial area UK and overseas

Meadow Cottage, Church Street, Beckley, Oxford OX3 9UT

Correspondent Miss E J Reis, Trustee

Trustees *John S Reis; Simon C Hogg; Miss Elizabeth J Reis.*

Information available Full accounts were provided by the trust.

General The trust supports large UK charities, many of which are regular beneficiaries. It would prefer to give new grants to locally-based organisations in Oxfordshire.

In 1998/99 the trusts income was £92,000 including £51,000 from investments, all of which are held in Henry Boots & Sons Plc and £18,000 from Gift Aid donations. It gave 13 grants totalling £93,000 and ranging from £1,200 to £15,000.

The largest grant of £15,000 went to NSPCC. Other large grants went to Mental Health Foundation and Shelter (each £10,800), Save the Children and Sense (each £10,000) and Sightsavers International (£8,000). Other grants included those to Sequal Trust (£6,800), Coventry Cathedral (£4,000), Extracare (£3,000), Brainwave (£2,000) and IMPS (£1,200).

Applications In writing to the correspondent.

Salo Bordon Charitable Trust

Jewish, health-related

£68,000 (1997/98)

Beneficial area Worldwide

78 Corringham Road, London NW11 7EB
Tel. 020 8458 5842
Correspondent S Bordon, Trustee

Trustees *S Bordon; Mrs L Bordon; M Bordon; D Bordon; M Bordon.*

Information available Full accounts were on file at the Charity Commission.

General The trust makes grants mainly to Jewish organisations, for social welfare and religious education. In 1998/99 the trust had an income of £338,000 and an expenditure of £114,000. Further information for this year was unavailable.

In 1997/98 its income was £313,000, including £200,000 from donations. After making grants of £68,000 and other expenditure, the surplus was transferred to the trust's capital account, which totalled £4.6 million at the year end.

Over 170 grants were made during the year, mostly of £100 or less. The largest grants were £8,100 to Society of Friends of the Torah, £6,700 to Mir Charitable Trust and £5,600 to Beis Yisroel Trust. A further 11 grants were made of £1,000 or more. All the beneficiaries were Jewish, with the exception of a few health-related charities, which received small grants.

Applications In writing to the correspondent.

The A Bornstein Charitable Settlement

Jewish

£107,000 (1997/98)

Beneficial area UK and Israel

Levy Gee, 66 Wigmore Street, London W1H 0HQ
Tel. 020 7467 4000
Correspondent Peter Musgrave

Trustees *N P Bornstein; M Hollander.*

Information available Full accounts were on file at the Charity Commission up to 1997/98.

General Unfortunately we have been unable to update the following information since the last edition of this guide.

The trust had an income of £264,000 in 1997/98 and made grants totalling £107,000. Over £80,000 was given in four grants: £43,000 to Shaare Zedek Hospital, £20,000 to Friends of Care of the Needy of Jerusalem, and £10,000 each to Friends of Yad Sarah and UJA Federation.

There were 10 smaller grants, of which the smallest was £100 to Save the Children Fund.

Applications In writing to the correspondent.

The Harry Bottom Charitable Trust

Religion, education, medical

£105,000 (1999)

Beneficial area UK, with a preference for Yorkshire and Derbyshire

Westons, Queen's Buildings, 55 Queen Street, Sheffield S2 1DX
Tel. 0114 273 8341 **Fax** 0114 272 5116
Correspondent D R Proctor

Trustees *J G Potter; G T Edwards; Prof. H F Woods; J M Kilner.*

Information available Accounts were on file at the Charity Commission, but without a list of grants.

General The trust states that support is divided roughly equally between religion, education and medical causes. Within these categories grants are given to:

- religion – small local appeals and cathedral appeals
- education – universities and schools
- medical – equipment for hospitals and charities concerned with disability.

In 1998/99 the trust had assets of £3.5 million and an income of £195,000. It gave £105,000 in grants which were broken down as follows:

Medical	£23,000
Religious	£26,000
Other	£55,000

Grants usually range from £200 to £10,000 although occasionally larger grants up to £20,000 have been given. No further information on the beneficiaries was available.

Exclusions No grants to individuals.

Applications In writing to the correspondent.

The A H & E Boulton Trust

Evangelical Christian

£111,000 (1997/98)

Beneficial area Worldwide

Moore Stephens, 47–49 North John Street, Liverpool L2 6TG

Tel. 0151 236 9044

Correspondent J Glasby

Trustees *Mrs J R Gopsill; F P Gopsill.*

Information available Full accounts were on file at the Charity Commission up to 1997/98.

General We have been unable to update this entry since the last edition.

The trust mainly supports the erection and maintenance of buildings to be used for preaching the Christian gospel, and teaching its doctrines. The trustees can also support other Christian institutions, especially missions in the UK and third world.

In 1997/98 it had an income of £176,000 from assets of £3 million. Grants totalled £111,000, with the two largest donations of £25,000 each going to Jireh Evangelical Church and Liverpool City Mission. Other larger grants went to Emmaus Bible School and Bethesda Church (each £15,000), Slanuk Gospel Association (£6,000) and Charles Thompson Mission (£5,000). A further 10 grants of £1,000 or more were listed in the accounts including those to Bible Society, Feba Radio, Gideons International, Leprosy Mission and NSPCC.

Applications In writing to the correspondent. The trust tends to support a set list of charities and applications are very unlikely to be successful.

The P G & N J Boulton Trust

Christian

£63,000 (1998/99)

Beneficial area Worldwide

28 Burden Road, Moreton, Wirral CH46 6BQ

e-mail email@pgnjbt.org.uk
website www.pgnjbt.org.uk

Correspondent Miss N J Boulton, Chair

Trustees *Miss N J Boulton, Chair; L J Marsh; A L Perry; Mrs S Perry.*

Information available Full accounts were on file at the Charity Commission.

General The trust gives a substantial proportion of its support to Christian missionary work; it also supports the areas of poverty relief, medical research, healthcare and disability. It gives preference to smaller charities where 'a relatively small gift can make a significant difference'.

In 1998/99 the trust had assets of £1.8 million and an income of £99,000. Grants totalled £63,000. Other expenditure included property costs of £17,000 and administration of £7,500.

The 16 grants of £1,000 or more were listed in the accounts. The larger grants were £12,000 to Elim Pentecostal Mission Fund, £6,500 to Intercessors for Britain and £4,800 to Just Care. Grants ranging from £1,000 to £3,000 included those to African Enterprise, International Red Cross, Open Doors and Worldwide Christian Outreach. Smaller grants totalled £17,000. Information was not given on the beneficiaries.

Exclusions No grants to individuals.

Applications In writing to the correspondent. Owing to the number of applications received the trustees cannot acknowledge all of them. Successful applicants will be contacted within two months.

The Bowerman Charitable Trust

General

£195,000 to organisations (1997/98)

Beneficial area Preference for West Sussex

Champs Hill, Waltham Park Road, Coldwatham, Pulborough, West Sussex RH20 1LY

Tel. 01798 831205

Correspondent D W Bowerman, Trustee

Trustees *D W Bowerman; Mrs C M Bowerman; Mrs J M Taylor; Miss K E Bowerman; Mrs A M Downham.*

Information available Accounts were on file at the Charity Commission, but without a written report.

General Unfortunately we have been unable to update this information since the last edition. The trust makes grants towards church activities, the arts, medical charities, youth work and charities concerned with relief of poverty and the resettlement of offenders. There is a preference for church-based organisations and local projects in West Sussex, especially in the Pulborough area.

In 1997/98 the trust had assets of £3.7 million. These are mainly fixed assets, including a violin with a market value of £254,000. The income was £241,000 and expenditure £254,000 including donations totalling £227,000. Grants to organisations totalled £195,000 and grants to five individuals totalled £33,000. Other expenditure included management charges, property expenses and rent collection charges.

Grants to 19 organisations of £1,000 or more were listed in the accounts; smaller grants totalled £3,200. The largest grant by far to an organisation was £100,000 to Chichester Cathedral Millennium Endowment Trust. Other larger grants were £15,000 to English Chamber Orchestra, £11,000 each to Chichester Cathedral Trust and St Margaret's Trust, £10,000 to Titus Trust, £7,600 to Royal College of Music and £7,100 to Newbury Festival.

Other organisations supported included Music at Boxgrove (£3,000), Chelsea Festival (£1,500), The Rocking Horse Appeal (£1,200), with £1,000 each to Keep Safe Project, St James' School and Turning Point. Of the organisations listed 11 had also received a grant in the previous year.

Applications In writing to the correspondent. The trustees said that they are bombarded with applications and unsolicited applications will not be considered.

The Bowland Charitable Trust

Young people, education, general

£226,000 (1997)

Beneficial area UK, with a preference for north west England

TDS House, Lower Phillips Road, Whitebirk Estate, Blackburn BB1 5TH

Tel. 01254 676921 **Fax** 01254 676950

Correspondent Mrs Carol Fahy

Trustees *H A Cann; R A Cann; D L Walmsley.*

Information available Full accounts were on file at the Charity Commission.

General In 1999 the trust had an income of £93,000 and an expenditure of £150,000. Unfortunately, no further information for this year was available and this information is repeated from the last edition of this guide.

The trust has general charitable purposes but focuses its support on the 'promotion of educational character forming activities for young people'.

In 1997 it had an income of £113,000, virtually all from donations received. Grants totalled £226,000, nearly all of which was given in five grants to regular beneficiaries. These were Lancaster University (£150,000), Brantwood (£37,000), Nazareth Unitarian Chapel (£25,000), Unitarian Millennium Appeal (£10,000) and Blackburn Cathedral (£1,300). A total of £2,900 was given in smaller grants.

Applications In writing to the correspondent, to be considered at any time.

The Harold and Alice Bridges' Charitable Foundation

General

£93,000 (1997/98)

Beneficial area UK, with a preference for Cumbria and Lancashire

Messrs Senior Calveley & Hardy, Solicitors, 8 Hastings Place, Lytham FY8 5NA

Correspondent R N Hardy, Trustee

Trustees *R N Hardy; J W Greenwood; The Royal Bank of Scotland plc.*

Information available Full accounts were on file at the Charity Commission.

General In 1998/99 the trust had an income of £84,000 and an expenditure of £81,000. Unfortunately, no further information for this year was available and this information is repeated from the last edition of this guide.

The trust concentrates its giving almost exclusively on projects operating in Lancashire from north of the Ribble Valley to the South Lakes. The trustees also favour locally-based projects with a strong element of community benefit and participation, where there has been a degree of fundraising from other community sources. They prefer to contribute to capital costs rather than running expenses.

In 1997/98 the trust had assets of £2.1 million, an income of £87,000 and grants totalled £93,000.

The largest grants were £5,000 each to St Martin's College – Lancaster and Derian House Children's Hospice and £4,000 to Sue Ryder Foundation. Lancaster Nuffield Hospital received £2,500 with seven grants of £2,000 each, given to Abbeyfield Lakeland – Hartley House, Burton Recreation Trust, Disabled Living – Manchester, Fraser Hall – Cowan Bridge, Ladyhulme Community Centre, 5th Lancashire Scout Beaver Cub Pack and Preston & North Lancashire Blind Welfare.

A further 79 grants were virtually all for either £500 or £1,000, given to a range of organisations such as Preston Cruse Bereavement Care, British Stammering Association, Homeless in Blackpool, Kirkby Lonsdale Bowling Club, Morecambe Youth Band, Army Benevolent Fund and Three Owls Bird Sanctuary and Reserve.

Applications In writing to the correspondent, followed by completion of a standard application form.

The British Council for Prevention of Blindness (*also known as* SEE – Save Eyes Everywhere)

Prevention and treatment of blindness

£436,000 see below (1998/99)

Beneficial area Worldwide

12 Harcourt Street, London W1H 1DS

Tel. 020 7724 3716
e-mail bcpb@globalnet.co.uk

Correspondent David Tant, Director

Trustees *Miss Jackie Boulter; Andrew Elkington; Gerard Frost; Richard Porter; Lady Wilson.*

Information available Full accounts were on file at the Charity Commission.

General The BCPB's mission statement is 'to help prevent blindness and restore sight in the UK and developing world by:

* funding research in UK hospitals and universities into the causes and treatments of the major eye diseases
* supporting practical treatment programmes and research in the developing world
* promoting vital skills, leadership, awareness and demand for the expansion of community eye health in the developing world through the education of doctors and nurses within communities.'

The trust's policy is to divide its support equally between projects in the UK and abroad. Grants are given to hospitals, universities and health centres both in the UK and in developing countries. Grants are also given to individuals through the Boulter Fellowship Awards, see below. Grants are usually for a maximum of £40,000 and given for a maximum of three years.

In 1998/99 the trust had assets of £72,000. It had an income of £298,000, from donations (including Gift Aid), legacies and covenants totalling £100,000 and a National Lottery grant of £190,000 for a specfic project. Grants totalled £436,000 to 17 organisations, including two Lottery funded projects. (In the previous year, the grant total was much lower at £163,000.)

Together with the International Centre for Eye Health, BCPB has received Lottery funding for the International Community Eye Health project. It is to be awarded £385,000 over three years to develop community eye health programmes. These are to be run in Colombia, India, Pakistan, South Africa, Nigeria and Tanzania. The programme involves training in six health centres. After the three years it is intended that the six centres will continue to run their own training courses independently although continuing support will be available from the UK. During 1998/99 the project received £171,000 of the funding.

The Department of Ophthalmology & Vision Sciences, Queens University Belfast also received Lottery funding via the trust of £19,000. This was for research on blood retinal barrier breakdown in Diabetic Retinopathy. Six other grants were given by the trust to the International Centre for Eye Health for different research projects around the world. These grants totalled £101,000 and ranged from £8,900 to £38,000. Two hospitals received support, in Cambodia and Malawi.

Six further grants were given to UK organisations, totalling £109,000 and ranging from £11,000 to £44,000. The beneficiaries were University Hospital Nottingham, Institute of Child Health London, the Universities of Aberdeen, Plymouth and Oxford and Queen's University Belfast for research into Glaucoma.

The Boulter Fellowship Awards received £10,000 (the same amount was given in the previous year). Each year two health workers receive a grant to cover tuition fees and living costs enabling them to study at the International Centre for Eye Health in London.

International Centre for Eye Health received three grants in 1997/98 for different projects, but apart from the Fellowship Awards the other grants were not recurrent from the previous year.

Exclusions All except projects directly concerned with research into blindness prevention or restoration of sight. 'We do **not** deal with the individual welfare of blind people in the UK.'

Applications Application forms are available from the correspondent. An initial pro forma must be completed prior to submission of the formal application and must be received no later than the first Monday in June. The deadline for completed applications is the last Friday in July. All projects are subject to a review process and a shortlist made at a meeting in October. All successful grants are awarded in February, unless otherwise stated.

British Record Industry Trust

Musical education

£762,000 (1999)

Beneficial area UK

BPI, 25 Saville Row, London W1X 1AA

Tel. 020 7851 4002 **Fax** 020 7851 4010
e-mail general@bpi.co.uk
website www.brittrust.co.uk

Correspondent Maggie Crowe, Administrator

Trustees *Sam Alder; Paul Burger; John Craig; Rupert Perry; Rob Dickins, Andrew Yeates.*

Information available Information was provided by the trust.

General The trust was established in 1989 and is entirely funded by contributions from the music industry and related organisations in the UK. Its mission is 'to encourage young people in the exploration and pursuit of educational, cultural or therapeutic benefits emanating from music'.

In 2000 grants were given to BRIT School for Performing Arts, British Medicine Performing Arts Trust, Chicken Shed, Drugscope, Heart 'n' Soul, Music in Prisons, Nordoff Robbins Music Therapy Centre and The Princes Trust. Further information was not yet available.

In 1999 the trust had assets of £2 million. Income totalled £1.1 million, made up of: Gift Aid donations of £850,000 from BRIT Awards Limited, including £200,000 from their Abbamania project; other donations from music organisations totalling £193,000; and an interest and investment income of £45,000. Administration and management fees were very low at £22,000. Grants totalling £762,000 were given to seven organisations, four of which were supported in the previous year. Grants were given as follows (1998 figures in brackets where applicable):

Brit School for the Performing Arts and Technology	£260,000	(£120,000)
Nordoff Robbins	£260,000	(£80,000)
National Foundation of Youth Music	£200,000	
Institute for the Study of Drug Dependency	£25,000	(£25,000)
Heart 'n' Soul	£7,200	
Avenues Youth Project	£5,000	(£2,000)
Fairbridge in Kent	£5,000	

Several of the trustees are directors of organisations which donated large sums to the trust; several were also directors of organisations which received large grants.

Exclusions No bursaries or grants to individuals. No capital funding projects are considered. Only registered charities are supported.

Applications In writing to the correspondent.

The Britland Charitable Trust

Christian

£95,000 (1999)

Beneficial area UK and worldwide, with some preference for London

20 Henderson Road, Wandsworth, London SW18 3RR

Tel. 020 7353 2500

e-mail jamiecolman@compuserve.com

Correspondent J M P Colman, Trustee

Trustees *J M P Colman; S E Colman; G D O Bell.*

Information available Full accounts were on file at the Charity Commission.

General This trust makes grants towards the advancement of Christianity, including support for Christian mission work, and Christian education and training.

In 1999 the trust had an income of £77,000, £58,000 of which was donated by family members and those well-known to them. Grants to 11 organisations and 2 individuals totalled about £95,000, which was also the total expenditure of the trust.

A major grant of £90,000 was given to Nehemiah Project to help it 'realise its vision to develop a Christian programme for the rehabilitation of drug and alcohol abusers'. Zambesi Trust received two grants totalling £4,600, whilst smaller grants of between £250 and £500 were given to nine organisations such as Care Trust, Impact Schools Team, Movement for Christian Democracy and SFI Football Fund. Grants were also given to a student and a vicar.

In 2000 the trust planned to assist the parish of St Mark Battersea Rise to modernise their church hall to provide dedicated ministry and teaching facilities equipped for the 21st century.

Applications In writing to the correspondent.

The Britten-Pears Foundation

Promotion of the work of Benjamin Britten and Peter Pears, the arts particularly music by living composers

£252,000 (1997/98)

Beneficial area UK, with a preference for East Anglia

Unit 4g Leroy House, 436 Essex Road, London N1 3QP

Tel. 020 7359 5552 **Fax** 020 7288 0252
e-mail britten@verger.demon.co.uk
website www.britten-pears.co.uk

Correspondent Ruth Orchard, General Director

Trustees *Marion Thorpe, Chair; Dr Colin Matthews; Noel Periton; Hugh Cobbe; Peter Carter; Michael Berkeley; Sir Robert Carnwath; Prof. Rhian Samuel; Mark Fisher; Dr John Evans; Dr Donald Mitchell.*

Information available Accounts were on file at the Charity Commission, but without a grants list.

General Unfortunately we have been unable to update the following information since the last edition of the guide.

The foundation was set up 'to promote the musical works and writings of Benjamin Britten and Peter Pears and the principles of musical education and performance developed by them'. It aims to promote the arts in general, particularly music, by way of grants to other charities or those whose objects are

of charitable intent, for commissions, live performances and, occasionally, recordings and innovatory musical education projects. It also makes grants to educational, environmental and peace organisations. Grants normally range from £100 to £2,500.

The foundation owns and finances the Britten-Pears Library at Aldeburgh, and supports the Britten-Pears School for Musical Studies at Snape and the annual Aldeburgh Festivals in June and the autumn. Its annual income largely derives from the royalties from the performance worldwide of the works of Benjamin Britten, and is channelled to the foundation through its trading subsidiary, Britten Estate Ltd by deed of covenant.

In 1997/98 grants totalled £252,000. Unfortunately further information for this year was not available.

In 1996/97 the foundation had assets of £11 million and an income of just over £1 million (almost £800,000 being the net income from the trading subsidiary). Direct charitable expenditure totalled £551,000. This was broken down as follows:

Grants	£326,000
Britten-Pears Library	£157,000
Red House Complex	£67,000

Grants included £167,000 to Aldeburgh Foundation, £70,000 in annual grants and £89,000 in other grants. Recipients of grants over £1,000 included Chester Summer Music Festival, Drake Music Trust, London Sinfonietta, Music Libraries Trust, National Appeal for Music Therapy, Scottish Chamber Orchestra, Trestle Theatre Company and UEA Environmental.

Exclusions General charitable projects; general support for festivals other than Aldeburgh; requests from individuals for bursaries and course grants other than for Britten-Pears School; travel costs; purchase or restoration of musical instruments or equipment, and of buildings other than at Snape Maltings/ Aldeburgh.

The foundation does not consider applications for support for performances or recordings of the works of Benjamin Britten, of whose estate it is the beneficiary. Subsidy for works by Britten which, in the estate's view, need further promotion, can be sought from The Britten Estate Ltd, which is a subsidiary trading company.

Applications In writing to the correspondent. Trustees meet in January, May and October. Applications should be sent for consideration by the middle of the preceding month. Five copies of any application should be sent.

The Broadfield Trust

Education

£210,000 (1994/95)

Beneficial area UK

c/o H L B Kidsons, Elgar House, Holmer Road, Hereford HR4 9SF

Tel. 01432 352222

Correspondent Ann Sheldon, Accountant

Trustees *Hon. E R H Wills; J R Henderson; Sir A C G Ponsonby; P N H Gibbs; C A H Wills; P J H Wills.*

Information available Full accounts were on file at the Charity Commission.

General In 1998/99 the trust had an income of £201,000 and an expenditure of £139,000. This information was available on the Charity Commission's database but unfortunately the accounts were not yet in the public file. The following is repeated from the last three editions of this guide.

The main beneficiary of this trust in recent years has been Farmington Trust. In fact in 1994/95 it received £208,000 out of a grant total of £210,000. However, in previous years substantial grants have also been given to other organisations.

In 1993/94 Farmington Trust received £238,000 with £40,000 given to the Roberts Centre, £7,000 to Balliol College, £3,500 to Our Lady's Convent Senior School and £2,000 to Manchester College.

The assets of the trust stood at £3.9 million in 1994/95.

Exclusions No grants to individuals.

Applications In writing to the correspondent.

The Bromley Trust

Human rights, conservation

£225,000 (1998/99)

Beneficial area Worldwide

Ashley Manor, King's Somborne, Stockbridge, Hampshire SO20 6RQ

Tel. 01794 388241 **Fax** 01794 388264

Correspondent Keith Bromley, Trustee

Trustees *Keith Bromley; Anna Home; Alan P Humphries; Lady Anne Prance; Anthony Roberts; Lady Ann Wood.*

Information available Full accounts were provided by the trust.

General The aims and objects of the trust are to make grants to charitable organisations which:

'a) combat violations of human rights, and help victims of torture, refugees from oppression and those who have been falsely imprisoned

b) help those who have suffered severe bodily or mental hurt through no fault of their own, and if need be their dependants: try in some small way to off set man's inhumanity to man

c) oppose the extinction of the world's fauna and flora and the destruction of the environment for wildlife and for mankind worldwide.'

The trust's objectives are narrow and it hardly ever departs from them. By far the greater part of the income goes to charities that are concerned with human rights; a comparatively small proportion is given to charities concerned with the preservation of the world environment. In general, conservation interests are limited to the preservation of rainforests and national and international conservation issues, not local projects. One-off grants are occasionally made, but are infrequent. Grants are given to UK-registered charities only.

The trust's declared policy is to give larger amounts to fewer charities rather than spread its income over a large number of small grants. Consequently the trust is slow to add new charities to its list. The trust's mainstream charities normally receive their grants in two half-yearly payments for a period of not less than three years, barring unforeseen circumstances.

The mainstream charities (as at April 2000):

Medical Foundation for the Care of Victims of Torture

The Redress Trust

Anti-Slavery International

Survival International

Prisoners of Conscience Appeal Fund

Amnesty International (UK Section) Charitable Trust

Ockenden International

Asylum Aid

Prisoners Abroad

Prison Reform Trust

Writers & Scholars Educational Trust

Minority Rights Group

Justice Educational & Research Trust

Childhope

International Childcare Trust

Koestler Awards Trust

Institute of Psychiatry – Istanbul Human Rights Centre

Karuna Trust

Womankind

Worldwide

Inside Out Trust

Kurdistan Human Rights Project

Population Concern

Marie Stopes International

Greenpeace Environmental Trust

Durrell Wildlife Conservation Trust

Reserva Ecologica de Guapi Açu (REGUA) (WorldWide Land Conservation Trust)

Birdlife International

Fauna & Flora Preservation Society

British Butterfly Conservation Society

Wildfowl & Wetlands Trust

Wildlife Conservation Research Unit

Countryside Restoration Trust

Aldeburgh Productions

Manic Depression Fellowship

Orchard Vale Trust

Prisoners' Education Trust

The New Bridge

The Hardman Trust

Penrose Housing Association.

The assets of the trust in 1998/99 were £7.6 million (see below) and its investment income totalled £176,000. Grants totalled £225,000 of which £168,000 was given to the regular beneficiaries above. Five one-off donations were given, they were to: Regua – previously known as Serro do Mar Reserva Ecologica (£23,000); three organisations already on the list – Medical Foundation for the Care of

Victims of Torture (£15,000), Amnesty International (£10,000) and The Redress Trust (£5,000); and University of Guelph, Canada (£4,000). A further £4 million was added to the endowment fund during the year, following gifts from the founder. This should lead to a rise in the trust's future annual income and the trustees estimate it is likely to be £300,000 to £330,000 in 2000/2001.

Exclusions No grants for individuals, expeditions or scholarships.

Applications In writing to the correspondent, but note above. The trustees meet twice a year in April and October, applications should be received the previous month. Urgent appeals may be dealt with at any time.

The David Brooke Charity

Youth, medical

£73,000 (1998/99)

Beneficial area UK

26 Briars Close, Pangbourne, Berkshire RG8 7LH

Correspondent D Brooke, Trustee

Trustees *D Brooke; J R Chamberlain; P M Hutt; N A Brooke.*

Information available Full accounts were on file at the Charity Commission.

General The trust supports youth causes, favouring disadvantaged young people, particularly through causes providing self-help programmes and outdoor activity training. Grants are also given to medical organisations.

In 1998/99 the trust had assets of £2 million generating an income of £82,000, a figure much less than in the previous year when it received a donation of £118,000. After administration and management costs of £17,000, grants were given to 29 organisations and totalled £73,000.

Grants ranged from £750 to £4,500 (Finchale Training Centre). Grants were given to a variety of UK and local groups concerned with children's welfare including £3,800 to Scout Association with £3,000 each to Arthritis Research Campaign, Camphill Village Trust, Fortune Centre for Riding Therapy, RNLI, RSPB and Royal College of Surgeons of England, £1,000 to Amelia

Trust Farm and £750 each to British Stammering Association and Berkshire Girl Guides.

Applications The correspondent stated that the trust's annual income is not for general distribution as it is committed to a limited number of charities on a long-term basis.

The Palgrave Brown Foundation

Education, medical, service/ex-service

£74,000 (1998/99)

Beneficial area UK

c/o Barnes Roffe, 24 Bedford Row, London WC1R 4HA

Tel. 020 7831 6393

Correspondent Donald Dooley

Trustees *A P Brown; I P Brown.*

Information available Full accounts were on file at the Charity Commission.

General Grants are given primarily for educational, medical or service/ex-service organisations.

In 1998/99 the trust had assets of £1.4 million generating an income of £233,000. Grants totalled £74,000, with 13 organisations receiving at least £1,000, 4 of which were supported in the previous year. The largest grant was £40,000 to Queens College, Oxford, over half the grant total. Other educational grants included £5,000 to Shrewsbury School Foundation (much less than they have received in recent years) and £2,000 to Oxford University Development Programme.

A range of UK medical organisations were supported including Marie Curie Cancer Care (£4,000) and Parkinson's Disease Society and National Asthma Campaign (£2,000 each). Grants were also given towards service organisations such as Greensleeves Home Trust (£5,000) and British Limbless Ex-Servicemen's Association and Royal British Legion (£2,000 each). A grant of £1,000 was also given to Shadingfield Parochial Church Council.

Exclusions No grants to individuals.

Applications No unsolicited applications.

Bill Brown's Charitable Settlement

Health, social welfare

£74,000 (1998/99)

Beneficial area UK

Payne Hicks Beach, 10 New Square, Lincoln's Inn, London WC2A 3QG

Tel. 020 7465 4300

Correspondent G S Brown, Trustee and Solicitor

Trustees *Percy W E Brown; Graham S Brown; Anthony J Barnett.*

Information available Full accounts were on file at the Charity Commission.

General In 1998/99 the trust had assets of £1.1 million generating an income of £72,000. Grants totalling £74,000 were made to 13 organisations, 10 of which received grants in the previous year. Administration and management costs totalled £11,000.

There were four grants of £10,000 each, given to Macmillan Cancer Relief, Imperial Cancer Research Fund, Leonard Cheshire Foundation and Salvation Army.

Eight grants were for between £2,000 and £5,000 and were given to Alzheimer's Disease Society, Barnardos, John Chilton Charitable Trust, Linden Lodge Charitable Trust, National Association for Colitis & Crohn's Disease, National Children's Home, Princess Alice Hospice and Twickenham & District Association for Mental Health. One small grant of £500 was given to Children with Leukaemia.

Applications In writing to the correspondent, including as much detail as possible. Applications are considered every six months. The trust states that nearly all of its funds are allocated to charities known to the trust and new applications have little chance of receiving grants.

Sir Felix Brunner's Sons' Charitable Trust

General

£76,000 (1998/99)

Beneficial area UK, with a preference for Oxfordshire

Flat 4, 2 Inverness Gardens, Kensington, London W8 4RN

Tel. 020 7727 6277

Correspondent T B H Brunner, Trustee

Trustees *J H K Brunner; T B H Brunner; H L J Brunner.*

Information available Full accounts were on file at the Charity Commission.

General Although UK charities are supported, the trust mainly supports local organisations or local branches of UK charities. Grants are given throughout the UK, although there is a preference for the Oxfordshire area. Most grants are recurrent.

In 1998/99 the trust had assets of £3.2 million producing an investment income of only £67,000. Grants totalled £76,000.

Grants are given for a wide range of causes, which in 1998/99 included St Mary's Millennium Appeal (£10,000); with £5,000 each to Mental Health Research, Oxfordshire Victoria County History Trust and Rugby Science School Appeal; £2,500 each to Knolly's Chapel Charitable Trust, Ashmolean Museum, Burford Priory and Relate Oxfordshire; and £1,000 each to Rotherfield Grey's Village Hall and British School at Rome.

Applications In writing to the correspondent.

Brushmill Ltd

Jewish

£217,000 (1995/96)

Beneficial area Worldwide

Cohen Arnold, 13–17 New Burlington Place, Regent Street, London W1S 2HL

Tel. 020 7734 1362

Correspondent Stanley Davis

Trustees *J Weinberger; Y Getter; Mrs E Weinberger.*

Information available Full accounts were on file at the Charity Commission up to 1991/92, since when the accounts have not included a list of grants.

General Unfortunately we have been unable to update the following information since the last edition of this guide.

In 1995/96 the trust had an income of £134,000, virtually all from Gift Aid. Grants totalled £217,000, but unfortunately, no grants list was available since that for 1991/92.

In 1991/92 the trust had an income of £158,000, down from £283,000 the previous year. Grants totalled £186,000, a slight rise from £167,000 the previous year.

All the grants were to Jewish organisations, the largest to Bais Rochel (£34,000), Friends of Yeshivas Shaar Hashomaim (£15,000) and Holmleigh Trust (£14,000).

Applications In writing to the correspondent.

Buckingham Trust

Christian, general

£132,000 to organisations (1998/99)

Beneficial area UK and worldwide

Messrs Foot Davson & Co., 17 Church Road, Tunbridge Wells, Kent TN1 1LG

Tel. 01892 549955

Correspondent David J Hanes, Trustee

Trustees *D J Hanes; D H Benson; R W D Foot; P R Edwards.*

Information available Full accounts were on file at the Charity Commission.

General In 1998/99 the trust had assets of £689,000 and an income of £164,000 (a 25% increase on the previous year), largely from gifts and donations. Grants to over 200 charities totalled £84,000, grants to 43 churches £48,000 and £6,600 was given to more than 35 individuals.

Grants to charities in 1998/99 were given to UK Christian organisations or similar local groups in London. Beneficiaries included Tearfund (£8,400), Watford New Hope (£2,300) and The Gideons (£1,500). Grants were also given to churches all over the country, including

Lancaster (£4,500), Cambridge (£3,400) and Llandrindond (£2,700).

Applications Unsolicited applications are not considered.

The Bulldog Trust

Arts, medical, youth, general

£130,000 (1998/99)

Beneficial area Worldwide, with a preference for the south of England

Messrs Hoare Trustees, 37 Fleet Street, London EC4P 4DQ

Tel. 020 7353 4522

Correspondent Richard Hoare, Trustee

Trustees *Richard Hoare; Messrs Hoare Trustees.*

Information available Full accounts were provided by the trust.

General In 1998/99 the trust had assets of £4.5 million and a high income of £921,000, including donations of £691,000. The trust had administration costs of only £11,000 and gave grants totalling £130,000. There were 44 grants of at least £1,000, with £23,000 being given in smaller grants.

Although grants are given for general purposes, there appears to be a preference for the arts, health and youth. Grants are given throughout the UK, but most support is given to projects in the south of England.

The largest grants of £10,000 each were given to Brendon Care and Princes Trust. Other grants included £5,000 each to Basingstoke YMCA, Music at Winchester and Royal Opera House, £3,000 to Rescue A Child, £2,300 to New Shakespeare Company Ltd, £1,500 to Theatre 28, £1,200 to London Marathon Ltd and £1,000 each to Kent College, Royal Court Theatre and St John Ambulance.

A number of universities were also supported, with £2,500 given to Edinburgh University and £1,000 each to the universities of Manchester, Nottingham and Oxford.

Exclusions No grants are given to individuals or to unsolicited applications.

Applications In writing to the correspondent, there are no application forms. However, please note that unsolicited applications are not acknowledged and are unlikely to be successful.

The Burden Trust

Christian, welfare, medical research, general

£191,000 (1999/2000)

Beneficial area UK and overseas

Little Clandon, West Clandon, Surrey GU4 7ST

Tel. 01483 222561 **Fax** 01483 224187

Correspondent Malcolm Tosh, Hon. Secretary

Trustees *Dr M G Barker, Chair; R E J Bernays; A C Miles; Prof. G M Stirrat; Bishop of Southwell; M C Tosh.*

Information available Full accounts were provided by the trust.

General The trust operates in accordance with various trust deeds dating back to 1913. These deeds provide for grants for medical research, hospitals, retirement homes, schools and training institutions, homes and care for the young and people in need. The trust operates with an adherence to the tenets and principles of the Church of England.

In 1999/2000 the trust had assets of £4.9 million and an income of £244,000. It gave grants totalling £191,000 to 28 organisations. The largest of £45,000 went to Burden Neurological Institute, regularly the major beneficiary. Other larger grants went to Trinity College, Bristol (£18,000), Langham Research Scholarships (£14,000), Oxford Centre for Mission Studies (£12,000), with £10,000 each to Theological College, Vaux-sur-Seine and Association for Theological Education by Extension, Bangalore. The remaining grants ranged between £1,000 and £9,000. Among the organisations to benefit were All Nations Christian College, London Bible College, Overseas Missionary Fellowship, Research into Ageing and Torch Trust for the Blind.

The majority of grants awarded each year are recurring with only five 'new' beneficiaries in 1999/2000. In addition to the above grants, the trust made provision in 1999 for £500,000 to be paid towards funding research costs of Burden Chair in Clinical Neurosciences at the University of Bristol, £75,000 of this was paid in 1999/2000.

The report highlighted that in addition to those causes supported during 1999/2000 about 480 applications for grants were received, 77 of which were not eligible.

Applications In writing to the correspondent. Financial information is required in support of the project for which help is requested. No application is responded to without an sae.

Recipients of recurring grants are notified each year that grants are not automatic and must be applied for annually.

Applications are considered at the annual trustees' meeting.

The Clara E Burgess Charity

Children

£321,000 (1998/99)

Beneficial area UK and worldwide

The Royal Bank of Scotland plc, Private Trust and Taxation, PO Box 356, 45 Mosley Street, Manchester M60 2BE

Tel. 0161 236 8585

Correspondent The Senior Trust Officer

Information available Full accounts were provided by the trust.

General This recently established trust makes grants to registered charities where children are the principal beneficiaries of the work. Grants are towards 'the provision of facilities and assistance to enhance the education, health and physical well-being of children particularly (but not exclusively) those under the age of 10 years who have lost one or both parents'. Within these boundaries grants can be made to the following causes: education/training, overseas projects, disability, social welfare, hospitals/hospices, medical/ health and medical research.

In 1998/99 its assets totalled £11 million and the income was £600,000. The assets have risen from the estate of the late Douglas Burgess. Trustees fees totalled £87,000 related to 'direct charitable matters' and other trustee fees and management and administration costs totalled £55,000. Grants totalled

£321,000, presumably the majority of the income was transferred to the assets. Grants to 33 organisations ranged from £500 to £45,000.

The largest grants went to National Children's Bureau (£45,000), Winston's Wish (£40,000) with £25,000 each to Barnardos, Save the Children Fund and Selby District Peter Pan Nursery. Seven grants were given ranging from £10,000 to £20,000 including those to Stockdales (£20,000), Starlight Children's Foundation and Children's Country Holidays (each £15,000), Rainbow Centre – Bristol (£13,000) and Jane Lane Jump for Joy Association (£10,000).

Nine grants ranging from £3,000 to £7,000 included those to Dyslexia Institute Bursary Fund (£7,000), Scottish Adoption Association (£5,400) and The Children's Adventure Trust (£3,000). A further nine grants of £1,000 to £2,000 included Open Door Centre – Carrickfergus, Relief Fund for Romania and Young Minds. Three grants of £500 each were given to Butterflies Children's Charity, Sense and Shard End Youth Centre.

Exclusions No grants to non-registered charities.

Applications On a form available from the correspondent. The trustees meet to consider grants in February, May, August and November and applications should be received in the month before those meetings. The trust states that applications should be as brief as possible: the trustees will ask for any further information they require.

The Hon. Dorothy Rose Burns Will Trust

Education, medicine, general

£172,000 to organisations (1997/98)

Beneficial area UK

Fladgate Fielder, Trustees' Solicitor, 25 North Row, London W1R 1DJ

Tel. 020 7323 4747

Correspondent A J M Baker

Trustees *Lady Balfour of Burleigh; Christopher Campbell; Prof. Bernard Cohen; Miss Ann Minogue; Lady Tumin.*

Information available Full accounts were on file at the Charity Commission.

General Unfortunately we have been unable to update the information for this entry since the last edition of this guide.

The policy of this trust is principally to support causes in the following areas:

* In education, by supporting Atlantic College with scholarships for Jamaican students and to assist other educational establishments.
* Also in education, combining this with artistic and cultural activity (in memory of the late Baron Duveen, the settlor's father as well as the settlor), giving six travelling scholarships each year to students at the Slade School of Art and supporting the Duveen section of the Donaldson Library there.
* In medicine, supporting certain hospitals, medical charities and research.
* Supporting other charitable organisations, mainly in the fields of arts, youth and Jamaica.

In 1997/98 the assets of the trust totalled £915,000 and the income was £50,000. Grants were made totalling £209,000 including £37,000 to and on behalf of Duveen Scholars. Just over half the grants were recurrent.

The largest grants, all of which received similar grants the previous year, went to United World College of the Atlantic (£27,000), Slade School of Art (£16,000), Royal Postgraduate Medical School (£10,000) and Attlee Foundation (£7,500). Other grants ranged from £500 to £6,000 with beneficiaries including Acorn Healing Trust, Camden Arts Centre, Foundation for Human Potential, Jamaica Orchestra for Youth, Pushkin Prizes in Scotland, Scope, Technology Colleges Trust and South Bank Centre.

Exclusions No applications from individuals are considered.

Applications In writing to the correspondent at any time.

The Arnold James Burton 1956 Charitable Settlement

General

£252,000 (1998/99)

Beneficial area UK, with a preference for Yorkshire and worldwide

Trustee Management Ltd,
19 Cookridge Street, Leeds LS2 3AG

Correspondent Keith Pailing

Trustees *A J Burton; J J Burton; M T Burton.*

Information available Full accounts were on file at the Charity Commission.

General The trust was set up in 1956 by A J Burton. In 1998/99 the trust had assets of £5 million, an income of £214,000 and grants totalled £252,000.

The trustees' report states that they give preference to registered charities relating to Jewish charities, medical research, education, social welfare and heritage. The report also states that the trust was expected to operate for 50 years. In practice, the trust supports charities already known to the trustees and is not interested in new applications.

Grants of £1,000 or more were listed in the accounts (totalling £218,000). The largest grants were £25,000 to Cookridge Cancer Centre Appeal and £13,000 to Trinity College. Seven grants of £10,000 each were given to Berkshire School, Brain Research Fund, Community Security Trust, Corda, Leeds Jewish Board of Guardians, Marie Stopes International and Royal College of Surgeons of England.

Grants ranging from £2,500 to £8,100 included those to British Technion Society, British Trust for Conservation Volunteers, Leeds Civic Trust, Institute of Psychiatry, JNF and York Millennium Mystery Plays. Most grants ranged from £1,000 to £2,000 and included those to Care International, Dyslexia Institute, Harrogate Hebrew Congregation, Leeds Jewish Welfare Board, Research into Ageing and Sight Savers International.

The grants list shows some preference for organisations in Yorkshire, particularly Leeds.

Exclusions No grants to individuals.

Applications In writing to the trust managers. However, the trust states that its funds are fully committed to charities already known to the trustees and new applications are not invited. Unsuccessful appeals will not necessarily be acknowledged.

The R M Burton Charitable Trust

Jewish charities, social welfare, education, the arts, especially in Yorkshire

£312,000 (1998/99)

Beneficial area England, with a preference for the Yorkshire and Humber area, particularly Leeds; also Israel

c/o Trustee Management Ltd,
19 Cookridge Street, Leeds LS2 3AG

Correspondent The Trust Manager

Trustees *Raymond M Burton; Pamela N Burton; Arnold J Burton.*

Information available Full accounts were on file at the Charity Commission.

General A very wide range of charities are assisted. Grants vary from a few hundred pounds to £100,000 and many are made to organisations previously supported by the trust. There is a strong preference for Yorkshire and the former county of Humberside, with about a third of the grants given in this area.

The trust was established in 1956 by Raymond Burton and for 50 years from that date its income may be used to make grants for charitable purposes. After this period the trust's assets will be given to the founder's descendants. The trust states, however, that the founder has powers to bring forward the wind-up of the trust and this has in part been done in the last year (1999/2000). The trust states that is assets in 1999/2000 are reduced to just over £1 million with an income below £50,000. At least half of the grant-aid goes to Jewish causes with special consideration also given to arts, education and social welfare causes.

In 1998/99 the trust had assets of £5.7 million and an income of £294,000. Grants totalled £312,000, 66 donations over £1,000 were listed in the accounts totalling £273,000. The largest grant of £100,000 went to Joint Jewish Charitable Trust.

The next largest grants were £11,000 to West London Synagogue and seven grants of £10,000 including those to Cookridge Cancer Research Centre Appeal, Friends of the Hebrew University of Jerusalem and Leeds Jewish Welfare Board.

Grants ranging from £3,000 to £5,000 included those to Community Security, University of York, Ryedale Arts and Yorkshire & Humberside Arts Council, with grants ranging from £1,000 to £2,500 going to Abbeyfield York Society, Harrogate Hebrew Congregation, Leeds Festival Chorus, Voluntary Action Leeds, The Woodland Trust and University of Hull. Smaller grants were not listed.

Exclusions Grants are not given to local charities outside Yorkshire or London, individuals or to new charities where their work overlaps with already established organisations which are supported by the trust.

Applications In writing to the correspondent at any time. The trustees try to make a decision within a month. Negative decisions are not necessarily communicated.

The Bill Butlin Charity Trust

General

£84,000 (1998/99)

Beneficial area UK

3rd Floor, Eagle House, 110 Jermyn Street, London SW1Y 6RH

Tel. 020 7451 9000

Correspondent The Secretary

Trustees *R F Butlin; Lady Sheila Butlin; P A Hetherington; T Watts; F T Devine; S I Meaden; T H North.*

Information available Full accounts were on file at the Charity Commission.

General This trust was established by Sir William E Butlin in 1963; it has a preference for organisations working with children, especially those who are disabled, and older people. The trust has a list of regular beneficiaries, to which only a few charities may be added each year. In 1998/99 13 of the 22 groups receiving a grant had been supported in the previous year.

In 1998/99 the trust had assets of £2.3 million generating an income of only £116,000. Grants to 22 organisations totalled £84,000, while the trust had high administration charges of £30,000.

While grants ranged from £500 to £20,000, most tend to be up to £5,000. The larger grants were given to Canadian Veteran's Association UK (£20,000) and Jessie May Trust (£10,000). Recurrent grants included £5,000 each to Barnardos - Queen's Road Bradford Appeal (the last of three grants) and St Wilfrid's Hospice (the last of five grants). Other grants included £5,000 to British Institute for Brain Injured Children, £3,000 to Victims of Violence and £2,000 to Grand Order of Water Rats.

Grants are available to individuals for welfare purposes.

Applications In writing to the correspondent. Trustees usually meet twice a year.

The Christopher Cadbury Charitable Trust

Nature conservation, general

£55,000 (1999/2000)

Beneficial area UK, with a strong preference for the Midlands

New Guild House, 45 Great Charles Street, Queensway, Birmingham B3 2LX

Tel. 0121 212 2222

Correspondent Roger Harriman, Administrator

Trustees *Roger V J Cadbury; Dr C James Cadbury; Mrs V B Reekie; Dr T N D Peet; P H G Cadbury; Mrs C V E Benfield.*

Information available Regular annual accounts were on file at the Charity Commission.

General In 1999/2000 the trust had assets with a market value of £1.6 million and an income of £68,000. Grants totalled £55,000. The trustees have drawn up a schedule of commitments covering 14 charities which they have chosen to support. These charities can receive up to a maximum of £49,000 over a period of five years. Any surplus funds will be given to six other grant-making charitable trusts.

The largest grants made were as follows: Royal Society for Nature Conservation for different projects (£16,000), Playthings Past Museum Trust (£7,500), Fircroft College (£5,500), Croft Trust and Norfolk Wildlife Trust (£5,000 each) and Worcestershire Wildlife Trust (£4,000).

Recipients of smaller grants included Survival International (£1,000), Selly Oak Nursery School (£500) and St Augustine's Church, Edgabaston (£250).

Applications Unsolicited applications are unlikely to be successful.

The Edward & Dorothy Cadbury Trust (1928)

Health, education, arts

£100,000 (1999/2000)

Beneficial area Preference for the West Midlands area

Elmfield, College Walk, Selly Oak, Birmingham B29 6LE

Tel. 0121 472 1838

Correspondent Mrs M Walton, Secretary

Trustees *Mrs P A Gillett, Chair; Dr C M Elliott; Mrs P S Ward.*

Information available Full accounts were on file at the Charity Commission.

General The trust supports registered charities only, with a special preference for health, education and the arts in the West Midlands area. The size of grants vary but most are within the range of £250 to £1,000. Ongoing funding commitments are rarely considered.

During 1999/2000 a total of 136 grants were made totalling £100,000. Assets totalled £3.6 million (of which 55% was shares in Cadbury Schweppes plc) and the income was £130,000. The trust stated in its report that it is continuing with its policy of making fewer larger grants, although this is relative as the majority of its grants are under £1,000. Grants of £1,000 and above were given to 25 organisations. The largest was £9,000 to Avoncroft Museum of Buildings. Other larger grants went to Christian Aid (£7,400), Age Concern – Bromsgrove and Camphill Village Trust (each £5,000), Bromsgrove Festival (£3,800), Bromsgrove Bereavement Counselling

(£3,000) and Centre for Black and White Partnership (£2,000). The 12 grants of £1,000 included those to Birmingham Friendship Housing, Coventry Cathedral, Families Against Tobacco and Alcohol, Kids and National Playbus Association.

The remaining 111 grants of under £1,000 included those to Action Force Volunteers, Design & Manufacture, Dystonia Society, Gap Activity Project, Help the Aged, Memorial to Women World War 2, Mobility Advice Line, St Martin's in the Bull Ring and Sandwell Community Care.

Exclusions No grants to individuals.

Applications To the correspondent in writing, giving clear, relevant information concerning the project's aims and its benefits, an outline budget and how the project is to be funded initially and in the future. Up-to-date accounts and annual reports, where available, should be included. Applications can be submitted at any time but three months should be allowed for a response. Applications that do not come within the policy as stated above will not be considered or acknowledged.

This entry was not confirmed by the trust but was correct according to information on file at the Charity Commission.

The George Cadbury Trust

General

£265,000 (1999/2000)

Beneficial area Preference for the West Midlands, Hampshire and Gloucestershire

New Guild House, 45 Great Charles Street, Queensway, Birmingham B3 2LX

Tel. 0121 212 2222

Correspondent R Harriman, Administrator

Trustees *Peter E Cadbury; Annette L K Cadbury; Robin N Cadbury; Sir Adrian Cadbury; Roger V J Cadbury.*

Information available Full accounts were on file at the Charity Commission.

General The trust was set up in 1924 and maintains a strong financial interest in the Cadbury company. In 1999/2000 the trust had assets of £8 million and an income of £307,000. Grants totalled £265,000 and ranged from £5 to £43,000.

The largest grants went to Symphony Hall (Birmingham) Ltd Organ Appeal (£43,000) and Birmingham Settlement Centenary Appeal (£25,000). Other larger grants ranged from £5,000 to £7,000 and included those to Bower Trust, Edith Cadbury Nursery School, Marine Aid and about four other Cadbury charitable trusts. Grants tend to be recurring. Information on smaller grants was not available.

Exclusions No support for individuals for projects, courses of study, expeditions or sporting tours. No support for overseas appeals.

Applications In writing to the correspondent. Please note that very few new applications are supported.

The George W Cadbury Charitable Trust

Population control, conservation, general

£171,000 (1999/2000)

Beneficial area Worldwide

New Guild House, 45 Great Charles Street, Queensway, Birmingham B3 2LX

Tel. 0121 212 2222

Correspondent Roger Harriman, Trust Administrator

Trustees *Mrs C A Woodroffe; Mrs L E Boal; P C Boal; Miss J C Boal; N B Woodroffe; Miss J L Woodroffe.*

Information available Full accounts were on file at the Charity Commission.

General In 1999/2000 the trust had assets of £6.1 million generating an income of £267,000. Grants totalled £171,000. After administration expenses of £18,000, the trust had a surplus of £78,000. Grants were given in the following geographical areas:

UK	70%
USA	20%
Canada	10%

The trust has general charitable purposes with a bias towards population control and conservation. Family planning and welfare causes received £22,000 during the year.

Altogether 81 grants were given, with 34 of £1,000 and above, the largest grants were £12,000 each to West Chester Children's Association and Haverford College, both in the USA and £11,000 to World Development Movement. Other larger grants ranged from £7,000 to £11,000, mostly given in the USA including Doctors Without Orders, Food for Surival, Gay Mens Health Crisis Inc., Hospice of the North Shore and New York City Ballet Combinations Fund. Other beneficiaries included Planned Parenthood Federation of Canada and Worldwide Fund for Nature UK. Beneficiaries of smaller grants were not listed.

Exclusions No grants to individuals or non-registered charities, or for scholarships.

Applications In writing to the correspondent. However, it should be noted that trustees' current commitments are such that no unsolicited applications can be considered at present.

The Cadogan Charity

General

£522,000 (1996/97)

Beneficial area UK, with a strong preference for Kensington & Chelsea and Central London

The Cadogan Office, 18 Cadogan Gardens, London SW3 2RP

Tel. 020 7730 4567

Correspondent Mr J L Treves, Secretary

Trustees *Rt Hon. Earl Cadogan; Countess Cadogan; Dowager Countess Cadogan; Viscount Chelsea.*

Information available Full accounts were on file at the Charity Commission.

General Unfortunately we have been unable to update the following information since the last edition. In 1996/97 this trust's assets stood at £2.2 million and its income for the year was £696,000. Grants totalled £522,000.

The largest grants went to Royal Veterinary College (£60,000), St Wilfrids (£50,000), Docklands Settlement

(£45,000), NSPCC (£25,000) and Covent Garden Royal Opera House Appeal (£20,000). Four organisations received £15,000: Christ Church Primary School, Imperial Cancer Research Fund, Leukaemia Research Fund and WNCCC Cancer Aware; £12,000 was given to St Mary's Church Birnam; and grants of £10,000 each went to Chelsea & Westminster Hospital – Arts Project, Great Ormond Street Hospital – Epilepsy Monitoring Suite and St David's College Development Appeal.

About 100 smaller grants were made of £500 upwards, also to a wide range of organisations. Those listed under 'A' were Age Concern, Alexandra Rose Day, Almshouses Association, Alzheimer's Research Trust, Animal Health Trust, Artist's General Benevolent Institution and Atlantic Salmon Trust.

Exclusions No grants to individuals.

Applications In writing to the correspondent, who states: 'Please note that contributions are given to a regular list of charities.'

The D W T Cargill Fund

Religious, medical, older people, general

£200,000 (1996/97)

Beneficial area UK, with a preference for West Scotland

190 St Vincent Street, Glasgow G2 5SP

Tel. 0141 204 2833

Correspondent Norman A Fyfe, Trustee

Trustees *A C Fyfe; W G Peacock; N A Fyfe; Mrs M E Graham.*

Information available Information was provided by the trust.

General In 1996/97 the trust had assets of £5.8 million and an income of £230,000. It gave grants totalling £200,000. Over 80% of the income is usually distributed in Scotland. The trust supports religious causes, medical charities, help for older people and general charitable purposes. A large proportion of the income is given in annual grants. These are reviewed each year and the proportion varie; they can comprise over 50% of the grants. One-off grants normally range from £1,000 to

71

£5,000. The categories in 1996/97 were as follows:

Category	%
Local charitable causes	42
Health and medical	40
Older people	7
Religion	4
Lifeboat services	4
Young people	3
Miscellaneous	1

Examples of beneficiaries were not available.

Exclusions No grants are made to individuals.

Applications In writing to the correspondent, supported by up-to-date accounts. Trustees meet quarterly.

Carlee Ltd

Jewish

£210,000 to organisations and individuals (1996/97)

Beneficial area Worldwide

6 Grangecourt Road, London N16 5EG

Correspondent Mrs A Stroh, Secretary

Trustees H Grunhut; Mrs P Grunhut.

Information available Accounts were on file at the Charity Commission, but without a list of grants and only a very brief narrative report.

General Unfortunately we have been unable to update the following information since the last edition of this guide.

In 1996/97 the trust's assets totalled £793,000 and it had an income of £214,000, comprised of rental income and donations received. Grants totalled £210,000. The trust supports Jewish causes and individuals in need, for example, Talmudical scholars, widows and their families. Unfortunately, no other information was available on the beneficiaries.

Applications In writing to the correspondent.

This entry was not confirmed by the trust but was correct according to information on file at the Charity Commission.

The Carmichael-Montgomery Charitable Trust

United Reformed Church, general

£55,000 to organisations (1999/2000)

Beneficial area UK

3 Bear Close, Henley-in-Arden, Warwickshire B95 5HS

Tel. 01564 793561

Correspondent Mrs N Johnson, Trustee

Trustees Mrs W G Baker; D J Carmichael; Miss B Exley; K Forrest; D M Johnson; Mrs N Johnson; Revd M G Hanson; P J Maskell; Mrs S Nicholson.

Information available Accounts were on file at the Charity Commission but without a grants list since 1995/96.

General The main purpose of this trust is to make grants to United Reformed Churches. Grants are normally for capital expenditure and not usually for 'running' expenses, or salaries. In addition, the trustees make small grants to individual young people, who are known either to the trustees or their contacts. The trust would only support organisations which fall outside its criteria if there is a personal contact with one of the trustees.

In 1999/2000 the trust gave 42 grants totalling £62,000, broken down as follows: 24 grants to United Reform Churches totalled £41,000; 10 grants to trusts and societies ranging from £250 to £5,000 totalled £14,000; and 8 grants to individuals totalled £7,100. Unfortunately, further information for this year was not available.

The latest grants list available was for 1995/96 when £49,000 was given in 39 grants. Grants totalling £28,000 were given to 16 United Reformed Churches. Other grants ranged from £200 to £5,000. Beneficiaries included several churches and also Harry Guntrip Memorial Trust (£5,000), The Oasis Appeal (£2,000), The Sports Centre – Moussa Conteh for a project in Sierra Leone (£1,000) and Newcastle College Chaplaincy (£500). Three clergymen received grants totalling about £4,000 and grants to other individuals totalled £600.

Exclusions Grants are not made to medical charities.

Applications In writing to the correspondent. The trustees normally meet in April and October and applications should be submitted in March and September. An sae is not necessary, since the trust does not acknowledge ineligible applications.

The Carpenters' Company Charitable Trust

Education, general

£83,000 to organisations (1998/99)

Beneficial area UK

Carpenters' Hall, 1 Throgmorton Avenue, London EC2N 2JJ

Tel. 020 7588 7001

Correspondent The Clerk

Trustees V F Browne; M R Francis; P C Osborne; D R Stuckey.

Information available Full accounts were on file at the Charity Commission.

General This trust's income is mainly comprised of donations from the Carpenters' Company. In 1998/99 it had an income of £215,000 and grants totalled £227,000.

The trust makes grants in the areas listed below:

EDUCATION

Building crafts college and technical education	£75,000
Educational grants, scholarships and prizes*	£78,000

OTHER CHARITABLE PURPOSES

Richard Wyatt's Almshouses	–
Other donations and gifts*	£74,000
Masters' Gift	£750

Grant-making to general charitable organisations is covered in the two categories marked with an asterisk, and descriptions of these follow.

Educational grants, scholarships and prizes

'Craft grants' were given to 38 individuals and totalled £69,000, about half of this was given to individuals at Building Crafts College. Six organisations also received support, they were: City of London Schools (£2,500), King Edward's School, Witley (£2,000), City of London Freeman's School (£1,500), Carpenter's

Road School (£1,100), Osbourne Fund – an annual award for a student at the Guildhall School of Music and Drama (£1,000) and Exchange Scholarships (£500).

Other donations and gifts

These totalled £74,000, 42 grants of £1,000 and over were listed in the accounts. The largest was £20,000 to Carpenters and Docklands Centre. Other larger grants went to Bayfordbury Pinetum (£5,000), HMS Norfolk Welfare Fund (£4,500), St Paul's Cathedral (£2,500), The Lord Mayor's Appeal and Luton Day Centre for the Homeless (£2,000 each) and Royal Hospital Chelsea (£1,100).

Grants of £1,000 each included those to All Hallow's Church, Alzheimer's Disease Society, Ex-Services Mental Welfare Society, Falkland Islands Memorial Chapel, Listening Books, Macmillan Cancer Relief, Princess Royal Trust for Carers, RNLI, Sail Training Association, Somerset Sustainable Housing, Tate Gallery and Waverley Youth Project. Smaller grants totalled £1,600.

Applications In writing to the correspondent, although the trust states that unsolicited applications are not invited.

The Leslie Mary Carter Charitable Trust

Conservation/ environment, welfare

£84,000 (1998)

Beneficial area UK, with a preference for Norfolk and Suffolk

Birketts, 24–26 Museum Street, Ipswich IP1 1HZ

e-mail sam.wilson@birketts.co.uk

Correspondent S R M Wilson, Trustee

Trustees *Miss L M Carter; S R M Wilson.*

Information available Accounts were on file at the Charity Commission.

General The trust has a preference for nature conservation and wildlife, it also supports welfare organisations. It also favours organisations in Norfolk or Suffolk. Grants generally range from £500 to £5,000.

In 1999 the trust had assets of £2 million, an income of £144,000 and gave grants totalling £67,000. The largest grants were of £6,000 each to Alzheimer's Research Trust and Multiple Sclerosis Society. Grants of £5,000 each went to Action Research, Broughton House Home, Field Studies Council, KGFS, RNIB for Talking Books, RSPB for Dingle Marshes, St Johns Church Clacton and WRNS Benevolent Fund.

Exclusions No grants to individuals.

Applications In writing to the correspondent. Telephone calls are not welcome. There is no need to enclose an sae unless applicants wish to have materials returned.

The Catholic Charitable Trust

Catholic organisations

£58,000 (1998)

Beneficial area America and Europe

Messrs Vernor Miles & Noble, 5 Raymond Buildings, Gray's Inn, London WC1R 5DD

Tel. 020 7242 8688

Correspondent J C Vernor Miles, Trustee

Trustees *J C Vernor Miles; R D D Orr; W E Vernor Miles.*

Information available Accounts were on file at the Charity Commission.

General The trust supports traditional Catholic organisations in America and Europe. In 1998 the trust had assets of £1.7 million and an income of £31,000. A total of £58,000 was given in 15 grants ranging from £1,000 to £15,000. The largest grants went to Society of Saint Pius X (£15,000) and Worth School (£10,000). Other grants included White Sisters (£4,000), The Carmelite Monastery – Carmel, California (£3,000), St Joesph's Catholic Primary School and Society of the Grail (each £2,000) and Ealing Abbey (£1,000). Of the grants, 10 were recurrent.

Exclusions No grants to individuals.

Applications In writing to the correspondent.

The Cattanach Charitable Trust

Homelessness, disability

£134,000 (1998/99)

Beneficial area UK, with a preference for Scotland

The Royal Bank of Scotland plc, Private Trust & Taxation, 2 Festival Square, Edinburgh EH3 9SU

Tel. 0131 523 2648 **Fax** 0131 228 9889

Correspondent Mrs Rhona Muirhead, Senior Trust Officer

Trustees *The Royal Bank of Scotland plc; Col. C H K Corsar; Lord MacLay; F W Fletcher; A R Thomson.*

Information available Full accounts and information was provided by the trust.

General The trust's objectives are the relief of poverty, advancement of education and religion and other purposes which benefit the community. However, the trust has two current themes which will be in operation until 2002, these are homelessness (with a focus on young homeless people under 30) and assisting people who are disabled to achieve their full potential. The themes for 2002 – 2007 will be adopted at the trustees' meeting in June 2000. Preference is given to organisations with a Scottish connection. In addition, the trust will consider any appeals from charities named in the trust deed and any appeals they consider extraordinary. An appeal is regarded as extraordinary if it is urgent, addresses an especially compelling need and will be of direct benefit to those the trust seeks to help.

The trust prefers to fund specific projects either entirely, or with a significant contribution, rather than make small contributions to large projects. It prefers not to commit to permanent funding of long-term projects. Grants usually range from £2,000 to £10,000. Occasionally larger grants are given.

In 1998/99 the trust had assets of £6.4 million, with over £500,000 added to the capital during the year. The income was £240,000. A total of £134,000 was given in 30 grants. The largest grant of £11,000 to ECSH. Three grants of £10,000 each went to Ex-Services Mental Welfare, Glasgow Simon Community and LEAD Scotland.

Other grants included those to Barnardos (£7,000), Big Issue and Samaritans (£5,000 each), Pollockshaws After School Service (£4,500), Princes Trust and Thistles Foundation Centre (£3,000), West of Scotland Children's Society (£2,000) and National Blind Children's Society (£1,000). Only one grant was under £1,000, that was £600 to Freespace.

Eight grants were recurrent from the previous year. The trust includes in its report a listing of all grants made since it was established in 1992. Out of the six years, one charity, SSPCA, has received grants in five years totalling £63,000 while two charities have received grants in four years: Children 1st and Ex-Services Mental Welfare, totalling £98,000 and £19,000 respectively.

Exclusions Only registered charities can receive support. Grants will not be given to fund salaries of staff already in post. Appeals which do not fall into the current themes of homelessness and disability will only be considered if they are urgent and directly benefit those the trust seeks to help.

Applications In writing to the correspondent. It would be helpful to the trust if the following details are included:

* the exact purpose of the grant
* how much is required and how the budget has been worked out
* how the project will be monitored and evaluated
* what other money has been raised and applied for
* a short history of the organisation's aims and functions
* the charity registration number and tax exemption number if one is available
* a copy of the most recent annual report and financial statement
* please also advise if the charity is subject to any investigation by the Charity Commission, Scottish Charities Office or Inland Revenue.

Trustees meet at the end of June and December each year, applications should be sent three months prior to these meetings. Appeals after this deadline will only be considered if they are extraordinary.

The Joseph & Annie Cattle Trust

General

£237,000 to organisations (1998/99)

Beneficial area Worldwide, with a preference for Hull and East Yorkshire

Morpeth House, 114 Spring Bank, Hull HU3 1QJ

Tel 01482 211198 **Fax** 01482 211198

Correspondent R C Waudby, Administrator

Trustees *Joan A Collier; Michael T Gyte; Roy Waudby.*

Information available Full accounts were on file at the Charity Commission.

General The object of the charity is to provide for general charitable purposes by making grants, principally to applicants in the Hull area. Older people and people who are disabled or underprivileged are assisted wherever possible, and there is a particular emphasis on giving aid to children with dyslexia.

The trust's investment income for 1998/99 increased by 8% to £368,000 and the assets rose to £7.4 million. The total income was £396,000 which included a donation of £28,000. Administration expenses were very low at £5,200. Under the terms of the trust deed, 20% of net income (£73,000 in 1998/99) is capitalised. 526 applications for grants were received during the year, of which 248 were approved totalling £298,000; £237,000 of this went to organisations and £61,000 to individuals.

The 75 grants of £1,000 or more were listed in the accounts, 1 was given to an individual and 3 to organisations on behalf of individuals. At least half the grants were given in Hull and the surrounding area. The largest grants were £21,000 to Hull & East Riding Institute for the Blind for a minibus, £20,000 to Brocklehurst Neurosurgical Fund, £10,000 each to Holy Trinity Appeal and Sobriety Project and £6,000 to Godfrey Robinson Home for the Disabled. Grants of £5,000 each went to British Red Cross for Crisis in Central America Appeal, Cottingham Tigers RLFC, Disability Aid for Abilitynet, Hull Compact Ltd and St

Mark's Scout Group with Riding for the Blind receiving £4,500.

The remaining grants listed were for £1,000 to £3,000. They included those to Children with Leukaemia, Depression Alliance, Help an Orphan Ministeries in Malawi, Hull CVS, Hull Fish Trades Boys' Club, North Bransholme Community Association, Pooh Bear Reading Association Society, Royal National Mission to Deep Sea Fishermen, Sailors Families Society, Samaritans, St Nicholas Parish Withernsea and Sick Childrens Trust.

Exclusions Generally no educational grants are given.

Applications In writing to the correspondent. Meetings are usually held on the third Monday of each month.

The Thomas Sivewright Catto Charitable Settlement

General

£200,000 (1998/99)

Beneficial area Worldwide

Clarebell House, 5–6 Cork Street, London W1X 1PB

Correspondent Miss Ann Uwins

Trustees *Hon. Mrs Ruth Bennett; Lord Catto; Miss Zoe Richmond-Watson.*

Information available Full accounts were on file at the Charity Commission.

General In 1998/99 the trust had assets of £6.4 million, a significant increase from £3.3 million in the previous year. This was due to the receipt of a legacy from The Estate of the Honourable Isabel Ida Gordon Catto of £3.7 million. A further £149,000 was given from the legacy to the income fund and grants totalled £200,000 compared to £79,000 the year before. Grants ranging from £50 to £20,000 were given to 177 organisations, of which 103 received less than £1,000.

The largest grants of £20,000 each went to Christian Aid, YWCA and YWCA World Office. Six grants were given of £2,500 to £5,000, including Minchinhampton Centre for the Elderly and Royal Hospital for Neuro-disability

(£5,000 each), Royal Scottish Academy of Music & Drama (£3,000) and Panos Institute Botswana Project (£2,500).

Grants of £1,000 or £2,000 were given to 68 organisations, including Asthma Allergy & Inflammation Research, Hurricane Appeal Central America, Macmillan Cancer Relief, Nottingham Trent University for Skin Cancer Research, RNLI, Royal Surrey County Hospital Children's Unit, West Wittering Memorial Hall and YWCA Scottish National Council.

Smaller grants included those to Aberdeen Children's Society, Alone in London, Breast Cancer Campaign, Friends of Amberley Ridge School, The Dyslexia Institute, Gingerbread, The Horn of Africa Charity, Lupus UK, Martlets Hospice, National Back Pain Association, Royal Scottish Society for Prevention of Cruelty to Children, St Peter's Church Guestwick and Voluntary Service Overseas.

Exclusions The trust does not support non-registered charities, expeditions, travel bursaries etc. or unsolicited applications from churches of any denomination. Grants are unlikely to be considered in the areas of community care, playschemes and drug abuse, or for local branches of UK organisations such as scout groups.

Applications In writing to the correspondent, including an sae.

The Wilfrid & Constance Cave Foundation

Conservation, animal welfare, health, welfare
£140,000 (1998/99)
Beneficial area UK

New Lodge Farm, Drift Road, Winkfield, Windsor SL4 4QQ
Tel. 01344 890351
Correspondent Mrs Lorraine Olsen
Trustees F Jones, Chair; Mrs T Jones; Mrs J Pickin; Revd P Buckler; M D A Pickin; Mrs J Archer; R Walker; Mrs M Payne.
Information available Full accounts were on file at the Charity Commission.

General The trust supports local and UK organisations for general charitable purposes. Grants in 1998/99 were of between £150 and £20,000, although most of the grants were between £1,000 and £5,000. In 1998/99 the trust had assets of £2.1 million generating an income of £92,000. Grants to 59 organisations totalled £140,000. Administration and management costs totalled £18,000.

The largest grant was £20,000 to Camp Mohawk, which often receives large grants from the trust. Grants were also given to Royal Agricultural Benevolent Institution (£15,000), Wey & Arun Canal Trust (£6,000), Save The Family Trust (£5,000), Nuneaton Equestrian Club (£3,500), St Margaret's Hospice (£3,000), Clwyd Special Riding Trust and Ocean Youth Club (£1,000 each) and Rarebreed Survival Trust (£150).

Applications In writing to the correspondent a month before trustees' meetings held twice yearly in May/June and October/November.

The B G S Cayzer Charitable Trust

General
£81,000 (1998/99)
Beneficial area UK

Cayzer House, 1 Thomas More Street, London E1W 1YB
Tel. 020 7553 8224
Correspondent Ms Jeanne Cook
Trustees Peter N Buckley; Peter R Davies.
Information available Full accounts were on file at the Charity Commission.

General In 1998/99 the trust had assets of £1.8 million and an income of £83,000. Grants totalled £81,000, including 18 grants of over £1,000.

The largest grant was given to Feathers Club Association (£35,000), which also received the largest grant in the previous year. Other grants were of up to £6,500 (Royal Horticultural Society) and were given for general charitable purposes, although there appears to be a preference for: medical charities such as Lady Elizabeth Lowe Leukaemia Trust (£5,000) and British Dyslexia Association (£1,300); and the arts including Longholm Music Festival (£2,000) and Royal Academy of Music (£1,000).

Grants were given to local organisations such as Royal College of Surgeons at Edinburgh (£2,000) and Birmingham Royal Ballet School (£1,000), as well as to UK groups including RNLI and St John Ambulance (£1,000 each).

Exclusions No grants to organisations outside the UK. Unsolicited appeals will not be supported.

Applications In writing to the correspondent, although the trust tends to support only people/projects known to the Cayzer family or the trustees.

The Chamberlain Foundation

General
About £100,000 to organisations (1998/99)
Beneficial area UK

Devon House, The Green, Winchmore Hill, London N21 1SA
Tel. 020 8882 9366
Correspondent Ms C L Elmer
Trustees Mrs M J Spears; Mrs G M Chamberlain; G R Chamberlain; A G Chamberlain; Mrs S J Kent; Mrs C M Lester; Mrs L A Churcher.
Information available Full accounts were on file at the Charity Commission.

General In 1998/99 the trust's assets totalled £3.1 million (up from £2.8 million the year before). It had an unusually high income of £415,000 from investments and grants totalled £161,000. In 1997/98, which was a more typical year, the trust had an income of £119,000 and gave grants of £113,000. In 1998/99 the trust divided its giving as follows.

Individuals
Gifts were made to 25 individuals totalling £49,000.

Donations
Grants were given to 37 organisations and 2 individuals, totalling £98,000. It gave an exceptional gift of £50,000 to The Farmhouse in Bucquoy. There were 10 grant given ranging from £1,500 to £3,800 including those to Parkinson's Disease Society, The Ripple Down House Trust, Seven Rivers Cheshire Home, Tourette Syndrome Association Headquarters, Winged Fellowship and

75

the Worshipful Company of Needlemakes.

Grants of £1,000 each went to 15 organisations, including Pace Centre, National Institute of Conductive Education, Boys' Brigade in Enfield 10th Company, Tools for Self Reliance – Middlesbrough and Young Minds. Smaller grants included those to Brainwave, CRUSE and Morning Star Trust. Two grants totalling £5,500 were made to individuals.

Education

A limited number of education grants were given, totalling £13,000. Six grants were given to individuals with the only grants to organisations being £5,000 to Birdham Church of England School and £500 to Christ's Hospital.

Applications In writing to the correspondent. However, the trust states that it is proactive in choosing beneficiaries and the amount available for unsolicited applications is limited. Unsolicited applications are not acknowledged. The trustees meet at least twice a year.

The Chapman Charitable Trust

General

£201,000 (1999/2000)

Beneficial area UK

Crouch Chapman, 62 Wilson Street, London EC2A 2BU

Tel. 020 7782 0007   **Fax** 020 7782 0939

Correspondent Roger S Chapman, Trustee

Trustees *Roger Chapman; John Chapman; Richard Chapman; Bruce Chapman; Guy Chapman.*

Information available Full accounts were provided by the trust.

General The trust was established in 1963 by the late Mrs Marjorie Chapman, whose two sons, with two of her grandsons and one great grandson, are the present trustees. A wide range of charities are supported, with many grants given to health and welfare causes.

In 1998/99 the trust had assets of £5.4 million and an income of £157,000, all of which was given in 120 grants. Grants ranged from £500 to £20,000.

Accounts for 1999/2000 were not available at the time of going to print. However, information about the grants was available. Grants totalled £201,000 and were broken down as shown in the table.

Grants ranged from £500 to £10,000. The main beneficiaries were Aldeburgh Productions which received two grants totalling £20,000 and Field Studies Council (Malham Tarn) which received two grants totalling £15,000. The following organisations received two grants totalling £10,000: Methodist Homes for the Aged, NCH Action for Children, Pesticides Trust, Queen Alexandra Hospital Home and St Bridget's Cheshire Home. Other beneficiaries receiving sizeable grants, from £1,000 to £4,000 (in one or two grants) included Association of Wheelchair, Iris Fund, Living Paintings Trust, National Playing Fields Association, South Bank Centre and Winged Fellowship Trust.

Smaller grants included those to Cambridge Sculpture Workshops, Interplay Theatre Trust, National Library for the Blind, Resources for Autism, Soil Association and Writers News (for Young Writers).

A few of the grants were recurrent from the previous year.

Exclusions No grants to individuals.

Applications In writing at any time. The trustees currently meet to consider grants twice a year at the end of September and March. They receive a large number of applications and regret

that they cannot acknowledge receipt of them. The absence of any communication for six months would mean that an application must have been unsuccessful.

The Charities Fund

Health, disability

£258,000 (1996/97)

Beneficial area UK

Sovereign Health Care, Royal Standard House, 26 Manningham Lane, Bradford, West Yorkshire BD1 3DN

Tel. 01274 729472   **Fax** 01274 722252

Correspondent The Secretary

Trustees *G McGowan; E E Sunderland; E Bentham; S Benson; J Hellawell; S N Johnson; L Morgan.*

Information available Full accounts were on file at the Charity Commission.

General Unfortunately we have been unable to update the following information since the last edition of this guide.

This trust is funded by donations received under the Gift Aid scheme from the investment income of The Hospital Fund of Bradford. Its objects are to provide amenities for hospital patients and to make grants to charities 'for the relief and assistance of needy sick and elderly people'.

In 1996/97 it had an income of £271,000 (including £193,000 from the Hospital Fund of Bradford) and made grants totalling £258,000. Grants were divided in the trust's annual report, as follows:

Grants to hospitals	£1,000
Grants to associations and institutions	£234,000
Grants to hospices	£12,000
Nurses training grants	£11,000

Donations over £1,000 were listed in the report and were made to 41 organisations. The largest grant by far was £42,000 to War on Cancer. Grants of £10,000 were made to Lord Mayor's Appeal, Rainbow Appeal, Sue Ryder Foundation and Stepping Stones.

Other grants listed ranged up to £7,500 and included £6,500 to Cancer Support Centre, £5,000 each to St Gemma's Hospital and West Yorkshire MS Therapy Centre, £4,500 to Arthritis and

THE CHAPMAN CHARITABLE TRUST – GRANT DISTRIBUTION				
	1999/2000		1998/99	
Category	No. of grants	Total	No. of grants	Total
Culture and recreation	15	£37,000	7	£23,000
Education and research	7	£25,000	6	£22,000
Environment and heritage	11	£16,000	10	£5,500
Health	7	£5,000	10	£21,000
Religion	2	£6,000	4	£3,000
Social Services	91	£112,000	83	£94,000

Rheumatism Council and £2,000 each to Bowling Special School and Cerebral Palsy Children's Charity.

A number of beneficiaries had also received grants in the previous year.

Applications In writing to the correspondent.

The Chase Charity

Social welfare, heritage, the arts

£492,000 (1998/99)

Beneficial area UK, with a special interest in rural areas

2 The Court, High Street,
Harwell, Didcot, Oxfordshire OX11 0EY

Tel. 01235 820044

Correspondent Ailsa Holland

Trustees *Gordon Halcrow, Chair; Mrs R A Moore; Ninian Perry; Alexander Robertson; Ann Stannard; Dodie Carter.*

Information available Full accounts were provided by the trust along with a booklet entitled 'How to apply for a grant'.

General The charity was founded in 1962 by a small group of people influenced by the work of a philanthropist, it has three broad areas of interest:

Historic buildings
This includes:

• churches; grants are to small rural parish churches of architectural and historical merit. There must be evidence of local support for the appeal

• almshouses; the trustees prefer to help historic almshouses in rural areas

• other buildings; the trustees will sometimes consider small, interesting buildings in rural areas, but they give priority to historic buildings which are of use to the community.

Promoting the arts in rural areas
They will consider requests from small touring dance, theatre and opera groups for help with one-off costs, and in certain circumstances, producing or running costs.

The trustees would like everybody to be able to enjoy, and where possible participate in the arts, particularly those who live in isolated areas or who are disabled. The trustees recognise the therapeutic value of such involvement, but only support projects which also pursue excellence.

Social welfare
This is an important area of the trustees' work. They are aware that in times of hardship marginalised groups are the most vulnerable. Therefore, the trustees aim to help projects working with the following groups: 'frail elderly people', people with special needs wishing to live independent and fulfilling lives, young people who are in trouble or at risk of getting into trouble, fragile communities – particularly those outside urban areas, vulnerable families and homeless people (only in rural areas). The charity's two previous annual reports detail how penal affairs along with addiction have been removed from their funding list. Another change has been to focus grant-giving to homelessness solely on projects working in rural areas. There was considerable change for this charity in 1998/99. Since 1968 administration has been linked to that of the Lankelly Foundation (see *A Guide to Major Trusts Volume 1*). The two trusts have always remained separate and independent but for the first time the Lankelly Foundation has made a grant of £250,00 to the charity to distribute to organisations working in the arts and heritage. This sum will be distributed within The Chase Charity's existing guidelines with two exceptions. Firstly, there will be a maximum grant of £20,000 available for the capital costs of heritage projects; and secondly organisations based in London will be eligible for a grant.

Last year saw an increase in the grant range from £500 – £5,000 to £1,000 – £10,000. Furthermore the charity decided that it was unrealistic to try to channel funds only to innovative projects when some organisations were struggling to keep going with regard to running costs and salaries. As a result, it was agreed to offer multiple grants, giving help for more than one year at a time. Subsequently they made 30 grants over £5,000, 5 grants towards salary costs, 5 grants over a 2 year period and two over three years. The charity believes that this way of giving also allows them to develop a more rewarding relationship with the grant recipient.

In 1998/99 the charity had assets of £5.5 million and and income of £528,000. It gave 69 grants totalling £492,000. Due to The Lankelly Foundation Arts & Heritage Grant this more than doubled the grantmaking capacity seen in 1997/98.

The grants were broken down as follows:

Almshouses	£25,000	(2 grants)
Arts/community arts	£199,000	(21 grants)
Children & young people	£25,000	(6 grants)
Community welfare	£42,000	(4 grants)
Conservation & museums	£45,000	(5 grants)
Disabilities & special needs	£37,000	(5 grants)
Historic buildings	£37,000	(13 grants)
Homelessness	£37,000	(5 grants)
Neighbourhood work	£28,000	(5 grants)
Older people	£19,000	(2 grants)

Historic buildings
Groups to benefit included: The Church of St Peter and St Paul, Thruxton, Hampshire which received £6,000 towards the cost of internal repair work; All Saints Church, Claverley, Shropshire which received £2,400 to help with repairs to the tower; and St Augustine's Church, Brookland, Kent which received £1,500 towards the cost of creating additional space for community use.

Arts
Beneficiaries included: Performing Arts Lab, Chiddingstone, Kent which received £30,000 towards the cost of Playwrights labs; Ledbury Amateur Dramatic Society, Herefordshire, which received £15,000 towards the cost of building a new theatre; and Norwich Puppet Theatre which received £5,000 towards the cost of a rural tour in autumn 1999.

Social welfare
Groups to benefit included: One Parent Families, York which received £8,000 over two years to help with the running costs of a two year project to develop support groups for lone parents; Barnabas House, Kings Lynn which received £8,000 towards the cost of replacing equipment and to help with the start up costs of a new hostel for homeless women; West Kirby Citizens Advice Bureau which received £3,000 to help with the cost of upgrading the office; and Isle of Ely Youth Forum, Ely, Cambridge which received £2,000 to help with the cost of running a community building for young people.

Exclusions Grants are not made to individuals, including students. Large UK organisations and their branches fall outside the guidelines. Revenue or salary support is only given in exceptional cases. The trustees do not contribute to large appeals or circular letters.

Applications The trust outlined its applications procedure as follows:

'When we receive your letter, if we think we can help, we may seek more information from you and ask you to write back at a stated time (we do not use application forms). If you reply, usually two or three months before the trustees meet, one of the staff will arrange to visit you or meet you at our office. If you have applied to a Lottery Board for the same need, your request will not be considered until after you have heard from the Board. As soon as possible after the trustees' meeting the staff will write to you with the decision; if a grant is agreed, you will be informed of any conditions attached to it.

'We reply to all letters we receive, except for circular letters, and the trustees see summaries of all the applications.

'What we need from you:

- Your initial letter should describe briefly what you do and why you need our help.
- You should describe the origins and status of your organisation e.g. is it a company, charity or co-operative.
- You should enclose your annual report and accounts

'You should answer the following questions:

- How much do you need to raise in total?
- How soon do you need to raise it?
- How much have you already raised?
- Who has given you that money?
- Are you waiting to hear from any other sources of funding
- Have you applied to the Lottery? If so, which Board(s) and for how much?'

Trustees' meetings are held in February, May, September and November.

The Children's Research Fund

Child health research

£216,000 (1998/99)

Beneficial area UK

668 India Buildings, Water Street, Liverpool L2 0RA

Tel. 0151 236 2844 **Fax** 0151 258 1606

Correspondent H Greenwood, Chair

Trustees *H Greenwood, Chair; Dr G J Piller; Prof. J Lister; Rt Hon. Lord Morris of Manchester; E Theobald; G W Inkin; H E Greenwood.*

Information available Full accounts were on file at the Charity Commission.

General The trust supports research into children's diseases, child health and prevention of illness in children at institutes and university departments of child health. The policy is to award grants, usually over several years, to centres of research. It will also support any charitable project associated with the well-being of children.

In 1998/99 the trust had assets of £1.3 million and an income of £198,000. A total of £216,000 was given in 11 grants. The largest grants were £45,000 to University of Liverpool – Department of Paediatrics, £32,000 to Great Ormond Street Hospital and £25,000 each to the Great Ormond Street Hospital Institute of Child Health and University of Southampton – Therapist course. The remaining grants were all to different UK universities, ranging from £650 to £23,000. Five of the grants were recurrent.

Exclusions No grants for capital projects.

Applications Applicants from child health research units and university departments are invited to send in an initial outline of their proposal; if it is eligible they will then be sent an application form. Applications are considered in March and November.

The Childs Charitable Trust

Christian

£295,000 (1997/98)

Beneficial area Worldwide

2–4 Saffrons Road, Eastbourne, East Sussex BN21 1DQ

Tel. 01323 417944

Correspondent D Martin, Trustee

Trustees *D N Martin; R H Williams; A B Griffiths.*

Information available Full accounts were on file at the Charity Commission.

General The objects of the trust are the furtherance of the Gospel of God, education, the relief of poverty and other charitable causes. The principal object is the furtherance of the Gospel of God and the trustees are actively involved in supporting and encouraging all Christian people and societies to achieve this goal. There is a preference for large-scale projects in the UK and abroad and ongoing support is given to some long-established Christian organisations.

In 1997/98 the trust had assets of £6.8 million and an income of £480,000. Grants totalled £295,000. The 28 grants of £1,000 and more were listed in the accounts. A further 72 smaller grants were given totalling £16,000.

The largest grant of £90,000 was given to Mission Aviation Fellowship for the purchase of a light aircraft for use in Christian humanitarian work in Africa. Other large grants included: £60,000 to Home Evangelism; £27,000 to Latin Link towards both establishing a Christian training centre and an orphanage in Ecuador for children whose parents have died of AIDS; Christian Hospital Radio (£15,000); Russian Ministries (£12,000); to Scripture Gift Mission (£10,000) and The Lord's Work Trust (£5,250).

Grants ranging from £1,000 to £3,000 included those to Apostolic Church – Zimbabwe, Bible Society, Faith Mission, Holy Trinity Pregnancy Crisis Centre and Through the Roof.

Applications In writing to the correspondent.

The Chownes Foundation

General

£75,000 to organisations (1998/99)

Beneficial area UK

The Courtyard, Beeding Court, Steyning, West Sussex BN44 3TN

Tel. 01903 816699

Correspondent John Woodman

Trustees *Charles Stonor, Chair; Abbot of Worth; Mrs U Hazeel.*

Information available Full accounts were on file at the Charity Commission.

General The objectives of this trust are the advancement of religion, the advancement of education among the young, the amelioration of social problems and the relief of poverty amongst older people and the former members of Sound Diffusion PLC who lost their pensions when the company went into receivership.

In 1998/99 the trust had assets of £34,000 and an income of £115,000 from Gift Aid donations from the company's directors. Grants totalled £98,000 including six grants to individuals totalling £23,000. Unfortunately no grants list was provided. In the past most beneficiaries have been based in the south of England.

Exclusions Applicant organisations must fit into the above criteria.

Applications In writing to the correspondent.

J A Clark Charitable Trust

Health, education, peace, preservation of the earth, the arts

£169,000 to organisations (1999/2000)

Beneficial area UK, with a preference for south west England

PO Box 1704, Glastonbury, Somerset BA16 0YB

Correspondent Mrs Pauline Grant, Secretary

Trustees *Lancelot Pease Clark; John Cyrus Clark; Thomas Aldham Clark; Caroline Pym, Aidan J R Pelly.*

Information available Full accounts were on file at the Charity Commission.

General The trust was established in 1992. It is concerned with projects oriented towards social change in areas of health, education, peace, preservation of the earth and the arts. Quaker organisations are also well supported. The trustees are particularly interested in supporting the work of small, new or innovative projects.

In 1999/2000 the trust had assets of £8.2 million and an income of £254,000. Grants totalled £169,000.Further information was not availabl forthis year.

In 1998/99 grants totalled £108,000. The largest grant was £19,000 given to Cyrus Clark Charitable Trust. Other large grants included those to Watershed Arts Fund (£8,500), CJC Bursary (£6,000), Jubilee 2000 Coalition and Network Foundation (£5,000 each), Somerset Trust for Integrated Health Care (£3,000) and Street Football Club (£2,000). Smaller grants of between £140 and

£1,000 were also given and included those to Association of Charitable Foundations, Fairtrade Foundation, Prisoners Education and Somerset County Council.

Exclusions No support for independent schools (unless they are for special needs), conservation of buildings or for individuals.

Applications The trust does not seek unsolicited appeals or acknowledge receipt of them. However, all applications are considered and a small number (less than five a year) are contacted with a view to the trustees considering a formal application. The trustees meet to consider grants in March and October each year and applications should be submitted in July and December.

The Roger & Sarah Bancroft Clark Charitable Trust

Quaker, general

£68,000 to organisations (1997)

Beneficial area UK and overseas, preference for Somerset

40 High Street, Street, Somerset BA16 0YA

Correspondent Marianne Ramsey

Trustees *Exleanor C Robertson; Mary P Lovell; Stephen Clark; S Caroline Gould; Roger S Goldby.*

Information available Full accounts were on file at the Charity Commission, but only up to 1997 in September 2000.

General Unfortunately we have been unable to update the following information since the last edition.

The objects of the trust are general charitable purposes with particular reference to:

- Religious Society of Friends and associated bodies
- charities connected with Somerset
- education (for individuals).

In 1997 the trust's assets were £2.2 million of which £1.7 million comprised shares in C & J Clark Ltd. The income for the year was £51,000 and grants totalled £82,000, including £68,000

to organisations and £14,000 to individuals.

A total of 142 organisations were supported. Seven beneficiaries received two or three grants during the year. The vast majority of grants were for less than £1,000, with 58 for £100. The largest three grants were all given to Trustees of Long Sutton Courthouse Charity and totalled £24,000.

Grants of £2,000 each were given to Britain Yearly Meeting of Friends – Swarthmoor Hall Appeal, Oxfam, Quaker Peace Service and The Hickman (Friends Boarding Home of Concord Quarerly). Other organisations supported included a number of local charities throughout the UK, although particularly in the Somerset area, including charities concerned with health and disability, Quaker charities and United Reformed, Baptist and Anglican churches.

Applications In writing to the correspondent. There is no application form and telephone calls are not accepted. Trustees meet about three times a year. Applications will be acknowledged if an sae is enclosed.

This entry was not confirmed by the trust but was correct according to information on file at the Charity Commission.

The Cleopatra Trust

Health, welfare, disability, homelessness, addiction, underprivileged children, environment

£228,000 (1998)

Beneficial area Mainly UK

Charities Aid Foundation, Kings Hill, West Malling, Kent ME19 4TA

Tel. 01732 520081

Correspondent Mrs Barbara Davis, Information Manager

Trustees *Charles Peacock; Mrs Bettine Bond; Dr Clare Peacock.*

Information available Full accounts were on file at the Charity Commission.

General The trust has common trustees with two other trusts, Dorus Trust and Epigoni Trust (see separate entries) with which it also shares the same aims and polices. All three trusts are administered by Charities Aid Foundation (CAF). Generally the trusts support different organisations each year.

The trust makes grants in the following areas:

- mental health
- cancer welfare/education – not research
- diabetes
- physical disability – not research
- homelessness
- addiction
- underprivileged children.

There is also some preference for environmental causes. It only gives grants for specific projects and does not give grants for running costs or general appeals.

In 1998 the trust had assets of £2.9 million (£3.5 million in the previous year) and an income of £267,000. It gave £228,000 in 47 grants. Administration charges to CAF were low at £588, which also received a grant of £2,500. The largest grants of £10,000 each went to nine organisations, including: Centrepoint, Foundation for Conductive Education, Macmillan Cancer Relief, National Osteoporosis Society, Sense and Society for Horticultural Therapy.

Other large grants included Royal Association for Disability & Rehabilitation (£8,000), City Road Youth Counselling (£7,000) and Remap GB (£6,500). There were 13 grants of £5,000 each including those to Colchester YMCA, Dystonia Society, Positively Women and Soil Association. The remaining grants ranged from £500 to £4,000 and included those to Health Action for the Homeless (£4,000), Cardinal Hume Centre (£3,000), Help the Hospices (£2,000), Queen Elizabeth Hospital Childrens Fund (£1,000) and Disability Initiative (£500).

Exclusions Grants are not given to individuals, non-registered charities or for medical research. Organisations with a local or regional focus are not normally supported.

Applications On a 'funding proposal form' available from the correspondent. Applications should include a copy of the latest annual report and audited accounts. They are considered twice a year in mid-summer and mid-winter. Organisations which have received grants from this trust, Dorus Trust or Epigoni Trust should not reapply in the next two years. Usually, funding will be considered under only one of these trusts.

Clover Trust

Older people, young people

£481,000 (1999)

Beneficial area UK and overseas, with a slight preference for West Dorset

Suite 7, Herbert Pepper & Rudland, Accurist House, 44 Baker Street, London W1U 7BD

Tel. 020 7486 5535

Correspondent G F D Wright

Trustees *N C Haydon; S Woodhouse.*

Information available Accounts, but lacking both the required grants list and narrative report, were on file at the Charity Commission.

General This trust supports organisations concerned with health, disability, children and Catholic activities. However, most grants are given to a 'core list' of beneficiaries and the trust states: 'the chances of a successful application from a new applicant are very slight, since the bulk of the income is earmarked for the regular beneficiaries, with the object of increasing the grants over time rather than adding to the number of beneficiaries.' Grants are given towards general charitable running costs, although no grants are given towards building work. Unsolicited applications which impress the trustees are given one-off grants, although only a tiny percentage of the many applications are successful.

In 1999 the trust had assets of £4.6 million and an income of £376,000. Grants to 82 organisations totalled £481,000. Grants ranged from £500 to £30,000.

The largest grants were £30,000 to Action for the Crippled Child and £20,000 each to British Red Cross, Cafod, Downside Settlement and Little Sisters of the Poor.

Exclusions The arts, monuments and non-registered charities are not supported.

Applications In writing to the correspondent. Replies are not given to unsuccessful applications.

Clydpride Ltd

Jewish charities, general

£287,000 (1997/98)

Beneficial area Not known

144 Bridge Lane, London NW11 9JS

Correspondent L Faust, Secretary to the Trustees

Trustees *L Faust; D Faust; T Faust.*

Information available Accounts up to 1997/98 only, and then without a grants list or a narrative report, were on file at the Charity Commission in September 2000.

General In 1998/99 the trust had an income of £169,000 and a total expenditure of £221,000. The income of this trust has been decreasing in recent years. In 1997/98, when the trust had a rental income of £248,000, grants totalled £287,000. It is not known how much was given in grants in 1998/99.

The objectives are to 'advance religion in accordance with the Jewish Orthodox faith, relief of poverty and general charitable causes'.

Applications The trust states that unsolicited applications are not entertained.

The Francis Coales Charitable Foundation

Historical

£108,000 (1999)

Beneficial area UK, especially Bedfordshire, Buckinghamshire, Hertfordshire and Northamptonshire

The Bays, Hillcote, Bleadon Hill, Weston-super-Mare, Somerset BS24 9JS

Tel. 01934 814009 **Fax** 01934 814009 **e-mail** fccf45@hotmail.com

Correspondent T H Parker, Administrator

Trustees *J Coales, Chair; H G M Leighton; A G Harding; E Viney; Revd B H Wilcox; H M Stuchfield.*

Information available Full accounts were on file at the Charity Commission.

General The trust provides grants for the repair of old buildings which are open to the public, for the conservation of monuments, tombs, hatchments, memorial brasses etc. Preference is given to churches and their contents in Buckinghamshire, Bedfordshire, Northamptonshire and Hertfordshire, although grants are made for church monuments irrespective of location.

Grants can also be made towards the cost of archaeological research and related causes, the purchase of documents or items for Records Offices and Museum and the publication of architectural and archaeological books or papers.

In 1999 the assets of the trust stood at £1.8 million and the income for the year was £105,000. Grants approved totalled £108,000 and ranged from £75 to cover the costs of illustrations for a publication to £10,000 for the conservation of a monument in Exton, Rutland.

Larger grants included £5,000 to Society for the Protection of Ancient Buildings to fund 'Craft Fellowship' and £4,000 for the conservation of a monument in Fawley, Buckinghamshire. Nearly two-thirds of the grants were between £1,000 and £3,000. About half the grants are towards building repairs, for example, for repairs to stonework, towers, rooves, windows etc. Other grants included those for bell repairs, conservation of monuments, brasses and wall paintings and for various publications e.g. article on the excavation of Pershore Abbey.

Exclusions No grants for buildings built before 1875, hospitals or hospices. Ecclesiastical buildings cannot receive grants for 'domestic' items such as electrical wiring, heating, improvements or re-ordering.

Applications On a form available from the correspondent.

Applications should include a quotation for the work or the estimated cost, details of the amount of funds already raised and details of funds appliedfor and other bodies approached. Applications for buildings or contents should include a copy of the relevant part of the architect/conservator's specification showing the actual work proposed. 'Photographs showing details of the problems often speak louder than words'.

The trust also states that receiving five copies of any leaflets or statements of finance is helpful so that each trustee can have a copy in advance of the meeting. Trustees normally meet twice a year to consider grants.

The Coates Charitable Settlement

Medical, health, welfare, education

£214,000 (1996/97)

Beneficial area UK, with a preference for Leicestershire

KPMG, Peat House, 1 Waterloo Way, Leicester LE1 6LP

Tel. 0116 256 6000

Correspondent M A Chamberlain, Trustee

Trustees *W C Coates; Ms B M Coates; M A Chamberlain.*

Information available Full accounts are on file at the Charity Commission.

General Unfortunately we have been unable to update the following information since the last edition.

The trust was established in 1992. It supports medical, health, welfare and educational causes.

In 1996/97 it had assets of £442,000 and an income of £25,000. It gave four grants totalling £214,000. The largest was £125,000 to Macmillan Cancer Relief Green Ribbon Appeal. The other grants were: £41,000 to Glenfield Hospital Department of Cardiology, £35,000 to Royal Leicestershire Rutland & Wycliffe Society for the Blind and £13,000 to Leicester Charity Organisation Society – Palliative Care Project.

Exclusions No support for individuals.

Applications In writing to the correspondent.

John Coates Charitable Trust

Arts, children, medical, environment, general

£286,000 (1998/99)

Beneficial area UK

40 Stanford Road, London W8 5PZ

Tel. 020 7938 1944

Correspondent Mrs P L Youngman

Trustees *Mrs McGregor; Mrs Kesley; Mrs Lawes; Mrs Youngman.*

Information available Accounts were on file at the Charity Commission.

General In 1998/99 the trust had assets of £6 million generating an income of £276,000. Grants to 59 organisations totalled £286,000. The trust spent £8,000 on administration, with an additional £48,000 for investment management.

In 1998/99 grants of between £500 and £10,000 were given both to UK organisations and local charities for a variety of causes, with a preference for the arts, children, environment and medical.

Grants given to the arts included Shakespeare's Globe Theatre (£10,000) and Welsh National Opera (£5,000). Grants to children's charities included Great Ormond Street Hopital (£10,000), Purcell School (£5,000) and Youth for Britain (£1,000). Environmental groups receiving support included National Trust (£10,000), National Playing Fields Association (£5,000), Farms for City Children (£1,000) and Barn Owl Trust (£500). Medical organisations benefiting included International Spinal Research and Royal Hospital for Neuro-Disability (each £10,000), and Cancer Research Centre and Cancer Resource Centre (each £5,000). Other grants were given to Chichester Cathedral and Sail Training Association (each £10,000), RNLI (£5,000).

Exclusions Grants are given to individuals only in exceptional circumstances.

Applications In writing to the correspondent. Small local charities are visited by the trust.

Andrew Cohen Charitable Trust

Jewish

£81,000 (1998/99)

Beneficial area UK

Wood Hall Lane, Shenley, Hertfordshire WD7 9AA

Correspondent Mr & Mrs Cohen

Trustees *Andrew L Cohen; Wendy P Cohen.*

Information available Accounts were on file at the Charity Commission, but without a grants list or a narrative report.

General In 1998/99 the trust had assets of £397,000 and an income of £24,000. Grants totalled £81,000 with administration charges just £39.

An up-to-date grants list was unavailable, although in the past grants have ranged from £25 to £126,000 and have been given to JIA, Oxford University L'Chaim Society, Scope Jewish Trust and Imperial Cancer Research.

Applications The trust does not respond to unsolicited applications. It states that its funds are fully committed for the next couple of years and that generally grants are made to organisations that have been previously supported and new applications are unlikely to be successful.

The Denise Cohen Charitable Trust

Health, welfare, arts, humanities, education, culture, Jewish

£88,000 (1997/98)

Beneficial area UK

Paisner & Co., Bouverie House, 154 Fleet Street, London EC4A 2JD

Tel. 020 7353 0299 **Fax** 020 7583 4897
e-mail mpaisner@paisner.co.uk

Correspondent M D Paisner, Trustee

Trustees *Mrs Denise Cohen; M D Paisner; Sara Cohen.*

Information available Full accounts were on file at the Charity Commission.

General In 1997/98 the trust's assets totalled £1.2 million, it had an income of £43,000 and grants were made to 87 charities totalling £88,000. While the trust lists its grants under the following headings in its annual report, beneficiaries include a number of Jewish charities.

Health and welfare
There were 57 charities were supported with grants totalling £42,000, making this the largest category. The main grants were £10,000 to Jewish Deaf Association, £6,300 to Child Resettlement Fund, £5,300 to Nightingale House – Home for Aged Jews and £3,000 to Norwood

Ravenswood. Five grants were made of between £1,000 and £1,500, including those to Chai Lifeline, Foundation for Human Potential and National Schizophrenia Fellowship. The remaining grants were mainly to non-Jewish organisations.

Arts and humanities
Grants totalling £36,000 were made to 12 organisations. The bulk of this was given in the largest grant made in 1997/98: £27,000 to Royal Opera House Trust. Other grants of £1,000 to £1,400 were made including those to Almeida Theatre Co., Designer Crafts Foundation, Israel Music Foundation, The National Gallery Trust and Royal National Theatre.

Education and cultural
Grants totalling £9,400 were made to 16 organisations. These included £2,000 to British Friends of the Council for a Beautiful Israel, £1,900 to Central Synagogue, £1,500 to Western Marble Arch Synagogue and £1,100 to Ben Gurion University Foundation. The remaining grants were all for less than £1,000 and were to Jewish organisations.

Applications In writing to the correspondent.

The Vivienne & Samuel Cohen Charitable Trust
(*also known as* The Charitable Trust of 1965)

Jewish, education, health and welfare

£124,000 (1998/99)

Beneficial area UK and Israel

9 Heathcroft, Hampstead Way, London NW11 7HH

Correspondent Dr Vivienne Cohen, Trustee

Trustees *Dr Vivienne Cohen; M Y Ben-Gershon; G D Cohen; D H J Cohen; J S Lauffer.*

Information available Full accounts were on file at the Charity Commission.

General The majority of the trust's support is to Jewish organisations. In 1998/99 the trust had assets of

£2.9 million and an income of £114,000. Grants totalled £124,000. Of the 121 grants given, only the 7 largest were listed in the accounts. All but one of the beneficiaries were Jewish organisations.

The largest donation was £31,000 to Maaleh Nievo Synagogue. The other grants listed were £13,000 to Maaleh Hatorah School, £10,000 each to British Friends of Sarah Herzog Memorial Hospital, Jerusalem Foundation and World Jewish Relief, £5,500 to B'Nei B'Rith and £5,000 to Variety Club. Six of these grants were recurrent from the year before.

Smaller grants totalled £40,000 but no information was available on the beneficiaries.

Exclusions No grants to individuals.

Applications In writing only, to the correspondent.

Col-Reno Ltd

Jewish

£51,000 (1997/98)

Beneficial area UK, Israel, USA

15 Shirehall Gardens, Hendon, London NW4 2QT

Tel. 020 8202 7013 **Fax** 020 8202 6459

Correspondent Mrs C Stern, Trustee

Trustees *M H Stern; A E Stern; Mrs C Stern.*

Information available Full accounts were on file at the Charity Commission.

General In 1998/99 the trust had an income of £77,000 and an expenditure of £55,000. Unfortunately this was the only information available at the Charity Commission, the full accounts were not yet in the public file.

The trust appears to support only Jewish organisations, with a preference for medical aid organisations and education.

In 1997/98 its assets totalled £331,000 and it had an income of £86,000 from rent on its properties. Grants totalled £51,000 (£29,000 in the previous year). The largest grant £20,000 went to Agudas Yisroel of California. Other larger grants included those to JSSM (£8,100) and Friends of Yeshivas Beis Yisroel (£4,000).

A grant of £6,600 was also made to SOFOT, which is a charity voucher scheme, and was allocated two thirds to

Jewish charities and one third to general charities mainly in the medical field.

The remaining grants ranged between £120 and £2,300.

Applications In writing to the correspondent.

John Coldman Charitable Trust

General, Christian

£61,000 (1999)

Beneficial area UK, with a preference for Edenbridge in Kent

Polebrook, Hever, Edenbridge, Kent TN8 7NJ

Tel. 020 7578 7000

Correspondent D Coldman, Trustee

Trustees D J Coldman; G E Coldman; C J Warner.

Information available Accounts were on file at the Charity Commission, but without a narrative report.

General The trust gives grants to community and Christian groups in Edenbridge, Kent and UK organisations whose work benefits that community such as children's and medical charities.

In 1999 the trust had assets of £33,000 and an income of £61,000, mostly from Gift Aid donations. Grants totalled £33,000. A grants list was not available.

Previous beneficiaries included British Liver Trust, Care and Action for Children with Handicaps, Croydon Colorectal Cancer Appeal, Cypress Junior School, League of Friends – Edenbridge Hospital, Marie Curie Cancer Care, NSPCC, Oasis Trust India and St Peter's Church – Hever.

Applications In writing to the correspondent.

The John & Freda Coleman Charitable Trust

People with disabilities, technical education for young people

£53,000 (1999/2000)

Beneficial area UK, with a preference for Surrey and Hampshire

Tanglewood, Bullbeggars Lane, Woking, Surrey GU21 4SH

Tel. 01483 762289

Correspondent John Round, Administrator

Trustees J P Coleman, Chair; P B Spark; Mrs F M K Coleman; L P Fernandez; A J Coleman; P H Coleman; B R Coleman.

Information available Full accounts were on file at the Charity Commission.

General The trust aims to provide 'an alternative to an essentially academic education, to encourage and further the aspirations of young people with talents to develop manual skills and relevant technical knowledge to fit them for satisfying careers and useful employment. The aim is to develop the self-confidence of individuals to succeed within established organisations or on their own account and to impress upon them the importance of service to the community, honesty, good manners and self discipline'.

In 1999/2000 the trust had assets of £1.1 million and an income of £102,000. Grants totalled £53,000.

The largest grant was £20,000 to RNIB which regularly receives a large grant from the trust. No further information for this year was available. In 1998/99 other beneficiaries included First Partnership, Lord Mayors Treloars Trust, Sayers Croft, Surrey Science and Technology Regional Office and Understanding Industry.

Exclusions No grants are made to students.

Applications In writing to the correspondent.

The Sir Jeremiah Colman Gift Trust

General

£91,000 (1998/99)

Beneficial area UK, with a preference for Hampshire especially Basingstoke

Malshanger, Basingstoke, Hampshire RG23 7EY

Correspondent Sir Michael Colman, Trustee

Trustees Sir Michael Colman; Lady Judith Colman; Oliver J Colman; Cynthia Colman; Jeremiah M Colman.

Information available Accounts were provided by the trust, but no report or grants list was included.

General The trust has special regard to:

* advancement of education and literary scientific knowledge
* moral and social improvement of people
* maintenance of churches of the Church of England and gifts and offerings to the churches
* financial assistance to past and present employees/members of Sir Jeremiah Colman at Gatton Park, J & J Colman Ltd or other clubs and institutions associated with Sir Jeremiah Colman.

In 1998/99 the trust had assets of £2.1 million and an income of £104,000. Grants totalled £91,000 and were broken down as follows:

Annual grants	£56,000
Extra grants	£4,000
Special grant	£31,000

Further information on the beneficiaries was not available.

In 1997/98 grants totalled £82,000. Most of the grants given are recurrent, and most organisations received the same amounts as they have over recent years. Most awards are for under £1,000, with an emphasis on Hampshire, particularly Basingstoke. Grants to the UK charities generally seem to go to the bigger, well-known ones.

Only 8 of the 164 annual grants were for £1,000 or more including those to Basingstoke & North Hampshire Medical Trust, Church of England Pensions Fund, National Art Collections Fund and Skinners Company School for Girls.

The 'special' grants included £7,000 for 'new appeals' given in grants ranging from £50 to £1,000. Recipients included Almshouses Association, Claybury Trust, Hampshire Musicspace Trust and Volunteer Reading Help. £19,000 was given in 'long-term payments' to charities receiving grants for three to five years and ranging from £150 a year to £5,000 a year. Beneficiaries include Ark Facility, Herbal Research Phytotherapy, Police Foundation and Wessex Children's Hospice.

The 12 'extra' grants ranged from £50 to £1,000, with a range of charities supported.

Applications 'The funds of the trust are fully committed and any unsolicited applications are most unlikely to be successful.'

The Colt Foundation

Occupational and environmental health research

£344,000 to organisations (1998/99)

Beneficial area UK

New Lane, Havant, Hampshire PO9 2LY
Tel. 023 9249 1400   Fax 023 9249 1363
Correspondent Miss Jacqueline Riley
Trustees *Jerome O'Hea, Chair; Mrs Mary Ault; Timothy Ault; Mrs Clare Gilchrist; Mrs Patricia Lebus; Walter McD Morison; Alan O'Hea; Peter O'Hea. Prof. D Denison and Prof. D Coggon act as Scientific Advisers.*
Information available Report and accounts with grants list and narrative explanation of grants and grant-making policy.

General Grants are made to support organisations and post-graduate students for research into occupational and environmental medicine. Donations to organisations vary from a few thousand pounds to £100,000 and may be repeated over two to five years. Beneficiaries are well established research institutes (awards to individuals are made through such), usually already well known to the foundation

The trust was established in 1978 by the O'Hea family with an initial gift of a 30% stake in the Colt Group ltd. Its original and current purpose is 'the promotion and encouragement of research into social, medical and environmental problems created by commerce and industry'.

In 1998/99 the foundation had assets totalling £11.7 million from which £539,000 in income was generated. Fourteen grants amounting to £344,000 were made to organisations and a total of £144,000 was awarded to an unknown number of students. Grants to universities and other organisations for scientific research received 70% of the funds (81% in the previous year) and grants to students or for the benefit of students in higher education received 30% (19% in the previous year). Of the organisations, some had been supported in the previous year and most have long-term funding relationships with the trust. The largest grants were to the National Heart and Lung Institute (£108,000), Institute of Occupational Health (£54,000), St George's Hospital Medical School (£33,000) and Imperial College of Science, Technology & Medicine (£27,000). Grants ranging from £10,000 to £22,000 went to six organisations including those to Back Pain Association and Napier University. Other grants ranged from £1,600 to £6,000 including those to Hearing Research Trust (£6,100), University of Newcastle (£4,300) and Colt Foundation Day (£1,600).

The trust has stated: 'We are interested in research into the causes of illnesses resulting from conditions at the place of work and in the wider environment. Such conditions are rarely, if ever, the sole cause, but we are interested if these are a significant factor. We are only interested where the science is of the highest quality and the subject is relevant to human welfare. We prefer to be the sole source of finance in a project. We never contribute to the general funds of another charity and we do not support overseas projects simply because we have not got the resources to assess or supervise them. We aim to help not only with money, but from the experience of our scientific advisors, and of our trustees, to make a constructive input. We support students for higher degrees in related subjects. In the case of PhDs in a scheme with the Faculty of Occupational Medicine, which is advertised annually in January, and for MScs through the medium of certain university departments. We do not make grants directly to students.'

Exclusions Grants are not made for:
• the general funds of another charity;
• projects overseas.

Applications To the correspondent. Trustees meet in May and November and applications may be submitted at any time.

The Comino Foundation

Education

£315,000 (1998/99)

Beneficial area UK

29 Hollow Way Lane, Amersham, Buckinghamshire HP6 6DJ
Tel. 01494 722595
Correspondent Alan C Roberts, Administrator
Trustees *Norman P Bailey; Mrs A Comino-Jones; J A C Darbyshire; Dr W E Duckworth; Prof. John Tomlinson.*
Information available Full accounts were on file at the Charity Commission.

General The Comino Foundation is an educational charity and has two main purposes:

• to promote the awareness that it is industry and commerce that produce the basic goods, services and resources on which the well-being and quality of life of all of us depend

• to promote a clearer understanding of the basic processes involved in getting results, and thus improve people's power and will to create opportunities and achieve their purposes.

The foundation's vision is 'that people in Britain should live more fulfilled lives within a prosperous and responsible society. The foundation contributes to the realisation of this vision through its educational activities by: a) encouraging and enabling groups and individuals to motivate and empower themselves and to develop progressively their potential for the benefit of themselves and others, and b) encouraging a culture which affirms and celebrates both achievement and responsible practice in industry and commerce.'

In 1998/99 the trust had assets of £7.8 million, generating an income of only £270,000. Grants totalled £315,000. Of the 16 organisations receiving grants 12 were also supported in the previous year. Administration and management costs totalled £98,000 including £39,000 in administrator's fees and expenses and £36,000 in investment manager's fees.

Grants included £70,000 for a GRASP dissemination project. GRASP (Getting Results and Solving Problems) is a registered trademark of the Comino Foundation and offers a structure for thinking about getting high-quality results. 'It introduces pattern design and method into this thinking. It helps to develop a clearer understanding of the process of achieving results and a more creative way of operating to enable the achievement of those results.' £28,000 was also given to King Alfred's College, Winchester (GRASP approach).

Large grants were given to various educational institutions including Dudley Educational Services and Liverpool John Moores University (£30,000 each), and University of Warwick (£29,000). Smaller grants were given to Institute of Directors HUB Initiative (£19,000), Pace Centre (£14,000), Potential Trust (£8,000) and Police Ethics Network (£2,100).

Exclusions No grants to individuals or general appeals.

Applications In writing to the correspondent.

Gordon Cook Foundation

Education and training

£364,000 (1997/98)

Beneficial area UK

Hilton Place, Aberdeen AB24 4FA

Tel. 01224 283704 **Fax** 01224 485457
e-mail i.b.brown@norcol.ac.uk

Correspondent Mrs Irene B Brown, Administrative Officer

Trustees *Prof. B J McGettrick; Dr P Clarke; D A Adams; Dr W Gatherer; J Marshall; C Skene; D S C Levie.*

Information available Full accounts and guidelines were provided by the trust.

General This foundation was set up in 1974 and is dedicated to the advancement and promotion of all aspects of education and training which are likely to promote 'character development' and 'citizenship'. The following information is taken from the foundation's own leaflet.

'In recent years, the foundation has adopted the term 'Values Education' to denote the wide range of activity it seeks to support. This includes:

- the promotion of good citizenship in its widest terms, including aspects of moral, ethical and aesthetic education, youth work, cooperation between home and school, and coordinating work in school with leisure time pursuits

- the promotion of health education as it relates to values education

- supporting relevant aspects of moral and religious education

- helping parents, teachers and others to enhance the personal development of pupils and young people

- supporting developments in the school curriculum subjects which relate to values education

- helping pupils and young people to develop commitment to the value of work, industry and enterprise generally

- disseminating the significant results of relevant research and development.`

The view of the trustees is that the work of the foundation should:

- invest in people and in effective organisations

- have an optimum impact on the educational and training system, and consequently on children and young people in life and work.

In November 2000 the trust stated: 'Current assets stand at £8.5 million generating an income of around £300,000 each year. The foundation currently supports a number of projects, including 'Consultations' organised by Institute of Global Ethics; Professional Ethics; Business Ethics; Enterprise Ethics; and Values Education in the Four Home Nations.'

In 1997/98 the assets of the trust stood at £8.5 million generating an income of £294,000. Grants totalled £364,000 with three organisations receiving grants for more than one project. Northern College received grants for four projects totalling £38,000, St Andrew's College received £26,000 for three projects and Scottish CCC received £10,000 for two projects. There were 24 other grants of which by far the largest was £100,000 given to the University of Ulster. Other larger grants included those to Norham Foundation (£30,000), University of Glasgow (£22,000) and Citizenship Foundation and Health Education Board for Scotland (both £20,000).

A range of organisations received smaller grants of £1,000 up to £18,000 including Skene Enterprise Awards, Grampian Heart Campaign, Western Isles Council, Scottish Parents Consultative Forum, Moray House Institute and Launchpad Summer Events. About half the organisations supported also received a grant the previous year and £190,000 was already committed for the following year.

Exclusions Individuals are unlikely to be funded.

Applications In accordance with announced programmes and invitations to tender, the trusts welcomes applications. Forms may be obtained from the correspondent.

The Mansfield Cooke Trust

Evangelical Christian work

£94,000 (1998/99)

Beneficial area Worldwide

PO Box 201, West Malling, Kent ME19 5RS

Correspondent Nigel A M Cooke, Trustee

Trustees *Nigel A M Cooke; B O Chilver.*

Information available Full accounts were provided by the trust.

General Nearly all grants are for some form of evangelical work – missions, youth work, scripture etc. Grants are given locally, to UK charities and overseas, to causes with which the trustees have personal contact. Other applications are not considered.

In 1998/99 the trust had assets of £93,000 and an income of £112,000, mainly from donations. A total of £94,000 was given in 41 grants ranging from £100 to £21,000. The largest grants went to Tearfund (£21,000), Worthing Tabernacle (£16,000), Operation Mobilisation (£7,500), Africa Inland Mission (£5,500) and International Christian Colleges (£5,000).

Smaller grants included Crusaders Union, Luis Palau Evangelistic Association, John Grooms Association for the Disabled, Keswick Convention and Treasures in Heaven Trust.

Applications The correspondent states that the trust is 'established for specific purposes related to the personal contacts of the trustees' and that 'funds are fully committed and that applicants should not waste their time or ours by writing'. There would therefore seem little point in applying to this trust unless you have personal contact with a trustee.

The Cooks Charity

Catering, general

£100,000 (1997/98)

Beneficial area UK

The Old Deanery, Deans Court, London EC4V 5AA

Tel. 020 7593 5043

Correspondent M C Thatcher, Clerk & Solicitor

Trustees *M V Kenyon; A W Murdoch; H F Thornton.*

Information available Accounts were on file at the Charity Commission.

General The trust was established in 1989 primarly to support educational and welfare projects concerned with people involved in catering, and then any charitable purposes in the City of London. The trust stated that the grant total is currently around £150,000.

In 1997/98 the trust had assets of £2.5 million and an income of £207,000, including a donation of £131,000 from the Worshipful Company of Cooks. Grants to four organisations totalled £100,000.

Grants were given to Bournemouth University (£50,000) and Hackney College (£30,000), both of which appear to be receiving ongoing support. The other two grants were given to Hotel and Catering Benevolent Society (£15,000) and Research into Ageing (£5,000). Grants have also been given to Academy of Culinary Arts, British Heart Foundation, Broderers Trust, St John Ambulance and PM Club.

Applications In writing to the correspondent. Applications are considered in spring and autumn.

The Cooper Charitable Trust

Medical, disability, Jewish

£65,000 (1997/98)

Beneficial area UK

Portrait Solicitors, 1 Chancery Lane, London WC2A 1LF

Tel. 020 7320 3888

Correspondent The Trustees

Trustees *Mrs S Roter; Miss J S Portrait; Ms M Hockley.*

Information available Accounts were on file at the Charity Commission with a very brief narrative report.

General The trust was originally endowed with shares in Lee Cooper plc, which was taken over by Vivat Holdings plc. These shares were sold in 1990/91 and the assets of the trust are now invested in government stocks.

In 1997/98 the trust had assets of £1.9 million and an income of £133,000. Grants totalled £65,000 and management and administration costs came to £5,500. Grants ranged from £1,000 to £18,000 and were given to 20 organisations. There was a strong preference for medical charities, particularly those concerned with children.

About a quarter of all grants were given to Jewish organisations. The largest grants went to St Mark's Research Foundation (£18,000), Children's Liver Disease Foundation (£16,000), Paul Strickland Scanner Centre Appeal (£9,000), Jewish Care (£6,000) and Norwood Ravenswood (£2,000).

The remaining grants were all of £1,000 and included those to Association for Children with Life Threatening or Terminal Conditions, British ORT, Children's Transplant Foundation, Jewish Child's Day, Manchester Jewish Community Care and Open Door. Five were recurrent from the previous year.

Applications In writing to the correspondent.

The Alice Ellen Cooper-Dean Charitable Foundation

General

£316,000 (1998/99)

Beneficial area UK, with a preference for Dorset

c/o Messrs Preston & Redman Solicitors, Hinton House, Hinton Road, Bournemouth BH1 2EN

Tel. 01202 292424

Correspondent Douglas J Neville-Jones, Trustee

Trustees *Miss Sylvia A M Bowditch; Maurice A Edwards; Rupert J A Edwards; Douglas J E Neville-Jones.*

Information available Full accounts were on file at the Charity Commission.

General This trust aims to relieve poverty, distress and sickness, and advance education and religion. Both local organisations and UK-charities are supported. The trust gives half its grants to organisations in Dorset. The trust had assets of £6 million generating an income of £456,000 in 1998/99. After high administration and management costs of £117,000 resulting from the management of its large property portfolio, the trust gave 78 grants totalling £316,000. Grants ranged from £500 to £25,000.

The trust supports a number of medical organisations, with the largest grants being given to St John Ambulance and MRI Critical Care Appeal (£25,000 each). Other medical grants included those to Breakthrough Breast Cancer Appeal Dorset and Wessex Cancer Care (£10,000 each), British Red Cross, Dorset Branch (£5,000) and MIND (£1,000).

Children's charities are also heavily supported with grants being given to Dorset Youth Association (£10,000), Bournemouth YMCA (£5,000) and NSPCC and Save The Children Fund (£1,000 each).

Arts charities in Dorset included those to Bournemouth Music Competitions Festival (£5,000) and Bournemouth Orchestra and Dorset Opera (£1,000 each). Other grants were given to organisations including Woodland Trust Stoke Abbott Project (£15,000), Devon and Dorset Regiment Museum

Development Fund (£5,000) and Age Concern Bournemouth (£1,000).

Exclusions No grants to individuals.

Applications In writing to the correspondent. The trust has stated that its funds are fully committed and that unsolicited applications have little chance of success.

The Marjorie Coote Animal Charity Fund

Wildlife and animal welfare

£102,000 (1999/2000)

Beneficial area Worldwide

Barn Cottage, Lindrick Common, Worksop, Nottinghamshire S81 8BA

Tel. 01909 562806

Correspondent Sir Hugh Neill, Trustee

Trustees *Sir Hugh Neill; Mrs J P Holah; N H N Coote.*

Information available Full accounts were on file at the Charity Commission.

General The trust was established in 1954 for the benefit of five named charities and any other charitable organisation which has as its main purpose the care and protection of horses, dogs or other animals or birds.

The trustees concentrate on animal health and research and on the protection of species, whilst continuing to apply a proportion of the income to general animal welfare, including sanctuaries. The trustees give ongoing support, subject to annual review, and also 'one-off' grants to organisations requiring funds for specific projects.

In 1999/2000 the trust had assets of £2.7 million generating an income of £108,000. A total of £102,000 was given in 20 grants.

Recurrent grants were given to 17 organisations, with the largest being £45,000 to Animal Health Trust (which received the same amount in the previous year). Other regular beneficairies included Friends of Conservation (£6,000), Guide Dogs for the Blind (£5,000), PDSA National and Sheffield (£3,500 each), Wildfowl and Wetlands Trust (£2,000), Devon Horse and Pony

Sanctuary (£1,500) and Shalpa Animal Sanctuary (£1,000), all of which receive similar-sized grants each year.

One-off grants were £5,000 to University of Edinburgh Department of Veterinary Clinical Studies and £1,000 to SPANA, which also received £1,000 in the previous year.

Exclusions No grants to individuals.

Applications In writing to the correspondent. Applications should reach the correspondent during September for consideration in October/November. Urgent one-off applications for a specific project can be considered between meetings, although most applications are held over until the next meeting.

The Coppings Trust

General

£123,000 (1998/99)

Beneficial area UK

44a New Cavendish Street, London W1G 8TR

Correspondent Clive M Marks, Trustee

Trustees *C M Marks; Dr R M E Stone; T P Bevan.*

Information available Full accounts were on file at the Charity Commission.

General This trust does not respond to unsolicited applications, with its funds fully allocated in advance.

The trust states that its 'principal aims and objectives ... are centred around human rights, be it for immigrants aid, the welfare of prisoners, or the victims of torture and anti-personnel mines. Family welfare therapy, care for disadvantaged youths, the aged and refugees are also the concern of the trustees. The trust also supports the literary and educational interests of the late settlor.'

In 1998/99 the trust had assets of £2.1 million and an income of £62,000, including a repayment of £20,000 from a £500,000 loan previously made to Manor House Trust (of which Dr Stone is also a trustee). After high administration and management costs of £26,000, grants to 12 organisations totalled £123,000.

The largest grants were £18,000 each to Charta Mede and Jewish Library Trust.

Other grants included £15,000 to London Music for a concert for children with disabilities, £10,000 to Emmanus UK for a homeless project, £5,000 to Beech Tree School for an extension and £500 to Jewish Museum for general funding.

Applications The 1998/99 accounts stated: 'The trustees are at present considering a number of applications already placed before them. Because of the heavy existing demands made, the trustees are concentrating on those projects already know to them'.

The trust has previously stated: 'As funds are not available for new projects, the trustees do not feel justified in allocating administrative costs to responding to applications.'

The Duke of Cornwall's Benevolent Fund

General

£127,000 to organisations (1998/99)

Beneficial area UK

10 Buckingham Gate, London SW1E 6LA

Tel. 020 7834 7346

Correspondent Angela Wise

Trustees *Earl Cairns; W R A Ross.*

Information available Full accounts were on file at the Charity Commission.

General The fund receives donations from the Duke of Cornwall (Prince Charles) based on amounts received by the Duke as Bona Vacantia (the casual profits of estates of deceased intestates dying domiciled in Cornwall without kin) after allowing for costs and ex-gratia payments made by the Duke in relation to claims on any estate.

The fund's objectives are:

- the relief of people in need
- provision of almshouses, homes of rest, hospitals and convalescent homes
- advancement of education
- advancement of religion
- advancement of the arts
- preservation for the benefit of the public of lands and buildings.

In 1998/99 the trust had assets of £2.8 million and an income of £158,000 (£60,000 of which was donated by Duke of Cornwall). Grants were given to 163 organisations and totalled £127,000. Grants were also given to three individuals totalling £3,200. The fund had administration and management costs of only £520.

Grants were given to environmental groups such as Henry Doubleday Research Association and Soil Association (£7,500 each), Rare Breeds Survival Trust (£5,000) and National Trust (£2,000).

Medical grants included MRI Critical Care Appeal (£5,000) and Cotswold Care Hospice and Macmillan Cancer Relief (£3,000 each).

Arts grants included Lake District Art Gallery and Museum Trust (£5,000), Heligan Gardens Trust (£3,000) and Museum of Rural Life (£1,000).

Educational grants included £8,000 to Prince of Wales Institute of Architecture and £3,000 to University of Plymouth. Other grants included £2,000 to Duloe Parish Church and £1,000 to Family Care.

Applications In writing to the correspondent. Applicants should give as much detail as possible, especially information of how much money has been raised to date, what the target is and how it is to be achieved.

The Sidney & Elizabeth Corob Charitable Trust

Jewish charities, arts, general

£235,000 (1998/99)

Beneficial area UK

62 Grosvenor Street, London W1K 3JF

Correspondent Ms S A Wechsler, Trustee

Trustees *S Corob; E Corob; J Cook; J V Hajnal; Ms S A Wechsler.*

Information available Full accounts were on file at the Charity Commission.

General The trust gives most of its largest grants for specifically Jewish causes, for scholarships more than welfare. The rest of the grants were given

to a range of causes with a preference for education and established arts organisations.

In 1998/99 the trust had assets of £2 million and an income of £88,000. Grants totalled £235,000, of which 40, of £1,000 and more, were listed in the accounts. The largest grants were £40,000 to Oxford Centre for Hebrew & Jewish Studies, £27,000 to University College London and £23,000 to Hope Charity. Other large grants went to Jewish Care (£13,000), Chief Rabbinate Charitable Trust (£10,000), Community Security Trust (£7,000), Norwood Ravenswood (£6,500) and Institute of Advanced Legal Studies and Pegasus Scholarship Trust (each £6,000).

Grants to non-Jewish organisations ranging from £3,000 to £5,000 included Princes Youth Business Trust, Royal Academy of Arts and Royal National Theatre. Jewish organsiations supported included Jewish Association for Business Ethics and UKJAID.

Grants ranging from £1,000 to under £3,000 went to 22 organisations, including: non-Jewish organisations such as British Museum Development Trust, Dermatrust and Lord Mayors Appeal for Leuka 2000; and Jewish organisations such as Anglo-Israel Association, Judaism Today Trust and London Jewish Chaplaincy.

Grants of less than £1,000 totalled £26,000, the beneficiaries were not listed.

Exclusions No grants to individuals or non-registered charities.

Applications In writing to the correspondent.

The Cotton Trust

Relief of suffering, elimination and control of disease, people who are disabled and disadvantaged

£191,000 (1999/2000)

Beneficial area UK and overseas

PO Box 211, Southam, Warwickshire CV47 2WX

Correspondent I C Stilwell

Trustees *Not known.*

Information available Full accounts were filed at the Charity Commission, but without a narrative report.

General The trust's policy is the relief of suffering; the elimination and control of diseases; and helping disabled and disadvantaged people of all ages. Grants are given for defined capital projects (excluding building construction and the purchase of new buildings). Running costs and salaries are only considered in exceptional cases. In 1999/2000 the trust had an income of £207,000 and grants totalled £191,000. No information was available on beneficiaries.

Exclusions Grants are only given to UK-registered charities which have been registered for at least one year. No grants to animal charities, individuals, students, further education, travel, expeditions, conservation, environment, arts, new building construction or the purchase of new buildings.

Applications In writing to the correspondent with latest accounts, evidence of charitable status, detailed budget, timetable and details of funds raised. Trustees meet in March and September. The closing date for applications is two months before each meeting.

The Country Landowners Charitable Trust (CLACT)

Disabled facilities and training

£61,000 (1999)

Beneficial area England and Wales only

The Elms, Everton, Sandy, Bedfordshire SG19 2JU

Tel. 01767 692050   **Fax** 01767 683546

website www.clachartiabletrust.org.uk

Correspondent A L Pym and Mrs R A Pym, Directors

Trustees *A N G Duckworth-Chad; A H Duberly; G E Lee-Steere.*

Information available Full accounts were provided by the trust.

General The trust was founded in 1980. It helps to provide facilities for people who are disabled to take part in country sports and recreation and training in agriculture and horticulture. It also promotes education in the countryside for children and young people who are disadvantaged. It prefers to support smaller projects where a grant from the trust can make a 'real contribution to the success of the project'. It gives grants for specific projects or items rather than for ongoing running costs.

In 1999 the trust had assets of £270,000 and an income of £68,000 mainly from donations of CLA members and the fundraising efforts of county branches. A total of £61,000 was given to 26 projects. Grants ranged from £1,000 to £4,900. Details of these beneficiaries were not available.

In 1998 when grants totalled £112,00, beneficiaries included Chilterns Multiple Sclerosis Society, Countryside Foundation, Country Trust Dergoed Farm Project, Eye on the Wild, Food & Farming Education Service, FWAG, Hull Disabled Sailing Group and Painshill Park Trust.

Exclusions No grants to individuals.

Applications In writing to the correspondent. Trustees meet four times a year.

The Augustine Courtauld Trust

General

£82,000 (1999/2000)

Beneficial area UK, with a preference for Essex

Red House, Colchester Road, Halstead, Essex CO9 2DZ

Correspondent Richard Long, Clerk

Trustees *Revd A C C Courtauld, Chair; Lord Bishop of Chelmsford; Lord Braybrook; J Courtauld; Lord Tanlaw; Lady Braybrook.*

Information available Full accounts were on file at the Charity Commission.

General This trust gives grants for expeditions and general charitable purposes, mostly to organisations in Essex.

In 1999/2000 this trust had assets of £1.3 million and an income of £135,000.

Grants to 87 organisations totalled £83,000.

The grants list was split into two sections, general and expeditions. Three grants were given for expeditions: £7,000 to Gino Watkins Memorial Fund, £750 to Royal Geographical Society and £500 to Friends of Scott Polar Research Institute.

General grants were given to 84 organisations, 73 of which were of £1,000 or less. The larger grants were given mainly to organisations in Essex including Friends of Essex Churches (£9,000), Essex Association of Boys' Clubs (£4,000), YMCA Chelmsford Branch (£2,500) and Little Haven Children's Hospice Appeal (£1,500). Smaller grants included: £1,000 each to Age Concern Essex, Barn 'n' Bus Southend-on-Sea and Ocean Youth Club as bursaries for people in Essex; £500 each to Colchester Furniture Project, Jubilee Sailing Trust, Ipswich Women's Aid and five schools in Essex; and £250 each to Association of British Contemplatives, Clockwise Centre – Clacton-on-Sea and Halstead Day Centre.

The trust also gives the Augustine Courtauld Award of £1,000, awarded to Rural Community Council of Essex in 1999/2000, which also received a grant of £250 to cover administration expenses.

Exclusions No grants to individuals. No grants to individual churches for fabric repairs or maintenance.

Applications In writing to the correspondent. Applications are considered in spring and late autumn, although in 1999/2000 a grant of £500 was given to Essex Voluntary Association for the Blind between meetings.

The Lord Cozens-Hardy Trust

Medicine, health, welfare, general

£64,000 (1999/2000)

Beneficial area UK and overseas, with a preference for Merseyside and Norfolk

PO Box 29, Fakenham, Norfolk NR21 9LJ

Correspondent The Trustees

Trustees *Hon. Beryl Cozens-Hardy; Hon. Helen Phelps; J E V Phelps; Mrs L F Phelps.*

Information available Full accounts were on file at the Charity Commission.

General The trust supports a few UK charities in the fields of medicine, health and welfare and local groups in Merseyside and Norfolk. It gives both one-off and recurrent grants.

In 1999/2000 the trust had assets of £2 million. It had an income of £75,000, of which £64,000 was given in 110 grants. Grants ranged from £100 to £12,000, although the average grant was just under £600. The largest grants went to BMA Medical Education Trust (£12,000) and PCC Cley (£7,200). Other grants included £500 to St John Ambulance – Merseyside and £250 each to British Heart Foundation, Mencap, Norfolk Guides, Norfolk Scouts and RNIB.

Applications In writing to the correspondent before December. The main distribution list is prepared in January. Telephone calls are not invited.

The Craps Charitable Trust

Jewish, general

£112,000 (1998/99)

Beneficial area UK, Israel

3rd Floor, Bryanston Court, Selden Hill, Hemel Hempstead HP2 4TN

Correspondent The Trustees

Trustees *J P M Dent; C S Dent; L R Dent.*

Information available Full accounts were on file at the Charity Commission.

General This trust supports the same 14 Jewish and medical charities each year.

In 1998/99 the trust had assets of £1.9 million, generating an income of £65,000. Grants totalled £112,000.

The largest grants went to Joint Jewish Charitable Trust (£31,000), Jewish Care (£20,000) and Friends of the Federation of Women Zionists (£16,000). Most grants ranged from £1,000 to £4,000. Organisations supported include Arthritis and Rhuematism Council and British Friends of Haifa University (£4,000), and Motor Neurone Disease Association and Scopus (£2,000). One smaller grant of £75 was given to Society for the Protection of Nature in Israel. The size of grants to each group is similar each year.

Applications The trust states that 'funds of the trust are fully committed and the trust does not invite other applications'.

Criffel Charitable Trust

Welfare, health, Christianity

£136,000 (1998/99)

Beneficial area UK and overseas

Hillfield, 4 Wentworth Road, Sutton Coldfield, West Midlands B74 2SG

Tel. 0121 308 1575

Correspondent Mrs Juliet E Lees, Trustee

Trustees J C Lees; Mrs J E Lees; Mrs J I Harvey.

Information available Accounts were provided by the trust but without a grants list.

General In 1998/99 the trust's assets totalled £1.3 million, it had an income of £52,000 and grants totalled about £136,000. There was a deficit for the year of £84,000.

A grants list was not included with the accounts, but the following breakdown of grants was given:

Advancement of Christianity	£65,000
Relief of sickness	£17,000
Relief of poor and needy	£19,000
Miscellaneous	£35,000

It was not clear from the accounts whether any grants were made to individuals. No further information was available.

Applications All funds are fully committed. The trust states that no applications are considered or acknowledged. It still receives an average of ten applications a week, none of which can receive support.

The Violet and Milo Cripps Charitable Trust

General

£71,000 (1998/99)

Beneficial area UK

Slaughter and May, 35 Basinghall Street, London EC2V 5DB

Tel. 020 7600 1200

Correspondent The Clerk

Trustees Lord Parmoor; Anthony J R Newhouse; Richard J Lithenthal.

Information available Full accounts were on file at the Charity Commission.

General In 1998/99 the trust had assets of £240,000 and an income of £15,000. Grants to 11 organisations totalled £71,000. The trust often gives more in grants than it receives in income.

The largest grants in 1998/99 were £20,000 each to Howard League and Prison Reform Trust, both of which have received similar grants in recent years. Other large grants were given to Amnesty International (£10,000) and Multi A Ltd (£5,000). Grants ranging from £1,000 to £3,000 included those to Sutton Veny CE School (£3,000), Finecell Work (£2,500) and Order of Malta Volunteers (£1,000).

Applications In writing to the correspondent.

The Cross Trust

Christian work

£90,000 to organisations (1998/99)

Beneficial area UK and overseas

Bourbon Court, Nightingale Corner, Little Chalfont, Buckinghamshire HP7 9QS

Tel. 01494 765428

minicom 01494 541800

Correspondent The Trustees

Trustees M S Farmer; Mrs J D Farmer; D J Olsen.

Information available Full accounts were on file at the Charity Commission.

General The funds of the charity are directed to charities and individuals carrying out Christian work overseas and

in the UK, especially for education and training. However, the funds are fully committed for the foreseeable future.

In 1998/99 the income was £81,000, mostly from covenants and Gift Aid. Grants totalled £101,000 and included £11,000 to individuals (£200 of which was from a restricted fund). The largest grant of £40,000 went to George Whitefield College, a C of E theological college in South Africa, for the new building fund. A further 10 grants were given, the larger going to The Rock Foundation (£12,000), The Toy Box Charity towards a new freehold building and Wychwood School (£10,000 each) and The E Ivor Hughes Education Foundation (£4,700). The other six grants were all for under £3,500. Grants to individuals included support for Christian work, overseas students and school fees.

Applications No unsolicited applications are supported, with funds already fully committed.

The Dennis Curry Charitable Trust

Conservation, general

£152,000 (1998/99)

Beneficial area UK

Messrs Alliotts, 5th Floor, 9 Kingsway, London WC2B 6XF

Tel. 020 7240 9971

Correspondent N J Armstrong, Secretary to the Trust

Trustees M Curry; Mrs A S Curry; Mrs M Curry-Jones; Mrs P Edmond.

Information available Accounts were on file at the Charity Commission with a very brief narrative report.

General The trust has general charitable objects with a special interest in the environment and education; occasional support is given to churches and cathedrals. The four trustees receive a share of the distributable income, with grants listed in the accounts under the relevant trustee. Several organisations receive grants from more than one trustee. Examples of grants below show the total amount each organisation received.

In 1998/99 the trust had assets of £3.3 million and an income of £122,000. A total of £152,000 was given in 13 grants. The main beneficiary was the Natural History Museum which received £20,000 for the Palaentology Department and £15,000 for the Banks Archive Project. Other large grants went to Galapagos Conservation Trust (£22,000), National Trust – Snowdon Appeal (£20,000) and Itchenor Memorial Hall (£15,000). Grants of £10,000 each were given to Council for National Parks, Satrosphere, Woodland Trust and Wycombe Imaging Appeal and £7,000 went to Geological Society. Four of these grants were recurrent from the previous year.

Smaller grants went to National Youth Wind Orchestra (£2,500) and Raleigh International (£250).

Applications In writing to the correspondent.

The Manny Cussins Foundation

Older people, children, health, Jewish, general

£51,000 (1998/99)

Beneficial area Mainly UK, with some emphasis on Yorkshire

c/o Freedman, Ross, 9 Lisbon Square, Leeds LS1 4LY

Correspondent Arnold Reuben, Chair

Trustees *A Reuben, Chair; A Cussins; A J Cussins; J Cussins; Mrs A Reuben.*

Information available Full accounts were on file at the Charity Commission.

General The trust's objects are as follows: to support the welfare and care of the elderly; welfare and care of children at risk; health care in the Yorkshire region and abroad; charities in Yorkshire and the former county of Humberside; and charitable need amongst Jewish communities in the UK and abroad.

In 1998/99 the trust had assets of £959,000, up from £893,000 in the previous year. It had an income of £99,000 and gave 39 grants totalling £51,000. It appears that the trust is using its surplus income to increase its capital fund, for future capital projects. Grants ranged from £20 to £8,000, although half were under £1,000.

The largest grant was £8,000 to Manny Cussins House which also received the largest grant in the previous year. Other larger grants went to Angels International (£5,300), Bramley & Rodley Community (£4,000), St George's Crypt (£3,000) and Leeds Jewish Welfare Board (£2,600). Grants ranging from £1,000 to £2,000 were given to 14 organisations, including British Heart Foundation, Cot Death Society, Manny Cussins Diabetics Centre, Jewish National Fund – Charitable Trust, St Gemma's Hospice, World Jewish Relief and Whizz Kidz.

Smaller grants included those to Lifeline for the Old (£600), The Community Shop Trust (£300), Yorkshire and Humberside Chaplaincy Board (£150) and Hadassah Lodge (£20). Half the grants were recurrent from the previous year. The trust usually, but not exclusively, supports registered charities.

Exclusions No support for personal applications for the benefit of individuals.

Applications The correspondent states that applications are not sought as the trustees carry out their own research.

The Daily Prayer Union Charitable Trust Ltd

Evangelical Christian

£57,000 (1998/99)

Beneficial area UK

10 Belitha Villas, London N1 1PD

Correspondent Sir Timothy Hoare, Trustee

Trustees *Right Revd T Dudley-Smith, Chair; Revd G C Grinham; Canon J Tiller; Sir T Hoare; Revd R J B Eddison; Mrs E Bridger; Mrs A Thompson; Mrs F M Ashton; Mrs R K Harley; Revd D Jackman.*

Information available Accounts were on file at the Charity Commission, but without a list of grants.

General The trust supports evangelical Christian causes. In 1998/99 it had assets of £155,000 and an income of £60,000. Grants totalling £57,000 were broken down as follows:

General	£42,000
Education	£6,600
Training	£8,600

Grants ranged from £1,000 to £7,000. Larger grants included those to Monkton School (£7,000), Fan Fare – New Generation (£3,000), IFES (£2,500), Oak Hill College and Society for International Mission (£2,000 each) and Dagenham Church (£1,500). Grants of £1,000 each went to 13 recipients, including both organisations and individuals.

Applications The trust supports causes already known to the trustees. Unsolicited applications are unlikely to be successful. Trustees meet at different times throughout the year, usually around February, June and October.

The Daiwa Anglo-Japanese Foundation

Anglo-Japanese relations

£314,000 to organisations and individuals (1999/2000)

Beneficial area UK, Japan

Daiwa Foundation Japan House, 13–14 Cornwall Terrace, London NW1 4QP

Tel. 020 7486 4348   **Fax** 020 7486 2914
e-mail office@daiwa-foundation.org.uk
website www.daiwa-foundation.org.uk

Correspondent Prof. Marie Conte-Helm, Director General

Trustees *Lord Roll of Ipsden, Chair; Y Chino, Vice Chair; Lady Adrian; Sir Alec Broers; Lord Carrington; Nicholas Peter Clegg; Hiroaki Fujii; Tomoaki Kusuda.*

Information available An information leaflet was available from the foundation. Full accounts were on file at the Charity Commission.

General The foundation was established in 1988 through a generous donation made by Daiwa Securities, to promote understanding between the UK and Japan in the cultural, professional, academic and artistic fields. The foundation has three objectives:

* the advancement of UK and Japanese citizens' understanding of each other's peoples and culture

* awarding scholarships and maintenance allowances for UK or Japanese students to travel abroad to pursue education

• making grants to institutions involved in promoting education in the UK or Japan, or research into cultural, historical, medical and scientific subjects and the publication of such research.

In 1999/2000 the trust had assets of £40 million and an income of £1.6 million. Charitable expenditure totalled £1.1 million and administration and management fees £234,000, spent on the centre's library and holding seminars and conferences. Grants totalled £314,000.

The grants list was divided into the following catergories:

Grants given in the UK
Japanese Language
Four grants were given totalling £12,000, including £5,000 to Association for Language and Learning (ALL) to fund the first two years of the newly established Japanese Language Committee and £1,500 to British Association for Teachers of Japanese (BATJ) to cover the costs of printing the BAJF journal.

Japanese Studies
A total of £97,000 was given in 20 grants, the largest went was £15,000 to Birbeck College, London, towards a lectureship in Japanese History (last instalment of a five year grant). There were 14 grants of £1,000 each for annual student exchanges at schools. The foundation has entered into an arrangement with Connect Youth International (part of the British Council) which now processes applications for school and youth exchanges related to Japan.

Professional and academic exchanges
A total of £56,000 in 18 grants including £7,500 to the UK/Japan Research and Development Group for Ageing, Disability and Rehabilitation (RADGADAT) in order to advance areas of development in relation to ageing and £5,000 to Links Japan towards the costs of a week long visit by a delegation from the Shimin (civil) Forum 21 Non Profit Organisation centre to study the structure of the voluntary sector in the UK.

Art
There were 31 grants totalling £53,000, including £2,000 each to Tate Gallery towards the costs of a pilot scheme to send two British Artists on three months residencies in Japan, World Haiku Festival and to West Country Craftsmen of UK-Japan for members to travel to Japan to put on an exhibition in

Okayama and to acquire experience of Japanese traditional crafts.

Grants given in Japan
Professional and academic exchanges
A total of £63,000 was given in 27 grants of between £1,000 and £3,000 to allow Japanese citizens to visit the UK for academic or medical research.

Art
There were 15 grants totalling £32,000 including £1,000 each towards the visit of Ganjiro Nakamura (Kabuki actor) to London for a public discussion at the Globe Theatre and to Theatre Planning Network Kansai to hold a workshop on the Alexander Technique.

The foundation also awards the Daiwa Adrian Prizes every three years to joint teams of British and Japanese scientists engaged in collaborative research. (In December 1998 four prizes totalled £50,000.)

Applications On a form available via e-mail, fax or post from the correspondent. Deadlines for applications are 30 November to be considered in January, 31 March to be considered in May and 31 July to be considered in September.

Applications from Japan should contact Ken Machida at Daiwa Anglo-Japanese Foundation, Daiwa Securities, Kabuto-cho Building 9F, 1–1–9 Nihonbashi Kayabacho, Chuo-ku Tokyo 103-0025.

Michael Davies Charitable Settlement

General
£56,000 (1999/2000)

Beneficial area UK

Lee Associates, 5 Southampton Place, London WC1A 2DA

Correspondent K Hawkins

Trustees *M J P Davies; G H Camamile.*

Information available Accounts were on file at the Charity Commission, but without a grants list.

General In 1999/2000 the trust had assets of £146,000 and an income of £5,800. This income was significantly less than the 1998/99 income of £185,000, mainly because the trust usually receives a large donation from Richard Rogers

Architects Ltd on 30 June which was given earlier in 1999, and included in the 1998/99 accounts. However, the 1999/2000 grant total of £56,000 was consistent with the amount given in previous years.

Unfortunately, no list of grants was available since 1996/97 when grants of up to £10,000 were given to organisations including Arkwright Arts Trust, Family Holiday Association, Royal Albert Dock Trust, St John Ambulance, Save the Children and Uphill Ski Club.

Applications In writing to the correspondent.

The Leopold De Rothschild Charitable Trust

Arts, Jewish, general
£79,000 (1996/97)

Beneficial area UK

Rothschild Trust Corporation Ltd, New Court, St Swithin's Lane, London EC4P 4DU

Correspondent Miss Norma Watson

Trustees *Rothschild Trust Corporation Ltd*

Information available Accounts were on file at the Charity Commission.

General Unfortunately we have been unable to update the following information since the last edition of the guide. The trust gives most of its support to the arts and has some preference for Jewish organisations, with limited support to other causes covering heritage, welfare, medical and children.

In 1996/97 the income was £62,000 and grants totalled £79,000 with the largest to English Chamber Orchestra and Music Society (£25,000). Other larger grants included £5,200 to American Museum in Britain and £5,000 each to Child Southbank Foundation, Jewish Child Day and Saddlers Wells. Most grants were for £1,000 or less.

Applications In writing to the correspondent.

The Miriam K Dean Refugee Trust Fund

Third world development

£156,000 (1999)

Beneficial area Mainly Tanzania and India (including Tibetan refugees)

7 Hillside, Whitchurch,
Hampshire RG28 7SN

Tel. 01256 895181 **Fax** 01256 895060
e-mail brian@btims.freeserve.co.uk

Correspondent Brian Tims

Trustees *Trevor Dorey; Val Dorey; Hugh Capon; Jill Budd; Gina Livermore.*

Information available Full accounts were on file at the Charity Commission.

General In 1999 the trust had assets of £268,000 and an income of £153,000, including £117,000 in legacies and donations. One-off and recurrent grants totalled £156,000 and were given to:

- People in Tanzania (£26,000 – three grants including £21,000 to the Diocese of Zanzibar and Tanga and £2,900 to Hospital Teule, Muheza)

- Tibetan refugees in North India (£36,000 – four grants including £13,000 to Mussoorie, Tibetan Homes Foundation and £19,000 to ApTibet)

- People in South India (£88,000 – three grants including £47,000 to Brother James Kimpton and £15,000 to Centre for Disabled Children, Naarasaraopel).

Exclusions The trust states they are unable to award major block grants to organisations in the UK or Europe. No grants are given to individuals for Operation Raleigh or other overseas trips.

Applications The trust does not wish to receive any applications. Its funds are fully committed to projects/organisations already known to the trustees. However, when grants are given, they can be processed quickly with one grant being given by return of post.

The Debmar Benevolent Trust

Jewish

£194,000 (1998/99)

Beneficial area UK

86 Princess Street, Manchester M1 6NP

Tel. 0161 236 4107

Correspondent M Weisz, Secretary

Trustees *M Weisz; G Klein; H Olsberg.*

Information available Full accounts were on file at the Charity Commission.

General Grants are given towards the advancement of the Orthodox Jewish Faith and the relief of poverty. In 1998/99 the trust gave grants of up to £30,000, although most grants were less than £1,000.

In 1998/99 the trust had assets of £2 million and an income of £531,000. The trust spent over £130,000 on overheads. Grants to 136 organisations totalled £194,000.

The largest grants were given to Square Foundation (£30,000), Gevuras Ari Academy Trust (£16,000) and Tomchei Shargei Zion (£15,000). Other grants included £10,000 to Telz Academy Jerusalem, £7,000 to Friends of Assos Chessed, £5,000 to Format Charitable Trust and £1,000 to Manchester Kollel. The trust also gave 112 smaller grants.

Applications In writing to the correspondent.

The Dellal Foundation

General, Jewish

£251,000 (1998/99)

Beneficial area UK

14th Floor, Bowater House,
68 Knightsbridge, London SW1X 7LT

Tel. 020 7299 1406

Correspondent S Whalley, Administrator

Trustees *J Dellal; E Azouz; J Azouz; G Dellal.*

Information available Full accounts were on file at the Charity Commission, but with only a brief narrative report.

General The trust states that it continues to give 'a significant proportion of the grants towards charities whose aim is the welfare and benefit of Jewish people'.

In 1998/99 the trust had assets of £2.2 million and an income of £147,000. Management and administration costs were very low at £1,000. A total of £251,000 was given in 25 grants. The largest grants were £100,000 to Tel Aviv Foundation and £59,000 to Aleph Society Trust. Other larger grants were £20,000 to Community Security Trust and £10,000 each to Institute of Contemporary Jewish Studies, Jewish Care, Naima JPS Redevelopment, Rescue a Child (two grants of £5,000 each) and St John's Hospice.

Eight grants of £1,000 to £5,000 included those to Hampstead Shteibel, Jewish Memorial Council, Jewish Policy Research and The Pain Relief Foundation. Smaller grants ranged from £170 to under £1,000 and included those to British Heart Foundation, Cerebral Palsy Care, Daybreak and Medical Aid for Iraqi Children.

Applications In writing to the correspondent.

The Delves Charitable Trust

Environment, conservation, medical, general

£188,000 (1999/2000)

Beneficial area UK

New Guild House, 45 Great Charles Street, Queensway, Birmingham B3 2LX

Tel. 0121 212 2222

Correspondent Roger Harriman, Trustee

Trustees *Mary Breeze; John Breeze; George Breeze; Dr Charles Breeze; Elizabeth Breeze; Roger Harriman.*

Information available Information was provided by the trust.

General The policy of the trust is to allocate most of the annual income by way of annual subscriptions to a variety of charities. Currently about 40 charities receive an annual grant. This list is reviewed once a year in July. In 1999/2000 the trust had assets of £6.9 million and an income of £236,000 with grants totalling £188,000.

Most grants are in the fields of environment/conservation and medicine. The largest grants were to British Heart Foundation (£19,000), Sequal (£10,000), Intermediate Technology and WaterAid (£10,000 each), Liverpool School of Tropical Medicine (£9,000), Edith Cadbury Nursery School and Quaker Peace and Service (£9,000 each), Macmillan Cancer Relief (£6,800) and DEC Mozambique Floods Appeal (£6,000).

The remaining grants ranged from £250 to £5,000, with the six beneficiaries of £5,000 being Abbeyfield Society Nationwide, Action Research for the Crippled Child, Alzheimer's Disease Society, LEPRA, Medical Foundation for the Victims of Torture, Parkinson's Disease Society, Relatives Association, Richmond Fellowship and Woodland Trust. Most of these organisations also received grants in the previous year.

Exclusions Sponsorships and personal educational grants.

Applications 'The funds of the trust are currently fully committed and no unsolicited requests can therefore be considered'.

The Dent Charitable Trust

Jewish, general

£94,000 (1999/2000)

Beneficial area Worldwide

109 Elgin Crescent, London W11 2JF

Correspondent J P M Dent, Trustee

Trustees *J P M Dent, Miss C S Dent; Miss L R Dent.*

Information available Full accounts were on file at the Charity Commission.

General The trust has a list of eight Jewish organisations that it prefers to support. After this it will consider other charities in the UK and elsewhere, especially those concerned with agriculture, arts, children and medicine.

In 1999/2000 the trust had assets of £1.6 million and an income of £91,000. Grants totalled £94,000.

The main grants were given to British Technion Society (£30,000), Friends of the Hebrew University (£14,000) and Jerusalem Foundation (£10,000), all of which are regularly supported. Other grants included £5,000 each to Sarah Herzog Memorial Hospital and Shaare Zedek Medical Centre and £3,000 each to CBF World Jewish Relief, Mind and Save the Children Fund.

Applications The trust states that 'no further applications for funds can be considered'.

The Richard Desmond Charitable Trust

General

£219,000 (1999)

Beneficial area Worldwide

The Northern and Shell Tower, City Harbour, London E14 9GL

Tel. 020 7308 5255

Correspondent Gary Suckling

Trustees *R C Desmond; Mrs J Desmond.*

Information available Accounts were on file at the Charity Commission, but without a narrative report or a grants list.

General In 1999 the trust had an income of £210,000 and expenditure of £219,000, all of which was given in grants ranging from £100 to £25,000.

Beneficiaries of the larger grants included British Forces Foundation, Chemical Dependency Centre, Child in Crisis, Children with Leukaemia, Variety Club and World Jewish Relief.

Applications In writing to the correspondent.

Alan and Sheila Diamond Charitable Trust

Jewish, general

£56,000 (1999/2000)

Beneficial area UK

Bright Grahame Murray, 124–130 Seymour Place, London W1H 6AA

Tel. 020 7402 5201

Correspondent P Rodney, Trustee

Trustees *A Diamond, Chair; J Kropman, Vice Chair; Mrs S Diamond; P Rodney.*

Information available Accounts were on file at the Charity Commission but without a description of the trust's policy.

General In 1999/2000 the trust's assets totalled £1.3 million, it had an income of £58,000 and grants were made totalling £56,000. Information on the beneficiaries was not available.

About two thirds of the trust's grant-making is to Jewish organisations, with the rest to a range of causes. In 1997/98 grants totalled £70,000. The major grants were £12,000 to both Community Centre in Israel Project and Youth Aliyah and £10,000 to Girton College – Cambridge. Other larger grants were £7,600 to British School of Osteopathy, £5,600 to Anglo Israel Association, £4,000 to Jewish Care and £3,200 to Norwood Ravenswood.

A further five grants ranged between £1,000 and £2,500 including those to Community Security Trust and Holocaust Educational Trust. A total of 62 grants of less than £1,000, totalled £9,000.

Applications In writing to the correspondent. However, the trust states that it will not consider unsolicited applications and trust funds for the next few years are already allocated.

The Dinam Charity

International understanding, general

£117,000 (1995/96)

Beneficial area Worldwide

Thomas Edgar Church Adams, 5 East Pallant, Chichester, West Sussex PO19 1TS

Tel. 01243 786111

Correspondent The Trustees

Trustees *Hon. Mrs M M Noble; Hon. Mrs G R J Cormack; Hon. E D G Davies; J S Tyres.*

Information available Accounts were on file at the Charity Commission, but without a full list of grants since 1988/89.

General Unfortunately we have been unable to update the following information since the last edition of this guide.

In 1995/96 the trust had an income of £178,000. Grants totalled £117,000, including £91,000 to David Davies Memorial Institute, regularly the main beneficiary.

The most recent list of grants on file at the Charity Commission is for 1988/89 when the grant total was £131,000. As usual the largest grant was to David Davies Memorial Institute (£70,000) while another regular beneficiary, Welsh Centre for International Affairs, received £25,000. Other larger grants were £6,500 to Christian Aid and £2,500 to Caldecott Community.

A further 58 grants were made ranging from £50 to £1,500. About 20% of grants were for overseas aid/development including £1,000 to Oxfam Nicaraguan Hurricane Disaster Appeal and £500 to WaterAid. A further 20% went to organisations in Wales including Blaenau Ffestiniog Memorial Hospital (£1,000) and Montgomery County Music Festival (£500). Other beneficiaries included UK and local charities, especially those concerned with animal welfare, children and youth.

Exclusions Grants are only given to registered charities. No grants to individuals.

Applications Applications can be made at any time. Unsuccessful applicants will not be notified unless an sae is enclosed with the application.

The Dinwoodie (1968) Settlement

Postgraduate medical education and research

£56,000 (1998/99)

Beneficial area England

5 East Pallant, Chichester PO19 1TS

Tel. 01243 786111 **Fax** 01243 532001

Correspondent The Clerk to the Trustees

Trustees W A Fairbairn; Dr J M Fowler; E W Gillison; Miss C Webster.

Information available A detailed report and accounts were on file at the Charity Commission.

General The trustees set out to 'assist ... postgraduate medical education, primarily by improvements to the buildings of independently controlled

Postgraduate Medical Centres (PMCs) and by enabling a limited number of postgraduates to widen their knowledge through medical research and by obtaining appropriate experience in hospitals overseas'. They also state that they will continue their 'policy of identifying and supporting significant projects in the field of medical education and research'. The trust only gives grants to projects in England.

The maximum grant towards a PMC project in any one area is normally £1 million. The largest grant given so far is just over £1 million to Stafford's PMC. All funds available for distribution until 2003 have been earmarked for specific projects which are expected to be successfully completed.

In 1998/99 the trust had assets of £4.5 million and an income of £427,000. Administration and management costs were high at £55,000, including £40,000 in legal fees. With many projects still being negotiated, the grant total for 1998/99 was limited to £56,000.

Exclusions Anything falling outside the main areas of work referred to above. The trustees do not expect to fund consumable or equipment costs or relieve the NHS of its financial responsibilities.

Applications In writing to the correspondent. The trustees state they are proactive rather than reactive in their grant-giving. Negotiating for new PMCs and monitoring their construction invariably takes a number of years. The trust's funds can be committed for three years when supporting major projects. The accounts contain detailed reports on the development of centres under consideration.

The Dorus Trust

Health, welfare, disability, homelessness, addiction, underprivileged children, environment

£238,000 (1998)

Beneficial area Mainly UK

Charities Aid Foundation, Kings Hill, West Malling, Kent ME19 4TA

Tel. 01732 520081 **Fax** 01732 520001

Correspondent Barbara Davis, Information Manager

Trustees Charles Peacock; Mrs Bettine Bond; A M Bond.

Information available Full accounts were on file at the Charity Commission.

General In 1999 the trust had an income of £186,000 and its total expenditure was £200,000. This information was available on the Charity Commission database but not yet in the public file. The following is repeated from the last edition of the guide.

The trust has common trustees with two other trusts, Cleopatra Trust and Epigoni Trust (see separate entries) with which it also shares the same aims and polices. All three trusts are administered by Charities Aid Foundation (CAF). Generally the trusts support different organisations each year.

The trust makes grants in the following areas:

- mental health
- cancer welfare/education – not research
- diabetes
- physical disability – not research
- homelessness
- addiction
- underprivileged children.

There is also some preference for environmental causes. It only gives grants for specific projects and does not give grants for running costs or general appeals.

In 1998 the trust had assets of £2.8 million (£3.5 million in the previous year) and an income of £267,000. Administration charges to CAF were low at £588, CAF also received a grant of £2,500.

The trust gave 28 grants totalling £238,000. The largest grant was £15,000 to UK Foundation for the South Pacific. Seven grants of £10,000 each went to Ace Centre Advisory Trust, Barnardos and National Back Pain Association. Other large grants went to National Autistic Society (£9,000), Christian Lewis Trust (£8,000) and HAPA Ltd (£6,000). Grants of £5,000 each went to 18 organisations including Happy Days Childrens Charity, Head Injuries Trust for Scotland, Learning Through Landscapes Trust, Maternity Alliance Educational & Research Trust and St John Ambulance National HQ.

Smaller grants ranged from £500 to £4,000 and included those to Scottish Association for Mental Health (£4,000), National Association for Victim Support Schemes (£3,000), Parentline (£2,500), Support Dogs (£2,000), Scottish Council on Alcohol (£1,000) and National Schizophrenia Fellowship (£500).

Exclusions Grants are not given to individuals or non-registered charities or for medical research. Local organisations are not usually supported.

Applications On a 'funding proposal form' available from the correspondent. Applications should include a copy of the latest annual report and audited accounts. They are considered twice a year in mid-summer and mid-winter. Organisations which have received grants from this trust, The Dorus Trust or the Epigoni Trust should not reapply in the next two years. Usually, funding will be considered under only one of these trusts.

The George Drexler Foundation

Medical research, education, older people

£72,000 to organisations (1998/99)

Beneficial area UK

PO Box 338, Granborough, Buckinghamshire MK18 3YT

Correspondent Mrs Carol Phillips, Trustee

Trustees *Mrs L M Dresher; Mrs C A Phillips.*

Information available Full accounts were on file at the Charity Commission.

General Established by the late George Drexler in 1959, the trust's grant-making still reflects the founder's wishes, making grants to UK organisations, individuals involved in further education and impoverished former employees of the Ofrex Group.

However, the 1998/99 annual report stated: 'in view of their limited experience in assessing individual claims, the trustees have decided to limit the proportion of income to be allocated to educational grants and instead to increase grants to other relevant charities.'

In 1998/99 the foundation had assets of £5.5 million and an income of only £208,000. After administration and management fees of £21,000 – including £9,000 in trustees' fees – the trust gave

grants to organisations and individuals totalling £72,000.

Grants were divided in the trust's annual report, as follows:

Charities	£72,000
Educational: to individuals and a school	£15,000
Payments for relief of poverty	£67,000

In total, 17 charities received support, with the largest grants being £10,000 to Radcliffe Medical Foundation – Critical Care Initiative, and the smallest £550 to Pewsey Day Care Centre. Other grants included £6,000 to RNLI, £5,000 to Imperial Cancer Research Fund, £4,000 each to Abbeyfield Development Team and RSPCA and £2,000 to Myasthenia Gravis Association. The foundation also gave £5,000 each to both the London and Royal Philharmonic Orchestras.

Applications In writing to the correspondent. Please note, the trust states that 'an sae is essential, otherwise there will not be an acknowledgment'.

The Dumbreck Charity

General

£107,000 (1998/99)

Beneficial area Worldwide, especially the Midlands

Messrs PricewaterhouseCoopers, Temple Court, 35 Bull Street, Birmingham B4 6JT

Tel. 0121 265 5000

Correspondent Mrs P M Spragg

Trustees *A C S Hordern; Miss B Y Mellor; H B Carslake.*

Information available Full accounts were on file at the Charity Commission.

General In 1998/99 the trust had assets of £3.4 million and an income of £101,000. Grants to 137 organisation totalled £107,000. Grants were generally of between £500 and £1,000, although up to £5,000 in certain circumstances. The trust gives to UK charities and those local to the Midlands.

New grants were given to 28 organisations totalling £26,000. These included British Red Cross – Central American Fund (£5,000); Birmingham and Midland Institute Centenary Fund Appeal (£2,000); £1,000 each to Mark Davies Injured Riders Fund, Triumph

Over Phobia and Worcestershire Wildlife Trust; £500 each to County Air Ambulance Trust, Dyslexia Institute and Mouth and Foot Painting Artists; and £250 to Swan Lifeline.

The other 109 grants were given to organisations which are on what is effectively an annual subscription list of charities the trust supports. Some of the groups receiving a new grant may be added to this list and receive regular assistance from the following year onwards. Whilst the recipients of these grants rarely changes, the amounts given vary each year. The accounts divide the grants list into the following categories:

Animal welfare/conservation
UK
There were 15 grants given totalling £12,000, including Brooke Hospital for Animals Cairo (£3,000), International League for Protection of Horses (£1,000) and RSPB (£500).

Local
Seven grants totalled £5,800 including Birmingham Dogs Home (£1,000) and Rugby Animal Trust (£750).

Children's welfare
UK
Six grants totalled over £5,000 including Save the Children Fund (£2,000), NSPCC (£1,000) and Farms for City Children (£500).

Local
Five grants totalled £4,000 including Leamington Boy's Club (£1,000), Barnardos – West Midlands and West Midlands Autistic Society (£500 each).

Elderly people and people with mental/physical disabilities
UK
Grants totalling £6,300 went to 11 organisations, including RNIB (£750), and Age Concern and Deafblind UK (£500 each).

Local
A total of £21,000 was given in 27 grants, including Birmingham Royal Institute for the Blind (£2,000), Myton Hospice (£1,500), Warwick Old People's Friendship Circle (£1,000), Midland Society for the Blind (£750) and MSA for Midland People with Cerebral Palsy (£500).

Medical
UK
There were 12 grants given totalling £6,500 including National Asthma Campaign (£750), Bone Marrow Appeal and Injured Jockey's Fund (each £500).

Local
Nine grants totalled £8,000 including St Mary's Hospice Birmingham (£2,000),

British Red Cross Association branches in West Midlands and Hereford & Worcester (each £1,000), National Association for Crohn's and Colitis (£750) and Coventry Hospitals Charity (£500).

Miscellaneous
UK
Nine grants totalled £5,800 including British Field Sports Association (£1,000), RNLI (£750) and Hunt Servants Benefit Society and SSAFA (£500 each).

Local
Eight grants totalled £5,500 including Relate – Worcestershire Marriage Guidance (£1,000), Avoncroft Museum Development Team (£750) and No Panic (£500).

Applications In writing to the correspondent. The trustees meet annually in April/May. Unsuccessful applications will not be acknowledged.

The Dwek Family Charitable Trust

General, Jewish

£55,000 (1998/99)

Beneficial area UK, with a preference for Manchester

Suite One, Courthill House, 66 Water Lane, Wilmslow, Cheshire SK9 5AP

Tel. 01625 549081

Correspondent J C Dwek, Trustee

Trustees *J C Dwek; J V Dwek; A J Leon.*

Information available Brief accounts, with no grants list, narrative report or details of the address or trustees, were on file at the Charity Commission.

General In 1998/99 the trust had assets of £511,000 and an income of £55,000, including a donation of £15,000 from Penmarric Plc. Grants totalled £55,000 and the trust had other expenses of £260. No further information was available.

In the past mainly Jewish charities have been supported with beneficiaries including CIAO Manchester, Delamere Forest School, JNF Charitable Trust, Jewish Cultural Centre, Manchester Jewish Social Services and North Cheshire Jewish School.

Applications In writing to the correspondent.

The Dyers' Company Charitable Trust

General

£188,000 (1998/99)

Beneficial area UK

Dyers Hall, Dowgate Hill, London EC4R 2ST

Tel. 020 7236 7197

Correspondent The Clerk

Trustees *H D M Morley-Fletcher; Lt Col M A Marshall; G F Rothwell; J N Leuchars; Sir Ralph Verney; Lord Blake; H T Cadbury-Brown; C A Cooper; J L Crockatt; Dr C Wynn Parry; Sir Thomas Macpherson; R S Skilbeck; R M S Goodsall; Dr P R V Tomson; J Aitkinson; P J Q Back; M W M Rowlandson; M Horton Ledger; P G Mathieson; Dr D Blackburn; F A Onians; R S Brook; J R Vaizey; R A Leuchars; E R Verney; C A Cripps; R P Back; E A M Lee.*

Information available Full accounts were on file at the Charity Commission.

General In 1998/99 the trust had assets of £3.1 million generating an income of £116,000. Grants to 97 organisations totalled £188,000 and were given in the categories shown below.

Crafts
Nine grants of between £300 and £30,000 totalled £81,000. Grants were given towards education and training in the crafts and included £30,000 to Society of Dyers and Colourists for a Directory of Colourants, £20,000 to University of Leeds, £10,000 to Textile Conservation Centre and £300 to Royal College of Needlework. £1,000 was also given in grants to Society of Dyers and Colourists students.

Education and young people
15 grants of between £500 and £23,000 totalled £38,000. Grants were given towards the development of young people, largely in the form of grants to educational establishments and youth organisations. Beneficiaries included Norwich School (£23,000), Harrogate Unit Sea Cadet Corps (£2,000), Castle Quay Project – Stockton-on-Tees (£1,000) and National Playing Fields Association (£500).

Health and welfare
27 grants of between £100 and £2,000 totalled £23,000. Grants were given to UK and local appeals, including Lord Mayor's Appeal for Leuka 2000 (£2,000), and East Anglia's Children Hospices and Pace Centre (£1,000 each). Two grants were also given to Arthritis and Rheumatism Council, £1,000 to the Bury St Edmonds branch and £500 to the Petersfield branch.

Local community/inner London
15 grants of between £250 and £5,000, but usually up to £750, totalled £20,000. Grants were given to educational establishments including Boutcher CE Primary School – Bermondsey (£5,000) and Homerton House School – Hackney (£2,000). Grants were also given to local organisations including City Road Youth Counselling (£500) and Downside Club for Young People (£250).

The arts
19 grants of between £250 and £2,500 totalled £16,000. Grants were given towards musical development and museums, including National Maritime Museum (£2,500), Royal Overseas League Music Competition (£1,500), Chelsea Opera Group (£1,000) and Young Concert Artists Trust (£500).

Services
Grants were given to Reserve Forces Ulysses Trust (£2,500) and RNLI – City of London Branch (£500).

The church
Grants of £500 each were given to Historical Churches Preservation Trust and St Andrew's – Oxshott.

Other grants
Eight grants of between £250 and £2,000 were given for general charitable purposes and totalled £6,800. These included £2,000 to Swan Sanctuary – Egham, £1,000 to Chelsea Physic Garden and £250 to Hertfordshire Association for the Care and Resettlement of Offenders.

Applications The trust does not welcome unsolicited applications.

The Earth Love Fund

Community-based rainforest conservation projects, Artists for the Environment (AFTE) Festival

£29,000 (1999/2000)

See below

Beneficial area UK and overseas

9 Standingford House, Cave Street, Oxford OX4 1BA

Tel. 01865 200208 **Fax** 01865 209091
e-mail earthlove@gn.apc.org
website www.earthlovefund.com

Correspondent Su Jordan

Trustees *Nicholas H Glennie-Smith; Ivan Hattingh; Edward Posey.*

Information available Full accounts were on file at the Charity Commission.

General The trust is a UK-based charity which workks through the arts to raise awareness and funds for community-based rainforest conservation projects worldwide. The fund was set up in 1989 by three individuals from the music Fraternity, the founders' contacts have enabled them to gain the support of top international artists. In 1996 ELF was awarded the United Nations Global 500 award for outstanding practical achievements in the protection and improvement of the environment.

The fund also coordinates Artists for the Environment (AFTE), an awareness-raising programme, through which small grants of up to £500 are offered to local community arts throughout the UK for the annual AFTE Festival.

In 1999/2000 grants totalled £25,000. In addition, over £3,000 was given in AFTE grants.

In 1998/99 the fund gave a total of more than £99,000 in 20 grants in support of conservation projects. The list of beneficiaries does not include the purpose of each grant. Over £3,000 was given in small AFTE grants; these were not listed separately by the fund. Beneficiaries of other grants included: Imaflora Brazil (£51,000); Forest Peoples Programme (£5,000); Honduras Hurricane Appeal (£3,500); TReeS and *Rainforest Alliance (£2,500 each); Venezuela Transmission Line and Oxfordshire Woodland Trust (£1,000 each). *previous beneficiary.

Applications 'Please contact Earth Love Fund at the address above.'

The Ebenezer Trust

Evangelical Christianity, welfare

£68,000 (1998/99)

Beneficial area Worldwide

31 Middleton Road, Shenfield, Brentwood, Essex CM15 8DJ

Tel. 020 7303 3022

Correspondent N T Davey, Trustee

Trustees *Nigel Davey; Ruth Davey.*

Information available Full accounts were provided by the trust.

General The trust gives grants to Evangelical Christian charities for education, medical, religion and welfare purposes.

In 1998/99 the trust had assets of £465,000 and an income of £380,000. Grants totalled £68,000. Although grants ranged from £42 to £20,000, 34 of the 50 grants were of less than £1,000.

The largest grant was £20,000 to Brentwood Baptist Church, with £6,700 also given to Tearfund. Other grants were given to Pilgrims Hatch Baptist Church (£3,300), Scripture Union (£2,200), Servants Fellowship International (£1,600), Medical Foundation for the Victims of Torture (£300), Word of Life (£250) and Treasures in Heaven Trust (£50).

Applications The trust states that they 'are most unlikely to consider unsolicited requests for grants'.

The Ecological Foundation

Environment/conservation

£173,000 (1999)

Beneficial area Worldwide

Lower Bosneives, Withiel, Bodmin, Cornwall PL30 5NQ

Tel. 01208 831236 **Fax** 01208 831083

Correspondent J Faull, Director

Trustees *The Marquis of Londonderry; John Aspinall; R Hanbury-Tenison; Edward Goldsmith.*

Information available Full accounts were on file at the Charity Commission.

General The foundation supports projects which it has set up either itself or chosen to sponsor. Income is raised from donations for the specific projects and is therefore all restricted. In 1999 the trust had income of £170,000 and gave grants totalling £173,000. The largest grant of £86,000 went to World Rainforest Programme. Other larger grants went to Outsider's Guide (£31,000), Trade Investment & Environment Project (£21,000), Public Outreach (£17,000) and Global Commons Institute (£15,000). Chapter Seven (Tinkers Bubble) received £3,500. Four of the grants were recurrent. Other grants totalled £80.

Applications In writing to the correspondent, but note the above.

The Gilbert & Eileen Edgar Foundation

General – see below

£71,000 (1999)

Beneficial area UK (and a few international appeals)

c/o Chantrey Vellacott DFK, Prospect House, 58 Queens Road, Reading RG1 4RP

Tel. 0118 952 4700

website www.cvdfk.com

Correspondent Penny Tyson

Trustees *A E Gentilli; J G Matthews.*

Information available Full accounts were on file at the Charity Commission.

General The settlor expressed the desire that preference be given to the following objects:

- the promotion of medical and surgical science in all forms
- helping people who are young, old or in need
- raising artistic taste of the public in music, drama, opera, painting, sculpture and the fine arts
- the promotion of education in the fine arts
- the promotion of academic education
- the promotion of religion
- the promotion of conservation and heritage, facilities for recreation and other leisure-time activities.

There is a preference for smaller organisations 'where even a limited grant may be of real value'. The majority of grants are around £500 each. Many of the organisations supported are regular beneficiaries. In 1999 the trust had assets of £1.8 million and an income of £92,000. A total of £71,000 was given in 113 grants. These were broken down as shown in the table.

Care and support was further broken down:

Children and young people:
21 grants totalling £8,800

Older people:
5 grants totalling £1,800

People with special needs:
37 grants totalling £16,000

This category receives the most applications. Its areas of support are quite broad and can include disability, people suffering from chronic medical disorders, refugees, those suffering from the tragedy of war, homelessness, natural disasters and poverty.

Examples of grants given under each category are shown below.

Medical and surgical research
Most grants were for £500 each including those to Breast Cancer Campaign and Leukaemia Research Fund. Smaller grants included Cardiac Fund – Battle Hospital (£300) and Meningitis Research Foundation (£250). Of the grants made, 13 grants were recurrent from the previous year.

Care and support
Children and young people
There were 15 grants given of £500 each, including those to Aberlour Childcare Trust, ChildLine and Women Caring Trust for Children in Northern Ireland. The remaining grants were £250 each, for example, to Breakout Children's Holidays. All but three of the grants were recurrent.

Older people
Grants ranging from £250 to £500 included those to Alzheimer Scotland, Counsel and Care for the Elderly and New Horizon Trust. People with special needs: One grant of £1,000 went to

Disasters Emergency Committee – Kosovo Crisis. 24 grants of £500 each included those to Action for Blind People and DEMAND – Design & Manufacture for Disability. The remaining grants were of £250 each, beneficiaries included Arthritis Care and Disability Law Service.

Fine Arts
Larger grants were given under this category with £3,000 to Royal National Theatre and £1,000 to English National Ballet. Smaller grants of £250 or £500 included those to Artists General Benevolent Institution and Music for the Blind.

Education in fine arts
Scholarships were given, to three Royal Academies: of the arts; dramatic art and music. One was of £9,000 and the others for £5,000 each. All of the grants were recurrent.

Academic education
Four grants went to Wolverhampton Grammar School (£1,500), Royal National College for the Blind (£500) and £250 each to St Loye's College Foundation and Royal School for the Blind, Leatherhead. They were all recurrent.

Religion and recreation, including conservation
The largest grant was £2,000 to Holy Cross Church in Ramsbury. Seven grants of £500 each included those to Atlantic Salmon Trust, Camp Mohawk and Survival for Tribes People. Four grants of £250 each included those to Jubilee Sailing Trust and Northamptonshire Association of Youth Clubs.

Exclusions Grants for education in the fine arts are made by way of scholarships awarded by academies, no grants are made directly to individuals in this regard.

Applications In writing to the correspondent. There are no application forms.

The Edinburgh Trust, No 2 Account

Education, service, scientific expeditions
£61,000 (1998/99)
Beneficial area UK and worldwide

Buckingham Place, London SW1A 1AA
Tel. 020 7930 4832
Correspondent Paul Hughes
Trustees *Sir Brian McGrath; C Woodhouse.*

Information available Full accounts were on file at the Charity Commission.

General In 1998/99 the trust's assets totalled £1.4 million and it had an income of £68,000, mostly from investments. Grants totalled £61,000, of which £15,000 was given towards the armed services with the remainder going towards education. The trust also makes grants towards 'scientific expeditions'. The trust appears to favour the areas of wildlife and nature conservation, preservation of historic buildings, youth and outdoor pursuits, and in some cases medical and health-related causes.

Donations were listed under the following headings:

Civilian annual
Grants were given to 32 organisations, of which 28 were between £200 and £300. The largest grants were £2,700 to Edwina Mountbatten Trust, £1,500 to Royal Life Saving Society and £1,300 to Romsey Abbey. Other beneficiaries included British Red Cross Society, LEPRA Children's Account and Galapagos Conservation Trust.

Service organisations
A total of 24 grants were made. The largest were £2,500 each to British Commonwealth Ex-Servicemen's League, King George Fund for Sailors and Royal Marines General Fund, £1,750 to King Edward VII Hospital for Officers and £1,500 to SSAFA No. 1 Account. The other grants were all for between £200 and £300.

Non-annual
Grants were given to 26 organisations. The largest, of £2,500 each, were given to The Award Scheme, London Federation of Clubs for Young People, Outward Bound Trust and PPT for Windsor and Maidenhead, followed by a grant of £2,000 to St George's House and

---

THE GILBERT & EILEEN EDGAR FOUNDATION
GRANT DISTRIBUTION IN 1999

Category	No. of grants	Total £
Medical and surgical research	22	10,000
Care and support	63	27,000
Fine arts	9	6,800
Education in fine arts	3	19,000
Academic education	4	2,500
Religion and recreation, including conservation and heritage	12	6,500

International Sacred Literature Trust. Most of these grants were recurrent from the previous year. Nine other grants were of £1,500, with the majority of the remainder for £100 to £500, including 14 grants towards scientific expeditions.

Exclusions No grants to individuals, only scientific expeditions are considered with the backing of a major society. No grants to non-registered charities.

Applications In writing to the correspondent. The trustees meet to consider grants in April each year, and applications must be submitted by January.

The W G Edwards Charitable Foundation

Care of older people

£133,000 (1998/99)

Beneficial area UK

Wedge Property Co. Ltd, 123A Station Road East, Oxted, Surrey RH8 0QE

Tel. 01883 714412 **Fax** 01883 714412

Correspondent S K Phillips, Trustee

Trustees *Mrs Margaret E Offley Edwards; Prof. Wendy D Savage; S K Phillips.*

Information available Full accounts were on file at the Charity Commission.

General The trust gives a few grants each year to organisations concerned with the care of older people. In 1998/99 the trust had assets of £2 million, consisting of shares in the Wedge Property Co. Ltd. Three of the trustees are also directors and shareholders of the company. The income in 1998/99 was £143,000 and grants totalled £133,000.

Four grants were given. The largest of £50,000 went to Lillian Faithfull Homes. Age Concern, Tower Hamlets, received £40,000. (It has also received large grants in the last two years and the trust has committed a further £30,000 to be given in the following year.) Friends of the Elderly received £38,000 and Shennington School received £5,000. A commitment of £5,000 was made to St Richard's Hospice for 1999/2000.

Applications In writing to the correspondent.

The Eighty-Eight Charitable Trust

General

£98,000 (1999/2000)

Beneficial area Worldwide

Messrs Pannell Kerr Foster, Pannell House, 1a Charter Court, Newcomen Way, Colchester CO4 4YA

Tel. 01206 854485

Correspondent Ms Latimer, Accountant

Trustees *Guy Hannen; Mrs Brigid Hannen.*

Information available Full accounts were on file at the Charity Commission.

General In 1999/2000 the trust had assets of £1.2 million generating an income of £70,000. Administration and management costs totalled £21,000. Grants totalling £98,000 were made to 18 organisations.

The largest grants went to Foresight (£30,000), Peterborough Cathedral Trust (£25,000), Leonard Cheshire Foundation (£15,000) and Green Turtle Cay Foundation (£10,000). Other grants ranged between £500 and £5,000 including those to Marie Curie Cancer Care (£5,000) and Ngini Kanel Foundation for Cambodia (£2,000).

Applications In writing to the correspondent.

The George Elias Charitable Trust

Jewish, general

£145,000 (1998/99)

Beneficial area Some preference for Manchester

Elitex House, Moss Lane, Hale, Altrincham, Cheshire WA15 8AD

Tel. 0161 928 7171

Correspondent N G Denton, Charity Accountant

Trustees *G H Elias; Mrs D Elias; E C Elias; S E Elias.*

Information available Accounts were on file at the Charity Commission, but without a grants list.

General This trust states it gives grants to charities supporting educational needs and the fight against poverty, as well as organisations promoting the Jewish faith. In practice, grants are only given to Jewish groups.

In 1998/99 the trust had assets of £333,000 and an income of £197,000. Grants totalled £145,000.

No grants list was included in the accounts for 1998/99, but in the previous year, when grants totalled £110,000, the largest grant was £35,000 to JNF Charitable Trust. Other grants included British Friends of Omoley (£10,000), Charity Associates Manchester (£7,000), Format Charitable Trust (£4,500), Hale and District Hebrew Congregretion (£3,900) and Academy Rabbinical Research (£250).

Applications In writing to the correspondent. Trustees meet monthly.

The Ellinson Foundation Ltd

Jewish

£220,000 (1998/99)

Beneficial area Worldwide

Messrs Robson Laidler & Co, Fernwood House, Fernwood Road, Jesmond, Newcastle upon Tyne NE2 1TJ

Tel. 0191 281 8191

Correspondent Gerry Crichton

Trustees *C O Ellinson; Mrs E Ellinson; A Ellinson; A Z Ellinson; U Ellinson.*

Information available Full accounts were on file at the Charity Commission.

General The trust supports hospitals, education and homelessness in the UK and overseas, usually with a Jewish teaching aspect. It regularly supports organisations such as boarding schools for boys and girls teaching the Torah.

In 1998/99 the trust had assets of £528,000 and an income of £219,000, including £55,000 in covenants. Grants totalled £220,000, with 87 of the 141 recipients having been supported in the previous year.

The largest grants were given to Friends of United Institution of Arad (£30,000), Emuno Education Centre (£26,000), Yeshiua L'Zeihim – Gateshead (£25,000) and Yeshiua Athereth – Israel (£23,000). Other large grants included those to

Friends of Neve Yerusholayim (£15,000), SOFT (£8,500), Tree of Life College – Elz Ohr Seminar (£5,000) and Gateshead Talmudical College (£2,100). Of the 141 grants, 118 were of £1,000 or less including £250 to Sunderland Kollel, £200 to Notzar Chessed, £100 to BLBH Gemach Fund, £50 to Beth Jacob Seminary Trust and £10 to Dushinskey Trust.

Applications In writing to the correspondent. However, the trust generally supports the same organisations each year and unsolicited applications are not welcome.

Elman Charitable Trust

Jewish charities
About £300,000
Beneficial area UK and Israel

Laurence Homes Eastern Limited, 14 Ruskin Close, Chilton Hall, Stowmarket, Suffolk IP14 1TY

Correspondent K Elman, Trustee

Trustees *Charles Elman; Colin Elman; Kenneth Elman.*

Information available Accounts for 1996/97 with a grants list, but no narrative report, was on file at the Charity Commission in September 2000.

General In autumn 2000 the trust stated that it had about £300,000 to distribute in grants each year. The majority of the grants are given in Israel to organisations such as schools and hospitals. Jewish charities in the UK are also supported. Most grants are recurrent. Examples of grants were not available.

The latest grants list available relates to 1996/97 when grants totalled £260,000. Although 31 awards were made, all to Jewish charities, about 80% of total grant giving went to just four organisations: Emunah Women's Organisation in Israel (£96,000); Friends of Asraf Harofeh Medical Centre and Jewish Care (£50,000 each); and Nir Yisrael Educational Trust (£11,000).

Other grants went to Friends of OHR Samayach (£6,000), Our Future – the poor of Herzelia (£5,300) and £5,000 each to British Friends of Aleh and Ohel Moshe Synagouge (£5,000 each).

Exclusions Grants are not usually given to individuals.

Applications In writing to the correspondent.

The Elmgrant Trust

Education, arts, social sciences, ecology and environment
£63,000 to organisations (1999/2000)
Beneficial area UK, with a preference for Devon and Cornwall

The Elmhirst Centre, Dartington Hall, Totnes, Devon TQ9 6EL

Tel. 01803 863160

Correspondent Mrs M B Nicholson, Secretary

Trustees *Marian Ash; Lord Young of Dartington; Sophie Young; Maurice Ash.*

Information available Full accounts were available at the Charity Commission.

General This trust has general charitable purposes, but in particular aims to encourage local life through education, the arts and social sciences. Although there is a preference for south west England, grants are also awarded throughout the UK. Fellowships are given to individuals over 30 who live in Devon or Cornwall (see *The Educational Grants Directory*).

In 1999/2000 the assets were £2.5 million and the income was £128,000. Administration and management fees were a high £35,000. Grants to 70 organisations totalled £63,000, and grants to 130 individuals totalled £43,000. They were broken down as follows (1998/99 figures in brackets):

Retraining grants	£33,000	(£36,000)
Education and educational research	£28,000	(£37,000)
Arts and arts research	£18,000	(£27,000)
Social sciences and scientific grants	£13,000	(£11,000)
Pensions, donations and compassionate grants	£15,000	(£15,000)

Organisations receiving grants included Institute of Community Studies (£13,000), Park School (£4,000),

Dartington Hall Trust (£2,800), Fight Against Addiction Dependency and Special Trustees of Middlesex Hospital for a teenage cancer ward (£2,000 each) and University of Plymouth (£1,300).

Exclusions The following are not supported: large scale national organisations; postgraduate study, overseas student grants, expeditions and travel and study projects overseas; counselling courses (other than fellowships); also renewed requests from the same (successful) applicant within a two-year period.

Applications In writing to the correspondent, giving full financial details and, where possible, a letter of support. Meetings are usually held in March, June, September and December. Applications need to be received by February, May, August and November.

Fellowship applications are considered only in response to local annual advertisements in March/April, and on completion of an application form.

Elshore Ltd

Jewish
£78,000 (1998/99)
Beneficial area Worldwide

10 West Avenue, London NW4 2LY

Tel. 020 8203 1726

Correspondent H Lerner, Trustee

Trustees *H M Lerner; A A Lerner; S Yanofsky.*

Information available Accounts were on file at the Charity Commission, but without a full written report or a grants list.

General This trust appears to make grants solely to Jewish organisations. In 1998/99 it had assets of £47,000 and an income of £126,000, mostly from donations. Grants totalled £78,000, with administration and management costs totalling just £620. A grants list was not included with the accounts for this year.

Further information has been unavailable since 1994/95, when grants to 40 beneficiaries totalled £178,000. The larger grants were £26,000 to Eminor Educational Centre and £20,000 to Cosmon Belz. Grants of £10,000 were given to 10 organisations, including Gur Trust and Marbeh Torah Trust. Most other grants were less than £1,000, although some were for up to £8,000.

Applications In writing to the correspondent. The trustee stated they did not wish to be included in this guide and refused to confirm the above information.

The Vernon N Ely Charitable Trust

Christian, welfare, disability, children and young people, overseas

£81,000 (1997/98)

Beneficial area Worldwide, with a preference for London Borough of Merton

Grosvenor Gardens House, 35–37 Grosvenor Gardens, London SW1W 0BY

Tel. 020 7828 3156

Correspondent Derek Howorth, Trustee

Trustees J S Moyle; D P Howorth; R S Main.

Information available Accounts were on file at the Charity Commission, but without a list of grants.

General In 1998/99 the trust had an income of £108,000 and an expenditure of £92,000. Unfortunately, no further information for this year was available.

The trust makes grants to Christian, welfare, disability, children, youth and overseas charities. Its 1997/98 annual report stated that the trust's policy had been reviewed during the year and it had been decided that the number of beneficiaries each year would be reduced, with larger grants being made.

In 1997/98 the trust had an income of £111,000. In the previous year, the income totalled £556,000 when the trust received a very large one-off dividend in connection with the takeover of Elys (Wimbledon) Plc, in which the whole of the trust fund had been invested. All the trustees were also directors of Elys.

The trust had £107,000 available for distribution and grants were made totalling £81,000. At the year end, assets held as cash at the bank, totalled £1.6 million. A list of grants was not available for that year although the trust

stated in its annual report that 'plans are well advanced' to donate £350,000 towards constructing a new IT block at Merton College of Further Education: 'Vernon Ely Information Technology Block'. The trust also plans to set up a bursary to fund Vernon Ely Tennis Scholarship.

In 1995/96, before the trust had reviewed its policy, it made 69 grants including 58 of less than £1,000. Grants show a preference for Merton and included £6,100 to Cottage Homes, £3,700 to London Playing Fields Association, £2,100 to Merton Voluntary Association for the Blind, £1,200 to British Red Cross Society and £1,000 each to Oxfam, Royal Marsden Cancer Appeal and Save the Children Fund. Beneficiaries of smaller grants included Merton WelCare Association, RSPCA Wimbledon and District, Second Hook Scout Group and Wimbledon Community Association.

Applications In writing to the correspondent.

The Emerton-Christie Charity

Health, welfare, disability, arts

£71,000 (1998/99)

Beneficial area UK

2 New Square, Lincoln's Inn, London WC2A 3RZ

Tel. 020 7421 4800   **Fax** 020 7421 4850

Correspondent The Trustees

Trustees A F Niekirk; D G Richards; Dr N A Walker.

Information available Full accounts were provided by the trust.

General The Emerton Charitable Settlement was established in 1971 by Maud Emerton, with additional funds subsequently added by Vera Bishop Emerton. In April 1996, it became the Emerton-Christie Charity following a merger with another trust, The Mrs C M S Christie Will Trust.

In 1998/99 it had assets totalling £2.4 million and an income of £68,000. Grants totalled £71,000 and were given to 35 organisations. The largest grant was £10,000 to Harnhill Centre for Christian Learning to reduce the interest free loan which the organisation had borrowed from the trust. Most grants were to

health, welfare and disability causes, with a couple to arts organisations.

Other larger grants included Royal College of Music (£5,000), RNLI (£4,000), BACUP and Woodlands Hospice Charitable Trust (£3,000 each) and Save the Children Fund (£2,500).

Two-thirds of the grants were between £1,000 and £1,500. Examples included Canine Partners for Independence, Disability Aid Foundation, Helen Arkell Dyslexia Centre, The Farm in the Forest Respite, NSPCC, Second Chance and Sense. About 10 grants were recurrent from the previous year.

Exclusions No support for international charities or non-registered charities.

Applications In writing to the correspondent.

The Emmandjay Charitable Trust

Social welfare, medicine, youth

£257,000 (1998/99)

Beneficial area UK, with a special interest in West Yorkshire

PO Box 88, Otley, West Yorkshire LS21 3TE

Correspondent Mrs A E Bancroft, Administrator

Trustees John A Clegg; Mrs Sylvia Clegg; Mrs S L Worthington; Mrs E A Riddell.

Information available Full accounts were on file at the Charity Commission, but without a grants list.

General The trust was established in 1962 by Frederick Moore, his wife Elsie, and their daughter and son-in-law, Sylvia and John Clegg 'as a token of gratitude for the happiness given to them by their late daughter and grand-daughter'. It is a time charity: all remaining capital will be distributed to the descendants of the family in 50 years from 1962, or 21 years from the death of the last survivor of the descendants of George V, whichever is the sooner.

The trust gives 'most particularly to help disadvantaged people but many different projects are supported – caring for the disabled, physically and mentally handicapped and terminally ill, work with young people, medical research. The trust likes projects which reach a lot of people. The trustees are keen that grants are actually spent'.

In 1998/99 the trust had assets of £3.7 million generating an income of £249,000. Grants totalled £257,000. No grants list was included in the accounts, although it contained a breakdown of the areas in which it gives grants as follows:

	1998/99	(1997/98)
Hospices, terminally ill, care	£62,000	(£20,000)
Youth activities, schools	£37,000	(£45,000)
Medical research	£36,000	(£36,000)
National charities	£32,000	(£53,000)
Special overseas appeals	£25,000	(£500)
Special schemes, workshops, disability	£23,000	(£13,000)
Homeless	£15,000	(£16,000)
Local community groups	£9,200	(£9,800)
Hospital appeals	£7,000	(£2,000)
Social services, probation services	£4,800	(£6,000)
Counselling services	£3,100	(£2,300)
Children's charities and care	£2,000	(£5,500)
Housing associations	£500	(£700)
Advice centres	£450	(£1,900)
Church, religious activities	£150	(£1,800)
Miscellaneous donations	nil	(£2,800)

Exclusions 'The trust does not pay debts, does not make grants to individual students, and does not respond to circulars.' Grants are only given, via social services, to individuals who live in Bradford.

Applications In writing to the correspondent.

The Englefield Charitable Trust

General, in Berkshire

£364,000 (1999/2000)

Beneficial area UK, with a special interest in Berkshire

Englefield Estate Office, Theale, Reading RG7 5DU

Tel. 01734 302504 **Fax** 01734 323748

Correspondent A S Reid, Secretary to the Trustees

Trustees *Sir William Benyon; James Shelley; Mrs Elizabeth Benyon; Richard H R Benyon; Mrs Catherine Haig.*

Information available Report and accounts with full grants list were provided by the trust.

General Around 100 grants are made to registered charities, most of them based in Berkshire. The amount donated varies from £100 up to around £50,000 with most around £1,000. The trustees say they do not have a preference for any particular charitable fields. Although a wide variety of causes are supported, many are Christian.

The trust was founded in 1968 by the settlor, and current trustee, Sir William Benyon. In addition to grant-making, the trust also provides low cost and retirement housing. The latter cost the trust £45,000 in 1999/2000.

By April 2000 the trust's assets totalled £11 million and income of £445,000 had been generated in the financial year. Grants totalled £364,000.

There were 109 grants given, of which 84 were for £1,000 and above. The largest grant of £50,000 was given to University of Reading for their Department of Agriculture, with £1,000 also being given to their 2000 Books Projects. Other sizeable grants went to St Mary the Virgin – Reading (£17,000), Christian Community Action and Douglas Martin Trust (£15,000 each) and £11,000 each to Berkshire Community Trust and Theale Green Community School.

Other benficiaries included Elstree 150th Anniversary Campaign and St Mark's Church – Englefield (£10,000 each), NCH Action for Children (£5,000), Frilsham Appeal for Ancient Church Railings (£3,500), Chelsea Physic Garden (£2,500), Colon Cancer Concern and Wexham Gastrointestinal Trust (£2,000 each), Newbury YMCA and Sense (£1,500 each) and £1,000 each to British Dyslexia Association and Relate Reading. Smaller grants were given to Bible Reading Fellowship, Heritage Education Trust, Raleigh International and Rhino Rescue Trust (£500 each), NSPCC (£300), Abbeyfield House Appeal (£250) and Newbury Spring Festival (£100).

Exclusions No individual applications for study or travel and no grants to non-registered charities.

Applications In writing to the correspondent stating the purpose for which the money is to be used and accompanied by the latest accounts. Applications are considered in March and September.

The Epigoni Trust

Health, welfare, disability, homelessness, addiction, underprivileged children, environment

£228,000 (1998)

Beneficial area Mainly UK

Charities Aid Foundation, King's Hill, West Malling, Kent ME19 4TA

Tel. 01732 520081

Correspondent Mrs Barbara Davis, Information Manager

Trustees *Charles Peacock; Mrs Bettine Bond; Michael Bond.*

Information available Full accounts were on file at the Charity Commission.

General The trust has common trustees with two other trusts, Cleopatra Trust and Dorus Trust (see separate entries) with which it also shares the same aims and polices. All three trusts are administered by Charities Aid Foundation. Generally the trusts support different organisations.

The trust makes grants in the following areas:

- mental health
- cancer welfare/education – not research
- diabetes
- physical disability – not research
- homelessness
- addiction
- underprivileged children.

There is also some preference for environmental causes. It only gives grants for specific projects and does not give grants for running costs or general appeals.

In 1998 the trust had assets of £2.9 million (£3.5 million in the previous year) and an income of £270,000. It gave £228,000 in 52 grants. Administration charges to CAF were low at £588, CAF also received a grant of £2,500. The largest grants were of £10,000 each, given to seven organisations, including Chichester Cathedral (Millennium Endowment Appeal), Dial UK, Muscular Dystrophy Group of GB & Northern Ireland and National Society for Epilepsy.

Other large grants went to Opportunities for People with Disabilities and Training for Life Ltd (£7,000 each) and Aidis Trust and Scottish Society for Autistic Children (£6,000 each). Grants of £5,000 each went to Children Say Charity, Find your Feet Ltd, National Missing Persons Helpline and Singalong Group.

Smaller grants, ranging from £500 to £3,500 included those to Shared Care UK (£3,500), Blind Business Association Charitable Trust (£2,500), Scottish Council on Alcohol (£2,000), Psoriatic Arthropathy Alliance and Wales Council for the Deaf (£1,000 each) and Pearsons Holiday Fund (£500).

Exclusions Grants are not given to individuals or non-registered charities or for medical research. Normally, only organisations with a UK-wide focus are supported.

Applications On a 'funding proposal form' available from the correspondent. Applications should include a copy of the latest annual report and audited accounts. They are considered twice a year in mid summer and mid autumn. Organisations which have received grants from this trust, Cleopatra Trust or Dorus Trust should not reapply within two years. Usually, funding will be considered under only one of these trusts.

The Equity Trust Fund

Welfare of professional performers and stage managers

£340,000 (1999/2000)

Beneficial area UK

222 Africa House, 64 Kingsway, London WC2B 6AH

Tel. 020 7404 6041

Correspondent The Secretary

Trustees *Jean Ainslie; Hugh Manning; Miltons John; Jeffrey Wickham; Nigel Davenport; Gillian Raine; Peter Plouviez; Derek Bond; Frank Williams; Norman Mitchell; Ian McGarry; John Barron; Colin Baker; Barbara Hyslop; John Johnston; Roy Marsden; Annie Bright; Graham Hamilton; Harry Landis; Frederik Pyne; Rosalind Shanks; Johnny Worthy; Frank Hitchman.*

Information available Accounts were on file at the Charity Commission, but without a full list of grants.

General The fund is a benevolent fund for professional performers and stage managers and their dependants. It offers help with welfare rights, gives free debt counselling and information and can offer financial assistance to those in genuine need. It also has an education fund to help members of the profession with further training provided they have at least 10 years, professional adult experience.

Professional theatre venues and theatre companies can approach the fund to see if they are eligible for consideration. It is not general policy to help with production costs. Projects which are going to provide long-term benefits to members of the profession are more likely to be considered.

In 1999/2000 the assets of the trust were £9.2 million, the income was £405,000 and direct charitable expenditure was £258,000. This was broken down as follows (1998/99 figures in brackets):

Theatre grants	£37,000	(£39,000)
Education grants	£124,000	(£101,000)
Welfare and benevolence	£86,000	(£52,000)
Loans – provisions and write-offs	£6,100	(£28,000)

No further details of grants were given in the accounts, but a list of the current outstanding loans was included in the 1998/99 accounts. The main loan was £113,000 to the Actors' Centre, with others ranging from £700 to £15,000 to theatres throughout the UK.

Exclusions No grants to amateurs or non-professional performers, non-professional theatre companies, multi arts venues, community projects or projects with no connection to the professional theatre.

Applications In the first instance please call the office to ascertain if the application is relevant. Failing that, submit a brief letter outlining the application. A meeting takes place about every six to eight weeks. Ring for precise dates. Applications are required two weeks beforehand.

The Euroclydon Trust

Christian

£66,000 (1997/98)

Beneficial area UK and worldwide

UKET, PO Box 99, Loughton, Essex LG10 3QJ

Tel. 020 8502 5600

Correspondent The Stewardship Services

Trustees *UKET.*

Information available Full accounts were on file at the Charity Commission.

General In 1997/98 the trust's assets totalled £1 million. It had an income of £54,000 from investments and grants to 16 organisations totalled £66,000. Most, if not all, the beneficiaries were Christian organisations.

The largest grants were £12,000 to Missionary Aviation Fellowship, £5,800 to Covenanters, £2,600 to Timothy Trust, £2,500 each to Echoes of Service and Ambassadors for Christ (India) and £1,800 to London Institute. Other grants ranged from £300 to £1,500. Most grants were recurrent.

Applications The trust states that applications are not invited.

The Alan Evans Memorial Trust

Preservation, conservation

£92,000 (1998/99)

Beneficial area UK

Coutts & Co., Trustee Deparment, 440 Strand, London WC2R 0QS

Tel. 020 7753 1624/1257

Correspondent The Trust Manager

Trustees *Coutts & Co.; John W Halfhead; Mrs D Moss.*

Information available Full accounts were on file at the Charity Commission.

General The objects of the trust 'are to promote the permanent preservation, for the benefit of the nation, of lands and tenements (including buildings) of beauty or historic interest and as regards land, the preservation (so far as practicable) of the natural aspect, features and animal and plant life'.

In 1998/99 the trust had assets of £3.3 million and an income of £110,000. Administration and management costs were a high £44,000. Grants totalled £92,000 and were categorised as follows:

£14,000	in respect of land
£56,000	to churches
£22,000	in respect of the environment

The accounts included a list of the 48 grants of £1,000 and more, which totalled £77,000. Grants were given to various UK and local countryside, environmental and restoration organisations. Beneficiaries included RSPB (£8,500), National Trust – Snowdonia (£5,000), Devon Wildlife Trust (£3,000), Countryside Restoration Trust (£2,500), Carstairs Countryside Trust (£2,000), Woodland Trust (£1,500) and Mugdock Trust (£1,000). Grants were also given to 34 churches and cathedrals throughout the country, although there was a preference for Wales.

Exclusions No grants to individuals or for management or running expenses, although favourable consideration is given in respect of the purchase of land and restoration of buildings. Grants are given to registered charities only. Any appeal falling outside the trust criteria will not be acknowledged.

Applications In writing to the correspondent stating why the funds are required, what funds have been promised from other sources, for example, English Heritage, and the amount outstanding. Trustees normally meet three times a year, although in urgent cases decisions can be made between meetings.

The Eventhall Family Charitable Trust

General

£113,00 (1998/99)

Beneficial area Preference for the north of England

23 Beeston Road, Sale, Cheshire M33 5AQ

Correspondent L H Eventhall, Chair

Trustees *Leon Eventhall, Chair; Corrine Eventhall; David Eventhall.*

Information available Grants information was provided by the trust. Accounts were on file at the Charity Commission, but without a grants list.

General In 1998/99 the trust had assets of £992,000 and a healthly income of £241,000. Grants to 85 charities totalled £113,000.

The largest grant was £73,000 to Heathlands Village and the trust also made a commitment to provide major funding for a refurbishment in 1999/2000. Other larger grants included those to JJCT (£10,000), Guide Dogs for the Blind (£3,200), Aish Hatorah (£2,600), Red Nose Day (£2,000), Community Security Trust (£1,600) and Greibach Memorial and South Manchester Synagogue (each £1,500). Smaller grants included M B Foundation Charity (£500), Sale Ladies Society (£250), ChildLine, Clitheroe Wolves Football Club and Only Foals and Horses Sanctuary (each £100), Shelter (£50), RNLI (£25) and International Wildlife Coalition (£10)

Exclusions No grants to students.

Applications In writing to the correspondent, however please note, the trust stated in July 1999 that it 'has entered into commitments for the next three years which will absorb approximately 95% of its income and [it] will, therefore, only have a very limited amount of funds available'. Telephone calls are not received by the trust. Trustees meet monthly to consider grants. A self-addressed is appreciated (stamp not necessary). Unsuccessful applicants will not receive a reply.

The Beryl Evetts & Robert Luff Animal Welfare Trust

Animal welfare

£63,000 (1998/99)

Beneficial area UK

294 Earls Court Road, London SW5 9BB

Tel. 020 8954 2727

Correspondent Michael Lock

Trustees *R C W Luff; Sir R Johnson; M Tomlinson; Mrs J Tomlinson; R P J Price; Lady Johnson; Ms G Favot.*

Information available Full accounts were on file at the Charity Commission.

General Unfortunately we were unable to update the information for this entry since the last edition of this guide.

The principal objective of the trust is the funding of veterinary research and the care and welfare of animals. It appears to make substantial commitments to a few organisations over several years, whether to build up capital funds or to establish fellowships. The trust gives priority to research projects and bursaries. In practice, the trust supports the same beneficiaries each year.

In 1998/99 the largest grant was a donation of £26,000 to the Royal Veterinary College's Beryl Evetts and Robert Luff Fellowship.

The Animal Health Trust received £25,000 towards the establishment of a Small Animals Orthopaedic Unit. In addition, a first grant payment of £10,000 was made for the establishment of a Clinical Neurology Unit.

Grants totalled £63,000 from an income of £87,000. The assets stood at £1.3 million. Beneficiaries of smaller grants included the National Equine and Smaller Animals Defence League (£1,000).

Applications 'No applications thank you.' The trust gives grants to the same beneficiaries each year and funds are often allocated two years in advance.

The Fairway Trust

General

£58,000 (1998/99)

Beneficial area Worldwide

The Gate House, Coombe Wood Road, Kingston-upon-Thames, Surrey KT2 7JY

Correspondent Mrs J Grimstone, Trustee

Trustees *Mrs Janet Grimstone; Mrs K V M Suenson-Taylor.*

Information available Full accounts were on file at the Charity Commission.

General The trust's objects are to support:

- universities, colleges and schools in the UK and abroad

- religious purposes (including the promotion of religion and supporting clergy)
- clubs and recreational facilities for children and young people
- preservation and maintenance of buildings of particular interest
- scholarships, grants and loans to postgraduates and undergraduates.

Social welfare charities are also supported.

In 1998/99 the trust had assets of £31,000 and an income of £66,000, £64,000 of which came from donations. After nominal expenses of £600, the trust gave 27 grants totalling £58,000.

The largest grants were £10,000 each to British and Internaional Sailor's Society, Family Education Trust and Riverside Housing Association. Many of the organisations receiving large grants have previously been supported by the trust. Other grants ranged from £1,000 to £5,000 and were given to a variety of causes including Boys' and Girls' Clubs of Northern Ireland, Kingston Arts Council, National Drug Prevention Alliance, St John The Baptist – Romanian Account and Welsh National Opera. A grant to £1,000 was also given to a student at Manchester University.

Applications In writing to the correspondent.

This entry was not confirmed by the trust but was correct according to information on file at the Charity Commission.

Famos Foundation Trust

Jewish

£66,000 (1998/99)

Beneficial area UK and overseas

4 Hanover Gardens, Salford M7 4FQ

Correspondent Rabbi S M Kupetz, Trustee

Trustees *Rabbi S M Kupetz; Mrs F Kupetz.*

Information available Accounts were on file at the Charity Commission, but without a grants list and only a very brief narrative report.

General In 1998/99 the trust's assets totalled £738,000, it had an income of £69,000 and grants totalled £66,000. Grants of up to £5,000 were given. The

trust supports a wide range of Jewish organisations, including those concerned with education and the relief of poverty. Many grants are recurrent. Unfortunately further information was not available.

Exclusions No grants to individuals.

Applications In writing to the correspondent, at any time. The trust does not accept telephone enquiries.

The Lord Faringdon First & Second Charitable Trusts

Medical, general

£138,000 (1998/99)

Beneficial area UK

The Estate Office, Buscot Park, Faringdon, Oxfordshire SN7 8BU

Tel. 01367 240786 **Fax** 01367 241794 **e-mail** estbuscot@aol.com

Correspondent J R Waters, Secretary

Trustees *Hugh S S Trotter; Anthony D A W Forbes; Hon. James H Henderson.*

Information available Full accounts were on file at the Charity Commission.

General The two trusts were in the process of amalgamation at the time of going to print. The new trust will be called Lord Faringdon Charitable Trust. It is expected to be in operation by 2001. The trusts have identical objects, which are:

- educational and scholarships grants
- hospitals and the provision of medical treatment for the sick
- purchase of antiques and artistic objects for museums and collections which have public access
- care and assistance of people who are elderly or infirm
- development and assistance of arts and sciences, physical recreation and drama
- research into matters of public interest
- relief of poverty
- support of matters of public interest
- maintaining and improving the Faringdon Collection.

Lord Faringdon First Charitable Trust
In 1998/99 the trust had assets of £3.4 million and an income of £66,000. It gave £84,000 in seven grants. A large grant of £50,000 was given to Buscot Centenary and Millennium Fund, which also received £30,000 the year before. The

other grants went to The Friends of St Denys (£15,000), Institute of Cancer Research (£6,000), Peper Harrow Foundation and Wildlife Network (£5,000 each), The Pedro Club (£2,000) and Langley House Trust (£1,000). One other grant was recurrent from the previous year.

Lord Faringdon Charitable Trust
In 1998/99 the trust had assets of £2.1 million and an income of £58,000. It gave £54,000 in 10 grants. The largest were of £10,000 each and went to Royal Choral Society and The Royal Horticultural Society. Six grants of £5,000 each went to The Children's Hospital – Bristol, Kew Foundation, RAFT, Reed's School, St Luke's Hospice and Tommy's Campaign. The other grants went to Edwina, Countess Mountbatten Trust (£3,000) and Leicester Chorale (£1,000). One grant was recurrent from the previous year.

Applications In writing to the correspondent.

Samuel William Farmer's Trust

General, education

£56,000 (1999)

Beneficial area Mainly Wiltshire

Tanglewood, 33 The Fairway, Devizes, Wiltshire SN10 5DX

Correspondent Mrs J Simpson

Trustees *V H Rendell, Chair; D Gauntlett; J Waight; P G Fox-Andrews; D Brockis.*

Information available Full accounts were on file at the Charity Commission.

General The trust was established for: the benefit of poor people who through ill health or old age are unable to earn their own livelihood; for educational purposes; and for the benefit of hospitals, nursing and convalescent homes or other similar objects.

In 1999 it had assets of £2.1 million and an income of £75,000. Grants totalled £56,000, divided as follows:

Annual grants	£7,000
Infirm, elderly and long service workers	£1,300
Special grants	£48,000

The annual grants went to Royal Agricultural Benevolent Institution and

Royal United Kingdom Beneficient Association (both £3,000) and Barnardos (£1,000). Special grants went to 11 organisations. The largest were of £10,000 each to ILC and Wiltshire Community Foundation. Other larger grants went to Ramsbury School (£8,000), St Francis School (£5,200), Wiltshire Air Ambulance (£3,000) and Devizes Museum and The Merchants House Trust (each £2,500). The remaining three grants were of £2,000 each and went to Monkton Combe School, Old Dauntseians Association and Oundle School Fund. Two grants were recurrent from the previous year.

Applications In writing to the correspondent. Trustees meet in April and October.

Farthing Trust

Christian, general

£119,000 (1997/98)

Beneficial area UK and overseas

48 Ten Mile Bank, Littleport, Ely, Cambridgeshire CB6 1EF

Correspondent Heber Martin, Trustee

Trustees C H Martin; Mrs E Martin; Miss J Martin; Mrs A White.

Information available Accounts were on file at the Charity Commission, but without a grants list.

General In 1998/99 the trust had an income of £292,000 and a total expenditure of £153,000. This information was available on the Charity Commission database, unfortunately the accounts were not yet in the public file. The following is repeated from the last edition of the guide.

In 1997/98 the trust had assets of £998,000 and a total income of £115,000, including £17,000 in donations. Grants totalled £119,000 and were categorised by the trust as follows (1997 figures in brackets):

Category	£	(£)
Education	12,000	(4,400)
UK churches	21,000	(23,000)
UK Christian causes	11,000	(11,000)
UK general charities	6,300	(4,900)
Local	1,500	(3,400)
Christian workers	26,000	(7,100)
Individuals in need	4,400	(900)
Overseas Christian missions	20,000	(28,000)
Overseas Christian causes	16,000	(10,000)
Overseas general charities	1,300	(2,500)

No further details on the charities to benefit were given by the trust.

Priority is given to those personally known to the trustees or recommended by those personally known to the trustees.

Applications Applications and enquiries should be made in writing to the correspondent. Applicants will only be notified of refusal if an sae is enclosed. There would seem little point in applying unless a personal contact with a trustee is established.

The Fidelity UK Foundation

General

£213,000 (1999)

Beneficial area UK and Europe

Windmill Court, Millfield Lane, Lower Kingswood, Surrey KT20 6RB

Tel. 01737 837842 **Fax** 01737 837850

Correspondent Miss Jacqueline Guthrie

Trustees B R J Bateman, Chair; E C Johnson; M P Cambridge; A J Bolton; R Milotte; R Millar.

Information available Guidelines for applications were provided from the trust. Accounts were on file at the Charity Commission, but with a grants list or a narrative report.

General The foundation gives for general charitable purposes, although it has a preference for addiction awareness and prevention, arts and culture, community development and services, conservation and preservation, disability (particularly concerned with children), education and health initiatives focusing on developing cures and treatment for long term, disabling diseases.

The trust gives grants to registered charities and some exempt charities, such as certain schools. It will fund programme support, special projects, development and capital campaigns, although grants are not available for costs additional to the core purposes of the charity such as advertising, and the trust will not support the entire cost of a project. Particular preference is given to organisations or projects in Kent, Surrey and central/City of London. It can also consider applications from European charities.

In 1999 the trust had assets of £5.7 million and an income of £1.5 million. This is a dramatic increase from the year before, the assets have more than doubled (£2.4 million in 1998) and the income is five times greater (£300,000 in 1998). Grants totalled £213,000. A grants list was not provided.

Grants may be given in kind rather than cash, and the foundation promises to match any donations made by staff members who raise money on behalf of other charities.

Exclusions Grants are not made to sectarian or political organisations, private schools or individuals, nor for scholarships, corporate memberships, video or film projects, sponsorships or participation in benefit events. The foundation will not generally make multi-year pledges and will not normally award grants to any organisation in successive years.

Applications In writing to the correspondent. Applications should include summary of proposal, organisation history and objectives, description of request and rationale, project budget, other funders and status of each request, operating budget and recent financial statements. Guidelines for applicants are available from the trust. Applications will be replied to within three months.

The trust states it receives more applications than it can fund, so some worthy causes cannot be supported.

The Doris Field Charitable Trust

General

£229,000 (1997/98)

Beneficial area UK, with a preference for Oxfordshire

Morgan Cole Solicitors, Buxton Court, 3 West Way, Oxford OX2 0SZ

Tel. 01865 262600

Correspondent Georgina Cheetham

Trustees N A Harper; W G S Crouch; J Cole; Mrs W Church.

Information available Full accounts were on file at the Charity Commission.

General One-off and recurrent grants are given to large UK organisations and small local projects for a wide variety of causes. The trust also makes a number of grants to young individuals with learning difficulties and disabilities to buy computers and also a number of small grants to playgroups and local Oxfordshire groups.

In 1997/98 the trust had assets of £4 million generating an income of £164,000. Grants to 90 organisations totalled £229,000, 43 of which were recurrent from previous years.

The largest grant was £109,000 to New Marston Pastoral Centre, a recurrent grant given since 1994/95. Other large grants included £10,000 to Volunteer Reading Help and £5,000 to Wolvercote Scout Hut, both also regular beneficiaries. Smaller recurrent grants have been given to Appleton with Eaton Parish Council (£1,000) and PDSA (£300). One-off grants were also given to Friends of Ormerod Schools and Marie Curie Cancer Care (£2,500 each), Woodfarm Youth Club (£500) and Dovecot Centre (£250).

Applications On a form available from the correspondent. Applications are considered in November.

The Finnart House School Trust

Jewish children and young people in need of care

£129,000 (1998/99)

Beneficial area Worldwide

5th Floor, 707 High Road, North Finchley, London N12 0BT

Tel. 020 8445 1670 **Fax** 020 8446 7370 **e-mail** finnart@anjy.org

Correspondent Peter Shaw, Clerk

Trustees *Dr Louis Marks, Chair; Robert Cohen; Jane Grabiner; Hilary Norton; David Fobel; Lilian Hochhauser; Jane Leaver; Dr Amanda Kirby; Mark Sebba.*

Information available Full accounts were provided by the trust.

General The trust supports the relief of children and young people who are of the Jewish faith and aged 21 and under. It particularly helps those who are disaffected; disadvantaged socially and economically, through illness or neglect;

and those who are in need of care and education.

In 1998/99 the trust had assets of £4.6 million, an income of £176,000 and gave £129,000 in 22 grants. Grants of over £2,000 were made to 21 organisations, of which 14 were recurrent; other grants totalled £2,000. The largest went to Ashalim Children's Village (£20,000), Manchester Jewish Foundation (£12,000) and £10,000 each to J F S Comprehensive School and Hamifal. All but the latter had received grants of different amounts in the previous year.

The other grants listed ranged from £2,000 to £7,000 and included Keren Klita (£6,000), Beit Issie Shapiro and Jewish Lads' and Girls' Brigade (£5,000 each) and Chamah (£2,500) – all of which were recurrent from the previous year. New grants included Shalva (£7,000), Jerusalem College of Technology (£6,000), Fun Lodge and Moral (each £4,000) and Children at Risk and Magen Avraham (each £3,000).

Exclusions No grants to individuals.

Applications There is an application form, which needs to be submitted together with a copy of the latest annual report and accounts.

The Sir John Fisher Foundation

General

£169,000 (1997/98)

Beneficial area UK, with a preference for the Furness peninsula

8-10 New Market Street, Ulverston, Cumbria LA12 7LW

Tel. 01229 583291

Correspondent R F Hart Jackson, Trustee

Trustees *D P Tindall; R F Hart Jackson; Mrs D S Meacock.*

Information available Full accounts were on file at the Charity Commission.

General The trust states that it gives grants to charities concerned with the Furness peninsula and local branches of UK charities. Grants are also made to UK

and international groups concerned with the shipping industry, medicine, the navy or military and music or theatre.

In 1997/98 the trust had assets of £187,000 and an income of £276,000, including a donation of £215,000 from James Fisher & Sons and £4,000 from Barrow Housing Company Ltd. Grants to 111 local and national charities totalled £169,000. Administration and management costs were high at £27,000 (that is £243 per grant given).

Grants to a wide range of 90 local organisations in Cumbria totalled £133,000 (including £6,500 in seven grants to groups in Liverpool). The largest of these grants were £25,000 to Lancaster University (Sir John Fisher Chair) and £10,000 to Hospice of St Mary of Furness. Grants are given to small local organisations such as Furness Drug Concern (£5,500), Dallan School (£4,000), Copeland Talking Newspaper (£500) and Cumbria Drama Festival (£100). Grants were also given to local branches of UK charities such as Samaritans of Furness (£5,500), Citizens Advice Bureau in Barrow (£5,500) and Ulverston (£5,000), Ocean Youth Club North West (£3,100), Multiple Sclerosis Society Barrow and District (£200) and RNLI (£100). Grants were also given to seven groups in Liverpool for similar purposes, including £500 each to British Lung Foundation Liverpool, River Mersey Inshore Rescue Team and Liverpool School of Medicine. Eight individuals received grants ranging between £250 and £500 totalling £2,300.

Grants to 21 national organisations totalled £36,000. The largest of these grants were given to Worshipful Company of Shipwrights (£12,000) and Foundation of Coagulation and Thrombosis at Dundee University (£10,000). Most of the national grants were of less than £1,000 and were given to organisations including Electronic Aids for the Blind, Mission for Seamen, Trinity House Maritime Museum, Voluntary Services Overseas and Welsh Initiative for Conductive Education. One individual received a grant for £2,500.

Exclusions Grants are not given to students.

Applications In writing to the correspondent. Trustees usually meet in May and November.

Marc Fitch Fund

See below

£105,000 to organisations (1997/98)

Beneficial area UK

Flat 7, Murray Court, 80 Banbury Road, Oxford OX2 6LQ

Tel. 01865 553369

Correspondent Roy Stephens, Director and Secretary

Trustees A Bell, Chair; The Duke of Norfolk; Hon. N Assheton; Prof. J P Barron; A J Camp; Prof. C R Elrington; Dr J I Kermode; Prof. D M Palliser.

Information available Full accounts were on file at the Charity Commission.

General The trust makes grants for 'publication of research in archaeology, historical geography, history of art and architecture, heraldry, genealogy, surnames, catalogues of and use of archives (especially ecclesiastical), conservation of artefacts and other antiquarian, archaeological or historical studies'.

In 1997/98 the fund had assets of £3.8 million and an income of £229,000, including a publishing income of £25,000. After 'charity related expenses' of £52,000, publishing costs of £33,000 and administration and management expenses of £15,000, the fund gave grants to organisations totalling £105,000, and £35,000 to individuals.

The largest grants were given to the universities of Leicester (£28,000) and Liverpool (£18,000). Other grants were given towards publications, research and societies including Historic Towns Trust (£5,000), Winchester Excavations Society (£4,000), Buildings Book Trust (£3,000), Local Population Studies (£2,000) and British Archaeological Society and Suffolk Records Society (£1,000 each). Many of the organisations supported had also received grants in the previous year.

Applications In writing to the correspondent. The trustees meet twice a year to consider applications.

The Fitton Trust

Social welfare, medical

£83,000 (1998/99)

Beneficial area UK

Phoenix House, 9 London Road, Newbury, Berkshire RG14 1DH

Tel. 01635 571009

Correspondent Penningtons, Trustees' Solicitor

Trustees Dr R P A Rivers; D M Lumsden; D V Brand.

Information available Accounts were on file at the Charity Commission, but without a list of grants.

General In 1998/99 the trust had an income of £107,000. Grants totalled £83,000 and its total expenditure was £103,000. Further information about the size and beneficiaries of grants was not available.

In previous years the trust has supported social welfare and medical charities.

Exclusions No grants to individuals.

Applications In writing to The Secretary, The Fitton Trust, PO Box 649, London SW3 4LA. The trust states: 'no application is considered unless accompanied by fully audited accounts. No replies will be sent to unsolicited applications whether from individuals, charities or other bodies.'

The Earl Fitzwilliam Charitable Trust

General

£69,000 (1999/2000)

Beneficial area UK, with a preference for in Cambridgeshire, Northamptonshire and Yorkshire

Estate Office, Milton Park, Peterborough PE6 7AH

Tel. 01733 267740

e-mail thompo@webleicester.co.uk

Correspondent Michael Thompson, Secretary to the Trustees

Trustees Sir Philip Naylor-Leyland; Lady Isabella Naylor-Leyland.

Information available Full accounts were provided by the trust.

General The trust was established by the Rt Hon. Earl Fitzwilliam in 1975 with £10,000 and land valued (for stamp duty) at £450,000. Further land was added in 1980, valued at £513,000. The trust tends to favour charities which benefit rural communities, especially those with a connection to Cambridgeshire, Peterborough, South Yorkshire and Malton in North Yorkshire where the Fitzwilliam family have held their landed estates for many centuries. In1999/2000 the trust had assets of just over £4 million and an income of £195,000. Grants totalled £69,000 (£71,000 in 1998/99); £92,000 was spent on the upkeep of the estate (£68,000 in 1998/99).

The accounts listed 35 grants of £1,000 or more. Most grants appear to be one-off. The largest grant of £4,000 went to Dore Old School Appeal (Sheffield). The remaining grants were all between £1,000 and £2,500. Some UK charities and many local organisations were supported, the latter predominantly in the areas mentioned above. Examples included those to Peterborough Council for Voluntary Service, St Mathew Housing (Peterborough), Etton Church (Peterborough), St Mary's Priory (Old Malton), Cavendish Fellowship in Hip Surgery, The Church Housing Trust, University of Reading, Croft Community (Malton) and Edith Cavell Hospital (Peterborough).

Exclusions No grants to individuals.

Applications In writing to the correspondent. Trustees meet about every two months.

The Rose Flatau Charitable Trust

Jewish, social welfare

£123,000 (1998/99)

Beneficial area UK

5 Knott Park House, Wrens Hill, Oxshott, Leatherhead KT22 0HW

Tel. 01372 843082

Correspondent M E G Prince, Trustee

Trustees M E G Prince; A E Woolf; N L Woolf.

Information available Accounts were on file at the Charity Commission with only a brief narrative report.

General The trust supports charities concerned with health and older people and Jewish organisations.

In 1998/99 the trust had assets of £1.6 million and an income of £61,000. It gave £123,000 in 42 grants. The largest of £15,000 went to Norwood Ravenswood Foundation which also received the same amount in the previous year. Other large grants were £6,000 to Anglo Jewish Association and 12 grants of £5,000 each including those to CRISIS, Queen Elizabeth Fund for the Disabled, Winged Fellowship Trust and World Jewish Relief. Other grants ranged from £1,000 to £2,500, including those to British Trust for Conservation Volunteers, Wizo (£2,000), Age Concern and Help the Hospices (each £1,000).

Applications The trust states: 'No further applications can be accepted as the income available is fully committed.' No application forms are available. There are no set dates for trustees' meetings.

Florence's Charitable Trust

Education, welfare, sick and infirm

£119,000 (1997/98)

Beneficial area UK, with a preference for Lancashire

E Sutton & Sons, PO Box 2, Riverside, Bacup, Lancashire OL13 0DT

Tel. 01706 874961

Correspondent R Barker, Secretary to the Trustees

Trustees *C C Harrison, Chair; R Barker; A Connearn; G D Low; M Thurlwell; J Mellows; R D Uttley.*

Information available Full accounts were on file at the Charity Commission.

General In 1998/99 the trust had an income of £108,000 and an expenditure of £315,000. Unfortunately, no further information for this year was available and this information is repeated from the last edition of this guide.

In 1997/98 the trust had assets of £1.5 million and an income of £122,000, almost all of which was given in grants.

Grants are categorised under three main headings: education (£59,000), sick and infirm (£34,000) and other public benefits (£11,000). One grant of £10,000

was given to Age Concern – Rossendale under the category 'Aged'. A further £6,100 was given to individuals in death grants.

There were 29 grants given in the education category, of which 26 were to schools in Lancashire. The largest went to St Anne's C of E Primary School (£3,000) and Alder Grange School (£2,300). The other grants to schools were all for £2,000. Other organisations supported were Life Education Trust for Lancashire, Rawtonstall Tutorial Centre and Young Enterprise Trust. All but one of the grants were recurrent.

The 'sick and infirm' category included 17 grants with the largest being £10,000 to Superscan Appeal. Other larger grants went to Mobility Trust (£7,000), Sense (£3,000) and Liverpool Society for the Blind and Multiple Sclerosis Society (each £2,000). Smaller grants ranged from £250 to £1,500 including those to Disability Sports, RNIB Dewsbury, East Lancashire Deaf Society and Christie's Hospital.

In the other public benefits category, the 22 grants ranged from £250 to £1,700. Five local branches of the Samaritans were supported as well as a range of other causes, such as Bacup Amateur Operatic Society, Bowland Pennine Mountain Rescue, Lancashire Crimestoppers and Shawforth Drum Majorettes.

Applications In writing to the correspondent.

The Gerald Fogel Charitable Trust

Jewish, general

£57,000 (1997/98)

Beneficial area UK

Morley & Scott, Lynton House, 7–12 Tavistock Square, London WC1H 9LT

Tel. 020 7387 5868

Correspondent J Clay, Accountant

Trustees *J G Fogel; B Fogel; S Fogel; D Fogel.*

Information available Accounts were on file at the Charity Commission.

General Unfortunately we have been unable to update the information for this entry since the last edition of this guide.

The trust stated in its annual report that its policy is 'to make a wide spread of grants'. In practice it appears to support mainly Jewish organisations.

In 1997/98 the trust's assets totalled £970,000 and it had an income of £60,000, half of which was from donations received. Grants were made to 64 organisations totalling £57,000. Only 23 beneficiaries, which received grants of £1,000 or more, were listed in the accounts.

The largest grants were £10,000 to Jewish Care, £8,500 to Norwood Ravenswood, £4,000 to Jewish Child's Day, £2,500 to The Constable Educational Trust and £2,000 to Jewish Marriage Council. The remaining grants listed were all for £1,000 and included those to non-Jewish beneficiaries such as Imperial Cancer Research, Jack's Pack, King Edward VII's Hospital for Officers, Macmillan Cancer Relief, Marie Curie Cancer Care, St John's Hospice and Variety Club.

Applications In writing to the correspondent.

The Follett Trust

Welfare, education, arts

£65,000 (1998/99)

Beneficial area UK

17 Chescombe Road, Yatton, North Somerset BS19 4EE

Tel. 01934 838337

Correspondent M D Follett, Trustee

Trustees *Martin Follett; Ken Follett; Barbara Follett.*

Information available Full accounts were on file at the Charity Commission.

General The trust's policy is to:

- give financial assistance to organisations in the field of education and individual students in higher education including theatre
- support organisations concerned with disability and health
- support trusts involved with writers and publishing
- respond to world crisis appeals for help.

For its income the trust relies almost entirely on regular donations from its trustees, which in 1997/98 totalled £80,000. Grants totalled £65,000, including a small number to individuals. Grants ranged from £50 to £15,000.

The largest grants went to Canon Collins Trust (£15,000) and University College London Development Fund (£10,000). Other larger grants included those to Stevenage CAB (£5,900), Edinburgh Book Festival (£5,800), Laban Centre (£3,000) and Oxfam (£1,200). Grants of £1,000 each included those to Amnesty International, Artsline, Community Heart, New Horizon Youth Centre, Roebuck Junior School, Save the Rhino International and Stevenage Community Trust.

Smaller grants included those to Gwent Cancer Support (£500), Hertfordshire and Bedfordshire Pastoral Foundation (£100) and Parkinson's Disease Society (£50).

Applications The trust states, 'A high proportion of donees come to the attention of the trustees through personal knowledge and contact rather than by written application. Where the trustees find it impossible to make a donation they rarely respond to the applicant unless an sae is provided'.

The Football Association National Sports Centre Trust

Play areas, football
£663,000 (1996)
Beneficial area UK

16 Lancaster Gate, London W2 3LW
Tel. 020 7262 4542
Correspondent M Day, Secretary to the Trustees
Trustees *K St J Wiseman, Chair; W T Annable; A W Brett; A D McMullen; E M Parry.*

Information available Full accounts were on file at the Charity Commission up to 1996.

General Unfortunately we have been unable to update this entry since the last edition of this guide.

In 1996 the trust's assets totalled £2.7 million and income was £1.4 million, mainly from Gift Aid donations from the Football Association. Grants were made totalling £663,000.

The trust's 1996 annual report states that the principal activity of the trust is 'the preservation and protection of the physical and mental health of the community; and the provision, in the interests of social welfare and with the object of improving the conditions of life for the persons for whom the facilities are primarily intended, of facilities for recreation and other leisure time occupations which shall be available to members of the public at large'.

In practice the trust appears to make grants in two areas:

a) towards hard surface play areas

b) to 'grass roots' football clubs.

Grants were given to 16 hard surface play areas in 1996, with applicants including councils, sports clubs and community associations. These grants totalled £294,000.

The remaining grants, totalling £369,000 were given in grants up to £5,000, to football clubs.

Applications In writing to the correspondent.

The Football Association Youth Trust

Sports
£153,000 (1996/97)
Beneficial area UK

9 Wyllyotts Place, Potters Bar, Hertfordshire EN6 2JD
Tel. 01707 651840
Correspondent M Appleby, Secretary
Trustees *K St J Wiseman, Chair; W T Annable; A W Brett; A D McMullen; E M Parry.*

Information available Accounts were on file at the Charity Commission, but without a grants list.

General Unfortunately we have been unable to update the following information since the last edition of this guide.

The principal activity of the trust continues to be the organisation or provision of facilities which will enable pupils of schools and universities in the UK to play association football or other games and sports including the provision

of equipment, lectures, training colleges, playing fields or indoor accommodation. In addition, the trust has organised or provided facilities for physical recreation in the interests of social welfare in the UK for people under 21 who need such facilities. Schools and in particular, the English Schools Football Association and the Universities and City Football Associations are major beneficiaries. A range of projects and events have been supported, an increasing number of which have been small donations to schools and clubs. Beneficiaries must be under 21 unless they are in full-time education.

In 1996/97 the trust had an income of £601,000 including a £500,000 Gift Aid donation from the Football Association. The assets have increased to £2.2 million and grants during the year totalled £153,000.

The largest grant was £51,000 to English Schools FA, with £7,500 each to the Independent Schools FA and British University Sports Association. Cambridge and Oxford University FC each received £4,000 and £12,000 was listed as 'payments to other institutions'.

Applications In writing to the correspondent. Grants are made throughout the year. There are no application forms, but a copy of the most recent accounts should be sent.

This entry was not confirmed by the trust but was correct according to information on file at the Charity Commission.

The Forbes Charitable Trust

Learning disabilities
See below
Beneficial area UK

9 Weir Road, Kibworth, Leicestershire LE8 0LQ
Tel. 0116 279 3225 **Fax** 0116 279 6384
e-mail carecentral@freeuk.com
Correspondent J B Shepherd, Secretary to the Trustees
Trustees *Colonel R G Wilkes; Major Gen. R L S Green; J C V Lang; E J Townsend; N J Townsend.*

Information available Full accounts were on file at the Charity Commission.

General The foundation was set up 'to make long-term provision for adults with learning disabilities'. In 1998/99 the trust's assets totalled £1.7 million and it had an income of £95,000. During the year the trust also sold the Broadhoath estate for £1.1 million which was £308,000 in excess of the valuation recorded in the foundation's books. Due to this unexpected excess, the trust made a commitment of a special donation of £250,000 to CARE Fund (Hand-in-Hand Appeal), a recently launched appeal for a new community centre for people with learning difficulties to be built in Kent. This donation was in addition to a commitment made in 1995/96 to pay £300,000 over a period of five years to the same project – all of which was paid this year.

Other grants made in 1998/99 totalled just over £15,000; they were £10,000 to Voice UK, £2,500 each to Great Ormond Street Hospital Children's Charity and Robert Owen Foundation and £250 to Carers' Relief Service – Holiday Respite Scheme.

In 1997/98 the trust had an income of £94,000 and made grants totalling £53,000 to CARE Fund – Shangton Silver Appeal (£50,000) and £1,000 each to Acorn Housing Trust, Douglas Farm Group – Riding for the Disabled and Challenge – Belfast.

Applications In writing to the correspondent.

The Oliver Ford Charitable Trust

Mental disability, housing

£104,000 (1999/2000)

Beneficial area UK

Messrs Macfarlanes, 10 Norwich Street, London EC4A 1BD

Tel. 020 7831 9222

Correspondent Matthew Pintus

Trustees *Derek Hayes; Lady Wakeham; Martin Levy.*

Information available Information was provided by the trust.

General The objects of the trust are to educate the public and advance knowledge of the history and techniques of interior decoration, the designs of fabric and other decorative materials and landscape gardening with particular reference to Oliver Ford's own work. Income not used for these purposes is

used for the Anthroposophical Society of Great Britain, Camphill Village Trust, Ravenswood Foundation or any other village or home for people with mental disabilities which is not state-subsidised.

In 1999/2000 the assets stood at £1.9 million and the total income was £114,000 following the sale of shares. Grants totalled £104,000.

The trust provided a summary of donations made over the last six years. Grants have been given each year to students at Kingston Maurward College (£11,000 in 1999/2000) and Victoria & Albert Museum (£25,000).

Grants were given to 11 other organisations, only 3 of which were new to the trust. The smallest grant was for £200 to Break and the largest £25,000 to Croft-Care Trust. Other recipients included Greenacre Farm Communities, Roy Kinnear Foundation, Martha Trust, and National Autistic Society.

Applications In writing to the correspondent. Trustees meet in March and October.

Fordeve Ltd

Jewish, general

£351,000 (1997/98)

Beneficial area UK

c/o Gerald Kreditor & Co., Tudor House, Llanvanor Road, London NW2 2AQ

Correspondent J Kon, Trustee

Trustees *J Kon; Mrs H Kon.*

Information available Accounts were on file at the Charity Commission, without a grants list and with only a brief narrative report.

General The trust makes grants to Jewish causes and for the relief of need. In 1997/98 it had assets of £385,000 and an income of £130,000, including £107,000 in donations. Grants totalled £351,000 (up from £138,000 in the previous year). Unfortunately further information was not available about the beneficiaries of, or size of, grants made.

Applications In writing to the correspondent.

Four Acre Trust

Respite care and holidays, vocational guidance, health disability, social housing

£254,000 (1999/2000)

Beneficial area Worldwide

Ardale Tower, Clockhouse Lane, North Stifford, Grays, Thurrock RM16 5UN

Tel. 01375 397600 **Fax** 01375 397600
e-mail info@fouracretrust.org.uk
website www.fouracretrust.org.uk

Trustees *Mary A Bothamley; Jennifer J Bunner; John P Bothamley; Robert Carruthers.*

Information available Accounts were provided by the trust but without a list of grants.

General The trust's area of interest is worldwide. It has several guiding principles, these are to:

- give preference to areas which are disadvantaged

- favour projects which will contribute to the preservation and development of a free and stable society

- give preference to projects which are innovative, developmental, designed to make a practical impact on a particular problem or need and reflect the principles of market forces; especially in the case of local projects, preference is given to those which demonstrate active local participation and support self-help

- attach importance to the assessment and dissemination of the results of work it has funded, so that others may benefit.

The trust makes grants under four specific categories:

Repsite care and holidays
Support for: holidays, holiday centres, refuges, carer support and respite, subsidised holidays

Guidance in choice of vocation
Support for: counselling for work training, employment generation, foyer schemes

Relief of health disability at low unit cost
Support for: cataract operations, immunisation programmes, prostheses

Social housing
Support for: provision of land and premises for social housing.

The trust states that it is currently keen to support holidays for those who would not normally have one. It has a preference for supporting capital costs but does give grants for revenue funding. The trust was formed in 1995 and a large part of its income is derived from a company within the construction industry. In 1999/2000 it had an income of £749,000 and gave grants totalling £254,000. The property fund to be used by other charities (see below) had increased to £464,000. Further information for this year was not available.

In 1998/99 the trust had assets of £2 million and an income of £824,000, including £698,000 in donations and gifts. Direct charitable expenditure totalled £228,000 including £22,000 depreciation of property used for charitable purposes, £125,000 rental income foregone – Brighton YMCA and £85,000 in charitable grants.

No further information was available on the grants made. However, it was stated in the trustees' report that the trust had built up relationships with about 20 charities and it is likely that they will continue to support these organisations if they provide satisfactory applications.

'A major project for the trust was the purchase of Ardale, a former community home, in Thurrock, Essex. This will be updated, converted and extended into a new community in partnership with a number of leading and local charities.' The project aims to provide sites and buildings for registered charities at 'highly discounted prices'. The project has been delayed, it appears because of Thurrock Council taking a long time to deal with the planning application. The trust states that new guidlelines by the Charity Commission (which the trust welcomes), make rural and urban regeneration and the relief of unemployment clearly charitable objects. The trust can now show the project's costs as charitable expense in future accounts. It states: 'A large part of the trust's expenditure in the coming year is likely to be made on this project as well as continuing support of other charities.'

Exclusions The trust does not support the following:

- animal welfare
- arts
- basic services (as opposed to imaginative new projects) for people who are disabled or elderly
- commercial publications
- conferences or seminars
- direct replacement of statutory funding

- establishing funds for scholarships or loans
- expeditions
- general appeals
- heritage
- hospices
- individuals
- individual parish churches
- large UK charities which enjoy wide support, including local branches of UK-charities
- medical (including research), general healthcare or costs of individual applicants
- night shelters
- overseas travel, conference attendance or exchanges
- performances, exhibitions or festivals
- projects concerning drug abuse or alcoholism
- religious activities
- science
- sports
- stage, film or television production costs
- university or similar research.

The trust does not make loans, or give grants retrospectively. Grants are not given towards any large capital, endowment or widely distributed appeal. It would consider a specific item, or project, if it formed part of a large appeal.

Applications In writing to the correspondent. Trustees meet in March, June, September and December. Applications should be kept brief and received two months before the meeting.

The Fox Memorial Trust

General

£108,000 to individuals and organisations (1998/99)

Beneficial area UK

Hangover House, 3 Burford Lane, East Ewell, Surrey KT17 3EY

Fax 020 8393 1222

Correspondent Mrs C Hardy, Administrator

Trustees *Miss S M F Crichton; Mrs F M F Davies; Miss A M Fox; Miss C H Fox.*

Information available Accounts were on file at the Charity Commission with a grants list but including only a very brief narrative report.

General The trust was established in 1970 with general charitable purposes. The trust does not describe its work in its annual report. However, the grants list shows a preference for education and health and welfare causes. Mainly UK organisations are supported.

In 1998/99 the trust had assets of £1.6 million (up from £1.3 million the year before). It had an income of £114,000, with grants totalling £108,000, of which £30,000 went to individuals. The largest grants to organisations were £2,000 to City of London Sinfonia and £1,000 each to Alzheimer's Disease Society, The Barn Owl Trust, Blond McIndoe Centre for Medical Research and Lord Mayor's Appeal.

All the remaining grants ranged from £100 to £800, but were mostly for £500. Examples of beneficiaries include Association of Wheelchair Children, Cardon Housing Youth Project, Disabled Living Foundation, Discovery Dockland Trust, Fight for Sight, Forget Me Not Cancer Appeal, Go to the Nations Ministry, International Spinal Research Trust, Muscular Dystrophy Group, Oasis Children's Venture, St John's Hospice, Samaritans, Victim Support and York Minster Fund.

Applications In writing to the correspondent.

The Timothy Franey Charitable Foundation

Children, health, education, arts

£126,000 (1998/99)

Beneficial area Mainly UK, with a small preference for south east London, about 10 per cent overseas

32 Herne Hill, London SE24 9QS

Tel. 020 7274 3383

Correspondent T Franey, Trustee

Trustees *T Franey; S Richmond; P Morrison.*

Information available Accounts were on file at the Charity Commission, but without a grants list.

General The trust helps children who are sick and underprivileged and supports causes in south east London concerned with health, education and the arts.

In 1998/99 the foundation had assets of £524,000 and an income of £39,000. Grants totalled £126,000 (with administration and management charges of £5,300).

No grants list was included in the 1998/99 accounts, although the narrative report stated that a grant of £50,000 was given to NCH Action for Children and £11,000 was given to Hopes and Homes for Children to establish a children's home in the Ukraine. A list of grants has not been included with the accounts since 1995/96 when beneficiaries included Dulwich College Bursary Appeal, Kings Appeal and Malcolm Sargent Cancer Fund for Children.

The trust has decided that because of the large amount of applications it receives and the resulting administration burden and costs it will now only support charities which it has worked with in the past.

Exclusions No grants to individuals. The trust stated 'we mainly support registered charities, or work with them in funding specific situations and projects'.

Applications In writing to the correspondent. However, the trust no longer accepts new applications (see above).

The Jill Franklin Trust

Overseas, welfare, prisons, church restoration

£101,000 (1999/2000)

Beneficial area Worldwide

78 Lawn Road, London NW3 2XB

Tel. 020 7722 4543 **Fax** 020 7722 4543
e-mail lawnroad@cableinet.co.uk

Correspondent Norman Franklin, Trustee

Trustees *Andrew Franklin; Norman Franklin; Sally Franklin; Sam Franklin; Tom Franklin.*

Information available Full accounts were on file at the Charity Commission.

General The trust states it has about £70,000 a year to spend, including

committed funds. Grants are given in the following areas:

- counselling (by volunteers not by professionals) particularly the recruiting and training of volunteers
- advice, training, employment and self-help groups to support people with a mental illness or learning difficulties, and their carers
- respite care and holidays (UK only). Grants for holidays are only given where there is a large element of respite care, and are given to registered charities only, not individuals
- special development projects in the Commonwealth with low overheads
- organisations helping and supporting refugees coming to, or already in, the UK
- the restoration (not improvement) of churches of architectural importance and occasionally to other buildings of architectural importance.

Grants are also given towards the resettlement of offenders including young offenders, and work with prisoners and their families. Grants of up to £200 are also given towards the education and training of prisoners. For these grants, the prisoners themselves should apply.

In 1999/2000 the trust had an income of £106,000 including donations, up from £82,000 in 1998/99. Grants totalled £101,000 and were broken down as follows:

Size of grants	No. of grants	Total
£200 or less to prisoners	90	£12,000
£249 or less (other grants)	28	£2,500
£250 – £499	23	£6,200
£500 – £999	106	£53,000
£1,000	13	£13,000
over £1,000	4	£15,000

Beneficiaries included Camden City Islington and Westminister Bereavement Services (£9,000), Rathbone CI (£1,500) and £1,000 each to British Deaf Association, Inside Out Trust, Medical Foundation for Victims of Torture and Prisoners Abroad and Winged Fellowship.

Exclusions Grants are not given to:

- both branches of UK organisations and its centre (unless it is a specific grant, probably for training in the branches)
- building appeals or endowment funds
- encourage the 'contract culture', particularly where authorities are not funding the contract adequately
- religious organisations set up for welfare, education etc., of whatever religion, unless the users of the service

are from all denominations, and there is no attempt whatsoever to conduct any credal propaganda or religious rituals
- restoration
- 'heritage schemes'
- animals
- students or any individuals or for overseas travel
- medical research.

Applications In writing to the correspondent, including the latest annual report, accounts and budget. The trustees tend to look more favourably on an appeal which is simply and economically prepared rather than glossy, 'prestige' and mailsorted brochures. Many worthy applications are rejected simply due to a lack of funds.

The Gordon Fraser Charitable Trust

Children, young people, environment, arts

£130,000 (1999/2000)

Beneficial area UK, with some preference for Scotland

Holmhurst, Westerton Drive, Bridge of Allan, Stirling FK9 4QL

Correspondent Mrs M A Moss, Trustee

Trustees *Mrs M A Moss; W F T Anderson.*

Information available Full accounts were provided by the trust.

General Currently the trustees are particularly interested in supporting children/young people in need, the environment and visual arts (including performance arts). Most grants are given within these categories. The trust states that 'applications from or for Scotland will receive favourable consideration, but not to the exclusion of applications from elsewhere'.

In 1999/2000 the trust had assets of £2.8 million and an income of £149,000. A total of £130,000 was given in 196 grants, ranging from £100 to £6,000. The grants list includes several health charities, these may receive grants especially for work with children/young people.

Grants of £1,000 or more were given to 33 organisations. The largest grants of £6,000 each went to Aberlour Childcare Trust and Ballet West; £5,500 went to Scottish Museums Council; and £5,000 each to Kilmartin House Trust and MacRobert Arts Centre.

Other large grants went to Artlink Central (£3,600), London Children's Flower Society and Royal Scottish National Orchestra (£3,000 each), Byre Theatre (£2,500), Borderline, Edinburgh Festival Society and National Trust for Scotland (£2,000 each) and Mansfield Traquair Trust and Scottish Opera (£1,500 each).

There were 19 grants of £1,000 and 177 for smaller amounts. Smaller grants included those to Acorn Centre Youth Project, Arts is Magic, British Stammering Association, Edinburgh Green Belt Trust, Friends of the Earth Scotland, Glasgow Sculpture Studies, KIDS Hull Family Centre, No Panic, Parkinson's Disease Society of the UK, RSPB and Woodland Trust.

Over a third of the grants were recurrent from the previous year.

Exclusions No grants to individuals or to organisations which are not registered charities.

Applications In writing to the correspondent. Applications are considered in January, April, July and October. Grants towards national or international emergencies can be considered at any time. All applicants are acknowledged; an sae would therefore be appreciated.

The Joseph Strong Frazer Trust

General

£405,000 (1998/99)

Beneficial area England and Wales only

Scottish Provident House, 31 Mosley Street, Newcastle Upon Tyne NE1 1HX

Tel. 0191 232 8065

Correspondent The Secretary

Trustees *Sir William A Reardon Smith, Chair; D A Cook; R H M Read.*

Information available Full accounts were on file at the Charity Commission.

General In 1998/99 the trust had assets of £10 million and an income of £491,000. Management and administration costs totalled £182,000, including £59,000 in property repairs. Grants totalled £405,000. Recipients cover a wide variety of fields and are based all over England and Wales (the trust appears to be one of a very few in this book to have a specific interest in Wales).

The awards were categorised as follows:

	1998/99	(1997/98)
Health and medicine	£101,000	(£97,000)
Medical research	£72,000	(£62,000)
Education	£69,000	(£90,000)
Culture, sport and recreation	£63,000	(£61,000)
Social services and relief	£52,000	(£50,000)
Welfare services and relief	£28,000	(£27,000)
Religion	£21,000	(£19,000)

Grants of over £2,000 went to 25 organsiations, totalling £95,000, with the largest given to: Mea Trust (£7,000), All Hallows Development Trust (£6,000) and Alzheimer's Research Trust and Cardiac Research and Development Trust (£5,000 each). Other large grants included £4,000 each to Boar Bank Nursing Home, Royal Merchant Navy School Foundation, Salvation Army Cardiff and Welsh National Opera, £3,000 each to Cystic Fibrosis, Downside Settlement and King Alfred School and £2,500 each to National Youth Jazz Orchestra, RNLI branches in City of London and Tynemouth, Samaritans and Wildlife and Wetlands Trust.

77 grants of £2,000 each were given to: about 40 UK organisations including Army Benevolent Fund, Multiple Sclerosis Society, Prison Reform Trust and Research into Ageing; about 20 local charities and local branches of UK organisations in Wales including Barnardos Wales and West Region, Bobath Cyrmu, British Red Cross branches in Cardiff and Gwent, Royal Welsh Fusiliers Museum Fund and Welsh Epilepsy Unit Support Fund; and various local charities and branches throughout England including Contact London, Iris Fund – Tyne & Wear, Northern Counties School for the Deaf and Tyne and Wear Play Association. Grants of under £1,000 totalled £156,000.

Exclusions No grants to individuals.

Applications In writing to the correspondent. Trustees meet twice a year, usually in March and September. Application forms are not necessary but it is helpful if applicants are concise in their appeal letters which must include an sae if acknowledgement is required.

The Louis Freedman Charitable Settlement

General

£13,000 (19998/99)

Beneficial area UK

c/o 25 Chargate Close, Burwood Park, Walton-on-Thames, Surrey KT12 5DW

Correspondent F H Hughes, Trustee

Trustees *Mrs V Freedman; F H Hughes.*

Information available Full accounts are on file at the Charity Commission.

General In 1998/99 the trust had assets of £2.7 million and an income of £90,000. Grants totalled only £13,000, with admininstration costs totalling £5,700. The trust has two main purposes, one is to build up an endowment fund for a significant project or donation to be made in memory of the trust's founder. Its over aim is to make grants for general charitable purposes.

It made 18 grants during the year, ranging from £100 to £5,000. The largest grants went to St Mark's Hospital (£5,000), Liver Research (£3,500) and Action on Addiction (£1,500). Smaller grants included those to British Racing School, Children's Country Holidays, Food Lifeline, Listening Books, Milton Abbey School, Puppy Lifeline and Victim Support.

In the previous year a very large grant of £954,000, was given to the Burnham Health Promotion Trust. This expenditure was largely covered by a Gift Aid donation received the previous year, of £958,000. Smaller grants were also given and £40,000 was transferred to a specific fund established to provide funds for a building project at Burnham Upper School. The aim was to accumulate £160,000 to fund this project.

Exclusions No grants to individuals. Only registered charities are considered for support.

Applications There is no application form. Applications should be in writing to the correspondent. They will be acknowledged if an sae is enclosed.

The Charles S French Charitable Trust

Community projects, disability, children and youth

£162,000 (1999/2000)

Beneficial area UK, in practice north east London and south west Essex

169 High Road, Loughton, Essex IG10 4LF
Tel. 020 8502 3575
Correspondent R L Thomas, Trustee
Trustees *W F Noble; R L Thomas; D B Shepherd.*
Information available Accounts were on file at the Charity Commission, but without a grants list.

General Established by Charles S French in 1959 the trust has a policy of supporting primarily local charities, which have continued to be mainly in north east London and south west Essex, specifically for children and the local community.

In 1999/2000 the trust had assets of £6.3 million and an income of £201,000. Grants totalled £162,000.

The grants, although not detailed by beneficiary, were categorised as follows (1998/99 figures in brackets):

	1999/2000	(1998/99)
youth	32%	(22%)
education and sport	19%	(19%)
community projects	17%	(17%)
disability	10%	(17%)
hospices and medical	10%	(11%)
older people	6%	(8%)
music, art and wildlife	6%	(6%)

Exclusions Registered charities only.

Applications In writing to the correspondent, including a copy of the latest accounts.

The Freshfield Foundation

Not known

£805,000 (1998/99)

Beneficial area UK

2nd Floor, Macfarlane & Co., Cunard Building, Water Street, Liverpool L3 1DS
Tel. 0151 236 6161
Correspondent Peter Turner
Trustees *P A Moores; A Moores; Mrs E J Potter.*
Information available Full accounts were on file at the Charity Commission.

General The trust was established in 1991 and received assets of £1.6 million. In 1998/99, the trust had assets of £5.1 million, up from £3.1 million the year before. It has been accumulating income since it was set up and has only recently began to make grants in 1997/98.

It approved grants totalling £805,000 in 1998/99 (£389,000 in 1997/98), of which £729,000 was paid out in the year in seven grants. Management and administration costs were low at £1,250. The largest grant was of £500,000 and was given to Moores Family Charity Foundation (which has now wound up). Other grants were £50,000 to Janatha Stubbs Foundation, which is a grant-making trust and has an entry in this guide (*see separate entry*); £44,000 to The Ostepathic Centre for Children; £40,000 each to Friends of the Earth and Sustrans; £30,000 to Centre for Tomorrow's Company; and New Economics Foundation (£25,000).

Applications In writing to the correspondent.

The Friarsgate Trust

Health and welfare of young and older people

£52,000 (1998/99)

Beneficial area UK, with a strong preference for East and West Sussex, especially Chichester

5 East Pallant, Chichester, West Sussex PO19 1TS

Tel. 01403 214500
Correspondent Miss Amanda King-Jones, Trustee
Trustees *R F Oates; Miss Amanda King-Jones.*
Information available Accounts were on file at the Charity Commission.

General The trust was established to support education of children whose parents are in need and orphans, including support for camps, playing fields etc., welfare of people in need and older people and other charitable causes. UK charities and local organisations are supported, in practice there is strong preference for East and West Sussex, especially Chichester.

In 1998/99 the trust had assets of £2.5 million generating an income of only £60,000 (2.4%). Grants totalled £52,000 and went to 44 organisations while one individual received £250. The largest grants were of £2,600 and went to Arthritis and Rheumatism Council, Children Family's Trust, Friends of Chichester Hospitals, Institute of Ophthalmology and St Christopher's Fellowship. A further 26 grants ranged from £1,000 to £2,100 including those to British Epilepsy Association, Chichester CAB, Chichester Marriage Guidance Council, St Wilfred's Hospice, Sea Cadets – Navy League, West Sussex Association for the Blind and YMCA.

Beneficiaries of smaller grants included Chichester and Bognor Regis Victim Support Group, King Edward VII Hospital and 'Not Forgotten' Association.

Exclusions Local organisations outside Sussex are unlikely to be supported.

Applications In writing to the correspondent. Applicants are welcome to telephone first to check they fit the trust's criteria.

The Frognal Trust

Elderly, blind, disabled, ophthalmological research, environmental heritage

£57,000 (1998/99)

Beneficial area UK

c/o Charities Aid Foundation, Kings Hill, West Malling, Kent ME19 4TA
Tel. 020 7353 1234

Correspondent Mrs Philippa F Blake Roberts, Trustee

Trustees *Mrs P F Blake Roberts; J P van Montagu; P Fraser.*

Information available Full accounts were provided by the trust.

General The trust particularly supports charities working in the fields of residential facilities and services, cultural heritage, hospices, nursing homes, ophthalmological research, conservation, heritage, parks, and community services. Its current policy is to make modest grants to as many qualifying charities as possible. Funding can be given for up to two years.

In 1998/99 the trust had assets of just under £2 million and an income of only £54,000. It gave £57,000 in 73 grants. Management and administration costs totalled £2,900, of which £1,700 went to the Charities Aid Foundation which administers the trust. Grants of £1,000 or more went to 13 organisations. The grants list shows a strong preference for charities concerned with health and disabilities, especially visual impairment. There was also some preference for conservation. The largest were £3,500 each to Central & Cecil Housing Trust and Society for the Study of Inborn Errors of Metabolism. Other large grants included Camphill Community Clanabogan (£3,000), Wessex Children's Hospice Trust (£2,500), Alzheimer's Disease Society and Royal Horticultural Society (£1,500 each) and seven grants of £1,000 each including those to Action on Elder Abuse, Civic Trust, East Sussex Association for the Blind and Universities Settlement in East London.

The remaining grants ranged from £400 to £750. They included Age Concern Hackney, Bristol Tinnitus Association, Disabled Living, Doncaster Partnership of Carers (PEACE), Edinburgh Family Service Unit, Focus on Blindness, Meningitis Research Foundation, North Pennines Heritage Trust, Oxford MIND, Southwark Playgrounds Trust, Visual Impairments Services and West Midlands Urban Wildlife Trust Ltd.

Exclusions The trust does not support charities concerned with animal welfare, the advancement of religion or charities for the benefit of people outside the UK. No grants are given for educational or research trips.

Applications In writing to the correspondent. Applications should be received by January, April, August or October, for consideration at the trustees' meeting the following month.

Gableholt Limited

Jewish

£84,000 (1991/92)

Beneficial area UK

4 Queensway, Hendon, London NW4 2TN

Tel. 020 8202 1881

Correspondent Solomon Noe, Governor

Trustees *S Noe; Mrs E Noe; C Lerner.*

Information available Accounts were on file at the Charity Commission and only up to 1991/92 in September 2000, but without a list of grants.

General In 1991/92 the trust had assets of £1.7 million, an income of £201,000 and gave grants totalling £84,000. Up-to-date information is not available on this trust. Unfortunately, the trust is choosing to ignore its legal obligations to provide information and be publicly accountable. The information below is identical to that in the last four editions of this guide.

Set up as a limited company in 1978, the trust grants practically all its donations to Jewish institutions, particularly those working in accordance with the Orthodox Jewish faith. The company's grant total does not truly reflect its wealth, whether it be the income of £201,000 or its assets of £1.7 million. Most of this has been achieved because of the company's large property holdings, though the last set of accounts shows a move into listed investments.

Some examples of the 32 beneficiaries include: Rachel Charitable Trust (£34,000) and Friends of Harim Establishment, Gur Trust and Torah Venchased Le'Ezra Vasad (£10,000 each). At the other end of the scale there were many smaller donations, including Mengrah Grammar School (£100), Afula Society (£40), Child Resettlement (£22) and Friends of the Sick (£10).

This last set of accounts saw a dramatic drop in grant total, from £270,000 in 1990/91, though as there seems no apparent financial reason behind this perhaps the total has risen again in subsequent years.

Applications In the past this trust has stated that 'in the governors' view, true charitable giving should always be coupled with virtual anonymity, and for this reason they are most reluctant to be a party to any publicity. Along with suggesting that the listed beneficiaries

might also want to remain unidentified, they also state that the nature of the giving (to Orthodox Jewish organisations) means the information is unlikely to be of much interest to anyone else. Potential applicants would be strongly advised to take heed of these comments.

The above information was not confirmed by the trust, but was correct according to the Charity Commission.

The Horace & Marjorie Gale Charitable Trust

General

£70,000 (1997/98)

Beneficial area UK, mainly Bedfordshire

Garner Associates, 138 Bromham Road, Bedford MK40 2QW

Tel. 01234 354508

Correspondent Gerry Garner

Trustees *G D Payne, Chair; J Tyley; J Williams; P H Tyley; K Fletcher.*

Information available Full accounts were on file at the Charity Commission.

General In 1999/2000 the trust had an income of £83,000 and an expenditure of £87,000. Unfortunately, the trust's accounts were being prepared at the time of publication, and the following information is repeated from the previous edition of this guide.

The trust gives support in three areas:

- for churches and church ministries, with emphasis on Bunyan Meeting Free Church, Bedford and the ministries of the Baptist Union in England and Wales
- donations to charities and organisations active in the community life of Bedford and Bedfordshire
- donations to UK charities and organisations active in community life.

The investments of just over £500,000 were increased by a further £200,000 from bank deposits in 1997/98. The income during the year was about £78,000 and the trust aims to make grants totalling about £70,000 each year. In 1997/98 these were categorised as follows:

Churches – £17,000

By far the largest grant was £9,000 to Bunyan Meeting Free Church. Five organisations received £1,000: The Baptist Union - Home Mission Fund, Baptist Missionary Society, Bedfordshire Baptist Trust, Hertfordshire & Bedfordshire Media Trust and St Luke's Church, Bedford. There were six other grants in this category all for £500.

Local charities – £36,500

A total of 28 grants were made in this category, with 19 for £1,000. The larger grants were to Bedford Hospitals Trust Endowment Fund Maxillo Facial Unit (£5,000), Abbeyfield Society and Bedford City Housing Association (£3,000 each), and £2,000 each to Bedford Modern School – R G Gale Prize fund, Bedfordshire Crime Beat and Samaritans – Bedford.

General charities – £17,000

All the grants in this category were for £1,000 and went to health and disability charities such as Arthritis and Rheumatism Council, Lady Hoare Trust, Migraine Trust and Whizz-Kidz.

While over half the grants in the first category were recurrent, only a couple of the grant recipients in the other two categories had benefited the previous year.

Exclusions Grants are rarely given to individuals.

Applications In writing to the correspondent. Grants are distributed once a year and applications should be made by September, for consideration in November.

Garrick Club Charitable Trust

Probably arts, children in London

Perhaps £300,000 a year, but see below

15 Garrick Street, London WC2E 9AY

Tel. 020 836 1737

Correspondent The Secretary

Information available Information was provided by the trust.

General The trust was established by the members of the Garrick Club in London in 1998. It was expected to be endowed with about £4 million from the proceeds of selling the Winnie the Pooh copyright to the Disney organisation. The deal had not yet been completed at the time of going to print, but the trust hoped that completion was 'imminent'. It is expected that the areas of work will be support for disadvantaged children in the East End of London, something close to A A Milne's heart and also arts organisations, particularly the performing arts, reflecting the interests of the Garrick Club.

Since it was established two years ago the trust has been receiving applications so there is likely to be high competition for funds when they are available.

Applications The trust was not yet in operation as this book went to print.

Garvan Limited

Jewish

£234,000 (1995/96)

Beneficial area UK

Flat 9, Windsor Court, Golders Green Road, London NW11 9PP

Tel. 020 8458 1125

Correspondent S Ebert

Information available Only a balance sheet was on file at the Charity Commission.

General This trust makes grants to Jewish organisations. In 1998/99 the trust had assets of £259,000. Unfortunately no other information about this trust, such as an income, expenditure, grants information, narrative report, details of activities, details of the trustees or even an address for the trust, was included in the accounts.

The public screens at the Charity Commission stated that in 1998/99 the trust had an income of £178,000 and a total expenditure of £95,000. In 1995/96, the last year for which a grants total was available, the trust had a similar income to this year and gave grants totalling £234,000, no information was available on the beneficiaries.

Applications In writing to the correspondent.

The Gertner Charitable Trust

Jewish

£188,000 (1996/97)

Beneficial area Worldwide

Fordgate House, 1 Allsop Place, London NW1 5LF

Tel. 020 7224 1234

Correspondent Mrs Michelle Gertner, Trustee

Trustees *Moises Gertner; Mrs Michelle Gertner; Eugene Moshan.*

Information available Full accounts were on file at the Charity Commission.

General Unfortunately we have been unable to update the following information since the last edition of the guide. In 1996/97 the trust's asset totalled £1.7 million and its income, mainly from donations, totalled £353,000. Grants were made to 55 organisations totalling £188,000. About a third of the grants appear to be ongoing, although they can vary in size from year to year.

The principal grant was £86,000 to American Friends of Yad Haron. Other larger grants were £18,000 to Tzemach Tzedek, £13,000 to Bais Yechiel and £10,000 each to Emuna Educational Centre and Torah and Chesed Limited. Grants to 12 organisations ranged between £1,200 and £6,000 and the remainder were all for £1,000 or less.

Applications In writing to the correspondent.

The Gibbins Trust

General, but see below

£68,000 (1998/99)

Beneficial area England (with a preference for Sussex) and Wales. Charities operating in Scotland or Northern Ireland are not considered

c/o Thomas Eggar Church Adams, 5 East Pallant, Chichester, West Sussex PO19 1TS

Tel. 01243 786111   **Fax** 01243 775640

Minicom 30300 Chichester

Correspondent R F Ash, Trustee

Trustees *R S Archer; R F Ash; Mrs P M Archer.*

Information available Guidance notes for applicants reprinted below. Full accounts were provided by the trust.

General The trustees' objective is to support charities active in the relief of hardship and disability particularly those aimed at young people and older people. Other areas supported include charities for medical research and holidays for people who are disabled. The general policy is to assist charities which are small to medium-sized. The trust gives to UK organisations and charities based in Sussex and the surrounding area.

In 1998/99 the trust had assets of £912,000 generating an income of £53,000. After high administration and management costs of £14,000, the trust gave 77 grants totalling £68,000. A third of the beneficiaries were also supported in the previous year.

Grants were given to groups working with people with disabilities, including Dogs for the Disabled (£700); DeafBlind UK (£600); £300 each to National Ankylosing Spondilitis Society and Talking Books Library; and £250 to Handicapped Anglers Trust. Children's charities included British Red Cross Adventure Holidays (£600), National Association of Toy and Leisure Libraries (£300) and £250 each to CHICKS (Country Holidays for Inner City Kids) and Hope and Homes for Children. Elderly organisations included Council and Care for the Elderly (£600) and Methodist Homes for the Aged (£250). Other grants included £300 each to Contact and Council for Music in Hospitals.

About a quarter of all grants made were to organisations in Sussex, in particular local disability groups, including local branches of UK charities. They included East Sussex Association for the Blind (£600), Crossroads Caring for Carers – Lewes and West Sussex Association for the Disabled (£250 each) and Sussex Multiple Sclerosis Treatment Centre (£100). Grants were given to various elderly organisations and homes including £10,000 to Sussex Housing Association for the Aged and £600 each to the branches of Age Concern in East and West Sussex. Local Christian establishments receiving support included Chichester Cathedral (£1,000) and Revelation Church – summer playschemes (£250). Local children's charities included Sussex Association of Boys' Clubs (£600), Hove's Air Cadets

(£250) and Chichester Youth Adventure Trust (£100).

Exclusions No grants are given to individuals and only very rarely to charities for animal welfare or for the preservation of buildings or other heritage appeals.

Applications The trust has stated that it 'is no longer considering applications and is going to be wound up in the near future'.

The Gibbs Charitable Trusts

Methodist
£71,000 (1998/99)
Beneficial area UK

8 Victoria Square, Bristol BS8 4ET

Correspondent Dr John N Gibbs, Trustee

Trustees *Sheila Gibbs, Chair; Andrew Gibbs; Dr John N Gibbs; Dr James M Gibbs; Juilet Gibbs; Celia Gibbs; Elizabeth Gibbs; John E Gibbs; Patience Gibbs; Simon E Gibbs; William M Gibbs.*

Information available Full accounts were on file at the Charity Commission.

General The trust divides its grant-giving into three areas:

1) innovative work undertaken by Methodist churches and organisations

2) other Christian causes, especially of an ecumenical nature

3) wider charitable aims, especially in creative arts, education and international concern.

In 1998/99 the trust had assets of £2.5 million and an income of £97,000. It had exceptionally low administration expenses, of £588. It gave 47 grants, totalling £71,000, and broken down as follows:

Category	No. of grants	Total
Methodist work	30	£22,000
Other Christian causes	12	£23,000
Other causes	5	£12,000

Methodist work
This category was divided into:

Methodist churches, circuits and districts
£14,000 was given in total to 20 churches, ranging from £300 to £2,000. A further

£1,000 was given in smaller grants, the beneficiaries were not listed.

Other Methodist bodies
Nine grants were given, ranging from £250 to £8,000. The largest grants went to Queen's College Taunton Millennium Appeal (£8,000) and £5,000 each to The Amelia Farm Trust and NCH Action for Children. Other beneficiaries included British Methodist Youth Choir (£1,000) and DEG – Child Foundation (£250).

Other Christian groups
Grants were given to 12 organisations ranging from £100 to £12,000, 12 organisations were supported. The largest grant went to Jubilee 2000. Other large grants included those to Keston Institute (£3,000), Jasperian Theatre Company (£1,000), Art and Christian Enquiry (£600), Wooton-under-Edge United Church (£500) and Oasis (£100).

Other causes
Five grants were given: Botton Village and Oxfam (£5,000 each), Dorothy L Sayers Society with Radius (£1,000), Tadworth Court Children's Trust (£500) and Lassallian Developing World Project (£200).

The trust has set up a Ministerial Training Fund with £100,000 in response to the expenses that trainee Methodist ministers will increasingly have to meet. The whole fund is to be distributed during the next few years (from autumn 1999).

Exclusions A large number of requests are received by the trust from churches undertaking improvement, refurbishment and development projects, but only a few of these can be helped. In general, churches which are selected are usually Methodist churches about which trustees have particular knowledge.

Individuals and animal charities are not supported.

Applications The trust has no application forms, requests should be made in writing to the correspondent. The trustees meet three times a year, at Christmas, Easter and late summer. Unsuccessful applicants are not normally notified. The trustees do not encourage telephone enquiries or speculative applications. They also state that they are not impressed by applicants that send a huge amount of paperwork.

Simon Gibson Charitable Trust

General

£348,000 (1998/99)

Beneficial area UK, with a preference for Norfolk, Suffolk, South Wales or Central London

Hill House, 1 Little New Street, London EC4A 3TR

Correspondent Bryan Marsh, Trustee

Trustees *Bryan Marsh; Angela Homfray; George Gibson.*

Information available Report and accounts with full grants list but no analysis of grants or grant-making was on file at the Charity Commission.

General Around 100 mostly small and repeated grants are made each year to a broad variety of charities. Beneficiaries are often UK charities, or local organisations in Norfolk, Suffolk, South Wales or Central London.

The trust was established in 1975 by George Simon Gibson, son of George Cock Gibson whose trust can be found in *A Guide to Major Trusts Volume 1*. By the year ending April 1999 its assets totalled £15 million which generated an income of £491,000. Grants totalled £348,000. Running costs were a notably low £4,500, just over a penny per £1 donated.

There were 123 donations made in the year, of which 72 were recurrent from the previous year. The average grant was £2,800. The majority of the awards (106) ranged between £1,000 and £3,000 with nearly half for £2,000. The largest awards – two of £20,000, went to Tower Hamlets Summer University and Welsh Livery Guild Charitable Trust. Three other awards of £10,000 each went to Cancer Research Campaign, Ely Cathedral Appeal Fund and Hospice of the Marches.

Other larger beneficiaries included 10 grants of £5,000 each, examples of recipients were Cystic Fibrosis Trust, Llancarfan Parish Church and Save the Children Fund.

Approximate breakdown of grants:

Welfare	36%
Children/young people	26%
Medical	12%
Church	9%
Animal welfare	5%
Arts and culture	5%
International	2%
Miscellaneous	6%

Several of the recipients in the welfare group were 'profession' charities such as the Army Benevolent Fund (£2,000), Mission to Seamen (£2,000) and Sailors Family Soceity (£1,000). A large number of both the medical and welfare grants went to organisations involved with people with disabilities. Examples of these included Brain Injury Rehabilitation and Development and PHAB Wales (£2,000 each) and John Groom Association for the Disabled (£1,000). Other beneficiaries included Princess Royal Trust for Carers – Greenwich (£3,000), Samaritans (£2,000) and Relate – Newmarket (£1,000).

Grants to 'Children/young people' included a number of donations to schools, amongst these were £2,000 to St Theresa's RC Primary School, £1,000 to Cheltenham Ladies College and three in Newmarket. Others went to the National Playing Fields Association (£3,000), Drive for Youth and Oasis Children's Venue (£2,000 each) and First Exning Boy Scouts Troop (£1,000).

Examples from the other categories include Blue Cross Animal Centre Cambridge, Exning Church and Midland Narrow Boat Project.

Exclusions No grants for individuals.

Applications In writing to the correspondent. Telephone calls should not be made. The trust has no application forms. It acknowledges all applications but does not enter into correspondence with applicants unless they are awarded a grant. The trustees meet in May and applications should be received in March.

The GNC Trust

General

£86,000 (1998)

Beneficial area UK

c/o Messrs PricewaterhouseCoopers, Cornwall Court, Cornwall Street, Birmingham B3 2DT

Tel. 0121 200 3000

Correspondent Mrs P M Spragg, Agent to the Trustees

Trustees *R N Cadbury; G T E Cadbury; Mrs J E B Yelloly.*

Information available Full accounts were on file at the Charity Commission.

General The trust is divided into two distinct funds; charitable appeals are settled by R N Cadbury and G T E Cadbury out of the Main Fund, and Mrs J E B Yelloly settles appeals from a separate fund.

In 1998 the trust had assets of £2.5 million generating an income of £81,000. A total of £86,000 was given in 70 grants, 49 of which were for less than £1,000.

The trust supports a variety of causes. Animal charities receiving grants included Brook Hospital for Animals (£1,700), World Wildlife Fund (£150), RSPB (£100) and Barn Owl Trust (£50). Medical organisations supported included St John Opthalmic Hospital (£2,900), Association for Spina Bifida and Hydrocephalus (£2,500), National Asthma Fund (£250), Macmillan Cancer Relief (£100) and British Psychological Society (£40). Countryside groups included Woodland Trust – Owl Appeal (£500), Countryside Educational Trust (£100), National Trust (£65) and Field Studies Trust (£45).

Other beneficiaries included British and International Sailors' Society and National Institution for Conductive Education (£15,000 each), National Youth Ballet (£5,500), League of Venturers Search and Rescue (£5,000), Sail Training Association and St Enodoc Church Organ Fund (£1,000 each), Elgar Birthplace Appeal (£240) and Birmingham Royal Ballet and St James Church Spire Appeal (£100 each). Grants were given to three branches of St John Ambulance; £400 to Oxfordshire, £350 to the general appeal and £90 to Northamptonshire.

Exclusions Only very occasionally are grants made to individuals. National appeals are not favoured, nor are most London-based charities.

Applications In writing to the correspondent.

The Sydney & Phyllis Goldberg Memorial Charitable Trust

Medical research, welfare, disability

£57,000 (1998/99)

Beneficial area UK

Coulthards Mackenzie, 17 Park Street, Camberley, Surrey GU15 3PQ

Correspondent M J Church, Trustee

Trustees *H G Vowles; M J Church; C J Pexton.*

Information available Full accounts were on file at the Charity Commission.

General The income for the trust comes from its investments which are mainly held in Syona Investments Limited. Phyllis Goldberg initially bequeathed her shareholding in Syona Investments Limited to the trust and since then the trust has bought the balance of the shares. In 1998/99 the trust had assets of £1.8 million and an income of £56,000. Grants totalling £57,000 were given to eight organisations, five of which were supported in the previous year.

The largest grant was £11,000 to Children of St Mary's Intensive Care Department of Child Health. Other grants included £7,500 to Dystonia Society for research into the relief of sickness, £7,000 to Institute of Child Health to carry out research into child leukaemia at Great Ormond Street Hospital, £6,000 to Elliott Comprehensive School to fund a library for children with disabilities and £5,000 to Handicapped Adventure Playground Association Limited.

Applications In writing to the correspondent. Telephone requests are not appreciated. Applicants are advised to apply towards the end of the calendar year.

The Golden Bottle Trust

General

£435,000 (1997/98)

Beneficial area UK

C Hoare & Co, 37 Fleet Street, London EC4P 4DQ

Tel. 020 7353 4522

Correspondent The Secretariat

Trustees *Messrs Hoare Trustees.*

Information available Accounts are on file at the Charity Commission, but without a grants list for the latest year.

General In 1995/96 the trust had an exceptional income of almost £1.5 million including £1.35 million from donations. The grant total remained at a similar level to previous years, £204,000, with the donations received adding to the assets of the trust which therefore rose considerably from under £1 million to £2.27 million. The grant total has since increased substantially, in 1997/98 rising to £435,000.

Unfortunately, no grants list was included with the accounts since that for 1993/94 when the trust gave 177 grants totalling £141,000. 22 grants were for £1,000 and 20 were for over £1,000. A wide range of organisations were supported.

Exclusions No grants for individuals or organisations that are not registered charities.

Applications In writing to the correspondent, who stated 'trustees meet on a monthly basis, but the funds are already largely committed and, therefore, applications from sources not already known to the trustees are unlikely to be successful'.

The Golden Charitable Trust

Catholic, Jewish, preservation, conservation

£93,000 (1998/99)

Beneficial area UK, preference for Sussex

Little Leith Gate, Angel Street, Petworth, West Sussex GU28 0BG

Tel. 01798 342434

Correspondent Lewis Golden, Secretary to the Trustees

Trustees *Mrs S J F Solnick; J M F Golden.*

Information available Full accounts were on file at the Charity Commission.

General The trust appears to have a preference in its grant-making for organisations in Sussex, in particular Petworth. There is also a preference for organisations in the field of the preservation and conservation of historic articles and materials. In 1998/99 the trust had assets of £445,000 and an income of £108,000, including £91,000

from donations. After minimal expenses of £118, 17 grants were given totalling £93,000, 12 of which were of £1,000 or less.

The largest grants included £50,000 to Petworth Cottage Nursing Home, £15,000 to Lodge Hill Trust, £10,000 to National Manuscripts Conservation Trust and £7,500 to London Library, all of which received the same amount in the previous year. Other grants included £5,000 to Leconfield Hall, £1,000 each to Guild Care, Listening Books, Petworth Festival and Wiener Library Endowment Trust, £250 to British Council of the Shaare Zedec Medical Centre, £100 each to Royal Signals Museum and Special Trustees of UCH and £70 to Parish Church of St Mary the Virgin, Petsworth.

Applications In writing to the correspondent.

The Jack Goldhill Charitable Trust

Health, arts, welfare

£78,000 (1997)

Beneficial area UK

Flat 85 Kensington Heights, 91–95 Campden Hill Road, London W8 7BD

Tel. 020 7727 4326

Correspondent Jack Goldhill, Trustee

Trustees *G Goldhill; J A Goldhill.*

Information available Full accounts were on file at the Charity Commission.

General In 1999 the trust had an income of £80,000 and an expenditure of £88,000. Unfortunately, no further information for this year was available and this information is repeated from the last edition of this guide.

In 1997 the trust had assets of around £400,000, including property, which generated an income of about £80,000.

A total of £78,000 was given in 77 grants, ranging from £30 to £27,000. Most were for £3,500 or less, including a number of 'Friends of…' payments.

The largest grants were £27,000 to Jack Goldhill Sculpture Award Fund and £18,000 to Jewish Care. No other grant was above £3,500 with recipients of £1,000 or more including Atlantic Collage, Inclusion, Joint Jewish Charitable Trust, Royal London Hospital,

Tate Gallery, Tricycle Theatre Company and West London Synagogue.

Exclusions No support for individuals or new applications.

Applications The trustees have a restricted list of charities to whom they are committed and no unsolicited applications can be considered.

Good Deed Foundation

Health, children

£85,000 (1999)

Beneficial area UK

c/o Manro Haydan Trading,
1 Knightsbridge, 4th Floor,
London SW1 7LX

Tel. 020 7823 2200 **Fax** 020 7823 1333

Correspondent Alan McCormack, Financial Manager

Trustees C J Smith; M Weiss; A J Winter.

Information available Accounts were on file at the Charity Commission with a grants list, but only a brief narrative report.

General In 1999 the trust had assets of £178,000 which have risen from minus £79,000 in the previous year. It had a large income of £342,000 presumably used to rebuild the assets, with the remaining £85,000 distributed in grants.

The trust has general charitable purposes but appears to have a preference for health charities especially those concerned with children. Most of the grant total was given in five large grants. They were £25,000 each to Cedar School for general purposes and to an individual for a life-saving operation. Two grants of £10,000 each went to Heartbeat Charity Concert and Tommy's Campaign and £5,000 was given to Wessex Children's Heart Circle.

Applications In writing to the correspondent.

The Good Neighbours Trust

People who have mental or physical disabilities

£79,000 (1999)

Beneficial area UK

16 Westway, Nailsea, Bristol BS48 2NA

Correspondent P S Broderick, Secretary to the Trustees

Trustees G V Arter, Chair; J C Gurney; R T Sheppard; P S Broderick.

Information available Financial statements were provided by the trust and guidance notes which are produced for applicants (shown under 'exclusions' and 'applications').

General The present policy of the trust is to principally support activities which benefit people who are physically or mentally disabled. It mainly gives one-off grants for low cost specific projects e.g. purchase of equipment or UK holidays for people who are disabled. In 1999 the trust had assets of £2.7 million and an income of £92,000. A total of £79,000 was given in 161 grants ranging from £200 to £2,500. The grants were divided into local grants which were mainly given in the Greater Bristol area and UK grants (which received the majority of the grants) were given mostly to locally based groups throughout the UK.

Local grants totalled £22,200 and 40 organisations were supported with nearly three-quarters of the grants being given in Bristol and most of the other grants given to groups in Bath, Gloucestershire and Somerset.

Seven grants were given of £1,000 or more. The Townfield Trust received two grants, for its Churchtown Centre, Cornwall project (£2,500) and for its VOICE project (£2,000). Scope and Patchway – Bristol received £1,500 and four grants of £1,000 each included those to National Eye Research Centre at Bristol Eye Hospital and St Peter's Hospice. Smaller grants included those to BIME (Bath Institute of Medical Engineering) Royal United Hospital Bath; Bristol Mind; Dystonia Society, London; Wildfowl and Wetlands Trust in Gloucestershire; and Woodspring Association for the Blind, Weston-Super-Mare.

UK grants of £1,000 or more went to 12 organisations. They included Help the Hospices, London (£2,500), Churchtown

Centre, Bodmin (£2,000) and nine grants of £1,000 each including those to Canine Partners for Independence Hampshire; Disability Network UK, St Helens; Linn Moor Residential School in Aberdeen; and The Children's Appeal, Sheffield Children' Hospital CHRIS Fund.

Smaller grants included those to Angus Special Playscheme, Montrose; Autism, London; Camp Quality UK, Exmouth; Dream Holidays, Surrey; Kings Mill School, Driffield; Merseyside Thursday Club, Liverpool; PHAB Wales; Rehab Scotland; Skelton Social Skills Centre, PTA, Cleveland; Style Acre Friends, Oxfordshire; Treasure Trove, Barry; and Wirral Autistic Society.

Exclusions Support is not given for:
- overseas projects
- general community projects*
- individuals
- general education projects*
- religious and ethnic projects*
- projects for unemployed and related training schemes*
- projects on behalf of offenders and ex-offenders
- projects concerned with the abuse of drugs and/or alcohol
- wildlife and conservation schemes*
- general restoration and preservation of buildings, purely for historical and/or architectural purposes.

* If these projects are mainly or wholly for the benefit of people who have disabilities then they will be considered.

Ongoing support is not given, and grants are not usually given for running costs, salaries, research and items requiring major funding. Loans are not given.

Applications The trust does not have an official application form, appeals should be made in writing to the Secretary, at any time. The trust asks that the following is carefully considered before submitting an application: Appeals must:
- be from registered charities
- include a copy of the latest audited accounts available (for newly registered charities a copy of provisional accounts showing estimated income and expenditure for the current financial year)
- show that the project is 'both feasible and viable' and, if relevant, give the starting date of the project and the anticipated date of completion
- include the estimated cost of the project, together with the appeal's target-figure and details of what funds have already been raised and any fundraising schemes for the project.

The trustees states that 'where applicable, due consideration will be given to evidence of voluntary and self-help (both in practical and fundraising terms) and to the number of people expected to benefit from the project'. They also comment that their decision is final and 'no reason for a decision, whether favourable or otherwise, need be given' and that 'the award and acceptance of a grant will not involve the trustees in any other commitment'.

Mike Gooley Trailfinders Charity

Mainly cancer research

£773,000 (1999/2000)

Beneficial area UK

Trailfinders Ltd, 9 Abingdon Road, London W8 6AH

Tel. 020 7938 3143   **Fax** 020 7937 6059

Correspondent Louise Bretton

Trustees *M D W Gooley; Mrs B M Gooley; T P Gooley; M Bannister.*

Information available Accounts were on file at the Charity Commission, but without a full narrative report or a list of grants.

General The founder of this charity, after whom it is named, is the owner of Trailfinders Limited, and the charity receives a donation from the company each year. The trust's policy is to make larger grants to fewer organisations. Grants are only made for research purposes and the trust is currently concentrating on cancer research. Large grants are often given over three to five years.

In 1999/2000 the trust had an income of £1.7 million and gave grants totalling £773,000. Two very large grants were given, they were £500,000 to Cancer Research Campaign (the third instalment of a four year commitment totalling £2.5 million) and £200,000 to Prostate Cancer Charity (third instalment of a four year commitment totalling £600,000). Another grant of £51,000 went to St George's House. The remaining £23,000 was given in small, one-off grants. The small grants are usually to organisations connected with the company or its staff.

In 1997/98 the trust bought a sports ground, as an investment for the charity, valued in the assets at the end of the year at £721,000. During 2001 the trust is using its income to invest in the sports ground and will not be making new grants. It expects to be making grants again in the following year. It has pledged £2 million to Imperial Cancer Research Fund.

Exclusions Grants are not made to overseas charities or to individuals.

Applications In writing to the correspondent. The trust is not expecting to make new grants until 2002, applications should be sent from September 2001.

The Grace Charitable Trust

Christian

£252,000 (1998/99)

Beneficial area UK

Rhuallt House, Rhuallt, St Asaph, Denbeighshire LL17 0TG

Tel. 01745 583141

Correspondent Mrs G J R Payne, Trustee

Trustees *Mrs G J R Payne; E Payne; Mrs G M Snaith; R B M Quayle.*

Information available Full accounts were on file at the Charity Commission.

General In 1998/99 the trust had assets of £306,000 and an income of £312,000, £202,000 of which was derived from donations. Grants totalled £252,000 with management and administration costs totalling only £2,000.

A grants list was not included in the accounts, although in the past grants have ranged from £1,000 to £6,800. Grants have been given to: Christian charities including Cheatle Trust, Gideons International, Operation Mobilisation and Saltmine Trust; and non-Christian organisations including Electrical & Electronic Industries Benevolent Fund, Jubilee Trust, NAYC and St Kentigerns Hospice.

Applications The trust states, 'applications for grants or donations are not considered'.

The Graff Foundation

General

£66,000 (1999)

Beneficial area UK and worldwide

6–7 New Bond Street, London W1Y 9PE

Correspondent Anthony D Kerman, Trustee

Trustees *Laurence Graff; Francois Xavier Graff; Anthony D Kerman.*

Information available Full accounts were on file at the Charity Commission.

General In 1999 the trust had assets of £1.2 million, an income of £71,000 and grants totalled £66,000. Management and administration costs were only £39. Nine grants were given, with the largest grant of £62,000 going to Gemological Institute of America which appears to regularly be the main beneficiary. Other grants ranged from £250 to £1,800 and went to Barnardos (£1,800), with £500 each to Jewellery Students Fund, NPH Trust Fund (Virginia Pinto Memorial Fund), Teenage Cancer Trust and UNICEF, £350 to The Red Cross and £250 to Norwood Ravenswood. Three grants were recurrent from the previous year.

Applications In writing to the correspondent.

The Reginald Graham Charitable Trust

Children, medical, education

£62,000 (1997/98)

Beneficial area UK

Charles Russell, 3–10 New Fetter Lane, London EC4A 1RS

Tel. 020 7203 5000

Correspondent Suzanne Marriott, Solicitor

Trustees *Reginald Graham; Mrs Melanie Boyd; Michael MacFadyen; David Eric Long.*

Information available Full accounts were on file at the Charity Commission.

General In 1998/99 the trust had an income of £75,000 and an expenditure of £52,000. Further information was not yet available for this year at the time of going to print. The following is repeated from the last edition.

In 1997/98 the trust supported 61 different organisations with grants totalling £62,000. The income for the year was £64,000.

By far the largest grant was £30,000 to Pembroke College which also received £16,000 the previous year. Grants of £1,000 to £5,000 were given to 10 organisations including Education Trust, King Edward VII's Hospital for Officers, King George Fund for Sailors, NSPCC, Oxford University Tennis Club, Pyschiatric Rehabilitation Association, Prince's Trust, Royal Academy Trust, Royal British Legion and Wellbeing. Seven of these had also received a grant the previous year.

The smaller grants ranged from £25 upwards and were given to a wide range of beneficiaries.

Exclusions No grants to individuals, only charitable organisations are supported.

Applications The trust stated that it currently has a number of charities which receive regular support and they are not considering new applications at present. It is anticipated that this will be the case until January 2002 at the earliest.

The Grahame Charitable Foundation

Jewish

£166,000 (1998)

Beneficial area UK and worldwide

5 Spencer Walk, Hampstead High Street, London NW3 1QZ
Tel. 020 7794 5281 **Fax** 020 7794 0094
Correspondent Mrs S Brooks
Trustees *Gitte Grahame; Jeffrey Greenwood; Leo Grahame.*
Information available Accounts were on file at the Charity Commission, but without a grants list.

General The trust's objects are to advance education, relieve poverty and advance religion anywhere in the world.

In practice, it appears to make grants to these ends mainly to Jewish charities. Each year small grants are made to a handful of non-Jewish welfare and medical charities.

In 1998 the trust's assets totalled £286,000. It had an income of £184,000, including £104,000 in covenants and donations and £46,000 in rent. Grants totalled £166,000. Unfortunately, for several years now, the trust has not provided a grants list.

The last information available on grants was relating to 1996, when the trust made 120 grants totalling £81,000. The largest grants were £15,000 to Child Resettlement Fund, £10,000 to Jerusalem College and £5,000 each to Bais Ruzin Trust and Share Zedek. Most grants were for £500 or less. The only non-Jewish beneficiaries were Operation Wheelchairs (£150) with £100 each The Samaritans, Scope and Sue Harris Bone Marrow Transplant.

Exclusions No grants to individuals.

Applications In writing to the correspondent. Trustees meet to consider grants in January, April, July and October.

The Grand Order of Water Rats Charities Fund

Theatrical, medical equipment

£76,000 (1999)

Beneficial area UK

328 Gray's Inn Road, London WC1X 8BZ
Tel. 020 7278 3248 **Fax** 020 7278 1765
e-mail water.rats@virgin.net
Correspondent John Adrian, Secretary
Trustees *Wyn Calvin; Declan Cluskey; Roy Hudd; Paul Daniels; Keith Simmons.*
Information available Full accounts were on file at the Charity Commission.

General The trust was established to assist members of the variety and light entertainment profession and their dependants who, due to illness or age, are in need. The fund also buys medical equipment for certain institutions and also for individuals who have worked with or who have been closely connected

with the same profession. The trust is mainly funded by donations.

In 1999 the trust had an income of £248,000 and a total expenditure of £110,000. Grants totalled £76,000.

In 1997, the last year in which grant information was available, the largest grants went to Cause for Hope (£11,000), Bud Flanagan Leukaemia Fund (£6,700) and Queen Elizabeth Hospital for Children (£3,000). There were six grants of between £1,000 and £2,000 including those to Actors Church Union, British Legion Wales and Northwick Park Hospital.

Exclusions No grants to students.

Applications In writing to the correspondent. The trustees meet once a month.

The Green Foundation

General, social welfare, Jewish

£124,000 (1999/2000)

Beneficial area UK

7 Astra Centre, Harlow, Essex CM20 2BG
Tel. 01279 727790
Correspondent D R Green, Trustee
Trustees *Mrs Toby Lawson, Chair; Mrs Kate Birk; Richard Green; David R Green.*
Information available Full accounts were on file at the Charity Commission.

General The trust gives grants for general charitable purposes, although there is a preference for Jewish, medical and children's causes, and particularly groups concerned with two or more of these causes.

In 1999/2000 the trust had an income of £65,000 and used its income and its assets to give grants totalling £124,000. In the previous year, the trust had assets of £41,000, an income of £110,000 and gave grants totalling £101,000. The trust regularly receives the majority of its income from donations.

Most of the largest grants were given to Jewish organisations. Beneficiaries included Norwood Ravenswood (£20,000), Jewish Care and Oxford Synagogue & Jewish Centre (£10,000 each), Joint Jewish Charitable Trust (£6,000) and Scopus Jewish Educational

Trust (£4,000). Smaller Jewish grants included £700 to Craven Walks Charitable Trust and £100 to Jewish Child's Day.

Medical organisations supported included Felsenstein Medical Research Centre (£20,000), North London Hospice and Royal National Institute for the Blind (£5,000 each), Cancer and Leukaemia in Children – CLIC (£2,400), Deafblind UK (£1,500), Friends of the Sick (£200) and Natural Medicines Society (£20).

Grants to children's charities included £300 each to Child Resettlement Fund and Children with Leukaemia Trust, £250 to Movement for Non-Mobile Children and £100 to Action for Children Charitable Trust.

Other grants included £250 to City Ballet, £100 to Salvation Army, £50 each to Help the Aged and Oxford Playhouse Trust and £15 to Education Otherwise Association.

Applications The trustees meet to consider grants in June and in December. Unsuccessful applications are not acknowledged or notified.

The Barry Green Memorial Fund

Animal welfare

£133,000 (1998/99)

Beneficial area UK, with a preference for Yorkshire and Lancashire

Fitzgerald-Harts, Claro Chambers, Boroughbridge, York YO51 9LD

Tel. 01423 322312 **Fax** 01423 324480

Correspondent The Clerk to the Trustees

Trustees *Richard Fitzgerald-Hart; Mark Fitzgerald-Hart.*

Information available Full accounts were on file at the Charity Commission.

General The trust was created under the Will of Mrs E M Green. It supports animal welfare charities concerned with the rescue, maintenance and benefit of cruelly-treated animals and also the prevention of cruelty to animals. There is a preference for small, local charities.

The trustees' report states 'the trustees are always willing to consider applications for assistance provided they fall strictly within the objects of the

charity and are also prepared to try and offer assistance to those charities which have fallen into financial difficulty, provided that they will take realistic steps to overcome their problems and there is a reasonable prospect of them being able "to get back on their feet"'.

In 1998/99 the assets amounted to £1.2 million and the income was £197,000. Management and adminstration costs totalled £111,000 – mostly property expenses. A total of £133,000 was given in 59 grants. The largest grant was £30,000 to PDSA. Other larger grants were £12,000 to Winslade Wildlife Sanctuary and £5,000 each to Assisi Appeal Fund and The Blue Cross. Most grants (48) ranged from £1,000 to £3,000, beneficiaries included Animal Lifeline, Devon Horse and Pony Sanctuary, Fife Cat Shelter, Hedgehog Rescue and Wildlife in Need.

Seven smaller grants included Diana Dickinsons Sanctuary for Elderly Cats (£500) and Hull & East Riding Boxer Rescue (£250).

Applications In writing to the correspondent.

The Gresham Charitable Trust

General

£78,000 (1997/98)

Beneficial area UK

92 Bell Lane, Little Chalfont, Amersham, Buckinghamshire HP6 6PG

Tel. 01494 762224

Correspondent F G A Flynn

Trustees *R Taylor; P S Vaines.*

Information available Full accounts were on file at the Charity Commission.

General The trust mainly supports UK charities, with a few grants to local causes where it is based.

In 1998/99 the trust had assets of around £1 million and an income of £75,000. Grants totalled around £78,000. No grant information was available at the time of publication.

Examples of previous beneficiaries included Age Concern, Barnardos, John Groom's Association for the Disabled, four Methodist causes including one church in Little Chalfont, Oxfam, Royal Society for the Prevention of Accidents,

St Dunstan's and Scout Association (2nd Amersham Common Scout Group). Many of the grants were recurrent.

Applications 'The funds are fully committed and applications are only considered from organisations approached by the trust.' Unsolicited applications are not acknowledged.

Grimmitt Trust

General

£206,000 (1998/99)

Beneficial area UK

Grimmitt Holdings, Woodgate Business Park, Kettles Wood Drive, Birmingham B32 3GH

Tel. 0121 421 7000

Correspondent David W Everitt, Trustee

Trustees *P W Welch; Mrs M E Welch; D W Everitt; J S Sykes; D C Davies; P B Hyland; M G Fisher; C Hughes Smith; C Humphreys; Dr C Kendrick; Dr D Owen.*

Information available Full accounts were on file at the Charity Commission.

General Grants are given to organisations in the Birmingham area. Local branches of UK organisations are supported, but larger UK appeals are not supported.

In 1998/99 the trust had assets of £516,000 and an income of £274,000, including Gift Aid payments of £197,000 from Grimmitt Holdings Limited.

Grants totalled £206,000 and were broken down as follows:

	1998/99	(1997/98)
Cultural and educational	£59,000	(£32,000)
Disability	£56,000	(nil)
Community	£37,000	(£33,000)
Children and youth	£22,000	(£19,000)
Medical and health	£12,000	(£24,000)
Overseas	£11,000	(£9,700)
Older people	£5,100	(£1,900)
Benevolent	£4,600	(£13,000)

Grants over £2,000 were listed in the accounts. The largest grant of £56,000 was given to Sense. Other grants included £10,000 to St Basil's Centre, £7,500 to CBSO – Taking Music into Schools, £5,000 to Royal Birmingham Society of Artists, £4,100 to Getting Older Dressage Society, £3,500 to WaterAid, £2,500 to Canterbury Festival, £2,200 to Triangle

Day Centre and £2,000 each to Black Country Museum and City of Birmingham Symphony Orchestra. Many of these organisations have also been supported in recent years.

Applications In writing to the correspondent.

The Grocers' Charity

General – see below

£258,000 (1998/99)

Beneficial area UK

Grocers' Hall, Princes Street, London EC2R 8AD

Tel. 020 7606 3113 **Fax** 020 7600 3082 **e-mail** anne@grocershall.co.uk

Correspondent Miss Anne Blanchard, Charity Administrator

Trustees *Directors of The Grocers' Trust Company Ltd (about 30).*

Information available Available from the trust: annual accounts; annual report with list of grants (for £750 or more), detailed narrative breakdown of grants/ grant-making and guidelines for applicants.

General About half of the charitable budget is reserved each year to make awards to a few independent schools with which the charity has strong links. The balance is given to charities working in the following fields: relief of poverty with an emphasis on young people, disability, medicine, the arts, heritage, the church and older people. The current emphasis is on the first two categories. Both capital or revenue projects are supported and grants are usually one-off.

The charity says: 'The Grocers' Charity is the charitable arm of the Grocers' Company, one of the senior livery companies of the City of London. Although the Grocers' Company has an historic tradition of dispensing monies to diverse charitable causes, it was not until 1968 that the charity itself was formally established. It is administered by the

Grocers' Trust Company Ltd.

'The charity is funded by its own investments (current value £7.8 million) together with a regular grant from the Grocers' Company (£60,000) and the income from covenants and donations made by members of the Grocers' Company (£45,000).'

In 1998/99 the charity had assets of £7.9 million and an income of £355,000. Grants totalled £258,000, slightly lower than usual due to large grants being made in the previous year totalling £352,000. Of the 1,006 applications received only 120 were successful. Grants were broken down as shown in the table.

The trust details several projects supported under each category. Grants of £750 or more are listed, and the number and total of smaller grants is given.

Education
Grants went to various independent schools for bursaries and scholarships.

Relief of poverty/disadvantaged young people
Grants of £750 or more were given to 20 organisations. The largest of £5,000 went to VSO which the charity has been supporting since its foundation in the 1960s. The grants helped five volunteers to work in developing countries. Comeback received £2,500; this project helps ex-offenders and long-term unemployed people to enter the workplace. Other grants included £3,800 to Samaritans for a Youth Outreach Programme, £1,000 each to Birmingham Settlement, Fairbridge and Robin Hood Gardens & Training Trust and £750 each to Children's Country Holidays and Second Chance. 14 grants of less than £750 were given.

Disability
18 grants of £750 or more were given, up to £2,000. Examples included Cambridge House & Talbot for their Only Connect project, an arts/education programme for

people with severe learning disabilities (£2,000). Studio on the Green in Selkirk received £750 for The Studio's Go for It Dance Company which enables young people and adults who are disabled to participate in music and dance. Other grants included those to Refresh (£1,500) and Cystic Fibrosis Holiday Fund for Children (£1,000). A further 11 grants of less than £750 were given.

Churches
Annual grants are given in support of the clergy livings that are under the patronage of the Grocers' Company. Grants were made to the PCCs of these parishes totalling £11,000. Two other grants were listed; they were The Charity of Dame Margaret Slaney (£1,100) and Oundle Parish Church Northamptonshire (£1,000). Five smaller grants were given.

Medicine
Seven grants of £750 and above were given. The largest grant of £5,000 went to The Lord Mayor's Appeal for Leuka 2000 for a new leukaemia unit at Hammersmith Hospital in West London. £2,000 was given to the The Haven Trust which is a new charity aiming to create a series of drop-in centres for breast cancer sufferers and their families. Other grants included £1,000 each to Calibre and The Orchid Cancer Appeal. Seven donations under £750 were also given.

Heritage
Six grants ranging from £1,000 to £2,500 were given and six smaller grants. Beneficiaries included Chichester Cathedral Restoration Trust (£2,500), Sir John Soane Museum (£2,000) and City of London Endowment for St Paul's Cathedral (£1,000).

The arts
Eight grants ranging from £750 to £1,500 were given. The largest grant went to London Festival of Chamber Music which takes music into the community. LAMDA received £1,000 for the Student Hardship Fund. Other grants included those to British Youth Opera and Tate Gallery of Modern Art. Seven smaller grants were given.

Older people
Two grants of £1,000 each went to Royal Hospital Chelsea and The Universal Beneficent Society. Two smaller donations were awarded.

General
Three grants under £750 were given.

Exclusions Only UK-registered charities are supported. Individuals cannot receive grants directly, although grants can be given to organisations on

THE GROCER'S CHARITY GRANT DISTRIBUTION IN 1998/99			
Category	No. of grants	Total £	%
Education	28	140,000	54
Relief of poverty, especially young people	34	34,000	13
Disability	29	25,000	10
Churches	8	15,000	6
Medicine	14	15,000	6
Heritage	11	13,000	5
The arts	13	11,000	4
Older people	4	3,000	1
General	3	1,100	1

their behalf. Support is rarely given to the following unless there is a specific or long-standing connection with the Grocers' Company:

- cathedrals, churches and other ecclesiastical bodies
- hospices
- schools and other educational establishments
- research projects.

Applications In writing to the correspondent on the charity's official headed notepaper. Full details of the project or projects referred to in the application and a copy of the latest audited accounts and annual report should be included. The receipt of applications is not acknowledged but all receive notification of the outcome. They are considered in January, April, June and November and should be received two months before the relevant meeting. Informal enquiries are welcome by telephone or e-mail to the correspondent.

Unsuccessful applicants are advised to wait a year before reapplying. Successful applicants should wait for at least two years before reapplying.

The GRP Charitable Trust

Jewish, general

£179,000 (1998/99)

Beneficial area UK

Kleinwort Benson Trustees Ltd, PO Box 191, 10 Fenchurch Street, London EC3M 3LB

Tel. 020 7956 6600 **Fax** 020 7626 6319

Correspondent The Secretary

Trustees *Kleinwort Benson Trustees Ltd.*

Information available Full accounts were on file at the Charity Commission.

General The G R P of the title stands for the settlor, George Richard Pinto, a London banker who set up the trust in 1968. Virtually all the grants are given to Jewish organisations.

In 1998/99 the trust had assets of £3.5 million and an income of £146,000, £100,000 of which came from donations. Kleinwort Benson Trustees Ltd received £8,200 for their services. Grants totalling £179,000 were given to 17 organisations, 13 of which were supported in the previous year.

The largest grant was £125,000 to Oxford Centre for Hebrew and Jewish Studies, who have also received a large proportion of the grant total in previous years. After other sizeable grants of £24,000 to Jerusalem Foundation and £6,600 to Anglo-Israel Foundation, grants ranged between £100 and £5,000. Beneficiaries included Council of Christians and Jews (£5,000), Institute of Jewish Policy Research (£2,000), B'nai B'rith Hillel Foundation and SCOPUS (both £1,000), Haifi University (£500), Chicken Shed Theatre Company (£250) and £100 each to Down's Syndrome Association and Norwood Ravenswood Appeal.

Exclusions No grants to individuals.

Applications In writing to the correspondent. However, the trustees prefer to provide medium-term support for a number of charities already known to them, and unsolicited applications are not acknowledged. Trustees meet annually in March.

The Walter Guinness Charitable Trust

General

£122,000 (1998/99)

Beneficial area UK and overseas, with a preference for Wiltshire and Hampshire

Biddesden House, Andover, Hampshire SP11 9DN

Correspondent The Secretary

Trustees *Hon. F B Guinness; Hon. Mrs R Mulji; Hon. Catriona Guinness.*

Information available Accounts were on file at the Charity Commission.

General The trust was established in 1961 by Bryan Walter, the second Lord Moyne, in memory of his father, the first Lord Moyne. Most grants are given to a number of charities which the trust has been consistently supporting for many years.

The assets of the trust stood at £3.9 million in 1998/99 generating an income of £143,000. A total of £122,000 was given in 163 grants, ranging from £50 to £10,000. The largest grants were £10,000 each to Enham Trust and St

James' Church Ludgershall Restoration Fund. Other larger grants went to UNIPAL (£9,000), Marlborough College Appeal (£5,000), Project Ability (£3,000) and Royal Academy Trust (£2,500). Grants from £1,000 to £2,000 included those to Asylum Aid, Disasters' Emergency Committee (Sudan Crisis), Global Cancer Concern, NCH Action for Children, Queen Elizabeth's Foundation for Disabled People, Raleigh International and Wiltshire Community Foundation.

Smaller grants ranging from £50 to £800 but mostly of £500, included those to Anti-Slavery International, British Red Cross, Drug and Alcohol Foundation, Help the Aged, Lytham St Anne's & Fylde YMCA, Prison Reform Trust, Royal Academy of Music, Scottish Wildlife Trust, Victim Support in Wiltshire and Yately Industries for the Disabled. Previously the trust has stated, 'We are unlikely to be able to support anything unless there is a personal connection, a local connection or unless the organisation has previously been supported by our trust'.

Exclusions No grants to individuals.

Applications In writing to the correspondent. The trust states it is unable to respond to unsuccessful applications.

The Gunter Charitable Trust

General

£97,000 (1998/99)

Beneficial area UK

c/o Forsters, 67 Grosvenor Street, London W1X 9DB

Correspondent S J Atkinson

Trustees *J de C E Findlay; H R D Billson.*

Information available Full accounts were on file at the Charity Commission.

General The trust gives grants to local and UK organisations, although there appears to be a preference for Scotland. Grants are given to a wide range of organisations, although there appears to be a preference for the countryside, medical and wildlife causes.

In 1998/99 the trust had assets of £2.6 million generating an income of £103,000. Grants ranging from £100 to

£8,800 were given to 80 organisations and totalled £97,000.

Countryside charities supported included Association of the Protection of Rural Scotland (£1,800), Countryside Workshops (£500) and Council for the Protection of Rural England (£300). Medical grants included Liverpool School of Tropical Medicine (£8,800), British Red Cross (£2,200), St Columba's Hospice (£2,000), Multiple Sclerosis Society (£1,000) and Wessex Medical Trust (£800). Wildlife groups included Scottish Wildlife Trust (£1,300), Hampshire & Isle of Wight's Wildlife Trust Limited (£250) and Wildlife Hospital's Trust (£100). Other grants included Crossroads – Glasgow (£7,900), Refugee Council (£3,500), Shelter Scotland (£3,300), Amnesty International (£1,000) and Prisoners Abroad and Royal National Mission for Deep Sea Fishermen (both £300).

Applications In writing to the correspondent, but please note, the trust states that unsolicited applications are not responded to.

Haberdashers' Eleemosynary Charity

Unemployed, homeless, disabled, terminally sick, excluded youth

£315,000 (1998/99)

Beneficial area UK and City of London

Haberdashers' Company, 39–40 Bartholomew Close, London EC1A 7JN

Tel. 020 7606 0967 **Fax** 020 7606 5738 **e-mail** charities@haberdashers.co.uk

Correspondent B J Blair, Assistant Clerk for the Charities

Trustees *Haberdashers' Company.*

Information available Accounts were on file at the Charity Commission, included in the consolidated accounts of the Haberdashers' Company Charities.

General The charity gives all its grants for the relief of need, hardship or distress. Under this criteria the charity makes grants to charities concerned with:

- helping unemployed and homeless people to find jobs or improve their

education or skills and to find more stable accommodation

- supporting carers, enabling people who are chronically sick, disabled or elderly to stay in their own homes or helping older people to find the best residential or nursing homes for their needs if they are no longer able to live independently

- caring for the terminally ill and hospices, although most help of this nature is given through national umbrella organisations

- helping young people who are excluded or 'at risk' to become integrated with society as 'useful citizens'

- providing holidays for people who are chronically sick, disabled or elderly

- providing employment training and placement for people who are disabled.

Grants are all one-off and generally range from £500 to £1,000.

In 1998/99 the trust had assets totalling £7 million and an income of £267,000. Grants totalled £315,000 and were broken down as follows:

	1998/99	(1997/98)
Arts & sport	–	(£1,000)
Christianity and the Church	£8,400	(£13,000)
Disadvantaged people	£229,000	(£145,000)
Education & training	£14,000	(£11,000)
Healthcare	£49,000	(£64,000)
Young people	£14,000	(£2,400)
Miscellaneous	£1,000	(–)

Grants of over £1,000 were listed in the accounts. These ranged from £2,000 to £75,000 and were given to 15 charities. The largest of £75,000 went to Centrepoint Soho. Other large grants went to St Catherine's Church Hatcham Community Project (£50,000), St Mary's NHS Trust (£25,000), St John the Baptist Church Hoxton (£20,000) and £10,000 each to The Globe Centre, Mental Health Foundation and National Association of Voluntary & Non-maintained Special Schools.

Smaller grants included £5,000 each to Christ Church Brixton, Startlight Children's Foundation and Sail Training Association, £3,300 to Royal College of Needlework, £3,000 to Guildhall School of Music & Drama and £2,000 each to DEC Kosovo Crisis Appeal and The Sea Cadets.

The Haberdashers' Eleemosynary Charity is the largest of 46 different charitable funds administered by the Haberdashers' Company. Most of the other trust funds

administered by the Haberdashers' Company are reputed to be very small, although there are several of note, including the Thomas Arno Bequest (*see separate entry*).

Exclusions No grants to individuals unless Freemen of the Haberdashers' Company or the City of London. No grants to organisations not involved with the relief of poverty.

Applications In writing to the correspondent, with a copy of your latest annual report and accounts, up-to-date financial information, and other information illustrating your aims and activities.

The Alfred Haines Charitable Trust

Christian, health, welfare

£156,000 (1998/99)

Beneficial area Worldwide, with a preference for the West Midlands

c/o Bloomer Heaven, 33 Lionel Street, Birmingham B3 1AB

Tel. 0121 236 0465

Correspondent The Trustees

Trustees *G L H Moss; A L Gilmour.*

Information available Accounts were on file at the Charity Commission, but without a grants list.

General The trust prefers to support specific projects and concentrates on helping smaller charities based in Birmingham and the immediate surrounding area. Most support is for local organisations helping people to improve their quality of life. Grants are generally one-off, although projects may be funded annually for up to three years. The trust prefers to make grants towards specific items and does not give to large appeals.

Projects overseas or outside the West Midlands, whether Christian or not, will only be considered where the applicants are known to a trustee or are recommended by someone known to a trustee who has first hand knowledge of the work.

In 1998/99 the trust had assets of £2.5 million and an income of £92,000. Grants totalled £156,000, with a further

£14,000 being paid in support costs and £9,200 in management and administration charges. No grants list was provided, but grants were broken down as follows.

- Family support and counselling (including salaries, training costs, centres, families at risk) 21 grants totalling £43,000

- Humanitarian and Christian overseas aid (including healthcare, childcare, water provision, education, literacy) 20 grants totalling £42,000

- Youth work, workers and support activities (including salaries, expenses of voluntary workers, educational literature) 25 grants totalling £24,000

- Care for people who are disabled or elderly (including equipment, transport, life skills training, salaries and expenses) 12 grants totalling £18,000

- Work with the homeless (including salaries, centre costs, resettlement) Eight grants totalling £11,000

- Holidays for disadvantaged children and teenagers (including disabled and deprived children and one parent families) Seven grants totalling £5,800

- Activities for and care of underprivileged children (including playschemes, after schools clubs, salaries, training counsellors) Five grants totalling £4,000.

Further information on the beneficiaries was not available. In 1997/98 grants were generally between £100 and £5,000; the only exception was a grant to Cornerstone (£20,000). The grants list included the purpose of each grant.

To illustrate the types of organisations supported, the following were the beneficiaries listed under 'm': Malachi Community Trust (£1,000 for lighting equipment for youth productions); Malvern Hills Homeless Young Adults Trust (£1,000 support for staff salaries); Manna House Counselling Service (£1,000 for a counselling room and office equipment); Manor Farm Outreach project (£1,000 towards a schools worker); Maranatha Ministries (£1,000 for strategy breaks for professionals); Merseyside Council for Voluntary Service (£1,000 for work with young homeless people); Midland County Sports Society for the Disabled (£1,000 for travelling expenses for disabled athletes and contributions to a computer); Mission Aviation Fellowship (£2,500 to airlift medical supplies in Tanzania); and MSA

(£1,500 for day care for people with cerebral palsy).

Exclusions No support for:

- activities which are primarily the responsibility of central or local government or some other responsible body
- animal welfare
- church buildings – restoration, improvements, renovations or new ones
- environmental – conservation and protection of wildlife and landscape
- expeditions and overseas trips
- hospitals and health centres
- individuals, including students. On the rare occasions that individuals are supported, the person has to be recommended by someone known to the trustees and the funding should be of long-term benefit to others
- large national charities; it is unusual for the trust to support large national charities even where there is a local project
- loans and business finance
- medical research projects
- overseas appeals (see above)
- promotion of any religion other than Christianity
- school, universities and colleges
- purely evangelistic projects.

Applications In writing to the correspondent, including: a brief description of the activities of the organisation; details of the project and its overall cost; what funds have already been raised and how the remaining funds are to be raised; a copy of the latest accounts including any associated or parent organisation; any other leaflets or supporting documentation, quoting reference 'DSC'. Trustees meet bi-monthly to consider written applications for grants. Replies are only sent where further information is required. No telephone calls or correspondence will be entered into for any proposed or declined applications.

Successful applicants are required to complete an official receipt and produce a report on the project, usually after 10 months. Successful applicants are advised to leave at least 10 months before applying for further support.

The Hamamelis Trust

Ecological conservation, medical research

£71,000 (1999/2000)

Beneficial area UK, but with a special interest in the Godalming and Surrey areas

c/o Penningtons, Highfield, Brighton Road, Godalming, Surrey GU7 1NS

Tel. 01483 791800

Correspondent Mrs F Collins

Trustees *Michael B Fellingham; Dr Adam F M Stone; Robert Rippengal.*

Information available Full accounts were provided by the trust.

General The trust was set up in 1980 by John Ashley Slocock and enhanced on his death in 1986. The main areas of work are medical research and ecological conservation. Grants are distributed to these areas of work equally. Occasionally grants are made to other projects. Preference is given to projects in the Godalming and Surrey areas.

In 1999/2000 the trust had assets of £3 million and an income of £81,000. A total of £71,000 was given in 24 grants.

Grants ranged from £1,000 to £5,000 and beneficiaries included Arthritis Research Campaign, BTCV, Blond McIndoe Research Unit, Farming and Wildlife Advisory Group, Guy's Hospital HRT Research Unit, Kent Wildlife Trust, Staffordshire Wildlife Trust and University of Oxford Department of Plant Science.

Exclusions Projects outside the UK are not considered. No grants to individuals.

Applications In writing to the correspondent. All applicants are asked to include a short summary of the application along with any published material and references. Unsuccessful appeals will not be acknowledged.

Medical applications are assessed by Dr Adam Stone, one of the trustees, who is medically qualified.

The Helen Hamlyn 1989 Foundation

Older people, health

£236,000 (1998/99)

Beneficial area UK

PO Box 7747, London SW3 6XF

Correspondent The Trustees

Trustees *Lord Hamlyn; Lady Hamlyn; Lord Owen; Prof. Kevin M Cahill.*

Information available Full accounts were on file at the Charity Commission.

General The trust makes grants to enable people who are elderly, sick and 'infirm' to 'live full and satisfying lives in the community'. Related to Helen Hamlyn's profession as a designer, grants are given to organisations which use design skills to improve the environment of older people.

In 1998/99 the trust had assets of £5.1 million and an income of £208,000. Grants to 10 organisations totalled £236,000, and were listed in the annual report as follows:

Design

Grants under this category went to £128,000 to RCA – Helen Hamlyn Research Centre, £83,000 to Design Age and £5,000 to RSA New Design for Old.

Other

Grants went to £15,000 to Fulbright Foundation, £6,000 to St Mungo's and £1,000 each to Charity Search, Neighbourly Care – Southall, RUKBA Trust, Sense and Southern Focus.

Applications In writing to the correspondent.

This entry was not confirmed by the trust but was correct according to information at the Charity Commission.

The Handicapped Children's Aid Committee

Equipment for children with disabilities

£265,000 (1998)

Beneficial area UK

Amberley Lodge, 13 Beechwood Avenue, Finchley, London N3 3AU

Tel. 020 8346 1147

Correspondent P Maurice, Treasurer

Trustees *R Adelman; J Bonn; P Maurice.*

Information available Accounts were on file at the Charity Commission but only up to 1997, and without a grants list.

General The committee was set up in 1961 to support organisations concerned with children who are disabled or under-privileged.

In 1998 the trust had assets of £977,000 and an income of £278,000. Grants totalled £265,0oo. No further information for this year was not available.

No grants list was included with the 1997 accounts, although the report did include the following statement: 'During the year, applications for help were received from hospitals, homes, special schools and from families and social workers on behalf of individual children. Appeals are investigated and once validity is established and approval given by the committee, money is allocated to purchase requirement's.

Applications In writing to the correspondent.

The Lennox Hannay Charitable Trust

Health, welfare, general

£350,000 (1998/99)

Beneficial area UK

RF Trustee Co. Ltd, Ely House, 37 Dover Street, London WC1S 4NJ

Tel. 020 7409 5685

Correspondent The Trust Manager

Trustees *RF Trustee Company Ltd; Walter L Hannay; Caroline F Wilmot-Sitwell.*

Information available Full accounts were provided by the trust.

General In 1998/99 the trust had assets of £11.5 million and an income of £339,000. Grants totalled £350,000. Although many grants are made to the same charities each year, none are promised or guaranteed. The trust listed 50 grants of £2,000 and above. 24 smaller grants totalled £25,000 but were not listed. Most recipients were UK health, welfare or disability charities, with a few grants to local organisations e.g. Oxford & District Sports & Recreation for the Disabled and North Cotswold Voluntary Help Centre.

The largest grant of £47,000 went to Health Unlimited, which received the same amount in the previous year. Eight grants of £10,000 plus were given, including those to Margaret Pike Foundation (£20,000), Sue Ryder Foundation (£16,000), Save the Children Fund (£15,000), British Deaf Association (£14,000), Barnardos (£12,000) and Ex-Services Mental Welfare Society (£10,000).

Grants from £2,000 to £9,000 included those to Tibet House Trust (£9,000), Help the Aged (£8,000), Herefordshire MIND (£5,000), Sense (£4,000), Animal Health Trust (£3,000) and £2,000 each to British Lung Foundation, King Edward VII Hospital, Riding for the Disabled and St John's Hospice.

Applications In writing to the correspondent. Applications need to be received by February as trustees meet in March.

The Kathleen Hannay Memorial Charity

Health, welfare, Christian, general

£206,000 (1998/99)

Beneficial area UK

RF Trustee Co. Ltd, Ely House, 37 Dover Street, London WC1S 4NJ

Tel. 020 7409 5685

Correspondent The Trust Manager

Trustees *Enid Hannay; Simon Weil.*

Information available Full accounts were provided by the trust.

General In 1998/99 the trust had assets totalling £6.2 million and an income of £190,000. It gave 48 grants totalling £206,000 (in 1997/98 it gave 47 grants totalling £181,000). Many grants are recurrent but the trust does not commit to ongoing support. Grants are given mainly to health, welfare and Christian charities.

Six grants were for £10,000 or more. The beneficiaries were Handel House Trust Ltd (£20,000), NSPCC (£13,000), £11,000 each to Children's Aid Direct, Red Hall Christian Centre and SANE; and £10,000 to Oxford Foundation for Ethics and Communications in Health Care Practice.

Other grants included those to The Samaritans (£9,000), Fight for Sight (£7,000), Barnardos (£5,000), Parent Network (£4,000), London Playing Fields Society (£3,000), Church Missionary Society (£2,000) and Oxford University Boat Club Trust Endowment Fund (£1,000).

Smaller grants ranging from £500 to £600 all went to six parochial church councils.

Exclusions No grants to individuals or non-registered charities.

Applications In writing to the correspondent. Applications need to be received by February as trustees meet in March.

The Haramead Trust

Welfare, children's welfare, health education
£284,000 (1998/99)

Beneficial area UK and overseas with a preference for Leicestershire

Park House, Park Hill, Gaddesby, Leicestershire LE7 4WH

Fax. 01664 840908

Correspondent M J Linnett, Trustee

Trustees *Mrs W M Linnett; M J Linnett; R H Smith; D L Tams.*

General In 1998/99 the trust had assets totalling £120,000, down from £389,000

in the previous year. It had an income of £16,000 from investments, in 1997/98 the trust had an income of £986,000, mostly from donations. Grants totalling £284,000 were given using both income and capital funds. (In 1997/98 grants totalled £601,000).

The trust gives grants for people in need, children's welfare and education about health. During the year it supported 19 organisations with grants ranging from £1,000 to £50,000. The largest grant of £50,000 went to DePaul Trust. Other large grants went to Leicester YMCA (£33,000), British Red Cross (£25,000) with four grants of £20,000 each to Shelter, Crisis, Rainbows and NSPCC.

Six grants ranging from £10,000 to £15,000 included those to 28th Leicester Wigston Scout Group, Menphys and Save the Children. Six grants ranging from £1,000 to £7,000 included those to Age Concern, Help the Aged and Intercare. Of all the grants, five were recurrent from the previous year.

Applications In writing to the correspondent.

The Harbour Charitable Trust

General
£155,000 (1998/99)

Beneficial area UK

22 York Terrace, Regents Park, London NW1 4PT

Tel. 020 7935 7440

Correspondent Mrs B B Green, Trustee

Trustees *Mrs B B Green; Mrs Z S Blackman; J F Avery Jones.*

Information available Accounts were on file at the Charity Commission, but without a list of grants.

General The trust makes grants for the benefit of childcare, education and health research and to various other charitable organisations. In 1998/99 it had assets of £1.7 million and an income of £318,000.

Management and administration costs were very high, amounting to 40% of the income at £126,000. These costs included £111,000 interest on a bank loan (£62,000 in the previous year). Grants totalled £155,000 and were categorised by the trust as follows (1997/98 figures in brackets):

Healthcare	£49,000	(£84,000)
Joint Jewish Charitable Trust	£43,000	(£53,000)
L'Chaim Society	£23,000	(£43,000)
Education	£15,000	(£15,000)
Childcare	£3,900	(£7,300)
Other	£22,000	(£46,000)

No further information was available on the charities supported.

Exclusions Grants are given to registered charities only.

Applications In writing to the correspondent.

The Harbour Foundation

Jewish, general
£112,000 (1998/99)

Beneficial area Worldwide

11 Curtain Road, London EC2A 3LT

Tel. 020 7456 8180

Correspondent The Trustees

Trustees *S R Harbour; A C Humphries; Z S Blackman; S Green; B B Green.*

Information available Accounts were on file at the Charity Commission, but without a grants list.

General The principal activities of the trust are providing relief among refugees and the homeless, advancement of education, learning and research, and to make donations to any institution established for charitable purposes throughout the world.

The following is taken from the 1998/99 trustees' report:

'The main thrust of the foundation's current and future charitable programme comprises two areas of activities which are, to some extent, complementary.

'The first is the support and development of technology-based education for the community. This support is directed both to university level and to those who have been failed by the educational system especially in the inner boroughs of London. Rapid and continual innovation in this field and the attraction and retention of highly qualified teaching staff necessitate a high level of financial support on a consistent and ongoing basis. A carefully phased release of donations by the foundation to education providers at the leading edge acts as an incentive for them to maximise performance and enables them to plan ahead with some degree of confidence. It is therefore essential to continue to build up reserves of the foundation to a level sufficient to ensure a reliable high level of financial support to such providers.

'The second strand of activity is also mainly aimed at the inner boroughs of London where it is intended to provide funds to improve the physical environment in deprived areas. This will be directed to the development of run down space, both open and constructed, for community use. Again this activity will require a high level of financial support and, therefore, also necessitates an expansion of the foundation's reserves.'

In 1998/99 the trust had assets of £6.1 million and an income of £1.2 million. Grants totalled £112,000, with management and administration costs high at £70,000, although the trust receives a rental and trading income which may account for this large figure.

Despite having a detailed and comprehensive narrative report, the trust provides no grants list or details of type or size of grants in their accounts.

Applications In writing to the correspondent.

The Harebell Centenary Fund

General, education, medical research, animal welfare

£72,000 (1999)

Beneficial area UK

1 Dean Farrar Street, London SW1U 0DY

Tel. 020 7222 8044

Correspondent Ms P J Chapman

Trustees *J M Denker; M I Goodbody; F M Reed.*

Information available Full accounts were on file at the Charity Commission.

General This trust has a particular interest in the promotion of neurological and neurosurgical research and the relief of sickness and suffering amongst animals.

The current policy is to concentrate on making donations to charities which do

not receive widespread public support and to keep the trust's administration expenses to a minimum. For this reason the trustees have decided to support only registered charities and not individuals. Unsolicited applications are not requested, as the trustees prefer to make donations to charities whose work they have come across through their own research.

The assets of the trust in 1999 stood at £2.7 million, an increase of £900,000 from the year before. The income for the year was £641,000 which included a large gift of £545,000 which was transferred to the capital fund (in the previous year the income was £72,000, all from investments). Administration costs were £12,000.

A total of £72,000 was given in 26 grants. The largest grant of £14,000 was given to the Royal Hospital for Neurodisability. Most grants (22) were of £2,500, beneficiaries included The Blackie Foundation, DEMAND, HITS – Head Injuries Scotland, Macmillan Cancer Relief, NSA Wildlife Sound Trust, St Joseph's Hospice – Hackney and the University of Dundee. Three grants of £1,000 each went to PACE, The Dyslexia Institute and The Shakespeare Hospice. Seven grants were recurrent from the previous year.

Applications In writing to the correspondent, unsolicited applications will no longer be replied to, unless accompanied by an sae. As trustees meet in March and November, applications need to be received by February or October.

Harnish Trust

Christian

£82,000 to organisations (1998/99)

Beneficial area Worldwide

The Riverbank, Reybridge, Lacock, Wiltshire SN15 2PF

Correspondent Jill Dann, Trustee

Trustees *Jill Dann; Jennifer R Paynter.*

Information available Full accounts were on file at the Charity Commission.

General The trust supports Christian activity and education worldwide, including charities, voluntary organisations and individuals. The trust is currently distributing its income and

capital funds. It is not known why this is the case or if the trust intends to distribute all its funds. In 1998/99 the trust had assets of £533,000, an income of £14,000 and grants totalled £102,000.

A total of 81 grants were given to both organisations and individuals. They ranged from £50 to £10,000. The largest grants of £10,000 each went to Cheltenham and Gloucester College Development Trust, The Lambeth Fund and one individual. Grants of £1,000 or more were given to 30 organisations including those to Scripture Union (£4,000), Bristol International Students Centre (£2,500), Tearfund and Trinity College Bursary Fund (£2,000 each) and Church Urban Fund and Living Waters (£1,000 each).

Smaller grants included those to World Vision (£600), Jubilee Trust and Olive Branch (£500 each), Women on the Move (£100) and Monkton Christian Union (£50).

Grants were given to 21 individuals totalling £20,000.

Applications Unsolicited applications are not considered.

The Charles Harris Charitable Trust

Education, general

£86,000 (1998/99)

Beneficial area UK

Philip Harris House, 1a Spur Road, Orpington, Kent BR6 0PH

Tel. 01689 875135

Correspondent A R Bull, Managing Executive

Trustees *C W Harris; Lady Harris; A R Bull.*

Information available Full accounts were on file at the Charity Commission.

General This trust has the same trustees and correspondent as both The Martin Harris Charitable Trust and The Peter Harris Charitable Trust. They all support projects of education, study and research, but can also make grants for more general charitable purposes. Some beneficiaries received grants from more than one trust in 1998/99 (Weitzman Institute Foundation receiving the same amount from all three). It is difficult to anticipate with all the trusts whether their grant-making will stay at the same level in future years.

In 1998/99 the trust had assets of £6,000 and an income of £51,000, mostly from donations. Grants totalling £86,000 were given to five organisations as follows:

Weitzman Institute Foundation £63,000

South Bromley Hospice £13,000

Henshaws Society for the Blind £5,000

Leuka 2000 £5,000

Bromley Autistic Trust £1,300

Applications In writing to the correspondent. Please note, the trust states that the funds are fully committed for the next five years.

The Martin Harris Charitable Trust

Education, general

£415,000 (1998/99)

Beneficial area UK

Philip Harris House, 1a Spur Road, Orpington, Kent BR6 0PH

Tel. 01689 875135

Correspondent A R Bull, Managing Executive

Trustees *C W Harris; Lady Harris; A R Bull.*

Information available Accounts were on file at the Charity Commission.

General This trust has the same trustees and correspondent as both The Charles Harris Charitable Trust and The Peter Harris Charitable Trust (see separate entries). They all support projects of education, study and research, but can also make grants for more general charitable purposes. Some beneficiaries received grants from all three trusts in 1998/99 (Weitzman Institute Foundation receiving the same amount from all three). In 1998/99 the trust had assets of £68,000 and an income of £17,000. Grants to nine organisations totalled £415,000 using both income and capital funds to make grants. The trust's assets fell from £466,000 to £68,000 during the year.

The grants were £250,000 to Animal Health Trust, £63,000 to Weitzman Institute Foundation, £25,000 each to Oxford Centre for Hebrew & Jewish Studies and Politeia, £13,000 to South Bromley Hospice and £10,000 each to Dementia Relief Trust, Hospice in the Weald, St Mary's Goudhurst and WellBeing.

Applications In writing to the correspondent. Please note, the trust states that the funds are fully committed for the next five years.

The Peter Harris Charitable Trust

Education, general

£104,000 (1998/99)

Beneficial area UK

Philip Harris House, 1a Spur Road, Orpington, Kent BR6 0PH

Tel. 01689 875135

Correspondent A R Bull, Managing Executive

Trustees *C W Harris; Lady Harris; A R Bull.*

Information available Accounts were on file at the Charity Commission.

General This trust has the same trustees and correspondent as both The Charles Harris Charitable Trust and The Martin Harris Charitable Trust. They all support projects of education, study and research, but can also make grants for more general charitable purposes. Some beneficiaries received grants from more than one trust in 1998/99 (Weitzman Institute Foundation receiving the same amount from all three).

In 1998/99 the trust had an income of £7,100 and gave seven grants totalling £104,000. During the year assets fell from £140,000 to just £43,000.

Grants were given to Weitzman Institute Foundation (£63,000), YMCA Housing Association (£22,000), Philharmonia Appeal (£6,000), Leuka 2000 (£5,000), Harris Manchester College (£4,700), Woodlea Primary School (£3,000) and South Bromley Hospice (£400).

Applications In writing to the correspondent. Please note, the trust states that the funds are fully committed for the next five years.

The R J Harris Charitable Settlement

General

£165,000 to organisations (1998/99)

Beneficial area UK, with a preference for west Wiltshire, with particular emphasis on Trowbridge, north Wiltshire, south of the M4 and Bath and environs

c/o Thrings & Long Solicitors, Midland Bridge, Bath BA1 2HQ

Tel. 01225 340099

Correspondent J J Thring, Secretary

Trustees *H M Newton-Clare, Chair; T C M Stock; J L Rogers; A Pitt.*

Information available Accounts were provided by the trust, but no list of grants or breakdown of grants was included.

General The trust deed of 1969 directs the trustees to use the income for 40 years for charitable purposes as they see fit. Both individuals and organisations can be supported. In 1998/99 the trust had assets of £1.8 million and an income of £80,000. Grants totalled £170,000, of which £65,000 was payable from income and £105,000 payable from the capital. Of the grants payable from the income, £4,900 went to individuals and the remainder to organisations. No grants list or breakdown of grants was given.

In 1997/98, grants totalled £73,000, payable from the income. 90 grants were given of between £100 and £5,000. The trust supports mainly south west-based organisations in the area defined above. Very few grants are given to large, well-known UK charities. Grants were categorised by the trust as shown below.

Category	Total	%
Medical and mental health	£11,600	16
The arts	£6,700	9
Education	£6,100	8
Youth organisations and projects	£4,500	6
Social welfare and disabled people	£31,500	43
Building restoration and general environment	£6,200	8
Ex-Bowyers staff	£6,700	9

No further details on the grants was available.

Applications In writing to the correspondent. Trustees meet three times each year. An sae is required.

The M A Hawe Settlement

General

£522,000 (1996/97)

Beneficial area UK, with a preference for Lancashire

94 Park View Road, Lytham St Annes, Lancashire FY8 4JF

Tel. 01253 796888

Correspondent M A Hawe, Trustee

Trustees *M A Hawe; Mrs G Hawe; Marc G Hawe.*

Information available Full accounts are on file at the Charity Commission.

General In 1996/97, the trust had assets of £5.2 million and an income of £271,000. Donations during the year were an exceptionally high £522,000. This was due to a grant of £486,000 to Kensington House Trust Ltd.

This company was established to run a property bought by the trust in 1993, as accommodation on a short stay basis for young homeless people. It now also provides furniture and equipment to people in need, shelter for victims of domestic violence and holidays for terminally ill people and for deprived children. In 1996/97, a large grant was given to the company to buy another property in Blackpool.

No other grant was above £3,000 with mainly local welfare causes receiving support.

The latest accounts for the trust also gave a nine-year summary of donations made. Over this period, out of a total of £1.2 million given in grants, £827,000 has been given to Kensington House Trust. Other major beneficiaries have been Trinity - The Hospice in the Fylde (£100,000), Fylde Coast Women's Refuge (£28,000) and BBC Children in Need (£27,000).

Applications In writing to the correspondent.

The Hawthorne Charitable Trust

General

£146,000 (1997/98)

Beneficial area UK, especially Hereford and Worcester

c/o Messrs Baker Tilly, 2 Bloomsbury Street, London WC1B 3ST

Tel. 020 7413 5100

Correspondent Roger Clark, Trustee

Trustees *Mrs A S C Berington; R J Clark.*

Information available Full accounts were on file at the Charity Commission.

General In 1998/99 the trust had an income of £110,000 and an expenditure of £141,000. Unfortunately, no further information for this year was available and this information is repeated from the last edition of this guide.

In 1997/98 the trust had assets of £5.2 million and an income of £151,000. Grants totalled £146,000.

The largest grants were £10,000 to Haven Trust, £5,000 each to Dyson Perrins Museum, Edward's Trust, Macmillan Cancer Relief and Society of Friends of Little Malvern Priory and £3,000 each to both Downside Abbey Trustees for St Wulstan's and Malvern Hills Citizens Advice Bureau. Most of the remaining grants were for £2,500, with just a few for smaller sums.

A wide range of organisations were supported particularly health and welfare causes, but also charities concerned with animal welfare, disability, heritage and young people. Examples include Alzheimer's Research Trust, Animal Welfare Foundation, British Wheelchair Sports Foundation, Child Poverty Action Group, Hearing Dogs for the Deaf, Iris Fund and Worcester Cathedral Appeal Trust.

Exclusions Grants are given to registered charities only. No grants to individuals.

Applications In writing to the correspondent, including up-to-date accounts. Applications should be received by October for consideration in November.

The Haydan Charitable Trust

Jewish, general

£74,000 (1997)

Beneficial area UK

4th Floor, 1 Knightsbridge, London SW1X 7LX

Tel. 020 7823 2200

Correspondent Wendy Miller

Trustees *Christopher Smith; Irene Smith; Anthony Winter.*

Information available Full accounts were on file at the Charity Commission.

General In 1999 the trust had an income of £50,000 and an expenditure of £70,000. The trust states that it gives recurrent grants to a few organisations and does not invite applications. Unfortunately, no further information for this year was available and the following is repeated from the last edition of this guide.

This trust was set up in 1990 and it has a clear relationship with its namesake company, Haydan Holdings Ltd, who in 1997 loaned the trust £53,000. In 1997 the trust had an income of only £337, and the assets were listed as having a deficit of £59,000. The trust owns 100 shares in Radlake Limited, a tennis centre with associated leisure facilities, of which two of the trustees are directors and which was purchased by the trust with the intention of its net profits being transferred to the trust. Radlake Limited, however, has ceased to trade and the shares are not worth anything.

The trust has continued to make grants, which in 1997 totalled £74,000. Two ongoing grants were made and a number of new charities were also supported. Grants were listed in the trust's annual report as follows: £33,000 to Cedar School for Disabled Children, £25,000 to The Nordoff Robbins Music Therapy Centre, £10,000 to Kisharon, £2,000 each to Cancer Research Campaign and Tommy's Campaign and £1,700 in miscellaneous grants.

Exclusions No grants are given for projects overseas.

Applications Unsolicited applications are not considered.

The Haymills Charitable Trust

Education, medicine, welfare, youth

£78,000 to organisations (1998/99)

Beneficial area UK, but particularly the west of London and Suffolk, where the Haymills group is sited

Empire House, Hanger Green, Ealing, London W5 3BD

Tel. 020 8991 4309

Correspondent I W Ferres, Secretary

Trustees *G A Cox, Chair; E F C Drake; I W Ferres; A M H Jackson; K C Perryman; J A Sharpe; J L Wosner; W G Underwood.*

Information available Accounts were on file at the Charity Commission.

General The trustees' report states: 'the trustees regularly review their policy, aiming to make the best use of the funds available by donating varying amounts to projects which they believe are not widely known and thus are likely to be inadequately supported. Their main support is to registered charities operating in areas known to them, especially those lying in and to the west of London and in Suffolk.

'Grants fall into four main categories:

Education: grants to schools, colleges and universities

Medicine: grants to hospitals and associated institutions and to medical research

Welfare: primarily to include former Haymills' staff, and to those who are considered to be 'in necessitous circumstances' or who are otherwise distressed or disadvantaged

Youth: support for training schemes to assist in the education, welfare and training of young people.

'No personal applications for support will be considered unless endorsed by a university, a college or other appropriate authority. Each year, a limited number of applicants can be considered who can show that they are committed to further education and training preferably for employment in the construction industry.'

In 1998/99 assets stood at £2 million and the income was £122,000, including £45,000 in Gift Aid donations and £60,000 in dividends from Haymills Group. Grants totalled £83,000, including £5,400 to individuals, and were categorised as follows:

Educational
A total of £16,000 was given in 11 grants. They were given to various educational establishments, especially towards scholarships. The largest beneficiary was Merchant Taylor's Company which received £10,000 for their Dudley Cox Bursary Fund and £1,000 for their Dudley Cox Awards for engineering, design and technology. Other grants included £3,000 towards a prize fund at Hammersmith and West London College, £2,000 towards a student advice centre at Thames Valley University and £500 to Anglia Polytechnic University for the Haymills Building Management Scholarship.

Medical
There were 14 grants given totalling £14,000. Grants were mainly given to hospitals and hospital appeals, although grants were also given towards research. Beneficiaries included Central Middlesex Hospital League of Friends (£2,200), Great Ormond Street Children's Hospital (£1,700), Mount Vernon Paul Strickland Scanner Appeal (£1,200), Marie Curie Cancer Care (£700), Royal London Hospital (£500) and Cystic Fibrosis Trust (£250).

Youth and welfare
Grants were given to 41 organisations and 6 individuals totalling £52,000. Beneficiaries included British Red Cross Hurricane Mitch Appeal (£6,000), Raleigh Trust (£3,500) Inter Action – HMS President and Middlesex Young People's Club (£3,000), Salvation Army (£2,000), Mencap (£1,000) and Canine Pets for Independence and Sea Cadets Norwich (£500 each). Grants of between £560 and £1,400 were given to six Haymill's pensioners.

Applications In writing to the correspondent, but see note above. Trustees meet at least twice a year, usually in March and October. Applications are not acknowledged.

May Hearnshaw's Charity

General

£77,000 (1998/99)

Beneficial area UK

The Law Partnership, City Plaza, 2 Pinfold Street, Sheffield S1 2GU

Tel. 0114 270 0999

Correspondent David Law, Trustee

Trustees *David Law; Jack Rowan.*

Information available Full accounts were on file at the Charity Commission.

General This trust was set up by the will of the late May Hearnshaw who died in 1988. It was her wish that the trust be used for the promotion of education, advancement of religion and relief of poverty and sickness.

The trust supports UK charities or local charities working in the South Yorkshire or North Midlands area. It mainly supports organisations with a limited number of grants given to individuals recommended by known charities.

In 1998/99 the trust had assets of £2.1 million generating an income of £77,000, all of which was given in grants. Further expenditure on management and administration totalled £17,000, over a fifth of the income. The grants were categorised as follows.

Relief of poverty and sickness
Under this category £59,000 was given in 20 grants, ranging from £500 to £10,000. The largest grants went to Childrens Appeal – Children's Hospital (£10,000), Cavendish Centre (£7,000) and Alzheimer's Disease Society (£5,000). Seven grants of £3,000 each included those to British Heart Foundation, Down's Syndrome Association and St Luke's Hospice. Seven grants of £2,000 each included those to Age Concern Sheffield and WellBeing. Smaller grants went to MENCAP (£1,300) and two grants of £500 each went to Disability Aid Fund on behalf of indivduals. Eight of the grants were recurrent from the previous year.

Advancement of religion
One grant of £2,000 was given to Methodist Homes.

Promotion of education
One individual received a grant of £650.

Other
Nine grants totalled £16,000, ranging from £500 to £3,000. The largest grants of

135

£3,000 each went to NSPCC and RNIB. Five grants ranging from £1,000 to £2,000 included those to Ability Net (for a new centre), Disability Sport England, National Trust and New Era Housing Association. Two of these grants were recurrent from the previous year. One grant of £500 went to Ability Net on behalf of an individual.

Exclusions No grants directly to individuals, but small grants can be made to known charities to assist in the relief of specified individuals.

Applications Unsolicited applications are counter-productive. The trustees usually decide on and make grants twice a year. They do not consider appeals, preferring to use other agencies.

The Michael & Morven Heller Charitable Foundation

University and medical research projects

£98,000 (1998/99)

Beneficial area Worldwide

8–10 New Fetter Lane,
London EC4A 1NQ

Tel. 020 7415 5000

Correspondent The Administrator

Trustees *Michael Heller; Morven Heller; Pearl Livingstone.*

Information available Accounts and a separate grants list were on file at the Charity Commission.

General This trust states it supports specific projects relating to medical research, science and educational research and gives significant donations to universities for research purposes and in particular medical research. In practice, there appears to be some preference for Jewish organisations.

The trust states: '[The trustees] are aware that there are presently few private charities in the UK which can make large donations that exceed £50,000. To enable them to make such donations, the trustees propose to accumulate and retain in hand sufficient reserves for this purpose.'

In 1998/99 the trust had assets of £2.3 million and an income of £191,000. Grants totalled £98,000.

No grants list was included in the accounts, which stated: 'The trustees consider that as this is a private charitable trust to which no public funds have been contributed, the disclosure of such information would serve no useful purpose and would, in certain circumstances be likely to prejudice the furtherance of the purposes of the charitable trust and the recipient. Full details of these grants will be supplied to the Charity Commission.'

However, the Charity Commission included a list of grants over £1,000 in the publicly available file. The largest grant of £15,000 went to Marie Curie Cancer Care. Other large grants included: £13,000 in three grants to University College London; £11,000 in two grants to Leuka 2000; and £8,100 in two grants to St Catherine's College. Other recipients included Beth Shalom Holocaust Memorial Centre (£7,500), Friends of Hebrew College (£6,100), FMRC Charitable Trust (£5,000), Tel-Aviv Foundation for Children at Risk (£4,000), Association Advancement of Cancer Therapies (£3,100) and WellBeing (£1,000). In total, 22 grants of over £1,000 were given.

Exclusions No support for individuals.

Applications In writing to the correspondent.

The Simon Heller Charitable Settlement

Medical research, science and educational research

£226,000 (1998/99)

Beneficial area Worldwide

8–10 New Fetter Lane,
London EC4A 1NQ

Tel. 020 7415 5000

Correspondent The trustees

Trustees *M A Heller; Morven Heller; S H Trust Co Ltd.*

Information available Accounts were on file at the Charity Commission. No grants list was available since 1996/97.

General This trust was established in 1972 and funds specific projects relating to medical research, science and educational research. This usually involves making large grants to universities for research purposes, particularly medical research. In practice, there appears to be some preference for Jewish organisations.

The trust states: '[The trustees] are aware that there are presently few private charities in the UK which can make large donations that exceed £50,000. To enable them to make such donations, the trustees propose to accumulate and retain in hand sufficient reserves for this purpose.'

In 1998/99 the trust had assets of £3.7 million and an income of £250,000. Grants totalled £226,000.

No grants list was included in the accounts, which stated: 'The trustees consider that as this is a private charitable trust to which no public funds have been contributed, the disclosure of such information would serve no useful purpose and would, in certain circumstances be likely to prejudice the furtherance of the purposes of the charitable trust and the recipient. Full details of these grants will be supplied to the Charity Commission'.

However, the Charity Commission included a 1996/97 grants list in the publicly available file. Grants were given solely to Jewish charities. Beneficiaries included British Techion Society, Jewish Care, Norwood Ravenswood, SCOPUS, BC Shaare Zedek and World Jewish Relief.

Applications In writing to the correspondent.

Help the Homeless Ltd

Homelessness

£69,000 (1998/99)

Beneficial area UK

Babmaes House (fifth floor),
2 Babmaes Street, London SW1 6HD

Tel. 020 7925 2582 **Fax** 020 7925 2583

Correspondent T Kenny, Secretary

Trustees *F J Bergin, Chair; T S Cookson; L A Bains; M McIntyre; T Rogers; R Reed.*

Information available Full accounts were provided by the trust.

General The trust makes small grants to smaller or new voluntary organisations, who are registered charities, for items of capital expenditure directly related to the provision of housing for people who are single and homeless.

In 1998/99 the trust had assets of £1.2 million and an income of £49,000, including £860 in donations. After spending £14,000 on administration and management, and £2,600 on fundraising and publicity costs, the trust gave 26 grants totalling £69,000.

The trust aims to give large grants to major organisations working with the homeless. In 1998/99 these were given to National Homeless Alliance (£20,000) and Emmaus (£10,000). Other grants rarely exceed £2,000, and typical examples include £2,000 each to Brick by Brick to buy furniture for their development of 11 flats, Patchwork Community Housing Association to reposition their offices to create a private interview and counselling area and YMCA Northampton to purchase an industrial washing machine and tumble dryer, £1,400 to Liverpool Student Community Action to buy kitchen equipment for a project to provide practical support to people in Liverpool who are street homeless and £1,000 to Kenward Trust to create a second lounge at one of their residential care and counselling homes for people with addiction problems.

Exclusions Charities with substantial funds are not supported. No grants for revenue expenditure such as ongoing running costs or salaries etc.

Applications The trust states 'you need to provide us with information about your organisation, its aims, how it works and how it intends to continue to meet those aims in the future. You will also be asked to send us a copy of your most recent audited reports and accounts'.

Trustees meet to consider grants four times a year. There should be a minimum period of two years between the receipt of a grant and a subsequent application.

Help the Hospices

Hospices
£528,000 (1997/98)

Beneficial area Predominantly UK

34–44 Britannia Street, London WC1 9JG

Tel. 020 7278 5668 **Fax** 020 7278 1021

Correspondent David Praill, Chief Executive

Trustees *Duchess of Norfolk; Michael Bayley; Ronald Giffin; Dr Peter Griffiths; Dr Andrew Hoy; Dr George Mitchell; Mrs Hilary McNair; Sam Willis; Mick Thorpe.*

Information available Full accounts and guidelines were provided by the trust.

General The charity aims to enhance the provision of palliative care for people who are terminally ill. It does this by: supporting major projects likely to have a significant effect on care; enhancing the skills of those providing the care; and supporting the organisations within which the care takes place.

It has focused its activities on helping the independent voluntary hospices.

The criterion for any application is that it will help to improve the quality of care given to patients in need of specialist/palliative care and their families. Innovative schemes are considered on their own merits, but applications for support of unestablished therapies are unlikely to be approved.

Where grants are made subject to the remainder of the funding being found from other sources, documentary evidence must be provided to confirm such other support before release of the trust's grant. Grants for courses or items of less than £75 are not normally provided.

Projects for which funding is available:

* Education and training (date and venue always to be given) – ENB and similar courses. If the course is directly relevant to the applicant's work and status a contribution towards the fee is often granted, particularly to voluntary hospice units. Academic courses (diplomas and degrees), if directly relevant, may be supported up to 50% of the fee with a ceiling of £750 for each of the first two years only. Conferences, attendance fees may be paid to enable applicants to attend conferences, the topic of which is

directly relevant to the applicant's work and status.

* Projects to improve management, audit and fundraising, a contribution is sometimes made.

* Minor items of equipment (including educational) which are not 'fundraising attractive' can be considered.

* Minor refurbishment requirements in special circumstances.

* Pump priming new posts and services. Occasionally funding towards the first year of a key post is made after detailed consideration of the request. There must be a written guarantee of the availability of follow-up funding, a written endorsement of the hospice chair and a copy of the most recent audited accounts.

* Research projects. Funding is only given for original research projects which are innovative.

* Occupational and recreational activities for the enjoyment of patients and staff (music, painting, mime etc.).

Grants totalled £528,000 in 1997/98, of which £465,000 was in grants of over £1,000. The largest were to IMPACT (£43,000), National Council for Hospice and Specialist Palliative Care Services (£35,000), St Ann's Hospice – Cheadle (£21,700), Association for Hospice Management (£21,500), Hth/Cruse (£21,000) and Association of Hospice Voluntary Service Co-ordinators (£20,000). Most of the remaining grants were made to local hospices throughout the UK.

A further £179,000 was awarded to 566 individuals to assist them with the payment of course fees. These included grants to staff working in independent hospices, NHS staff and others such as Marie Curie Cancer Care and Sue Ryder staff. Nursing staff, doctors, social workers and hospital administrators all benefited.

Exclusions The following limitations apply:

* Attendance at overseas courses or conferences is not normally supported.
* Accommodation, subsistence and locum expenses are not granted.
* Travel costs are only considered in excess of £75 for second class return rail, coach, or shuttle air, for one return journey only during a course or training attachment.
* If Help the Hospices is giving substantial support to the costs of a course or conference attendance fees are not granted in addition.

• Where training courses or conferences are organised by a hospice, attendance by the hospice's own staff or volunteers will not be considered for grants.
• Applications by Macmillan nurses pump primed by CRMF are not eligible and should be made to CRMF.
• Applications for capital costs and general running costs are not accepted.

Applications On a form available from Anne Garley at the above address. The grants committee meets every six weeks, and applications should be received four weeks beforehand.

The Christina Mary Hendrie Trust for Scottish & Canadian Charities

Older people, youth, general

£81,000 (1999)

Beneficial area Scotland and Canada

48 Castle Street, Edinburgh EH2 3LX

Tel. 0131 220 2345

Correspondent George R Russell WS

Trustees G A S Cox; Mrs A D H Irwin; C R B Cox; J K Scott Moncrieff; Miss C Irwin; Maj. Gen. A S H Irwin; R N Cox; A G Cox.

Information available Information was supplied by the trust.

General The trust was established in 1975 following the death in Scotland of Christina Mary Hendrie. The funds constituting the trust originated in Canada. Grants are distributed to charities throughout Scotland and Canada, although the majority is now given in Scotland. There is a preference for charities connected with young or older people, although other groups to receive grants include cancer charities.

Grants in 1999 totalled £81,000. Grants normally range from £1,000 to £5,000. Unfortunately there was no information on the beneficiaries supported.

Exclusions Grants are not given to individuals.

Applications In writing to the correspondent. The trustees meet twice a year, usually in March and November, to consider grants.

Philip Henman Trust

General

£57,000 (2000/2001)

Beneficial area Worldwide

17 Victoria Avenue, Lancaster LA1 4SY

e-mail info@pht.org.uk
website www.pht.org.uk
Correspondent Dave Clark, Trustee
Trustees J C Clark; D J Clark; J Duffy.

Information available Information was provided by the trust, including comprehensive guidelines for applicants, most of which are reproduced below.

General The trust's guidelines state: 'The trust was set up in 1986 with equity left by the late Philip Henman. The original aim was to continue funding causes supported by Philip Henman during his lifetime. After ten years the trustees felt a need to restructure the trust and a consultant was brought in to recommend more effective grant-giving'.

The trust makes grants towards a range of causes and splits its grant-making as follows:

Long-term grants	70%
One-off grants	20%
Grants to its own projects	10%

Long-term grants

The trust makes grants 'to organisations requiring partnership funding for projects lasting between three and five years. These grants are split into annual payments (normally between £3,000 and £5,000 a year) with a maximum total of £25,000. Once the grant has been approved the organisation will be guaranteed an annual grant for the duration of the project, as long as receipts and reports are sent back to the trust.

'The trust only has resources to guarantee an average of two new long-term grants a year, and therefore it is important to be sure any project fits our criteria before applying. Successful applications are normally those that prove the following, that the:

• project is being run professionally by an established UK-registered charity

• project will start and finish within five years
• funding from the trust is important to the project
• project will provide a lasting beneficial impact to the people or environment it seeks to help
• project is being partly funded by other sources. Voluntary work and central office administration costs can be counted as other source funding.

One-off grants

'Grants of up to £1,000 are made and aimed at unique projects normally initiated by individuals or small UK-based charities. Once a grant has been given the individual or organisation is then not eligible to apply for a further one-off grant for five years.

'Successful applications are normally those that prove the following, that the:

• application is specific about the way the grant will be used
• grant will make a substantial difference to the project
• applicant can prove an ability to make the project work
• project will make lasting positive changes to the people or environment it involves
• project is not entirely funded by the grant. Voluntary work and office administration costs count as alternative funding.'

The trust gives an annual grant to Folly Gallery, a community arts centre set up in part using funds left by Philip Henman. Each trustee also has their own account to make small one-off grants of between £10 and £500 to local charities.

In 2000/01 grants were given to 13 organisations totalling £57,00. Only two of these were new grants, they were £1,000 each to Motability and Peper Harrow Foundation. Recurrent grants included: £5,000 each to Bridge Trust, NCH Action for Children, WaterAid and Winged Fellowship; Jubilee Sailing Trust (£4,000); Sight Savers International (£3,300); and WaterAid (£1,000).

Exclusions 'There are no restrictions on which organisations can apply as long as they are a UK-registered charity.'

Applications The trust asks that a small form is completed and sent with a description of your project to the correspondent. The form requires the following information: your name, the name of your organisation, its Charity Commission number, its address and postcode, the type of grant you are seeking (one word/short sentence), the amount requested and the project length (long-term applicants only).

To apply for a one-off grant or long-term grant you should write a one or two page description of the project respectively, with an attached budget. The trust states: 'Any other information about your organisation and annual accounts is useful for an assessment of your organisation carried out by our secretary, but will not be forwarded to our trustees for consideration of the grant'.

The trustees meet twice a year in March and October. Applications for long-term grants should be sent before 10 September for consideration at the October meeting and applications for one-off grants should be sent before 10 February for consideration at the March meeting.

'All applications will receive an acknowledgement that their application has been received and further note to indicate whether the application was successful or not. The trust receives far more worthy applications than it has funds available and therefore encourages applicants to make simple low cost project descriptions.'

The trust prefers charities to look at its website, where its guidelines for applications are published, before applying.

The Hesed Trust

Christian

£49,000 (1997/98)

Beneficial area UK and overseas

14 Chiltern Avenue, Cosby, Leicestershire LE9 1UF

Tel. 0116 286 2990

Correspondent G Rawlings, Secretary

Trustees *R Rawlings; B Shutt; R J Aubrey.*

Information available Accounts were on file at the Charity Commission, but without a narrative report or a list of grants.

General The trust supports Christian organisations. Grants are one-off and for up to £500 each. In 1998/99 the trust had an income of £50,000 and a total expenditure of £60,000. Further information was not available for this year at the time of going to print and the following information is repeated from the last edition of this guide.

In 1995/96 the trust's assets totalled only £24,000 and it had an income of £67,000, including £51,000 in donations. Expenditure totalled £71,000 and was listed in the accounts as follows:

Ministry support	£15,000
General and specific gifts	£9,600
Gifts to other charities	£32,000
Training support	£12,000

The rest of the expenditure comprised 'depreciation and bank charges'.

Applications In writing to the correspondent.

The Bernhard Heuberger Charitable Trust

Jewish

£70,000 (1998/99)

Beneficial area Worldwide

12 Sherwood Road, London NW4 1AD

Tel. 020 8807 5555

Correspondent H Heuberger, Secretary

Trustees *D H Heuberger; S N Heuberger.*

Information available Accounts were on file at the Charity Commission, but without a narrative report.

General The trust was established in 1986. In 1998/99 the trust had assets of £2.2 million and an income of £131,000. The trust had large management and administration costs of £46,000, including £30,000 on depreciation, overheads and repairs to properties, and £14,000 in salaries. Grants totalled £70,000.

The largest grants were £30,000 to Sage, £13,000 to Hendon United Synagogue, £10,000 to Shalva and £6,000 to Hendon Co-ordinated Charities (which also received £5,000 in the previous year). Other grants included Jewish Care (£2,000), World Jewish Relief (£1,500) and Vanessa Foundation (£1,000).

Applications In writing to the correspondent.

The Higgs Charitable Trust

General

£55,000 (1999)

Beneficial area UK, with a preference for the former county of Avon

Moger & Sparrow, 24 Queen Square, Bath BA1 2HY

Tel. 01225 444882 **Fax** 01225 445208

Correspondent A C Nash

Trustees *D W M Campbell; T W Higgs; Mrs L Humphries.*

Information available Accounts were on file at the Charity Commission.

General This trust makes grants mainly to UK charities and charities in the Avon area. In 1999 the trust had assets of £1.2 million and an income of £48,000. Administration and management charges were high at £12,000, a quarter of the trust's income. The accounts state it spent £55,000 on grants although the grants list only mentions three grants totalling £37,000, they were: £25,000 to TWJ Foundation, £10,000 to Skinner Company Lord Malmesbury Bounty and £2,000 to Jobson Foundation.

Applications In writing to the correspondent, not less than two months before the annual general meeting in November.

The Charles Littlewood Hill Trust

Health, disability, service, children (including schools)

£154,000 (1999)

Beneficial area UK, with an interest in Norfolk and Nottingham

Eversheds, 1 Royal Standard Place, Nottingham NG1 6FZ

Tel. 0115 950 7000 **Fax** 0115 950 7111

Correspondent The Trustees

Trustees *C W L Barratt; W F Whysall; T H Farr; N R Savory.*

Information available Full accounts were on file at the Charity Commission.

General The trust gives to children (including schools), disability, health and services. It supports UK organisations and local charities, including local branches of UK charities in Nottingham and Norfolk. This trust is connected to Charles Littlewood Hill Trust, with which it shares some of the trustees and has similar criteria.

In 1999 the trust had assets of £3.1 million generating an income of £147,000. Grants totalled £154,000. The accounts split the grants of over £1,000 into three categories

Nottingham

17 grants included Army Benevolent Fund – Nottinghamshire (£5,000), Nottingham Hospital League of Friends (£4,000), Nottingham Sea Cadet Unit (£3,000), Samaritans Nottinghamshire and Southwell Care Project (£2,000 each) with £1,000 each to Dovecoat and Scope's Rutland Hosue School.

Norfolk

11 grants including £50,000 to Norwich Cathedral and £11,000 to its Choir Endowment Fund, £5,000 each to East Anglia Art Foundation and Norwich & Norfolk Far East POWs, £3,000 to SSAFA Norfolk and £1,000 each to How Hill Trust Appeal and Scope NANSA.

UK

16 grants of £1,000 each including ASBAH, Ex-Services Housing Society, High Blood Pressure Foundation, Lady Hoare Trust, Police Foundation and Snowdon Award Scheme.

The trust also gave unspecified smaller grants totalling £7,300.

Exclusions Applications from individuals are not considered.

Applications In writing to the correspondent including the latest set of audited accounts. Unsuccessful applications will not be acknowledged. Trustees meet in March, July and November.

The Holly Hill Charitable Trust

Environmental education and conservation

£416,000 (1998/99)

Beneficial area UK

Flat 5, 89 Onslow Square, London SW7 3LT
Tel. 020 7589 2651
Correspondent M D Stanley, Trustee
Trustees *M D Stanley; A Lewis.*
Information available Full accounts were on file at the Charity Commission.

General This trust was established in 1995 to support environmental education and conservation.

In 1998/99 the trust had assets of £1.7 million and an income of £50,000. Grants totalling £416,000 were given to 16 organisations, 5 of which were supported in the previous year.

The largest grant was £303,000 to Imperial College, which received £40,000 in the previous year; there was no explanation why this year's grant was six times larger than the trust's income. Other large grants were £39,000 to Devon Wildlife Trust and £20,000 to University College - London. Other grants were from £2,000 to £7,000 and included those to Durrell Institute (£7,000), Mobility Trust (£5,000), St Mary's University College (£4,000), with £2,000 each to Notting Hill Housing Trust, Rain Forest Concern and Safe Ground.

Exclusions No grants to individuals.

Applications In writing to the correspondent. Applications need to be received in April and in September and trustees meet in June and in November.

Lady Hind Trust

General

£292,000 (1998)

Beneficial area England and Wales only, with a preference for Nottinghamshire and Norfolk

c/o Eversheds, 1 Royal Standard Place, Nottingham NG1 6FZ
Tel. 0115 950 7000

Correspondent W F Whysall, Trustee
Trustees *C W L Barratt; W F Whysall; T H Farr; N R Savory.*
Information available Full accounts were on file at the Charity Commission.

General This trust makes mainly one-off grants, for general charitable purposes. It appears to have some preference for supporting health and disability-related charities. This trust is connected to Charles Littlewood Hill Trust, with which it shares some of the trustees and has similar criteria.

In 1998 the trust had assets of £9.1 million generating an income of £331,000. Grants totalled £292,000 with £2,300 being spent on travelling expenses to visit applicants. A fee of £26,000 was paid to Eversheds. Grants of over £1,000 were listed in the trust's annual report according to geographical location, as shown below.

Nottinghamshire

A total of £139,000 was given in 55 grants, including £15,000 to Worcestershire and Sherwood Forest Regimental Memorial and Museum Appeal, £10,000 to Portland Training Centre for the Disabled, £5,000 each to Beaumont House Hospice Aid, Lincolnshire and Nottinghamshire Air Ambulance, University of Nottingham Student Hardship Fund, £3,000 to Winged Fellowship Trust and £1,000 each to Beeston Citizens Advice Bureau, Elizabeth Fry Family Centre, Kirkby Voluntary Centre, NSPCC – Nottinghamshire, RelateNottinghamshire Marriage Guidance and Stonebridge City Farm.

Norfolk

A total of £65,000 was given in 25 grants, including £10,000 to Norfolk & Norwich Association for the Blind and £5,000 each to Mencap Blue Sky Appeal, Norfolk Churches Trust and Princes Trust. Other grants included Norfolk Family Mediation Society (£4,000), Norfolk Eating Disorders Association (£3,000), Norwich School (£2,000) with £1,000 each to East of England Orchestra, Cruse – Norwich, Norwich YMCA and Outward Bound Trust Norfolk.

Elsewhere

A total of £54,000 was given in 38 grants, including £5,000 each to Maidwell Hall, Multiple Sclerosis Trust of Great Britain and Northern Ireland and Save the Children Fund; £2,000 each to Blesma, Mark Davies Injured Riders, Ear Foundation and Orchid Cancer Appeal; and £1,000 each to 31 organisations including AFASIC Overcoming Speech Impairments, Bath Institute of Medical

Engineering Limited, British Blind Sport, Missing Persons Helpline, National Schizophrenic Fellowship, Not Forgotten Association, Understanding Industry and Woodland Trust.

Grants of under £1,000 totalled £35,000.

Exclusions Grants are seldom made for parish church appeals unless they are within the counties of Norfolk or Nottinghamshire. Applications from individuals are not considered.

Applications Applications, in writing and with accounts, must be submitted two months in advance of meetings in March, June, September and December. Unsuccessful applicants are not notified.

The Stuart Hine Trust

Evangelical Christianity

£101,000 (1999/2000)

Beneficial area UK and overseas

'Cherith' , 23 Derwent Close, Hailsham, East Sussex BN27 3DA

Tel. 01323 843948

Correspondent Raymond Bodkin, Trustee

Trustees *Raymond Bodkin; Nigel Coltman; Amelia Gardner.*

Information available Information was supplied by the trust.

General The trust gives grants to evangelical Christian organisations which are supported by the trustees or by the settlor during his lifetime and which are known to the trustees.

In 1999/2000 the trust had an income of £146,000 and gave grants totalling £101,000. The most recent grants list on file at the Charity Commission was for 1995/96 when grants were made to 11 evangelical Christian organisations totalling £51,000. The bulk of the grant total in that year was given to Wycliff Bible Translators (£40,000). Other grants included £1,500 each to The Retired Missionary Aid Fund and Bible Text Publicity Mission and £1,000 each to Manchester City Mission, The Open Air Mission, FEBA Radio and Kingsway Trust.

Applications In writing to the correspondent, although please note, the trust states that 'unsolicited requests for

funds will not be considered'. The trustees meet to consider applications twice a year, in April and in November.

The Hinrichsen Foundation

Music

£74,000 grants approved
(1999/2000)

Beneficial area UK

10–12 Baches Street, London N1 6DN

Correspondent Mrs Lesley E Adamson, Secretary

Trustees *Prof. A Whittall, Chair; Mrs C E Hinrichsen; P Strang; K Potter; P Standford; S Walsh; J Dyer; Dr J Cross; Miss Linda Hirst; M Williams; T Berg.*

Information available Full accounts were on file at the Charity Commission.

General The trust states: 'The Hinrichsen Foundation is a charity devoted to the promotion of music. Although the objects of the trust are widely drawn, the trustees have decided for the time being to concentrate on assisting in the "written" areas of music, that is, assisting contemporary composition and its performance and musical research.'

In 1999/2000 the trust had assets of £69,000 and an income of £70,000, including a covenant of £65,000. Management and administration charges were £15,000, including the salary of a full-time secretary. During the year, 52 grants and one composition bursary were approved totalling £74,000. Both individuals and organisations received support.

The trust supports the public performance of living composers. Grants include those to performing ensembles for concerts and festivals. Grants are made retrospectively. Organisations supported include both UK organsiations and local groups throughout the UK.

The following are examples of grants either given or approved in 1999/2000. The largest was a grant of £15,000 to Huddersfield Contemporary Music Festival, which had also received £15,000 in the previous year, although the trust does not usually make grants of this size. A bursary of £10,000 was given to Wingfield Arts. Other grants ranged from £150 to Piano Circus to £3,000 to

London Sinfonietta. Other beneficiaries included Dartington International Summer School and Rainbow over Bath (each £2,000), East of England Orchestra (£1,400), Cheltenham Music Society (£1,000), Ensemble QTR (£750) and Sounds Positive (£500).

Exclusions The trust does not support study courses, including those at postgraduate level. Grants are not given for instruments, equipment or recordings.

Applications In writing to the correspondent. Grants are made after the completion of the project, whenever that is. The trustees meet to consider grants four times a year, usually in February, April, July and November.

Hobson Charity Ltd

Social welfare, education

£177,000 (1996/97)

Beneficial area UK

21 Bryanston Street, Marble Arch, London W1A 4NH

Tel. 020 7499 7050

Correspondent Mrs Deborah Clarke, Trustee and Secretary

Trustees *R F Hobson; Mrs P M Hobson; Sir Donald Gosling; Mrs Deborah Clarke.*

Information available Full accounts were on file at the Charity Commission.

General In 1998/99 the trust had an income of £308,000 and an expenditure of £674,000, unfortunately no further information was available for view in the public files at the Charity Commission. This entry was included in the last edition of this guide.

In 1996/97 the trust had an income of £139,000 and gave grants totalling £177,000. The largest went to British School of Osteopathy (£34,000), Tate Gallery (£33,000), Royal Academy of Music and John Grooms Association for Disabled People (each £25,000) with £10,000 each to British Youth Opera, British Youth Orchestra and Howard League.

Applications In writing to the correspondent.

The Hockerill Educational Foundation

Education, especially Christian education

£183,000 to organisations (1999/2000)

Beneficial area UK, with a preference for the dioceses of Chelmsford and St Albans

16 Hagsdell Road, Hertford, Hertfordshire SG13 8AG

Tel. 01992 303053   **Fax** 01992 425950

Correspondent C R Broomfield, Secretary

Trustees *Dr Shelia Hunter, Chair; Bishop of St Albans; Bishop of Chelmsford; Director of Education, Diocese of Chelmsford; Director of Education, Diocese of St Albans; Rt Revd J H Richardson; Ven. Trevor Jones; Rt Revd Dr Laurie A Green; Prof. Bernard Aylett; Mrs Margaret Helmore; Mrs Hannah Potter; Robert E Wood.*

Information available Full accounts were provided by the trust.

General The foundation's priorities are:

- education and training of teachers and others involved in education (particularly religious education)
- research and development of religious education
- support for other students in further and higher education (normally only to first degree level)
- those involved in non-statutory education, including adult and Christian education.

Grants are made to organisations for projects or research likely to enhance the Church of England's contribution to higher and further education or religious education in schools. Recurrent grants can be made, normally up to three years and not more than five years. Grants towards salaries will be made once a term or quarterly. Grants are also made to individuals (see *The Educational Grants Directory*).

About two thirds of the grant total is given to education work in the dioceses of Chelmsford and St Albans. These grants are applied for via the dioceses and are not open to general applications.

In 1999/2000 the trust had assets of £6.6 million and an income of £212,000. Grants totalled £211,000. Management and administration costs totalled £22,000.

Grants to organisations totalled £183,000, nearly all of which went to organisations within the two dioceses.

In the Diocese of Chelmsford, 11 grants were made totalling £89,000, ranging from £1,000 to £34,000. Examples include £9,500 towards salary costs for a diocesan youth officer and £1,000 towards a Millennium Pack for schools.

In the Dioceses of St Albans, 10 grants were made totalling £87,000, ranging from £2,900 to £21,000. Examples include £4,000 towards a Diocesan International Youth Festival and £5,000 to Barnibus Project to provide a mobile classroom for rural villages. Three grants were given to other projects totalling £6,600, they went to Luton Churches Educational Trust (£3,000), The National Society (£2,000) and Visible Communications to provide a video training for the deaf (£1,600). Grants to individuals totalled £29,000 (£48,000 in 1998/99).

Exclusions Grants are not given for general appeals for funds, 'bricks and mortar' building projects or purposes that are the clear responsibility of another body.

With regard to individuals, grants will not normally be considered from:

- teachers who intend to move out of the profession
- those in training for ordination or for other kinds of mission
- clergy who wish to improve their own qualifications, unless they are already engaged in teaching in schools and/or intend to teach in the future
- students of counselling, therapy or social work
- undergraduates or people training for other professions, such as accountancy, business, law or medicine
- people doing courses or visits abroad, including 'gap' year courses (except as an integral part of a course, or a necessary part of research)
- children at primary or secondary school.

Applications On a form available from the correspondent and submitted by 1 March each year. Results of applications will be communicated in the middle of May. Receipt of applications is not acknowledged. Applications which do not fit the criteria would not normally receive a reply.

The Edward Sydney Hogg Charitable Settlement

General

£69,000 (1998/99)

Beneficial area UK

Messrs Hoare Trustees, 37 Fleet Street, London EC4P 4DQ

Tel. 020 7353 4522

Correspondent The Secretary

Trustees *Messrs Hoare Trustees.*

Information available Full accounts were on file at the Charity Commission.

General In 1998/99 the trust had assets of £1.5 million and an income of £259,000, including £200,000 in funds added to the settlement. Grants to 28 organisations totalled £69,000.

The largest grants were of £5,000 and went to Countess Mountbatten House Campaign, Friends of Kent Churches, Guild of Air Pilots and Air Navigators, Irish Association Order of Malta, RUKBA and Shuttleworth Veteran Aeroplane Society. Other grants ranged from £500 to US$5,000 (around £3,100) and included £2,500 each to Learning for Life and St Bartholomew's Church of England Religious Education Foundation, £2,000 to Living Paintings Trust, £1,000 each to The Air League, Sussex PHAB and Youth Clubs Scotland and £500 to South Brent Old School Project.

Applications In writing to the correspondent. Trustees meet monthly.

The J G Hogg Charitable Trust

Welfare, animal welfare, general

£115,000 (1998/99)

Beneficial area Worldwide

Chantrey Vellacott DFK, Russell Square House, 10–12 Russell Square, London WC1B 5LF

Tel. 020 7509 9000

Correspondent C M Jones, Trustees' Accountant

Trustees *Sarah Jane Houldsworth; Joanna Wynfreda Hogg.*

Information available Full accounts were on file at the Charity Commission.

General The trust states that it has no set policy on the type of charity supported, but would give favourable consideration to those based primarily in the UK that support the relief of human and animal suffering.

In 1998/99 the trust had assets of £634,000 and an income of £196,000, including a donation of £172,000 from J G Hogg Children's Settlement. Grants to 16 organisations totalled £115,000.

Grants included £10,000 each to Canine Partners for Independence, Crisis and National Playbus Association, £7,500 each to Contact a Family, Deafblind UK, Refuge and Seeability, £5,500 to Oxfam and £5,000 each to Anglo-Peruvian Child Care Mission, Pace Centre, Quest, Scuba Trust and Woodland Camp.

Exclusions No grants to individuals.

Applications In writing to the correspondent.

The Holst Foundation

Arts

£197,000 (1998/99)

Beneficial area UK

179 Great Portland Street, London W1N 6LS

Tel. 020 77323 4000

Correspondent Peter Carter, Secretary

Trustees *Rosamund Strode, Chair; Noel Periton; Prof. Arnold Whittall; Peter Carter; Andrew Clements; Julian Anderson.*

Information available Full accounts were on file at the Charity Commission.

General The trust has two objects: firstly, to promote public appreciation of the musical works of Gustav and Imogen Holst; and secondly, to encourage and promote the study and practice of the arts.

In practice the trust tends to be proactive. Funds are available almost exclusively for the performance of music by living composers. An annual awards scheme is offered to performing groups who wish to commission new work. The trust has historical links with Aldeburgh in Suffolk and is a major funder of new music at the annual Aldeburgh Festival. It also promotes the recording of new music by means of substantial funding to the recording label NMC.

In 1998/99 the trust had assets of £2.1 million and an income of £371,000, including £273,000 from G & I Holst Ltd, a trading subsidiary. It made grants totalling £197,000, the including £96,000 to NMC to fund major recording projects.

There were 36 other grants of £1,000 or more, totalling £60,000, about half of these were recurrent from the previous year. A further 65 smaller grants were made totalling £27,000. Two further substantial donations were £13,000 to Opera North and £8,500 to SPNM.

The remainder of listed grants were in the range of £1,000 to £2,800, but were mostly for £1,000 beneficiaries included Birmingham Contemporary Music Festival, Cheltenham International Festival, Gogmagogs, Piano Circus, Purcell School, Roehampton Institute, Schubert Ensemble, University of York and Western Sinfonia.

Exclusions No support for the recordings or works of Holst that are already well supported. **No grants to individuals for educational purposes.**

Applications In writing to: The Grants Administrator, 43 Alderbrook Road, London SW12 8AD. Trustees meet four times a year. There is no application form. Seven copies of the application should be sent. Applications should contain full financial details and be as concise as possible. Funding is not given restrospectively.

P H Holt Charitable Trust

General

£318,000 (1998/99)

Beneficial area UK, with a preference for Merseyside

India Buildings, Liverpool L2 0RB

Tel. 0151 473 4693

Correspondent Roger Morris, Secretary

Trustees *K Wright, Chair; John Utley; John Allan; D Morris; Tilly Boyce; Christopher Stephens.*

Information available Full accounts were on file at the Charity Commission.

General The trust makes a large number of mostly small grants, about three quarters of them in Merseyside. This trust is a welcome and exceptional example of Liverpool shipping money staying in and around the city. Payments in 1998/99 were categorised as shown in the table.

In 1998/99 the trust had assets of £14.7 million and an income of £369,000, with a total of £318,000 given in 160 grants. Grants given under the category of 'Merseyside' accounted for 85% of the grant total this year.

Merseyside one-off grants

Two major grants were given, they were £100,000 to Liverpool School of Tropical Medicine for its Centenary Appeal and £50,000 to Age Concern Liverpool towards the initial running costs of its new Active Age Centre. Other grants were not greater than £5,000, the larger ones included The Big Issue in the North Trust and Liverpool Biennial of Contemporary Art (£5,000 each), University of Liverpool's Institute of Popular Music to conduct a feasibility study for an exhibition of Liverpool's musical heritage (£4,000) with £3,000 eacg to SNIP – Sefton Neighbourhood

P H HOLT CHARITABLE TRUST – GRANT DISTRIBUTION IN 1998/99				
	Total	Merseyside	'Holt tradition'	Elsewhere
Category	£	£	£	£
Community	44,000	37,000	4,900	1,900
Welfare	99,000	83,000	8,900	6,900
Education	133,000	125,000	1,800	6,000
Arts	20,000	19,000	1,500	0
Heritage	16,000	2,400	13,000	500
Environment	1,800	800	1,000	0
Medicine	4,500	1,500	0	3,000
Total committed in year	318,000	269,000	31,000	18,000

143

Initiative Project towards a partnership project to extend the use of information technology in Merseyside's voluntary sector and West Everton Community Council to support the development of services as its people's project. Other grants included those to Brouhaha International to help with the development of its annual international street theatre festival and associated training programme (£2,600), Riverside Housing Project to provide training equipment for the foyer project in Toxteth (£2,000) and £1,000 each to Africa Oyé!, Everyman Youth Theatre and Shelter.

Smaller grants included those to Liverpool CVS (£600), Elle FM (£500), Grove Park Parents' Support Group (£400) and Windows Project (£100).

Merseyside ongoing grants

The grants were divided into the same categories as listed above i.e. community, welfare etc. The largest grants were £10,000 to PSS, £7,500 to Liverpool Council of Social Service, £5,000 to Merseyside CVS and £2,500 to Merseyside Youth Association. Smaller grants included those to Birkenhead School, Bluecoat Arts Centre, Liverpool One Parent Families, Liverpool Parish Church and Merseyside Buildings Preservation Trust.

'Holt Tradition'

One-off grants were given to 12 organisations. The largest of £10,000 went to The Museum of London for its new Docklands Museum. Other grants included Lake District Art Gallery and Museum Trust (£2,000), Inter Faith Network (£1,000), Braille and Disability Aids Project (£400) and CMS Northwest (£100). The regular annual subscriptions are small and declining in number, often going to bodies with which the Holt families or businesses had a connection. They included Liverpool Domestic Mission Society, Mersey Mission to Seamen, Merseyside & Deeside Outward Bound, Merseyside International Network, Royal Liverpool Seamen's Orphans Insititution, RNLI – Port of Liverpool Branch and Sail Training Association – Merseyside.

Elsewhere

Grants given in this category are mainly to support the charitable work of the past and present employees of Ocean Group plc, the company which Philip Holt founded as The Ocean Steam Ship Company. Larger grants included those to Dukes Barn to help develop new outdoor activities and REMAP (£2,000 each), Mediation Dorset (£1,000), CRISIS (£750) and British Heart

Foundation (£300). Grants of £200 each went to 11 organisations including Age Concern Bracknell, Mailflight, Streatham Youth Centre and Ocean Youth Club. In addition Business in the Community, a regular beneficiary, received £5,000 and two grants of £1,000 each went to Royal Academy of Music and Royal College of Surgeons, both of which have previously been supported.

Exclusions No grants to individuals. Grants are not usually given to organisations outside Merseyside (see above for exceptions to this).

Applications In writing to the correspondent at any time.

The Homelands Charitable Trust

The New Church, health, social welfare

£217,000 (1998/99)

Beneficial area UK

c/o Alliotts, Ingersoll House, 5th Floor, 9 Kingsway, London WC2B 6XF

Tel. 020 7240 9971

Correspondent N J Armstrong, Trustee

Trustees D G W Ballard; N J Armstrong; Revd C Curry.

Information available Full accounts were on file at the Charity Commission.

General This trust is unusual in that both the capital and income, although administered as one, are allocated to individual settlors. It was established in 1962, the settlors were four members of the Curry family and the original endowment was in the form of shares in the Curry company. H F Curry, Revd Clifford Curry and Miss Elizabeth Curry are now deceased but four funds are maintained. One original settlor, Miss Freda Curry, has her own allocation each year, whilst two further parts are distributed by the Revd C Curry Junior and by the trustees as a whole.

The trust's objectives are 'to support a wide range of general charitable causes, together with special emphasis towards contributions to the general conference of the New Church, medical research, the care and protection of children and hospices'.

In 1998/99 the trust had assets of £4.5 million and an income of £235,000,

including a donation of £41,000 from the estate of Miss Elizabeth Curry. Grants to 75 organisations totalled £217,000.

The largest grants were £43,000 to General Conference of the New Church and £20,000 to Bournemouth Society of the New Church. Other grants ranged from £500 (Weston Lodge Charity) to £6,000 (Broadfield Memorial Trust) and included £5,000 to Oxfam, with £3,000 each to Action Research for the Crippled Child, Christian Aid, Manic Depression Fellowship, Prince's Trust and YMCA, £2,000 each to I-Can and International Society for the Protection of Animals, £1,000 to National Trust and £750 to RSPCA.

Exclusions No grants to individuals.

Applications In writing to the correspondent.

Sir Harold Hood's Charitable Trust

Roman Catholic

£305,000 (1998/99)

Beneficial area Worldwide

31 Avenue Road, St John's Wood, London NW8 6DS

Tel. 020 7722 9088

Correspondent Sir Harold Hood, Trustee

Trustees Sir Harold J Hood; Lady Ferelith R Hood; Kevin P Ney; Mrs Margaret Gresslin; Nicholas E True; Mrs A M True; Dom James Hood.

Information available Full accounts were on file at the Charity Commission.

General The trust supports Roman Catholic causes. In 1998/99 the trust had assets with a market value of £7.2 million. This is a large increase from the previous year when the assets were £4.8 million due to an addition to the funds and also a revaluation. Donations from Lady Hood and Sir Harold Hood totalling £1.1 million were added to the capital fund. The ordinary income for the year was £132,000. Grants totalled £305,000, of this £121,000 was from the income fund and £184,000 from the capital fund. Management and administration costs were low at under £5,000.

From the income funds 25 grants were made, of which 20 were recurrent from the previous year. Grants ranged from

£1,000 to £10,000. The largest included those to Hope Residential & Nursing Care – Cambridgeshire (£10,000), Aid to the Church in Need – Vietnam and Sacred Heart Church Frinton-on-Sea (£7,000 each), St Francis Leprosy Guild (£6,000) and St Anthony's Orphanage Diocese of Dundee (£5,000).

Smaller grants include those to Catholic Housing Aid Society, St Thomas Fund for the Homeless and St Francis Xavier's Church Liverpool.

From the capital funds, 15 grants were given, all but of one of which were recurrent. Grants ranged from £4,000 to £30,000. The largest went to Bourne Trust (£30,000), Downside Settlement and St Benedict's Abbey – Fort Augustus (£25,000 each), Craig Lodge House of Prayer (£20,000), Hospital St John & St Elizabeth (£17,000) and Coming Home Appeal Ace of Clubs (£12,000).

Other grants went to Housetop Centre (£9,000), Langsyde School Natal (£7,000), St Gregory's Charitable Trust (£5,000) and Westminster Cathedral Appeal (£4,000).

Exclusions No grants for individuals.

Applications In writing to the correspondent. Applications are considered in late November and need to be received by October.

The Hope Trust

Temperance, reformed Protestant churches

£88,000 (1997)

Beneficial area Worldwide, with a preference for Scotland

Drummond Miller, 32 Moray Place, Edinburgh EH3 6BZ

Tel. 0131 226 5151

Correspondent Carol Hope

Trustees *Revd Prof. D W D Shaw; Revd Prof. A C Cheyne; Very Revd Dr W J G McDonald; Prof. G M Newlands; Prof. D A S Ferguson; Revd G R Barr.*

Information available Accounts were provided by the trust.

General In 1998/99 the trust had an income of £74,000 and an expenditure of £61,000. Unfortunately, no further information for this year was available and this information is repeated from the last edition of this guide.

This trust was established to promote the ideals of temperance and Protestant church reform through education and the distribution of literature.

In 1997 it had an income of £119,000 and made grants totalling £88,000. Larger grants included those to World Alliance of Reformed Churches (£8,500), Leith Drug Prevention Group towards running a drop-in centre (£5,500), Church of Scotland Priority Areas Fund (£5,000), Scottish Reformation Society (£3,900) and National Bible Society and Presbyterian Church of East Africa (each £2,000). Other grants range from £100 upwards. In addition £14,000 was given to postgraduate theology students.

Exclusions No funding for trips abroad, or refurbishment of property.

Applications In writing to the correspondent.

The Cuthbert Horn Trust

Environment, older people

£49,000 (1998)

Beneficial area UK

Royal & Sun Alliance Trust Co. Ltd, Phoenix House, 18 King William Street, London EC4N 7HE

Tel. 020 7800 4188 **Fax** 020 7800 4180

Correspondent S P Martin

Trustees *Alliance Assurance Company Ltd; A H Flint.*

Information available Full accounts were provided by the trust.

General The trust's main aims are to support charities helping older people and charities undertaking practical work in supporting the conservation and preservation of the environment. In 1998 the trust's assets totalled £1.1 million. It had an income of £245,000 including £158,000 from the sale of investments with the rest from both investment income and rent. Grants totalling £49,000 were made to 16 charities. In addition, £15,000 was transferred to the endowment fund.

The largest grant of £10,000 went to Council and Care, which also received the largest grant in the previous year. The remaining grants ranged from £1,000 to £5,000 and included those to: Centre for

Alternative Technology (£5,000); Africa Educational Trust (£4,000); £3,000 each to Cotswold Canals Trust, The Island Trust and Farms for City Children; £2,000 each to The Gaia Trust, Pesticide Trust and The Safe Charitable Trust; and Society for Environmental Improvement (£1,000).

Half the grants were recurrent from the previous year.

Exclusions No grants are made to individuals.

Applications There are no application forms to complete; applicants should provide in writing as much background about their charity or cause as possible. Applications need to be received by September as the trustees meet in October.

Mrs E G Hornby's Charitable Settlement

General

£59,000 (1998/99)

Beneficial area UK, with some preference for London

Kleinwort Benson Trustees Ltd, PO Box 191, 10 Fenchurch Street, London EC3M 3LB

Tel. 020 7475 6600 **Fax** 020 7626 6319

Correspondent N R Kerr-Sheppard, Secretary

Trustees *N J M Lonsdale; Mrs P M W Smith-Maxwell; Kleinwort Benson Trustees Limited.*

Information available Full accounts were on file at the Charity Commission.

General In 1999/2000 the trust had an income of £49,000 and an expenditure of £67,000. Further information for this year was not available at the time of going to print.

In 1998/99 the trust had an income of £53,000. Grants from capital funds totalled £25,000 and from income funds £34,000. Its assets at the year end totalled £1.3 million (£1.4 million in the previous year). In total 25 grants were made including a few to charities based in London. A number of grants went to previous beneficiaries.

From the income account, 21 grants were made totalling £34,000. The largest grants were to Countryside Foundation (£13,000), followed by St Richard's Hospice (£3,000), Macmillan Cancer Relief (£2,500), Irish Draught Horse Society (£1,800) and Martin House Children's Hospice (£1,500).

Other grants from the income account ranged between £250 and £1,000 and included those to Battersea Dogs Home, Foundation for the Study of Infant Deaths, London Federation of Clubs for Young People, Queen Mary's London Clothing Guild and Romanian Challenge Appeal.

Grants from the capital account were £17,000 to Friends of the Elderly and Gentlefolk's Help, £3,000 each to St Christopher's Hospice and St Michael's Hospice Development Trust and £2,000 to Population Concern.

Exclusions Individuals are not supported.

Applications In writing to the correspondent. The trust's current policy is to accumulate all the written appeals received, and to consider them on their individual merits when they meet annually, for distribution in April. Only successful applicants are notified.

Hospital Saturday Fund Charitable Trust

Medical, health

£100,000 to organisations (1999/2000)

Beneficial area Mainly UK and Ireland

24 Upper Ground, London SE1 9PD

Tel. 020 7928 6662 **Fax** 020 7928 0446
e-mail trust@hsf.co.uk

Correspondent K R Bradley, Administrator

Trustees L I Fellman, Chair; A F Tierney; K R Bradley; Miss D O Denton; P P Grant; Miss I Racher; Mrs D A Young.

Information available Full accounts were provided by the trust.

General The trust was formed in 1987 to take over the discretionary grant-making activities of the Hospital Saturday

Fund, thereby maintaining the aims and ideals of the founders of the fund.

The trust aims to support a wide variety of hospitals, hospices and medically-associated charities for care and research. Several welfare charities were supported. The policy of not supporting an organisation two years in succession has been continued, unless there are exceptional circumstances. It also gives grants to individuals whose health problem has entailed financial hardship or towards the cost of a special piece of equipment because of disability or to make life easier. Six sponsorships were given to people undertaking additional studies in connection with a medically related career.

In 1999/2000 the trust has assets of £158,000 and an income of £123,000, mainly from donations and gifts (£110,000 from the Hospital Saturday Fund). Grants totalled £109,000, they were broken down as follows:

Category	Total	No. of grants
Charities, hospitals and hospices	£100,000	188
Sponsorship	£1,100	9
Individuals	£7,500	89

All grants, except two, were of £500. They were divided geographically, as follows.

UK
Grants were given to 50 charities. One larger grant of £2,000 was given to Council for Music in Hospitals. Other grants went to Birth Defects Foundation, Fight for Sight, PHAB and Prostate Cancer Charity.

South East and London
16 hospitals and 25 other charities received grants. Charities included Community Action Network – London, Magic Lantern and Yateley Industries for the Disabled.

South West, Wales and the Channel Islands
Seven hospitals and nine charities, the latter included Greenacre Farm Community Ltd, Jersey Hospice Care and Wiltshire Air Ambulance.

Midlands & North
Nine hospitals were supported and eight other charities. Grants to charities included BREAK – Norfolk, St Leonard's Hospice – York and Woodbridge Gateway Club, Suffolk. Scotland: grants were given to 11 hospitals including a larger grant of £1,000 to Glasgow Royal Infirmary. In addition 11 charities were supported, beneficiaries included Ayrshire Hospice, Body Positive –

Strathclyde and Scottish Society for Autistic Children.

Northern Ireland and the Isle of Man
Two hospitals were supported and three other organisations: Heartbeat – Northern Ireland, Kelly Fog Memorial Fund – Isle of Man and National Schizophrenia Fellowship – Northern Ireland.

Republic of Ireland
Eight hospitals were supported and 32 other organisations received grants. Examples included Ard Aoibhainn Day Care Centre – Wexford, Children in Hospital Ireland, Housing Association for Integrated Living and Irish Wheelchair Association – Dublin.

Overseas
Two organisations received grants, they were Commonwealth Society for the Deaf and Royal Commonwealth Society for the Blind.

Applications Hospitals, hospices and medically-related charities are invited to write detailed letters or to send a brochure with an accompanying letter. There is a form for individuals to complete available from the personal assistant to the trust administrator.

The Hudson Foundation

General

£284,000 (1997/98)

Beneficial area UK, with a preference for the Wisbech area

12–13 The Crescent, Wisbech, Cambridge PE13 1EP

Tel. 01945 584113

Correspondent A D Salmon, Trustee

Trustees P A Turner; M A Bunting; H A Godfrey; A D Salmon.

Information available Full accounts were on file at the Charity Commission.

General The trust makes grants for general charitable purposes, although in practice groups caring for people who are elderly or infirm are more favourably supported. Grants are given mostly to organisations in the Wisbech area.

In 1997/98 the trust had an income of £76,000 and a total expenditure of £286,000. Grants totalled £284,000.

In 1996/97, when grants totalled £93,000, the largest grants were £41,000 to Royal

Fleet Club, £26,000 to Wisbech Grammar School, £7,500 to Wisbech Angle Centre and £6,000 to Imperial War Museum. Grants were both one-off and ongoing. Other past beneficiaries have included Alexandra Trust, Chatham Historic Dockyard, Ely Diocesan Board of Finance, National Trust and Wisbech Swimming Club.

Applications In writing to the correspondent. Applications are considered throughout the year.

The Huggard Charitable Trust

General

£209,000 (1997/98)

Beneficial area UK, with a preference for Wales

Blacklands Farm, Five Mile Lane, Bonvilston, Cardiff CF5 8TQ

Correspondent S J Thomas, Trustee

Trustees G J Davies; Mrs E M Huggard; T R W Davies; S J Thomas.

Information available Accounts were on file at the Charity Commission up to 1997/98, but without a narrative report or recent grants list

General Unfortunately we have been unable to update the following financial information since the last edition of this guide.

In 1997/98 the trust's assets totalled £1.6 million, it had an income of £103,000 and grants totalled £209,000. This resulted in a deficit for the year of £106,000. In 1996/97 the trust received £225,000 in donations from R J Huggard Contractors Limited (now wound up), creating a surplus of £197,000.

The trust informed us that it has supported a wide variety of organisations, including some major projects in south Wales which have received substantial funding. These included Amelia Trust Farm in the Vale of Glamorgan, Penrhys Community Partnership in the Rhondda Valley and Cardiff Action for the Single Homeless. For the future the trustees wish to concentrate on a specific list of organisations (about 80) whom they will support, and therefore do not seek applications from others.

Applications Please see above.

The Humanitarian Trust (*also known as* The Michael Polak Foundation)

Education, health, social welfare, Jewish

£44,000 (1998/99)

Beneficial area Worldwide, mainly Israel

27 St James Place, London SW1A 1NR

Correspondent Mrs M Myers, Secretary

Trustees M Jacques Gunsbourg; Lord Rothschild; P Halban.

Information available Full accounts were on file at the Charity Commission.

General The trust was founded in 1946. In the early years donations were made overwhelmingly to educational causes in Israel. Nowadays the trust is giving to a wider range of causes, still mainly Jewish, but some smaller grants are given to non-Jewish organisations.

In 1998/99 the trust had assets of £3.6 million and an income of £91,000. Grants totalled £44,000. No further information was available for this year.

In 1997/98 the trust had assets of over £3 million and an income of only £81,000. It gave grants totalling £56,000 including £4,000 in grants to individuals, which are only given via institutes of further education (see *The Educational Grants Directory*).

Grants were broken down as follows:

Academic and educational
A tota of £32,000 was given in 30 grants. By far the largest grant was, and is usually, to the Friends of the Hebrew University of Jerusalem (£10,000). Ben Gurion University received £2,000 towards a Community Action Group. All other grants were from £200 to £700 and included Open University and other universities all over England, which may have been for individuals.

Medical and charitable
Eight grants were given totalling £7,000, the largest being to Michaelson Institute for the Prevention of Blindness, Hadassah (£3,000) and Shaare Zedek Medical Centre, a regular beneficiary (£1,500). The other grants were for £200 or £500.

Social service
There were 16 grants given totalling £16,000. This heading is usually dominated by support to the Jerusalem Foundation (usually grants of around £5,000). Other beneficiaries included New Israel Fund, Norwood Child Care and CBF World Jewish Relief.

Exclusions Awards are only given for academic purposes and not given for travel, overseas courses, fieldwork or the arts (such as theatre, dance, music, fashion, journalism etc.). They are intended only as supplementary assistance and are to be held concurrently with other awards. One-off grants to individuals only up to a maximum of £200 as a final top-up for fees.

Applications In writing to the correspondent for consideration at trustees' meetings in March and November.

Miss Agnes H Hunter's Trust

Social welfare

£254,000 (1999/2000)

Beneficial area UK with a preference for Scotland

Robson McLean WS, 28 Abercromby Place, Edinburgh EH3 6QF

Correspondent Mrs Jane Paterson, Grants Administrator

Information available Information, but with no grants list, was supplied by the trust. A leaflet about the trust is available from the above address.

General The trust was established in 1954. The main aims of the trust are to support:

* charities for blind people in Scotland
* people who are disabled
* training and education for people who are disadvantaged
* research on the cause, relief or cure of cancer, tuberculosis or rheumatism.

These aims are currently being pursued in the following areas: children and family support, youth development, older people, homelessness, physical and mental illness and the environment.

The trustees are highly selective and priority is given to Scottish projects. The trustees review their policies periodically and areas of interest may change.

Grants range from £500 to £8,000, although they are usually not higher than £5,000. In 1999/2000 the trust gave 67 grants totalling £254,000. Further information was not available for this year.

Its capital assets in property and investments were valued at £3.4 million in 1997/98. In that year 55 grants totalling £224,000 were approved. A grants list was not provided.

Exclusions No grants to individuals nor to organisations under the control of the UK government.

Applications In writing to the correspondent.

Hurdale Charity Limited

Jewish

£394,000 (1997/98)

Beneficial area Worldwide

54–56 Euston Street, London NW1 2ES

Tel. 020 7387 0155 **Fax** 020 7388 4758

Correspondent Paul Finn

Trustees *M Oestreicher; Mrs E Oestreicher.*

Information available Accounts were on file at the Charity Commission, but without a grants list.

General In 1997/98 the trust had assets of £539,000 and an income of £424,000, including donations of £180,000. Grants totalled £394,000.

No grants information was included in the accounts, but the report stated it had 'continued its philanthropic activities in support of religious, educational and other charitable institutions'. The trust supports Jewish organisations which are seen to uphold the Jewish way of life, both in the UK and overseas.

In 1994/95 grants totalled £197,000, most were for £2,000 or more. The largest went to Imrei Chaim College (£28,000), Gemilas Chesed & Endowment of Bride Bridal Society (£21,000) and Mesifta Talmudical College (£17,000).

Applications In writing to the correspondent.

The Idlewild Trust

Performing arts, culture, restoration & conservation, occasional arts education

£110,000 (1999)

Beneficial area UK

54–56 Knatchbull Road, London SE5 9QY

Tel. 020 7274 2266 **Fax** 020 7274 5222

Correspondent Mrs Angela Freestone, Administrator

Trustees *Lady Judith Goodison, Chair; Mrs A S Bucks; M H Davenport; J C Gale; Mrs A C Grellier; Mrs F L Morrison-Jones; A Ford.*

Information available Full accounts and annual report were on file at the Charity Commission.

General The trust was founded in 1974 by Peter Brissault Minet, who had previously set up the Peter Minet Trust (see separate entry). Its policy is to support charities concerned with the encouragement of performing and fine arts and preservation for the benefit of the public of lands, buildings and other objects of beauty or historic interest. Occasionally support is given to bodies for educational bursaries in these fields or for conservation of the natural environment. The trust prefers to support UK charities and it is unlikely to support a project of local interest only.

In 1999 the trust had assets of £4.2 million and an income of £190,000. It received 789 appeals, many of which were outside the trust's terms of reference. It approved 50 grants totalling £110,000. Grants ranged from £500 to £5,000 (41 of which were between £1,000 and £3,000).

Grants were categorised in the trust's annual report as follows:

Category	No. of grants	Total
Education in the arts	7	£11,000
Performing arts	13	£20,000
Museum and galleries	5	£15,000
Preservation, restoration	14	£34,000
Fine art	5	£14,000
Conservation	6	£17,000

The largest grants were £5,000 each to Landmark Trust, Royal College of Music and Spitalfields Heritage Centre and £4,000 each to Regional Furniture Society and Horniman 2000. Grants ranging

from £1,000 to £3,000 included those to Birmingham Contemporary Music, Carlisle Cathedral, Council for Music in Hospitals, Dr Johnson's House, Kent Wildlife Trust, Opera Della Luna, Tie Break Theatre and Woodland Trust. Three grants given were under £1,000, they went to Bath Preservation Trust (£900), Philharmonia Orchestra (£750) and Foundation for Community Dance (£500).

Exclusions Grants to registered charities only. No grants are made to individuals. The trust will not give to:

- repetitive UK-wide appeals by large charities
- appeals where all, or most of, the beneficiaries live outside the UK
- local appeals unless the artistic significance of the project is of more than local importance
- appeals whose sole or main purpose is to make grants from the funds collected
- endowment or deficit funding.

Applications On a form available from the correspondent. Applications should include the following information:

- budget breakdown (one page)
- most recent audited accounts
- a list of other sponsors, including those applied to
- other relevant information.

Potential applicants are welcome to telephone the trust on Tuesdays or Wednesdays to discuss their application and check eligibility. Trustees meet twice a year in March and November.

All eligible applications, which are put forward to the trustees, are acknowledged, other applications will not be acknowledged unless an sae is enclosed. Applications from organisations within twelve months of a previous grant will not be considered.

The Iliffe Family Charitable Trust

Medical, disability, heritage, education

£284,000 (1999/2000)

Beneficial area UK

Barn Close, Yattendon, Berkshire RG18 0UY

Correspondent Miss Julia Peel

Trustees *N G E Petter; G A Bremner; Lord Iliffe; Hon. Edward Iliffe.*

Information available Full accounts were on file at the Charity Commission.

General The trust gives grants towards groups concerned with medical, disability, heritage and education. The bulk of grants made from the trust are to charities already known to the trustees, to which funds are committed from year to year. Other donations are made for a wide range of charitable purposes.

In 1999/2000 the trust had assets of £1.9 million and an income of £146,000. Grants totalled £284,000. Further information for this year was not available.

In 1996/97 grants totalling £106,000 were made to 57 organisations, ranging from £50 to £25,000, although most were for £500 or less. The largest grants were £25,000 to Macmillan Cancer Relief, £10,000 to Oasis Appeal and £8,800 to Berkshire Community Trust. Other grants ranged up to £5,000 and included: £3,000 to Oriel College, Oxford; £1,000 each to CAMVET and Yattendon and Frilsham Christian Stewardship; £500 each to NSPCC and The Missions to Seamen; £250 each to Red Cross and Whizz-Kidz; and £150 to NABS.

Exclusions No grants to individuals and rarely to non-registered charities.

Applications In writing to the correspondent. Only successful applications will be acknowleged. Grants are considered at ad hoc meetings of the trustees, held throughout the year.

The Inlight Trust

Religion

£151,000 (1998/99)

Beneficial area UK

P O Box 2, Liss, Hampshire GU33 6YP

Correspondent Mrs Judy Hayward

Trustees *Sir Thomas Lucas; Michael Collishaw; Michael Meakin; Alan Thompson; Richard Wolfe; Wendy Collett.*

Information available Full accounts were provided by the trust.

General The trust makes grants for the advancement of religion only. It states that its funding priorities are 'To make donations on an undenominational basis to charities providing valuable

contributions to spiritual development and charities concerned with spiritual healing and spiritual growth through religious retreats'.

Grants are usually one-off for a specific project or part of a project. Bursary schemes may also be supported.

In 1998/99 the trust's assets totalled £2.3 million, it had an income of £200,000 and six grants were made totalling £151,000 (four grants totalled £116,000 in 1997/98).

Grants were: £45,000 to Jamyang Buddhist Centre London SE11, £38,000 each to Holy Island Project – Dumfriesshire and White Eagle Lodge, £15,000 to Hamblin Religious Trust, £10,000 to Acorn Christian Healing Trust – Bordon and £5,000 to Throssel Hole Buddhist Abbey – Scottish Buddhist Priory.

Exclusions Core funding or salaries are rarely considered. Non-registered charities are not supported. No grants are made to individuals, including students, or to large UK organisations. Grants for church buildings are seldom made.

Applications In writing to the correspondent including details of the need the intended project is designed to meet plus an outline budget and the most recent available annual accounts of the charity. Only applications from eligible bodies are acknowledged. Applications must be accompanied by a copy of your trust deed or of your entry in the Charity Commission register. Only successful applicants are informed.

Grants are considered at trustees' meetings four times a year in March, June, September and December and applications should be submitted two months before those meetings.

The Inman Charity

Social welfare, disability, older people, hospices

£241,000 (1999)

Beneficial area UK

Payne Hicks Beach, 10 New Square, Lincoln's Inn, London WC2A 3QG

Tel. 020 7465 4300

Correspondent A L Walker, Trustee

Trustees *Inman Charity Trustees Ltd: G W Mathews; P J H Shepherd; A L Walker; Miss B M A Strother; N J Wingerath.*

Information available Full accounts were on file at the Charity Commission.

General The trust states that it 'maintains a list of charitable organisations which it regularly supports and the list is reviewed half-yearly at the meeting of the directors. Surplus income funds are distributed to other charitable organisations during the year'.

The trust aims to disburse £250,000 a year, including an annual bursary to Uppingham School (£14,000). This grant stands outside its main areas for support – disability, medical, research, older people and hospices.

In 1999 the trust had assets of £5.4 million generating an income of £254,000. Grants totalled £241,000. Most grants were of either £3,500 or £7,000, with some for less. Grants were divided as follows:

Disability charities
Grants included £7,000 each to Crossroads and Queen Elizabeth Foundation for the Disabled and £3,500 each to British Wheelchair Sports Foundation, Disabled Living Foundation and Invalids at Home.

Medical organisations
Those supported included £7,000 each to Ottery St Mary Hospital League of Friends Community Help Scheme and St Francis Hospice – Havering-atte-Bower, £3,500 each to Hartlepool & District Hospital and Imperial Cancer Research Fund, £1,500 to Action for ME and £1,000 to Dyslexia Institute Bursary.

Older people's organisations
Grants included £7,000 each to Counsel and Care and National Benevolent Fund for the Aged, £1,000 each to Contact the Elderly and Polish Day Centre for the Elderly and grants to Age Concern branches in London (£7,000) and Westminster (£3,500).

Other grants
Theseincluded £7,000 each to Ex-Services Mental Welfare Society, Family Holiday Association, Samaritans and Victim Support, £4,000 to Eaves Housing for Women and £2,500 to London Voluntary Service.

Exclusions No grants to individuals.

Applications In writing only to the correspondent, including up-to-date reports and accounts. Trustees meet half-yearly usually in March and September.

149

The Inverforth Charitable Trust

General

£205,000 (1999)

Beneficial area Almost entirely the UK

The Farm, Northington, Alresford, Hampshire SO24 9TH

Correspondent E A M Lee, Secretary and Treasurer

Trustees *Elizabeth Lady Inverforth; Rt Hon. Lord Inverforth; Hon. Mrs Jonathan Kane; Michael Gee.*

Information available Full accounts were available from the trust (at a cost of £5).

General The trust supports a range of UK charities, particularly 'small nationals'. Unlike many trusts, it gives unconditional grants to help with core costs and general income requirements in preference to capital costs.

In 1999 the trust had assets of £4 million and an income of £187,000. A total of £205,000 was given in 197 grants, these were broken down as follows:

Churches, heritage	4%
Disability and older people	13%
Health (including mental health)	38%
Hospices	3%
Music and the arts	17%
Youth and education	7%
Other (including a very few international grants)	18%

The categories received very similar percentages in the previous year.

The largest grant of £15,000 went to National Asthma Campaign which received the same amount in the previous year. The next largest grants were of £2,000 or £2,500 and went to 13 charities, including British Lung Foundation, Centrepoint, Missions to Seafarers, Samaritans, Spitalfields Festival and Terrence Higgins Trust.

The remaining 183 grants of £500, £1,000 or £1,500 included those to Arthritis Care, British Youth Opera, ChildLine, Fairbridge, John Grooms Association for Disabled People, National Playbus Association, Plantlife, Trestle Theatre Company, Trinity Hospice and Youth Clubs UK.

A proportion of the charities supported receive regular grants although no commitments are made. The trust states that it receives many applications which fall outside its criteria.

Exclusions Grants are not given to small or localised charities, churches, village halls, schools, etc; (if your name includes the word 'community' or a relevant place name in your title you are unlikely to qualify). Other exclusions are:

- animal charities
- branches or subsidiary charities
- individuals
- advertisers, fundraising events
- non-charities.

No application will be reconsidered within 12 months of its last submission to the trust.

Applications In writing to the correspondent at least one month before meetings. No special forms are necessary, although accounts are desirable. A summary is prepared for the trustees, who meet quarterly in March, June, September and early December. Replies are normally sent to all applicants; allow up to four months for an answer or grant. The correspondent receives over 1,000 applications a year, and advises of a high failure rate for new applicants.

The Ireland Fund of Great Britain

Welfare, community, education, peace and reconciliation, the arts

£143,000 unrestricted funds (1998)

Beneficial area Ireland and Great Britain

8–10 Greyfriars Road, Reading, Berkshire RG1 1QE

Tel. 0118 956 9111 **Fax** 0118 950 5519

Correspondent Mrs Jacqueline Wherlock, Executive Secretary

Trustees *Bryan Hayes, Chair; Josephine Hart; Hon. Kevin Pakenham; Dr Tony O'Reilly; John Riordan; Gavin O'Reilly.*

Information available Full accounts were on file at the Charity Commission.

General The fund was set up in the late 1980s. Its objects are to 'alleviate the problems in Ireland, to improve British-Irish friendship and to help the less fortunate Irish in Great Britain and Ireland, North and South'. Half the money raised by the Ireland Fund of Great Britain is allocated in Ireland, both North and South, and decisions about its disbursement are made by the Central Advisory Committee of the parent body – The Ireland Funds in Dublin. The other half is allocated in Great Britain to organisations of the Irish community, or those working with them.

In 1999/2000, 59 grants were distributed, the amounts were not available or the grant total at the time of going to print. The grants were divided into British-based (38 grants, 22 of which were given to London organisations) and Irish-based (21 grants). Examples of British-based organisations include: Bosco Youth Club, Celtic Connections, Comhaltas Ceoltoiri Eireann, Irish in Britain Representation Group, Irish World Heritage Centre, London Irish Women's Centre and South London Family Service Unit. Grants to Irish-based projects included those to Achill Deserted Village Project (Westport), Corduff Centre for the Unemployed (Dublin), Dillon's Cross Project (Cork), Foreglen Youth Club (Dungiven), Newman Institute (Belfast), Strabane & District Playclub, The Tyrell Trust (Kildare) and Women on the Move (Derry).

In 1998 the fund's total income was £549,000 of which £446,000 was raised through various functions. Grants totalled £228,000, of which £143,000 was unrestricted and the remaining £85,000 was restricted. The main grants are usually for £5,000 to £10,000 and most others are for £2,000 to £5,000, though smaller grants are also given. The grants actually paid during the year were given in several categories as outlined below.

Art
Four grants totalling £8,500: Club Cheoil and Culra (Comhaltas Eireann-Britain) each received £3,000, with £2,000 to Coventry Irish Friendship Development and £500 to TARA CCE.

Peace and reconciliation
Two grants totalling £5,000: Community Dialogue received £3,000 and British Irish Association £2,000.

Education
Six grants totalling £24,000, with by far the largest grant to the Lawlor Foundation (£10,000). Other grants, of £1,500 to £4,000, included those to Bannside Children's Group, Huddersfield Irish Association, Irish Employment and Training Consortium and Youth Against Racism in Brent.

Alleviation of poverty/community care
21 grants were made totalling £111,000. The largest grants were given from the

restricted fund, they were to CORE Project (£52,000) and Jack and Jill Foundation (£25,000). The largest grants from the unrestricted funds went to Cherry Orchard Equine Centre (£10,000) and Safe Start Foundation (£6,700). Other beneficaries included £6,000 each to Belvedere Youth Club, Breakfree, Horizon Halfway House and West Kirby Community Project; Camden Elderly Irish Network (£3,500); Irish Community Care Merseyside (£2,000) and Kilburn Irish Pensioners Club (£500).

A further 16 grants were approved during the year but remained unpaid at the year end.

Applications In writing to the correspondent. Applications should be received by February or August for consideration in March or October.

The Irish Youth Foundation (UK) Ltd

Irish young people

£265,000 (1998/99)

Beneficial area UK and Ireland

The Irish Centre, Blacks Road, Hammersmith, London W6 9DT

Tel. 01895 823711

Correspondent Heather Kerr

Trustees *Mary Clancy, Chair; Polly Devlin; H Farrell; F Gormley; F Hucker; P Kelly; D Murray; J O'Hara; Nessa O'Neill; N Smurfit; Colin McNicholas; Bernard McNicholas; Sean O'Neill.*

Information available Full accounts were on file at the Charity Commission.

General The trust's main aim is to support youth projects in Britain that assist young Irish emigrants and also to support emigration related programmes in Ireland.

Previous guidelines have given the following information, it is not known whether these are still relevant.

The trust is for the benefit of young Irish people, especially those that are disadvantaged and are in need. It raises funds and makes grants in order to:

- provide and organise centres for educational training and research into youth and child development

- support projects tackling the immediate problems of deprived children, unemployed young people, disadvantaged youth and children, alcohol abuse and crime, violence and vandalism

- aid preventative programmes for young people and children which promote their personal growth and development

- develop facilities and amenities for young people and children and provide equipment

- undertake 'pilot' action research programmes aimed at developing effective means of resolving youth and children problems

- promote standards of excellence among programmes for young people and children

- strengthen, expand and replicate programmes 'that work'.

'The foundation is concerned with supplementing state aid. We are not in the business of substituting it. We are not in the business of replacing funding lost as a result of cutbacks in statutory support. However, we may consider offering interim support, provided that you are taking steps to resolve your long-term funding situation by exploring new sources and examining the impact of these changes on your services and structures.

'We give priority to small organisations working directly with young Irish people at community level, which do not have the ability to fundraise for themselves. Larger or national organisations will only be eligible for funding if they can demonstrate that the project to be funded either breaks new ground in the given field and/or will significantly benefit small community-based projects benefiting young Irish people.

'The foundation considers requests for:

1. programme development grants, i.e. grants to enhance existing programmes or to develop new ones.

2. seeding grants, i.e. grants to help start up projects, especially ones of an innovatory nature. While salaries are not funded, in certain circumstances contributions towards salary costs may be considered.

3. grants to upgrade premises/equipment.

4. small grants.

'In general no more than one grant will be given to any one organisation in one year. However, in certain special

circumstances commitment to a particular project may extend beyond one year, subject to continuous review.'

In 1998/99 the foundation had an income of £174,000 including £155,000 in donations received. Grants totalled £265,000. No list of grants was included with the accounts on file at the Charity Commission.

The grants list available was that for 1994/95, when the trust had an income of IR£827,000 with IR£206,000 from activities/events and IR£561,000 from contributions. Grants totalled IR£454,000, of which IR£442,000 was allocated for disbursement in the next year, categorised by the trust as follows:

Programme development grants
IR£15,000 (four grants). Beneficiaries received grants of £3,000 to £5,700 and were APIC Centre, Belvedere Youth Club, Peace Corps and Vietnamese Association.

Special projects
IR£25,000 (two grants). £15,000 was given to the National Youth Federation and £10,000 to the Bridge Project Ltd.

Research projects
IR£25,000 (two grants). Two research projects were funded by the trust, one analysing the current service situation for children and young people in Northern Ireland, the other a study of services for the 5-20 year age group. Prior to this year, the trust benefited only the 14-25 age group.

A further IR£250,000 was earmarked for projects and programmes yet to be assessed in the categories: special projects for disadvantaged young people, travellers projects, enterprise/employment, drugs/HIV/AIDS, arts and drama, outdoor activities, exchanges and children's projects.

UK larger grants
IR£71,000 (14 grants) with a further IR£30,000 to be allocated to four of the supported projects, following further assessment and evaluation. These grants ranged from £2,000 to £8,000 with recipients including Irish Commission for Prisoners Overseas, Islington Women's Counselling Centre, Luton Irish Advice Bureau, Safe Start Foundation and Sheffield Gypsy & Traveller Support Group.

UK small grants
IR£26,000 (23 grants). These were for £1,500 or less with beneficiaries including Chester Aid to the Homeless, Harehills Irish Music Project – Leeds, Irish Community Care Merseyside and London Traveller Youth Work Forum.

151

Exclusions The foundation generally does not support: projects which cater for people under 12 years or over 21 years of age; individuals; general appeals; work in the arts, museums, or of an environmental nature; academic research; educational bursaries; as a substitute for state support; alleviation of deficits already incurred; services run by statutory/public authorities; and major capital appeals.

Applications In writing to the correspondent, requesting an application form. The application period is short. Applications are considered in November and all applicants notified in January. Applications are assessed on the following requirements: need; continuity; track record/evaluation; disadvantaged young people; innovativeness; funding sources; and budgetary control.

The Ironmongers' Quincentenary Charitable Fund

General

£78,000 (1998/99)

Beneficial area UK

Ironmongers' Hall, Barbican, London EC2Y 8AA

Tel. 020 7606 2725

Correspondent Mrs C Maude

Trustees *Worshipful Company of Ironmongers.*

Information available Full accounts were on file at the Charity Commission.

General Set up under trust deed in 1964, the fund's assets stood at £1.8 million in 1998/99. Its income for the year was £112,000 and grants totalled £78,000. These were divided as follows:

Crafts
Grants totalling £9,900 included those to Hetley Studios (£3,500), Glasgow School of Art for a bursary (£2,500) and Voluntary Service Overseas (£2,400).

Universities and industry
A total of £17,000 was given. Six universities were supported, five received £2,400, and £3,000 was given to Oxford University. In addition, British Institute of Foundrymen – Jubilee Awards received £1,700.

National Trust and other restoration
Grants totalled £33,000. The National Trust received a grant of £12,000 for Erdigg. Other grants were £19,000 to Birchwood School and £2,000 to Royal College of Arms.

Other organisations
A total of £18,000. There were 10 grants listed ranging from £1,000 to £2,100. Beneficiaries included Arkwright Scholarship, Deafblind UK – London, Dockland Sailing & Watersports Centre, Guildhall School of Music & Drama, Hayward Adventure Playground, Inside Out Trust, Lord Mayor's Appeal Leuka 2000 and Trinity Hospice. Smaller grants totalled £3,500.

Applications Applicants should send a brief outline of their work including an sae. The trust will send an application form to those which fit its criteria. The committee meets twice a year in March and October, applications should be received before the end of January and the end of August.

J A R Charitable Trust

Roman Catholic, education, welfare

£53,000 (1998/99)

Beneficial area Worldwide

Vernor Miles & Noble, 5 Raymond Buildings, Gray's Inn, London WC1R 5DD

Tel. 020 7242 8688

Correspondent Philip R Noble, Trustee

Trustees *Philip R Noble; Revd William Young; Revd Paschal Ryan.*

Information available Full accounts were on file at the Charity Commission.

General The trust states in its annual report that it makes grants towards: Roman Catholic missionaries, churches and other causes; education for people under 30; and food and clothing for people over 55 who are in need. In practice, the trust gives regular grants to support mainly Roman Catholic organisations.

In 1998/99 the trust's assets totalled £2.3 million, it had an income of £51,000 and made 52 grants totalling £53,000. A number of beneficiaries received more than one grant during the year. Grants ranged from £200 to £5,000.

Westminster Cathedral 1995 Charitable Trust was the main beneficiary and received two grants of £5,000 each. Grants of £2,000 each went to Diocese of Brentwood, Schools at Somerhill Charitable Trust, Ursuline Convent and Ursuline Sisters. Grants of £1,000 went to 23 organisations including Archdiocese of Liverpool, Cardinal Hume Centre, Diocese of Middlesbrough, Dyslexia Association, LIFE, Westminster Cathedral Night Shelter and White Sisters.

Smaller grants included those to Brentwood Children's Society, Crisis at Christmas, St Joesph's Hospice and Winged Fellowship.

Applications In writing to the correspondent. Please note that the trust's funds are fully committed to regular beneficiaries and it states that there is very little, if any, for unsolicited appeals.

The J R S S T Charitable Trust

See below

£45,000 (1999)

Beneficial area UK

The Garden House, Water End, York YO30 6WQ

Correspondent Mrs Joy Boaden

Trustees *Archibald J Kirkwood, Chair; David T Shutt (Lord Shutt of Greetland), Vice Chair; Trevor A Smith (Lord Smith of Clifton); David A Currie (Lord Currie of Marylebone); Christine J Day; Christopher J Greenfield; Diana E Scott; Pam Giddy.*

Information available Full accounts were on file at the Charity Commission.

General The trust was originally endowed by the non-charitable Joseph Rowntree Reform Trust Ltd (see *A Guide to the Major Trusts Volume 1*). The trust will consider and sometimes instigate charitable projects which related specifically to the work of The Joseph Rowntree Reform Trust Ltd in supporting the development of an increasingly democratic and socially-just society in Great Britain.

In 1999 the trust had assets of £3.5 million and an income of £166,000. After administration and management expenses of £52,000 (nearly a third of their income), grants to 21 organisations totalled £45,000.

The seven grants of over £1,000 were given to European Policy Forum (£15,000), Coeur (£10,000), Council of the Isles – British and Irish Project (£9,000), Engender (£2,200), Democratic Audit regarding House of Lords Reform (£2,100), Campaign for Quality Television (£1,500) and Northern Ireland Educational Foundation (£1,000).

Applications The trustees meet quarterly. They do not invite applications.

The Dorothy Jacobs Charity

Jewish care, medical

£63,000 (1999)

Beneficial area UK

Heywards, St George's House, 15 Hanover Square, London W1R 0HE

Tel. 020 7629 7826

Correspondent R H Moss, Trustee

Trustees *R H Moss; A M Alexander.*

Information available Accounts were on file at the Charity Commission, but without a grants list or a narrative report.

General The trust was established in 1989 to provide 'relief of sickness by provision of medical aid and undertaking of medical research, advancement of education and relief of the elderly and infirm'. It was set up to support 15 nominated charities – three hospitals, four Jewish charities, three cancer-related charities, and five others: Arthritis and Rheumatism Council, BBC Children in Need, British Red Cross, Oxfam and Scope. Other charities are rarely supported.

In 1999 the trust had assets of £811,000 generating an income of £28,000. Grants totalled £63,000, although information about these grants was not available.

Applications In writing to the correspondent, but note the comments above.

The J P Jacobs Charitable Trust

Art, community, health, religion, research, youth

£103,000 (1998/99)

Beneficial area UK, with a preference for Merseyside, and overseas

Newstead, Beaconsfield Road, Woolton, Liverpool L25 6EJ

Tel. 0151 428 6207

Correspondent Grahame Young

Trustees *D B Swift; Mrs P E Swift.*

Information available Accounts were on file at the Charity Commission, up to 1995/96.

General The trust supports art, community, health, religion, research and youth projects. Some overseas development causes are also supported usually through a Christian or Jewish organisation. There is a preference for charities with a Merseyside connection. ; The trust states: 'some income is accumulated with the intention of making larger donations'

In 1998/99 the trust had assets of £1.8 million generating an income of £109,000. Grants to 71 organisations totalled £103,000.

The largest grant was £50,000 to National Museums and Gallaries on Merseyside. Other sizeable grants were £7,500 to Lake District Art Gallery and £5,000 each to Charis and New Israel Fund of Great Britain. Grants of £2,000 each were given to Liverpool Old Hebrew Congregation, Schools Council UK and Veximage, £1,500 to King David Foundation and £1,000 each to 16 organisations including ChildLine, Howard League for Penal Reform, Jubilee 2000 Coalition, Liverpool School of Tropical Medicine, Muncaster Conference, Macmillan Cancer Relief, One World Action, Shelter and YMCA. 47 smaller grants of between £50 and £500 were also given.

Exclusions No support for individuals.

Applications The trusts funds are fully committed and new applications cannot be considered.

The Ruth & Lionel Jacobson Trust (Second Fund) No 2

Jewish, medical, children, disability

£111,000 (1998/99)

Beneficial area UK, with a preference for the North East

High Wray, 35 Montagu Avenue, Gosforth, Newcastle upon Tyne NE3 4JH

Tel. 0191 285 1245

Correspondent Mrs I R Jacobson, Trustee

Trustees *Irene Ruth Jacobson; Malcolm Jacobson.*

Information available Full accounts were provided by the trust.

General The trust supports UK charities and organisations based in the north east of England. The trust states that it supports the advancement of Jewish religious education and healthcare charities. In 1998/99 the trust had assets of £1.2 million and an income, after management and administration, expenses of £60,000. The trust gave over 140 grants totalling £111,000. About 30 of the beneficiaries also received grants the previous year.

The main grants made were £25,000 to Northumbria Calvert Trust, £13,000 to Joint Jewish Charitable Trust, £10,000 each to Tyneside Foyer Appeal and United Jewish Israel Appeal and £5,000 to University of Newcastle upon Tyne Development Trust Appeal.

Other larger grants were £2,500 each to Centre for Advanced Rabbinics, Juvenile Diabetes Foundation, Northern Pine Tree Trust and St Oswald's Hospice, £2,100 to Gateshead Jewish Boarding School, £2,000 to Breast Cancer Campaign Newcastle RVI and £1,000 each to Dance City and The Royal Grammar School Peter Taylor Fund. The remaining grants ranged between £50 and £500.

The trust states that it receives many more applications than it is able to support. Local charities outside the north east of England are supported whenever possible.

Exclusions No grants for individuals. Only registered charities will be supported.

Applications In writing to the correspondent. Please enclose an sae. Applications are considered every other month.

The John Jarrold Trust

Arts, churches, enviornment/conservation, third world, social welfare, medical research

£207,000 (1999/2000)

Beneficial area Worldwide, with a preference for Norfolk

Messrs Jarrold & Sons, Whitefriars, Norwich NR3 1SH

Tel. 01603 660211

Correspondent Brian Thompson, Secretary

Trustees *Members of the Jarrold family: R E Jarrold, Chairman; A C Jarrold; P J Jarrold; Mrs D J Jarrold; Mrs J Jarrold; Mrs A G Jarrold; Mrs W A L Jarrold.*

Information available Full accounts were on file at the Charity Commission.

General The trust supports a wide range of organisations including churches, medical, arts, environment/ conservation, welfare and overseas aid. There is a preference for charities in Norfolk. Also, it prefers to support specific projects rather than contribute to general funding.

In 1999/2000 the trust had assets of £1.5 million and an income of £175,000. Grants totalled £207,000.

The four largest donations were recurrent grants to local organisations, they were Norwich School (£13,000), Norwich Cathedral Trust (£12,000), East Anglia Art Foundation (£10,000) and East Anglia Sports Park (£8,500). Other grants included £6,500 to Norfolk & Norwich Festival, £5,000 each to Action Arthitis, Northern Ballet School and Thorpe St Andrew School and £2,500 to Royal College of Surgeons.

In 1998/99 just over 20% of the grants to organisations were of £1,000 to £2,500, examples include ActionAid, Adapt, The Christian Fellowship, Ely Cathedral,

National Meningitis Trust, Norwich & District CAB, Roman Catholic Diocese of East Anglia, RNIB and Wulugu Project. The majority of the grants, 70%, were of smaller amounts. Beneficiaries included Childwise, The Geographical Association, Peepham Housing Trust, Poetry-next-the Sea, NCH Action for Children and Norfolk Opera Players.

Exclusions Educational purposes that should be supported by the state will not be helped by the trust.

Applications Applications should be in writing and reach the correspondent before the trustees' meetings in January and July.

Rees Jeffreys Road Fund

Road and transport research and education

£303,000 (1999)

Beneficial area UK

13 The Avenue, Chichester, West Sussex PO19 4PX

Tel. & Fax 01243 787013

Correspondent B Fieldhouse, Secretary

Trustees *P W Bryant, Chair; D Bayliss; Dr S Glaister; M N T Cottell; Mrs June Bridgeman; Sir James Duncan; W H P Davison; M J Kendrick.*

Information available Report and accounts with full grants list, exploration of grants, and descriptions of the trust's history and objects.

General The fund gives financial support to research and other projects designed to improve the safety and beauty of public highways. Grants vary from £1,000 to over £100,000, spread over a few years, and are mostly made for research and/or academic study (though the fund has stated that the maximum is now £70,000).

It was established in 1950 by the sole settlor, the late William Rees Jeffreys. Mr Rees Jeffreys was a 'road enthusiast' and was described by Lloyd George as 'the greatest authority on roads in the United Kingdom and one of the greatest in the world'. The fund is just one legacy of a life-time dedicated to the improvement of roads; Rees Jeffreys was the author of an historical and autobiographical record of sixty years of road improvement (The King's Highway, published 1949) which

is introduced with the words 'I early knew my mission in life'. Ironically, given the conquering of the road by the petrol engine and cycling's shift off-road, he was also a very keen cyclist.

At the close of 1999 the fund totalled £8.6 million and generated income of £270,000. The fund 'gives financial support for research to improve the quality and efficiency of roads and their use by vehicular traffic, cyclists, pedestrians and public transport. Grants for individual projects range from £1,000 to £70,000 and include academic study and improving the roadside environment.

The trust's priorities are:

- Education of transport professionals, largely through financial support for teaching staff and bursaries for postgraduate studies. The trust is concerned aboyt the supply of trained professionals and has launched a study of future requirements.

- Stimulating research into all aspects of roads, road usage and road traffic – this commands a large share of the trust's budget. The trust develops its own research programmes as well as responding to proposals from recognised agencies and researchers. Proposals are accessed against prevailing transport issues, e.g. environmental questions, congestion, modal choice and resource development.

- Roadside environment. Applications for the provison of roadside rests are welcome, while support for the work of country wildlife trusts fro improving land adjoining main roads is also maintained. The trust is not normally able to buy land or to fund improvements to roads, footpaths or cycle tracks.

The trust will supports projects and pump-priming for longer term ventures for up to a maximum of five years. Operational or administratvie staff costs are rarely supported. In almost all cases applicants are expected to provide or arrange match funding.

In 1999 the trust's grants were divided as follows:

Education: bursaries and support for universities	£173,000
Research and other projects	£98,000
Physical projects: roadside rests and land adjoining	£50,000

Education
This category was further divided as follows: £156,000 for academic posts and

studentships – general; £16,500 in support of PhD research; and £1,000 in Prizes.

Research and other projects
Grants were given to 11 organisations and 1 individual, ranging from £3,000 to £35,000. The largest grant went to Transport Skills for the Next Millennium, a sponsored project. Other grants included: £10,000 to The Motorway Achievement for the employment of a part-time historian for two years to help record this archive; £5,000 to RNIB to help develop and produce a prototype electronic wayfaring system for people who are blind or partially sighted; £4,500 to Sustrans for updating or printing the Safe Routes to Schools information sheets; and £3,000 to Global Action Plan – a contribution for the addition of a transport module tot he existing portfolio on energy, waste and water.

Physical projects
Grants to 10 organisations ranged from £2,000 to £10,000. Two grants of £10,000 each went to North York Moors National Park towards its park and ride scheme and Moorsbus Interchange at Sutton Park, and to Highways Agency for help with rest facilities at Pottersbury on the A5. A grant of £5,000 was given to National Urban Forestry Unit to help with greening the M62 in West Yorkshire and M65 in East Lancashire (two year grant). Six wildlife trusts received grants of either £3,000 or £5,000 for specific areas.

Exclusions Operational and administrative staff costs are rarely considered.

Applications There is no set form of application for grants. Brief details should be submitted initially. Replies are sent to all applicants.

The Jenour Foundation

General
£105,000 (1998/99)

Beneficial area UK, with a special interest in Wales

Blenhein House, Fitzalan Court, Newport Road, Cardiff CF2 1TS

Tel. 029 2048 1111

Correspondent Sir Peter Phillips, Trustee

Trustees Sir P J Phillips; G R Camfield.

Information available Full accounts were on file at the Charity Commission.

General In 1998/99 the trust had assets of £2.3 million generating an income of £87,000. Grants to 35 organisations totalled £105,000.

The largest grants were £8,000 each to Cancer Research Campaign and Red Cross International, £7,000 to Wales Millennium Centre and £6,000 each to Atlantic Centre and Provincial Grand Lodge of Monmouth. Grants were given to UK organisations such as Save the Children Fund (£4,000), Barnardos (£3,000), Army Benevolent Fund (£2,500) and Leukaemia Research Fund (£1,000). Local charities and local branches of UK charities in Wales included National Museum of Wales and NSPCC Cardiff Central Committee (£3,500 each), RNLI Welsh District (£2,000), Bridgend YMCA Gymnastics Club (£1,500) and Welsh National Opera (£1,000). Maes Y Dyfar, which received £1,000, was the only organisation which were not also supported in the previous year.

Exclusions No support for individuals.

Applications Applications should be in writing and reach the correspondent by February for the trustees' meeting in March.

The Jephcott Charitable Trust

Alleviation of poverty in developing countries, general
£137,000 (1999/2000)

Beneficial area UK, developing countries overseas

Gappers Farm, Membury, Axminster, Devon EX13 7TX

Correspondent Mrs Meg Harris, Secretary

Trustees Mrs M Jephcott, Chair; Dr P Davis; Judge A North; Mrs A Morgan.

Information available Full accounts were on file at the Charity Commission.

General In the trust's 1998/99 annual report it states that it is particularly interested in giving grants for start-up costs. Previously it has stated that its priorities are population control, education, health and the environment. Grants are usually for a specific project or part of a project. Core funding and/or salaries are rarely considered. 'Pump-priming' donations are offered – usually grants to new organisations and areas of work. As well as being reactive (responding to applications) the trust is becoming increasingly proactive.

The trustees are flexible in their approach, but take the following into account when considering a project:

- the ability to evaluate a project. With overseas projects local involvement is thought to be essential for ongoing success
- the involvement of a third party e.g. ODA, NGOs, National Heritage
- financial: level of administration costs, reserves held within the group etc.
- whether the project is basic or palliative; whether it is one-off or ongoing
- to what extent the organisation helped themselves.

In 1999/2000 the trust's assets stood at £4.6 million giving an income of £143,000. A total of £137,000 was given in 23 grants, ranging from £750 to £14,000. The largest grants were £14,000 to Woodside Sanctuary and £10,000 each to ADESA, Mozambique Schools Fund and Winter Comfort. Other recipients included Institute of Cultural Affairs Development Trust (£9,500), Archbishop Joseph Cababa Ssunga Health Centre (£7,500), World Medical Trust (£6,000), Alpha School (£5,000), Charles Darwin Project (£3,000) and Anglo-Peruvian Child Care Mission (£2,500). The three smaller grants went to St Batholomew's Anglican Church (£1,000), University of Brighton (£950) and Miyana Community Centre – Uganda (£750).

Seven of the beneficiaries were also supported in the previous year.

Exclusions No grants to individuals, including students, or for medical research. No response to general appeals from large, UK organisations nor from organisations concerned with poverty and education in the UK. Core funding and/or salaries are rarely considered.

Applications Guidelines and application forms are available on request and receipt of an sae. Applications can be made in writing at any time to the correspondent. Trustees meet twice a year (in April and October) and must have detailed financial information about each project before they will make a decision.

Jewish Child's Day

Jewish children in need or with special needs

£408,000 (1998/99)

Beneficial area Worldwide

5th Floor, 707 High Road,
North Finchley, London N12 0BT

Tel. 020 8446 8804 **Fax** 020 8446 7370
e-mail jcd@anjy.org
website www.jewishchildsday.co.uk
Correspondent P Shaw, Executive Director

Trustees *Mrs Joy Moss, Chair; Mrs Amanda Ingram; Mrs Virginia Campus; Stephen Moss; The National Council.*

Information available Full accounts were on file at the Charity Commission.

General The trust was established in 1947 to encourage Jewish children in Britain to help less fortunate Jewish children who were survivors of the Nazi holocaust. Now it supports projects benefiting Jewish children in the UK or overseas. It disburses funds raised itself through appeals.

Preference is given to children with disabilities and special needs. Grants generally range from £500 to £3,000 and can be given towards the cost of equipment or a project directly benefiting children.

In 1998/99 (1997/98 figures in brackets) the trust had assets of £589,000 (£515,000) and an income of £626,000 (£508,000) of which £606,000 (£489,000) was received in contributions. After administration and fundraising costs of £174,000 (£167,000) the trust gave £408,000 (£266,000) in grants, although £250,000 was from restricted funds.

The grants were broken down as follows:

	1998/99	(1997/98)
Israel	£254,000	(£230,000)
Great Britain	£38,000	(£35,000)
Other	£116,000	(£1,100)

There were 62 grants of £500 or more listed in the accounts. The largest were

£103,000 to Children of Chenobyl, £88,000 to Shalva, £22,000 to Hamifal – Educational Children's Homes, £11,000 to Micha Society for Deaf Children – Tel Aviv and £11,000 each to Delamere Forest School. Other grants included Youth Aliya (£8,500), Hai Friends of Hematology (£6,900), Bayit Lekhol Yeled Be Yisrael (£5,000), Manchester Jewish Federation (£4,400), Association for Research into Stammering in Childhood (£3,000), Side by Side Kids Ltd (£3,100), Israel Folk Dance Institute (£2,000), The Wolfson Hillel Primary School (£1,500), Ezrath Nashim Hospital (£1,400), Beth Jacob Kindergartens (£1,000) and The Speech and Language Learning Centre (£500).

Smaller grants totalled £822.

Exclusions Individuals are not supported. Grants are not given towards general services, building or maintenance of property or staff salaries.

Applications There is an application form which needs to be submitted together with a copy of the latest annual report and accounts and any supporting information. The trustees meet to consider applications twice a year, usually in March and September/October, applications should be submitted two months earlier. The trust states 'if you require any advice as to the eligibility of your application or assistance in preparing it please do not hesitate to contact us and we shall be happy to help'.

The H F Johnson Trust

Christian education

£68,000 (1999)

Beneficial area Worldwide, but mainly the UK

4 Parkgate Close, Kingston upon Thames, Surrey KT2 7LU

Correspondent Dennis Colby, Trustee

Trustees *Dennis Colby; Miss Nancy B Johnson.*

Information available Full accounts were on file at the Charity Commission.

General Established by trust deed in 1962, the trust's main object is the advancement of the Christain faith.

In 1999 the trust had assets of £984,000 and an income of £132,000, this came mainly from rental income from

properties owned by the trust. Grants totalled £68,000.

The majority of the trust's grant fund each year (£46,000 in 1999) goes on the School Bible and Book Project. The trust listed nine other organisations which received grants in the year, four of which had been supported in the previous year. The largest of these was £5,000 to Tearfund. Two grants of £2,000 each went to Scripture Union and Manna Trust and £1,500 each went to Crusade for World Revival and St Paul's Church Kingston Hill. Grants of £1,000 went to Elim Pentecostal Church, CRIBS Trust, London Emmanuel Choir and Saltmine Trust.

An undisclosed number of smaller grants under £500 were made. Those going to Christian institutions totalled £5,200 and those to Christian evangelists totalled £1,600.

Applications The trust stated that it only supports organisations and individuals which are personally known to the trustees and requests that you do not write in.

The Lillie C Johnson Charitable Trust

Children, young people who are blind or deaf, medical

£189,000 (1997/98)

Beneficial area UK, with a preference for the West Midlands

Heathcote House, 136 Hagley Road, Edgbaston, Birmingham B16 9PN

Tel. 0121 454 4141

Correspondent Victor M C Lyttle, Trustee

Trustees *Victor Lyttle; Peter Adams.*

Information available Full accounts were on file at the Charity Commission.

General In 1988/89 the trust received £1.6 million from the estate of Miss L C Johnson. It mainly supports charities concerned with children or young people and medical causes.

In 1997/98 the trust had assets of £4.6 million and an income of £191,000. Grants totalled £189,000. A third of the beneficiaries were based in Birmingham and the West Midlands.

The larger grants were £30,000 each to Birmingham Heartlands Hospital - Children's Development Centre and University of Birmingham Tinnitus Research and £10,000 to Sense. Other grants included Royal British Legion Poppy Appeal (£8,500), Heart of England School (£8,000), Pulse (£3,500), Birmingham Children's Hospital Appeal and County Air Ambulance (£2,000 each), Barnardos (£1,500) and Cornerstone, Mencap and St Peters Junior School (£1,000 each).

Exclusions No support for individuals.

Applications Applications are only considered from charities which are traditionally supported by the trust.

The J E Joseph Charitable Fund

Jewish

£107,000 (1998/99)

Beneficial area UK, with a preference for London, the Far East, Israel and Palestine

6 Lyon Meade, Stanmore, Middlesex HA7 1JA

Tel. 020 7289 8780   **Fax** 020 7289 8780

Correspondent Roger J Leon, Secretary

Trustees *F D A Mocatta; J H Corre; P S Gourgey; J S Horesh; S Frosh; D Silas.*

Information available Full accounts were available at the Charity Commission.

General Unfortunately we have been unable to update the following information since the last edition of this guide.

The trust was established for the benefit of Jewish communities; relief of poverty; relief of suffering of poor Jews; advancement of education and the Jewish religion; and other purposes beneficial to Jewish communities. Grants are only given to or through Jewish organisations. In 1995/96 the trust decided to regularise its grant-making in the following proportions:

Home organisations	55%
Israeli charities	35%
Eastern charities	5%
Sundry requests	5%

In 1998/99 the trust had assets of £3.8 million and an income of £100,000. Grants totalled £107,000 and were broken down by the trust as shown in the table.

'The trustees believe it inappropriate to disclose the names of grantees, being other charities and individuals.'

Applications In writing to the correspondent.

The Lady Eileen Joseph Foundation

General

£65,000 (1998/99)

Beneficial area UK

8 Baker Street, London W1M 1DA

Correspondent Mrs J M S Sawdy, Trustee

Trustees *Mrs J Sawdy; T W P Simpson; Mrs N J Thornton.*

Information available Full accounts were on file at the Charity Commission.

General The trust was registered in 1987. The accounts for 1998/99 show that the trust had assets of £970,000 and an income of £52,000. It gave grants totalling £65,000.

The main grants were to Help the Hospices (£50,000), Tower Hamlets College Voluntary Fund (£5,000), Community Security Trust (£2,500), Cancer BACUP (£2,000) and Laughton School Association (£1,200). The trust also gave an unspecified number of grants of under £1,000 each.

Applications In writing to the correspondent, although the trust states that unsolicited requests will not be considered.

The Jungels-Winkler Charitable Foundation

Visually impaired – generally and in the arts

About £100,000 (1999/2000)

Beneficial area UK

Herbert Smith, Exchange House, Primrose Street, London EC2A 2HS

Tel. 020 7374 8000   **Fax** 020 7374 0888

Correspondent J R Wood, Trustee

Information available Information was provided by the trust.

General Grants are towards projects or charities for the benefit of people who are visually impaired, with some preference for those charities which are arts-related. The trustees are proactive in deciding which organisations benefit.

In 1999/2000 grants totalling around £100,000 were made, with most of the total going in three donations of around £30,000 each.

Applications In writing to the correspondent. Please note, the trust states that the funds are fully committed until the end of 2001.

THE J E JOSEPH CHARITABLE FUND GRANT DISTRIBUTION 1998/99			
Category	Range £	No. of grants	Total £
Home – general	0–5,000	7	15,000
	5,001–10,000	4	26,000
Home – schools	0–5000	5	20,000
Eastern	0–5,000	2	2,500
	5,001–10,000	1	6,500
Israeli	0–5,000	8	22,000
	10,001–15,000	1	13,000
Individuals & sundry	0–5,000	5	3,000

The Anton Jurgens Charitable Trust

Welfare, general

£304,000 (1996/97)

Beneficial area UK

c/o Saffery Champness, Fairfax House, Fulwood Place, Grays Inn, London WC1V 6UB

Tel. 020 7405 2828

Correspondent M J Jurgens, Trustee

Trustees C V Jurgens, Chair; A H Jurgens; Miss B W Jurgens; E Deckers; M J Jurgens; F Jurgens.

Information available Accounts were on file at the Charity Commission, but without a narrative report.

General In 1998/99 the trust had an income and a total expenditure of £349,000. Further information for this year was not available at the time of going to print.

In 1996/97 the trust had assets of £6.5 million, generating an income of £299,000. Over 50 grants to a variety of disability and social welfare groups totalled £304,000. Grants ranged from £500 to £50,000 and averaged between £2,000 and £5,000. Just under half the grant giving was concentrated on three beneficiaries: Princes Trust and Fairbridge Mission (each £50,000); and St John, Berkshire – care in the community (£25,000).

Other beneficiaries included: Woodland Trust (£15,000); Combat Stress (£13,000); Aidiss Trust and The Treloar Trust (£10,000 each); Carpaid Trust (£5,000); £2,000 each to Hope Nursery, The Quaker Opportunity Group and Handicapped Adventure Playground Association; The Broadway Trust (£1,000); and Durham County Probation Service (£500).

Applications In writing to the correspondent. Applications are considered in April and October and should arrive at least one month in advance.

The Bernard Kahn Charitable Trust

Jewish

£236,000 (1998/99)

Beneficial area UK and Israel

18 Gresham Gardens, London NW11 8PD

Correspondent Bernard Kahn, Trustee

Trustees Mrs C B Kahn; B Kahn; S Fuehrer.

Information available Accounts were on file at the Charity Commission.

General In 1998/99 the trust had assets of £2.3 million and an income of £229,000, including £39,000 in donations from the Kahn family. Grants to 63 organisations totalled £236,000. Over half of the grants were of under £1,000.

The largest grants were £60,000 to Yeshivat Margenita d'avrohom, £25,000 each to Ohr Somayach College and Orthodox Council of Jerusalem and £20,000 each to Gevurath Ari Academy and Tels Academy. Other grants included £7,000 to Gateshead Jewish High School, £5,000 to Friends of Religious Settlement, £1,750 to Hasmonean High School, £800 to Woodstock Sinclair Trust, £250 to Enuno EC and £75 each to Finchley Road Synagogue and Marbeh Torah Trust.

Applications In writing to the correspondent.

The Stanley Kalms Foundation

Jewish charities, general

£291,000 (1996)

Beneficial area UK and overseas

c/o Titmuss Sainer Decheot, 2 Sarjeants Inn, London EC4Y 1LT

Correspondent Miss O Morgan

Trustees Stanley Kalms; Pamela Kalms; Stephen Kalms.

Information available Accounts up to 1996 were on file at the Charity Commission. A list of grants was included but without a narrative report.

General Established in 1989, this charity states its objectives as the encouragement of Jewish education in the UK and Israel. Other activities include support for the arts and media and other programmes, secular and religious.

Total assets of the charity amounted to £1.8 million in 1996, with incoming resources at £68,000. The annual report and accounts shows that 56 grants were given in 1996 totalling £291,000. Grants were mainly to Jewish organisations (social and educational) with grants also going to the arts, education and health. Most of the grants were for less than £5,000, with the largest being for over £100,000 and the smallest for £1,000. About a quarter of the grants are repeated from previous years.

Examples of the larger grants include: Immanual College (£102,000), Institute for Policy Research (£25,000), Shalom Hartman Institute (£21,000), Ravenswood Foundation (£17,000), Community Security Trust and Nightingale House (each £13,000), Royal Opera House (£12,000), Institute for Jewish Policy Research (£11,000), Economic Education Trust and the Mencap Challenge Fund (each £10,000).

Other smaller examples include British Friends of Art Museums in Israel (£4,000), Jewish Care (£2,000), Jewish Marriage Council (£2,000), National Opera Studio (£1,000), Kings Diabetic Fund (£1,000) and Kings Appeal (£1,000).

Applications In writing to the correspondent, but note that most of the trust's funds are committed to projects supported for a number of years.

The Boris Karloff Charitable Foundation

General

£77,000 (1998/99)

Beneficial area Worldwide

Peachey & Co., 95 Aldwych, London WC2B 4JF

Tel. 020 7316 5200

Correspondent The Trustees

Trustees Ian D Wilson; Geoffrey F Hill; Peter A Williamson.

Information available Full accounts were on file at the Charity Commission.

General This foundation was set up in 1985, by Evelyn Pratt (Karloff), wife of the famous horror actor Boris Karloff (whose real name was William Henry Pratt). When Evelyn Pratt died in June 1993 she bequeathed over £1.4 million to the assets of the foundation.

In 1998/99 the trust had assets of £1.8 million and an income of £89,000. Grants to 17 organisations totalled £77,000.

Grants were given to acting charities including £10,000 each to Actors Charitable Trust, Cinema & Television Benevolent Fund and Royal Theatrical Fund and £1,000 to Garrick Theatre Altrincham. Medical organisations supported included Imperial Cancer Research Fund (£5,000), Deafblind UK (£4,000) and Partially Sighted Society (£1,000). Other grants included £15,000 in two grants to Wiltshire Community Foundation – Ken Barrington Cricket Scheme (£5,000), Salisbury Samaritans (£3,000), Salisbury and District Council for Voluntary Workers (£1,000) and Little Sisters of the Poor (£500).

Applications In writing to the correspondent.

The Kasner Charitable Trust

Jewish

£144,000 (1997/98)

Beneficial area UK and Israel

Kimberley House, 172 Billet Road, London E17 5DT

Tel. 020 8527 8812

Correspondent Josef Kasner, Trustee

Trustees *Josef Kasner, Chair; Mrs Elfreda Erlich; Baruch Erlich.*

Information available Full accounts were on file at the Charity Commission.

General In 1998/99 the trust had an income of £54,000 and an expenditure of £257,000. This information was available on the Charity Commission database but unforunately the accounts were not yet available in the public file. The following is repeated from the last edition.

In 1997/98 this trust's assets totalled £1.3 million and it had an income of £555,000 which was unusually large because of the receipt of one-off dividends of £516,000 from investments. Over 200 donations were made totalling £144,000, most of which were for £200 or less.

Larger grants were to Gevurath Ari Academy Trust (£38,000), Telz Academy Trust (£30,000), Torath Moshe Educational and Charitable Trust (£10,000), Friends of Menovah Grammar School and Tiferes Yakov – Gateshead (£5,000) and Emunoh Educational Centre (£4,000).

Applications In writing to the correspondent.

The Michael & Ilse Katz Foundation

Jewish, general

£110,000 (1998/99)

Beneficial area Worldwide

Parke & Co., The Counting House, Trelill, Bodmin, Cornwall PL30 3HZ

Tel. 01208 851814   **Fax** 01208 851813
e-mail osman.azis@virgin.net

Correspondent Osman Azis, Trustee

Trustees *Norris Gilbert; Osman Azis.*

Information available Full accounts were on file at the Charity Commission.

General The trust was established in 1971, by Michael R Katz and Ilse P Katz. The main grants are usually to Jewish organisations, many of which are regular beneficiaries, although grants can differ in size.

In 1998/99 the trust had assets of £1.8 million and an income from investments of £44,000. Grants totalled £110,000.

Grants included those to British Friends of Neve Shalom (£25,000), Bournemouth Orchestra (£16,000), Community Security Trust (£8,000), Norwood Ravenswood (£5,000), Holocaust Education Trust (£3,500), New Israel Fund of Great Britain (£2,000), Wiener Library Endowment (£1,300) and Jews' Temporary Shelter (£1,000). One grant of £300 was also given to an individual.

Most of the smaller grants in the past have been to UK medical/disability or welfare charities. We cannot confirm that this is still the practice of the trust, since grants to organisations under £1,000 are no longer listed in the report.

Applications In writing to the correspondent.

The C S Kaufman Charitable Trust

Jewish

£65,000 (1998/99)

Beneficial area UK

162 Whitehall Road, Gateshead, Tyne & Wear NE8 1TP

Correspondent C S Kaufman

Trustees *I I Kaufman; J Kaufman.*

Information available Full accounts were on file at the Charity Commission.

General In 1998/99 the trust had assets of £248,000 and an income of £74,000, including £7,000 in donations. Grants to 89 organisations totalled £65,000.

The largest grants were £13,000 to Society of Friends of Torah, £7,000 to Friends of Harim and £6,000 to Friends of Knesset Yehuda. Other grants included Gatesheaad Foundation for Torah (£3,100), Glasgow Kollel (£1,800), Toldos Aharon (£1,300), Friends of Ponevez (£800), Craven Walks (£6,600), Bais Hatalmud Gateshead (£60) and Project Seed (£50).

Applications In writing to the correspondent.

This entry was not confirmed by the trust but was correct according to information on file at the Charity Commission.

The Mendel Kaufman Charitable Trust

Jewish charities

£444,000 (1993/94)

Beneficial area UK, especially the north east of England

c/o Cohen Arnold & Co, 13–17 New Burlington Place, Regent Street, London W15 2HL

Tel. 020 7734 1362

Correspondent Cohen Arnold & Co

Trustees *Z M Kaufman; I I Kaufman; J Kaufman.*

Information available Accounts up to 1993/94 only were on file at the Charity Commission in September 1998 and even then without a list of grants.

General The last set of accounts available for this trust are those for 1993/94 which were audited only in April 1996. As usual, they are skeletal, with no notes nor a list of grants. The following is reprinted from the previous edition:

The trust supports Jewish organisations, with a preference for the north east of England, especially the Gateshead area. In 1993/94 the trust had assets of nearly £3 million, but this value includes all its investments at cost instead of at market value. One of the liabilities of the trust is a loan for over £1 million, but with no explanation in the accounts about its purpose. This loan accounts in part for the high administration expenses (19% of income) which included £111,000 for bank charges and interest.

The trust had an income of £604,000 in 1993/94 generated mainly from property revenue (£401,000) and donations received (£122,000). A total of £444,000 was distributed in grants, lower than the total in 1992/93 (£509,000). There is no known reason why this trust should not disclose any information about its charitable activities.

Applications In writing to the correspondent.

The Kennel Club Charitable Trust

Dogs

£213,000 (1998/99)

Beneficial area UK

1 Clarges Street, Piccadilly, London W1Y 8AB

Tel. 020 7518 1050

e-mail mwetherell@the-kennel-club.org.uk

website www.the-kennel-club.org.uk

Correspondent Mrs Mary Wetherell, Secretary

Trustees *M J R Stockman, Chair; Brigadier R J Clifford; B J Hall; W R Irving; M Townsend.*

Information available Full accounts were on file at the Charity Commission.

General The trust describes its objects as 'science, sentiment and support'. It supports the furthering of research into canine diseases and hereditary disorders of dogs and also organisations concerned with the welfare of dogs in need and those which aim to improve the quality of life of humans by promoting dogs as practical or therapeutic aids. The trust gives both ongoing and one-off grants.

The trust has assets of £573,000 and an income of £115,000. Grants totalled £213,000 and were divided into 'research project support' which received £189,000 and 'donations' totalling £24,000. Grants ranged from £500 to £95,000. Animal Health Trust received the largest grant of £95,000 to support the work of their Genetics Co-ordinator and also £25,000 for an Epidemiological Study. Other larger grants went to University of Edinburgh – mitral valve endocardiosis research (£26,000), University of Bristol – canine gastro-enterology research (£25,000) and University of Glasgow – molecular genetic study of canine cancer (£12,700).

The largest non-research grant was £10,000 to Dogs for the Disabled. Other donations included those to PDSA and Swedish University of Agricultural Sciences (each £5,000), Blue Cross (£2,500) and RSPCA (£500). Two grants of £3,000 each were given to Royal College of Veterinary Surgeons for bursaries for veterinary nurses.

In March 2000 the trust launched an appeal to raise £1 million over two years.

Exclusions The trust does not give grants directly to individuals. Veterinary nurses can apply to the Royal College of Veterinary Surgeons where bursaries are available, see above.

Applications In writing to the correspondent. The trustees meet three times a year.

Kleinwort Benson Charitable Trust

Arts, conservation, inner cities, medical, young people, welfare

£278,000 (1998)

Beneficial area UK, with some preference for east London

PO Box 560, 20 Fenchurch Street, London EC3P 3DB

Tel. 020 7623 8000

e-mail Jennifer.Emptage@dresdnerkb.com

Correspondent Miss J A Emptage, Administrator

Trustees *Kleinwort Benson Trustees Ltd.*

Information available Full accounts were provided by the trust.

General The trust supports organisations concerned with medical, welfare, youth, conservation, inner cities and the arts. Most grants are given to UK organisations although some preference is given to projects in east London where it also operates a volunteering programme.

The 1998 report states that 'sympathetic consideration was given to charities with which staff members of the Dresdner Kleinwort Benson Group had an active involvement. Three special donations of £12,500 each were made to charities selected via ballot by employees of the Dresdner Kleinwort Benson Group'. In 1998 these went to Atlantic College, Children's Head Injury Trust and Parkinson's Disease Society.

In 1998 the income totalled £267,000 of which £250,000 came by Gift Aid from Kleinwort Benson Limited. Grants to 177 organisations totalled £278,000. Large grants included £14,000 to Tommy's Campaign; £10,000 each to East London Small Business Charity, Hackney City Farm and Newham Community Renewal Progamme – Homeless Young People's Project; £8,000 to English National Opera; £6,700 each to Business in the

Community; and £5,000 to United Kingdom Historic Building Preservation Trust.

Half of the grants were between £1,000 and £3,000 and recipients included Bankers Benevolent Fund, Centrepoint, English Martyrs School, Friends of the Elderly, Imperial Cancer Research Fund, London Lighthouse, NSPCC, National Youth Orchestra of Great Britain, Sight Savers International, Tower Hamlets Education Business Partnership and Woodland Trust.

Smaller grants include those to Addaction, Anglo-Chilean Society, Coopers' Livery Housing Fund, Dementia Relief Trust, Hackney Music Development Trust, Mare Street Citizens Advice Bureau, National Literacy Trust, Rehearsal Orchestra, St Mary-Le-Bow Church Young Homeless Project and Workroute.

Many of the grants to UK organisations may be recurrent as the trust states that it supports 'national charities with which we have a long-standing relationship'.

Exclusions No grants to individuals or local church appeals.

Applications In writing to the correspondent. Trustees meet quarterly in March, June, September and December.

The Kobler Trust

Arts, Jewish, medical

£333,000 (1998/99)

Beneficial area UK

Lewis Silkin, Windsor House, 50 Victoria Street, London SW1H 0NW

Correspondent Joanne Evans, Trustee

Trustees *Joel W Israelsohn; Antoine Xuereb; Andrew H Stone; Joanne L Evans.*

Information available Full accounts were on file at the Charity Commision.

General In 1998/99 the trust had assets of £4.5 million and an income of £217,000. After administration and management costs of £23,000, grants totalling £333,000 were given to 56 organisations, 16 of which were supported in the previous year.

The largest grant was £60,000 to Friends of Amutat Avi (Beit Issie Shapiro). Other sizeable grants included £25,000 to Crusiad, £20,000 each to Chicken Shed Theatre, Covent Garden Festival, Jewish

Care and Royal Academy of Music and £15,000 to BACUP.

Other grants ranged from £200 to £13,000. Arts organisations supported included Tricycle Theatre Company Limited (£13,000), Pavilion Opera Education Trust (£12,000), Magic Mirror Theatre Company Limited (£5,000) and British Youth Theatre (£1,000). Jewish beneficiaries included £2,000 each to Jewish Blind and Disabled and Norwood Ravenswood. Medical grants included Express Link Up (£10,000), FACTS (£4,000) and Jewish Aids Trust (£2,000).

Exclusions Grants are only given to individuals in exceptional circumstances.

Applications In writing to the correspondent.

The Kurt and Olga Koerner Charitable Trust

Conservation, environment, education

£90,000 (1999)

Beneficial area UK, with a strong preference for Scotland and Sussex

39 Sloane Street, London SW1X 9LP

Tel. 020 7235 9560   **Fax** 020 7235 9580

Correspondent Mrs E Owen, Administrator

Trustees *Lisbet Koerner; Joseph Leo Koener; Sigrid M E Rausing; Märit Rausing.*

Information available Full accounts were provided by the trust.

General Established in 1997, the trust has no guidelines. The trust has stated previously that 'donations have broadly been to organisations involved with conservation and care of the environment. The trust has also made some educational donations.' The trust has a preference for Scotland and Sussex.

Grants made in 1999 were not explained in the trustees report. A list of grants was available and showed a strong preference for Scotland and for projects concerned with the environment and education. In 1999 the trust had assets of £986,000 and an income of £72,000. A total of £90,000 was given in 18 grants. The largest grant was of £30,000 to Francis Holland School

Trust. Four grants of £10,000 each went to Big Brothers & Sisters UK, The Parnham Trust, Soil Association and Sustrans. Other large grants were £5,000 each to Association of Art Historians, Royal Botanic Garden (Edinburgh) and Trees for London and £2,500 to STIRK.

Smaller grants ranged from £50 to £500, including those to Homes for a Future, Let the Children Play, Kinlochleven Youth Group, Lochaber & District Fisheries Trust, The Pesticides Trust and West Highland Museum. Eight of the grants (mainly the smaller ones) were recurrent from the previous year when they received similar amounts.

Exclusions No grants to individuals.

Applications In writing to the correspondent. Trustees meet twice a year in May and November. The trust states that it is administered on a part-time voluntary basis and due to the large number of applications received it is unable to reply to all applicants.

The Kohn Charitable Trust

Scientific and medical projects, the arts – particularly music, education, Jewish charities

£356,000 (1998)

Beneficial area UK

14 Harley Street, London W1N 1AA

Correspondent Dr R Kohn, Chair to the Trustees

Trustees *Dr Ralph Kohn, Chair; Zahava Kohn; Anthony A Forwood.*

Information available Full accounts were on file at the Charity Commission.

General The trust was founded by Ralph and Zahava Kohn in 1991 to support general charitable causes, but primarily education, the Jewish religion, the relief of poverty, the care of people who are sick and mentally ill, and medical research.

In 1998 the trust's assets totalled £2.4 million. It had an income of £51,000 (£243,000 in the previous year which included £200,000 in Gift Aid donations). Grants totalled £356,000 (£123,000 in 1997/98) including 14 of £1,000 or more which were listed in the accounts. Smaller grants totalled £8,300.

The largest grant by far was £200,000 to The Royal Society. Other large grants went to Academy of Medical Services (£50,000), Wigmore Hall International Song Competition (£36,000), The Bach Pilgrimage (£25,000) and £10,000 each to North West London Jewish Day School and The Vega Science Trust.

Grants ranging from £1,000 to £5,000 included those to Foundation for Science and Technology, The Medical Art Society, Hasmonean High School, Joint Jewish Charitable Trust, Rudolf Kempe Society and Sage.

Applications In writing to the correspondent.

The Neil Kreitman Foundation

Jewish charities, arts

£298,000 (1996/97)

Beneficial area UK and Israel

Citroen Wells (Chartered Accountants), 1 Devonshire Street, London W1W 5DR

Tel. 020 7304 2000

Correspondent Eric Charles, Trustee

Trustees *Roger Kreitman; H Kreitman; Mrs S I Kreitman; Eric Charles.*

Information available Accounts were on file at the Charity Commission up to 1996/97, but without a narrative report.

General The trust makes about 15 grants each year. Practically all funds go to charities previously assisted by the foundation. The beneficiaries come from a variety of charitable fields, but the large grants (which account for most of grant expenditure) are usually made to cultural institutions.

The foundation was set-up in 1974 by Neil Kreitman. Its practices, stated in the 1996/97 report, are as follows: 'The foundation generally supports projects in the fields of culture, education, health and welfare. The foundation makes grants to registered charities only and to organisations which are exempt ... and which are based in the UK.'

The foundation's day to day activities are administered by its accountants as it employs no staff. Its trustees are solely responsible for the consideration and authorisation of the donations made. It is the usual policy of the trustees to make awards from the accumulated fund only.

In 1996/97 the assets of £5.8 million generated an income of £294,000. Grants totalling £298,000 were given to 14 organisations, 13 of which had been supported in the previous two years. As in the two previous years, the largest donation of £180,000 went to Ashmolean Museum (£152,000 in 1995/96). Other large grants were to Ancient India and Iran Trust (£30,000) and British Library (£25,000). These three grants accounted for 81% of grant expenditure.

Other beneficiaries included Corpus Inscriptionum Iranicum (£13,000), The Onaway Trust (£11,000), RELEASE (£10,000), International PEN Foundation (£5,000), Queen Elizabeth Fund for the Disabled (£2,800) and £2,000 each to British Heart Foundation, Multiple Sclerosis Society, NSPCC and Sargent Cancer Fund for Children. All of these organisations received the same amount in the previous year. The only new beneficiary was Henry Spink Foundation (£1,000).

Exclusions No grants to individuals.

Applications In writing to the correspondent.

The Heinz & Anna Kroch Foundation

Medical research, severe poverty or hardship

£72,000 (1998/99)

Beneficial area UK

PO Box 17, Worsley, Manchester M28 2SB

Tel. 0161 793 4201 **Fax** 0161 793 4201
e-mail hakfso@hotmail.com

Correspondent Mrs H Astle, Administrator

Trustees *Ms Ann Carol Kroch; Dr A Kashti; Christopher Richardson; Peter English; Daniel Lang.*

Information available Accounts were on file at the Charity Commission, but without a list of grants.

General The foundation gives grants to new and existing medical research projects. It supports about five/six projects each year, the amount given varying according to funds available. It also supports individuals suffering severe financial hardship who also have ongoing medical problems (applications must be made through welfare agencies – see *A Guide to Grants for Individuals in Need*).

In 1998/99 the trust had assets of £2.2 million and an income of £90,000. It gave grants totalling £71,000 but unfortunately a grants list was not included with the accounts.

Exclusions Students of any kind, churches or holidays. Funds for refurbishing hospitals and newly created care homes are not supported. Project funding is not given.

Applications Appeals are considered on a regular basis, usually every two or three months, depending upon the number of applications waiting at any one time. Applications for medical research should include details of the research, cost of the project and any further relevant information; they should be no more than four pages long. Applications always receive a reply, please include an sae.

The Kulika Charitable Trust

Sustainable agriculture, poverty alleviation and development, environment/ conservation

£115,000 to organisations (1998/99)

Beneficial area East Africa, ,mainly Uganda, and some support in the UK

4 The Mount, Guildford, Surrey GU2 4YN

Tel. 01483 563567 **Fax** 01483 562505
e-mail uk@kulika.org

Correspondent Andrew Jones

Trustees *D J Burnstone; Miss P A M Brenninkmeyer; T A Brenninkmeyer; Mrs M M E Wentworth-Stanley; A J van Amelsvoort; Dr C P Peacock; Mrs S Errington; Langersal Limited.*

Information available Accounts were provided by the trust with a report and grants list.

General The trust continued to concentrate its work in the following four main areas in 1998/99:

- provision of educational scholarships to students for East Africa, and in particular, Uganda

- development of a training and awareness programme in sustainable agriculture for farmers and others from East Africa, in particular Uganda

- support for poverty alleviation and development projects in East Africa, in particular Uganda

- support for environmental and conservation projects in the UK and East Africa.

Most of the trust's expenditure is committed to the first two of these areas. In 1998/99 £253,000 was given to individuals in the form of educational grants and scholarships and £199,000 was spent on the Sustainable Agriculture Programme.

In total the trust had assets totalling £5 million. It had an income of £406,000, (the income of £2.3 million in 1997/98 was due to the unusually high level of fundraising in that period). Grants to organisations totalled £115,000 and were listed in the accounts as follows:

General charitable	£14,000
Overseas project aid	£72,000
Sustainable agriculture	£29,000
Conservation	–

Beneficiaries of grants in excess of £1,000 were listed in the trustees' report. The Kulika Charitable Trust in Uganda received six grants totalling almost £90,000, areas to benefit included project work, core costs, sustainable agriculture and training. Other grants listed were: £15,000 to Bannabikira Daughters of Mary; £10,000 to World University Service (UK), towards the cost of administering their Campus Scholarship Scheme; and £3,000 to Child Welfare & Adoption Society (Uganda).

The trust's annual report stated that they wish to continue supporting similar projects at a similar financial level to those funded in 1998/99. It also stated that because of the need to fund work in Uganda, the trust again made no grants to projects designed to improve and conserve the environment (1996/97: £5,000; 1997/98: nil).

Applications In writing to the correspondent. The trustees meet to consider grants three times a year.

The Christopher Laing Foundation

General

£104,000 (1998/99)

Beneficial area UK

c/o Ernst & Young, 400 Capability Green, Luton LU1 3LU

Tel. 01582 643126

Correspondent P J Claessen, Accountant

Trustees *Christopher M Laing; Donald Stradling; Peter Jackson; Diana C Laing.*

Information available Full accounts were provided by the trust.

General The trust was founded in 1979. The trustees make a large number of gifts to a variety of charities in areas such as welfare, education and the environment. In 1998/99 it had an income of £175,000 and assets of £5.3 million. After administration expenses of £18,000, grants were made totalling £104,000. Each year the trust's largest grant is to Charities Aid Foundation to handle the administration of smaller grants, £40,000 in 1998/99. No grants list was provided for these donations.

A further 15 grants were made to registered charities totalling £64,000, the largest of these being £17,000 to The Lord Taverners, while National Playing Fields Association and Rugby Science Schools Appeal received £10,000 each. Smaller grants included those to NSPCC (£5,000), The Wildside Trust (£2,500) and Leeds Grammar School (£1,000).

The charity states that it has received an increasing number of requests for help and only a small proportion of the requests can be fulfilled.

Exclusions Donations are only made to registered charities.

Applications In writing to the correspondent.

The David Laing Foundation

Children, families, disability, environment

£156,000 (1999/2000)

Beneficial area Worldwide

The Studio, Mackerye End, Harpenden, Hertfordshire AL5 5DR

Correspondent David E Laing, Trustee

Trustees *David Eric Laing; John Stuart Lewis; Richard Francis Barlow; Frances Mary Laing.*

Information available Information was provided by the trust.

General In 1999/2000 the trust had assets of £4 million and an income of £134,000. General administration and accountancy costs were high at £21,000 and grants totalled £156,000. Small gifts were made out of funds deposited with the Charities Aid Foundation, totalling £65,000, further details on individual grants was not available.

The trust confirmed that it has continued its policy of making a large number of gifts to a wide and varied number of charities. Its policy is to support charities concerned with children, broken homes, people who are physically and mentally disabled, and also the environment, arts and animal welfare.

Exclusions No grants to individuals.

Applications In writing to the correspondent. Trustees meet in March, June, October and December, although applications are reviewed weekly.

The Martin Laing Foundation

General

£175,000 (1998/99)

Beneficial area UK and worldwide

c/o Ernst & Young, 400 Capability Green, Luton LU1 3LU

Tel. 01582 643126

Correspondent P J Claessen, Accountant

Trustees *Sir John Martin Laing; Donald Stradling; Brian O'Chilver; Edward Charles Laing.*

Beneficial area UK and worldwide.

Information available Full accounts were provided by the trust.

General This trust makes grants t a wide variety of charities. In 1998/99 the assets were worth £4.6 million and generated an income of £193,000. Grants totalling £175,000 were distributed, including payments for small grants

163

through the Charities Aid Foundation (£90,000).

Other grants were listed in the trust's annual report as follows:

Business in the Community	£10,000
Macmillan Cancer Relief	£10,000
Marine Stewardship Council	£25,000
NSPCC	£5,000
Westminster Pastoral Foundation	£10,000
WWF – UK	£25,000

Applications The trust states 'The trustees receive an enormaout and increasing number of requests for help. Unfortunately the trustees are only able to help a small proportion of the requests and consequently they limit their support to those charities where they have a personal connection or interest in their activities'.

The Lambert Charitable Trust

Health, welfare, Jewish, arts

£114,000 (1998/99)

Beneficial area UK and Israel

18 Hanover Street, London W1R 9HG

Tel. 020 7499 7899

Correspondent M Lambert, Trustee

Trustees M Lambert; Dr H P Lambert; H Alexander-Passe.

Information available Full accounts were on file at the Charity Commission.

General The trust's primary objective is to further charitable purposes relatin to the Jewish faith. In 1998/99 the trust had assets of £2.6 million and an income of £103,000.

In the year, 141 grants totalling £114,000 were made, they were borken down into the following areas:

Category	Total	No. of grants
Charitable purposes in Israel	£20,000	24
Jewish faith in the UK	£26,000	23
Other charitable purposes	£68,000	94

Over 20 organisations recieved donations of over £1,000. the largest grant of £10,000 was given to Jewish Care and £5,000 each wnet to THET and UCL Medical School. Among the five organisations receiving grants of £2,000 were Ben Gurion Universtiy Foundation, British Friends of the Rambah Medical Centre and Centadiary Committee. Donations of £1,000 were made to 16 charities, among thosse to benefit were British Council of the Shaare, Leonard Cheshire Foundation, Kisharon Day School, League of Jewish Women and Zedek Medical Centre.

The remainder of grants were in the range of £250 to £750. Grants included £750 each to British ORT, Lodon Philharmonic Orchestra and Save the Children Fund, £500 each to Anglo Jewish Association and JNF Charitable Trust and £250 each to British Stammering Associaion and Rainbow Song.

Applications In writing to be received by the correspondent before July for payment by 1 September.

The Langdale Trust

Social welfare, Christian, medical, general

£90,000 (1996/97)

Beneficial area Worldwide, but with a special interest in Birmingham.

c/o Lee Crowder, 39 Newhall Street, Birmingham B3 3DY

Tel. 0121 236 4477

Correspondent M J Woodward, Trustee

Trustees T R Wilson; Mrs T Whiting; M J Woodward.

Information available Accounts were on file at the Charity Commission.

General Unfortunately we have been unable to update the following information since the last edition of this guide.

The trust was establishded in 1960 by the late Antony Langdale Wilson. In 1996/97 the trust had assets of £3 million and an income of £101,000. It gave 41 grants totalling £90,000. There is a preference for local charities in the Birmingham area and those in thefileds of social welfare and health, especially with a Christian context.

Grants ranged from £500 to £5,000, with over half of the grants for £1,000 to £2,000. The largest grant of £5,000 went to the Bible Society. Other larger grants included £4,000 each to Help the Aged, Save the Children Fund and United Christian Broadcasters Ltd and £3,000 each to Council for the Protection of Rural England, Old Farmstead Art Project, Samaritans and YMCA Birmingham.

Applications In writing to the correspondent. The trustees meet in October.

The Richard Langhorn Trust

Sport for children (see below)

£50,000 (1997)

Beneficial area UK and overseas

Administration, Harlequins Rugby Football Club, Stoop Memorial Ground, Langhorn Drive, Twickenham TW2 7SX

Correspondent Bindy Lockheart

Trustees Ms G Bell; K Bray; S Langhorn; P Winterbottom; T York.

Information available We were unable to see the accounts for this trust.

General The trust makes grants towards sports charities for the benefit of children only, particularly in the areas of rugby, sailing, basketball and skiing. Grants can also be made to individuals.

In 1997 the trust had an income of £150,000 and grants were made totalling £50,000. Further information was not available.

Applications In writing to the correspondent.

The Langley Charitable Trust

Christian, general

£11,000 (1995)

Beneficial area UK, with a preference for the West Midlands, and worldwide

Wheatmoor Farm, 301 Tamworth, Sutton Coldfield, West Midlands B75 6JP

Correspondent J P Gilmour, Trustee

Trustees J P Gilmour; Mrs S S Gilmour.

Information available Full accounts were on file at the Charity Commission.

General Unfortunately we have been unable to update the following information since the last edition of this guide.

The trust makdes grants to evangelical Christian organisations and to other charities in the fields of welfare, medicine and health. It makes grants in the UK and worldwide, but appears to have some preference for the West Midlands.

In 1997 the trust had an income of £414,000. Its total expenditure was £209,000, but information about how much of this was given in grants was not available.

The most recent year for which accounts were available on file at the Charity Commission was 1995, when the trust had an income of £145,000 and donations totalled £12,000, including three grants to individuals totalling £1,200.

Larger grants were made to Holy Trinity Church (£3,000), Birmingham Bible Institution (£2,300) and London Bible College and Send a Cow (£1,000 each). Other grants ranged from £20 to £600 and included those to Teen Challenge, Sutton Coldfield Baptist Church, United Christian Broadcasts and NSPCC.

Exclusions No grants to animals or birds.

Applications In writing to the correspondent.

The R J Larg Family Charitable Trust

Education, health, medical research, arts particularly music

About £100,000 (1999/2000)

Beneficial area UK but generally Scotland, particularly Tayside

Messrs Thorntons WS, 50 Castle Street, Dundee DD1 3RU

Tel. 01382 229111 **Fax** 01382 202288

Correspondent N Barclay

Trustees R W Gibson; D A Brand; Mrs S A Stewart.

Information available Information was provided by the trust.

General The trust has an annual income of about £127,000. Grants, which totalled about £100,000 in 1999/2000, ranged between £250 and £6,000 and were given to a variety of organisations.

These included organisations concerned with cancer research and other medical charities, youth organisations, university student's associations and amateur musical groups.

Beneficiaries of larger grants included: High School, Dundee (£6,000 for the cadet force and £5,000 for the Larg Scholarship Fund); Whitehall Theatre Trust (£4,000); Macmillan Cancer Relief – Dundee and Sense Scotland Children's Hospice (each £2,500); and £2,000 to Rachel House.

Exclusions Grants are not available for individuals.

Applications In writing to the correspondent. Trustees meet to consider grants in February and August.

Largsmount Ltd

Jewish

£154,000 (1996/97)

Beneficial area UK and overseas

Cohen Arnold & Co Accountants, 267 Durham Road, Gateshead, Tyne & Wear NE9 5AD

Correspondent The Trustees

Trustees *Z M Kaufman; Mrs Z M Kaufman; C S Kaufman.*

Information available Accounts were on file at the charity commission.

General Unfortunately we have been unable to update the following information since the last edition of this guide.

This trust supports orthodox Jewish charities.

In 1996/97 it had assets of £1.5 million and had an income of £293,000, including £161,000 donations received. Grants totalled £154,000, but no

information was available as to the organisations supported.

Applications In writing to the trustees.

Rachel & Jack Lass Charities Ltd

Jewish, children, education, medical research

£154,000 (1997/98)

Beneficial area England, Scotland and Wales

15 Neville Drive, London N2 0QS

Tel. 020 8446 8431 **Fax** 020 8458 4578

Correspondent Leonard Lass, Governor

Trustees *Leonard Lass; Sally Lass.*

Information available Accounts were on file at the Charity Commission.

General The trust gives primarily to Jewish charities preferring those involved with children, education and medical research.

In 1997/98 the trust had an income of £163,000, all but £2,500 of which was from donations received. Grants totalled £154,000. Grants over £900 were listed in the accounts and were made to 15 organsations, other smaller donations totalled £12,000 but were not listed separately. Some were to non-Jewish causes.

Five grants were made over £10,000, the largest grant was £22,000 to Ravenswood Foundation. Grants of £20,000 each went to Yesodey Hatorah Schools, Yeshira Horomo Talmudical College and Telz Talmudical Academy & Talmud Torah Trust and £12,000 to Mogen David Adom. Grants of £10,000 each went to Emuno Educational Centre, Cosmon (Belz) Limited, Friends of Harim Establishments and Gevurath Ari Torah Academy Trust.

Other grants ranging from £900 to £1,500 included Jewish Care, Youth Aliyah and Life Hospital Trust.

Exclusions No grants to students.

Applications In writing to the correspondent.

The Lauffer Family Charitable Foundation

Jewish, general

£176,000 (1998/99)

Beneficial area Worldwide, i.e. UK (including Isle of Man and Channel Islands), Canada, Australia, New Zealand, The Union of South Africa, Pakistan, Sri Lanka, any other country in the British Commonwealth, the State of Israel and USA

18 Norrice Lea, London N2 0RE

Tel. 020 8455 8877

e-mail bethlauffer@lineone.net

Correspondent J S Lauffer, Trustee

Trustees *Mrs R R Lauffer; J S Lauffer; G L Lauffer; R M Lauffer.*

Information available Accounts were on file at the Charity Commission.

General In 1998/99 the foundation had assets of £4.2 million, generating an income of £160,000. Grants totalling £176,000 were made to 139 organisations. The top 12 grants were listed in the accounts.

Project Seed received the largest donation of £25,000. British Friends of Somayach received £18,000 while Spiro Institute received £15,000. Grants of £5,000 each went to British Friends of Sarah Herzoy Memorial Hospital, Jewish Deaf Association, Shvut Ami and Jewish Learning Exchange, £4,000 to Menorah Foundation School, £3,000 to University of Cambridge and £1,000 to Jerusalem Foundation.

The remaining 127 grants totalled £88,000. The foundation supports many of the same organisations each year.

Exclusions No support for individuals.

Applications In writing to the correspondent.

The Mrs F B Laurence 1976 Charitable Settlement

Social welfare, medical, disability, environment

£132,000 (1998/99)

Beneficial area Worldwide

c/o Payne Hicks Beach, 10 New Square, London WC2A 3QG

Tel. 020 7465 4300

Trustees *M Tooth; G S Brown; D A G Sarre.*

Information available Full accounts were on file at the Charity Commission.

General The trust was established in 1976 by Mrs Florence Beatrice Laurence who died in 1982. By 1998/99 the assets had a market value of £2.8 million generating an income of £106,000. A total of £132,000 was given away in 125 grants. Donations went to a range of beneficiaries with some preference for social welfare, medical, disability and environment organisations. Grants mainly went to new charities.

Over 60 grants were made of over £1,000. By far the largest donation was for £20,000 which went to Institute of Neurology to support a research project in the area of post-stroke recovery of the optic nerve. Other larger grants went to Emmaus UK – Greenwich (£5,000), Lords (£2,500), Friends of Russian Children and MIND (£2,000 each) and Angels International (£1,500).

Grants of £1,000 went to Ability Net, Blond McIndoe Centre, Gurkha Welfare Trust, Friends of the Earth, National Meningitis Trust, RSPCA and Shelter. The remainder of grants were for under £1,000. Smaller grants of £750 each went to Woodland Trust, Centre for Brain Injury Rehabilitation and Prison Reform Trust; Camping Holidays for Inner-city Kids (£500); and St Mary's Social Action Centre (£250).

Exclusions No support for individuals.

Applications In writing to the correspondent. Applications will only be considered from UK-registered charities and they must be accompanied by a set of the latest accounts. Trustees meet twice a year.

The Kathleen Laurence Trust

General

£87,000 (1998/99)

Beneficial area UK

Trustee Department, Coutts & Co, P O Box 1236, 6 High Street, Chelmsford, Essex CM1 1BQ

Tel. 01245 292484

Correspondent The Manager

Trustees *Coutts & Co.*

Information available Full accounts were on file at the Charity Commission.

General In 1998/99 the assets stood at about £3.2 million with an income of only £98,000. This was given in 55 grants ranging from £500 to £4,000. The trust states that 'donations are given to a wide range of institutions, particularly favouring smaller organisations and those with specific requirements such as for the purchase of land, the restoration of cathedrals, churches or other buildings of beauty or interest to which the public can have access or for the specific raising of funds for an anniversary year'. Grants are also given towards organisations concerned with people who are ill or mentally or physically disabled.

The largest grants were to British Kidney Patient Association and IVCS (£4,000 each). Dreams Come True and Rinoht Special Trustees both received £3,000 each.

There were 24 grants of £2,000; 1 of £1,500; 18 of £1,000; and 7 of £500 were awarded. The larger grants included £2,000 each to Hope House, Imperial Cancer Research, National Asthma Campaign, Papworth Trust, Prince's Trust, Rainbow Trust and Wildside Trust and £1,000 each to Evelina Children's Hospital, Society at Work, SPADEWORK and Stroke Association. Organisations receiving smaller grants included ACTIVE, King Edward Grammar School and Ron Pickering Memorial Fund. A number of grants were recurrent from the previous year.

Exclusions No donations are made for running costs, management expenses or to individuals.

Applications In writing to the correspondent. Trustees meet quarterly, usually in February, May, August and November.

The Edgar E Lawley Foundation

Older people, disability, children, medical research

£160,000 (1999/2000)

Beneficial area UK, with a preference for the West Midlands

Hollyoak, 1 White House Drive, Barnt Green, Birmingham B45 8HF

Tel. 0121 445 3536 **Fax** 0121 445 3636

Correspondent Philip J Cooke, Executive Trustee

Trustees *Mrs M D Heath, Chair; J H Cooke; Mrs G V H Hilton; P J Cooke; Miss E Jacobs; Prof. J Caldwell; F S Jackson.*

Information available Full accounts were on file at the Charity Commission.

General The trust's primary objects are 'the making of grants to charitable bodies for provision of medical care and services to children and the aged, the advancement of medicine and for educational purposes'. There is a preference for the West Midlands.

In 1999/2000 the trust had assets of £3.6 million and an income of £177,000. Grants totalling £160,000 were made to 83 organisations.

Two substantial grants were made in the year, to Imperial College School of Medicine – also a major beneficiary in 1998/99 – towards equipment costs (£30,000) and Kings Fund towards a maternity care evaluation project (£24,000).

The remainder of grants were in the range of £500 to £5,000, but were mainly for £1,000 or £1,500. Recipients included £5,000 to Jigsaw; £1,500 each to 2 Care, Aidis Trust, Children Nationwide, Motability, Sense and Walsall Society for the Blind; and £1,300 to Calver Trust Kielder. 33 grants of £1,000 included those to Action for Kids Charitable Trust, Counsel & Care, Fight for Sight, Rainbow Trust Children's Charity and St Loye's Foundation. Grants of £500 each went to Stockport Cerebral Palsy Society and Wrexham PHAB Club.

Many grants were repeated from the previous year. A mix of local and UK organisations were supported.

Exclusions No grants to individuals.

Applications In writing to the correspondent in March or April.

The Lawlor Foundation

Social welfare, education, general

£116,000 (1999/2000)

Beneficial area Principally Northern Ireland, also Republic of Ireland, London and the home counties

Traceys Farm, Stanford Rivers, Ongar, Essex CM5 9QD

Tel. 01392 252184 **Fax** 01392 252184

Correspondent Mrs Carley Brown

Trustees *Virginia Lawlor; Kelly Lawlor; Martin Spiro; Frank Baker; K R P Marshall; Blanca Fernadez Drayton.*

Information available A comprehensive annual report and accounts were provided by the foundation.

General The foundation has four main objectives: 'support for organisations working with troubled adolescents (these organisations having an identifiable Irish component); social welfare and education in Ireland (or with an identifiable Irish component); educational grants for disadvantaged students with an Irish background; and projects underpinning the peace process in Ireland.' A number of donations also reflect the trustees' personal interests.

The trustees have a particular interest in promoting co-operation and mutual understanding between the peoples of Ireland, North and South. Currently the emphasis is on education. The principal beneficiaries include a number of Northern Irish educational establishments and individual students (who must have an Irish background), British-based organisations which support Irish immigrants, and vulnerable young people. Grants can be one-off or recurrent and can include core funding and salaries.

Grants to individuals range from £100 to £500 and to organisations from £250 to £10,000. The maximum length of support is normally three years, but schools are invited to re-apply at the end of this period.

In 1999/2000 the trust had assets of £2.4 million and an income of £96,000.

Grants totalled £116,000 and were broken down as follows:

Area	No. of grants	£
Britain	7	37,000
Northern Ireland	10	62,000
Republic of Ireland	1	7,500
British Isles	22	9,000

Category	No. of grants	£
Education	32	92,000
Social welfare	6	23,000
Peace and reconciliation	1	1,300
Women's interests	1	500

The largest grant was £21,000 to Shankhill Education Project in Belfast, which was set up three years ago by the foundation and is administered by the trustees. Three grants of £10,000 each went to Jesus College, Cambridge, a recurrent annual grant to help financially disadvantaged undergraduates from Northern Ireland; Brent Adolescent Centre, London, a recurrent annual grant to support core costs for the organisation which provides treatment and research into adolescent mental and emotional problems; and St Louise's College, Belfast to help financially disadvantaged former pupils at UK and Irish universities. Tullow Community School, County Carlow, received a £7,500 recurrent annual grant to help disadvantaged former pupils and support school projects and individual pupils.

Other grants ranged from £500 to £6,000 including those to: La Salle Boys' Secondary School, Belfast (£6,000); Irish Studies Centre, University of London (£5,000); Brandon Centre, London (£3,000); Lifeline, Belfast (£1,300); Tara Counselling Service, Omagh (£1,000); and Belfast Women's Training Services (£500).

Exclusions No grants are made in response to general appeals from large well-known organisations or from organisations outside the geographical areas of Ireland, London and the Home Counties. Grants are not normally made to the arts, medicine, the environment, expeditions, children's projects or international causes.

Applications By letter to the correspondent at any time, with a description of the project and a copy of the latest accounts. Preliminary telephone enquiries are welcomed. Applications will only be acknowledged if they relate to the trustees' general interests. The trustees normally meet in January, April, July and October.

Please note that the trust has many ongoing commitments which restrict the funds available for new applicants.

The Carole & Geoffrey Lawson Foundation

Jewish, general

£198,000 (1998/99)

Beneficial area UK

Stilemans, Munstead, Godalming, Surrey GU8 4AB

Tel. 01483 420757

Correspondent Geoffrey Lawson, Trustee

Trustees *Geoffrey C H Lawson; Hon. Carole Lawson; Harold I Connick.*

Information available Full accounts were on file at the Charity Commission.

General It is the trust's policy to consider appeals from charitable causes with a previous track record covering the welfare of children, relief of poverty and advancement of the arts and education. In addition, the trustees have a commitment to the work of Liver Research Trust and the re-building of Covent Garden.

In 1998/99 the trust had assets of £1.1 million and an income of £39,000. Grants totalled £198,000. It received approximately 50 applications in the year and gave to 17 organisations, 8 of which were supported in the previous year. The largest grants went to Royal Opera House Trust which received £54,000. Other substantial grants went to Liver Research Trust (£50,000), Young Minds (£30,000), Royal School for the Blind (£15,000) and Jewish Care (£10,000). Grants under £10,000 included Macmillan Cancer Relief (£8,000), Ze-er Argaman (£6,000), British ORT (£5,500) with £5,000 each to Yvonne Arnaud Theatre Trust, Community Security Trust and Greater London Fund for the Blind. Recipients of smaller grants include David Sheppard Conservation Foundation (£1,000), Commonwealth Jewish Trust (£500) and Spiro Institute (£250).

Exclusions No grants to local charities or individuals.

Applications In writing to the correspondent.

The Raymond & Blanche Lawson Charitable Trust

General

£150,000 (1998/99)

Beneficial area UK, with an interest in West Kent and East Sussex

28 Barden Road, Tonbridge, Kent TN9 1TX

Tel. 01732 352183 **Fax** 01732 352621

Correspondent Mrs P E V Banks, Trustee

Trustees *John V Banks; John A Bertram; Mrs P E V Banks.*

Information available Full accounts were on file at the Charity Commission. Some information and a grants list was provided by the trust.

General The trust has a preference for local organisations and generally supports charities within the following categories:

* scouts, guides, brownies, cubs etc.
* preservation of buildings
* hospices
* care in the community
* assistance for the blind
* armed forces benevolent funds.

In 1998/99 grants amounting to £150,000 were awarded to 85 organisations. About half of the organisations supported had received grants in the previous year.

By far the largest grant of £17,000 went to Abbeyfield Groombridge Society. Two grants of £10,000 each were awarded, these went to Age Concern and Maidstone Trust Kent River Walk. The next largest grant went to Kent & East Sussex Hospital Trust for £6,400. £5,000 each was given to Kent Air Ambulance Appeal, The Heart of Kent Hospice, Marden Memorial Hall, St George's Children's Community Project, Hospice in the Weald and Royal Society for Deaf Children.

About 50 other grants were made over £1,000. Beneficiaries included £3,000 each to Canterbury Oast Trust and Compaid Trust, £2,000 each to Wateringbury Guides & Scouts, NSPCC and Kent Association for the Blind, £1,500 to Vinters Park Trust and £1,000 each to Parenthood, Age Concern, YMCA Housing, Trinity Hospice, English Heritage, Carers First, Salvation Army and RNLI.

The remainder of grants were under £1,000, among those receiving grants were Heartline (£760); £500 each to Barnabas Trust, Singalong Group, Sparks, British Wireless for the Blind; and Queen Elizabeth Grammar School Appeal (£250).

Exclusions No support for churches or individuals.

Applications In writing to the correspondent.

The Lawson-Beckman Charitable Trust

Jewish, welfare, education, arts

£66,000 (1998/99)

Beneficial area UK

c/o Hacker Young, St Alphage House, 2 Fore Street, London EC2Y 5DH

Tel. 020 7216 4600

Correspondent M A Lawson, Trustee

Trustees *M A Lawson; J N Beckman.*

Information available Full accounts were on file at the Charity Commission.

General The report states that the trust gives grants for the 'relief of poverty, support of the arts and general charitable purposes'. Grants are allocated two years in advance. In 1998/99 the trust had assets of £1.4 million and an income of £120,000. Its expenses were only £3,000 and grants totalled £66,000, leaving a surplus of £51,000. The 34 grants awarded ranged from £200 to around £10,000, but were usually for about £1,000. They can be broken down as follows:

Health & welfare	£35,000	(14 grants)
Education & cultural	£28,000	(13 grants)
Arts & humanities	£3,000	(7 grants)

The trust mainly supports Jewish causes, with the largest grants being given to Jewish Care (£13,000), Maccabi Foundation and Norwood Ravenswood (£10,000 each) and Nightingale House and UCL Development Fund (£5,000 each). Other sizeable grants went to Youth Aligah (£4,000), British ORT (£3,000), Who Cares? Trust (£2,000) and SAGE (£1,000).

All other grants were generally for around £250 to £500 and were also mainly to Jewish organisations such as Aid for Alyn, Sotti Foundation and Zemel Choir. Non-Jewish beneficiaries included Arthritis Research, Cancer Research Campaign and MIND – Enfield.

Applications In writing to the correspondent, but please note that grants are allocated two years in advance.

The Leach Fourteenth Trust

Disability, general

About £80,000 (1998/99)

Beneficial area UK, with some preference for south west England and the home counties, and overseas

Nettleton Mill, Castle Combe, Nr Chippenham, Wiltshire SN14 7NJ

Correspondent Roger Murray-Leach, Trustee

Trustees *W J Henderson; M A Hayes; Mrs J M M Nash; Roger Murray-Leach.*

Information available Accounts were on file at the Charity Commission for 1997/98. Most of this information was provided by the trust.

General Unfortunately we were unable to update the following information since the last edition of this guide.

Although the trust's objectives are general, the trustees support mainly disability organisations. The trust has previously also had a preference for conservation (ecological) organisations. In practice there is a preference for the south west of England and the home counties. In 1998/99 the trust had assets of £2.4 million and an income of about £80,000, all of which was given in grants.

A few charities receive regular donations. The trustees prefer to give single grants for specific projects rather than towards general funding, and also favour small organisations or projects. The trust informed us that in recent years it has supported a local swimming pool appeal for autistic children and causes such as child bereavement care and cancer care. Grants are usually £500 to £10,000, but can be as large as £50,000.

In 1997/98 the largest grants were £5,500 to Plan International UK, £5,000 to

Deafblind UK – Changing Faces and £4,000 to Winston's Wish. In total 154 grants were made, and most of the others were above £1,000. Other beneficiaries of grants between £1,000 and £2,000 included British Wheelchair Sports Foundation (Stoke Mandeville), Gurkha Welfare, Royal Kinnear Trust, Isles of Scilly Museum Association, Hope and Homes for Children, Salvation Army, Dorothy House and Jersey Wildlife Preservation.

Exclusions Only registered charities based in the UK are supported (the trust only gives overseas via a UK-based charity). No grants to: individuals, including for gap years or trips abroad; private schools, unless for people with disabilities or learning difficulties; or for pets.

Applications In writing to the correspondent. Only successful appeals can expect a reply. A representative of the trust occasionally visits potential beneficiaries. There is an annual meeting of trustees in the autumn, but not necessarily to consider grants. Grants tend to be distributed twice a year.

The Leche Trust

Georgian art, music and architecture

£166,000 to organisations (1998/99)

Beneficial area UK

84 Cicada Road, London SW18 2NZ

Tel. 020 8870 6233   **Fax** 020 8870 6233

Correspondent Mrs Louisa Lawson, Secretary

Trustees *Primrose Arnander, Chair; Ian Bristow; Felicity Guinness; Simon Jervis; Robin Porteous; John Riddell; Simon Wethered.*

Information available Full accounts were on file at the Charity Commission.

General The trust was founded and endowed by the late Angus Acworth in 1950. Grants are normally made in the following categories:

- preservation of buildings and their contents, primarily of the Georgian period

- repair and conservation of church furniture, including such items as bells or monuments, but not for structural

repairs to the fabric – preference is given to objects of the Georgian period

- assistance to the arts and for conservation, including museums

- assistance to organisations concerned with music and drama

- assistance to students from overseas during the last six months of their doctoral postgraduate studies in the UK.

In 1998/99 the trust had assets of £6.5 million and an income of £220,000. After expenses of £53,000, it approved 59 grants totalling £223,000 (£57,000 went on grants to individuals). Grants ranged from £400 to £15,000. They can be broken down as follows:

Arts
34 grants totalling £70,000. Causes to benefit included Opera Circus (£5,000); Spitalfields Festival (£4,000); £3,000 each to The Georgian Concert Society, Operate and The English Concert; and Rising Roots Productions (£1,000).

Church furniture and monuments
14 grants totalling £40,000. Beneficiaries included St Andrew's Church, Powys (£10,000), St Cuthbert's Church, Devon (£8,000), Carlisle Cathedral – armoire, (£2,300) and St Mary's Church, Shropshire (£1,000).

Education, institutions and museums
Seven grants totalling £34,000. Among those receiving grants were National Opera Studio (£2,000 a year for three years), Tate Gallery, London (£5,000) and Royal Naval Museum (£3,000).

Historic buildings
Four grants totalling £21,000. Recipients included Chiswick House, London (£10,000 over two years), The Blue Coat School, Liverpool, (£4,000) National Trust for Scotland (£3,800) and Lady Margaret Hungerford, Wiltshire (£3,000).

Grants to individuals
Grants totalling £57,000. Beneficiaries receiving grants on behalf of individuals include London Academy of Music & Dramatic Art (£5,000 a year for three years), Central School of Ballet (£5,000), London Contemporary Dance School (£3,000) and five other grants to students ranging between £1,500 and £3,000.

Grants totalling £25,000 were made to 38 overseas students from 22 countries. The average grant was £660.

Exclusions No grants are made for: religious bodies; overseas missions; schools and school buildings; social welfare; animals; medicine; expeditions; UK students other than music students.

Applications In writing to the secretary. Trustees meet three times a year, in February, June and October and applications need to be received the month before the trustees meet.

The Arnold Lee Charitable Trust

Jewish, educational, health

£86,000 (1998/99)

Beneficial area UK

47 Orchard Court, Portman Square, London W1H 9PD

Tel. 020 7486 8918

Correspondent A Lee, Trustee

Trustees *A Lee; H Lee; A L Lee.*

Information available Full accounts were on file at the Charity Commission, but without an up-to-date grants list.

General The policy of the trustees is to distribute income to 'established charities of high repute' for any charitable purpose or object. The trust supports a large number of Jewish organisations.

In 1998/99 grants totalled £86,000. The trust had assets of £1.3 million and an income of £90,000, mostly from rent.

The lastest grants list filed at the Charity Commission was from 1997/98 when 63 grants were made totalling £89,000. The largest grant went to Joint Jewish Charitable Trust (£34,000). Other recipients of substantial grants included Project SEED (£7,500), Jewish Care (£6,500), Lubavich Foundations (£5,000), The Home of Aged Jews (£2,500) and Yesodey Hatorah School and Friends of Akim (£2,400 each).

Virtually all remaining grants were to Jewish charities and most were for around £500 or less. Recipients included The President's Club (£600), Gesher (£500), British Technion Society and Institute of Higher Rabbinical Studies (£250 each), Bolton Village Appeal Fund (£100) and Society of Friends of the Torah (£50).

Exclusions Grants are rarely made to individuals.

Applications In writing to the correspondent.

The Leigh Trust

Drug and alcohol rehabilitation, criminal justice, asylum seekers/ racial equality

£465,000 (1999/2000)

Beneficial area UK and overseas

Clive Marks and Company, 44a New Cavendish Street, London W1M 7LG

Tel. 020 7486 4663 **Fax** 020 7224 2942

Correspondent The Trustees

Trustees *Hon. David Bernstein; Dr R M E Stone; C Moorehead.*

Information available Information was provided by the trust.

General This trust was established in 1976. It makes grants to a variety of registered charities concerned with:

- drug and alcohol rehabilitation
- criminal justice
- asylum seekers/racial equality

It is the policy of the trustees to support those organisations which are in greatest need. In 1999/2000 the trust had assets of £4.6 million and an income of £134,000. The current policy is to distribute investment revenue and a proportion of capital gains. Grants were made totalling £465,000. The 20 largest grants were listed by the trust and totalled £289,000.

The major beneficiary was Inquest Charitable Trust which helps bereaved families and received two grants of £15,000 each over the year. Other substantial donations were made to Joint Council for the Welfare of Immigrants and Chemical Dependency Centre (£25,000 each), Rehabilitation of Addicted Prisoners (£22,000) and Refugee Council and Nelson House Recovery Trust (£20,000 each).

Other larger grants were £15,000 each to Public Concern at Work, EPRA (UK) and Prisoners Abroad and £12,000 to Paddington Development Trust. Nine grants of £10,000 each included those to Addiction Counselling World, Charities Evaluation Service, European Association for the Treatment of Addictions (UK), Institute for Citizenship, Penal Reform International (NACRO) and Tripscope. Unlisted grants under £10,000 totalled £176,000.

Exclusions The trust does not make grants to individuals.

Applications Initial applications should be made in writing to the registered office of the trust, enclosing most recent accounts and an sae. Applicants should state clearly on one side of A4 what their charity does and what they are requesting funding for. They should provide a detailed budget and show other sources of funding for the project. The charity may be requested to complete an application form. It is likely that an officer of the trust will wish to visit the project before any grant is made. Trustees' meetings are held quarterly.

The trustees can only respond favourably to very few applications.

The Mark Leonard Trust

Environmental education, youth, general

£142,000 (1999/2000)

Beneficial area Worldwide, but mainly UK

9 Red Lion Court, London EC4A 3EF

Tel. 020 7410 0330

Correspondent M A Pattison, Director

Trustees *Mrs Z Sainsbury; Miss J S Portrait; J J Sainsbury; M L Sainsbury.*

Information available Information was provided by the trust.

General The trust is one of the Sainsbury Family Charitable Trusts (see *A Guide to the Major Trusts Volume 1*) which share a common administration. The trust has a strong preference for environmental education and youth work. It favours projects which are innovative and can be successfully replicated or become self-sustaining.

In 1999/2000 the trust had assets of £6.2 million and an income of £747,000, the settlor made a donation of £519,000 which has been added to the expendable endowment. During the year the trustees approved 23 grants totalling £210,000, some of which were payable over more than one year; grants totalling £142,000 were actually paid. Approved grants were broken down into the following categories:

- Environment: £84,000 (nine grants between £1,000 and £38,000)

- Youth work: £115,000 (eight grants between £1,000 and £48,000)
- General: £12,000 (three grants between £2,000 and £5,000)

Environment

Grants are made for environmental education, particularly supporting projects displaying practical ways of involving children and young adults. The trustees rarely support new educational materials in isolation, but are more interested in helping pupils and teachers to develop a theme over time (such as renewable energy), perhaps combining IT resources for data gathering and communication with exchange visits and sharing of information and ideas between schools. The trustees are particularly interested in projects that enable children and young people to develop a sense of ownership of the project over time, and that provide direct support to teachers to deliver exciting and high quality education in the classroom. Among those to receive grants were:

Children's Play Council – £38,000 to help fund an internet-based initiative to encourage young people in issues of sustainable transport.

National Energy Foundation – £7,000 towards the PoweEd scheme to install small-scale renewable energy in 50 schools, and provide back-up support and educational resources.

Community Car-Share Network – £2,500 to carry out research, and find a solution to the insurance problems faced by community car-sharing projects.

Youth work

Grants are made for projects that: support the rehabilitation of young people who have become marginalised and involved in anti-social or criminal activities; extend and add value to the existing use of school buildings; and encourage greater involvement of parents, school leavers and volunteers in extra-curricular activities. Projects which benefited include:

Scotswood Area Strategy, Newcastle – £48,000 to fund and develop an Attendance Project which works with children who, for a variety of reasons, fail to attend school.

Schools Councils UK – £12,000 for a part-time training co-ordinator to support teachers and pupils wishing to establish school councils.

Leyton Orient Community Sports – £5,000 towards the sports educational package being delivered in nine secondary schools in the London borough of Hackney.

General

The three grants went to:

Goal UK – £5,000 for emergency work in East Timor

Interact – £5,000 to continue support for the recycling of computers largely for training purposes overseas

Rise Phoenix – £2,000 towards a proposed theatre tour of Kosovo.

Exclusions Grants are not normally made to individuals.

Applications Proposals are generally invited by the trustees. Unsolicited applications are discouraged and are unlikely to be successful, even if they fall within an area in which the trustees are interested. Last year the trustees met four times.

The Ralph Levy Charitable Company Ltd

Educational, medical, general

£178,000 (1998/99)

Beneficial area UK

14 Chesterfield Street, London W1X 7HF
Tel. 020 7499 9492
Correspondent C J F Andrews, Director
Trustees D S Levy; S M Levy; C J F Andrews.

Information available Accounts were on file at the Charity Commission, but without a grants list.

General The trust has general charitable purposes with a preference for education and medical organisations.

In 1998/99 the trust had assets of £1.1 million and an income of £64,000. A total of £178,000 was given in 69 donations. An educational project in Israel received 3 grants, the remaining 66 were given in the UK. One donation of £125,000 was made, this was substantially funded from the company's accumulated surplus of £1.1 million.

Exclusions No educational grants to individuals.

Applications In writing to the correspondent.

The Sir Edward Lewis Foundation

General

£69,000 (1997/98)

Beneficial area UK and overseas, with a preference for Surrey

Messrs Rawlinson & Hunter, Eagle House, 110 Jermyn Street, London SW1Y 6RH
Tel. 020 7451 9000
Correspondent M Harris, Trustee
Trustees R A Lewis; M Harris.

Information available Full accounts were on file at the Charity Commission.

General The trust was established in 1972 by Sir Edward Roberts Lewis. By 1997/98 it had assets of £6.5 million producing an income of £122,000. After expenses of £5,000, grants totalling £69,000 were awarded.

The trust has revised its policy and now plans to make one substantial donation every two or three years to an appropriate cause as well as smaller donations on an annual basis. Therefore it will not distribute all its income every year. The trustees prefer to support charities known personally to them and those favoured by the settlor. Of the 82 grants made in the year, 62 had been supported previously. The largest donation went to St Bartholomew's Church, Leigh for £4,000, with Institute of Economic Affairs and Royal British Legion receiving £3,000 each. Other larger grants were £2,000 each to King Edward VII's Hospital, SeeAbility and St Mary's 150th Anniversary Appeal with £1,500 each to Heatherley Cheshire Home, Music Trades Benevolent Society, Reeds School, Shipwrecked Fisherman's Society and St John Ambulance.

Grants of £1,000 were awarded to 23 organisations including Royal Academy of Music, Ex-Services Mental Welfare Society, St Francis Nursing Home and Great Ormond Street Children's Hospital.

The remainder of grants were in the range of £200 to £750, groups to benefit included Barnardos, Iris Fund, Motability, St Luke's Hospital for Clergy and Scope.

In 1996/97 a substantial donation of £100,000 was made to the Arthritis and Rheumatism Council.

171

Exclusions Grants are only given to charities, projects or people known to the trustees.

Applications In writing to the correspondent. The trustees meet every six months.

The Lindale Educational Foundation

Roman Catholic

£171,000 (1997/98)

Beneficial area UK and overseas

6 Orme Court, London W2 4RL

Correspondent J Valero

Trustees *Netherhall Educational Association; Greygarth Association; Dawliffe Hall Educational Foundation.*

Information available Full information was provided by the trust.

General The trust's objects are to make grants to advance the Roman Catholic religion and for educational purposes. In past years grants have been made to institutions which train priests. 'The trustees have committed funds available for some years ahead to a number of specific projects and causes which they know well.'

In 1997/98 the trust's assets totalled only £11,000. It is heavily reliant on covenanted donations for its grant-making and received £161,000 in the year. There were no administration costs during the year. Grants totalling £171,000 were awarded to five organisations, two of which were corporate trustees of the foundation.

Donations made in the year were:

- £86,000 to Collegio Romano della Santa Croce towards training priests
- £61,000 to Netherhall Educational Association for activities at Wickenden Manor, a centre for retreats and study activities
- £14,000 to Dawliffe Hall Educational Foundation
- £7,000 to Thornycroft Hall
- £3,500 to Dunreath Study Centre in Glasgow.

Applications In writing to the correspondent, but note the above comments.

The Lister Charitable Trust

Watersports

£15,000 (1998/99) **but see below**

Beneficial area UK

Windyridge, The Close, Totteridge, London N20 8PJ

Tel. 020 8445 4379 **Fax** 020 8445 3156
e-mail sarah.sharkey@talk21.com

Correspondent Mrs S J Sharkey

Trustees *Noel A V Lister, Chair; David A Collingwood; David J Lister; Benjamin P Cussons; Stephen J Chipperfield.*

Information available Full accounts were provided by the trust.

General The trust aims to help disadvantaged young people through watersport-based activities. The UK Sailing Academy is regularly supported.

In 1998/99 the trust had assets of £8.8 million generating an income of £320,000. Grants to seven organisations totalled £15,000. Administration expenses totalled £28,000. In the previous year grants totalled £244,000, the trust regularly has a large surplus income.

Grants were given to 3rd Totnes Sea Scouts (£7,500), UK Sailing Academy (£5,000), Sailability (£1,000), Lyford Cay (£620), Whizz-Kidz (£500), Treasury Cay Community Centre (£300) and Central America Fund (£100).

Exclusions Applications not related to watersports or from individuals are not considered or acknowledged.

Applications In writing to the correspondent. Applications are considered at any time of the year.

Harry Livingstone Charitable Trust

Jewish, general

£142,000 (1998/99)

Beneficial area UK

Westholme, The Springs, Park Road, Bowdon, Altrincham, Cheshire WA14 3JH

Tel. & Fax 0161 928 3232

Correspondent Jack Livingstone, Trustee

Trustees *J Livingstone; Mrs H Bloom.*

Information available Accounts were on file at the Charity Commission, with a very brief narrative report.

General This trust makes grants to Jewish organisations and also for general charitable purposes. In 1998/99 its assets totalled £1.2 million, it had an income of £54,000 and made grants totalling £142,000 (£12,000 in 1997/98 and £50,000 in 1996/97).

Grants were made to 10 organisations in the year. As has been the case in previous years, major grants were given to both Jack Livingstone Charitable Trust and Hannah Bloom Charitable Trust – presumably connected with the trustees of this trust – they received £65,000 each.

Other grants for the year were £4,000 to Norman Museum; £2,000 each to Heathlands and Southport New Synagogue; £1,000 each to Manchester Jewish Federation – Sale, Altrincham and District Spastics Association, Southport Jewish Convalescent and Aged Home and Alone in London and £250 to One to One Charity.

Applications The trust does not respond to unsolicited applications.

Jack Livingstone Charitable Trust

Jewish, general

£70,000 (1997/98)

Beneficial area UK and worldwide, with a preference for Manchester

Westholme, The Springs, Park Road, Bowdon, Altrincham, Cheshire WA14 3JH

Tel. & Fax 0161 928 3232

Correspondent Mrs Janice Livingstone, Trustee

Trustees *Mrs J V Livingstone; Mrs H Bloom.*

Information available Full accounts were on file at the Charity Commission.

General In 1998/99 the trust had an income of £127,000 and an expenditure of £81,000. This information was obtained from the Charity Commission database. Unfortunately further information for this year was not available in the public files and the following information is repeated from the last edition of this guide.

In 1997/98 the trust's assets totalled £1.5 million. It had an income from investments of £72,000. Grants were made to mainly Jewish organisations and totalled £70,000. Grants of £100 or more were made to 25 organisations, with the remainder totalling £630. It appears that the trust makes both one-off and ongoing grants.

The main beneficiary was JPAIME which received £50,000. Other larger grants were Ashten Trust (£5,000), Christies Hospital (£3,200), Community Security Trust (£2,500), DFS Extension Charitable Trust and Langdon College (£2,000 each) and Aish Hatora (£1,000).

Other grants ranged between £100 to £700, at least nine of these were to Jewish organisations, including Sale & District Hebrew Congregation, Tay Sachs Appeal, Tel Aviv University Trust and Beth Shalom Holocaust Memorial Centre. Non-Jewish beneficiaries included Emmanuel College in Cambridge, The Lords Taverners, North West Lung Centre and Royal Marsden NHS Trust.

Applications The trust does not respond to unsolicited applications.

Lloyd's Charities Trust

General

£425,000 (1999)

Beneficial area UK, with some interest in London

One Lime Street, London EC3M 7HA

Tel. 020 7327 1000 ext. 5925
Fax 020 7327 6368

Correspondent Mrs Linda Harper, Secretary

Trustees H R Dobinson, Chair; P Barnes; Lady Delves Broughton; A G Cooper; R Gilkes; G Morgan; M J Wade; A A Duguid.

Information available Full accounts were available at the Charity Commission.

General This charity was set up in 1953, and is the charitable arm of Lloyd's insurance market in London. Originally the trust was funded mainly by covenanted subscriptions from members of Lloyd's. By 1997 the majority of these covenants had expired, having a substantial impact on lowering the income of the trust. The trust in response

has adopted a new policy in their grant-giving, described below. Other sources of income are available. One member of Lloyd's left almost his entire estate of £800,000 to the trust in 1990. Lloyd's have also approved £250,000 of corporation funding a year over the next three years.

In 1999 the trust had assets of £2.7 million, its income was £725,000 and £320,000 was given in grants.

In 1998 Lloyd's chose five charities to receive a share of £200,000, these were Alzheimer's Research Trust, British Trust for Conservation Volunteers, Care International, Crimestoppers Trust (London) and Save the Children Fund. These five charities will be partners of Lloyd's for the next three years and no other grants will be made. In view of the change in policy the trust stated that they are unable to respond positively to other appeals received.

The 1999 report stated that the trustees were able to continue to support a number of ad-hoc appeals. In total, 31 out of 1100 appeals were supported totalling £120,000. It was agreed that where possible funds should be given to support specific projects such as the purchase of essential equipment. Grants were broken down as follows:

Social welfare	£44,000	(11 grants)
National medical	£56,000	(7 grants)
Children and youth	£11,000	(7 grants)
Environmental	£8,000	(6 grants)

The above information refers to the General fund. The grant-making policy and practice of three other funds are described below.

Lloyds Community Programme
The principal elements of this programme are support for programmes in the fields of education, training and enterprise. Increasingly, the programmed opportunities will focus and be involved in projects which help to shape and develop a sense of partnership.

In 1999 grants totalled £104,000, and were given mainly to London-based charities. Larger grants went to Tower Hamlets Education Business Partnership (£10,000 towards core funding and £15,000 in respect of Lloyd's sponsorship of the business mentoring scheme), East London Small Business Centre (£10,000 towards the cost of administering Lloyd's Loan Fund and £5,000 to fund training courses) and Business in the Community (£10,000). At the end of the year, £32,000 was carried forward to 2000.

Cuthbert Heath Centenary Fund
This fund provides bursaries at nine schools, each are allocated £6,600 a year. The nine participating schools are Aldenham, Bishops Stortford, Bradfield, Brighton, Charterhouse, Felsted, Reeds, Queenswood and Westminster.

Exclusions No grants for any appeal where it is likely that the grant would be used for sectarian purposes or to local or regional branches of charities where it is possible to support the UK organisation. Support is not given to individuals.

Applications In writing to the correspondent including a copy of the latest annual report and accounts.

Localtrent Ltd

Jewish, educational, poverty

£91,000 (1998/99)

Beneficial area UK, with some preference for Manchester

Lopian Gross Barnat & Co., Harvester House, 37 Peter Street, Manchester M2 5QD

Tel. 0161 832 8721

Correspondent A Kahan, Accountant

Trustees Mrs M Weiss; B Weiss; J L Weiss; P Weiss; S Feldman.

Information available Accounts were on file at the Charity Commission.

General The trust was established in 1983 for the advancement of the Jewish religion, education and the relief of poverty (probably among Jewish people). By 1998/99 it had assets of £243,000 and an income of £79,000. It gave grants totalling £91,000.

Major grants over £1,000 were listed in the accounts and went to 12 organisations. The largest was for £43,000 and went to Chasdei Yoel Charitable Trust. The only other grant over £10,000 went to Beis Minchas Yitzchak for £11,000.

Other grants went to Charity Association (M/C) Limited (£6,400), UTA (£3,700), Tzedoka Charity (£3,000), Rabbinical Research College (£1,600), Manchester Grammar School (£1,300) and Toras V'Chesed (£1,000). Various other donations totalled £11,000.

Applications In writing to the correspondent.

Insufficient.

The Locker Foundation

Jewish

£76,000 (1998/99)

Beneficial area UK and overseas

28 High Road, East Finchley, London N2 9PJ

Correspondent The Trustees

Trustees I Carter; M Carter; Miss S Carter.

Information available Full accounts were on file at the Charity Commission.

General This trust mainly supports Jewish organisations. In 1998/99 it had assets of £1.5 million and an income of £276,000 (£146,000 in 1997/98). It made nine grants totalling £76,000 (£58,000 in 1997/98). Management and administration totalled £14,000 with £2,500 going on trustees' fees. There was a surplus of £184,000 in the year.

The largest grant was £33,000 to Jewish National Fund. Grants of £15,000 each went to Society of Friends of Torah and Kahal Cassidim Bobov, both of which had been major recipients in the previous year. Other grants went to Jewish Care (£6,000), British Friends of Boys Town Jerusalem (£3,500), Yad Sarah (£3,000), BUGS and Craven Walk Charities Trust (£150 each) and Teenage Cancer Trust (£100).

Applications In writing to the correspondent.

The Loftus Charitable Trust

Jewish

£136,000 (1997/98)

Beneficial area UK and overseas

48 George Street, London W1H 5RF

Tel. 020 7486 2969

Correspondent A Loftus, Trustee

Trustees R I Loftus; A L Loftus; A D Loftus.

Information available Accounts were on file at the Charity Commission.

General The trust was established in 1987 by Richard Ian Loftus. Its objects are the:

- advancement of the Jewish religion
- advancement of Jewish education and the education of Jewish people
- relief of the Jewish poor.

In 1997/98 the trust had assets of £509,000 and an income of £291,000 (£50,000 from bank interest and £241,000 from donations received). After expenses of only £700, grants totalled £136,000. Grants of over £1,000 were listed in the accounts and went to 15 organisations. The largest was £30,000 to Community Accommodation Trust. Five other grants were made over £10,000: Habad Orphan Aid Society (£20,000); Jewish Care (£18,000); Joint Jewish Charitable Trust (£14,000); Lubarich Foundation (£13,000); and Community Security Trust (£11,000).

Other grants included Shaare Zedek (£6,300), United Synagogue (£3,900), Norwood Ravenswood (£3,000), Jewish Marriage Council (£2,000), Western Marble Arch Synagogue (£1,700) and £1,000 each to British Ort and Cosgrove Care. Sundry donations under £1,000 totalled £9,500.

Exclusions The trustees state that all funds are committed and unsolicited applications are not welcome.

Applications In writing to the correspondent, but see above.

London Law Trust

Children and young people

£173,000 (1998/99)

Beneficial area UK

Messrs Alexanders, 203 Temple Chambers, Temple Avenue, London EC4Y 0DB

Tel. 020 7353 6221 **Fax** 020 7583 0662 **e-mail** info@alexanders-solicitors.co.uk

Correspondent G D Ogilvie, Secretary

Trustees Prof. A R Mellows; R A Pellant; Sir Michael Hobbs.

Information available Full annual report and financial statements were provided by the trust.

General The trustees have power to make grants to any charitable area. However, they have continued with their long-standing policy of focusing on charities which support and develop children and young people in the three main areas shown below. Grants were broken down as follows:

1. preventing and curing illness and disability (6 grants totalling £25,000)
2. alleviating or reducing the causes or likelihood of illness and disability (31 grants totalling £85,000)
3. encouraging and developing the qualities of leadership and service to the community (25 grants totalling £63,000).

Within these categories the trustees tend to favour smaller research projects and new ventures.

In 1998/99 the trust had assets of £4.1 million and an income of £145,000. After management and general expenses of £39,000 the trustees made 62 grants totalling £173,000. The largest grant was for £10,000 but they tended to be in the range of £500 to £5,000. No grants were repeated from the previous year.

Recipients in the first category included Sheffield Children's Hospital (£5,000), National Eye Research Centre (£2,500) and ERIC (£2,000). Grants awarded in the second category include Body & Soul and The Farm in the Forest (£5,000 each), Family Heart Association (£2,500), The AT Society and Children's Head Injury Trust (£1,000 each) and Look (£500).

Recipients in the final category include Outward Bound who received the largest grant of £10,000, GAP (£5,000), The Excelsior Trust (£4,000), Youth in Action (£2,500), Air Training Corps (£1,500) and League of Venturers (£500).

Applications In writing to the correspondent. The trustees employ a grant adviser whose job it is to evaluate applications. Applicants are requested to supply detailed information in support of their applications. The grant adviser makes on-site visits to almost all applications.

The trustees meet twice a year to consider the grant adviser's reports. Most grants are awarded in the autumn.

The William & Katherine Longman Trust

General

£240,000 (1999/2000)

Beneficial area UK

Charles Russell, 8–10 New Fetter Lane, London EC4A 1RS

Tel. 020 7203 5000

Correspondent W P Harriman, Trustee

Trustees *W P Harriman; J B Talbot; A C O Bell.*

Information available Accounts were on file at the Charity Commission.

General In 1999/2000 the trust had assets of £5.1 million and an income of £148,000. Grants totalled £240,000 and were given to 51 organsiations, 28 of which were recurrent.

The largest grants were £15,000 each to Care, Knight Foundation, Lambeth Fund – Springboard and Tearfund and £10,000 to Sargent Cancer Care for Children. Most grants went to health and welfare charities, beneficiaries of smaller grants included APEX Charitable Trust, Actors' Charitable Trust, Down's Syndrome Association, FRAME, Iris Fund, Queen Mary's Sidcup NHS Trust, WWF UK and WaterAid.

Exclusions No grants to individuals.

Applications The trustees believe in taking a pro-active approach in deciding which charities to support and it is their policy to not respond to unsolicited appeals.

The C L Loyd Charitable Trust

General (but see below)

£88,000 (1998/99)

Beneficial area UK, with a preference for Berkshire and Oxfordshire

Betterton House, Lockinge, Wantage, Oxfordshire OX12 8QL

Tel. 01235 833265   **Fax** 01235 862422

Correspondent C L Loyd, Trustee

Trustees *C L Loyd; T C Loyd.*

Information available Full accounts were on file at the Charity Commission.

General The trust supports recognisable UK charities and local charities (in Berkshire and Oxfordshire), of which the trustees have first-hand knowledge that they are properly and efficiently run. Within these boundaries, grants can be given to a wide range of organisations involved in welfare, animals, churches, medical/disability, children/youth and education.

In 1998/99 the trust had assets of £2.6 million and an income of £118,000. Over 140 grants totalling £88,000 were given. Although many of these were repeat grants, a wide variety of new organisations were supported.

The trust gave 19 grants over £1,000. The Country Buildings Protection Trust was the largest beneficiary receiving 7 grants totalling £42,000. Others to benefit from larger grants included Vale and Downland Museum and Injured Jockeys' Fund (£5,000 each), Friends of Newbury Spring Festival (£3,000) and East Hendred Parochial Church Council (£1,200).

The bulk of remaining grants were in the range of £100 to £250, although some of the smaller grants were for £5 to £25. Grants included £250 to Cancer Research Oxford Appeal, Countess Mountbatten House and Royal Agricultural Benevolent Institution and £100 each to Ashmolean Museum, Oxfordshire County Scout Council, Royal British Legion, St Luke's Hospital for the Clergy and International League for Protection of Horses. Among the recipients of smaller grants were £50 each to Bibles for Children, Northmoor Trust and Girls Brigade, £25 to Friend of Friendless Churches and £20 to Reading YMCA.

Exclusions No support for individuals or medical research.

Applications In writing to the correspondent.

The Luck-Hille Foundation

Jewish, disability, children

£406,000 (1998/99)

Beneficial area UK and Israel

Devonshire House, 1 Devonshire Street, London W1N 2DR

Tel. 020 7304 2000

Correspondent J W Prevezer, Trustee

Trustees *Mrs Jill Luck-Hille; P M Luck-Hille; J W Prevezer.*

Information available Full accounts were on file at the Charity Commission.

General The foundation was established for general charitable purposes in 1975 by Jill Kreitman (now Mrs Luck-Hille), daughter of Hyman and Irene Kreitman (see entry for The Kreitman Foundation in *A Guide To Major Trusts Volume 1*).

Grants are made in the fields of education, health, disability and welfare. The trust makes grants to charities based in the UK, including non-registered charities. In 1998/99 assets were £5.2 million and the income £238,000. Four grants were made totalling £406,000. After management and administration costs of £56,000 there was an excess of £225,000. In 1997/98 the trust gave only £3,600 in grants leaving an excess of £198,000.

In 1998/99 Middlesex University received £400,000, the bulk of the grant fund. The foundation has entered into an agreement with this organisation for the construction and fitting out of a real tennis court. Under the terms of the agreement the foundation has agreed to provide funding for the project with the core grant being £1.3 million up to 2003. The three remaining smaller grants went to SPRITO Lifetime Learning (£5,000), Norwood Ravenswood (£1,000) and Parent Network (£250).

Exclusions No grants to individuals.

Applications To the correspondent in writing. The trustees seem to have a list of regular beneficiaries and it may be unlikely that any new applications will be successful.

Robert Luff Foundation Ltd

Medical research

£257,000 (1998/99)

Beneficial area UK

294 Earls Court Road, London SW5 9BB

Tel. 020 7373 7003 **Fax** 020 7373 8634

Correspondent M D Lock

Trustees *R C W Luff; Sir Robert Johnson; Lady Johnson; R P J Price; Ms G Favot; Mrs J Tomlinson.*

Information available Full accounts were on file at the Charity Commission.

General In 1998/99 the foundation had assets of £19.4 million from which it gained an income of £615,000. After taking into account a loss of £52,000 from its trading subsidiary, Futurist Light & Sound Ltd, the income was £563,000. Grants totalling £257,000 were given to 14 organisations, of which 13 had been supported in the previous year. The five organisations which received grants of more than £20,000 were Harpur Trust (£50,000), National Heart & Lung Institute (£45,000), Cystic Fibrosis Trust and St John Ambulance (both £30,000) and British Lung Foundation (£27,000).

Other grants went to Sheffield Health Authority and University College London Medical School (£16,000 each), National Asthma Campaign (£15,000) and British Scoliosis Research Foundation (£13,000). The remainder of grants were all for under £5,000, recipients included Northwick Park Luff Foundation Trust Fund and Royal Eastbourne Gold Club - Charity Toy Fund.

Applications The foundation makes its own decisions about what causes to support. It has stated that 'outside applications' are not considered, or replied to.

The Lyndhurst Settlement

Social problems, civil liberties, environment, conservation

£175,000 (1999/2000)

Beneficial area Usually UK, but overseas applications are considered if there is a strong civil liberty component

2nd Floor, 15–19 Cavendish Place, London W1G 0DD

Correspondent Michael Isaacs, Trustee

Trustees *Michael Isaacs; Anthony Skyrme; Kenneth Plummer.*

Information available Full accounts were provided by the trust.

General The policy of the trust is to encourage research into social problems with a specific emphasis on safeguarding civil liberties, maintaining the rights of minorities and protecting the environment which the trustees regard as an important civil liberty. The trustees prefer to support charities (both innovatory and long-established) that seek to prevent, as well as relieve, hardship.

Beneficiaries include not only civil liberty, immigration and penal reform organisations, but a number of birth control advisory centres, environmental and conservation groups, AIDS groups and homeless organisations.

In 1999/2000, the settlement had assets of £938,000 (£1.1 million in 1998/99) and an income of £75,000. Grants totalled £175,000. Out of about 1,000 requests received during the year it gave grants to 69 charities, 22 of which were supported in the previous year. It is the trustees' policy to maintain a level of distribution in excess of income. This will result in a decrease in the settlement's capital over coming years.

The grants listed between £500 and £8,000. Some of the environmental and heritage organisations supported were small local groups. Grants included Newland Furnace Trust (£3,000) and Oxfordshire Woodland Project (£2,000). The trustees believe that an essential element in the protection of the environment is the limitation of population growth. Grants in relation to this were given to Education for Choice,

Population Concern and Brook Advisory Council (£6,000 each).

The settlement was one of the first trusts to be concerned with the civil rights of prisoners. Grants included Howard League – for penal reform and Prisoners Abroad (£4,000 each) and Prison Reform Trust (£3,500).

Grants to minority groups were given in the UK and abroad and included Migrant Helpline (£8,000), Immigrants' Aid Trust (£4,000), Refugee Arrivals Project (£3,500) and Asylum Welcome (£2,000).

The settlement does not generally give grants to medical charities, but has given to organisations concerned with AIDS or HIV. Grants were given to Food Chain and Healing Circle (£2,000 each).

Further examples of grants were British False Memory Society (£3,000), Bristol Nightstop (£2,000), Age Concern Hackney (£1,500) and Summerfield Care & Repair Project and Luton Mediation (£1,000 each).

Exclusions No grants to non-registered charities or individuals. Medical or religious charities are not normally supported.

Applications Requests for grants should include a brief description of the aims and objects of the charity and must be in writing and not by telephone. Unsuccessful applications will not be acknowledged unless an sae is enclosed. Applications are considered throughout the year.

The Lyons Charitable Trust

Health, medical research, children

£49,000 (1998/99)

Beneficial area UK

Field Fisher Waterhouse, 35 Vine Street, London EC3N 2AA

Correspondent Mrs H Fuff

Trustees *M S Gibbon; Nick Noble.*

Information available Accounts were on file at the Charity Commission, but without a recent grants list.

General The trust in particular makes grants in the fields of health, medical research and children in need.

In 1998/99 the trust had an income of £104,000 and an expenditure of £52,000. Donations totalling £48,000 were made to six organisations. Further information was not available about the size or beneficiaries of grants in this year.

In 1994/95 the trust made grants totalling £53,000 to five organisations. Grants of £12,000 each were made to Great Ormond Street Hospital for Sick Children, The Florence Nightingale Fund, Printers Charitable Corporation and WWF with £5,000 to Terrence Higgins Trust.

Applications In writing to the correspondent.

The Sir Jack Lyons Charitable Trust

Jewish, arts, education

£106,000 (1998/99)

Beneficial area UK and overseas

c/o Sagars, 3rd Floor, Elizabeth House, Queen Street, Leeds LS1 2TW

Correspondent M J Friedman, Trustee

Trustees *Sir Jack Lyons; Lady Lyons; M J Friedman; J E Lyons; D S Lyons.*

Information available Full accounts were on file at the Charity Commission.

General This trust shows a particular interest in Jewish charities and also a consistent interest in the arts, particularly music. In 1998/99 the trust had assets of £1.9 million and an income of £142,000, £109,000 of which came from rents. After management and administration costs of £15,000, £106,000 was given in donations to 29 organisations.

The largest grant was £40,000 to British ORT. Other large grants went to Mount Sinai Centre Foundation (£12,000) and York University and Jewish Music Heritage Trust (£10,000 each). All of these organisations have been major beneficiaries in previous years.

Music, arts and education organisations to benefit included London Symphony Orchestra (£7,600), Royal Academy of Arts and City University (£2,500 each), London String Quartet Foundation (£1,500), University of Miami School of Music (£320) and York Early Music Festival (£300).

The trust also supports organisations working in aspects of social welfare, disadvantage and disability. Recipients in these areas included Jewish Community Foundation (£5,300), Age Endeavour Fellowship (£300), British Red Cross (£150) and Norwood Childcare (£100).

Exclusions No grants to individuals.

Applications In writing to the correspondent. In the past the trust has stated: 'In the light of increased pressure for funds, unsolicited appeals are less welcome and would waste much time and money for applicants who were looking for funds which were not available.'

The M & C Trust

Jewish, social welfare

£172,000 (1998/99)

Beneficial area UK

c/o Chantrey Vellacott DFK, Russell Square House, 10–12 Russell Square, London WC1B 5LF

Tel. 020 7509 9000   **Fax** 020 7463 8884

Correspondent A C Langridge, Trustee

Trustees *A Bernstein; Mrs J B Kemble; A C Langridge; Elizabeth J Marks; Rachel J Lebus.*

Information available Full accounts were provided by the trust.

General Since 1999 the trust's primary charitable objects have been Jewish causes and social welfare. In 1998/99 the trust had assets of £6 million and an income of £231,000. Grants totalling £172,000 were awarded to 17 charities, most of these were Jewish.

The largest grant went to Jerusalem Foundation (£50,000). Other recipients of large grants were Norwood Ravenswood (£30,000), Jewish Care (£25,000) and National Children's Orchestra (£10,000). Grants under £10,000 went to Friends of Israel Educational Trust and Jewish Marriage Council (£8,000 each), Institute for Jewish Policy Research (£5,000), Koestler Award Trust (£3,000) and Spiro Institute (£2,000). Non-Jewish beneficiaries included National Children's Orchestra (£10,000) and One World Action (£3,000).

The trust is connected with Quercus Trust, being under the same administration and having similar objectives. In 1999 the trustees agreed to transfer investments of £4 million to Quercus Trust.

The trust stated in autumn 2000 that 'funds are currently earmarked for existing projects'.

Exclusions No grants to individuals.

Applications In writing to the correspondent, but please note the above. In order to keep administration costs to a minimum, they are unable to reply to any unsuccessful applications.

The M D & S Charitable Trust

Jewish

£114,000 (1997/98)

Beneficial area UK

22 Overlea Road, London E5 9BG

Correspondent M D Cymerman, Trustee

Trustees *M D Cymerman; Mrs S Cymerman.*

Information available Full accounts were on file at the Charity Commission.

General In 1997/98 the trust's assets totalled £553,000 and it had an income of £191,000, derived from donations, gifts of property and investment income. Grants were made totalling £114,000. Grants of over £1,000 were given to 19 organisations and totalled nearly £105,000. Smaller, unlisted donations totalled £9,500.

The grants all appeared to be given to Jewish causes, with the largest grant of £18,000 going to Yeshivat Hechel Shimon Volozhin. Other larger grants went to Yershival Magen Avrohom and Tifrach Torah Centre (£13,000 each), Ponevez Aid and Benevolence Fund (£11,000) and Yershivat Gaon Yaakov (£10,000). Other recipients included Yeshivat Nechomos Isar Yisroel (£6,000), Yeshivat Ponevez (£5,500), Friends of Beth Jacob (£4,500), Yeshivat Netiot Avrohom Erlanger (£4,000) and Beis Yisroel Benevolent Fund (£3,500).

Applications In writing to the correspondent.

M N R Charitable Trust

Christian, general

£119,000 (1999)

Beneficial area UK, overseas

c/o Mazars Neville Russell, 24 Bevis Marks, London EC3A 7NR

Correspondent Bryan K H Rogers

Trustees *John S Mellows, Chair; Andrew N Russell; David E Ryan.*

Information available Full accounts were provided by the trust.

General The name of the charity was changed from the N R Charitable Trust in 1999. It was established in 1983 for the main purpose of receiving contributions from the partners of Mazars Neville Russell and making donations to charitable causes, especially those concerned with the advancement of the Christian faith.

During 1999 the charity had assets of just £13,000, the bulk of its £105,000 income came from Gift Aid donations from the participating partners in Mazars Neville Russell. Grants totalling £119,000 were made to 53 organisations. A list detailing the top 25 grants made over £1,000 was provided by the trust.

Grants of £15,000 each were made to International Needs for the Columbia Earthquake, Tearfund for work in Yemen and World Vision for the Kosovo Appeal. £10,000 went to Medina Valley Centre. Among the recipients of smaller grants were £5,000 each to IMPACT, Meningitis Research Foundation and Prison Fellowship, £4,000 to Chartered Accountants' Benevolent Fund, £2,500 each to Children Say Charity and International Substance Abuse & Addiction Coalition, £1,500 to Yorkshire Wildlife Trust and £1,000 each to Lloyds Community Programme and London First Millennium Projects Trust. There were 28 grants of less than £1,000, totalling £4,900, which made up the remainder of the grant total.

Exclusions No recurrent grants.

Applications Unsolicited applications will not normally be considered or acknowledged. Normally applications will only be considered from charities with which the partners of Mazars Neville Russell already have an active relationship.

The Madeline Mabey Trust

Medical research, children's welfare

£200,000 (1997/98)

Beneficial area UK, and UK-registered international charities

Floral Mile, Twyford, Reading RG10 9SQ

Tel. 0118 940 3921

Correspondent Joanna L Singeisen, Trustee

Trustees *Alan G Daliday; Bridget A Nelson; Joanna L Singeisen.*

Information available Accounts were on file at the Charity Commission, but without a list of grants, or a full narrative report.

General In 1997/98 this trust had an income of £139,000. The trust received two donations totalling £102,000 and a substantial balance was carried forward from the previous year. This resulted in a considerable increase in the number of donations the trustees were able to make. A total of 147 donations were made, amounting to £200,000.

The trust has stated that it makes grants principally, but not exclusively, towards medical research and children's welfare charities. Unfortunately a grants list was not included in the accounts, so we have no further information about the size or beneficiaries of grants.

'The trustees sought and obtained confirmation from the Charity Commission that donations could be made to charities registered in the UK but who apply some or all of their funds outside the UK'.

Applications In writing to the correspondent. Please note, unsuccessful applications are not usually acknowledged.

The Robert McAlpine Foundation

Children, social welfare, medical research

over £200,000 (1999/2000)

Beneficial area UK

Eaton Court, Maylands Avenue, Hemel Hempstead, Hertfordshire HP2 7TR

Correspondent Graham Prain

Trustees *David McAlpine; M H D McAlpine; Kenneth McAlpine; Cullum McAlpine; Adrian N R McAlpine.*

Information available Full accounts were on file at the Charity Commission for the years up to 1975/76 with the usual details of donations. Accounts are also available for 1983/84 and 1986/87 but details of grants are no longer included. The trust informed us in November 2000 that it had not filed accounts with the Charity Commission since the SORP was introduced. However, it had prepared three sets of accounts which would be approved at a trust meeting at the end of the year.

General In November 2000 the trust informed us that in recent years it had been giving around £200,000 each year to charitable causes. Unfortunately we have been unable to obtain further up-to-date information for this trust. The following information was included in the last edition of this guide.

The trust supports children, social welfare and medical causes, especially in relation to people who are elderly or deaf, and hospices, medical research and education in areas of urban deprivation. Under the latter category, the trust is currently only supporting one charity concerned with young unemployed people.

The most recent list of grants on file at the Charity Commission is that for 1975/76 when the trust gave a total of £55,000 to 28 organisations. Both UK and local charities received support, mainly in the field of social welfare.

Exclusions The trust does not like to fund overheads.

Applications In writing to the correspondent, at any time.

Macdonald-Buchanan Charitable Trust

General

£167,000 (1998)

Beneficial area UK

Rathbone Trust Ltd, 159 New Bond Street, London W1Y 9PA

Tel. 020 7399 0820

Correspondent Miss Linda Cousins

Trustees *Capt. John Macdonald-Buchanan; A J Macdonald-Buchanan; A R Macdonald-Buchanan; H J Macdonald-Buchanan; Mrs M C A Philipson.*

Information available Full accounts were on file at the Charity Commission.

General The Hon. Catherine Macdonald-Buchanan set up this trust in 1952 for general charitable purposes and endowed it with 40,000 shares in the then Distillers Company. The trust now has substantially more assets, spread over a wide range of investments, with a value of £3.2 million.

In 1998 the trust's income was £142,000, £21,000 was spent on administration and £167,000 was given in donations. About 135 organisations were supported, a large proportion of which were supported in the previous year. Only six grants were of £1,000 or more.

By far the largest donation was £54,000 to Carriejo Charitable Trust. Other larger grants went to British Racing School (£25,000), Historic Churches Preservation Trust and Orrin Charitable Trust (£15,000 each), National Horse Racing Museum (£3,300) and Chichester Cathedral Trust (£1,000). Two of the major recipients appear to be regular beneficiaries. The trust states that some UK charities are supported annually, although no commitment is given to the recipients.

About 100 grants were made for £500 with the remainder being for £100. These went to a wide range of organisations including health and welfare charities, service/ex-service organisations, conservation, heritage and horse riding. Specific recipients included 1940 Dunkirk Veteran Association, Age Concern (England), Barnardos, Injured Jockeys' Fund, Oxfam, Muscular Dystrophy Group, Rukba, National Asthma Campaign, Scope and National Trust.

Exclusions No grants to individuals.

Applications In writing to the correspondent, for consideration once a year.

The A M McGreevy No 5 Charitable Settlement

General

£290,000 (1997/98)

Beneficial area UK, with a preference for the Bristol and Bath area

KPMG, 100 Temple Street, Bristol BS1 6AG

Tel. 0117 905 4694

Correspondent Mike Haynes

Trustees *Avon Executor & Trustee Co; Anthony M McGreevy; David Johnstone; Charles Sommerville; Miss Elise McGreevy; Alfred Hill; Katrina McGreevey.*

Information available Full accounts were on file at the Charity Commission.

General The trust was established in 1979 by Anthony M McGreevy. In 1997/98 the assets were £1.7 million and the income £62,000. Grants totalling £290,000 were made to 12 organisations. Previous grants lists have shown a preference for charities based in the former county of Avon. This year a number of national organisations received substantial grants, although these may be regional branches.

By far the largest grant was £250,000 to Royal Hospital for Children. Other grants over £10,000 went to NSPCC (£16,000) ChildLine (£12,000) and SPA (£10,000).

The remainder of the grants were all for under £1,000. Organisations to benefit included Dolphin Society, Friends of the BADA Trust, Friends of the Royal Academy, Stroke Association and Victoria and Albert Museum.

Exclusions No support for individuals.

Applications In writing to the correspondent.

The Jack & Pat Mallabar Charitable Foundation

Medical, education

£1.6 million (1997/98)

Beneficial area UK

41 Orchard Court, Portman Square, London W1H 9PB

Tel. 020 7839 3899

Correspondent J M L Stone, Trustee

Trustees *J M L Stone; Sir Gordon Reece; Dr James Bevan.*

Information available Full accounts were on file at the Charity Commission.

General Unfortunately we have been unable to obtain up-to-date information for this trust, this entry was included in the last edition of *A Guide to the Major Trusts Volume 3*.

This trust, established in 1992, appears to have given regular large grants to Foundation of Nursing Studies, with most of its other support going to medical charities and educational establishments.

In 1997/98 the trust had an income of £77,000 but made donations far exceeding this using funds from its capital account, totalling £1.6 million. Its assets at the year end totalled £501,000, down from £2 million in the previous year. In the accounts for that year the trust anticipated that the trust would shortly distribute the balance of its assets.

In 1997/98, 20 grants were made with the largest being a phenomenal £754,000 to Foundation of Nursing Studies. Other larger grants were £314,000 to Ampleforth Abbey Trust, £127,000 to Christchurch – Oxford, £65,000 to Daughters of the Crown and £64,000 each to The 150th Anniversary Appeal and The Westminster Roman Catholic Diocese.

Three other regular beneficiaries also received grants, Downing College (£65,000), Radcliffe College (£25,000) and Centrepoint (£20,000). The remaining grants ranged between £1,000 and £21,000.

Exclusions No grants to individuals. Virtually all grants are to registered charities, though occasionally grants are made to organisations which are not.

Applications In writing to the correspondent. Due to the level of applications received, the trustees regret that they cannot respond to unsuccessful applications.

This entry was not confirmed by the trust but was correct according to information on file at the the Charity Commission.

Maranatha Christian Trust

Christian

£368,000 (1997/98)

Beneficial area UK and worldwide

68 Roslyn Gardens, Gidea Park, Essex RM2 5RD

Correspondent G P Ridsdale

Trustees *A C Bell; Revd L Bowring; Viscount Crispin Brentford.*

Information available Accounts were on file at the Charity Commission but without a list of grants.

General The trust makes grants towards the advancement of the Christian gospel in the UK and overseas.

In 1997/98 the trust's assets totalled £2 million, it had an income of £65,000 and grants were made totalling £368,000.

In 1996/97 grants totalled £215,000 including £27,000 to individuals. The largest grant was £30,000 to CARE Trust, and it also received a further grant of £5,000 towards its intern programme. Other larger grants included £10,000 each to Stewards Trust and Riding Lights and £7,500 to Portman House Trust.

Other grants mostly ranged from £1,000 to £5,000 and included £5,000 to Oasis Media, £4,000 to Clasp, £1,500 to Women in Mission and £1,000 each to Christians in Entertainment, Rewick Park Initiative – Rwanda, Southeast Asian Outreach – Rajana Craft Project Cambodia and Stepping Stones.

Applications In writing to the correspondent, but please note, the trust does not welcome unsolicited applications.

Marbeh Torah Trust

Jewish

£197,000 (1998/99)

Beneficial area UK and Israel

116 Castlewood Road, London N15 6BE

Correspondent M C Elzas, Trustee

Trustees *Moishe Chaim Elzas; Jacob Naftoli Elzas; Simone Elzas.*

Information available Accounts were on file at the Charity Commission, but without a list of grants.

General This trust makes grants to Jewish charities in the UK and Israel. Its objects are the furtherance of orthodox Jewish religious education and the relief of poverty. In 1998/99 its assets were £9,700 but it had an income made up of donations totalling £196,000. Grants totalled £197,000.

Unfortunately further information about the size and beneficiaries of grants was not available.

Applications In writing to the correspondent. The trust stated that 'demand constantly outstrips the income' and unsuccessful applicants will only receive a reply if an sae is enclosed.

The Stella and Alexander Margulies Charitable Trust

Jewish

£143,000 (1998/99)

Beneficial area UK

23 Grosvenor Street, London W1X 9FE

Correspondent M J Margulies, Trustee

Trustees *M J Margulies; M D Paisner.*

Information available Accounts were on file at the Charity Commission.

General The trust mainly gives to Jewish organisations but also makes some grants to other groups. In 1998/99 it had assets of £4.9 million, an income of £280,000 and made 22 grants totalling £143,000. The largest grant of £90,000 went to Joint Jewish Charitable Trust.

The Royal Opera House also received a substantial grant of £20,000. Grants of £5,000 each went to Save the Children Fund, Jerusalem Foundation and AISH.

Other donations included those to Huntingdon Foundation (£3,600), Remembering for the Future (£2,500), Y Meharash Engel Madomishi (£2,000), Friends of the Israel Opera (£1,800), British Red Cross Society (£1,400), Royal Academy Trust (£1,100) and £1,000 each to Community Security Trust, Hope Charity and Nightingale House.

Applications In writing to the correspondent.

This entry was not confirmed by the trust but was correct according to information on file at the Charity Commission.

The Hilda & Samuel Marks Foundation

Jewish, general

£238,000 (1997/98)

Beneficial area UK

1 Ambassador Place, Stockport Road, Altrincham, Cheshire WA15 8DB

Tel. 0161 941 3183 **Fax** 0161 927 7437
e-mail davidmarks@mutlypropities.co.uk

Correspondent D L Marks, Trustee

Trustees *S Marks; Mrs H Marks; D L Marks; Mrs R D Selby.*

Information available Full accounts were on file at the Charity Commission.

General Unfortunately we have been unable to update the following information since the last edition of this guide.

The trust supports principally Jewish organisations. In 1997/98 the trust had assets of £2.5 million and an income of £181,000. It gave 69 grants totalling £238,000.

The trust has a number of regular beneficiaries including Emunah Child Resettlement Fund (three grants totalling £51,000), Manchester Jewish Federation (two grants totalling £10,000) and Chai Lifeline (£3,000).

Other larger grants were £68,000 to BF/WD, £20,000 to Bournemouth Jewish Day School, £10,000 each to Global Cancer Concern and Norwood Ravenswood, two grants totalling £10,000 to Binoh of Manchester and two grants totalling £8,000 to Jewish Marriage Council.

The remaining grants ranged up to £5,000, including 46 for £1,000 or less.

Applications In writing to the correspondent. However, the trust has stated that it supports projects known to the trustees and unsolicited applications are not sought.

Michael Marks Charitable Trust

Arts, environment

£359,000 (1998/99)

Beneficial area UK and overseas

5 Elm Tree Road, London NW8 9JY

Tel. 020 7286 4633   **Fax** 020 7289 2173

Correspondent The Secretary

Trustees *Lady Marks; Prof. C White; Dr D MacDiarmid.*

Information available Full accounts were on file at the Charity Commission.

General The trust supports the arts (including galleries and museums), and environmental groups, with grants generally ranging from £200 to £25,000, although larger grants have been given.

In 1998/99 the trust had assets of £6 million and an income of £305,000. Grants totalling £359,000 were given to 33 organisations, 9 of which were supported in the previous year.

The largest grant was £60,000 to Scottish Poetry Library. Other large grants went to Pothenios Limited (£30,000), with £25,000 each to Ashmolean Museum (University of Oxford), Bodleian Library Oxford and Victoria & Albert Museum and £20,000 each to British Museum, Charleston Trust and Royal Collection Trust.

Other grants ranged from £200 to £15,000 and were given towards: the arts including Sir John Soare's Museum (£6,500), Theatre Museum (£5,000) and A1 Media Theatre (£300); Jewish organisations including Community Centre in Israel Project (£770), Greek Orthodox Charity Organisation (£350) and Middlesex New Synagogue (£200); and other groups including Polish Association of the Knights of Malta and Woodland Trust (£15,000 each) and London Hellenic Society (£850).

Exclusions Grants are given to registered charities only. No grant to individuals or profit organisations.

Applications In writing to the correspondent before July. Applications should include audited accounts, information on other bodies approached and details of funding obtained.

The Erich Markus Charitable Foundation

Medical, welfare, general

£128,000 (1999)

Beneficial area UK

Payne Hicks Beach, 10 New Square, Lincoln's Inn, London WC2A 3QG

Tel. 020 7465 4300

Trustees *Erich Markus Charity Trustees Ltd.*

Information available Full accounts were provided by the trust.

General Erich Markus died in 1979, leaving half of his residual estate to the trust. The original capital was made up of 355,000 ordinary 25p shares in Office & Electronic Machines Ltd. The trust has since diversified its holding and by 1999 had assets valued at just under £4 million. It supports medical and welfare causes.

The income for 1999 was £140,000 while administration and management of the foundation totalled £40,000. During the year £128,000 was given in 61 grants, many were recurrent from the previous year.

The largest grant of £10,000 went to Naima Jewish Preparatory School, also the major beneficiary in 1998. Other larger grants included £6,000 to Spanish & Portuguese Jews Home for the Aged and £4,000 each to Imperial Cancer Research Fund, Jewish Blind and Disabled, Nightingale House, Norwood Ravenswood, Royal Star and Garter Home, Samaritans, St Christopher's Hospice, Trinity Hospice and World Jewish Relief.

The remainder of the grants were mostly in the range of £1,000 to £3,500, but were for as little as £400. A range of small and large organisations were supported. Grants included: £3,500 to St Frances Hospice; £2,000 each to Camphill Village Trust, Kidney Research Aid Fund,

Sargent Cancer Care for Children, SSAFA and The Westminster Society for Mentally Handicapped Children and Adults – Erich Markus House; and £1,000 each to Alone in London, CommunicAbility, Dogs for the Disabled, Motability, Save the Children Fund and Youth Aliyah Child Rescue.

Smaller grants under £1,000 were £500 each to Age Concern – Westminister and Essex Voluntary Association for the Blind and £400 to Help Tibet.

Exclusions No grants to individuals.

Applications In writing to the trustees. Applications will only be considered if accompanied by a copy of the latest accounts. Trustees meet twice a year, usually in April and October.

Marr-Munning Trust

Overseas aid

£102,000 (1997/98)

Beneficial area Worldwide, mainly third world

9 Madeley Road, Ealing, London W5 2LA

Tel. 020 8998 9593

Correspondent D Gleeson

Trustees *Joan Honor; W Macfarlane; Mary Herbert; J O'Brien; C A Alam; Margaret Lorde.*

Information available Accounts were on file at the Charity Commission, but without a narrative report.

General In 1998/99 the trust had an income of £273,000 and an expenditure of £217,000. Unfortunately further information for this year was not available and the following information is repeated from the last edition of *A Guide to the Major Trusts Volume 3.*

The trust makes grants to overseas aid organisations mainly working in the third world. In 1997/98 its assets totalled £2.7 million and it had an income of £305,000 including £204,000 from rents and £38,000 from donations. Total expenditure was £267,000, including £94,000 spent on property maintenance and £102,000 given in grants.

Grants are listed in the accounts month by month, according to when they were distributed. The country where the beneficiary is based was also usually listed.

The largest grants were £10,000 each to Health Unlimited, Sense, Sound Seekers and UNICEF – North Korea and £7,500 to Impact – India. The remaining grants were for £5,000 or less.

Grants totalling £8,700 were made to a presumably connected charity, Marr-Munning Ashram, which is based in India. Other grants given in April 1997 included: £1,300 to Gram Niyojan – India, £1,000 each to Joe Holman Trust and Nilgiris Adivasi – both in India and £500 each to Fund for Human Need – Jamaica and Village Services – India.

Grants made in February were to a number of different countries: £5,000 each to Cambodia Trust and Save the Children Fund – Vietnam, £2000 each to Africa Now, Aid to Romania and Almsakin Hospital – Pakistan and £600 to Hope – Sri Lanka.

Applications In writing to the correspondent.

The Marsh Christian Trust

General

£114,000 (1998/99)

Beneficial area UK

Granville House, 132–135 Sloane Street, London SW1X 9AX

Tel. 020 7730 2626 **Fax** 020 7823 5225

Correspondent Lorraine McMorrow, Administrator

Trustees B P Marsh; A B Marsh; R J C Marsh; N C S Marsh.

Information available Full accounts and a copy of their triennial review were provided by the trust.

General The trust was established in 1981 and has increased steadily in size with each year. In 1998/99 it had an income of £142,000, assets of £3.5 million and made 225 grants totalling £114,000, 118 of these had been supported in the previous year. The financial report showed high administration costs of £67,000, but this can be accounted for by the proactive nature of the charity and the large number of small grants made.

Based on the 1994–97 report, in which time £491,000 was distributed, causes were supported in the following areas (percentage of grant fund allocation is shown in brackets):

Social welfare (20%)
Small donations went to charities helping people with physical and mental disabilities. Charities working amongst the young, the aged, the homeless, alcoholics and drug abusers were all supported as far as is possible, especially those displaying a Christian emphasis in their work.

Environmental causes/animal welfare (15%)
The trust has been a supporter of various organisations devoted to nature conservation and the well-being of wildlife, both within the UK and overseas. A particular project, Wildlife Information Network, which was previously an initiative of the Marsh Christian Trust, has now become fully independent and established itself within the Royal Veterinary College.

Healthcare and medical research (22.5%)
Much of the money distributed under this category went to hospices and other organisations working with people who are terminally ill. (The trustees try to avoid giving funds to hospitals in the belief that it is the responsibility of the local and national community to maintain these).

Education and training (9%)
Funding and training for children and adults with disabilities is a part of the trust's programme. The trust regularly makes grants to the Royal College of Music, English Speaking Union, Young Enterprise and Oxford Evangelical Research Trust among others. (The trustees try to avoid giving funds to ordinary schools, colleges or universities in the belief that it is the responsibility of the local and national community to maintain these.)

Arts and heritage (22.5%)
The trust gives support to a number of museums and galleries.(The trustees try wherever possible to avoid making donations to appeals for individual church buildings or cathedrals, believing that it is the responsibility of individual congregations and the church to maintain these.)

Overseas appeals (8.5%)
Examples of causes supported during the year include Voluntary Service Overseas, ActionAid and Royal Commonwealth Society for the Blind.

Miscellaneous (2.5%)
The Highgate Cemetery, Prisoners Abroad and Population Concern are examples of causes supported during the period.

The Marsh Awards Scheme Educational and literary awards ranging between £750 and £3,500 were also funded by the trust, 16 were given out during the period.

The trustees will normally only make grants to registered charities experienced within their chosen field of work. Long term core funding of appropriate work is the trust's normal approach, taking the form of money given on a recurring annual basis subject to yearly resubmission and review.

The size of donations normally ranges from £250 to £4,000 but can be as low as £10. In 1998/99, 20 grants over £1,000 were awarded, the largest going to Wildfowl Information Network (£4,000). Other recipients of larger grants were English Speaking Union (£3,000), Industry and Parliament Trust (£2,500) and Royal Academy of Arts (£1,000).

Grants under £1,000 included Cruse Bereavement Care (£800), Humane Research Trust (£750), British Institute for Brain-Injured Children (£600), The Broadway Trust and The Royal Geographical Society (£500 each), Birmingham City Mission (£400), Action for Kids (£400), The Salvation Army and Medical Aid for Poland Fund (£250 each), Cleeve Prior Heritage Trust (£150) and International Otter Survival Trust (£25).

Exclusions No grants to individuals or for building work. The trustees are not interested in single projects or sponsorship proposals.

Applications In writing to the correspondent, including a copy of the most recent accounts. The trustees currently receive about 8,000 applications every year, of which 7,800 are new. Decisions are made at monthly trustee meetings. The trustees attempt to visit each long-term recipient at least once every three years to review the work done, to learn of future plans and renew acquaintance with those responsible for the charity. Advice on fund-raising and other organisational problems is also offered free of charge by the trust.

The Charlotte Marshall Charitable Trust

Roman Catholic, general

£147,000 (1998/99)

Beneficial area UK

c/o C & C Marshall Limited, Ponswood, Hastings, East Sussex TN34 1YJ

Correspondent The Clerk

Trustees *Miss A M Cirket; Miss C C Cirket; K B Page.*

Information available Full accounts were on file at the Charity Commission.

General The trust supports educational, religious and other charitable purposes for Roman Catholics in the UK, and general charitable purposes.

In 1998/99 the trust's assets totalled £800,000 and it had an income of £161,000. Grants totalling £147,000 were made to 37 organisations, 34 of these had been supported in the previous year.

Larger grants went to St Mary Magdalen's Church (£20,000) and Cardinal Hume Centre and St Michael's Hospice (£10,000 each). Other substantial grants went to St Gregory Youth Project (£9,000), Sheffield Law Centre (£8,500), St Mary Star of the Sea (£8,000) and £6,000 each to St Richard's RC School and Sacred Heart Primary School. Other grants ranged between £1,000 and £5,000. Roman Catholic beneficiaries included CAFOD, Catholic Housing Aid and Little Brothers of Nazareth.

General grants included those to British Society of Music Therapy, Macmillan Cancer Relief, Intermediate Technology, The Depaul Trust, Merseyside Development Foundation, East Sussex Dyslexia Association, Shelter and Age Concern.

Applications In writing to the correspondent.

Marshall's Charity

Parsonage and church improvements

£741,000 (1997)

Beneficial area England and Wales

Marshall House, 66 Newcomen Street, London SE1 1YT

Tel. 020 7407 2979

Correspondent R Goatcher, Clerk to the Trustees

Trustees *M J Dudding; P R Thompson; and others.*

Information available Full report and accounts were on file at the Charity Commission.

General In 1999 the charity had an income of £1 million and an expenditure of £1 million, unfortunately no further information from this year was available for view in the public files at the Charity Commission, the following entry was included in the last edition of *A Guide to the Major Trusts Volume 1.*

The charity is established to support parsonages throughout England and Wales, to help with the upkeep of churches in Kent, Surrey or Lincolnshire, to build new churches and to support in particular the Parish of Christ Church, Southwark.

In 1997 the charity spent £741,000 on these purposes in 43 dioceses, including 212 grants for parsonage schemes, of which 113 included payment for security measures. Also, 68 churches were assisted, with 'special consideration being given to parishes in Urban Priority Areas'.

No grant appears to have been for more than £9,000 for a parsonage or £5,000 for a church, and indeed the latter figure is probably the usual maximum in both cases.

Exclusions No grants to churches outside the counties of Kent, Surrey and Lincolnshire, as defined in 1855.

Applications To the correspondent in writing. Trustees meet in January, April, July and October. Applications need to be sent by the end of January, April, July and October for consideration at the next meeting.

Marston Charitable Trust

General

£139,000 (1998/99)

Beneficial area UK

Clay Farm, Marston St Lawrence, Banbury, Oxfordshire OX17 2DA

Correspondent J B Sumner

Information available Full accounts were on file at the Charity Commission.

General This trust appears to support a range of charities, including some related to horse-racing. In 1998/99 its assets totalled £517,000 and it had an income of £16,000. Due to a transfer from the capital account of £120,000, the trust was able to make donations totalling £139,000.

Over 150 grants were made. Grants of £10,000 each were made to Animal Health Trust, Arthritis Care, British Red Cross, Cancer Research Campaign, DGAA Homelife, Home Farm Trust, Injured Jockeys Fund, Jockey Club Charitable Trust, Macmillan Cancer Relief and Racing Welfare Charities. Grants of around £5,000 each were made to Army Benevolent Fund, Hunt Servants Fund, Queen Elizabeth Foundation for the Disabled, Salvation Army and The Primrose Hospice.

The remaining grants were mostly for less than £100.

Applications In writing to the correspondent.

The Mason Porter Charitable Trust

Christian

£109,000 (1998/99)

Beneficial area UK, with a preference for Merseyside

Liverpool Council of Social Service (Inc.), 14 Castle Street, Liverpool L2 0NJ

Tel. 0151 236 7728

Correspondent Carol Chapman, Secretary

Trustees *Liverpool Council of Social Service (Inc.).*

Information available Full accounts were provided by the trust.

General In 1998/99 the trust's assets totalled £1.8 million generating an income of £95,000. Other income totalled £110,000 from donations. Grants were made totalling £109,000 and appear to have been given mostly to Christian causes.

The accounts only listed the 11 grants made over £1,000. The largest grants were £30,000 to Barcaple Christian Outdoor Centre, £27,000 to Cliff College and £10,000 to Greasby Methodist Church. Other grants under £10,000 went to: Just Care and Life Changing Ministries (£7,500 each); New Creations (£5,000); University of Lincolnshire & Humberside (£4,000); PPS (£2,000); and Crusade for World Revival and St Luke's Methodist Church, Hoylake (each £1,000). Four of the beneficiaries listed had also received grants in the previous year.

Unlisted grants under £1,000 totalled £13,000.

Applications In writing to the correspondent, although the trust only makes grants to charities known to the settlor and unsolicited applications are not considered.

The Leonard Matchan Fund Ltd

Social and medical welfare

£53,000 (1998/99)

Beneficial area UK

c/o 16 The Towers, Lower Mortlake Road, Richmond, Surrey TW9 2JR

Correspondent Ms Jeanne Sutherland, Secretary

Trustees *Ms B A Thompson; Ms S D Groves; Ms J E M Sutherland; K H Thompson; P A Rosenthal.*

Information available Full accounts were provided by the trust.

General Grants are given to registered charities in the UK including the Channel Islands.

In 1998/99 the trust had assets of £767,000 generating an income of

£60,000. Grants totalled £53,000 and were given to 23 organisations, 17 of which were supported in the previous year.

The largest grants were £5,000 to Exmoor Calvert Trust, £3,000 each to Alzheimer's Disease Society, Attlee Foundation, Children's Society, Helen House, Roy Kinnear Charitable Trust, Relate, Weston Spirit, Willow Trust and YMCA – Croydon and £2,000 each to Dystonia Society, Jersey Christmas Appeal, RAF Association – Jersey and Whizz-Kidz.

Other beneficiaries included Canine Partners for Independence and Deafblind UK (£1,500 each), Cancer BACUP and Salvation Army – Jersey (£1,000 each). with £500 each to British Wireless for the Blind Fund and Ryder-Cheshire Foundation.

Exclusions No grants to individuals.

Applications In writing to the correspondent.

The Maxwell Family Foundation

Disability/medical, welfare, conservation, education and animals

£143,000 (1999/2000)

Beneficial area UK

181 Whiteladies Road, Clifton, Bristol BS8 2RY

Correspondent E M Maxwell, Trustee

Trustees *E M Maxwell; P M Maxwell; R P Spicer.*

Information available Full accounts are on file at the Charity Commission.

General This trust was established in 1984, by Eric McLean Maxwell and as well as having general charitable purposes, its objects are the promotion of health, medical research, and the relief of people who are elderly, disabled or sick. Support for these objects is pursued on a national basis and in the main, from an established list with which the foundation has been involved for some years.

In 1999/2000 the assets stood at £2.1 million and the income was £114,000. Management and administration costs were £7,000 this included £3,000 to Mr P M Maxwell for administration servies. A total of 29 grants were made totalling

£143,000, 15 were recurrent from the previous year.

The largest grant was for £115,000 to Sense, enabling them to purchase a home in Bristol, now the permanent residence of five people with serious disabilities.

There were a further 25 grants ranging from £100 to £7,300. Larger grants included those to Royal International Flying Scholarships for the Disabled (£7,300), Deafblind UK, (£3,500) and Dean Forest Hoispice (£2,500) and £1,000 each to Newcastle Society for the Blind, Prostate Cancer Charity and Bristol Royal Infimary.

Among those organisations receiving smaller grants in the range of £100 to £750 were Army Benevolent Fund and Family Centre (deaf children).

Exclusions The trust states explicitly that there is no support for unsolicited applications. It clearly abides by this policy and we would urge readers who do not know the trustees personally not to write to the trust.

Applications Applications are neither sought nor acknowledged. There appears little purpose in applying to this trust as no application will be supported unless accompanied by a personal request from someone known by the trustees.

This entry was not confirmed by the trust but was correct according to information on file at the Charity Commission.

The Mayfield Valley Arts Trust

Arts, especially chamber music

£117,000 (2000/01)

Beneficial area Unrestricted, but with a special interest in Sheffield and South Yorkshire

c/o Irwin Mitchell, St Peter's House, Hartshead, Sheffield S1 2EL

Tel. 0114 276 7777 **Fax** 0114 275 3306 **e-mail** jellym@irwinmitchell.co.uk

Correspondent J M Jelly, Administrator

Trustees *A Thornton; J R Thornton; Mrs P M Thornton; D Whelton; D Brown.*

Information available Accounts were on file at the Charity Commission.

General The trust was set up to encourage art and artistic activities of a charitable nature, particularly 'music and the promotion and presentation of concerts and other musical events and activities'. The trust concentrates its support on recurrent beneficiaries: Music in the Round Festivals, Live Music Now!, York Early Music Festival, York Early Music Foundation, IMS Prussia Cove and Wigmore Hall. Any remaining funds are made available to established Chamber Music venues.

In 2000/01 the trust gave a total of nearly £117,000 in grants to six beneficiaries. These were Sheffield Chamber Music in the Round Festivals (£47,000), York Early Music Festival (£7,500), York Early Music Foundation (£20,000), Wigmore Hall (£25,000), Live Music Now! (£13,000 in three grants) and IMS Prussia Cove (£5,000).

In the previous year the trust gave a grant of £20,000 to Glyndebourne for the Children's Opera 'Zoë'.

Exclusions No grants to students.

Applications The trust states that no unsolicited applications are considered.

Melodor Ltd

Jewish, general

£149,000 (1998/99)

Beneficial area UK and overseas

148 Bury Old Road, Manchester M7 4SE

Correspondent Henry Neumann, Administrator

Trustees B Weiss; M Weiss; P Weiss; S Weiss; J L Weiss; H Weiss; R Sofer; W Neuman; F Neumann; H Neumann; M Neumann; E Neumann; M Friedlander; P Neumann; J Bleier; E Henry; R De Lange.

Information available Full accounts were on file at the Charity Commission.

General The principal objective of the company is the distribution of funds to religious, educational and similar charities. In 1998/99, as in previous years, all of its support went to Jewish organisations. The trust had assets of £727,000 and an income of £234,000, including £116,000 from the sale of property and £57,000 from rents. It gave grants totalling £149,000 (£182,000 in 1997/98 and £126,000 in 1996/97).

During the year 80 grants were made, many of these were recurrent from the previous year. The largest donation in the

year went to Yeshiva L'Zeirim for £30,000. Other grants over £10,000 went to Chasdei Yoel (£28,000), BCGCT (£16,000) and Beis Minchas Yitzchok (£14,000).

The remaining grants ranged from £150 to £4,500 and included those to Kollel Shomrei Hachomoth (£4,500), Belz – Manchester (£4,200), Jewish Senior Boys School (£1,800), Rabbanical Research College (£1,500), Magen Charitable Trust (£1,400) and Manchester Charitable Trust (£1,000). Grants under £1,000 included those to North Salford Synagogue (£750), Tiffereth Yaakov (£500), HTVC (£200) and Brookvale (£150).

Applications In writing to the correspondent.

Melow Charitable Trust

Jewish

£315,000 (1997/98)

Beneficial area UK and overseas

21 Warwick Grove, London E5 9HX

Tel. 020 8806 1549

Correspondent J Low

Trustees M Spitz; E Weiser.

Information available Accounts were on file at the Charity Commission, but with only a brief narrative report.

General This trust makes grants to Jewish charities both in the UK and overseas. In 1997/98 its assets totalled £408,000 and it had an income of £337,000 comprised mainly of donations received (£230,000) but also with £97,000 received from rents.

This year saw an increase in the trust's grant-making with awards totalling £315,000 compared with £148,000 in 1996/97. Grants ranged between £1,200 and £30,000 and were made to 34 organisations. A large number of new organisations, as well as some of those supported in the previous year, received grants. Larger grants were £31,000 to Shalom Torah Centre – USA, £30,000 to Yeshivas Chidushei Harim – Israel and £23,000 to United Talmudical Associates – USA.

Other larger grants went to Congregation Mosdos Toledos Aharon (£15,000), Yeshiva Horomoh Talmudical College

(£12,000), Dushinsky Trust (£11,000) and Satmar Gemach (£10,000).

Grants less than £10,000 went to Congregation Letev Lev – USA and Rabbi Pinet Memorial Fund (£8,000 each), Craven Walk Charitable Trust (£7,000), Yetev Lev Youth Club (£6,000), Toldos Yaakov Yost Institutions Trust (£5,300), British Jewish Heritage Society (£3,300), Beis Rochel School – Manchester (£2,300) and Rehabilitation Trust (£1,200).

Applications In writing to the correspondent.

Menuchar Ltd

Jewish

£115,000 (1997/98)

Beneficial area UK

Flack Stetson, Mattey House, 128–136 High Street, Edgware, Middlesex HA8 7EL

Tel. 020 8952 1986

Correspondent The Trustees

Trustees N Bude.

Information available Accounts were on file at the Charity Commission but without a list of grants since 1993/94.

General The main objects of the trust are the advancement of religion in accordance with the orthodox Jewish faith and the relief of people in need. In 1997/98 the trust had assets of £518,000 and an income of £86,000, of which £39,000 came from donations. Management and administration costs were low at £900 and grants totalled £115,000. No further information was available on the grants for this year.

All the grants in 1993/94 were to Jewish organisations, the largest being £18,000 to Friends of Harim Establishments, and £10,000 each to Woodstock Sinclair Trust and Friends of Seret Wiznitz. Over half the remaining grants were under £500. Grants were generally one-off.

Exclusions No grants to non-registered charities or to individuals.

Applications In writing to the correspondent.

Mercury Phoenix Trust

AIDS, HIV

£601,000 (1998/99)

Beneficial area Worldwide

The Mill, Mill Lane, Cookham, Berkshire SL6 9QT

Tel. 01628 527874

Correspondent Peter Chant

Trustees *M Austin; H J Beach; B H May; R M Taylor.*

Information available Accounts were on file at the Charity Commission, but without a list of grants. An information leaflet describing its work and listing some of the beneficiaries was provided by the trust.

General The trust was set up in memory of Freddie Mercury by the remaining members of the legendary rock group, Queen, and their manager. It makes grants to 'help relieve the poverty, sickness and distress of people with AIDS and HIV and to stimulate awareness and education in connection with the disease throughout the world'. The trust informed us in November 2000, that it is 'only funding projects with charities in developing countries during the year 2000 and, unless the policy changes, this will also be the case for 2001'.

Starting with the Freddie Mercury Tribute Concert for AIDS Awareness, the trust's fundraising activities have been spectacular. Income has been raised from, for example, a fan-initiated annual national street collection, a Queen album and from a ballet which was inspired by the music of Queen and Mozart.

The trust's information leaflet states: 'Applications for grants have come in from many countries around the world and collaboration has been realised with groups as far removed as the World Health Organisation to grass-root organisations run partly by voluntary workers in Uganda, Kenya, South Africa, Zambia, Nepal and India. The trust is following the latest developments in drug therapies and adapting funding policy to the changing needs of those affected by HIV/AIDS in the UK and elsewhere'.

In 1998/99 the trust's assets totalled £1.4 million with an income of £259,000, including £143,000 from Gift Aid and other donations. Grants totalled £601,000, resulting in a large deficit for the year.

Further information was not available in the accounts about the beneficiaries or

size of grants. However, the trust's information leaflet includes a list of over 200 previous beneficiaries. The following are examples: AIDS Fondet Denmark, All Hallows Hospital, Barnardos Broad Street Project, Bihar State Dalit Women's Organisation, Blackpool and Preston Body Positive, Buddies, Children with AIDS Charity, Foundation d'Aide Direct, HARASS – Hastings and Rother, Life AIDS Project, National AIDS Manual, Open Road, Rajasthan Mahila Kalyan Mandal, Rural Heal Mission, TASO – Uganda, World Medical Fund and Zambia Charitable Trust.

Applications In writing to the correspondent.

Midhurst Pensions Trust

General

£111,000 to organisations and individuals (1999/2000)

Beneficial area UK and overseas

The Cowdray Trust Limited, Pollen House, 10–12 Cork Street, London W1X 1PD

Correspondent Alan J Winborn

Trustees *The Cowdray Trust Limited.*

Information available Full accounts were on file at the Charity Commission.

General The Fourth Viscount Cowdray was the settlor of this trust, reflected in the fact that The Cowdray Trust Limited is a trustee and also represented in some of the grant beneficiaries (see below).

In 1999/2000 the trust had assets of £4.6 million and an income of £129,000. Grants were made totalling £111,000.

The largest grant of the year was £50,000 to Tibet House Trust; Ladaka School Project also received a substantial grant of £10,000. Other organisations supported in the past include King Edward VII Hospital – Midhurst and Viscount Cowdray's Charitable Trust. Individual pensions were made to a number of older people in the year, including those linked with the Cowdray family.

Exclusions No grants to individuals, other than those shown above.

Applications In writing to the correspondent. Unsuccessful applications will not be acknowledged.

The Miller Foundation

General, animal welfare

£161,000 (1999)

Beneficial area UK, with a preference for Scotland, especially the west of Scotland

c/o Maclay Murray & Spens, 151 St Vincent Street, Glasgow G2 5NJ

Tel. 0141 248 5011   **Fax** 0141 248 5819
e-mail asb@maclaymurrayspens.co.uk

Correspondent A Biggart, Secretary to the Foundation

Trustees *C Fleming-Brown; C C Wright; G R G Graham; J Simpson; C F R Fleming-Brown.*

Information available Information was provided by the trust.

General The trust supports the following:

- charities in Scotland, especially in the west of Scotland
- UK, animal welfare charities.

It will support a wide range of charities in Scotland. In 1999 grants totalled £161,000 and ranged from £1,000 to £2,000. Several grants were recurrent. Examples of beneficiaries were not available.

Exclusions No grants to individuals.

Applications On a form available from the secretary. Trustees meet twice a year to consider grants, in April and November. Applications should be received by the end of March and October respectively.

The Millfield Trust

Christian

£100,000 (1998/99)

Beneficial area UK and worldwide

Millfield House, Bell Lane, Liddington, Swindon, Wiltshire SN4 0HE

Tel. 01793 790181

Correspondent D Bunce, Trustee

Trustees *D Bunce; Mrs R Bunce; P W Bunce; S D Bunce; A C Bunce.*

Information available Full accounts were on file at the Charity Commission.

General This trust was set up to provide grants to Christian organisations, and has supported a number of missionary societies for the last 50 years. Grants are given solely to organisations known to the trust and new applications are not considered.

In 1998/99 the trust had assets of £145,000 and an income of £73,000, comprised of Gift Aid donations and investment income. Grants to 57 organisations totalled £100,000 and grants to individuals totalled £3,900.

The largest grants in 1998/99 were given to Tearfund (£25,000), Gideons International (£23,000) and Friends of Ridgeway School (£13,000). Other grants ranged from £50 to £3,200 and were given to a variety of causes including: Christian groups such as Scripture Union (£1,500), Church Army (£1,000), Japan Evangelistic Band (£300) and Christchurch Marlborough (£50); international relief and development organisations such as British Red Cross and Send a Cow (each £1,000) and UNICEF (£100); and UK charities catering for individuals such as Banardos, Help the Aged and NSPCC (£100 each). Many of the organisations supported have received similar sized grants in recent years.

Applications No replies to unsolicited applications.

The Millhouses Charitable Trust

Christian, overseas aid, general

£78,000 (1997/98)

Beneficial area UK and overseas

Medicos House, 79 Beverly Road, Hull HU3 1XR

Tel. 01482 320243

Correspondent Dr A W Harcus, Trustee

Trustees *Revd J S Harcus; Dr A W Harcus.*

Information available Accounts were on file at the Charity Commission, but without a narrative report or grants list.

General In 1998/99 the trust had an income of £55,000 and an expenditure of

£64,000. Unfortunately further information for this year was not available and the following information is repeated from the last edition of this guide.

Most of the grants given by this trust are recurrent. If new grants are made, they are usually to organisations known to the trustees.

In 1997/98 the trust's assets totalled £539,000. It had an income of £72,000 from both investments and Gift Aid donations. Grants totalled £78,000, but further information was not available about beneficiaries in that year.

In 1996/97 grants totalled £55,000 and were made to 40 organisations. The largest grant was £10,000 to Batah Foundation. Grants of £5,000 were made to six organisations including Amnesty International UK, Baptist Missionary Society, Christian Aid and NSPCC. Grants of £1,000 were made to five organisations including Bible Society, Child Hope UK and Children of the Andes. A grant of £750 was given to Ethiopiaid, other grants were all for £250.

Exclusions Grants are made to registered charities only, no grants to individuals.

Applications In writing to the correspondent, but note the comments above.

The Millichope Foundation

General

£186,000 (1998/99)

Beneficial area UK, especially the West Midlands and Shropshire

Millichope Park, Munslow, Craven Arms, Shropshire SY7 9HA

Correspondent Mrs S A Bury, Trustee

Trustees *L C N Bury; Mrs S A Bury; Mrs B Marshall.*

Information available Full accounts were on file at the Charity Commission.

General The trust makes donations to a wide range of different organisations including:

• UK charities
• local charities serving Birmingham and Shropshire
• conservation charities.

In 1998/99 the assets stood at £4.2 million, the income was £253,000, of which £52,000 came from donations. The 139 donations made totalled £186,000. Grants were in the range of £50 to £13,000, 85 of these were for £1,000 or more. A number of recipients had received grants in the previous year.

The largest grant of the year went to the Fauna & Flora Preservation Society. This organisation received two grants totalling £13,000 and has been the major beneficiary in previous years. The trust made six grants of £5,000, beneficiaries included Midlands Centre for Spinal Injuries Appeal, Oxfam Hurricane Appeal, National Trust and Save the Children Fund. Other larger grants included £3,500 to Royal Opera House Covent Garden; £2,500 to St Basil's Centre and National Institute of Conductive Education; and £1,000 each to Barnardos, Castle Vale Homestart, Centre of Earth, English Bridge, Relate and Royal Academy of Music Education.

Grants given locally in the Birmingham and Shropshire areas included: Birmingham City Mission (£1,000); with £500 each to Midland Youth Orchestra, Age Concern, Shropshire Family Mediation and Shropshire Youth Adventure Trust; and £50 to Shropshire Helping Hand.

Exclusions No grants to individuals or non-registered charities.

Applications In writing to the correspondent

The Minos Trust

Christian, general

£72,000 (1998/99)

Beneficial area UK and overseas

Deloitte & Touche, Leda House, Station Road, Cambridge CB1 2RN

Tel. 01223 460222   **Fax** 01223 363869

Correspondent S Midwinter, Trustee

Trustees *Revd K W Habershon; Mrs K W Habershon; S Midwinter.*

Information available Full accounts were on file at the Charity Commission.

General The trust gives most of its support to Christian charities in grants ranging up to £15,000. Remaining funds are given to other causes, with a preference for animals and wildlife, although these grants tend to be less than

£1,000. Many of the organisations receiving the larger grants are regularly supported by the trust.

In 1998/99 the trust had an income of £29,000 from investments and donations. About 100 grants were made totalling £72,000.

The largest grants were £10,000 each to Chichester Cathedral Trust and Tigers Club Project. Other large grants included Care Trust (£2,500), Tearfund (£2,000), Ashburnham Christian Trust (£1,500) with £1,000 each to Bible Society, Friends of the Elderly and Youth with a Mission. 80% of the grants were were under £1,000 and were given to Christian organisations in the UK and overseas including: Africa Christian Press (£400), Aid to Russian Christians (£300) and Gideons International (£100). Other grants included those to Worldwide Fund for Nature (£450) and Sussex Farming Wildlife Advisory Group and RSPB (£50 each).

Applications In writing to the correspondent, for consideration on an ongoing basis.

The Laurence Misener Charitable Trust

General, Jewish

£84,000 (1998/99)

Beneficial area UK

Messrs Bourner Bullock, Sovereign House, 212–224 Shaftesbury Avenue, London WC2H 8HQ

Tel. 020 7240 5821

Correspondent C A Letts

Trustees J E Cama; P M Tarsh.

Information available Full accounts were on file at the Charity Commission.

General In 1998/99 this trust had assets of £3 million and an income of £98,000. 27 grants were awarded in the year totalling £84,000, all of these were recurrent and appear to be ongoing commitments.

The largest donation was to Richard Dimbleby Cancer Fund for £8,200. Other larger grants were £5,900 each to Jewish Association for Physically Handicapped, Jewish Care and Home for Aged Jews –

Nightingale House and £5,000 to Robert Owen Foundation.

The 22 other grants ranged from £1,800 to £4,000. Beneficiaries included Age Concern, Blond McIndoe Centre, Devon County Association for the Blind, Imperial War Museum Trust, Jews' Temporary Shelter, Royal College of Surgeons, Sussex Stroke and Circulation Fund, SGHMS Haematology Research Fund and World Ship Trust.

Applications In writing to the correspondent.

The Victor Mishcon Charitable Trust

Jewish, social welfare

£62,000 (1998/99)

Beneficial area UK

21 Southampton Row, London WC1B 5HS

Correspondent P A Cohen, Trustee

Trustees Lord Mishcon; Lady Mishcon; P A Cohen.

Information available Full accounts were on file at the Charity Commission.

General The trust supports mainly Jewish charities, but also gives grants to general social welfare and medical/disability causes.

In 1998/99 it had assets of £1.6 million and an income of £92,000. Grants totalled £62,000, with £850 spent on management and administration.

Grants were made to 140 organisations in the year, over half of these were supported in the previous year. The largest grant was of £13,000 which went to JPAIME. Other larger grants went to Echoes Theatre Co. Ltd. (£5,000), Simon and Phillip Cohen Charitable Trust (£3,000), United Synagogue (£2,400), Joint Jewish Charitable Trust (£2,200), University College London (£2,000), Nightingale House (£1,700), British Centre of the Shaare Zedak (£1,400) and European Palestine Israel Centre (£1,000).

Most of the remaining grants were between £100 and £500. These were given to a range of causes, though they were predominantly Jewish, health and welfare. Recipients included Jewish Care,

Jewish Marriage Council, Friends of Jewish Youth, Cardiff United Synagogue, World Jewish Relief and Youth Alliyah. Non-Jewish beneficiaries included Action in Distress, Action for Blind People, British Red Cross, Centrepoint, NSPCC and World Cancer Research Fund.

Grants totalling £9,600 were given in 'donations for the relief of poverty'. Further information on these beneficiaries was not available.

Applications In writing to the correspondent.

The Mitchell Charitable Trust

Jewish, general

£84,000 (1998/99)

Beneficial area UK, with a preference for London

28 Heath Drive, London NW3 7SB

Tel. 020 7794 5668 **Fax** 020 7794 5680

Correspondent Ashley Mitchell, Trustee

Trustees Ashley Mitchell; Parry Mitchell; Elizabeth Mitchell; Hannah Lowy.

Information available Accounts were provided by the trust.

General The trust was established in 1984. In 1998/99 it had assets of £2 million (in shares in a wide range of companies) and an income of £74,000. Grants totalling £84,000 were made to 39 organisations, ranging from £16 to £25,000. 10 of the organisations supported had received grants in the previous year. The trust has general charitable purposes but in practice appears to have a strong preference for welfare charities, Jewish organisations and health charities.

The largest grant of £25,000 went to Jewish Care (the major beneficiary in recent years) with Norwood Ravenswood and World Jewish Relief both receiving £10,000 each.

A number of other charities received grants of between £1,000 and £5,000. Recipients included The Otto Schiff Housing Association (£5,000), Community Security Trust (£2,500) and St Giles Trust and The Spires Centre (£2,000 each). Grants of £1,000 each were given out to 12 organisations including ChildLine, Gifts in Kind UK, Spiro Institute and Westminster School.

Recipients of grants under £1,000 included Teenage Cancer Trust (£600); with £500 each to Action for ME, Changing Faces, Friends of Searchlight, Society of Voluntary Associations. Smaller grants included those to Action Aid (£200), The One to One Project (£100) and St Peter's Research Trust (£20).

Exclusions No grants to individuals or for research, education, overseas appeals or non-Jewish religious appeals. Applicants from small charities outside London are unlikely to be considered.

Applications In writing to the correspondent. Applications must include financial information. The trust does not reply to any applications unless they choose to support them. Trustees do not meet on a regular basis, thus applicants may not be advised of a grant for a considerable period.

The Mizpah Trust

General

£165,000 (1997/98)

Beneficial area UK

Foresters House, Humbly Grove, South Warnborough, Hook, Hampshire RG29 1RY

Correspondent A C O Bell, Trustee

Trustees A C O Bell; J E Bell.

Information available Full accounts were on file at the Charity Commission.

General In 1998/99 the trust had an income of £124,000 and an expenditure of £136,000. Unfortunately further information for this year was not available and the following information is repeated from the last edition of this guide.

The trust is proactive and makes grants to a wide range of organisations. In 1997/98 it had assets totalling £134,000 and its income was £96,000 including £50,000 in Gift Aid donations. Grants totalled £165,000. Three major grants were made during the year: £55,000 to Tearfund, £35,000 to Micah Trust and £30,000 to CARE.

Other grants were for up to £7,500 and included those to Lambeth Partnership, Brentford Settlement and Crusade for World Revival. All the beneficiaries

appeared to be Christian, with the exception of Guide Dogs for the Blind which received £2,500.

Applications The trust states that 'no applications will be considered'.

The Mole Charitable Trust

Jewish, general

About £78,000 (1995/96)

Beneficial area UK, with a preference for Manchester

2 Okeover Road, Salford M7 4JX

Tel. 0161 832 8721

Correspondent M Gross, Trustee

Trustees M Gross; D Z Lopian; Mrs L P Gross.

Information available Accounts were on file at the Charity Commission.

General In 1998/99 the trust had an income of £718,000 and expenditure totalling £317,000. This was taken from the Charity Commission database, further information was not yet available in the public files at the time of going to print. The following is repeated from the last edition of this guide.

In 1995/96 the trust had assets of £157,000 and an income of £204,000. It gave 39 grants totalling £78,000, leaving a surplus of £126,000. Most grants were to Jewish organisations, with a preference for those in Manchester. The trust also gave £23,000 in loans to the same type of organisations as above.

Grants ranged from £250 to £16,000, 17 of which were for £1,000 or more. The largest of these grants were to: Broom Foundation (£16,000) – a regular beneficiary; Vaad Hatzdoko Charitable Trust (£13,000); and Manchester Charitable Trust (£8,000) – another regular beneficiary. Other regular beneficiaries included Broughton Jewish Cassell Fox Primary School (£2,500) and Binoh of Manchester (£1,800). Grants under £1,000 were made to 22 organisations, including those to Manchester Jewish Benevolent Society, Manchester and Gateshead Talmudical Colleges and North Salford Synagogue.

Applications In writing to the correspondent.

The D C Moncrieff Charitable Trust

Social welfare, environment

£60,000 (1998/99)

Beneficial area UK and worldwide, with a preference for Norfolk and Suffolk

14 Stubbs Wood, Gunton, Lowestoft, Suffolk NR32 4TA

Correspondent L G Friston, Trustee

Trustees L G Friston; D J Coleman; A S Cunningham.

Information available Full accounts were on file at the Charity Commission.

General The trust was established in 1961. It supports a number of large, UK organisations, however it tends to concentrate on charities local to the Norfolk and Suffolk areas. Its two main areas of support are social welfare and the environment.

In 1998/99 it had an income of £60,000 and assets of £736,000. Grants to 55 organisations totalled £60,000. A significant number of beneficiaries had also received grants in the previous year. The largest grant of £6,000 went to the Church Army (Harleston House) while £3,000 each went to Friends of Lothingland Hospital and All Hallows Hospital. The trust also awarded 27 grants ranging from £1,000 to £2,500 and 25 smaller grants of £500. Social welfare charities to receive grants included St Luke's Hospital for the Clergy (£2,000), and NSPCC and East Suffolk Blind Association (each £500). Environmental organisations to benefit included Wiltshire Gardens Trust (£1,500), Suffolk Wildlife Trust (£1,000) and RSPB (£500). Grants also went to Lowestoft Girl Guides (£2,500) and Society for Lincolnshire History & Archaeology (£1,500).

Exclusions In May 2000 the trust stated that demand for funds exceeded available resources, therefore no further requests were currently being invited.

Applications In writing to the correspondent, though note the above.

George A Moore Foundation

General, mostly in Yorkshire and Isle of Man

£286,000 (1999/2000)

Beneficial area Principally Yorkshire and the Isle of Man but also some major UK appeals

Mitre House, North Park Road, Harrogate, North Yorkshire HG1 5RX

Correspondent Miss L P Oldham

Trustees *George A Moore; Mrs E Moore; J R Moore; Mrs A L James*

Information available Information and a grants list provided by the trust.

General The foundation's policy outline is as follows:

'The trustees select causes and projects from the applications received during the year and also independently research and identify specific objectives where they wish to direct assistance. The types of grant can vary quite widely from one year to another and care is taken to maintain a rough parity among the various fields covered so that one sphere of activity does not benefit unduly at the expense of another. Areas which are not or cannot be covered by official sources are favoured.

'The beneficial area is principally Yorkshire and the Isle of Man but consideration is given to some major national charities under certain circumstances.

'Grants are normally non-recurrent and the foundation is reluctant to contribute to revenue appeals. Approximately 75% of the grants made are £500 or below.

'Only registered charities are considered and the foundation rarely contributes seedcorn finance to newly-established organisations. Projects for young people (teenagers/young adults) are favoured, as are community care projects.'

Grants are generally for £1,000 or less, but most of grant expenditure goes in a few large grants of up to £100,000. Awards are usually one-off payments but many, including the large donations, go to organisations previously funded. Beneficiaries are charities working in a variety of fields, but particularly for people who are young, elderly or disabled.

In 1999/2000 the trust's assets totalled £6.9 million, generating an income of £617,000. Grants totalling £286,000 were made to 67 organisations, 19 of these grants were for £1,000 or more, with the two largest grants amounting to £220,000, or 77% of grant expenditure. These two awards were to St John Ambulance (£170,000) and LGI Community Chest Appeal (£50,000).

Other larger beneficiaries included Knaresborough Rotary Club Millennium Clock (£5,400), Welfare Fund HMS Illustrious (£4,300), Macmillan Cancer Relief Harrogate & District Appeal (£2,500) with £1,000 each to Age Concern Knaresborough, Barnardos, CHAS Housing Aid Centre, NSPCC, Re-Solv and Sick Children's Trust. The remainder of grants were in the range of £50 to £800, with most being for £500 or under. Beneficiaries included British Diabetic Association and Friends of St Edwards (£750 each), Tockwith & District Show (£600) and £500 each to British Wheelchair Sports Association, Cookridge Cancer Centre Appeal, Knaresborough Festival, Reach, Wetherby in Bloom and Wheatfields Hospice.

Smaller grants included those to Cot Death Society (£400); Pannal Cricket Club and UNICEF (£250 each); British Red Cross (£200); Macmillan Cancer Relief, RNIB and York Student Community Action (£100 each); and St Mary's Church Boston Spa (£75).

Exclusions No assistance will be given to individuals for courses of study, expeditions, overseas travel, holidays, or purposes outside the UK. Local appeals for UK charities will only be considered if in the area of interest. Because of present long-term commitments, the foundation is not prepared to consider appeals for religious property or institutions, or for educational purposes.

Applications In writing to the correspondent. No guidelines or application forms are issued. The trustees meet approximately four times a year, on variable dates, and an appropriate response is sent out after the relevant meeting.

The Nigel Moores Family Charitable Trust

Arts

£84,000 (1996/97)

Beneficial area UK, with some preference for Wales

c/o Macfarlane & Co., 2nd Floor, Cunard Building, Water Street, Liverpool L3 1DS

Correspondent P Kurthausen, Accountant

Trustees *J C S Moores; Mrs L M White; Mrs P M Kennaway.*

Information available Full accounts were on file at the Charity Commission.

General In 1998/99 the trust had an income of £189,000 and an expenditure of £272,000. Unfortunately further information for this year was not available and the following information is repeated from the last edition of this guide.

This trust's principal object is to make grants towards 'raising the artistic taste of the public, whether in relation to music, drama, opera, painting, sculpture'. Its secondary objects are to make grants 'in connection with the fine arts and academic education, the promotion of the environment, the provision of facilities for recreation or other leisure time occupations and the advancement of religion'.

In 1996/97 the trust's assets totalled £284,000. It had an income from donations of £91,000 and grants were made to 11 organisations totalling £84,000.

The largest grants were £21,000 to Tate Gallery – Liverpool, £20,000 to Landlife, £19,000 to The New Contemporaries (1988) Ltd and £15,000 to Massive Video. Other grants ranged from £500 to £4,000 and all but one were to Welsh organisations including Llantysilio School Foundation (£4,000), Pentrwf Community Association (£2,000) and Llangollen Pre-school Playgroup (£1,000).

Applications In writing to the correspondent.

Morgan Williams Charitable Trust

Christian, welfare

£108,000 (1995/96)

Beneficial area UK

95 Thurleigh Road, London SW12 8TY

Tel. 020 7606 1066

Correspondent K Costa, Trustee

Trustees *K J Costa; Mrs A F Costa.*

Information available Accounts were on file at the Charity Commission, but only up until 1995/96.

General Unfortunately we have been unable to update the following information since the last edition of this guide.

This trust appears to rely on annual donations to maintain its level of grant-giving. In 1995/96 it received donations of £102,000 and had a total income of £107,000. The main beneficiary is regularly Holy Trinity Church. Smaller grants were also given to individuals, Oasis Charitable Trust, St Barnabas Church and other Christian organisations, with only a few very small grants to other welfare charities. Less than a quarter of the grants were recurrent from the previous year.

Applications The trust states that only charities personally connected with the trustees are supported and absolutely no applications are either solicited or acknowledged.

The Oliver Morland Charitable Trust

Quakers, general

£107,000 (1999/2000)

Beneficial area UK

Thomas's House, Stower Row, Shaftesbury, Dorset SP7 0QW

Tel. 01747 853524

Correspondent J M Rutter, Trustee & Treasurer

Trustees *Priscilla Khan; Stephen Rutter; Joseph Rutter; Jennnifer Pittard; Kate Lovell; Charlotte Jones.*

Information available Accounts were on file at the Charity Commission.

General In 1999/2000 the trust had an income of £99,000 and gave grants totalling £107,000. The trustees state that the majority of funds are given to Quaker projects or Quaker-related projects, which are usually choosen through the personal knowledge of the trustees.

Grants were divided into the following categories:

Quaker projects and schools	£77,000
Health and social care	£16,000
International environment	£6,700
Animal and nature projects	£3,500
Other	£3,100

Applications The trustees meet twice a year, probably in May and November. The trust stated that it tends to give to the same charities each year and no funds are available for unsolicited applications.

The Morris Charitable Trust

Welfare, health, older people, education

£121,000 (1998/99)

Beneficial area UK and overseas, with a preference for Islington

Management Department, Business Design Centre, 52 Upper Street, Islington Green, London N1 0QH

Tel. 020 7359 3535   **Fax** 020 7226 0590

Correspondent The Chair's Secretary

Trustees *Mrs G Morris; J A Morris; P B Morris; A R Stenning.*

Information available Full accounts were provided by the trust along with a detailed grants list.

General The trust was founded in 1989 by the Morris Family, owners of the City Industrial Limited Group. These companies contribute a proportion of profits to fund charitable activity.

The object of the trust is to promote charitable causes, in particular to relieve people who are deprived, sick or elderly and advance education for public benefit. The trust supports national and international community charitable causes, however, there is a preference for making grants locally in the London borough of Islington.

In 1998/99 the trust's income was £103,000 (coming mainly from donated income) and its assets totalled £116,000. Grants totalled £121,000 and can be broken down as follows:

Local organisations

Grants totalling £81,000 were given to 57 organisations. The largest of £50,000 was given in Islington to William Tyndale School. Other larger grants included those to Sam Morris Centre Nursery (£5,000), Islington Police Summer Project (£2,200), Six Acres Tenants & Residents Association (£1,500) and Islington Arts Factory (£1,000).

The remainder of grants were in the range of £50 and £750, recipients included Andover Youth Trust (£700), Islington Mencap Services (£500), Colt's Football Club (£350) and St Stephen's Church (£250).

UK/International

A total of £40,000 was given in 183 grants. Two larger grants were given to Poole's Park School (£3,000) and Anne Frank Educational Centre (£1,000). The remainder of grants in this category were in the range of £50 and £800, but tended to be for smaller amounts under £250. Recipients included Norwood Ravenswood (£800), Tower Theatre (£500) with £250 each to Community Security Trust, Canonbury School Association and Children's Express and £100 each to Coronary Prevention Group, Headway, Help the Aged and Raleigh International.

Applications By application form, available from the correspondent.

Morris Family Israel Trust

Jewish

£167,000 (1998/99)

Beneficial area UK and Israel

Flat 90, North Gate, Prince Albert Road, London NW8 7EJ

Tel. 020 7722 0252

Correspondent Conrad J Morris, Trustee

Trustees *Conrad Morris; Ruth Morris; Sara Jo Ben Zvi; Elisabeth Pushett; David Morris.*

Information available Up-to-date accounts were provided by the trust.

General In 1998/99 the trust's assets totalled £44,000 and it had an income comprised of donations totalling £163,000. Grants totalled £167,000 (£173,000 in 1997/98).

About 90 grants were made, with the main one being £53,000 to Bet Haggai, followed by £11,000 to Elad. The remaining grants ranged between £15 and £6,100. Beneficiaries included Ascent Institute, Chana Jaffe, Jewish Student Information Centre, Our Jerusalem and Women in Green.

Applications In writing to the correspondent.

Ruth and Conrad Morris Charitable Trust

Jewish, general

£186,000 (1998/99)

Beneficial area UK and Israel

c/o Paul Maurice, MRI Moores Rowland, Mitre House, 177 Regent Street, London W1R 8BB

Tel. 020 7470 0000

Correspondent Conrad Morris, Trustee

Information available Accounts were on file at the Charity Commission, but with no narrative report.

General In 1998/99 the trust's assets totalled £77,000. However, it received an income of £204,000, mainly from donations. Grants were made mainly to Jewish organisations in the UK and Israel, totalling £186,000.

The accounts listed the largest 142 grants, further grants of £100 or less were also made, totalling £3,100.

The main beneficiaries were Lubaritch Foundation (£31,000), Morris Family Israel Trust (£25,000) and L'Chaim (£13,000). A further 37 grants were made over £1,000, recipients included SCOPUS (£9,000), Jill Dalyn (£6,000), SAGE (£5,000), Yesodey Hatorah (£4,500), BICC (£4,000), Joint Jewish Charitable Trust (£3,000) and Immanuel College and Nightingale House (£1,000 each).

Grants under £1,000 included Jerusalem Foundation, Jewish Learning Exchange and Youth Aliyah. Organisations among the small number of non-Jewish

beneficiaries were Cancer Research Campaign and Globe Cancer Research.

Applications In writing to the correspondent.

The Willie & Mabel Morris Charitable Trust

Medical, general

£90,000 (1997/98)

Beneficial area UK

Charles Russell, 8–10 New Fetter Lane, London EC4A 1RS

Tel. 020 7203 5269

Correspondent Alan Bryant

Trustees *Michael Macfadyen; Joyce Tether; Peter Tether; Hugh Jackson; Andrew Tether.*

Information available Full accounts were on file at the Charity Commission.

General The trust was established in 1980 by Mr and Mrs Morris. It was constituted for general charitable purposes and specifically to relieve physical ill-health, particularly cancer, heart trouble, cerebral palsy, arthritis and rheumatism. Grants are usually only given to registered charities.

In 1997/98 the trust had assets of £3.1 million and an income of £108,000. Grants totalling £90,000 were made to 66 organisation, 25 of these had received help in the previous year.

The largest grant of £12,000 went to St Thomas' Lupus Trust. Other large grants included those to Covent Garden Cancer Research Trust (£4,000), Muscular Dystrophy Group (£3,200), Adult Dyslexia Development Centre and Lane Fox 'Breath Taking' Fund (£3,000 each).

Other grants made included 16 of £2,000, 3 of £1,500 and 7 of £1,000, with the remainder being for under £1,000. These went mainly to medical organisations with beneficiaries including Arthritis Research Campaign, British Heart Foundation, Meningitis Research Foundation, The Stroke Association, British Polio Fellowship, Children with Leukaemia and Health Unlimited.

Non-medical beneficiaries included Royal Botanical Gardens Kew Foundation, Horse Rescue Fund, Raleigh

International, Royal British Legion, St Johns Church Restoration Fund and St Albans Cathedral Music Trust.

Exclusions No grants for individuals or non-registered charities.

Applications The trustees 'formulate an independent grants policy at regular meetings so that funds are already committed'.

The G M Morrison Charitable Trust

Medical, education, welfare

£120,000 (1999/2000)

Beneficial area UK

11/J Stuart Tower, 105 Maida Vale, London W9 1UH

Tel. 020 7289 0976

Correspondent G M Morrison, Trustee

Trustees *G M Morrison; N W Smith; J P S Thomson.*

Information available Full accounts were on file at the Charity Commission.

General Grants are given to a range of charities/organisations involved in education, medical research and welfare.

In 1998/99 the trust had assets of £7.9 million and an income of £210,000. After expenses of £29,000, the trust gave 205 donations totalling £120,000, the largest of which went to University of Aberdeen Development Trust (£10,000), Wolfson College (two grants totalling £6,000), Rugby School (two grants totalling £4,500), Royal Institution and Royal Society of Arts Endowment Fund (£2,000 each) and Royal College of Surgeons (£1,200).

It gave 13 grants of £1,000 to organisations such as Children's Family Trust, London Immunology Cancer Trust, University of Liverpool and YMCA.

The remainder of grants were in the range of £200 and £950. Recipients included Help the Hospices (£800), Alone in London and RNIB (£700 each), Anchor Trust (£500), Covent Garden Cancer Research Trust and Skin Treatment and Research Trust (£400 each), Home Farm Trust (£350) and

Police Dependants' Fund (£250). A small number of organisations outside the trust's usual areas of interest also received grants in the year. These included Royal Botanical Gardens – Kew, Royal Horticultural Society, RSPB and Missionaries of Africa. A number of PCCs also benefited.

Exclusions No support for individuals or for non-registered charities.

Applications In writing to the correspondent. Grants are distributed once a year in January. Please note, telephone applications are not considered.

Vyoel Moshe Charitable Trust

Not known

£317,000 (1997/98)

Beneficial area UK

2–4 Chardmore Road, London N16 6HX

Tel. 020 8806 2598

Correspondent J Weinberger, Secretary

Trustees *Rabbi M Teitelbaum; Rabbie J Meisels; Y Frankel; B Berger; S Seidenfeld.*

Information available Accounts were on file at the Charity Commission up until 1997/98, but without a list of grants or a narrative report.

General Unfortunately we have been unable to update information about this trust since the last edition of this guide. Furthermore, since there is very little information on file for this trust at the Charity Commission, we cannot confirm what its grant-making policy is.

In 1997/98 the trust's assets totalled only £20,000, its income, from donations, totalled £340,000. Grants were made totalling £317,000, resulting in a surplus, after other expenditure, of £21,000.

Applications In writing to the correspondent.

The Moss Charitable Trust

Christian, education, poverty, health

£166,000 to organisations (1999/2000)

Beneficial area Worldwide, with an interest in Dorset, Hampshire and Sussex

7 Church Road, Parkstone, Poole, Dorset BH14 8UF

Tel. 01202 730002

Correspondent P D Malpas, Chair

Trustees *A W Malpas; J H Simmons; A F Simmons; J L Simmons; P L Simmons.*

Information available Information was provided by the trust, but without a full grants list.

General The objects of the trust are to benefit the community in the county borough of Bournemouth and the counties of Hampshire, Dorset and Sussex, also the advancement of religion either home or overseas, and the advancement of education and the relief of poverty, disease and sickness.

To meet its objects, the trust provides facilities for contributors to give under deed of covenant, Gift Aid or direct giving and redistributes them according to their recommendations. The trustees also make grants from the general income of the trust.

In 1999/2000 the trust had an income of £412,000, of which £387,000 came from Gift Aid and covenants and was all restricted funds. Grants to organisations were made totalling £166,000, while £29,000 went to individuals. The 30 grants made over £1,000 were listed in the report. Of the organisations supported, 18 had received help in the previous year.

The largest grant was £35,000 to World Outreach. Other grants included those to Slavic Gospel Association (£10,000), Tearfund (£9,000), Stour Valley Community Church (£7,300), Scripture Union International (£6,100), Outreach to Kenya and Victory Outreach (£5,000 each), Emmanuel Christian Fellowship (£4,200), Blandford Youth Trust (£3,000), Bulgaria Support Fund (£2,000) and £1,000 each to Connect International, Madehurst PCC and Nightstop.

Applications No funds are available by direct application. Because of the way in which this trust operates they are not open to external applications for grants.

The Mount 'A' & Mount 'B' Charitable Trusts

General

Around £102,000 (1997/98)

Beneficial area UK, with a preference for Bristol and Jersey; and Italy

c/o PricewaterhouseCoopers, 9 Greyfriars Road, Reading RG1 1JG

Tel. 0118 959 7111

Correspondent The Trustees

Trustees *The Barbinder Trust.*

Information available Full accounts were on file at the Charity Commission.

General These two trusts seem effectively to operate as one. Their grants lists appear to more or less replicate each other and are very similar in size. We have been unable to see the Charity Commission file for the Mount B Charitable Trust, so the information for 1997/98 only relates to the Mount A Charitable Trust. It can probably be assumed that, as in most other years, any grants given by Mount A were also given by Mount B.

In 1997/98 the Mount A Charitable Trust had assets of £854,000 generating an income of £36,000. After expenses of £10,000, the trust made about 59 donations totalling £102,000. The trust has continued its support for organisations in Italy, Bristol and Jersey and about half the beneficiaries had been supported in the previous year. In the past the trust has stated that 'only appeals from children's charities are considered by the trustees'.

By far the largest grant was for £50,000 and went to the Jersey Opera House Restoration Appeal. Two other larger grants were made, going to Aphasia Trust (£18,000) and Famiglia Bordigaiana (£10,000). Grants over £1,000 went to WellBeing (£2,500); Jersey Drag Hunt – Pony Club (£2,000); and £1,000 each to British Heart Foundation, Family Nursing Association, NSPCC, St Michael's Prep School, Jersey Across

Group and University of Oxford Development and Trust Fund.

The remainder of grants were for under £1,000. Over half of these grants were for less than £250, but some were for as much as £800. Jersey organisations to benefit included Jersey Joint Christmas Appeal, Jersey Preservation Trust, Lion's Club of Jersey Swimarathon, Jersey Arts Council and Variety Club of Jersey. Organisations in Bristol to receive grants included Bristol Marriage Guidance Council, Bristol Young Men's Christian Society and Avon & Bristol Federation of Boys' Clubs. Italian beneficiaries in the year included Italian Cher Trust and Accademica Italiana. Other grants included those to Riding for the Disabled, Cot Death Society, Leukaemia Research, Scope, NCH Action for Children and Children with Cystic Fibrosis.

Applications In writing to the correspondent. Presumably a letter to either trust will be considered by both.

Mountbatten Festival of Music

Royal Marines and Royal Navy charities

£76,000 (1998/99)

Beneficial area UK

HMS Excellent, Whale Island, Portsmouth PO2 8ER

Tel. 01705 547205

Correspondent The Corps Secretary

Trustees *Commandant General Royal Marines; Chief of Staff; Chief Staff Officer Personnel.*

Information available Full accounts were on file at the Charity Commission.

General The trust was set up in 1993 and is administered by the Royal Marines. It raises funds from band concerts, festivals of music and beating retreat. Unsurprisingly, the main beneficiaries are service charities connected with the Royal Marines and Royal Navy. The only other beneficiaries are those hospitals or rehabilitation centres etc. which have recently directly aided a Royal Marine in some way and also Sargent Cancer Care for Children. Both one-off and recurrent grants are made.

In 1998/99 the trust's assets totalled £117,000 and its income was £194,000,

including £187,000 from fundraising. It made donations totalling £76,000 and spent £99,000 on fundraising expenses. The trust has two major fundraising events which raise the bulk of the trust's annual income: a concert in Royal Albert Hall in mid-February each year and the Beat Retreat Ceremony on Horse Guards Parade which is held every three to five years.

In total 30 organisations received grants, 28 of which were supported in the previous year. The largest grants were made to Malcolm Sargent Cancer Fund (£15,000) and The 1939 War Fund (£13,000), also the major beneficiaries in 1997/98. Other larger grants included those to RN Benevolent Trust (£5,500), King George's Fund for Sailors and Fleet Amenities Fund (£4,000 each), St Loye's Foundation (£3,500), Royal Marines Association (£3,000) and Metropolitan Police Benevolent Trust (£2,000). Grants of £1,000 were awarded to 10 recipients including RMR 50th Anniversary Fund, Wrens Benevolent Trust, Forces Mental Welfare, Royal British Legion, 'Not Forgotten' Society, Mission to Seamen and BLESMA.

Smaller grants of £250 or £500 went to Pembroke House, South West Children's Hospice, Hearing Concern, Exeter Hospice and Royal Sailor's Rest.

Applications In writing to the correspondent. Applications can be received at any time but distributions are normally made once a year, around May or June.

The Edwina Mountbatten Trust

Medical

£95,000 (1999)

Beneficial area UK and overseas

Estate Office, Broadlands, Romsey, Hampshire SO51 9ZE

Tel. 01794 518885

Correspondent John Moss, Secretary

Trustees *Countess Mountbatten of Burma, Chair; Noel Cunningham-Reid; Mrs Mary Fagan; Lord Farringdon; Lord Romsey; P H T Mimpriss.*

Information available Full accounts were on file at the Charity Commission.

General The trust was set up as a memorial to Edwina, Countess Mountbatten of Burma. Its main objects are:

1. Support for the St John Ambulance Brigade (of which she was superintendent-in-chief).

2. Support for Save the Children Fund (of which she was president).

3. Promotion and improvement of the art of nursing (she was patron or vice-president of a number of nursing organisations).

The trust supports specific projects rather than general running costs.

In 1999 the trust had assets of £3.6 million and an income of £108,000. Grants totalled £95,000 with administration expenses at £1,200.

St John Ambulance Brigade and Save the Children Fund received £30,000 each. The other grants went to Baby Lifeline, Burrswood Centre, Open Doors, Countess Mountbatten House and Countess Brecknock Hospice.

Exclusions No grants to individual nurses working in the UK for further professional training.

Applications In writing to the correspondent. The trustees meet once a year, generally in May or June.

The Mulberry Trust

General

£383,000 (1997/98)

Beneficial area UK, probably with a special interest in north east London and surrounding areas

Messrs Farrer & Co, 66 Lincoln's Inn Fields, London WC2A 3LH

Correspondent Charles Woodhouse, Trustee

Trustees *J G Marks; Ms A M Marks; C F Woodhouse.*

Information available Accounts were on file at the Charity Commission but without a full list of grants.

General In 1997/98 the trust had assets of £3.1 million and an income of £202,000, mostly gained from investments and Gift Aid contributions of £65,000.

The report states that 'during the year the trustees made grants to Credit Action, the Bugatti Trust and the British Sports Trust'. No further details were available about the size of grants or other beneficiaries. There is no full information about the grants made by this trust since 1991. At that time, the bulk of the grant total was spent in the area described above, with awards in Havering, Waltham Forest, Harlow and Chelmsford. There appeared then to be an interest in specifically Christian charities and in money advice.

The trust has said that it 'will not, as a matter of policy, consider favourably applications which are unsolicited'.

Applications See above.

The Edith Murphy Foundation

General

£247,000 (1998/99)

Beneficial area UK

Crane & Walton, 113–117 London Road, Leicester LE2 0RG

Tel. 0116 255 1901

Correspondent D L Tams, Solicitor

Trustees *Edith A Murphy; David L Tams; Pamela M Breakwell; Freda Kesterton; Jack Kesterson.*

Information available Accounts were on file at the Charity Commission.

General This trust was established in 1993. It supports organisations helping medical causes and people who are poor or in need. There is a strong preference for animal charities. In 1998/99 the income was £55,000 (£1.7 million in 1997/98, £1.6 million of which came from donations and gifts). The assets at the year end stood at £749,000. Grants to 10 organisations totalled £247,000, exceeding the foundation's income by £193,000 and deducted from the accumulated fund. The largest grant went to Leicester Animal Aid Association for £110,000. Two other substantial grants went to the Winged Fellowship Trust (£54,000) and National Kidney Research Fund (£50,000).

Other grants included £10,000 each to Leicester Children's Holiday Centre, Lord Mayor Scanner Appeal and Mainline Steam Trust. Smaller grants included those to Burleigh Houses for the Elderly

(£1,500), Glenfield Hospital Breast Care Appeal (£500), Aylestone Park Youth Football Club (£300) and Dr Hadwen's Trust (£250).

Applications In writing to the correspondent.

The Mutual Trust Group

Religion, education

£75,000 (1997)

Beneficial area Not known

12 Dunstan Road, London NW11 8AA

Correspondent B Weisz, Trustee

Trustees *A Weisz; B Weisz; M Weisz.*

Information available Very brief accounts were on file at the Charity Commission, with no narrative report or list of grants.

General In 1998 the trust had an income of £90,000 and an expenditure of £106,000, unfortuntely no further information was available for view in the public files at the Charity Commission. The following entry was included in the last edition of this guide

In 1997 the trust had an income of £87,000 and grants were made totalling £75,000. Grants are given for religious and educational activities. Unfortunately further information was not available about this trust.

Applications In writing to the correspondent.

This entry was not confirmed by the trust but was correct according to information on file at the Charity Commission.

MYA Charitable Trust

Jewish

£79,000 to organisations (1992/93)

Beneficial area Worldwide

4 Amhurst Parade, Amhurst Park, London N16 5AA

Tel. 020 8800 3582

Correspondent M Rothfield, Trustee

Trustees *Chaskel Rand; Myer Rothfield; Rabbi Abraham Sternbuch.*

Information available Accounts are on file at the Charity Commission.

General According to the Charity Commission database in 1997/98 the trust had an income of £127,000 and an expenditure of £54,000. Unfortunately further information for this year was not available for view in the public files and the following information is repeated from the last edition of this guide.

In 1992/93 the trust gave £79,000 in grants to organisations and £9,000 to individuals. It had a surplus of income over expenditure of £135,000 increasing the trust's assets to almost £300,000. A grants list was not included with the accounts.

Applications The correspondent has previously stated that all the trust's funds are fully committed.

The Willie Nagel Charitable Trust

Jewish, general

£94,000 (1998/99)

Beneficial area UK

3rd Floor, 10 Ely Place, London EC1N 6TY

Correspondent A L Sober, Trustee

Trustees *W Nagel; A L Sober.*

Information available Accounts were available at the Charity Commission, but without a full narrative report or a grants list.

General This trust's income comes mainly from donations and tends to vary from year to year, in 1998/99 totalling £80,000 (£245,000 in 1997/98 and £107,000 in 1996/97). Expenses were just £70 for the year and grants were made totalling £94,000. There was an excess of payments over receipts of £14,000.

A 1998/99 grants list was not available with the accounts held at the Charity Commission. The last one filed was from 1989/90, when grants totalled £52,000 and included the following larger grants: £20,000 to Friends of Wiznitz, £5,300 to Board of Deputies Charitable Trust, £5,000 to Victoria and Albert Museum, £3,800 to National Children's Home and £3,200 to Israel Music Foundation. Other grants ranged from £20 to £2,000 and were mostly for £100 or less.

The trust stated in its report that 'all income is fully spoken for'.

Applications In writing to the correspondent, but note the above.

The Naggar Charitable Trust

Jewish, general

£129,000 (1998/99)

Beneficial area Worldwide

61 Avenue Road, London NW8 6HR

Tel. 020 7834 8060

Correspondent Mr & Mrs Naggar, Trustees

Trustees *Guy Naggar; Hon. Marion Naggar.*

Information available Accounts were on file at the Charity Commission but with only a limited narrative report.

General The trust mainly supports Jewish organisations and a few medical charities. Arts organisations also receive some support.

In 1998/99 the trust had assets of £34,000 and the trust's income was £129,000, virtually all from Gift Aid donations. Grants totalling £129,000 were made to 38 organisations, about a third of these were supported in the previous year. The largest grant was £25,000 to Society of the Friends of Torah. Four other grants were made over £10,000, and went to Merephdi Foundation (£22,000), Tate Gallery Foundation (£20,000), Jerusalem Foundation (£19,000) and British Friends of the Art Museums of Israel (£13,000). Other larger grants went to Israel Philharmonic Orchestra Foundation (£5,000), Western Marble Arch Synagogue (£2,300) and AECC and Leuka 2000 (both £1,500).

The remaining 29 beneficiaries were for £1,000 or less with most being for under £500. Grants included £1,000 each to British Aid Committee Israel, Jewish Memorial Council and Lionel Rosenfeld Testimonial Fund. Other smaller donations went to Or Hachayim (£500), British Ort (£350), Marimonides Foundation and Max Adda Charitable Trust (£250 each), L'Chaim Independent Charitable Trust (£150), British Friends of Jaffa Institute (£100), JNF Charitable

Trust (£50) and Chasdei Moshe Zri Trust (£10).

Non-Jewish organisations to receive grants included Whitechapel Art Gallery, London Symphony Orchestra, Riding for the Disabled, Hampstead Theatre, After Adoption/Parents for Children and the Friends of Royal Academy.

Applications In writing to the correspondent.

The Elani Nakou Foundation

Education, international understanding

£224,000 (1998/99)

Beneficial area UK and overseas, but mostly Europe

c/o Kleinwort Benson Trustees, PO Box 191, 10 Fenchurch Street, London EC3M 3LB

Tel. 020 7475 5093

Correspondent Dr E Holm, Trustees

Trustees *Dr E Holm; Y A Sakellarakis; L St John T Jackson; H Moller.*

Information available Accounts were on file at the Charity Commission.

General The main aim of the trust is to advance the education of the people of Europe in each other's culture. The four trustees include two Danish people, one Briton and one Greek.

In 1998/99 the trust had assets of only £1,700, decreasing from £30,000 in the previous year. Its income of £211,000 was received from a connected charity, Nakou Charitable Trust. After expenses of £16,000, it gave grants totalling £224,000 (£79,000 in 1997/98). By far the two largest grants of the year went to 2000 Symposium Delphi (£100,000) and 1998 Symposium Institute of International Relations – Prague (£65,000). Grants of £5,000 and above included Danish Institute at Athens (£9,500), University College London (£7,500), University of Copenhagen Studieskolen (£5,300) and Hellenic Community Trust – London (£5,000).

Other smaller grants included Danish Greek Cultural Association Copenhagen (£4,900), 1996 Symposium Toledo and Ortega Y Gasset Foundation (£3,700 each), French Service Cultural

Copenhagen (£2,100) and Ry High School – Denmark (£1,100).

Applications In writing to the correspondent. Applications are considered in May.

The Janet Nash Charitable Trust

Medical, general

£96,000 to organisations (1998/99)

Beneficial area UK

Nabarro Nathanson, The Old Chapel, New Mill, Eversley, Hampshire RG27 0RA

Tel. 0118 973 0300

Correspondent R Gulliver, Trustee

Trustees *Ronald Gulliver; M S Jacobs; Mrs J M Bohanna.*

Information available Full accounts were on file at the Charity Commission.

General In 1998/99 the income of the trust was £242,000, mainly from donations and gifts received. The trust usually receives a large sum from City Electrical Factors Ltd under deed of covenant. Grants totalled £266,000, comprised of £170,000 to individuals and £96,000 to organisations.

By far the largest grant was £35,000 to Myton Hamlet Hospice. Other large grants went to Child Advocacy International (£20,000), Duke of Edinburgh's Award International Foundation (£15,000) and Acorns Children's Hospice (£10,000).

Other grants made included those to Macmillan Cancer Relief and Sense (£5,000 each), Dyslexia Institute (£4,000) and Child Victims of Crime (£1,300).

The trust supports a number of the same organisations each year. Also, in previous years some preference has been shown for causes in West Midlands and Warwickshire.

Applications In writing to the correspondent.

The National Catholic Fund

Catholic welfare

£197,000 (1999)

Beneficial area UK

39 Eccleston Square, London SW1V 1BX

Tel. 020 7630 8279 **Fax** 020 7630 5166

Correspondent Monsignor Arthur Roche, General Secretary

Trustees *Archbishops Michael Bowen, John Ward, Maurice de Murville, Patrick Kelly; Mrs Elspeth Orchard; John Gibbs.*

Information available Information was provided by the trust.

General The fund, formerly New Pentecost Fund, was established in 1968 and is concerned with 'the advancement of the Roman Catholic religion in England and Wales'. The trust achieves its objectives through the work of the 25 Committees of the Bishops' conference and various agencies such as the Catholic media office, each committee is concerned with a different area of the work of the church. Grants are only given to organisations which benefit England and Wales as a whole, rather than local projects.

In 1999 the trust had assets of £1.9 million and an income of £1.5 million, £785,000 of which was from diocesan assessments. The majority of its income was spent on running the General Secretariat, the Catholic Media and the Liturgy Committee, but £197,000 was also spent on Christian organisations (£481,000 in 1998). A total of 45 grants were awarded ranging from £200 to £30,000. Almost all beneficiaries receive a similar sized grant each year. These grants were broken down as follows:

Grants to organisations – 20 grants totalling £131,000 ranging from £200 to £30,000. Recipients included Young Christian Workers (£30,000), National Board of Catholic Women (£17,000), Diocesan Vocational Services and Movement of Christian Workers (£16,000 each), National Conference of Priests (£11,000) and Linacre Centre (£10,000). There were also nine grants of £2,000 to over £6,600 to organisations such as Catholic Housing Aid Society and Catholic Student Council.

'National expenses' – 12 grants totalling £67,000 ranging from £1,000 to £14,000. Most beneficiaries receive a similar sized grant each year. Recipients included Churches Commission on Mission

(£13,000), CTBI Racial Justice (£9,200), Universities (£6,500), Churches' Coordinating Groups for Evangelisation (£5,300) and CTBI Interfaith and CCEE (£4,300 each).

The largest grants went to Young Christian Workers (£30,000), National Board of Catholic Women (£17,000) and Diocesan Vocation Services and Movement of Christian Workers (£16,000 each). Other larger grants included National Conference of Priests (£11,000) and Linacre Centre (£10,000).

Exclusions No grants to individuals, local projects or projects not immediately advancing the Roman Catholic religion.

Applications In writing to the correspondent.

National Committee of The Women's World Day of Prayer for England, Wales, & Northern Ireland

Christian education and literature

£171,000 (1998)

Beneficial area UK and worldwide

Commercial Road, Tunbridge Wells, Kent TN1 2RR

Tel. 01892 541411 **Fax** 01892 541411

Correspondent Mrs Lynda Lynam

Trustees *The Officers of the National Committee.*

Information available Full accounts were on file at the Charity Commission.

General Unfortunately we have been unable to update the following information since the last edition of this guide.

The trust makes grants to charitable Christian educational projects and Christian organisations publishing literature and audio-visual material designed to advance the Christian faith.

The main object of the trust is to unite Christians in prayer, focused in particular on a day of prayer in March each year. The trust's income is mainly from donations collected at this event. After the trust's expenses, including the costs

of running the day of prayer, the income can be used for grant-making.

One-off grants are listed separately in the accounts and each year preference appears to be given to projects located in the country where the Day of Prayer was located, as follows:

1998	Madagascar
1999	Venezuela
2000	Indonesia
2001	Western Samoa
2002	Romania
2003	Lebanon

In 1998 the organisation had an income of £280,000. Its expenditure totalled £295,000, including £171,000 in grants.

One-off grants ranged from £500 to £10,000 and were given to 12 organisations. The largest two grants, each of £10,000, were made to The United Society for the Propagation of the Gospel (for use in Madagascar) and Vehivavy Kristiana Mpiara-Mivvaka (Madagascar WDP project). Other grants included £5,000 to Korean Women's World Day of Prayer, £2,500 to Study by Extension for All Nations International, £1,000 to Ecumenical Forum of European Christian Women and £500 to Mission Aviation Fellowship (materials on Madagascar).

Ongoing grants were made to 15 organisations, which received grants of the same amount the previous year. Grants included £27,000 to Feed the Minds, £26,000 to Bible Society, £22,000 to United Society for Christian Literature and £11,000 to Scripture Gift Mission. The remaining grants ranged from £1,000 to £8,000.

International donations were made to World Day of Prayer International Committee (£9,500) and World Day of Prayer European Committee (£200).

Other grants listed were those allocated by the committee for Welsh-speaking churches. There were 14 grants, ranging from £100 to £500, all to Welsh projects. Beneficiaries included Fellowship of Reconciliation and Peace (Wales), Bible Society (Wales), Christians Against Torture (Wales) and Cytun. A further £1,300 was given in total to various denominational publications.

Applications In writing to the correspondent.

The National Hospital Trust

Hospitals

£407,000 (1997)

Beneficial area UK

10 Philpot Lane, London EC3M 8AB

Correspondent MS G Catchpole, Administrator

Trustees *Sir Adrian Blennerhasset; Miss Beata Brookes; Prof. Sir Colin Berry.*

Information available Accounts are on file at the Charity Commission.

General The trust was set up in 1988 to distribute the income from the NHS Lotto. 'Donations must go to hospitals within the NHS, community care trusts, mental health establishments or ambulance services.' The funds may be given for equipment, supporting staff, research projects – the results of which should be published, and the development of new procedure.

Donations are up to a maximum of £250,000 each. In 1997, grants totalled £407,000 (up from £90,000 in 1995). The largest were £60,000 to Queens Medical Centre NHS Trust in Nottingham towards research into acute stroke imaging and £55,000 to Musgrave Park Hospital in Belfast towards the development of specialist equipment in the Gait laboratory. Other grants ranged from £230 to £50,000, but over half were for £10,000 or more.

The income figure was not available for this year. It varies, depending on the proceeds from the NHS Lotto.

Applications In writing to the correspondent. Please note, a copy of the trust's donations policy is available from the correspondent. Potential applicants should consider the criteria outlined in the policy, before making an application.

The National Manuscripts Conservation Trust

Conserving manuscripts

£83,000 (1999)

Beneficial area UK

National Preservation Office, The British Library, 96 Euston Road, London NW1 2DB

Tel. 020 7412 7048 **Fax** 020 7412 7796
e-mail npo@bl.uk
website www.bl.uk/services/preservation

Correspondent Alison Walker, Secretary to the Trustees

Trustees *Lord Egremont; B Naylor; C Sebag-Montefiore.*

Information available Full accounts were provided by the trust.

General Now in its tenth year of operation, the object of the trust is to make grants towards the costs of conserving manuscripts which are of historic or educational value, and of national importance.

Grants are available to record offices, libraries and other similar publicly-funded institutions including local authority, university and specialist record repositories, as well as to owners of manuscript material which is conditionally exempt from capital taxation or owned by a charitable trust. Grants are made towards the cost of repair, binding and other preservation measures, including reprography and may cover the cost of contract preservation and conservation or the salaries and related expenses of staff which are specially employed for the project, as well as expendable materials required for the project.

In 1999 the trust had assets of £1.8 million and an income of £151,000 (£85,000 from investment income and £66,000 from donations). Management and administration of the trust totalled £2,700. Grants totalling £83,000 were made to 12 organisations in the year.

The largest grant was made to Hythe Town Council for £20,000, towards the conservation of the Hythe Borough and Cinque Port Collection. Ancient India and Iran Trust received £6,300 towards the conservation of 11 Persian

manuscripts and the provision of acid-proof boxes. Royal Free Hospital and School of Medicine received £3,000 towards the conservation of minute books and other records of the hospital. Shropshire Records and Research Service received the smallest grant of £900 towards the conservation of the Haughmond Cartulary.

Since 1 April 1999 the trust has been administered from the National Preservation Office. From the same date, contributions from the Department of Culture, Media and Sport stopped. This was the first time the fund had not benefited from its financial support. It now looks solely to donations and investment income to finance grants. However, over the last few years the trust has been able to build up its assets (in 1997 they totalled £1.2 million, in 1998 £1.7 million) and its grant-making has not significantly reduced (in 1998 £109,000, in 1999 £83,000 – see above).

Applications Applications must be submitted on a form in the 'Guide to Applicants' which is available from the trust. Deadlines are 1 April and 1 October each year. The trust is willing to advise on potential projects and other possible sources of funding.

Nemoral Ltd

Jewish

£1.5 million (1998)

Beneficial area Worldwide

13–17 New Burlington Place, Regent Street, London W15 2HL

Tel. 020 7734 1362

Correspondent The Trustees

Trustees *C D Schlaff; M Gross; Mrs Z Schlaff; Mrs R Gross; M Saberski.*

Information available Full accounts were on file at the Charity Commission.

General This trust supports the Orthodox Jewish community in the UK and abroad. In 1998 it had assets of £1.3 million, its income of £1.2 million came mainly from Gift Aid donations of £1 million. Grants totalled £1.5 million, up from £556,000 in 1997.

The largest grant was for £815,000 to United Talmudical Associates, also the major beneficiary in the previous year. Other larger grants included Friends of Yeshiva Shaar Hashomayim (£200,000),

British Friends of Chazon Ish Institutions (£125,000), Friends of Tamir (£61,000), Bobov Hatzola Federation (£19,000) and Regentbrook Ltd. (£15,000).

Applications In writing to the correspondent.

Newby Trust Limited

Medical welfare, education and training, relief of poverty

£205,000 to institutions (1998/99)

Beneficial area UK

Hill Farm, Froxfield, Petersfield, Hampshire GU32 1BQ

Tel. 01730 827557 **Fax** 01730 827557

Correspondent Miss W Gillam, Secretary

Trustees *Mrs I S A Charlton; Mrs J M Gooder; Dr R D Gooder; Mrs A S Reed.*

Information available Full accounts and report were provided by the trust.

General The trust works throughout the UK to promote, in particular, medical welfare, training and education and the relief of poverty. The directors have a policy of selecting one category for support each year. Recent causes have included rural welfare in 1998/99 and the elderly in 1999/2000. In 2000/01 it will be children under the age of 11 with particular educational needs.

In 1998/99 the trust had an income totalling £567,000 and assets of £9.6 million. In all, 756 grants totalling £358,000 were made during the year, 567 for individuals (£153,000) and 189 to institutions (£205,000). The directors expect the same level of giving to continue in the foreseeable future. The following grants information is taken from the annual report for 1998/99.

Medical welfare

Grants totalled £39,000 (11% of grant expenditure). Six principal grants over £1,000 went to Anthony Nolan Bone Marrow Trust (£5,000), Camphill Village Trust – Croft Community and Medical Foundation for the Victims of Torture (£2,000 each), with £1,000 each to Birmingham Children's Hospital, Hope in the Valley Riding Group for Physically

Handicapped Children and Sheffield Children's Hospital.

There were 135 smaller grants, mostly for personal comforts to sufferers from various medical conditions, or as contributions towards more expensive items such as lifts and alterations to houses. Such grants are only made when applications are supported by a social worker's letter, and when the item is costed.

Education and training

Grants totalled £98,000 (27%). Out of more than 950 applications received, 142 grants were provided to schools and universities for individual students. The trust's general policy is to make grants available to those taking second degrees, to mature students, and to students from abroad whose circumstances have been affected by adverse events beyond their control (but not including students whose funds have been cut off by their own government). These grants were mostly between £250 and £1,000, including 10 for field trips. In addition, 20 grants were made to organisations, 4 ranging between £1,000 and £5,000 and 14 smaller grants. Recipients included Bedales School Grants Trust Fund, Ditchling Film Society and Ditchling Museum.

Relief of poverty

Grants totalled £64,000 (18%). This went mostly in 366 small grants for individuals and 39 donated to institutions for their own work. Most of the grants for individuals were payments of £120 made after application by a social worker.

Sundry gifts

Grants totalled £152,000 (42%). Under the special category for the year 'rural welfare' grants were made to 29 organisations. Recipients of larger grants included Ditchling Village Hall (£18,000), Parochial Church Council St. Margaret's Church, Ditchling (£11,000) and £10,000 each to Lanntair Arts Centre, Snainton Village Hall & Playing Fields and Westmeston Parish Room Trust. Other grants included £5,000 each to Age Concern – Cambridgeshire, Colonsay Village Hall Committee and Midhurst Community Bus Association and £2,000 each to The Friends of Ditchling and Ffestiniog Village Hall Management Committee. Grants of £1,000 each included those to 1st Ditchling Scout Group, The Benjamin Project, Chantry Residents Association, The Friends of Ditchling and Hay & District Dial-a-Ride.

A further 21 grants totalling £5,000 (14% of the grant total) were made to various organisations, in particular those working in the community e.g. for clubs, playgroups, community centres and village halls. Typically, help was provided towards kitchen and other equipment, toilets and lifts for people who are disabled, and general running costs.

Exclusions Funding is not provided for the following:

- CPE Law Exam
- BSc intercalated with a medical degree
- postgraduate medical/veterinary degrees in the first or second years
- courses which are outside of the UK.

In addition, first degrees are generally excluded.

Applications The secretary takes principal responsibility for most of the smaller grants for relief of poverty and medical welfare, the directors being responsible for the remaining grants, either at the twice-yearly meetings in November and March or in response to specific applications, especially educational grants.

Relief of poverty and medical welfare: applications on behalf of individuals are only acceptable if they are made by the social services or other similar bodies on an individual's behalf. Grants are restricted to a maximum of two per household.

Special category: applications are invited from registered charities by way of two A4 pages giving full particulars of the project, supported by annual report and/ or budget together with any photographs if relevant. The directors will award grants at their meetings in November and March each year.

Individuals (students) may apply in the form of a personal letter setting out their personal circumstances, supported by: a full cv, statement of financial situation, two letters of reference (preferably academic), and an sae. No reply is made without an sae.

Awards to students usually range from £150 to £1,000 (maximum). Cheques are made out to the educational institution and not to the individual student. It is recommended that applications intended for the start of a new academic year should be submitted at least four months in advance, preferably earlier. Very few grants are made in September and October.

The Richard Newitt Fund

Education

£76,000 (1998/99)

Beneficial area UK

Kleinwort Benson Trustees Ltd,
PO Box 191, 10 Fenchurch Street,
London EC3M 3LB

Tel. 020 7475 5093

Correspondent Chris Gilbert

Trustees *Kleinwort Benson Trustees Ltd; D A Schofield; Prof. D Holt; Baroness Diana Maddock.*

Information available Full accounts were on file at the Charity Commission.

General In 1998/99 the trust had assets of £2.5 million and an income of £78,000. Charitable donations of £76,000 were made during the year.

The trustees have selected a small number of educational institutions and donations are made directly to their student hardship funds. As in 1997/98 the University of Southampton was the largest beneficiary receiving over £38,000 in total; this can be broken down as follows:

Bursaries £18,000
Prize awards £3,500
Hardship awards £17,000

Other grants ranged from £1,700 to £4,400 with 11 institutions benefiting. These included University of Newcastle Upon Tyne, University of Durham, Bristol Old Vic Theatre School, North London University, Textile Conservation Centre, Royal Northern College of Music and Royal Veterinary College. Winchester School of Art was the only new recipient in 1998/99, the other organisations had received the same amount in the previous year.

Exclusions No grants to individuals.

Applications Trustees meet in June and applications need to be received by April.

Newpier Charity Ltd

Jewish, general

£129,000 (1998/99)

Beneficial area UK

Wilder Coe, Auditors, 233–237 Old Marylebone Road, London NW1 5QT

Correspondent Mark Saunders

Trustees *C Margulies; H Knopfler; R Margulies; S Margulies; M Margulies.*

Information available Accounts were on file at the Charity Commission, but without a list of grants.

General The main objectives of the charity are the advancement of the Orthodox Jewish faith and the relief of poverty. In 1998/99 it had an income of £412,000 including donations totalling £271,000 and rent received totalling £124,000. Grants totalled £129,000.

No grants list was included in the 1998/99 accounts. The last available list was from 1997/98 when grants were made to 23 organisations totalling £80,000. All the beneficiaries were Jewish organisations and nine had also received a grant the year before. The largest donation was to SOFT for redistribution to other charities (£23,000 was given in 1996/97).

Other larger grants were £17,000 to KID (£14,000 in 1996/997), £7,000 to Mesdos Wiznitz, £6,100 to BML Benityashvut, £5,000 to Friends of Biala (£1,500 in 1996/97) and £3,000 to Gateshead Yeshiva.

Applications In writing to the correspondent. The address given above is effectively a PO Box, from where letters are passed on to the trustees and telephone calls are not invited.

The Chevras Ezras Nitzrochim

Jewish

£175,000 (1998)

Beneficial area UK, with a preference for London

53 Heathland Road, London N16 5PQ

Correspondent H Kahan, Trustee

Trustees *H Kahan; K Stern; J Stern.*

Information available Accounts were on file at the Charity Commission, but without a grants list.

General 'The objects of the charity are the relief of the poor, needy and sick.' There is a preference for those living in Greater London, but help is also given further afield. Grants can also be made to individuals.

In 1998 the trust's assets totalled £1,000 and it had an income of £180,000 coming from funds raised by the trustees and voluntary helpers. Grants for the year totalled £175,000. Further information was unavailable about the beneficiaries and size of grants.

Applications In writing to the correspondent.

The Noel Buxton Trust

Child and family welfare, penal matters, Africa

£106,000 (1999)

Beneficial area UK, eastern and southern Africa

28 Russell Square, London WC1B 5DS

Correspondent Margaret Beard, Secretary

Trustees *Richenda Wallace, Chair; David Birmingham; Paul Buxton; Simon Buxton; Angelica Mitchell; Joyce Morton; Jo Tunnard; Jon Snow.*

Information available Full accounts and guidelines for applicants were provided by the trust.

General Grants are made for the following:

* the welfare of children in disadvantaged families and of children in care. This will normally cover families with children of primary school age and under, although work with children in care will be considered up to the age at which they leave care. (Grants are not given for anything connected with physical or mental disability or any medical condition.)

* the prevention of crime, especially work with young people at risk of offending; the welfare of prisoners' families and the rehabilitation of

prisoners; housing of any kind is excluded;

- education and development in eastern and southern Africa.

The trust seldom gives grants of more than £2,000 and often considerably less. Applications for recurrent funding over several years and for running costs are considered. Due to the size of grants, contributions are not normally made towards salary costs. The trust does not respond to appeals from large, well-supported UK charities, but welcomes appeals from small local groups throughout England, Scotland and Wales. Preference is given to areas outside London and south east England.

In 1999 the trust had assets of £2.5 million and an income of £69,000. Donations were made to 125 organisations totalling £106,000. Grants were distributed as shown below. The first category received a larger proportion of funds due to more applications in this area.

Welfare of disadvantaged children

A total of £43,000 was given in 71 grants (40% of fund), including those to Family Rights Group (£4,000), Asylum Aid (£3,000), Who Cares? Trust and Family Meditation – Cardiff (£1,500 each), Edinburgh Volunteer Tutors Organisation (£1,000), Home-Start – Telford & Wrekin (£600), Southampton Women's Aid (£500) and Parentline (£400).

Education and development in eastern and southern Africa

Grants totalling £33,000 were given to 31 organisations (32% of fund). Beneficiaries included One World Action – South Africa and UWESO UK Trust – Uganda; (£3,000 each); Harvest Help – Zambia (£2,500); CAMFED – Zimbabwe, Farm Africa – Tanzania and Y Care International (each £2,000); Institute of Commonwealth Studies – University of London (£900); Evergreen Trust – Zambia (£750); and UWESO UK Trust – Uganda (£500).

Penal matters

24 grants were given totalling £30,000 (28% of fund). Beneficiaries included Howard League (£3,000), TRAX Prisoners Wives & Families Society (£2,750), Centre for Crime & Justice Studies and Prisoners Abroad (£2,500 each), New Bridge and Prisoners Advice Service (£2,000 each), Prisoners' Educational Trust (£1,000) and Prison! Me! No Way! and Derbyshire Crimebeat (£500 each).

The trust was disappointed to find that 11 grants (nearly 10% of the total) were not acknowledged and some offers for a second grant were not taken up, and in one case not claimed. It also regularly receives more applications from organisations that are not eligible than from those which are.

Exclusions The trust does not give to: academic research; advice centres; animals; the arts of any kind; buildings; conferences; counselling; development education; drug and alcohol work; the elderly; the environment; expeditions, exchanges, study tours, visits, etc. or anything else involving fares; housing and homelessness; human rights; anything medical or connected with illness or mental or physical disability; anywhere overseas except eastern and southern Africa; peace and disarmament; race relations; youth (except for the prevention of offending); and unemployment.

Applications There is no application form and applications may be submitted at any time. They should include the organisation's charity registration number and the name of the organisation to which grants should be paid if different from that at the head of the appeal letter.

The following should be included with applications: budget for the current and following year; details of funding already received, promised, or applied for from other sources; and the last available annual report/accounts in their shortest available form. In order to reduce administration costs the trust does not acknowledge receipt of applications or reply to unsuccessful appeals. Every effort is made to communicate a decision on successful appeals as soon as possible (normally within six months).

The Norman Family Charitable Trust

General

£264,000 (1998/99)

Beneficial area Primarily south west England

14 Fore Street, Budleigh Salterton, Devon EX9 6NG

Tel. 01395 446699 **Fax.** 01395 446698

Correspondent R J Dawe, Trustee

Trustees *W K Norman; R J Dawe; Mrs M H Evans; M B Saunders; Mrs M J Webb.*

Information available Accounts provided by the trust.

General This trust continues to support a wide range of charities mainly in the south west of England. In 1998/99 the trust had assets of £5.2 million and an income of £914,000. The income was double that of the previous year due to the inheritance from the estate of P M Norman. All of the legacies, totalling £505,000, were given to the endowment fund. Income was also received from a Gift Aid payment from W K Norman to be transferred to the capital funds. Funds for distrubution were mostly from investments and totalled just under £300,000. After administration costs of £26,000, grants totalling £264,000 were made.

The trust listed 47 grants made over £1,000 totalling £183,000. The largest grant went to Blue Cross which received £50,000. Grants of £10,000 and over went to FORCE – Exeter (£20,000), Exeter Leukaemia Fund (£20,000) and Dr Hadwen Trust and Rest Haven (£10,000 each). Other recipients included Humane Research (£7,000), Exeter Hospicecare Endowment Trust (£5,000), Devon Air Ambulance (£3,000) Devon Horse and Pony Sanctuary (£2,000) and Woodside Animal Welfare Trust (£1,500). A further 28 grants of £1,000 were listed, these included Alone in London, Brainwave, Cinnamon Trust, Great Ormond Street Hospital, Staffordshire University Mobile Robotic Systems and YMCA – Exmouth. The trust also spent £17,000 on producing and distributing wooden products, mainly toys, to local charities.

Exclusions No grants to individuals and any charity which involves experimentation on live animals.

Applications In writing to the correspondent. The trustees meet quarterly to agree the distribution of grants.

The Norman Trust

General, young people

£180,000 (1999)

Beneficial area UK

c/o The Roundhouse, Chalk Farm Road, London NW1 8EH

Tel. 020 7424 9991 **Fax** 020 7424 9992

Correspondent Caspar Norman, Trustee

Trustees *T P A Norman; Mrs E A Norman; C J Norman*

Information available Information was provided by the trust.

General The trust is now only supporting one major project – The Roundhouse, therefore no money is available for any other unsolicited projects.

In 1999 the trust had assets of £6.2 million and an income of £180,000, most of which was spent on The Roundhouse.

Applications The trust is not currently entertaining or acknowledging applications.

The Duncan Norman Trust Fund

General

£56,000 (1998/99)

Beneficial area UK, with a preference for Merseyside

Liverpool Council of Social Service (Inc.), 14 Castle Street, Liverpool L2 0NJ

Tel. 0151 236 7728

Correspondent Roger Morris, Honorary Treasurer of LCSS

Trustees *J A H Norman; R K Asser; Mrs V S Hilton; Mrs C E Lazar; Liverpool Council of Social Service (Inc.).*

Information available Full accounts were provided by the trust.

General In 1998/99 the trust had assets of £2.3 million generating an income of £69,000. Grants totalled £56,000. The accounts listed the 16 grants of £1,000 or over, only 3 of which were over £2,000.

Merseyside beneficiaries included Royal School for the Blind – Liverpool (£5,000), West Kirby Residential School Roof Appeal (£2,000) and £1,000 each to Liverpool Cancer Information Centre and Merseyside and Cheshire Alcohol Services.

Grants given in the UK generally included £5,100 to National Trust and £1,000 each to British Red Cross, Roy Castle Lung Cancer Foundation and Universal Beneficent Society.

Applications In writing to the correspondent, although the trust only makes grants to charities known to the settlor and unsolicited applications are not considered.

The Normanby Charitable Trust

Social welfare, disability, general

£345,000 (1998/99)

Beneficial area UK, with a special interest in north east England

c/o Lythe Hall, Whitby, North Yorkshire YO21 3RL

Correspondent Miss J Moorhead

Trustees *Dowager Marchioness of Normanby, Chair; The 5th Marquis of Normanby; Lady Lepel Kornicka; Lady Evelyn Buchan; Lady Peronel Cruz; Lady Henrietta Burridge.*

Information available Full accounts were at the Charity Commission.

General The trust had assets of £8.9 million in 1998/99 which generated an income of £303,000. Donations totalled £345,000 and after further expenditure there was a deficit of £50,000 for the year. A total of 75 grants were made, ranging from less than £50 to £30,000. The largest grant of the year was for £30,000 and went to St Mary's Parish Church. A further 14 grants were of £10,000 or more, with £20,000 each going to Dunstan's, Captain Cook Schoolroom Museum and Warter C of E Primary School and £15,000 each going to Trinity URC Whitby Community Projects and Yorkshire Wolds Building Preservation Trust. Other substantial grants went to Lythe School Nursery Appeal (£12,000) and £10,000 each to Marrick Priory Appeal, Royal Free Hospital School of Medicine, Sir John Soanes's Museum Society and Camphill Village Trust.

The range of these grants show that it is not easy to characterise the interests of the trust. There appears to be a preference for social welfare, health and disability with an interest also in heritage, the arts and education.

Beneficiaries loosely in the areas of social welfare, health and disability included CRISIS and Shelter (£7,000 each) and £3,000 each to Age Concern, Home-Start UK and York Council for Voluntary Service.

Grants in the areas of heritage, the arts and education included Whitby Junior Jazz Band (£6,000), Youth Theatre Yorkshire (£700), York Oral History Society (£500), Yorkshire Youth Orchestra (£200) and Eskdale Festival of the Arts (two grants of £50 each).

Exclusions No grants to individuals, or to non-UK charities.

Applications In writing to the correspondent. Only successful applications will be acknowledged. Telephone calls are not encouraged. There are no regular dates for trustees' meetings.

The Northmoor Trust

General

£32,000 (1998/99)

Beneficial area UK

44 Clifton Hill, London NW8 0QG

Tel. 020 7372 0698 **Fax** 020 7372 4668

Correspondent Mrs Hilary Edwards, Secretary

Trustees *Viscount Runciman; Viscountess Runciman; Frances Bennett.*

Information available Full accounts were provided by the trust.

General The Northmoor Trust was established by Deed of Settlement in 1968. Grants are given for the relief of hardship, poverty or distress, whether directly or indirectly.

In 1998/99 the trust had assets of £3.4 million and an income of just

£32,000, due to low levels of dividends received. In the previous year, when assets totalled £3.3 million, the trust had an income of £80,000.

Grants totalling £30,000 (£91,000 in 1997/98) were made to six organisations. The largest grant of £9,000 went to FARE. Other grants ranging between £4,000 and £5,000 went to Inquest, ATD Fourth World, Vietnamese Mental Health Project, Kings Cross Homeless Project and St John's Wood Terrace Adventure Playground. Three of these organisations had received grants in the previous year.

Exclusions Grants are only made to organisations which one or more of the trustees have direct personal knowledge.

No grants to individuals, or organisations concerned with: religion, medicine or the arts. Occasionally grants are made to educational charities where the guiding criteria are met. The trust does not respond to general appeals.

Applications In writing to the correspondent, including the latest accounts and annual report, a list of the main sources of funding and a budget for the current year including details of other grant applications made. For first time applicants, a general description of aims and achievements to date and an outline of plans for future development. Applications should arrive by 31 January for preliminary consideration in March, decisions are made in May. Applicants may be visited or asked to provide additional information for the May meeting. The trustees may also visit applicants between the two meetings.

The trustees expect to receive a short report confirming how the grant was spent. No grants for more than one year can be made in the first instance, although the trust may extend grants over a period of several years where their criteria has been sufficiently met and repeat applications are accompanied by an account of how the previous grant was spent.

Norwood & Newton Settlement

Christian
£234,000 (1999/2000)
Beneficial area UK

126 Beauly Way, Romford, Essex RM1 4XL
Tel. 01708 723670
Correspondent David M Holland, Trustee
Trustees *P Clarke; D M Holland; W W Leyland.*
Information available Full accounts were on file at the Charity Commission.

General The trust supports Methodist and other mainline Free Churches and some other smaller UK charities in which the founders had a particular interest. As a general rule, grants are for capital building projects which aim to improve the worship, outreach and mission of the church.

Where churches are concerned, the trustees take particular note of the contribution and promised contributions towards the project by members of the church in question.

In 1999/2000 the trust had assets of £6.4 million and an income of £293,000. Grants totalling £234,000 were given in 60 grants ranging from £1,000 to £10,000. Over 70% of grants (43) were to Methodist churches engaged in the building of new premises, or in making improvements to their existing premises. Free churches received 12 grants with the remaining 5 going to other organisations. Grants to churches were given throughout the UK in areas ranging from Cornwall to Cumbria and Essex to Northern Ireland.

The other organisations supported were Community of the Prince of Peace (£5,000), Methodist Diaconal Order (£3,000), Woodlands Camp – Essex (£2,500), Havering Talking Newspaper (£2,000) and European Baptist History (£1,000).

Exclusions Projects will not be considered where an application for National Lottery funding has been made or is contemplated. No grants to individuals, rarely to large UK charities and not for staff/running costs, equipment, repairs or general maintenance.

Applications In writing to the correspondent. In normal circumstances, the trustees' decision is communicated to the applicant within seven days (if a refusal), and if successful, immediately after the trustees' quarterly meetings.

The Oakdale Trust

Social work, medical support, medical research, general
£129,000 (1998/99)
Beneficial area Worldwide, especially Wales

Tansor House, Tansor, Oundle, Peterborough PE8 5HS
e-mail oakdale@tanh.demon.co.uk
Correspondent Rupert Cadbury, Trustee
Trustees *B Cadbury; Mrs F F Cadbury; R A Cadbury; F B Cadbury; Mrs O Tatton-Brown; Dr R C Cadbury.*
Information available Full accounts were provided by the trust.

General The trust gives preference to Welsh charities engaged in social work, medical support groups and medical research. Some support is given to UK charities working overseas and to conservation projects at home and abroad. The average grant awarded is around £500.

In 1998/99 the assets of the trust stood at £4.3 million, with a large proportion still comprised of shares in Cadbury Schweppes plc. The income was £161,000 including £61,000 in donations received. A total of 144 grants totalling £129,000 were made (decreasing from £156,000 the previous year). Management and administration costs were very low at just £347. Over 60 grants were made in the range of £1,000 to £5,000 but were mostly for £1,000. Beneficiaries included BASIC, CARE International, Cities in Schools, Hospice of the Marches, Llandrindod High School, Marie Stopes International, Powys Challenge Trust, Tukes and Wellbeing.

A further 78 smaller grants of under £1,000 were also made. Recipients included Age Concern, Brainwave, Cae Dai Trust, Cystic Fibrosis Trust, People's Dispensary for Sick Animals, Powys Association of Voluntary Organisations,

Rhondda Against Illegal Drugs, Samaritans and Ysgol Crug Glass Project 2000. A number of organisations were supported in the previous year including Cinnamon Trust, DASH, Hearing Dogs for the Deaf, ORBIS and Simon Community.

Exclusions No grants to individuals, holiday schemes, sport activities, expeditions, church restoration or to appeals from charities outside Wales unless the work is international.

Applications No application form is necessary, but requests should be concise, quoting charity registration number, a summary of achievements, plans and needs, with a copy or summary of the most recent annual accounts. The trustees meet twice yearly, usually in April and September and requests should be submitted if possible before the start of these months.

'Owing to a lack of secretarial help and in view of the numerous requests we receive, no applications are acknowledged even when accompanied by a stamped addressed envelope.'

The Odin Charitable Trust

General

£191,000 (1998/99)

Beneficial area UK

PO Box 1898, Bradford on Avon, Wiltshire BA15 1YS

Correspondent Mrs M Mowinckel, Trustee

Trustees *Mrs S G P Scotford; Mrs A H Palmer; Mrs M Mowinckel.*

Information available Full accounts were on file at the Charity Commission.

General Unfortunately we were unable to update the following information since the last edition of this guide.

In 1998/99 the trust's assets totalled £3.1 million and it had an income of £165,000. Grants totalled £191,000 and administration and management costs totalled £7,600.

Although the objects of the charity are wide, the trust has a preference for making grants towards: furthering the arts; providing care for people who are disabled and disadvantaged; supporting hospices, the homeless, prisoners'

families, refugees, gypsies and 'tribal groups'; and furthering research into false memories and dyslexia.

The trustees are more likely to support small organisations and those, that by the nature of their work, find it difficult to attract funding.

The beneficiaries of grants and amounts given, vary widely from year to year, so the following examples of grants for 1998/99 should not be taken as representative of the trust's ongoing work. The largest grants made were £50,000 to Friends of Style Acre; £30,000 to British False Memory Society; £25,000 to Helen Arkell Dyslexia Centre; £16,000 to University of Central England; and £10,000 each to Crisis, University of Liverpool and Wessex Children's Hospice Trust.

Exclusions Applications from individuals are not considered.

Applications In writing to the correspondent.

The Ofenheim & Cinderford Charitable Trusts

Health and welfare, arts, environment

£376,000 (1998/99)

Beneficial area UK

Baker Tilly, Iveco Ford House, Station Road, Watford, Hertfordshire WD1 1TG

Tel. 01923 816400

Correspondent G Wright

Trustees *R J Clark; R McLeod.*

Information available Information was provided by the trust.

General These trusts operate in conjunction and have the same founder and trustees. It has been the practice for the two trusts to make their donations jointly, in proportion to funds available. However, last year some donations were made by The Cinderford Trust alone, and it is stated that this practice is likely to be repeated in future years.

The trusts made donations to a variety of mainly UK, high profile organisations in the fields of health, welfare, arts and the environment. The additional grants made by The Cinderford Trust also gave grants

within these areas. Organisations supported by both trusts this year were the same as for 1997/98.

In 1998/99 the Cinderford Charitable Trust had assets of £8 million and an income of £335,000. Grants totalled £326,000. The Ofenheim Trust had assets of £1.6 million and an income of £48,000. Grants totalled £50,000.

There are two grants lists in the accounts. One, totalling £266,000, lists the grants contributed by both trusts. These included eight grants of £12,000 each, given to St Winifred's Hospice Eastbourne, Save The Children Fund, Musicians' Benevolent Fund, Barnardos Home, World Wildlife Fund, Salvation Army, NSPCC and Scope. Other grants given were 16 of £7,500, 6 of £4,500, 4 of £3,000 and 6 of £1,800. Among those receiving donations were £7,500 each to Macmillan Cancer Relief, National Youth Orchestra of Great Britain, Royal Association in Aid of the Deaf and Dumb, National Art Collections Fund and King Edward VII Hospital, £3,000 each to Greater London Fund for the Blind and Centrepoint (Soho), £1,800 each to Wildfowl & Wetlands Trust, Friends of Eastbourne Hospitals and Royal Academy of Music.

The second list of 24 grants totalling £110,000 contains those made only by The Cinderford Charitable Trust. These showed some preference for smaller organisations based in the south of England, but also supported charities in Scotland and overseas. They included two grants of £15,000 each to Herstmanceux Community Hall and Shakespeare Globe Trust and £10,000 to The Royal Free Hospital School of Medicine. Grants ranging between £1,000 and £8,000 were given to a variety of organisations including The Dulwich Picture Gallery (£7,500), Royal Horticultural Society (£5,000), St Joseph's Pastoral Care and NCHT Developing Hospice Care in Kenya (£3,000 each), Moray Concert Brass Band (£2,000) and Home-Start UK (£1,000).

Applications In writing to the correspondent. Unsuccessful applications will not be acknowledged. Trustees meet in November and applications need to be received by October.

The Ogle Christian Trust

Evangelical Christianity

£135,000 (1999)

Beneficial area Worldwide

2 Park Farm Stables, Stopham Road, Pulborough, West Sussex RH20 1DR

Tel. 01798 874692

Correspondent Chris Fischbacher, Secretary

Trustees D J Harris, Chair; A I Kinnear; S Procter; Mrs F J Putley; C A Fischbacher.

Information available Accounts were on file at the Charity Commission but without a list of grants.

General In 1999 grants totalled £135,000. Funds are mainly directed to new initiatives in evangelism worldwide, support of missionary enterprises, publication of Scriptures and Christian literature and famine and other relief work.

Grants usually range up to £1,000. No further information was available.

Exclusions Applications from individuals are discouraged, those granted require accreditation by a sponsoring organisation. No grants are made for building projects.

Applications In writing to the correspondent, accompanied by documentary support and an sae. Trustees meet in May and November, but applications can be made at any time.

The Old Broad Street Charity Trust

General

£113,000 to organisations (1998/99)

Beneficial area UK and overseas

Eagle House, 110 Jermyn Street, London SW1Y 6RH

Tel. 020 7451 9000

Correspondent S P Jennings, Secretary

Trustees Mrs E J Franck; Mrs M Cartier-Bresson; A T J Stanford; P A Hetherington; C J Sheridan.

Information available Full accounts were provided by the trust.

General The objects of the trust are general. However, it was the wish of Louis Franck, the founder, that part of the income should be used to fund scholarships, preferably for UK citizens.

In 1998/99 the trust had assets of £2.2 million and an income of £94,000 (£915,000 in 1997/98 due to donations of £836,000 which were transferred to the capital funds). Grants totalled £153,000 (£40,000 of this went to the Louis Franck scholarship fund to support five students). Nineteen grants were made to organisations totalling £113,000, eight of these were recurrent from the previous year. The grants list showed some preference for arts/music causes.

The three largest grants went to Pour Que L'Espirit Vive (£30,000) and Art for the World and Royal College of Music (£10,000 each). Other recipients included L'Hopital Intercommunal de Creteil (£9,200); Bezirksfursorge, Saanen (£8,700); Byrd Hoffmann Foundation (£6,000); Elias Fawcett Trust (£5,000); International Menuhin Music Academy (£4,400); Square Rigger Trust (£2,500); and Bloomfield Early Learning Centre, Guy's Hospital (£2,300). Grants of £1,000 and under included those to Variety Club Children's Charity – School Marathon and Turquoise Leaf Project (Osal Nyingpo) Tibet (£1,000 each) and Tate Gallery Foundation (£650).

Exclusions The trustees only support organisations of which they personally have some knowledge.

Applications In writing to the correspondent. Unsolicited applications are not considered.

Old Possum's Practical Trust

Literary history

£142,000 (1999/2000)

Beneficial area UK and overseas

Baker Tilly, 2nd Floor, Exchange House, 482 Midsummer Boulevard, Central Milton Keynes MK9 2EA

Tel. 01908 687800

Correspondent Judith Hooper

Trustees Mrs Esme Eliot; Charles Willett; Brian Stevens.

Information available Full accounts were on file at the Charity Commission.

General The trust's objects are to support: the increase of knowledge and appreciation of any matters of historic, artistic, architectural, aesthetic, literary, musical, theatrical or scientific interest.

In 1999/2000 the trust made grants totalling £142,000 (£42,000 in 1998/99) out of income received in the previous year. In 1998/99 the trust had an income from Gift Aid donations of £195,000. The largest grants were £20,000 each to St Stephen's Church and Newnham College Library. Grants of over £3,000 were made to 13 organisations. Another 24 smaller grants were made, 2 were recurrent.

Exclusions No grants towards sport or to students seeking funding for overseas trips.

Applications In writing to the correspondent.

The John Oldacre Foundation

Research and education in agricultural sciences

£77,000 (1998/99)

Beneficial area UK

Woodlands, New Road, Minchinhampton, Gloucestershire GL6 9BQ

Tel. 01453 835486 **Fax** 01453 835486

Correspondent W J Oldacre, Trustee

Trustees W J Oldacre; H B Shonler; S J Charnock.

Information available Full accounts were on file at the Charity Commission.

General Grants are made to universities and agricultural colleges towards the advancement and promotion, for public benefit, of research and education in agricultural sciences and the publication of useful results.

In 1998/99 the trust's assets totalled £3.1 million and it had an income of only £91,000, including £58,000 from rent. Management and administration costs were £8,900 and six grants were given totalling £77,000. The main beneficiary, which appears to receive support on an ongoing basis, was the Royal Agricultural College, with a grant of £32,000 this year. Other grants repeated from the previous year were Harper Adams Agricultural College and University of Reading which received £10,000 each and Nuffield Scholarship Trust which received £7,500. Two further grants were awarded to University of Bristol (£12,000) and Wye College (£6,000).

Exclusions No grants towards tuition fees.

Applications In writing to the organisation.

Onaway Trust

General

£117,000 (1998)

Beneficial area UK, USA and worldwide

275 Main Street, Shadwell, Leeds LS17 8LH

Tel. 0113 265 9611

Correspondent J Morris, Trust Administrator

Trustees J Morris; Ms B J Pilkinton; A Breslin.

Information available Full accounts, with a detailed narrative report, were on file at the Charity Commission.

General This trust's objects are stated in its 1996/97 annual report as follows:

'To relieve poverty and suffering amongst indigenous peoples by providing seed grants for (small) self-help, self-sufficiency and environmentally sustainable projects.

'... These projects aim to make significant differences to the lives of the world's traditional/indigenous peoples who continue to struggle for both spiritual and physical survival in their own lands.

'... These [grants] empower the recipients to flourish and affirm the quality of their lives within traditional communities; thereby preserving invaluable knowledge, which might otherwise be lost to future generations.'

Additional, secondary objects are to make grants for the benefit of the 'world environment and animal welfare'.

In 1998 the trust's assets totalled £534,000 and its income was £175,000

including a donation of £122,000 from The Joseph Trust, which is a regular supporter. The three trustees listed above are also trustees of The Joseph Trust.

Grants totalling £117,000 were given to 38 new and ongoing projects (17 of the beneficiaries had been supported in the previous year). Grants were divided in the annual report between those given in the UK (£64,000) and those given in the USA (£53,000). At least six grants were made to individuals, towards, for example, travel costs and expenses. A further £31,000 was spent in management and administration costs.

The largest grants were £11,000 to Plenty Canada – First Environmental Midwifery Project, £9,000 each to Woodland Trust and Earth Action Network, £6,000 to Jeel Al Amal (Middle East), £5,500 to Forest Peoples Programme and £5,000 each to ApTibeT and Tibet Information Network. Other grants were mainly between £1,000 and £5,000. Animal welfare grants included £4,800 to Bird Sanctuary, £3,600 to Alaska Wildlife Alliance, £3,500 to Phillips Cat Sanctuary and £1,000 to Canine Partners for Independence. Other grants included £4,800 to Californian Indian Basket Weavers, £4,500 to Compassion in World Farming, £3,000 to the Society for Promoting Self-reliance, £2,000 to Shadwell Horticultural Training Project and £1,800 to Rainy Mountain Foundation.

Applications In writing to the correspondent, enclosing an sae.

The Raymond Oppenheimer Foundation

General

£118,000 (1998/99)

Beneficial area UK and worldwide

35 Ely Place, London EC1N 6TD

Tel. 020 7404 0069

Correspondent D Murphy, Trustee

Trustees Alec G Berber; David Murphy; Clifford T Elphick.

Information available Accounts were on file at the Charity Commission, but without a full narrative report.

General In 1998/99 this trust's assets totalled £852,000 and it had an income of

only £27,000. Grants were made to four organisations totalling £118,000.

The Stichting Mario Montessori 75 Fund received the bulk of the grant total with a donation of £62,000, it was also the main beneficiary in the previous year. Other grants were made to Oxford University (£50,000), Mario Montessori School Scholarship Fund (£6,000) and Imperial Cancer Research (£500).

Applications In writing to the correspondent.

The Orpheus Trust

Music, especially for people with disabilities, Orpheus Centre

£420,000 (1998/99)

Beneficial area UK

Trevereux Manor, Limpsfield Chart, Oxted, Surrey RH8 0TL

Correspondent Richard Stilgoe

Trustees Alex Armitage; Andrew Murison; Esther Rantzen; Revd Donald Reeves; Annabel Stilgoe; Holly Stilgoe; Jack Stilgoe; Joseph Stilgoe; Dr Jemima Stilgoe; Richard Stilgoe; Rufus Stilgoe.

Information available Full accounts were on file at the Charity Commission.

General The trust's objects are to relieve adults and children who are physically or mentally disabled (also those with mental illnesses) by the provision of facilities in the interests of social welfare for their recreation and leisure time occupation with the aim of improving their conditions of life and in particular to provide music and musical entertainment by:

- providing opportunities for the tuition of and performance by such people by the provision of training and of teachers and of the other necessary facilities

- bringing to such people a wider appreciation and involvement in the live performance of music and musical entertainment by assisting in the improving of facilities and access to existing and future concert halls, theatres and public buildings at which live performances of music can be held.

During the year the trust has seen the opening of the Orpheus Centre at Godstone, Surrey, a centre that offers long-term and short-term courses for disabled and non-disabled young people to enable them to develop their skills in the arts. The trust has pledged to donate most of its funds to this centre.

In 1998/99 the trust had assets of £2.8 million and an income of £390,000. A total of £440,000 was spent on music and arts courses of which £390,000 went to the Orpheus Centre. Other grants totalled £31,000. Three organisations received £11,500, they were Enabling for Music (£6,000); The Drake Research Project (£5,000); and Papworth Hospital (£500). Also, four individuals received grants totalling £20,000.

In the previous year £88,000 was given to 14 organisations in grants ranging from £50 to £25,000.

Applications In writing to the correspondent.

The Ouseley Trust

Choral services of the Church of England, Church in Wales and Church of Ireland

£152,000 (1999)

Beneficial area England, Wales and Ireland

127 Coleherne Court, London SW5 0EB

Tel. 020 7373 1950 **Fax** 020 7341 0043
e-mail 106200.1023@compuserve.com
website www.ouseleytrust.org.uk

Correspondent Martin Williams, Clerk to the trustees

Trustees *Prof. B W Harvey, Chair; Dr J A Birch; Dr L F Dakers; S M Darlington; N A Ridley; C J Robinson; R J Shephard; N E Walker; Revd A F Walters; Revd A G Wedderspoon; Sir David Willcocks; Dr J Rutter.*

Information available Full accounts were provided by the trust.

General The trust administers funds made available from trusts of the former St Michael's College, Tenbury. Its object is 'to promote and maintain to a high standard the choral services of the Church of England, the Church of Wales and the Church of Ireland'. This includes

the promotion of religious, musical and secular education for pupils connected to the churches and observing choral liturgy.

Grants awarded fall into six categories:

Courses, instruction
Grants will be awarded only where there is a clear indication that an already acceptable standard of choral service will be raised. Under certain circumstances grants may be awarded for organ tuition.

Endowment grants
Grants awarded will be paid in one sum to provide an immediate contribution to an endowment fund.

Fees – individual
Applications must be submitted by an institution. Grants awarded will be paid in one sum as an immediate contribution. The trustees may require an assurance that the sum offered will achieve the purpose for which help has been requested.

Music
Grants will be awarded only where the replacement of old, or the purchase of new music will render specific assistance to the promotion or maintenance of high choral standards.

Organs
Grants will not generally be awarded in this category. Applications may be considered if the organ is an instrument of particular significance and an integral element in a choral service of a high standard.

Other
Each application will be considered on its merits, keeping in mind the specific terms of the trust deed. Unique, imaginative ventures will receive careful consideration. The trust does not normally award further grants to successful applicants within a two-year period.

In 1999 the trust had assets of £3.2 million and an income of £144,000. It gave 30 grants totalling £152,000. These were categorised as follows:

Category	No. of grants	Total
Music	6	£4,700
Fees	11	£15,000
Endowments	9	£114,000
Organs	3	£13,000
Other	1	£5,000

The largest grants were given in the endowments category with £50,000 to St Alban's Cathedral, £25,000 to Rochester Cathedral and £10,000 to Ely Cathedral as well as smaller grants to Ripon Cathedral and Lincoln Cathedral. Other significant grants were £5,000 each to

Bayswater and Upper Norwood for organs and Salisbury Cathedral School and Wells Cathedral School for fees. Other grants were given to St John the Evangelist and St Matthew.

The trustees' policy is to continue making grants to cathedrals, choral foundations and parish churches throughout England, Wales and Ireland.

Exclusions Grants will not be awarded to help with the cost of fees for ex-choristers, for chant books, hymnals or psalters. No grants will be made for the purchase of new instruments nor for the installation of an instrument from another place of worship where this involves extensive reconstruction. Under normal circumstances, grants will not be awarded for buildings, cassettes, commissions, compact discs, furniture, pianos, robes, tours or visits.

Applications Applicants are strongly advised to obtain a copy of the trust's guidelines (either from the correspondent or their website) before drafting an application. Applications must be submitted by an institution on a form available from the correspondent. Closing dates for applications are 31 January for the March meeting and 30 June for the October meeting.

The Paget Charitable Trust (*also known as* Joanna Herbert-Stepney Charitable Settlement)

General – see below

£302,000 (1999/2000)

Beneficial area Worldwide

The Old Village Stores, Dippenhall Street, Crondall, Farnham, Surrey GU10 5NZ

Tel. 01252 850253

Correspondent Joanna Herbert-Stepney, Trustee

Trustees *Joanna Herbert-Stepney; Lesley Mary Blood; Mrs Joy Pollard.*

Information available Accounts, with a brief narrative report, were provided by the trust.

General The trust supports both UK and local charities for general charitable purposes, although there appears to be a preference for animals, children, Christian, environment, international aid and development, medical and welfare.

In 1999/2000 the trust had assets of £4.1 million and an income of £163,000. After high administration and management costs of £74,000, the trust gave grants to 162 organisations totalling £302,000, both the income and some of the capital were distributed. The largest grant was £50,000 to IEAL Bursary Fund.

Animal grants included £1,000 each to Dian Fossey Gorilla Fund, Humane Slaughter Association, Vetaid and World Society for the Protection of Animals.

Children's charities included Hope and Homes for Children (£12,000) and International Childcare Trust (£3,000), with £1,000 each to CHICKS, Child and Family Trust, ChildLine Midlands and Rockingham Estate Play Association, and £500 to Herts Charity for Deprived Children.

Environment included Royal Agricultural Benevolent Institute (£7,000), Soil Association and Tree Aid (£3,000 each), Energy Advisory Associates (£2,000), Traidcraft Exchange (£1,000) and Friends of the Earth Trust and Greenpeace Environmental Trust (£500 each).

International aid and development grants included ApTibeT (£12,000), Ellenor Foundation Romania Appeal (£10,000), Oxfam (£6,000), with £2,000 each to Ethiopiaid, Farm Africa, Medical Foundation for the Care of Victims of Torture and £1,000 each to Cambodia Trust and United Aid for Azerbaijan.

Medical grants included Global Cancer Concern (£2,000), with £1,000 each to Loughborough MS Society, RNIB, RNID and Mary Stevens Hospice and £500 to Friends of the Centre for Rehabilitation of the Paralysed.

Religious groups included The Church of St Mary-in-Charnwood (£10,000), Churches Commission on Overseas Students (£2,000), Quaker Social Action (£1,000) and St Andrew's Evangelical Mission (£500).

Welfare included £1,000 each to Caring for Life, Friends of the Young Deaf, Help the Aged and Research into Ageing and £500 each to Age Concern and Shelter.

Other grants included West of England School (£2,000) and MCVS Liverpool and Womankind (£1,000 each).

Exclusions Grants are normally given to registered charities only. The trust does not support individuals (including students), projects for people with mental disabilities, medical research or AIDS/HIV projects.

Applications In writing to the correspondent, there is no application form. The trustees meet in spring and autumn.

The Gerald Palmer Trust

Education, medical, religion, general

£130,000 (1999/2000)

Beneficial area UK, especially Berkshire

Eling Estate Office, Hermitage, Thatcham, Berkshire RG18 9UF

Tel. 01635 200268 **Fax** 01635 201077

Correspondent C J G Muir, Resident Agent

Trustees J M Clutterbuck; D R W Harrison; J N Abell; R Broadhurst.

Information available Information provided by the trust.

General The trust's main activity is the management of its Eling Estate, but it also gives grants to organisations.

The trust tends to support mainly UK education, medical and health-related charities together with a range of local charities in Berkshire.

In 1999/2000 33 grants were given ranging from £50 to £20,000. The two largest donations were £20,000 each to Prior's Court School and Russian Orthodox Church in Exile. Six grants of £5,000 were awarded, including those to Almshouse Association, AMREF, Enham Trust and Toynbee Hall.

Other grants were: £3,000 to Reading School New Library & Teaching Block Appeal; £2,500 to Newbury Spring Festival; £2,000 each to CRUSE, Eling Trust, Migratory Salmon Foundation, Understanding Industry and University of Liverpool; £1,000 to Federation of Children's Book Groups; £500 to United Response; and £50 to National Asthma Campaign.

In 1996/97 it had assets of £15 million and an income of £536,000 comprised mainly of income from the estate and woodland, but also including £69,000 investment income.

Expenditure on the estate and woodlands totalled £459,000 and £115,000 was given in grants.

Exclusions No grants to individuals or to small local charities geographically remote from Berkshire.

Applications In writing to the correspondent.

The Rudolph Palumbo Charitable Foundation

Education, relief of poverty, conservation, general

£434,000 (1992/93)

Beneficial area UK and overseas

37a Walbrook, London EC4N 8BS

Correspondent T H Tharby, Trustee

Trustees Lord Mishcon; Sir Matthew Farrer; Lady Palumbo; T H Tharby; J G Underwood.

Information available Accounts were on file at the Charity Commission only up to 1992/93.

General The foundation refused our request for an annual report and accounts and also appears to be neglecting to send these to the Charity Commission. It is still a registered charity (but see below) and is therefore legally obliged to send the report and accounts to the Commission and to make them available to the public. In June 1998 the foundation wrote:

'There is a major reorganisation due in this trust. It is also fully committed for at least the next two years. I would therefore suggest that reference to it is omitted for the time being from your directory so as to prevent the frustration of applicants whom we cannot respond to.'

While all this may be true, it is not an excuse for the foundation's neglect of its statutory obligations. The charity later told these editors: 'There is a legal question over the charitable status of the foundation and for the time being no grants are being made; watch this space.'

Applications In writing to the correspondent.

Panahpur Charitable Trust

Missionaries, general

£141,000 (1998/99)

Beneficial area UK, overseas (see below)

Jacob Cavenagh and Skeet, 6-8 Tudor Court, Brighton Road, Sutton, Surrey SM2 5AE

Tel. 020 8643 1166 **Fax** 020 8643 3467

Correspondent The Trust Department

Trustees *P East; Miss D Haile; Mrs E R M Myers; A E Perry.*

Information available Accounts were on file at the Charity Commission.

General The trust was established in 1911 from the will of Sydney Long Jacob. Grants are made towards Christian charities and other charities and individuals in the UK and overseas, especially Christian missionary organisations. The trust's annual report states that beneficiaries are generally already known to the trustees.

In 1998/99 the trust's assets totalled £4.4 million, it had an income of £191,000 and made grants totalling £141,000. The trust's annual report provided the following analysis of grants.

Geographical split:

Africa	£12,000
Britain	£74,000
Eastern Europe	£120
Far East	£5,000
India	£38,000
Israel	£50
Middle East	£3,000
Spain	£1,200
South America	£1,500

Categories:

Scripture distribution/ reading encouragement	£14,000
Relief work	£10,000
Missionary work (UK)	£25,000
Missionary work (overseas)	£71,000
Missionary welfare	£800
Work amongst students	£150
Direct preaching of the gospel	nil
Educational	£6,000
Ashburnham Christian Trust	£200
Christian retreats	£8,100

The trust made 86 grants in the year, 51 of which had been supported in the previous year. Over half of grants made were of £1,000 or more, with the largest going to Interserve for £13,000, also the major beneficiary in the previous year.

Other grants over £1,000 included Penhurst Retreat Centre (£8,500), Scripture Union (£8,000), Interhealth (£6,700), Bible Society (£6,500), Herbertpur Christian Hospital (£5,800), OMF (£5,200), Emmanuel Hospital Association and Oasis India (£5,000 each), North Kasai Mission (£4,800), Pyersingh Trust Fund – Redcliffe College (£4,000), All Nations Christian College (£3,000), COST (£2,500), Evangelical Alliance and London Bible College (£2,000 each) and School of Oriental and African Studies and YMCA Bolivia (£1,000 each).

About 30 grants were made for £100 and less. These included Age Concern, Chips, LSE Library, Old House Retreat, Tearfund and UCCF.

Applications In writing to the correspondent, although the trust informed us that applicants will not be successful unless they are already known to the trust.

The Frank Parkinson Agricultural Trust

British agriculture

£57,000 (1999)

Beneficial area UK

c/o Grant Thornton, St John's Centre, 110 Albion Street, Leeds LS2 8LA

Tel. 0113 245 5514 **Fax** 0113 246 5055

Correspondent Miss Janet Smith, Secretary to the Trustees

Trustees *Prof. J D Leaver, Chair; W M Hudson; J S Sclanders; C Bourchier.*

Information available Full accounts were provided by the trust with a detailed Guidelines for Grant Applications.

General The trust's principal object is the improvement and welfare of British agriculture. In 1999 its assets totalled £1.2 million and it had an income of £48,000. Management and administration costs totalled £9,600 and it made the following three grants totalling nearly £57,000:

* Royal Agricultural College, Cirencester – Information and Communications Centre (£30,000)
* Hartpury College, Gloucester – Learning Resources Centre (£25,000)

* Publishing Costs – A Tale of Two Trusts (£1,600, 50% of first payment).

Two of the recipients had been supported in previous years. Other recent beneficiaries Easton College – Norfolk, Wye College University of London – Library and Learning Resources Centre and Nuffield Farming Scholarship Trust.

The trust has committed to pay £70,000 over four equal payments, between 2000 and 2002, to University of Reading for a conference room in the Agriculture Building.

Exclusions The trust is not able to assist with financial help to any individuals undertaking postgraduate studies or degree courses.

Applications In writing to the correspondent. A detailed Guidelines for Grant Applications is available from the trust. The trustees meet annually in April.

'The Chairman has the authority to approve small grants between annual meetings, but these are only for minor sums and minor projects.'

The Samuel & Freda Parkinson Charitable Trust

General

£130,000 (1998/99)

Beneficial area UK

Pattinson & Scott, Trustees' Solicitors, Stonecliffe, Lake Road, Windermere, Cumbria LA23 3AR

Tel. 015394 42233 **Fax** 015394 88810

Correspondent J R M Crompton, Solicitor

Trustees *D E G Roberts; Miss J A Todd; J F Waring.*

Information available Accounts were on file at the Charity Commission.

General This trust was established in 1987 with £100. The fund stayed at this level until 1994/95 when £2.1 million worth of assets were placed in the trust on the death of the settlor.

In 1998/99 the trust's assets totalled £2.8 million and its income was £166,000. Grants were made totalling £130,000 and other expenditure totalled £40,000.

The founder of this charity restricted the list of potential beneficiaries to named charities of his choice and accordingly the trustees do not have discretion to include further beneficiaries, although they do have complete discretion within the stated beneficiary list.

In 1998/99 grants were given as follows: £30,000 to Salvation Army; £25,000 each to Church Army and Leonard Cheshire Foundation; £20,000 to RNLI; £15,000 to RSPCA; and £7,500 each to Animal Rescue Cumbria and Animal Concern. All of the organisations had been supported in the previous year.

Applications See above.

The Patrick Charitable Trust

Children, disability

About £154,000

Beneficial area UK, with a special interest in the Midlands

2 Water Court, Water Street, Birmingham B3 1HP

Correspondent M Kay, Trustee

Trustees J A Patrick; R L Patrick; M V Patrick; M Kay.

Information available Full accounts were on file at the Charity Commission.

General In 1998/99 the trust had an income of £151,000 and an expenditure of £412,000. Unfortunately further information for this year was not available and the following information is taken from the last edition of this guide.

Joseph Patrick lived in Worcester when he established the trust in 1962 for general charitable purposes. Donations are given to charities connected with children and people who are disabled. Grants can be one-off or ongoing.

In 1994/95 the trust had assets of £1.4 million generating an income of £88,000. Grants totalled £154,000, of which £115,000 was given to Stackpole Trust which regularly receives more than half of the grant total, with £500,000 committed to it over a few years. It is based in Pembrokeshire and provides recuperative holidays, field studies and leisure for people who are disabled or chronically sick.

The next largest grant was given to Joseph Patrick Memorial Trust (£32,000

and £77,000 over the previous two years). There were three grants of £1,000 each to Shaftesbury Society, Make a Wish Foundation and Disability Information Trust. The other grants were for £100 to £500 and included those to House Youth Unit, Children in Crisis, Jubilee Sailing Trust, Little Sisters of the Poor, Save the Children Fund and Stroke Association.

Applications In writing to the correspondent.

The Late Barbara May Paul Charitable Trust

Older and young people, medical care and research, preservation of buildings

£74,000 (1998/99)

Beneficial area UK, with priority to East Anglia

Lloyds TSB Private Banking Ltd, UK Trust Centre, The Clock House, 22–26 Ock Street, Abingdon, Oxfordshire OX14 5SW

Tel. 01235 554000

Correspondent Chris Shambrook, Trust Manager

Trustees Lloyds TSB Bank plc.

Information available Full accounts were on file at the Charity Commission with only a limited report.

General Lloyds TSB Bank plc is the sole trustee for this and two other trusts, each founded by a different sister from the Paul family. This trust is the largest and makes larger grants but they all appear to have very similar grant-making policies. There is a preference throughout the trusts for Suffolk and some organisations have been supported by all three trusts.

This trust has stated in recent years that it is increasingly focusing its grant-making on local organisations in East Anglia, and East Anglian branches of UK charities.

In 1998/99 the trust had assets of £585,000 and an income of £23,000. Grants were made to 55 organisations totalling £74,000. Donations were in the range of £500 and £5,000 but most were for £1,000. Many of the organisations

supported had received grants in the previous year.

The largest grant of £5,000 went to Whizz-Kidz, while two organisations received £3,000 each, Suffolk Preservation Society and Norfolk Millennium Trust for Carers. The 10 grants of £2,000 each included those to Essex County Youth Service, Bus Project, Shelter, One-to-One, East Suffolk Mines, Essex Voluntary Association for the Blind, Cancer Research Campaign and Norfolk & Norwich Scope. Six grants of £1,500 and more than thirty of £1,000 were made, recipients included Queen Elizabeth's Foundation for Disabled People, FNA, RNIB, British Red Cross, Tannington Church, Salvation Army, Macmillan Cancer Relief, Age Concern, Sargent Cancer Care for Children, Suffolk Association for Youth and Ipswich Scouts & Guides Council. Grants under £1,000 went to Rotary Club of Ipswich and Ipswich Disabled Advice (£750 each).

Applications In writing to the correspondent.

The Susanna Peake Charitable Trust

Disability, general

£66,000 (1999/2000)

Beneficial area UK, but an emphasis on Gloucestershire

Rathbone Trust Company Limited, 159 New Bond Street, London W1Y 9PA

Tel. 020 7399 0820   **Fax** 020 7399 0050
e-mail linda.cousins@rathbones.com

Correspondent The Secretary

Trustees Mrs Peake; D Peake.

Information available Full accounts were on file at the Charity Commission.

General This is another of the Kleinwort family trusts, a number of which have entries in A Guide to the Major Trusts Volumes 1 and 2. It was set up by Susanna Peake in 1981 for general charitable purposes. It has a preference for charities based in the Gloucestershire area. In addition, non-local appeals when received are accumulated and considered by the trustees annually. Although grants ranged from £100 to £5,000, most grants were of between £1,000 and £2,000.

In 1999/2000 the trust had assets of £2 million and an income of £78,000. Grants totalled £66,000. No further information for this year was available.

In 1998/99 grants to 32 organisations totalled £65,000. Grants of £5,000 each were given to Bobby Appeal – Hampshire and Life Education Centres, £4,000 went to Church of St James – Loughborough, £3,000 each to Chipping Norton Theatre Trust and Longborough Parents & Friends Association – Longborough School and £2,500 each to ATP Enterprise Development and North Cotswolds Voluntary Help Centre. Nine grants of £2,000 included those to Brainwave, Defeating Deafness and WaterAid. Smaller grants ranged from £100 to £1,000.

Exclusions No grants to individuals.

Applications In writing to the correspondent.

The Penny in the Pound Fund Charitable Trust

Hospitals, health-related charities

£98,000 (1999)

Beneficial area North west England, north Wales and parts of Scotland

Merseyside Health Benefits Council, 7 Sir Thomas Street, Liverpool L1 6HE

Tel. 0151 236 7051 **Fax** 0151 236 1915 **e-mail** karnold@medicash.org
Correspondent K Arnold, Finance Officer

Trustees *P B Teare, Chair; K W Monti; K Arnold; J E Brown; W C Gaywood*

Information available Accounts were on file at the Charity Commission.

General The charity was formed by a trust deed in 1968 and is under the control of Merseyside Health Benefits Council. This is a health benefits insurance company from which the trust receives donations. The trust has continued to support NHS hospitals and selected charitable organisations mainly in north west England (Cheshire, Cumbria, Lancashire and Merseyside), but also north Wales (Clwyd) and Scotland. It makes grants for equipment and amenities for patients and residents

which would not otherwise be available from public funds.

In 1999 the trust had assets of £109,000 and an income of £87,000, £71,000 of this came from donations and gifts. It made grants of £98,000; 41 grants totalling £85,000 went to NHS hospitals and 18 grants totalling £13,000 to other establishments.

Grants to NHS Hospitals

Grants over £10,000 went to Aintree Hospitals (£16,000) and Royal Liverpool and Broadgreen University Hospitals NHS Trust (£14,000). There were 11 grants in the range of £1,000 to £5,000 and 26 in the range of £500 to £1,000. Organisations to benefit included St Helens and Knowsley Hospitals (£5,000), Liverpool Women's Hospital NHS Trust (£2,000) and Mid Cheshire Hospitals (£1,500) and £750 each to Argyle & Clyde Acute Hospitals NHS Trust, Blackpool Victoria Hospital NHS Trust, Northumberland Mental Health NHS Trust and Walton Centre for Neurology NHS Trust.

Grants to other establishments

Larger grants went to MCVS, Liverpool (£2,000); Stockdales, Sale (£1,200) and Abbeyfield, Halycon House, Formby (£1,000). The 15 grants under £1,000 included Royal School for the Blind (£850), Hoylake Cottage School (£600), The Cassel Hospital Families Centre Appeal (£600) and Royal Manchester Children's Hospital (£500).

Applications In writing to the correspondent. Applications need to be received in July and trustees meet in October.

The Pennycress Trust

General

£64,000 (1997/98)

Beneficial area UK, with a preference for Cheshire and Norfolk

25 North Row, London W1R 1DJ
Tel. 020 7323 4747 **Fax** 020 7629 4414
Correspondent Mrs Doreen Howells, Secretary

Trustees *Lady Aline Cholmondeley; A J M Baker; C G Cholmondeley.*

Information available Accounts were provided by the trust, but did not include a list of grants.

General The trust's policy is to make donations to smaller charities and especially those based in Cheshire and Norfolk, with some donations to UK organisations.

In 1998/99 the assets of the trust stood at £2.3 million and the income was £75,000. Management and administration of the trust came to £9,800 for the year. Grants were made to 214 organisations totalling £61,000, mainly of sums of £200, £300 and £500, but with three of £1,000 and one of £2,000.

No grants list was provided with the accounts but in previous years about a quarter of the grants have been in each of the two preferred areas, with the remainder to UK charities. Beneficiaries have included organisations such as Cheshire Homes Stockport, Great Ormond Street Hospital, King's Lynn Preservation Trust, Norfolk Deaf Association, Prince's Trust Norfolk Appeal and Turning Point Chester.

Exclusions No support for individuals.

Applications In writing to the correspondent. Trustees meet twice during the year, usually in July and December. Applications need to be received by June or November.

The Mrs C S Heber Percy Charitable Trust

General

£55,000 (1997/98)

Beneficial area Worldwide with a preference for Gloucestershire

Rathbones, 159 New Bond Street, London W1Y 9PA

Correspondent Miss L J Cousins

Trustees *Mrs C S Heber Percy; Mrs J A Prest.*

Information available Full accounts were on file at the Charity Commission.

General In 1998/99 the trust had an income of £84,000 and an expenditure of £49,000. Further information for this year was not available.

In 1997/98 the trust had assets of £2 million and an income of £91,000. It gave 26 donations totalling £55,000.

Despite the stated preference for Gloucestershire, only two organisations in the grants list are obviously local (*). In addition to local appeals, non-local applications are accumulated and considered annually by the trustees.

Grants were made to Health Unlimited (£15,000), The Friends of the Aphrodisias Trust (two grants of £5,000 each and one of £2,500), Leukaemia Research and The Shakespeare Hospice Trust (£5,000 each), Bequia Hospital, British Light Horse Breeding Society and Mark Davies Injured Riders Fund (£3,000 each), League of Friends of Macintyre Tall Trees and Macmillan Cancer Relief (£1,000 each), Berkshire, Buckinghamshire and Oxfordshire Naturalist Trust (two grants of £500 each), Mencap (£250) and Cotswold School* and Gloucestershire Historic Churches Trust* (£200 each).

Exclusions No grants to individuals.

Applications The correspondent stated that unsolicited applications are not required.

The Philanthropic Trust

Homelessness, developing world, welfare (human and animal), environment, human rights

£106,000 (1998/99)

Beneficial area UK, Africa, Asia

Trustee Management Limited, 19 Cookridge Street, Leeds LS2 3AG

Correspondent The Trust Administrator

Trustees *Paul H Burton; Jeremy J Burton; Amanda C Burton.*

Information available Full accounts were provided by the trust.

General The trust was created in 1995 by P H Burton. Special consideration is given to institutions relating to the homeless, the developing world, welfare (both human and animal), the environment and human rights.

Total income for 1998/99 was £226,000, a decrease of £661,000 from the previous year when over £600,000 was added to the capital. Total expenditure increased by £68,000 to £112,000. Assets totalled £3.1 million. Charitable donations

increased by £65,000 to £106,000. Grants were in the range of £100 to £5,000, though most were for £1,000. A full list of grants was supplied by the trust, with the 12 'most significant' listed in the accounts, 5 of which had been supported in the previous year.

Big Issue Foundation received grants totalling £5,000. £4,000 each went to Barnardos, Centrepoint, NCH Action for Children, Refugee Council, Samaritans, St Christopher's Fellowship and St Mungo's. Child Hope, UNICEF and World Jewish Relief received £3,000 each and Community Self Build Agency received £2,500. Smaller grants went to Prisoners of Conscience Appeal Fund, Crisis and Power International Limb Project (£2,000 each), Brainwave, NSPCC and Notting Hill Housing Trust (£1,000 each) and Breakthrough Deaf Hearing Integration and National Back Pain Association (£500 each). A number of these organisations were also supported in the previous year.

Exclusions No grants for the arts, education, religious organisations, expeditions or individuals. Grants are given to UK-registered charities only.

Applications In writing to the correspondent. Unsuccessful appeals will not necessarily be acknowledged.

The Reginald M Phillips Charitable Foundation

Medical research, general

£136,000 (1997/98)

Beneficial area UK

National Westminster Bank plc, Financial & Investment Services, 153 Preston Road, Brighton BN1 6BD

Tel. 01273 545111

Correspondent The Manager

Trustees *National Westminster Bank plc.*

Information available Full accounts were on file at the Charity Commission.

General Unfortunately we have been unable to update the following information since the last edition of this guide.

The trust's annual report states that 'the majority of funds have been utilised in the field of research at Sussex University in cell cultures and into ageing diseases (Alzheimer's/Parkinson's). With the limited remaining funds, other smaller charities have benefited'.

In 1997/98 the trust had assets of £1.1 million and an income of £156,000 (much of which was from rent). Grants totalled £136,000, most of which went to to Trafford Foundation for research at Sussex University. Other grants were £1,500 to Brighton Sea Cadets and £250 to Help the Aged.

Applications In writing to the correspondent, but note the above. Applications are considered in April each year.

The Ruth & Michael Phillips Charitable Trust

General, Jewish

£91,000 (1998/99)

Beneficial area UK

Berkeley Square House, Berkeley Square, London W1X 5LE

Tel. 020 7491 3763 **Fax** 020 7491 0818

Correspondent M L Phillips, Trustee

Trustees *M L Phillips; Mrs R Phillips; M D Paisner.*

Information available Full accounts were on file at the Charity Commission.

General This trust's annual report stated that the trustees 'consider all requests which they receive and make such donations as they feel appropriate', however, it tends to makes grants mainly to Jewish organisations. Up until 1991/92, the grants list included all the organisations the trust had ever supported and the total amount each organisation had received. The main recipients were JPAIME, Phillips Family Charitable Trust and the Foundation for Education.

In 1998/99 the trust had assets of £1.1 million and an income of £163,000, £115,000 of which was received in a donation from J B Rubens Charitable Foundation. After administration costs of nearly £40,000, the trust gave grants totalling £91,000. The accounts listed the 20 largest donations, 15 of the beneficiaries had also received a grant in the previous year. The largest grants went to Joint Jewish Charitable Trust (£20,000), GRET (£15,000), Jewish Care (£6,000) and Jerusalem Foundation and Ravenswood Foundation (each £5,000).

There were 15 donations ranging from £700 to £3,000, recipients included: Lubavitch Foundation (£3,000); Variety Club Children's Charity Limited (£2,700); £2,500 each to British ORT, Immanuel College and Tel Aviv Foundation; B'nai B'rith Hillel Foundation (£1,500); £1,000 each to Holocaust Education Trust, Ohel Torah and Project Seed Europe; and Marble Arch Synagogue (£700). The only non-Jewish recipient listed was Royal National Theatre which received £1,000.

Applications In writing to the correspondent.

A M Pilkington's Charitable Trust

General

£130,000 (1999/2000)

Beneficial area UK, with a preference for Scotland

Carters, Chartered Accountants, Pentland House, Saltire Centre, Glenrothes, Fife KY6 2AN

Tel. 01592 630555

e-mail catersca@sol.co.uk
website www.catersca.co.uk

Correspondent G J Carter

Information available Information was provided by the trust.

General The trust supports a wide variety of causes in the UK, with few causes excluded (see below). In practice there is a preference for Scotland and probably half the grants are given in Scotland.

In 1999/2000 the trust had assets of £3.1 million and an income of £172,000. It gave grants to 146 charities totalling £130,000. There is a preference for giving recurring grants. Grants normally range from £500 to £1,500. Details on the beneficiaries were not available.

Exclusions Grants are not given to overseas projects or political appeals.

Applications In writing to the correspondent. Trustees meet in June

and December to consider grants, applications should be received by April and October respectively.

The Austin & Hope Pilkington Trust

General, see below

£548,000 (1998/99)

Beneficial area UK and overseas (see below)

PO Box 124, Bisley, Stroud, Gloucestershire GL6 7YN

Correspondent Mrs Penny Shankar, Trustee

Trustees Mrs J M Jones; Mrs P S Shankar.

Information available Full accounts were on file at the Charity Commission.

General Since 1995 this trust has decided to focus its wide-ranging funding in specific areas, but only on two or three in one year:

2000	Community, poverty and religion
2001	Youth and children, older people, medical
2002	Music and the arts, famine/overseas
2003	Community, poverty and religion

The trust stated that 'the majority of donations reflect these categories but rare exceptions can always be made for projects that have been supported by the trust for a number of years.'

In 1998/99 assets of £9.7 million generated an income of £300,000. A total of £548,000 was distributed amongst more than 100 organisations. This year it supported music and the arts and famine/overseas.

General – £388,000
The largest grant of £21,000 went to National Asthma Campaign with £15,000 going to Help the Hospices. Six grants of £10,000 included those to Care and Repair, Christian Aid, Fight for Sight, Help the Aged, London Connection and Who Cares? Trust. Among the 28 charities receiving £5,000 were Action on Elder Abuse, British Heart Foundation and Tree Aid.

Music and the arts – £62,000
Two grants went to Purcell School, one to purchase a flute and the other to fund two scholarships. A grant also went to the Royal Academy of Music to fund two

students. Other recipients included Artsline, Dorset Opera, Kaleidoscope Arts Group, Midland Youth Orchestra and Royal Academy of Arts.

Famine/overseas – £98,000
Grants included £20,000 each to British Red Cross – Kosovo Appeal and Care International UK – Kosovo Appeal and £10,000 each to Oxfam – Kosovo Appeal and British Red Cross – Hurricane Mitch Appeal. Other recipients included Farm Africa and Tearfund.

The trust stated that it 'continues to despair at the volume of applications received that do not fall within the funding priorities of the trust'. The more inappropriate applications received, 'the less time it has to consider those with real merit'.

Exclusions Grants only to registered charities. No grants to individuals or to purely local organisations.

Applications In writing to the correspondent. **Please note the selected areas for each year as given above.** Applications should include full budgets and annual accounts where appropriate. No correspondence will be entered into unless applications are successful, even if applicants send an sae. No application forms or guidelines are available.

The Cecil Pilkington Charitable Trust

Conservation, medical research, general on Merseyside

£146,000 (1998/99)

Beneficial area UK

PO Box 8162, London W2 1G

Correspondent A P Pilkington, Trustee

Trustees Sir A Pilkington; A P Pilkington; R F Carter Jones.

Information available Accounts were on file at the Charity Commission with a limited report.

General Grants have traditionally been mainly to conservation projects, medical research and Merseyside charities.

In 1998/99 the trust had assets of £6.4 million and an income of £203,000. Grants totalled £146,000. Grants were awarded to 48 organisations in the year, over twice the number awarded in 1996/97. A number of the beneficiaries had received help in the previous year. By far the largest grant was to Psychiatry Research Trust for £40,000. Other large grants were £10,000 each to Liverpool School of Tropical Medicine and St Helens and Knowsley Hospice and £5,000 each to Alzheimer's Research Trust, Mansfield College Oxford, Rare Breeds Survival Trust and Wildlife & Wetlands Trust.

The remainder of grants were in the range of £500 and £5,000, but were mainly for £1,000 or £2,000. Over half of the grants awarded went to conservation organisations. Beneficiaries in this area included British Trust for Conservation Volunteers, Church and Conservation Trust, Lancashire Wildlife Trust, Plantlife, Spadework and Green Alliance.

A wide range of organisations including arts, education, medical and welfare causes received help. Those to benefit included: Citadel Arts Centre, St Helens; Merseyside Young People's Theatre Company; Sunningwell School of Arts; St Helens Disability Network; St Helens Deaf; Huntingdon's Disease Association; and Nutgrove Primary School, St Helens.

Applications The trust does not accept unsolicited applications.

The Pilkington General Charity Fund

Welfare in north west England

£58,000 (1998/99)

Beneficial area UK, with a preference for Merseyside

PO Box 8162, London W2 1GF

Correspondent The Secretary

Trustees Dr Lawrence H A Pilkington; Arnold P Pilkington; Hon. Mrs Jennifer M Jones; Neil Pilkington Jones.

Information available Full accounts were provided by the trust.

General The trust gives grants to registered charities only, with a preference for the Merseyside area.

In 1998/99 the trust had assets of £1.6 million and an income of £61,000.

Grants to 69 organisations totalled £58,000, only 10 of which were of £1,000 or over.

Beneficiaries in Merseyside included YMCA – St Helens (£1,000), Citadel Arts Centre – St Helens and Liverpool One-Parent Families (£700 each), with £500 each to Groundwork Trust – St Helens, Knowsley & Sefton, Liverpool Lunchtime Theatre Limited, Merseyside Council for Voluntary Services, Merseyside Drugs Council, Royal Society for the Blind – Liverpool and Wirral Autistic Society and £200 to Sefton Children's Holiday Fund.

Local organisations outside Merseyside included Exeter University Postgraduate Medical School (£12,000 in two grants), Bath Institute for Medical Engineering and Cruse Bereavement Care – Preston Branch (£500 each) and St Patricks Church – Wigan (£300).

UK groups supported included Marie Stopes International (£1,600 in two grants), Mental Health Foundation (£1,500 in two grants), Alzheimer's Research Trust and Help the Aged (£1,000 each), National Missing Persons Helpline and Royal National Institute for the Blind (£700 each), £500 each to Deafblind UK, National Deaf Children's Association, Shelter, Talking Newspaper Association and Youth Clubs UK and £400 to Dystonia Society.

Exclusions No support for non-registered charities or individuals.

Applications In writing to the correspondent.

The Sir Harry Pilkington Trust

General

£92,000 (1998/99)

Beneficial area UK, with a preference for Merseyside, and worldwide

Liverpool Council of Social Service (Inc.), 14 Castle Street, Liverpool L2 0NJ

Tel. 0151 236 7728   **Fax** 0151 258 1153

Correspondent Carol Chapman

Trustees Liverpool Council of Social Service (Inc).

Information available Full accounts were provided by the trust.

General In 1998/99 this trust had assets of £5.4 million with an income from investments of £144,000. Grants for the year totalled £92,000.

Grants over £1,000 were listed in the accounts and were made to 15 organisations, with smaller grants totalling £4,300. There is a preference for organisations based in Merseyside.

The largest grant during the year was £24,000 to Liverpool CSS, which also acts as the trustees. Other substantial grants were £20,000 to St Helens Theatre Royal Trust Roof Appeal and £10,000 to Friends of Ravenscliffe School. Recipients of smaller grants were: £5,000 each to Arid Lands Initiative, Arms and St Helens UVO Community Trust; Knowsley Mayor's Appeal (£3,000); and The National Trust (£1,000).

Applications In writing to the correspondent, although the trust states that grants are only made to charities known to the settlor and unsolicited applications are not considered.

The Platinum Trust

Disability

£86,000 (1998/99)

Beneficial area UK

Regency House, 1–4 Warwick Street, London W1R 6RJ

Tel. 020 7439 8692

Correspondent P Panayiotou, Secretary

Trustees G K Panayiotou; A D Russell; C D Organ.

Information available Accounts were on file at the Charity Commission, but without a list of grants.

General The trust makes grants to disability organisations in the UK, with an emphasis on representative organisations. It was funded up until March 1993 by a four-year covenant. Funding from the settlor has continued, with annual donations of £100,000 committed until March 2000.

Grants are made to support 'a small number of key organisations, to be decided yearly, with which the trust has an established funding relationship'. Unsolicited applications from new applicants are therefore unlikely to be considered. If the trust wishes to continue funding a particular organisation, it will make the approach.

In 1998/99 the trust had assets of £127,000 and an income of £106,000, including a donation of £100,000 from the settlor. After administration costs of £23,000, grants totalling £86,000 were made. Three grants totalling £26,000 were given to BCODP, which often receives the largest grant. Other beneficiaries were CSIE (£18,000), The Alliance for Inclusive Education and Parents for Inclusion (£10,000 each) and POHWER (£5,000).

Other recipients in the past have included Disability Advice Centre, Disability Awareness in Action, Mockbeggar Theatre Company and Theatre Resource. Local organisations across the UK have also previously benefited, including Suffolk Artlink, Southampton Centre for Independent Living and Worcester and District Lifestyles.

Applications The trust does not accept unsolicited applications; all future grants will be allocated by the trustees to groups they have already made links with.

The Polden-Puckham Charitable Foundation

Peace and security, ecological issues, social change

£405,000 (1999/2000)

Beneficial area UK organisations for work at home and overseas

BM PPCF, London WC1N 3XX

Correspondent M Bevis Gillett, Secretary

Trustees *Candia Carolan; Harriet Gillett; David Gillett; Jenepher Gordon; Carol Freeman; Anthony Wilson; Heather Swailes.*

Information available Full accounts, guidelines and a booklet Review of Grant-Giving 1990–2000 provided by the trust.

General 'In its work the foundation aims to support projects that change values and attitudes that promote equity and social justice, and that develop

radical alternatives to current economic and social structures.'

It prefers to make grants available to small, pioneering organisations which find it difficult to attract funds from other sources. The foundation supports work in the following areas, with grants usually in the range of £1,000 to £15,000.

Peace
Development of ways of resolving international and internal conflicts peacefully, and of removing the causes of conflict.

Ecological issues
Work which tackles the underlying pressures and conditions leading towards global environmental breakdown; particularly initiatives which promote sustainable living.

Other areas
Human rights work, in particular where it is related to peace, ecological and women's issues. The trust has a long standing link with the Society of Friends.

In 1999/2000 the trust had assets of £13 million generating an income of £309,000. Administration expenses were high at £40,000, although this included the reasonable wages of a full-time secretary. Grants were awarded to 76 organisations totalling £405,000.

The largest grants were: £27,000 to Quaker Peace & Service, £20,000 of which was for core funding, the rest for their Quaker UN Office in Geneva; £25,000 to Millennium Peace Fund to contribute to their endowment; and £20,000 to Responding to Conflict for core funding.

Other major beneficiaries included Oxford Research Group (£14,000), Gaia Foundation (£12,000 in three grants), Centre for Conflict Resolution (£9,000 in two grants), Soil Association (£7,200), Environmental Transport Association's Slower Speeds Initiative (£7,000) and £5,000 each to Green Alliance Trust and Schumacher Society. Other grants included £4,000 each to The Civil Liberties Trust, Jubilee 2000 Coalition and Woodbrook College, £3,000 each to Cycle West and Traidcraft Exchange and £2,000 to British Irish Rights Watch. Smaller grants included those to Friends of Swanivar (£1,000), Living Village Trust (£750) and Winged Horse Trust (£700).

Many of the organisations supported have received help in previous years, grants are often given for core funding. Grants totalling £16,000 have been approved for 2000/2001 and £99,000 for 2001/2002.

Exclusions Grants to individuals; travel bursaries (including overseas placements and expeditions); study; academic research; capital projects (e.g. building projects or purchase of nature reserves); community or local projects (except innovative prototypes for widespread application); general appeals; and organisations based overseas.

Applications The trustees meet twice a year in spring and autumn; applications should be submitted by 15 February and 15 September respectively. Decisions can be made on smaller grants between these meetings. The foundation will not send replies to applications outside its area of interest. Up-to-date guidelines will be sent on receipt of an sae.

Applications should be no longer than two pages and should include the following:

- a short outline of the project, its aims and methods to be used
- the amount requested (normally between £500 and £5,000 over one to three years), the names of other funders and possible funders, and expected sources of funding after termination of PPCF funding
- information on how the project is to be monitored, evaluated, and publicised
- background details of the key persons in the organisation.

Please also supply:

- latest set of audited accounts
- a detailed budget of the project
- list of trustees or board of management
- names of two referees
- charity registration number
- annual report.

Applications outside of the trust's criteria will not receive a reply.

The George & Esme Pollitzer Charitable Settlement

Jewish, health, social welfare

£151,000 (1998/99)

Beneficial area UK

Saffery Champness, Courtyard House, Oakfield Grove, Clifton, Bristol BS58 2AE

Correspondent J Barnes, Trustee

Trustees *J Barnes; B G Levy; R F C Pollitzer.*

Information available Accounts were on file at the Charity Commission, but without a full narrative report.

General This trust gives the majority of its support each year to Jewish causes. However, it also supports a range of well known, UK organisations.

In 1998/99 the trust had assets of £2.6 million, an income of £101,000 and expenses of £6,800. Grants totalling £151,000 were given to 56 organisations, 21 of which had received a grant in the previous year.

The largest donation was £25,000 to Nightingale House. Other larger grants went to Ne Yisroel Educational Trust and Sunridge Housing Association (£15,000 each) and Princes Youth Business Trust and West London Synagogue (£10,000 each). Grants of between £2,000 and £5,000 went to 13 organisations including Breast Cancer Care, World Jewish Relief, SSAFA, Barnardos, BHHI, Jewish Children's Holiday Fund and St John Ambulance.

The remainder of grants were for £1,000. Non-Jewish organisations to benefit included Alzheimer's Research Trust, Cancer Care, Gingerbread, Listening Books, Macmillan Cancer Relief, RNIB, Scope, Mencap and Youth Clubs UK.

Exclusions Only registered charities are supported. No support for individuals for educational courses or overseas ventures, or for local hospices, homes etc.

Applications In writing to the correspondent.

Edith and Ferdinand Porjes Charitable Trust

Jewish, general

£229,000 (1998/99)

Beneficial area UK and overseas

Bouverie House, 154–160 Fleet Street, London EC4A 2JD

Tel. 020 7353 0299 **Fax** 020 7583 8621

Correspondent M D Paisner, Trustee

Trustees *M D Paisner; A H Freeman; A S Rosenfelder.*

Information available Full accounts were on file at the Charity Commission.

General This charity mainly supports Jewish organisations, but makes some significant grants to non-Jewish organisations as well. In 1998/99 this charity's assets totalled £2.3 million and it made grants totalling £229,000.

The largest grants in that year were £50,000 to Jews Free School, £25,000 to The Imperial War Museum Trust, £24,000 to The British Friends of the Council for a Beautiful Israel and £20,000 to The Jewish Museum. The remaining grants ranged between £500 and £14,000.

Smaller grants to Jewish organisations included £5,000 each to British Friends of Rabbi Steinsaltz and Yesodey Hatorah Grammar School, £2,500 to B'nai B'rith First and £1,500 to British Friends of OHEL Sarah.

Grants to non-Jewish organisations included £13,000 to NSPCC, £7,500 each to two Oxford colleges, £5,500 to Immigration Advisory Service and £4,000 to Queen Mary and Westfield College.

Applications In writing to the correspondent.

The John Porter Charitable Trust

Jewish, education, general

£63,000 to institutions (1998/99)

Beneficial area Worldwide, but mainly UK and Israel

79 Mount Street, London W1Y 5HJ

Tel. 020 7616 4700

Correspondent John Porter, Trustee

Trustees *Sir Leslie Porter; John Porter; Steven Porter; Peter Green.*

Information available Full accounts were on file at the Charity Commission.

General This trust makes grants to projects in the fields of education, culture, environment, health and welfare 'which encourage excellence, efficiency and innovation, and enhance the quality of people's lives'. It makes grants to registered charities and exempt charities.

Up until 1992/93 this trust had a regular surplus of income over expenditure enabling a solid asset base to be established. By 1998/99 the assets stood at £5.8 million generating an income of £172,000. Five grants to institutions were made totalling £63,000. Several beneficiaries have received ongoing support over a number of years including the trust's major project for the year Tel Aviv University Trust – Porter Super-Centre for Environmental and Ecological Studies which received £40,000. JPAIME - Daniel Amichai Education Centre also received further support of £7,000.

The other three grants went to Institute for Jewish Policy Research (£10,000) and Israel Music Foundation and Wiener Library (£3,000 each). One grant of £25,000 was given to an individual although the trust's policy normally excludes individuals.

Exclusions No grants to individuals.

Applications In writing to the correspondent.

The J E Posnansky Charitable Trust

Jewish charities, health, welfare

£296,000 (1998/99)

Beneficial area UK and overseas

c/o Baker Tilly, 2 Bloomsbury Street, London WC1B 3ST

Tel. 020 7413 5100 **Fax** 020 7413 5101

website www.bakertilly.co.uk

Correspondent P A Cohen, Trustee

Trustees *Lord Mishcon; P A Cohen; A V Posnansky; Mrs G Raffles; P A Mishcon; N S Posnansky; E J Feather.*

Information available Information was provided by the trust.

General The trust gives mainly to Jewish charities, grants are also made to social welfare and health charities.

In 1998/99 the trust had an income of £244,000 generated from assets of £6.2 million. Grants totalling £296,000 were given to 109 organisations, at least a third of these were recurrent from the previous year.

Nine grants were made over £10,000. Many of these larger grants went to Jewish charities, such as Jewish Aid Committee (£28,000), JPAIME (£25,000), £15,000 each to Society of Friends of the Federation of Women Zionists and General Jewish Hospital and

£13,000 each to Friends of the Hebrew University of Jerusalem and Norwood Ravenswood.

Grants to social welfare and health organisations included Save the Children Fund (£12,000), CARE International (£5,000), Macmillan Cancer Relief (£3,000), Terrence Higgins Trust (£2,500), Sue Ryder Foundation and Amnesty International (£2,000 each) with £1,000 each to Bromley Racial Equality Council, Help the Aged and UNICEF.

Applications To the correspondent. The trustees' meetings are held in May.

Premierquote Ltd

Jewish, general

£236,000 (1997/98)

Beneficial area Worldwide

Harford House, 101–103 Great Portland Street, London W1N 6BH

Tel. 020 8203 0665

Correspondent D Last, Trustee

Trustees *D Last; Mrs L Last; H Last; M Weisenfeld.*

Information available Accounts were on file at the Charity Commission, but without a list of grants.

General The trust was established in 1985 for the benefit of Jewish organisations, the relief of poverty and general purposes. In 1997/98 it had assets of £3.5 million and an income of £439,000 from investments. In previous years they have depended on one-off Gift Aid payments, which almost doubled their income in 1996/97. However, the trust is currently building up assets to allow for a more regular, sustainable level of giving in the future. Grants totalled £236,000 in 1997/98, but no information was available on the beneficiaries. The trustees stated in their report that they have a large, continually growing demand from institutions for grants and donations.

Applications In writing to the correspondent.

Premishlaner Charitable Trust

Jewish

£47,000 (1999/2000) but see below

Beneficial area UK and worldwide

186 Lordship Road, London N16 5ES

Correspondent C M Margulies, Trustee

Trustees *H C Freudenberger; S Honig; C M Margulies.*

Information available A 1999/2000 grants list was provided by the trust. Accounts up to 1998/99 were on file at the Charity Commission, without a full grants list.

General This trust was founded in 1995, its principal objects are:

- to advance orthodox Jewish education
- to advance the religion of the Jewish faith in accordance with the orthodox practice
- the relief of poverty.

In 1999/2000 the trust awarded 24 grants totalling £80,000, although one grant of £34,000 was returned. Grants included £20,000 to a Jewish educational organisation, £1,600 to Lev Efraim, £1,000 to Beth Jacob Primary School, two grants of £750 each to SOFT, two grants totalling £620 to Yeshuos Chaim Synagogue and £250 to Beis Ruzhin Trust. Many of these organisations were also beneficiaries in the previous year.

No other financial information for this year was available, although in 1998/99 the trust had assets of £428,000 and an income of £90,000, £51,000 of which came from donations and gifts.

Applications In writing to the correspondent.

The Primrose Trust

General

£147,000 (1998/99)

Beneficial area UK

Stable Mews, Everleigh, Wiltshire SN8 3EP

Correspondent M Clark, Trustee

Trustees *M G Clark; G E G Daniels.*

Information available Full accounts were on file at the Charity Commission.

General The trust was established in 1986 with general charitable purposes. In 1998/99 it had assets of £3.6 million and an income of £138,000. Grants for the year totalled £147,000. The trust made 21 grants, supporting a number of new organisations as well as some who had received help in the previous year.

The largest grant went to Winston's Wish for £15,000. Seven grants of £10,000 and eight of £5,000 were awarded. They included £10,000 each to Christian Lewis Trust, Dermatitis Trust, Francis House, Victim Support, Multiple Sclerosis Society and NSPCC and £5,000 each to AFB, Atworth Youth Club, London Sailing Project, Shelter Cymru and YMCA Cardiff.

The remainder of grants were under £5,000, beneficiaries included Fluency Trust (£3,500), Tregennys (£3,000), Rescue Foundation (£2,000) and WSPA (£1,000).

Exclusions Grants are given to registered charities only.

Applications In writing to the correspondent, including a copy of the most recent accounts.

The Prince of Wales's Charitable Foundation

See below

£387,000 (1998/99)

Beneficial area UK

The Prince of Wales Office, St James's Palace, London SW1A 1BS

Correspondent Stephen Lamport, Trustee

Trustees *Rt Hon. Earl Peel; Sir Michael Peat; Stephen Lamport; Mrs Fiona Shackleton.*

Information available Accounts were provided by the trust, only the four largest grants were listed.

General The trust principally continues to support charitable bodies and purposes in which The Prince of Wales has a particular interest.

217

During 1998/99 the total income of the trust was £972,000 including £525,000 net income from subsidiary companies, £255,000 from donations received and an investment income of £192,000. The foundation has two wholly owned subsidiaries, Duchy Originals Ltd and A G Carrick Ltd, from which most of its income is derived. To ensure an even flow of income for the foundation, £150,000 was transferred to the designated fund (part of the capital) during the year. The assets totalled £3.8 million.

The restricted fund is held by the foundation for the purpose of enabling United World Colleges (International) Ltd to provide scholarships to students to attend at the 10 United World Colleges located around the world.

Other grants were broken down into the following classifications:

Category	1999	1998
Animals	£11,000	£1,500
Armed services	£16,000	£1,000
Children and youth	£6,300	£1,300
Culture	£85,000	£49,000
Education	£57,000	£65,000
Environment	£52,000	£59,000
Hospices and hospitals	£56,000	£73,000
Medical welfare	£28,000	£100
Overseas aid	£18,000	£14,000
Restoration of churches and cathedrals	£23,000	£25,000
Social welfare	£36,000	£11,300

Only those grants of over £10,000 were listed in the accounts. They were to United World Colleges (£55,000), SANE Helpline (£20,000) and Soil Association and Temenos Academy (£15,000 each). Three of these had been supported at a similar level in the previous year.

Exclusions No grants to individuals.

Applications In writing to the correspondent.

Princess Anne's Charities

Children, medical, welfare, general

£167,000 (1997/98)

Beneficial area UK

Buckingham Palace, London SW1A 1AA

Correspondent Lt Col. T J Earl, Trustee

Trustees *Hon. M T Bridges; Commodore T J H Laurence; Lt Col. T J Earl; B Hammond.*

Information available Accounts were on file at the Charity Commission, with a list of grant recipients but not the amounts given.

General In 1998/99 the trust had an income of £151,000 and an expenditure of £160,000. Unfortunately further information for this year was not available and the following information is repeated from the last edition of this guide.

This trust was registered in 1979 with its main support for charities in which Princess Anne has a particular interest. In 1997/98 the trust made grants totalling £167,000. Further information was not available for this year.

In 1996/97 it had assets of £3.8 million which generated an income of only £153,000 while £27,000 was received in donations giving a total income of about £180,000. After expenses of £24,000, it gave 36 donations totalling £124,000, leaving a surplus of £32,000.

The trust categorised its grants as follows:

Social welfare	£44,000
Children and youth	£30,000
Environment	£26,000
Medical charities	£20,000
Ecclesiastical	£5,300

The most recent grants list included in the trust's file at the Charity Commission is for 1995/96, when grants totalled £111,000. Examples of beneficiaries were listed, but without the amounts given. They included Arthritis & Rheumatism Council for Research, Association of Combined Youth Clubs, British Executive Service Overseas, Butler Trust, Canal Museum Trust, Child to Child Trust, Farms for City Children, Jersey Wildlife Preservation Trust, Missions to Seamen, Princess Royal Trust for Carers and Save the Children Fund.

Exclusions No grants to individuals.

Applications Trustees meet to consider applications in January, and applications need to be received by November. 'The trustees are not anxious to receive unsolicited general applications as these are unlikely to be successful and only increase the cost of administration of the charity.'

The Priory Foundation

Health and social welfare, especially children

£198,000 (1998)

Beneficial area UK

The Priory, 54 Totteridge Village, London N20 8PS

Correspondent M Kelly, Trustee

Trustees *N W Wray; L E Wray; M Kelly; T W Bunyard.*

Information available Full accounts were on file at the Charity Commission.

General Unfortunately we have been unable to update the following information since the last edition of this guide.

The trust was established in 1987 to make donations to charities and appeals which directly benefit children.

In 1998 the trust had assets of £4.5 million, having increased from £2.1 million in 1995 following realised and unrealised gains on investments. Over 600 grants were given totalling £198,000.

The largest grants were to London Borough of Barnet for social needs cases (over £30,000), and over £5,000 each to ABCD, Birthright and MEP.

Most of the remaining grants were under £1,000 with beneficiaries including Action for Sick Children, ChildLine, Disability Aid Fund, East Belfast Mission, Sandy Gall's Afghanistan Appeal, Teenage Trust Cancer Appeal and Training Ship Broadsword. Most grants were one-off and given to UK organisations.

Applications In writing to the correspondent.

This entry was not confirmed by the trust but was correct according to information at the Charity Commission.

The Privy Purse Charitable Trust

General

£249,000 (1999/2000)

Beneficial area UK

Buckingham Palace, London SW1A 1AA

Tel. 020 7930 4832

e-mail privypurse@royal.gov.uk

Correspondent John Parsons, Trustee

Trustees *Sir M C Peat; G N Kennedy; J C Parsons.*

Information available Full accounts were on file at the Charity Commission.

General This trust gets most of its annual income from donations. In 1999/2000 it had assets of £2.8 million and an income of £349,000. Grants were made totalling £249,000 (£222,000 in 1998/99).

The following classifications were listed in the 1999/2000 annual report, with the amounts given in each category as follows.

Category	Total
Animals	£5,200
Armed services	£5,900
People who are blind	£2,400
Children and youth	£11,000
Cultural	£2,400
Disability	£2,900
Ecclesiastical	£107,000
Education	£62,000
Environment	£900
Ethnic and foreign	£50
Family welfare	£800
Hospices and hospitals	£4,700
Medical research	£2,000
Medical welfare	£3,900
Mental disability and illness	£1,600
Older people	£5,800
Overseas aid	£500
People who are deaf	£600
Restoration of cathedrals and churches	£7,100
Royal almonry	£3,800
Social welfare	£5,900
Sport	£3,100
Trades and professions	£7,500
Voluntary services	£1,600

The accounts listed the following five grants made over £10,000. The largest grant was for £51,000 and was given in the 'education' category to fund choristers' school fees. Three substantial grants were made in the 'ecclesiastical' category and went to Chapel Royal – St James's Palace (£36,000), Chapel Royal – Hampton Court Palace (£34,000) and

Sandringham Group of Parishes (£12,000). The final grant listed in the accounts was made in the 'education' category and was for the Queen's Chorister – Scholarship (£10,000).

In previous years beneficiaries have included a wide variety of UK and locally based organisations including Mayor of Windsor's Benevolent Fund, National Garden's Scheme Charitable Trust, Queen's Nursing Institute – Scotland Gardens, British Red Cross, Children's Country Holidays Fund, Dersingham Meals on Wheels, Liverpool School of Tropical Medicine, London Over-the-Border Church Fund, Motability, Norfolk Record Society, Royal College of Music and Shaw Trust.

Applications The trust makes donations to a wide variety of charities, but does not respond to appeals nor to grant applications.

The Puebla Charitable Trust

Community development work, relief of poverty

£103,000 (1999/2000)

Beneficial area Worldwide

Ensors, Cardinal House, 46 St Nicholas Street, Ipswich IP1 1TT

Tel. 01473 220022

Correspondent The Clerk

Trustees *J Phipps; M A Strutt.*

Information available Accounts were on file at the Charity Commission, but without a list of grants.

General The trust has stated that: 'At present, the council limits its support to charities which assist the poorest sections of the population and community development work – either of these may be in urban or rural areas, both in the UK and overseas'.

Grants are normally in the region of £5,000 to £20,000, with support given over a number of years where possible. Most of the trust's income is therefore already committed, and the trust rarely supports new organisations.

In 1999/2000 the trust's assets were £2.4 million. The income was £111,000 and the administration expenses were an exceptionally low £1,800. Grants totalled £103,000, but unfortunately, as in

previous years, no grants list was included with the accounts.

Exclusions No grants for capital projects, religious institutions, research or institutions for people who are disabled. Individuals are not supported and no scholarships are given.

Applications In writing to the correspondent. The trustees meet in July. The trust is unable to acknowledge applications.

Quercus Trust (*formerly* A Bernstein Charity Trust)

Arts, general

£125,000 (1999/2000)

Beneficial area UK

Radcliffes, 5 Great College Street, London SW1P 3SJ

Tel. 020 7222 7040   **Fax** 020 7222 6208

Correspondent T H R Crawley, Trustee

Trustees *Lord Bernstein of Craigwell; Thomas H R Crawley; Alan C Langridge; Kate E Bernstein; Lady Bernstein.*

Information available Full accounts were on file at the Charity Commission.

General In February 1999 the trustees declared by deed that distributions would in future be directed principally (but not exclusively) to the arts and any other objects and purposes which seek to further public knowledge, understanding and appreciation of any matters of artistic, aesthetic, scientific or historical interest.

In 1999/2000 the trust had assets of £7 million, an income of £164,000 and gave 21 grants totalling £125,000. The largest grants were to Old Theatre Trust (£29,000), Jerusalem Foundation (£26,000), Old Vic Theatre (£21,000), Artangel Trust (£15,000) and Royal Ballet School (£10,000). The remaining grants ranged from £200 to £5,600.

Applications In writing to the correspondent, but please note, the trust states: 'All of the trust's funds are currently earmarked for existing projects. The trust has a policy of not making donations to individuals and the trustees regret that, in order to keep administrative costs to a minimum, they are unable to reply to any unsuccessful applicants'.

The R V W Trust (Ralph Vaughan Williams)

British music, both contemporary and neglected music of the past

£219,000 (1998)

Beneficial area UK

16 Ogle Street, London W1W 6JA

Tel. 020 7255 2590   **Fax** 020 7255 2591

Correspondent Helen Faulkner, Secretary and Administrator

Trustees *Michael Kennedy, Chair; Lord Armstrong of Ilminster; Sir John Manduell; Mrs Ralph Vaughan Williams; Musicians' Benevolent Fund, Corporate Trustee.*

Information available Full accounts are on file at the Charity Commission.

General The trust makes grants towards the following (the amount paid in each category in 1998 in brackets):

- the public performance of musical works (including opera and concerts) (13 grants totalling £24,000)
- copying/publishing music (one grant of £1,000)
- music festivals (eight grants totalling £41,000)
- the advancement of public education in music (six grants totalling £86,000)
- publishing music books (nil)
- musicians and dependants in need (one grant of £1,000)
- musical education grants (24 grants totalling £65,000).

In 1998 the trust's assets totalled £1.5 million, it had an income of £396,000, mainly from royalties from the Performing Right Society, and its total expenditure was £301,000. In total, £219,000 was donated in 53 grants. There was a surplus of income over expenditure for the year of £95,000. Grants were in the range of £250 to £28,000 with the trust giving support to a number of previously supported projects as well as new ones.

Larger grants were £28,000 to Sir Thomas Armstrong Centenary CD, £25,000 to Huddersfield Contemporary Music Festival, £16,000 to Roberto Gerhard – Complete Mature Orchestra Music CDs,

£15,000 to British Music Information Centre, £13,000 to Society for the Promotion of New Music and £10,000 each to Vaughan Williams Memorial Library, National Opera Studio and William Walton Foundation – Ischia Summer School. Other grants went to Double Image, Music Past and Present, Gloucester Three Choirs Festival, Spitalfields Festival, Norwich and Norfolk Festival and London Guildhall University – Department of Musical Instrument Technology.

Exclusions No support for: government associated bodies or universities; schools of music; festivals with very large budgets; degree courses, except first Masters degrees in musical composition. No support for dance, vocal or drama courses.

Applications In writing to the correspondent, giving project details, at least one month before the trustees meet. Trustees' meetings are held in February, June and October. Masters in Music Composition applicants will only be considered at the June meeting, applications must be received by the end of April.

The Radcliffe Trust

Music, crafts, conservation

£469,000 (1998/99)

Beneficial area UK

5 Lincoln's Inn Fields, London WC2A 3BT

Tel. 020 7405 1234

Correspondent John Burden, Secretary to the Trustees

Trustees *Lord Cottesloe, Chair; Lord Quinton; Lord Balfour of Burleigh; Christopher J Butcher; Dr Ivor F Guest.*

Information available Accounts were on file at the Charity Commission.

General The Radcliffe Trust has developed a policy to support a very precise range of activities in music and the crafts, with a small margin to look at activities outside its main concerns. It has a distinguished history and was founded in 1714 by the will of Dr John Radcliffe, the most prominent physician of his day, who left the income from his property to fund the trust.

The following quotations are taken from the trust's 1997/98 report.

Music

'In the area of music they operate a scheme under which the Allegri Quartet make regular visits to a selected number of universities and other centres, giving concerts, master-classes and teaching sessions. As a further development of this scheme the trustees have appointed John Cooney as Composer-in-Association with the Allegri Quartet. The trustees have also initiated a highly successful series of specialist seminars in double-reed playing and on the technology of pianos. In addition the trustees make grants for classical music education, but they do not accept applications from individuals.'

Crafts

'In the area of crafts, the main thrust is the support of craft training among young people both at the level of apprenticeships (mostly but not exclusively, in cathedral workshops) and also at the post-graduate and post-experience levels. This can be by way of direct grants to employers, contributions to bursaries or other awards on offer to students or interns at appropriate training establishments, or support for the setting up of relevant new posts or courses at such institutions. For other grants, the trustees' main concern is to achieve a standard of excellence in crafts related particularly to conservation. The trustees monitor the progress of projects for which grants are made, particularly those which are spread over periods of more than one year, in which cases satisfactory progress reports are required as a condition of later instalments being paid.

'The trustees make small grants for the repair and conservation of church furniture, including bells and monuments. Such grants are made … through the Council for the Care of Churches … ; direct applications are not accepted. Grants are not made for structural repairs to church buildings, nor for organs.'

Miscellaneous

'Miscellaneous applications which do not fall within the above categories may be considered subject to availability of surplus income, but the following categories are excluded:

- construction, conversion, repair or maintenance of buildings
- grants directly to individuals for education fees and maintenance
- sponsoring musical and theatrical performances
- medical research
- social welfare
- support of expeditions.'

In 1998/99 the trust had a net income of £344,000 from assets of £10.6 million. Grants totalling £469,000 were made to 64 organisations, £200,000 of which came from reserves. Grants can be broken down as follows:

Crafts – £190,000 (30 grants)
Larger grants went to West Dean College (£21,000), Textile Conservation Centre (£16,000), Scottish Maritime Museum and Cathedrals Research Unit – York University (£11,000 each). Other grants went to: Meridian Trust Association (£7,000); British Library (£5,000); Orton Trust (£3,000); Chester Cathedral Library (£2,500); and National Glass Centre (£2,400).

Fellowships – £9,400 (one grant)
The trustees have for many years supported fellowships in history and philosophy. These are now being phased out.

Music – £128,000 (29 grants)
Grants of £10,000 and over went to Allegri String Quartet (£19,000), Birmingham Conservatoire (£15,000), University of Cambridge, Faculty of Music (£13,000) and Godstowe Preparatory School (£10,000).

Other grants went to City of Birmingham Symphony Orchestra (£7,500), National Federation of Music Societies (£3,000) and British Youth Opera (£2,500).

Miscellaneous - £142,000 (11 grants)
The major grant was given to the Bodleian Library for £125,000. Other grants went to Bardsey Island Trust (£5,000), Clavert Trust (£3,000), Royal Academy of Dancing (£500) and PCC St Mary's & St Giles (£25).

Exclusions No grants to individual applicants. No grants to non-registered charities, or to clear or reduce past debts. Please also see under 'Miscellaneous' in the 'General' section above.

Applications Applications for music grants are short-listed for consideration by a panel of musicians who make recommendations, where appropriate recommended applications are then placed before the trustees for decision. The music panel usually meets in March and October in advance of trustees' meetings in June and December and applications should be submitted in writing by the end of January and the end of August respectively to allow time for any further particulars (if so required) to be furnished.

Craft applications should be in writing, and submitted by the end of March to be considered for referral to the trustees' meeting in June and by the end of

September to be considered for referral to the trustees' meeting in December.

Applications for miscellaneous grants should be in writing and applications should be received by the end of April for consideration at the June meeting and by the end of October for consideration at the December meeting.

The Mark Radiven Charitable Trust

Jewish, general
£145,000 (1998/99)
Beneficial area Worldwide, with some preference for Manchester

Charles Frieze & Co., 12 Charlotte Street, Manchester M1 4HP
Tel. 0161 236 4521 **Fax** 0161 236 8457
Trustees S Friedland.
Information available Full accounts were on file at the Charity Commission.

General The trust mainly supports Jewish causes, with some preference for Manchester and also for Israel. In 1998/99 it had assets of £252,000 (£429,000 in the previous year) and an income of £8,600. Administration and management costs were high at £3,000, over a third of the trust's income. The grant total was £145,000, presumably using capital funds accounting for their dramatic reduction. In the previous year the trust had an income of £6,000 and gave grants totalling £103,000.

The largest grant of £108,000 was given to Joint Jewish Charitable Trust (over 12 times larger than the income of the trust), which also received the largest grant in the previous year (£25,000). Other large grants included those to Abraham Fund (£9,100), Delamere Forest School (£7,300), Yeshurun Hebrew Congregation (£6,300), Manchester Jewish Grammar School (£4,000), Dvar Yerushalm (£2,000) and Community Security Trust (£1,300). Many grants of under £1,000 were also made.

Applications In writing to the trustees.

The Rainford Trust

Social welfare, general
£152,000 (1998/99)

Beneficial area Worldwide, with a preference for areas in which Pilkington plc have works and offices, especially St Helens and Merseyside

c/o Pilkington plc, Prescot Road, St Helens, Merseyside WA10 3TT
Tel. 01744 20574
Correspondent W H Simm, Secretary
Trustees Mrs J Graham; A L Hopkins; Mrs A J Moseley; H Pilkington; Lady Pilkington; R E Pilkington; R G Pilkington; I S Ratiu; Mrs I Ratiu.
Information available Accounts were provided by the trust.

General The trust confirmed that its current policy is as follows:

'To consider applications from organisations that aim to enhance the quality of community life.

To help initiate and promote special projects by charitable organisations which seek to provide new kinds of employment. To assist programmes whose objects are the provision of medical care, including holistic medicine, the advancement of education and the arts, and the improvement of the environment.

Applications from religious bodies and individuals will be considered if they fall within the scope of these aims.

'Although the trust will continue to give preference to applications from St Helens (as stated in the trust deed), and from other main Pilkington UK areas, this does not prejudice the trustees discretion to help charities that operate outside these areas.'

In 1998/99 the total income was £264,000 gained through investment income and donations. The assets rose in the year to £5.4 million. The trust made 124 grants totalling £152,000, this includes the trust's continued support for Citadel Arts Centre (two grants totalling £73,000).

Other grants ranged from £500 to £3,000, with the larger grants to Bristol Cancer Help Centre (£3,000), The Royal Star and Garter Home and British Red Cross - Kosovo Appeal (£2,000 each) with £1,500 each to Addaction, Rainbow Trust and Koestler Award Trust. Grants of £1,000 were made to 17 organisations, recipients included Primary British Red Cross, Gingerbread, Winged Fellowship Trust, RefAid and Scottish European Aid.

The majority of the remaining grants were in the range of £500 to £750. Organisations to benefit included Iris Fund and Counsel and Care (£750 each), Westnell UK (£700), St Helens District Council for Voluntary Service (£600) and £500 each to Royal Liverpool University Hospitals, National Back Pain Association, Wirral Society of the Blind and Partially Sighted, APT Enterprise Development and Eating Disorders Association.

Exclusions No grants to individuals for educational purposes will be considered unless the individual is normally resident in St Helens.

Applications On a form available from the correspondent. Applicants may apply at any time. Only successful applications will be acknowledged.

The Peggy Ramsay Foundation

Writers and writing for the stage

£97,000 to organisations (1999)

Beneficial area British Isles

Harbottle & Lewis Solicitors, Hanover House, 14 Hanover Square, London W1R 0BE

Tel. 020 7667 5000 **Fax** 020 7667 5100

Correspondent G Laurence Harbottle, Trustee

Trustees *G Laurence Harbottle; Simon Callow; John Welch; Michael Codron; Sir David Hare; John Tydeman; Baroness McIntosh of Hudnall; Harriet Walter.*

Information available Full accounts were provided by the trust.

General This trust exists to help writers and writing for the stage. It was established from Peggy Ramsay's personal estate in accordance with her will. The objectives of the foundation are:

- the advancement of education by the encouragement of the art of writing
- the relief of poverty among those practising the arts, together with their

dependants and relatives, with special reference to writers

- any charitable purpose which may, in the opinion of the trustees, achieve, assist in, or contribute to, the achievement of these objectives.

In 1999 the trust had assets totalling £5.5 million and an income of £220,000. Its annual grant total of £193,000 was divided almost equally between individuals and organisations.

The main category of charitable support which the foundation offers is to writers for the stage who have individual problems and needs. The foundation supports writers who are very often successful but who cannot afford to continue writing because of day to day commitments. During the year £96,000 was spent on 44 people with varying needs, from providing computers to allowing writers time to work.

The second largest contribution is made through the Peggy Ramsay Play Award. The format of this has varied from year to year. For the first time in 1999 the award was divided between the production and the author of the play which won the award. Two authors were awarded £5,000 each for their plays, with the Tron in Glasgow receiving the main award of £35,000. The Foundation also supported a number of other awards and bursaries throughout the year including the Pearson Television Theatre Writers Scheme.

Apart from these major categories, theatres and producing managements have received help for projects which involve writing directly, workshops and management expenses which contribute to theatre writing. On two occasions companies were helped to engage literary managers to contribute to the quality of work available for production. Grants to producing companies are not usually made for production costs but are intended to facilitate new work, whether by commissions which could not otherwise be afforded or for supportive arrangements such as workshops or the salaries of literary managers.

About £97,000 was given to organisations, the trustees report listed 27 grants over £500. The largest grant of £10,000 went to Royal Court Theatre. Liverpool Lunchtime Theatre Ltd received the second largest grant of £5,700. Six grants of £5,000 went to New Shakespeare Company Ltd, Traverse Theatre, London Live, Polka Childrens' Theatre Ltd, Cleanbreak Theatre Company and London New Play Festival. The remainder of listed grants were in

the range of £500 to £4,000. Recipients included Theatre Machine Ltd (£4,000), Blackpool Grand Theatre (£3,000), Society of Authors and Bristol Old Vic (£1,000 each) and Forbidden Theatre Co. (£500).

£10,000 was given to young people's theatre on two occasions. This area has provided some difficulty for the trust. While recognising its importance educationally and as an introduction to professional theatre, the trustees are reluctant to support something which looks like production costs in adult theatre. The question of what further support might be given is a continuing debate.

Exclusions No grants are made for productions or writing not for the theatre.

Applications Applications should be made by writing a short letter, when there is a promising purpose not otherwise likely to be funded and which will help writers or writing for the stage. Grants are considered at four or five meetings during the year, although urgent appeals can be considered at other times.

The Joseph & Lena Randall Charitable Trust

Jewish, general

£159,000 (1998/99)

Beneficial area Worldwide

Berwin Leighton, Adelaide House, London Bridge, London EC4R 9HA

Correspondent The Trustees

Trustees *D A Randall; B Y Randall.*

Information available Accounts were on file at the Charity Commission, but without a list of grants.

General It is the policy of this trust to provide regular support to a selection of charities, providing important medical, educational and cultural facilities. In 1998/99 the trust's assets totalled £1.9 million, it had an income of £163,000 and grants totalled £159,000. In the year 39 donations were made, none below £500. The trust stated that '70% of awards went to organisations committed to relieving hardship, suffering and poverty among minorities', this probably refers mainly to Jewish charities.

Further information about beneficiaries and the size of grants made was unavailable for 1998/99. The most recent grants list was for 1995/96, when grants totalled £152,000 and beneficiaries included Jewish Philanthropic Association (£30,000), The Kerland Foundation 'Brainwave' (£7,000 – fifth donation out of seven), Glyndebourne Festival Society Appeal (£6,000 – last of four donations), British Diabetic Association (£4,000) and Institute for the Special Child (£500).

Exclusions No grants to individuals.

Applications In writing to the correspondent. The trust stated in their 1998/99 report that funds were fully committed, and they regretted that they were 'unable to respond to the many worthy appeals'.

The Ratcliff Foundation

General

£156,000 (1998/99)

Beneficial area UK, with a preference for the Midlands, north Wales and Gloucestershire

Ernst & Young, One Colmore Row, Birmingham B3 2DB

Tel. 0121 535 2000

Correspondent J B Dixon, Trustee

Trustees *Ms C M Ratcliff; E H Ratcliff; D M Ratcliff; J B Dixon; J M C Fea; Ms G M Thorpe.*

Information available Full accounts were on file at the Charity Commission.

General The trust was established in 1961 by Martin Rawlinson Ratcliffe. In 1998/99 it had assets of £3.2 million, with an income of £190,000 from investments and an additional £70,000 from F R Ratcliff Charitable Settlement. Management and administration costs were high at £33,000, over 10% of the income.

A total of £156,000 was given in 85 grants, ranging from £500 to £5,000. Larger grants included £5,000 to Cancer Research (Kemerton) Campaign, £4,500 to St Nicholas Church – Kemerton, with £3,000 each to Walsall Relate, Good Shepherd Trust, St John's Ladywood

Appeal, RBSA and Starlight Children's Foundation.

The accounts show the grants grouped under the name of each individual trustee. This may be due to the trustees preferring particular causes and living in different areas. Grants have shown an interest in health/disability, social welfare, children/youth, wildlife/conservation/environment and education causes. The trustees have a preference for Worcester/Gloucester, Birmingham/Midlands, Warwickshire and Wales.

Specific organisations to benefit include Birmingham City Mission, Burstow Park Riding for the Disabled, Dogs for the Disabled, Educational Theatre Services Ltd, Midland Youth Jazz Orchestra; National Meningitis Trust, RSPB, West Bromwich Boys' Club and Wheatley Out of School.

The foundation supported one special project in the year, £16,000 went to CRAB (Cancer Research at Birmingham).

Applications In writing to the correspondent.

The Eleanor Rathbone Charitable Trust

Merseyside, women, unpopular causes

£233,000 (1999/2000)

Beneficial area UK, with the major allocation for Merseyside; women-focused international projects

3 Sidney Avenue, Wallasey, Merseyside CH45 9JL

Correspondent Lindsay Keenan, Administrator

Trustees *Dr B L Rathbone; W Rathbone; Ms Jenny Rathbone; P W Rathbone; Lady Morgan.*

Information available Full information was provided by the trust.

General The trust concentrates its support largely on the following:

* charities and charitable projects focused on Merseyside (over 70% of beneficiaries in 1999/2000)

* charities benefiting women and unpopular and neglected causes but avoiding those with a sectarian interest

* special consideration is given to charities with which any of the trustees have a particular knowledge or association or in which it is thought Eleanor Rathbone or her father William Rathbone VI had a special interest.

Most grants are on a one-off basis, although requests for commitments over two or more years are considered.

In 1999/2000 the trust had assets of just over £6.3 million, producing an income of only £206,000. Grants to 134 organisations totalled £233,000. Grants ranged from £100 to £12,000 and were broken down as follows with specific beneficiaries shown beneath each category:

Merseyside charities – 96 grants
RUKBA (£12,000); Merseybeat Appeal – Liverpool Cardiothoracic Centre (£10,000); Save the Children Fund (£6,000); Young Person's Advisory Service (£5,000); Fairbridge in Merseyside (£3,500); Liverpool CAB (£2,000); Crossroads Care – St Helens and Wirral Autistic Society (£1,000 each); Merseyside Youth Association (£500); and Bluecoat School (£100).

International charities – 20 grants
Womankind Worldwide and Canon Collins Educational Trust for South Africa (£5,000 each); Music as Therapy (£3,000); Refugee Women's Legal Group (£2,000); Africa Now and Christian Aid (£1,000 each); and Tradecraft Exchange (£500).

Other UK/regional charities –18 grants
Gingerbread Northern Ireland (£3,000); Penrose Housing Association and Women's Therapy Centre (£2,000 each); Barnardos and New Bridge (£1,000 each); and Ealing Somali Welfare and Cultural Association (£500).

The grants list was made up of both previously supported and new organisations.

Exclusions Grants are not made in support of:

* any activity which relieves a statutory authority of its obligations

* individuals, unless (and only exceptionally) it is made through a charity and it also fulfils at least one of the other positive objects mentioned above.

The trust does not generally favour grants for running costs, but prefers to support specific projects, services or contribute to specific items.

Applications No application form, the trust asks for a brief proposal for funding including costings, accompanied by the latest available accounts and any relevant supporting material. It is useful to know who else is supporting the project.

To keep administration costs to a minimum, receipt of applications is not usually acknowledged, unless an sae is enclosed.

Trustees currently meet three times a year, dates vary.

The Märit and Hans Rausing Charitable Foundation

Architecture and other arts, children, medical and agricultural research, science, nature preservation

£269,000 (1999)

Beneficial area UK and worldwide

39 Sloane Street, London SW1X 9LP

Tel. 020 7235 9560 **Fax** 020 7235 9580

Correspondent Miss E Owen, Administrator

Trustees *Peter Hetherington; Prof. Anthony R Mellows; Sir John Sparrow; Philippa Blake-Roberts.*

Information available Full accounts were provided by the trust.

General The trustees will only consider applications for grants in the following fields:

Arts and national heritage
The preservation and enhancement of national and cultural heritage

Children charities (not individual cases)
• helping particularly gifted children to develop
• the protection of children from cruelty and abuse
• the prevention and relief of children who are disabled
• the encouragement of children and young people to study outside their own country (note: in this category preference will be given to those living in Eastern Europe)

Medical
• hospitals and hospices
• medical research

Sciences, social sciences and economics
The enhancement of the study and teaching of sciences, including economics.

Nature preservation
The conservation and preservation of wildlife in the countryside in the UK.

In 1999 the trust had assets of £1.7 million and an income of £349,000, of which £334,000 was the net income from a trading subsidiary (Alta Advisers Ltd). Grants totalling £269,000 were made to 26 charitable causes.

The largest grant was for £90,000 to Institute of Economic Affairs, which was also given the same amount in 1998 and was the only grant made from the designated fund. Other larger grants were to European Science and Environmental Forum and Burrswood Jubilee Appeal (£50,000 each) and £10,000 each to Caine Prize, Royal Navy Submarine Museum and Aleph Society.

The remainder of grants were in the range of £500 and £6,200. Recipients included Russian Arts Help, Listening Books, Reach, Sense, Orbis, Romney Marsh Research Trust, Pace Centre and Dystonia Society.

Applications In writing to the trustees. The trust states that 'due to the overwhelming number of applications received it is not always possible to send a response'.

The Roger Raymond Charitable Trust

General

£143,000 (1998/99)

Beneficial area UK

Sayers Butterworth, 18 Bentick Street, London W1M 5RL

Tel. 020 7935 8504 **Fax** 020 7487 5621

Correspondent R W Pullen, Trustee

Trustees *R W Pullen; P F Raymond; M G Raymond.*

Information available Accounts were on file at the Charity Commission with only a limited review and no list of grants.

General In 1998/99 the trust had assets of £5 million and an income of £200,000, of which £143,000 was given in grants. In previous years the trust had been split into a Main Fund and a No. 2 Fund, giving separate grants from each, however it now appears to have only one.

The principal beneficiary of the year, and of the previous year, was Bloxham School which received £108,000 – over 75% of the grant fund, (£75,000 in 1997/98). We have been unable to obtain further information about other beneficiaries and size of grants.

The last detailed grant information on file at the Charity Commission was from 1994/95 when the total amount given in grants by both funds was £140,000. The main grants were to Royal Commonwealth Society for the Blind (£5,000), ITDG (£4,500), Salvation Army (£4,000) and Samaritans and Leonard Cheshire Foundation (£3,000 each). It gave 33 grants of £1,000 to £2,300 which included those to Barnardos, British Heart Foundation, British Wheelchair Sports Foundation, ChildLine, Handy 1 Robotic Appeal, Isle of Purbeck Club, MIND, National Asthma Campaign, NSPCC, RNLI, Save the Children Fund, WaterAid, Woodlands Trust and WWF. The smallest grants were to Salvation Army (£580), Girl Guides Association and Scout Association (£500) and College of Law (£250). Many of these beneficiaries are regularly supported.

Applications The trust stated that applications are considered throughout the year, although funds are not always available.

The Rayne Trust

Jewish, general

£129,000 (1998/99)

Beneficial area UK

33 Robert Adam Street, London W1M 5AH

Tel. 020 7935 3555

Correspondent R D Lindsay-Rea, Secretary

Trustees *Lord Rayne, Chair; Lady Jane Rayne; R A Rayne.*

Information available Full accounts were on file at the Charity Commission.

General This trust is administered from the same office as the much larger Rayne Foundation (see *A Guide to the Major Trusts Volume 1*), and shares with that foundation the practice of giving a large number of relatively small grants. Since 1958 it has given away over £3 million.

In 1998/99 the trust had assets of £1.6 million and an income of £594,000. Administration costs came to only £3,600 and grants were made totalling £129,000.

Most beneficiaries were Jewish organisations and grants were made towards social welfare, older people, arts and young people. The report listed only those grants made over £1,000. The largest donation was for £26,000 to Home for Aged Jews, also the major beneficiary in the previous year. Other larger grants went to Winton Primary School (£15,000), West London Synagogue of British Jews (£13,000), Community Security Trust (£10,000) and Institute of Contemporary History and Weiner Library and Jewish Association for the Mentally Ill (£5,000 each).

Other organisations to benefit included Holocaust Educational Trust (£3,500), Jewish Care (£1,500) and Jewish Music Heritage Trust (£1,000).

Non-Jewish organisations to receive grants included Chicken Shed Theatre Trust (£2,800), English Chamber Orchestra and Music Society (£2,000) and Delamere Forest School (£1,000).

Other donations each of less than £1,000 totalled £14,000.

Exclusions No grants to individuals or non-registered charities.

Applications In writing to the correspondent.

The Albert Reckitt Charitable Trust

General

£69,000 (1999/2000)

Beneficial area UK

Southwark Towers, 32 London Bridge Street, London SE1 9SY

Correspondent J Barrett, Secretary

Trustees *Mrs S C Bradley, Chair; Sir Michael Colman; Mrs M Reckitt; Mrs G M Atherton; D F Reckitt; J Hughes-Reckitt; P C Knee; Dr A Joy.*

Information available Accounts were on file at the Charity Commission, but without a list of grants.

General In 1999/2000 the trust had assets of £1.7 million and an income of £81,000. Administration costs of the trust totalled £5,300 for the year. Grants are separated between subscriptions (annual grants) totalling £43,000 and donations (one-off) totalling £26,000.

The trust has a preference for UK organisations rather than local areas. Grants usually ranged from £250 to £750. Information on beneficiaries was not available.

Exclusions No grants for political or sectarian charities, except for Quaker organisations.

Applications In writing to the correspondent. Trustees meet in June/July and applications need to be received by March.

The C A Redfern Charitable Foundation

General

£199,000 (1998/99)

Beneficial area UK

PricewaterhouseCoopers, 9 Greyfriars Road, Reading, Berkshire RG1 1JG

Tel. 0118 959 7111

Correspondent *The Trustees*

Trustees *C A G Redfern; T P Thornton; S R Ward; Sir R A Clark; D S Redfern.*

Information available Full accounts were on file at the Charity Commission.

General This trust supports a wide range of organisations with some preference for those concerned with health and welfare.

In 1998/99 the assets of this trust stood at £4.7 million. The total income for the year was £231,000 and 61 grants were made totalling £199,000 (£250,000 in 1997/98). Over two-thirds of the organisations supported had received a grant in the previous year.

The largest grant was £30,000 to South Buckinghamshire Riding for the Disabled. Other large grants went to Saints and Sinners Club (£25,000) and Motor and Allied Trades Benevolent

Fund (£10,000). Awards included 14 grants of £5,000, 9 of £3,000 and 14 of £1,000. Grants included £5,000 each to Cancer Support Centre Wandsworth, Canine Partners for Independence, Seven Springs Play and Support Centre and Farms for City Children; £3,000 each to Campus Children's Holidays, CRUSE, RNIB and The De Paul Trust; and £1,000 each to British Red Cross, Help the Aged, Northwick Park Institute for Medical Research and NSPCC – Berkshire.

The remainder of grants were mainly for £250 or £500. Recipients included Fight for Sight, London Lighthouse, New Heart Start Appeal, RNLI, Save the Children Fund, Shelter and YMCA.

Applications The trust does not accept unsolicited applications.

The Christopher H R Reeves Charitable Trust

Food allergies, disability

£111,000 (1997)

Beneficial area UK

Hinwick Lodge Farm, Hinwick, Wellingborough, Northants NN29 7JQ

Tel. 01234 781090

Correspondent E M Reeves, Trustee

Trustees *E M Reeves; V Reeves; M Kennedy.*

Information available Full accounts were on file at the Charity Commission.

General In 1998/99 the trust had an income of £139,000 and an expenditure of £80,000. Unfortunately further information for this year was not available and the following information is repeated from the last edition of this guide.

The trust is holding about 75% of its income and capital for application in the limited area of food allergy and related matters. Nearly all the income in this section has already been committed to The Centre for Allergy Research and Environmental Health at University College London and to the production and distribution of a database of research references under the title of Nutritional and Environmental Medicine and Allergies Database.

New appeals related to food allergy and intolerance are invited and a response will be made to applicants.

The remaining 25% of the trust's income and capital will be held for general donations. The main area of interest is in disability. Donations will largely be made to charities already associated with the trust. Only successful applicants will receive a response.

In 1997 the assets of the trust stood at £3.6 million and generated an income of £137,000. Grants totalled £111,000 with £50,000 to University College London. The other substantial grant was £42,000 to Mother and Child Foundation. The other 19 grants ranged from £30 to £2,000, with most for £1,000. Beneficiaries included Bedfordshire Society for Autism, Highland Hospice, National Food Alliance, Northamptonshire Association for the Blind, Research into Ageing and Salvation Army.

Exclusions No grants for individuals, overseas travel and expeditions, animal charities, church/community hall/school appeals outside the north Bedfordshire area, overseas aid, children's charities, drugs/alcohol charities, mental health charities or education.

Applications In writing to the correspondent. Trustees meet five times a year in March, May, July, September and November.

This entry was not confirmed by the trust but was correct according to information on file at the Charity Commission.

REMEDI

Research into disability

£107,000 (1999/2000)

Beneficial area UK

The Old Rectory, Stanton Prior, Bath BA2 9HT

Tel. 01761 472662 **Fax** 01761 470662
e-mail g.coles_remedi@btinternet.com
website www.remedi.org.uk

Correspondent Lt Col Patrick Mesquita, Director

Trustees *Brian Winterflood, President; Dr A K Clarke, Chair; Alan Line; Dr A H M Heagerty; Dr A St J Dixon; David Hume; Dr I T Stuttaford; Rosie Wait.*

Information available Full information was provided by the trust.

General REMEDI supports pioneering research into all aspects of disability in the widest sense of the word, with special emphasis on the way in which disability limits the activities and lifestyle of all ages. There was a minor change of emphasis in 1998 with the trustees deciding to support fewer applications with substantially larger grants. They continue to favour applicants who wish to carry out innovative and original research and experience difficulty in attracting funding from the larger and better-known organisations. Collaboration with other charities working in the same field is actively encouraged to share the costs of research, provided it is undertaken in the UK. It will give grants for projects, equipment and therapy research.

In 1999/2000 the total income of the trust was £250,000, which came mostly from donations and deeds of covenants. Grants totalled £107,000 (£335,000 in 1998/99).

Projects which were to receive support in 2000 included: research into prostate cancer at St Mary's Hospital, London; new ways to vaccinate against Meningitis at University of Bristol; community memory clinics for Research Institute for the Care of the Elderly, Bath; and the experience of adults with learning disabilities and their carers in general hospitals at University of Edinburgh.

Exclusions Cancer and cancer-related diseases are not normally supported.

Applications By e-mail. Applications are received throughout the year. They should initially include a summary of the project on one side of A4 with costings. The chair normally examines applications on the third Tuesday of each month with a view to inviting applicants to complete an application form by e-mail.

The Rhodes Trust Public Purposes Fund

Oxford University, overseas, general

£2.7 million (1998/99)

Beneficial area UK and overseas

Rhodes House, Oxford OX1 3RG

Tel. 01865 270903 **Fax** 01865 270914

Correspondent Dr John Rowett, Secretary

Trustees *Rt Hon. William Waldegrave; Sir John Kerr; Sir Richard Southwood; Dr C R Lucas; Prof. R J O'Neill; Mrs R Deech; Miss R Hedley-Miller.*

Information available Full accounts were on file at the Charity Commission.

General The primary purpose for which the trust was established and for which it continues to be used and managed, is to provide scholarships to be allocated each year to enable students from selected countries of the Commonwealth, the USA and the Federal Republic of Germany, to spend two or three years on an undergraduate or postgraduate course of study at Oxford University.

The Public Purposes Fund, from which the trustees can appropriate property to the scholarship fund, can make grants for educational and other charitable purposes, in any part of the Commonwealth or the USA. The policy has been to restrict its use to educational purposes in Oxford University and Commonwealth countries in Africa and the Caribbean.

The combined income for 1998/99 was £6 million. The cost of maintaining the scholarship programme was £3.9 million and charitable donations from Public Purposes Fund amounted to £2.7 million. In addition, £75,000 was granted from the Scholarship Capital Reserve Fund and £44,000 from the South Africa Fund. At the year end, the assets stood at about £197 million.

The grants from Public Purposes Fund were broken down as follows:

	1999	1998
Oxford University	£1.3 million	£920,000
African and Commonwealth	£1.3 million	£588,000
Other	£41,000	£20,000

Oxford University grants
Nine grants were made including £862,000 to Rothermere America Institute, £250,000 to Oxford University Scholarships for overseas students, £90,000 to Oxford University Sports Committee and £50,000 to Erasmus Exchange Scheme.

African and Commonwealth
A total of 22 grants were given with 3 for £100,000 or more, these were University of Witwatersan Foundation (£517,000), Rhodes University – Eden Grove Centre (£274,000) and University of Cape Town – bursaries (£100,000). Other grants ranged from £5,000 to £61,000 and included Liverpool University's Diabetes

Education (£61,000), Valley Trust (£51,000), World University Service UK–Campus Scheme (£7,000) and African Book Collection Trust (£5,000).

Other
Four grants were made: £25,000 to British School in Rome, £10,000 to British Academy, £5,000 to Churches Commission on Overseas Student Hardship and £1,000 to the Round Table.

Exclusions Grants to institutions only. No grants to individuals.

Applications To the correspondent in writing. Trustees meet in June and November.

Daisy Rich Trust (*formerly* Charity of Miss Winifred Daisy Rich)

General

£125,000 (1999/2000)

Beneficial area UK, with a possible preference for the Isle of Wight

The Cranbourn Suite, 61 Upper James Street, Newport, Isle of Wight PO30 1LQ
Tel. 01983 521236
Correspondent Mrs J Williams, Secretary
Information available Accounts were on file at the Charity Commission, but without a grants list or narrative report.

General In 1999/2000 the trust's assets totalled £2.3 million and it had a net income of £111,000. It made grants totalling £125,000. Unfortunately a grants list was not included with the accounts. There is a possible preference for supporting organisations and individuals on the Isle of Wight.

Applications In writing to the correspondent.

Cliff Richard Charitable Trust

Spiritual and social welfare

£107,000 (1998/99)

Beneficial area UK

Harley House, 94 Hare Lane, Claygate, Esher, Surrey KT10 0RB
Tel. 01372 467752 **Fax** 01372 462352
Correspondent Bill Latham, Trustee
Trustees *Philip Parker; Bill Latham; Malcolm Smith.*

Information available Accounts were on file at the Charity Commission, but without a detailed breakdown of all donations, or a full narrative report.

General The trust was founded in 1969. In 1998/99 it had assets of £151,000 and had an income of £129,000, mainly from donations. Administration costs were low at under £200. Grants totalled £107,000.

The accounts listed three grants made by the trust, the largest was £50,000 to Leprosy Mission. The two other grants listed were to Genesis Arts Trust (£6,000) and Arts Centre Group (£5,000), both of which had been supported in the previous year. £46,000 was given in 'sundry donations', no further information was available on the size of these donations or the type of organisation they went to.

Exclusions Capital building projects, church repairs and renovations are all excluded.

Applications Applications should be from registered charities only, in writing, and for one-off needs. All applications are acknowledged. Grants are made in January, April, July and October.

The Muriel Edith Rickman Trust

Medical research, education

£109,000 (1998/99)

Beneficial area UK

12 Fitzroy Court, 57 Shepherds Hill, London N6 5RD
Tel. 020 8348 1448
Correspondent H P Rickman, Chair

Trustees *H P Rickman, Chair; M D Gottlieb; Raymond Tallis.*
Information available Full accounts were on file at the Charity Commission.

General The trust makes grants to medical research organisations towards equipment. The trust prefers to support physical disabilities than mental illnesses. A school is also supported by the trust.

In 1998/99 its assets totalled £120,000 and the income was £127,000, mainly from donations (£118,000). Grants totalled £109,000 and most were one-off.

Larger grants were £26,000 to Blond McIndoe Centre, £20,000 to Aberdeen University Appeal and £13,000 each to Royal Liverpool University Hospitals and British Retinitis Pigmentosa.

Other grants went to London Chest Hospital (£8,900), Research in Ageing (£6,000), Defeating Deafness (£5,100), Muscular Dystrophy Group (£3,400), War on Cancer (£2,500) and Juvenile Diabetes Foundation (£1,000).

The only grant repeated from the previous year was to Guide Dogs for the Blind (£250).

Applications In writing to the correspondent.

Ridgesave Limited

General, education

£475,000 (1998/99)

Beneficial area UK

13–17 New Burlington Place, Regent Street, London W1S 2HL
Correspondent *The Trustees*
Trustees *J L Weiss; Mrs H Z Weiss; E Englander.*
Information available Accounts were on file at the Charity Commission, but without a list of grants.

General This trust was set up to support organisations for education or other general charitable purposes. In 1998/99 it had assets of £2.6 million and its income was £438,000, nearly all from donations. Grants totalled £475,000, up almost £100,000 from the year before. Unfortunately a grants list was not included in the accounts.

Applications In writing to the correspondent.

227

The River Trust

Christian

£247,000 (1997/98)

Beneficial area UK, with a preference for Sussex

c/o Kleinwort Benson Trustees Ltd,
PO Box 191, 10 Fenchurch Street,
London EC3M 3LB

Tel. 020 7956 6600

Correspondent Chris Gilbert

Trustees *Kleinwort Benson Trustees Ltd.*

Information available Full accounts were on file at the Charity Commission.

General Gillian Warren formed the trust in 1977 with an endowment mainly of shares in the merchant bank Kleinwort Benson. It is one of the many Kleinwort trusts, several of which are included in *A Guide to the Major Trusts Volume 1* as well as this guide. The River Trust is one of the smaller of the family trusts; it supports Christian causes.

In 1997/98 the trust had assets of £480,000 and an income of £249,000, including £228,000 in donations. Grants were made totalling £247,000 (£191,000 in 1996/97 and £334,000 in 1995/96). Many of the 67 organisations supported had received help in the previous year, grants ranged from £1,000 to £47,000.

The largest grants were to Youth with a Mission (£47,000), Chasah Trust (£28,000), Dolphin Trust (£25,000), Timothy Trust (£12,000) and Care Trust (£11,000). Other grants over £1,000 went to Genesis Arts Trust and Scripture Union (£8,000 each), St Stephen's Society (£6,400), Challenge 2000 (£5,000), Prison Fellowship and Tearfund (£3,000 each) and March for Jesus (£2,000).

Recipients of the 17 grants of £1,000 included Deep Trust, Inter Health, New Directions Theatre Company Ltd and Quantock Christian Trust. Grants under £1,000 were made to 20 organisations including African Enterprise, Cuckfield Parochial Church, Lawrence Barham Memorial Church and Post Green Community Trust Ltd.

Exclusions Only appeals for Christian causes will be considered. No grants to individuals. The trust does not support 'repairs of the fabric of the church' nor does it give grants for capital expenditure.

Applications In writing to the correspondent. Unsolicited appeals are considered as well as causes which have already been supported and are still regarded as commitments of the trust. Only successful applicants are notified of the trustees' decision. Some charities are supported for more than one year, although no commitment is usually given to the recipients.

Riverside Charitable Trust Limited

Health, welfare, older people, education, general

£193,000 (1998/99)

Beneficial area Mainly Lancashire

c/o E Suttons & Sons, Riverside, Bacup,
Lancashire OL13 0DT

Tel. 01706 874961

Correspondent Barry J Lynch, Trustee

Trustees *B J Lynch; I B Dearing; J A Davidson; F Drew; H Francis; A Higginson; G Maden.*

Information available Accounts were on file at the Charity Commission.

General The trust's objects are to support the following: people who are poor, sick or older; education; healthcare; the relief of poverty of people employed or formerly employed in the shoe trade; and other charitable purposes.

In 1998/99 the trust had assets of £2.4 million and an income of £141,000. Grants totalled £193,000 which were broken down as follows: donations (£161,000); donations to retired footwear employees (£26,000); funeral expenses and death grants (£4,500); and Twenty Five Year Retired Members (£2,100).

A total of 155 'donations' were given ranging from £50 to £20,000, 129 of these were recurrent from the previous year. The largest grant of £20,000 went to Macmillan Cancer Relief. A further 50 grants were given ranging from £1,000 to £6,200. Beneficiaries included Cancer Research Campaign (£6,200), St Mary's Hospice and Rossendale Valley Domestic Violence Forum (£6,000 each), Hospice in Lancashire (£3,100), British Heart Foundation (£3,000), East Lancashire Contact Centre (£2,500) with £2,000 each to Stacksteads Junior Band, Cumbria Deaf Association and Barrow and District Society for the Blind and £1,500 to Alzheimer's Disease. Among the 21 organisations receiving £1,000 were Bacup Aged, Detached Families Worker Project, Furness Mountain Rescue, Marie Curie Cancer Care, NSPCC – South Cumbria and SCOPE.

Smaller grants under £1,000 included those to Arthritis Care – Rossendale, Kirkland Foundation, Lancashire Constabulary, Mayoral Charity Appeal and RSPCA – Woodside Animal Farm.

Exclusions No grants for political causes.

Applications In writing to the correspondent.

Robson Charitable Trust

General

£70,000 (1996/97)

Beneficial area UK

Midway Manor, Bradford-on-Avon,
Wiltshire BA15 2AJ

Tel. 01225 864269

Correspondent J A Robson, Chair

Trustees *J A Robson, Chair; Mrs G J Robson; R Barrett.*

Information available Accounts were on file at the Charity Commission, with a very brief narrative report.

General Unfortunately we were unable to obtain up-to-date information for this trust. The following entry is repeated from the last edition of this guide.

This trust was established in 1995 with 75,000 shares in the company Colleagues Direct Marketing Plc; 30,000 of these were sold in April 1996 to fund the trust's grant giving during the year. This left the assets standing at £140,000 at the year end.

In 1996/97 grants totalled just over £70,000 with £60,000 given to King Edward's School and £10,000 to the Princes Trust. The only other grants were for £200 each, given to Save the Children Fund and Teenage Cancer Trust.

Applications In writing to the correspondent. Please note, the trust states that it is not open to public applications and all funds are fully committed.

Rokach Family Charitable Trust

Jewish, general

£103,000 (1998/99)

Beneficial area UK

20 Middleton Road, London NW11 7NS

Tel. 020 8455 6359

Correspondent Norman Rokach, Trustee

Trustees N Rokach; Mrs H Rokach; Mrs E Hoffman; Mrs M Feingold; Mrs A Gefilhaus; Mrs N Brenig.

Information available Full accounts were on file at the Charity Commission.

General This trust supports Jewish and general causes in the UK. In 1998/99 its assets totalled £958,000. The trust's income was £195,000, mainly from rent on its properties. Grants totalled £103,000. Many of the same organisations were supported in 1997/98.

The largest beneficiary was Friends of Viznitz which received £55,000 – over half of the grant fund. This organisation had also received major support in previous years. Seven further grants were made over £1,000 including those to Craven Walk Charitable Trust (£12,000), Cosmon (Belz) Limited (£6,700), CMZ Trust (£4,900), Jewish Educational Trust (£3,000) and Finchley Road Synagogue (£1,300).

Other grants ranged from £100 to £800, but were mainly for amounts under £400. Recipients of smaller grants included Kisharon (£800), London Academy of Jewish Studies (£500), Ponervitz (£300), Friends of Belz and Kollel Shomrei Hachomoth (£250 each) and TTMH (£100). Donations under £100 totalled £4,400.

While there is a strong preference for Jewish organisations, in the past the trust has stated that smaller grants have been given to a wide range of organisations. They also informed us that non-Jewish charities regularly receive larger grants and include cancer research organisations and hospices.

Applications In writing to the correspondent.

The Helen Roll Charitable Trust

General

£98,000 (1998/99)

Beneficial area UK

Marches & Co., 3 Worcester Street, Oxford OX1 2PZ

Correspondent F R Williamson, Trustee

Trustees Jenny Williamson; Dick Williamson; Paul Strang; Christine Chapman; Terry Jones.

Information available Full accounts were provided by the trust.

General 'One of the trustees' aims is to support work for charities which find it difficult or impossible to obtain funds from other sources. Some projects are supported on a start-up basis, others involve funding over a longer term. The charities supported are mainly those whose work is already known to the trustees and who report on both their needs and achievements. Each year a handful of new causes are supported. However, the trust states that 'the chances of success for a new application are about 100–1'.

In 1998/99 the assets of the trust were £1.9 million and the income was £59,000. Grants totalled £98,000 and administration expenses £17,000. Of the 26 organisations which received grants, 19 had also benefited the previous year.

The grants list showed a preference for organisations based in the south of England particularly Oxford, with Oxford University Bodleian Library and Pembroke College Oxford receiving £8,000 each. Other larger grants went to Trinity College of Music (£7,500), Oxford University – Ashmolean Museum (£7,000), Friends of Home Farm Trust (£6,500), Purcell School (£6,000), Stroud Court Community (£5,500) and Sick Children's Trust – Sheffield and Dogs for the Disabled (£5,000 each).

A wide range of causes received support with recipients of other grants including Notting Hill Housing Trust (£4,000), National Association for Colitis and Crohn's Disease (£3,000), Friends of Animal League (£2,000), Action Against Men's Violence and Hunters Bar Infant School HAS (£1,500 each), Gerald Moore Prize (£500) and Medicalert (£300).

Exclusions No support for individuals or non-registered charities.

Applications In writing to the correspondent during the first fortnight in February. Applications to be kept short, ideally on one sheet of A4. Further material will then be asked of those who are short-listed. The trustees normally make their distribution in March.

The Sir James Roll Charitable Trust

General

£135,000 (1998/99)

Beneficial area UK

5 New Road Avenue, Chatham, Kent ME4 6AR

Tel. 01634 830111   **Fax** 01634 408891

Correspondent N T Wharton, Trustee

Trustees N T Wharton; B W Elvy; J M Liddiard.

Information available Full accounts were on file at the Charity Commission.

General The trust's main objects are the:

- promotion of mutual tolerance, commonality and cordiality in major world religions
- furtherance of access to computer technology as a teaching medium at primary school levels
- promotion of improved access to computer technology in community based projects other than political parties or local government
- funding of projects aimed at early identification of specific learning disorders.

In 1997/98 the trust's assets totalled £4 million, it had an income of £145,000 and grants were made totalling £135,000. Management and administration costs totalled £19,000.

A mix of new and previously supported causes received grants. In total, 84 grants were made, about a quarter of which were for over £1,000. The largest grant was £11,000 to RNIB. Six donations of £10,000 each included those to Crisis at Christmas, The Children's Society, The Pace Centre and St Clement PCC. Grants of £5,000 each went to Great Ormond Street Hospital Children's Charity, Open Age Project and British Polio Fellowship.

Two grants of £4,000, one of £2,500, two of £2,000 and eight of £1,000 were given. Recipients included National Missing Persons Bureau, Listening Books, Sense, Children's Country Holiday Fund, City Escape and Fifth Trust.

Smaller grants under £1,000 went to Oxfam, Scope, Willow Tree Sanctuary, 3H Fund, Hi Kent, Muscular Dystrophy Group, Prison Reform Trust and NSPCC.

Applications In writing to the correspondent.

The Cecil Rosen Foundation

Welfare, especially older people, infirm, people who are mentally or physically disabled

£233,000 (1998/99)

Beneficial area UK

118 Seymour Place, London W1H 1NP

Tel. 020 7262 2003

Correspondent M J Ozin, Trustee

Trustees *Mrs L F Voice; M J Ozin; A J Hart.*

Information available Accounts were on file at the Charity Commission without a list of grants and only a limited review of activities.

General Established in 1966, the charity's main object is the assistance and relief of the poor, especially older people, the infirm or people who are disabled.

In 1998/99 the trust had assets of £2.2 million and an income of £486,000. It gave grants totalling £233,000, administration costs were £4,700 for the year. Further information was not available about beneficiaries or the size of grants.

The last information on grants on file at the Charity Commission was from 1996/97. Beneficiaries in this year included The Cecil Rosen Charitable Trust which shares the same trustees as this trust (£60,000) and The Jewish Blind and Disabled Society (£40,000). Both of these organisations had also received large grants the year before.

According to the correspondent almost all the trust's funds are (and will always continue to be) allocated between five

projects. The surplus is then distributed in small donations between an unchanging list of around 200 organisations. 'Rarely are any organisations added to or taken off the list.'

Applications The correspondent stated that 'no new applications can be considered'. Unsuccessful applications are not acknowledged.

The Teresa Rosenbaum Golden Charitable Trust

Medical research

£301,000 (1999/2000)

Beneficial area UK

140 High Street, Edgware, Middlesex HA8 7LW

Tel. 020 8952 1414   **Fax** 020 8952 2424

Correspondent John Samuels, Trust Administrator

Trustees *T Rosenbaum; R Ross; R M Abbey.*

Information available Full accounts were on file at the Charity Commission.

General The trust supports medical research by supporting researchers from recognised research departments or institutes with proven records of achievement and excellence in their field.

Grants totalled £301,000 in 1999/2000 with donations of £5,000 or more given to Alzheimer's Disease Society, Arthritis Research Campaign, Defeating Deafness, Digestion Disorders Foundation, Fight for Sight, Imperial College School of Medicine, Julia Polak Lung Transplant Fund, Kings Medical Research Trust, Migraine Trust, Motor Neurone Disease Association, MS (Research) Trust, MS Society, Psychiatry Research Trust, Research into Ageing, Royal Free Hospital and Shaare Zedek Medical Centre.

Exclusions No support for individuals.

Applications In writing to the correspondent. 'The trustees are not medical experts and require short clear statements in plain English setting out the particular subject to be researched,

the objects and likely benefits, the cost and the time-scale. Unless a charity will undertake to provide two concise progress reports each year, they should not bother to apply as this is a vital requirement. It is essential that the trustees are able to follow the progress and effectiveness of the research they support.'

The Roughley Charitable Trust

General

£87,000 (1998/99)

Beneficial area UK, but mainly West Midlands

Crosby Court, 28 George Street, Hockley, Birmingham B3 1QG

Correspondent J R L Smith, Trustee

Trustees *Mrs M K Smith; G W L Smith; Mrs D M Newton; M C G Smith; J R L Smith.*

Information available Full accounts were on file at the Charity Commission.

General In 1998/99 the trust had assets of £2.2 million and an income of £113,000. Grants totalled £87,000 and were listed in the trust accounts under two headings shown below:

Annual grants

18 grants totalling £10,000, ranging from £28 to £3,000. The only recipients of £1,000 or more were St James Church (£3,000), Medical Foundation for the Care of Victims of Torture (£2,000) and Amnesty International UK Section Charitable Trust (£1,000). Of the smaller grants made, most were to charities in the West Midlands such as Birmingham Rathbone Society, Sutton Coldfield Handicapped Children's Association and Birmingham Botanical Gardens and Glasshouses.

Specific grants

24 grants were listed totalling £76,000 and were in the range of £50 to £25,000. The largest donations were to Emmaus Cambridge Expansion Appeal (£25,000), Birmingham Settlement (£15,000) and Midlands Arts Centre (£13,000). Other grants in this category went to Birmingham Symphony Hall Organ Fund (£5,000), Black Country Museum (£3,000), Phoenix Sheltered Workshop and Selly Oak Methodist Church (£1,000 each), Birmingham Institute for the Deaf and Churches Commission on Overseas

Students Hardship Fund (£500 each) and Macmillan Cancer Relief (£50).

Applications 'The funds are fully committed to charities known to the trustees; no further applications wanted.'

Rowanville Ltd

Orthodox Jewish

£428,000 (1999/2000)

Beneficial area UK and Israel

8 Highfield Gardens, London NW11 9HB

Tel. 020 8458 9266

Correspondent J Pearlman, Governor

Trustees *J Pearlman; Mrs R Pearlman; M Neuberger; M D Frankel.*

Information available Full accounts were on file at the Charity Commission.

General The objectives of the trust are 'to advance religion in accordance with the orthodox Jewish faith' and to support 'philanthropic religious and educational activities'. Only 'established institutions' are supported.

In 1999/2000 the trust carried assets of £1.7 million and had an income of £506,000, a large proportion of this came from Gift Aid and other donations. Grants totalled £428,000, (£355,000 in 1998/99). The trust tends to make a large number of recurrent grants each year, giving all of its support to Jewish organisations.

The largest grants were for school funding and went to Yesodey Hatorah Grammar School and Menorah Grammar School. Other larger grants went to Nayzar Chesed (£20,000), Yeshivas Shaarei Torah (£15,000), Centre for Advanced Rabbanics (£13,000) and Telz Talmudical Academy (£11,000).

In previous years other recipients have included Kahal Chasidim Bovov, Beer Arrohom (UK) Trust, Friends of Ohel Moshe, Gateshead Talmudical College, SOFOT, Pinto Talmudical Centre, Torah Educational Trust, North West London Shepardish Synagogue, Gur Trust, Marbeh Torah Trust and WIZO.

Applications The trust states that applications are unlikely to be successful unless one of the trustees has prior personal knowledge of the cause, as this charity's funds are already very heavily committed.

Joshua and Michelle Rowe Charitable Trust

Not known

£184,000 (1998/99)

Beneficial area Not known

84 Upper Park Road, Salford M7 4JA

Correspondent J Rowe, Trustee

Trustees *J Rowe; Mrs M B Rowe.*

Information available Very sparse accounts were filed at the Charity Commission, without a narrative report or grants list.

General In 1997/98 the trust had assets of just £73,000 and an income of £15,000 (in 1997/98 the trust had received £156,000 from Gift Aid contributions, increasing its income to £177,000). Grants totalled £184,000, there was a deficit of £168,000 for the year.

Despite the trust's large grant total, there was very little information on file at the Charity Commission. We do not have any indication of the trust's grant policy.

Applications In writing to the correspondent.

The Rowlands Trust

General (see below)

£223,000 (1999)

Beneficial area UK, but primarily the West Midlands, south Midlands and Gloucestershire

c/o Wragge & Co., 55 Colmore Row, Birmingham B3 2AS

Tel. 0121 233 1000 **Fax.** 0121 214 1099

Correspondent Michael Wells, Clerk to the Trustees

Trustees *A C S Hordern, Chair; G B G Hingley; C P Harris; K G Mason.*

Information available Full accounts and application guidelines were provided by the trust, some of which is printed below.

General This trust makes grants for 'research, education and training in the broadest sense so as to promote success' and to 'support charities providing for medical and scientific research, the services, the sick, poor, [disabled], elderly, music, the arts, the environment and the restoration and maintenance of Anglican church buildings'. The geographical area of benefit is the West Midlands and South Midlands, including Hereford and Worcester, Gloucester, Shropshire and Birmingham.

In 1997 the first year of operation of the trust, it had an income of £6.3 million, including a legacy from the founder of £6 million, which was transferred to the trust's capital account. Other income was £229,000 from the estate of H R Rowlands and £40,000 from investments. By 1999 the assets were £7.5 million and the income was £283,000. Management and administration costs were high at £34,000. Grants were made to 29 organisations totalling £233,000.

The two largest grants were £50,000 to Worcestershire Association for the Blind and £25,000 to Sunfield Chiuldren's Homes Ltd. The trust made a further seven grants over £10,000 including Bernard Issacs Memorial Fellowship and Friends of Birmingham Museums and Art Gallery (£15,000 each) and £10,000 each to Wrekin Community Safety Partnership, Sense and Herefordshire Mind.

Remaining grants were in the range of £1,000 to £7,500, recipients included Colwall Players (£7,500), £5,000 each to Fairbridge West Midlands, Acorns Children's Hospice Trust and King Edward VI Camp Hill School for Girls, St Basil's Centre Ltd and Elgar School for Music (£2,500 each) and Phoenix Sheltered Workshop (£1,000).

Exclusions No support for individuals or to charities for the benefit of animals. Generally, applications for revenue funding will not be considered.

Applications On a form available from the correspondent, a detailed guidelines for applicants for grants is also provided.

The trustees meet to consider grants four times a year.

231

The Russell Trust

General

£244,000 (1998/99)

Beneficial area UK with a preference for Scotland

Markinch, Glenrothes, Fife KY7 6PB

Tel. 01592 753311

Correspondent Mrs Cecilia Croal, Secretary

Information available Information was provided by the trust.

General The trust usually supports specific services or projects and prefers to give start-up grants for new initiatives. Grants were categorised as follows:

* St Andrews University archaeology
* National Trust for Scotland
* church
* music and the arts
* education
* youth work
* preservation work/conservation
* the Iona Community
* local causes
* general – ecology, museums, miscellaneous
* health and welfare.

Grants are one-off and usually range from £250 to £10,000. The average grant is £1,000.

In 1998/99 the trust had assets of £375,000 and an income of £300,000. Grants totalled £244,000.

Beneficiaries supported included Dance Base Appeal and Royal Society for Edinburgh for a conference on nature (£5,000 each). In the previous year Children 1st received a large grant for a phone-line providing counselling for both children and parents.

Applications On a form available from the correspondent.

The Audrey Sacher Charitable Trust

Arts, medical, care

£137,000 (1998/99)

Beneficial area UK

Acre House, 11–15 William Road, London NW1 3ER

Correspondent The Trustees

Trustees *S J Sacher; J M Sacher; M H Sacher.*

Information available Full accounts were on file at the Charity Commission.

General The trust states its main areas of work as the arts, medical and care. Grants are only made to charities known personally to the trustees.

In 1998/99 the trust had assets of £2.7 million and an income of £97,000. The trust made 52 grants in the year totalling £137,000, 16 of the organisations supported, including some of the main beneficiaries, had also received a grant in 1997/98.

The largest grants were £30,000 each to English National Ballet and Centrepoint, £20,000 to St Paul's Girls School and £10,000 to Anna Freud Centre. A further 17 grants were made over £1,000 including Royal Opera House (£8,000), Whizz-Kidz (£3,000), Chicken Shed Theatre Company (£2,800), Royal National Theatre (£2,100), Royal Academy of Dancing (£1,500) and National Gallery Trust (£1,000).

The remaining grants were for smaller amounts in the range of £50 to £500, but were mostly for £250 or less. Beneficiaries included: Royal Academy Trust (£500); £250 each to Aids Crisis Trust, Hearing Dogs for Deaf People, Save the Children Fund and Byam Shaw School of Art; British Youth Opera and Marie Curie Cancer Care (each £200); Notting Hill Housing Trust (£100); and Britto Foundation (£50).

Exclusions No grants to individuals or organisations which are not registered charities.

Applications In writing to the correspondent.

The Michael Sacher Charitable Trust

Jewish, general

£142,000 (1999/2000)

Beneficial area UK and Israel

Acre House, 11–15 William Road, London NW1 3ER

Correspondent Mrs Irene Wiggins, Secretary

Trustees *Simon John Sacher; Jeremy Michael Sacher; Michael Harry Sacher.*

Information available Accounts were on file at the Charity Commission but without a grants list since 1984/85.

General In 1999/2000 the trust had assets of £4.6 million and an income of £159,000. It gave grants totalling £142,000.

No grants lists was on file at the Charity Commission since that for 1984/85, when the trust gave £131,000 in grants. Grants given to non-Jewish organisations totalled less than £500 and were given to NSPCC, Leukaemia Research Fund and Kids. The main grants were to JPAIME (£101,000), Friends of the Hebrew University of Jerusalem (£12,000), Central British Fund (£5,000) and Hebrew University (£2,000). There were seven grants of £1,000 to £1,500, one for £750 to the Anglo-Israel Association and all other grants were for £10 to £500.

Applications In writing to the correspondent.

Dr Mortimer & Theresa Sackler Foundation

Arts, hospitals

£121,000 (1995)

Beneficial area UK

15 North Audley Street, London W1Y 1WE

Tel. 020 7493 3842

Correspondent Christopher B Mitchell, Trustee

Trustees *Mortimer Sackler; Theresa Sackler; Christopher Mitchell; Robin Stormonth-Darling; Raymond Smith.*

Information available Accounts were on file at the Charity Commission, but without a list of grants.

General In 1998 the trust had an income of £325,000 and an expenditure of £135,000. Unfortunately further information for this year was not available and the following information is repeated from the last edition of this guide.

The foundation was set up in 1985 by Mortimer Sackler of Rooksnest, Berkshire for general charitable purposes and 'the advancement of the public in the UK and elsewhere in the fields of art, science and medical research generally'. Under a four-year deed of covenant (ending 1991) the foundation received (unspecified) donations from Bard Pharmaceuticals Ltd, and the company also made a special donation of £667,000 in 1990/91.

The assets of the foundation were built up by these donations and in December 1995 stood at £3 million, of which £2.8 million was held as a balance at the bank. This only gave an income of £112,000, but the trust also received further donations of £1 million. After expenses of only £400, the trust gave £121,000 in grants.

Unfortunately, the trust did not include a grants list with the accounts, but did state that it is 'continuing its commitments to the National Gallery, Ashmolean Museum, Worcester College - Oxford and a new commitment to the Serpentine Gallery and the Louvre'. Its commitments over the next four years are, within one year (£299,000), two years (£230,000), three years (£133,000) and four years (£133,000).

Applications To the correspondent in writing, but see the reservations made above.

The Ruzin Sadagora Trust

Jewish

£123,000 (1997/98)

Beneficial area UK, Israel

269 Golders Green Road,
London NW1 9JJ

Correspondent I M Friedman, Trustee

Trustees *Israel Friedman; Sara Friedman.*

Information available Limited accounts were on file at the Charity Commission without a grants list since 1993/94.

General In 1997/98 the trust had assets of £654,000 and an income of £151,000, of which £103,000 came from donations. Grants totalled £123,000 for the year.

In its annual report the trustees stated that they continued to:

• fund the cost, upkeep and activities of Ruzin Sadagora Synagogue in London (£24,000)

• fund and support the parent and other associated and affiliated Sadagora institutions and other religious causes and charities (£123,000).

No further details were available about the size or number of the beneficiaries in 1997/98. The last grants list on file at the Charity Commission from 1993/94 saw the trust giving only to Jewish organisations.

Applications In writing to the correspondent.

This entry was not confirmed by the trust, but was correct according to information at the Charity Commission.

The Saddlers' Company Charitable Fund

General

£295,000 (1998/99)

Beneficial area UK, but mainly England in practice

Saddlers' Hall, 40 Gutter Lane,
London EC2V 6BR

Tel. 020 7726 8661/6 **Fax** 020 7600 0386

Correspondent Group Captain W S Brereton-Martin

Trustees *D S Snowden (Master) and 27 others who make up the Court of Assistants.*

Information available Annual report and financial statements were provided by the trust.

General In 1998/99 the charity had an income of £362,000 and assets of £8.5 million. It made grants totalling £295,000 in support of the City of

London, the saddlery trade, the equestrian world, education and general charitable activities. In order to structure the charity's grant-making policy the trustees have, for the past three years, focused on aiding smaller charities assisting people who are disabled. It was agreed that this policy should be continued in 1999. To meet the trust's policy, members of the livery are asked to visit a charity local to them and report on the charity's suitability to receive a grant. This is then considered by a grant committee whose recommendations are passed on to the trustees.

Significant grants went to Alleyn's School (£100,000), Riding for the Disabled (£28,000), Royal Veterinary College (£12,000) and Lord Mayor's Appeal for Leuka 2000 (£10,000). The trust supports many of the same charities each year such as Alleyn's School and Riding for the Disabled. After making these allocations, about one quarter of the remaining money is allocated to major UK charities working in all charitable sectors and about three quarters for responding to specific charitable appeals which are received throughout the year. Grants to major UK organisations included £1,800 to Royal British Legion and £1,000 each to Salvation Army, The Samaritans, Children's Heart Foundation and Motor Neurone Disease Association. Charitable appeals receiving help included Berkshire MS Therapy Centre Appeal (£1,500) and Phasels Wood Activity Centre – Diamond Jubilee Appeal (£1,000).

The trustees report points out that grants given in one year do not necessarily serve as a precedent for giving in subsequent years. The following is a breakdown of grants by category made in 1998/99:

Category	Total
City of London	£11,000
The equestrian world	£24,000
Education	£124,000
Disability	£97,000
Saddlery trade	£10,000
General charitable activities	£29,000

Exclusions Appeals by individuals for educational grants cannot be considered.

Applications By letter, with supporting background information. Grants are made in January and July, following trustees' meetings. Charities are asked to submit reports at the end of the following year on their continuing activities and the use of any grant received.

233

The Jean Sainsbury Animal Welfare Trust

Animal welfare

£201,000 (1999)

Beneficial area Mainly the UK, but overseas charities are considered

PO Box 469, London W14 8PJ

Correspondent Miss Ann Dietrich, Administrator

Trustees *Jean Sainsbury; Cyril Sainsbury; Colin Russell; Gillian Tarlington; James Keliher; Mark Spurdens; Jane Winship; Audrey Lowrie.*

Information available Financial statements along with a grants list were provided by the trust.

General The trust was established in 1982 with the objective of benefiting and protecting animals from suffering. Over £2.5 million had been donated by 1999. The policy of the trustees is to support smaller charities concerned with animal welfare and wildlife. Some organisations receive regular donations.

In 1999 the trust had an income of £295,000, assets of £8.7 million and made donations totalling £201,000 to 136 organisations. Grants ranged between £100 and £10,000.

Grants of £10,000 each went to Ashbourne and District Animal Welfare Society, North Clwyd Animal Rescue and Three Owls Bird Sanctuary and Reserve – South Yorkshire. Other recipients included Faith Animal Rescue – Norfolk (£7,500), Brent Lodge Bird & Wildlife Trust – Chichester (£6,000), Animals in Distress – Manchester (£5,300), Paz Animal – Colombia (£5,000), Terry Marsh Bird Rescue Service – Mansfield (£4,000) and Spear (Sue Pike Equine and Animal Rescue) – Warwick (£2,500). Grants of £1,000 each included those to Hearing Dogs for the Deaf – Oxford and Exotic Pet Rescue and Animal Aid – Aintree. Smaller grants went to Greek Cat Welfare Society (£500), Stalybridge Hedgehog Hospital Trust – Cheshire (£250) and Royal Veterinary College – Beaumont Animal Hospital (£100).

Before support is considered the trustees want to see the accounts and where possible visit the charities which are new to them. In 1998, 38 animal welfare organisations were visitied.

Exclusions No grants are made to individuals or non-registered charities and no loans can be given.

Applications In writing to the correspondent, including a copy of accounts. There are three trustees' meetings every year, usually in March, July and November.

St Gabriel's Trust

Higher and further religious education

£296,000 to organisations (1999)

Beneficial area Mainly in the UK, with an interest in the diocese of Southwark

Ladykirk, 32 The Ridgeway, Enfield, Middlesex EN2 8QH

Tel. 020 8363 6474

Correspondent Peter Duffell, Clerk

Trustees *Priscilla Chadwick, Chair; Colin Alves; Linda Borthwick; Revd Canon John Hall; Prof. Ben Pimlott; Shane Guy; Roger Harrison; Anne Lamb; Arthur Pendlebury-Green; Judith Roy.*

Information available Reports and financial statement were provided by the trust.

General The trust is concerned with the the advancement of higher and further education in one or more of the following ways by:

- promotion of the education and training of persons who are, or intend to become, engaged as teachers or otherwise in work connected with religious education

- promotion of research in, and development of, religious education

- promotion of religious education by the provision of instruction, classes, lectures, books, libraries and reading rooms

- granting of financial assistance to institutions of higher or further education established for charitable purposes only.

In 1999 the trust had an income of £686,000 (£465,000 from the sale of property) and assets of £6.3 million. Administration costs came to £19,000. Grants totalling £307,000 were made comprising of £202,000 in corporate

awards, £94,000 on the St Gabriel's Programme (see below), and £11,000 to individuals.

A total of 14 corporate grants were made in the year, the largest was £70,000 to Millennium Development Programme and College Centenary. Other grants over £10,000 went to: National Society to start up a website (£30,000); ACCT for RE Teachers Recruitment Initiative (£25,000); University of East Anglia for a Senior Research Associate (£19,000); London Diocesan Board for Schools for Collective Worship (£14,000); Stapleford Institute to develop new courses for teachers in Christian values (£12,000); and Professional Council for RE (£11,000). Seven grants in this category were supported in the previous year.

The trustees have committed funds for several corporate projects including:

(i) an initiative to recruit RE teachers, in conjunction with other trusts

(ii) Stapleford Institute to develop new courses for teachers in Christian values

(iii) assistance to the National Society's website

(iv) University of Exeter's the Biblos Project on Teaching the Bible.

The St Gabriel's Programme is an ongoing venture which has been run jointly with Culham College Institute; it has 'continued to develop thought and action in support of RE teachers'. The aim is to foster good practice in RE.

A sum of £11,000 was spent on personal awards to individuals in the year. These were given towards course fees and expenses for teachers taking part-time RE courses whilst continuing their teaching jobs. Occasional grants have been given to those undertaking specialist research which will clearly benefit the religious education world.

Exclusions Grants are not normally available for: any project for which local authority money is available, or which ought primarily be funded by the church – theological study, parish or missionary work – unless school RE is involved; and research projects where it will be a long time before any benefit can filter down into RE teaching. No grants are made to schools as such; higher and further education must be involved.

Applications In writing to the correspondent with an sae. Applications need to be received by the beginning of January, April or October as trustees meet in February, May and November.

St James's Place Foundation

(formerly J Rothschild Assurance Foundation)

Children

£341,000 (1999)

Beneficial area UK

J Rothschild House, Dollar Street, Cirencester, Gloucestershire GL7 2AQ

Tel. 01285 640302 **Fax** 01285 640436

Correspondent Gail Mitchell-Briggs, Secretary

Trustees *M Cooper-Smith; J Newman; Sir Mark Weinberg; M Wilson.*

Information available An annual report, comprehensive grants list and full application details were provided by the trust.

General The objective of the foundation is to raise money for distribution to organisations which meet its current theme. Since 1996 this has been 'Cherishing the Children'.

The following criteria are applicable whatever theme is current:

- applicants should be well-established registered charities with a proven track record, which have worthwhile objectives and are run efficiently and economically. Applications from individuals will not be considered

- applicants should be in respect of tangible projects or equipment with visible end results, rather than salaries, administration and running costs

- the project should help as many people as possible or, where this is not applicable, have a major impact on the lives of those helped

- UK charities only.

Under the 2000/2001 theme of 'Cherishing the Children' the foundation will consider applications for projects which are for the direct benefit of children aged 17 or under who have either:

- physical or mental disability

- life-threatening or degenerative illness.

The foundation will support established charities or special needs schools.

In 1999 the trust had net assets of £294,000. It had an income of £508,000 including Gift Aid payments from

St. James Place Capital plc of £218,000, covenants of £171,000 and fundraising of £106,000; investment income totalled only £2,000. The foundation made grants totalling £341,000, a 128% increase on 1998.

The annual report contained a detailed list of grants selected by the managing committee. These included: £10,000 to Cerebral Palsy Children's Charity to help equip a multi-sensory room; £9,500 to Lineham Farm Children's Centre to help improve existing facilities at the centre for children with disabilities and learning and behavioural problems; £7,600 to Ovingdean Hall School for children who are severely and profoundly deaf, towards IT equipment; £3,500 to MENCAP – Aldershot & District which provides a social and recreational facility for children aged between 5 and 10 with severe learning disabilities; £2,000 to Hartlepool Toy Library which encourages the learning development of children who are severly disabled; and £1,100 to Royal School for the Blind, Liverpool for a special chair for use with physiotherapists.

In order to promote more local interest in the foundation throughout the country, the regional offices of J. Rothschild Assurance plc made an additional 54 smaller grants, ranging between £100 and £1,000. Organisations to benefit include Joseph Holt's Christies Appeal and Acorn's Children's Hospice Trust (£1,000 each), Guide Dogs for the Blind, English Heritage and St Mungo's (£500 each), Rocking Horse Appeal (£250), MENCAP and Hope House Hospice (£200 each) and The Herschel House Trusts and Yateley Fire Station Alarm Initiative (£100 each).

Exclusions The foundation will not consider applications in relation to respite care or holidays.

The trust does not provide support for

- political, sectarian, religious and cultural organisations
- research projects
- sponsorship or advertising.

Applications All applications must be submitted on a fully completed application form and be accompanied by the latest audited report and accounts, together with any supporting explanatory documents as appropriate. The trustees meet quarterly.

St James' Trust Settlement

General

£186,000 (1998/99)

Beneficial area Worldwide

44a New Cavendish Street, London W1M 7LG

Tel. 020 7486 4663

Correspondent Richard Stone, Trustee

Trustees *Jane Wells; Richard Stone; Cathy Ingram.*

Information available Full accounts were on file at the Charity Commission.

General The trust's main aims are to make grants to charitable organisations that respond to areas of concern which the trustees are involved or interested in. In the UK, the main areas are social justice and in the USA, education, especially for the children of very disadvantaged families, and in community arts projects.

Grants are made by the trustees through their involvement with the project. Projects are also monitored and evaluated by the trustees.

In 1998/99 the trust had assets of £4.9 million. The income for the year was £121,000 and grants totalled £186,000. 11 grants were made in the UK totalling £141,000 and 12 in the USA totalling £45,000. Mostly new organisations were supported.

In the UK five organisations received £20,000 each: Charta Mede – towards racial equality; Dutch Pot Lunch Club – Afro-Caribbean Elderly Club; Ebony Steel Band Trust – working with people who are disabled; Reform Foundation – promotion of progressive Judaism; and World ORT Union for Ethiopian immigrant education. Other recipients included One World Action – third world projects (£10,000), Law Centres Education Trust for new computers (£4,000) and Mangrove Trust for community development with Afro-Caribbean groups (£2,000).

In the USA the grants included those to Theatre for a New Audience (£18,000), Fairhaven School – building funds (£4,600), Rachel Cooper Foundation – heart surgery for children (£4,400), Little Sisters of the Assumption – Young East Harlem (£1,900) and Mother's and Other's Environment Action (£600).

Applications 'The trust does not seek unsolicited applications to grants, the trustees do not feel justified in allocating administrative costs to responding to applications. If you do send an application you must send a stamped addressed envelope.'

Saint Sarkis Charity Trust

Armenian churches and welfare, disability, general

£204,000 (1999/2000)

Beneficial area UK and overseas

c/o Economic & General Secretariat Ltd, 98 Portland Place, London W1N 4ET

Tel. 020 7636 5313

Correspondent P A Lovatt, Secretary

Trustees *Mikhael Essayan; Boghos Parsegh Gulbenkian; Paul Curno.*

Information available Information provided by the trust.

General 'The principal objectives of the trust are the support of the Armenian Church of St. Sarkis in London and Gulbenkian Library at the Armenian Patriarchate in Jerusalem. In addition, the trustees support other charities concerned with the Armenian Community in the UK and abroad, and to the extent that funds are available, grants are also made to small registered charities concerned with social welfare and disability.'

The total income in 1999/2000 was £323,000 gained from assets of £7.4 million. Grants were made totalling £204,000.

Major grants were given to Armenian Church of Sarkis (£89,000) and The Armenian Patriarchate, Jerusalem (£70,000). Other grants included those to Centre for Armenian Information and Advice (£6,100), Prisoners Fellowship E & W (£5,400), London Armenian Poor Relief (£5,000), Trauma After Care Trust (£2,000) and grants of £1,000 or less totalling £26,000.

The trust has made a commitment to make a grant of around £111,000 towards the cost of tomography equipment at Sutp Pirgic Hospital in Turkey. It is anticipated that further substantial funds will be required for the repair and maintenance of the Armenian Church of Saint Sarkis.

Applications In writing to the correspondent. Trustees meet monthly.

The Saintbury Trust

General

£88,000 (1998)

Beneficial area Gloucestershire, West Midlands and Worcestershire; UK in exceptional circumstances

Hawnby House, Hawnby, Nr Helmsley, North Yorkshire YO62 5QS

Correspondent Mrs V K Houghton, Trustee

Trustees *Victoria K Houghton; Anne R Thomas; Jane P Lewis; Amanda E Atkinson-Willes; Harry O Forrester.*

Information available Information was provided by the trust.

General The trust gives grants for general charitable purposes, although the trust deed states that no grants can be given to animal charities. Grants are made to organisations in Gloucester, West Midlands and Worcestershire. Grants are only made in other parts of the UK in exceptional circumstances.

In 1998 the trust had assets of £2.9 million and an income of £78,000. Grants totalled £88,000.

The largest grant was £25,000 paid in two grants to National Institute of Conductive Education. Beneficiaries of other larger grants of between £5,000 and £15,000 included Emmanus Cambridge, RAPt, St Basil - Birmingham and Symphony Hall Birmingham. Smaller grants of between £200 and £500 included those to Birmingham Boys' and Girls' Clubs, City Hospital Breast Cancer Appeal, Homestart and Marriage Care – Gloucester.

Exclusions No grants to individuals or to animal charities. The trust stated that they do not respond to 'cold-calling' from organisations outside its main beneficial area, and groups from other parts of the UK are only considered if personally known to one of the trustees.

Applications In writing to the correspondent. Applications are considered in April and November and should be received one month earlier.

The Saints & Sinners Trust

Welfare, medical

£80,000 (1997/98)

Beneficial area UK

Lewis Golden & Co., 40 Queen Anne Street, London W1G 9EL

Tel. 020 7580 7313 **Fax** 020 7580 2179

Correspondent N W Benson, Trustee

Trustees *N W Benson; Sir Donald Gosling; P Moloney; N C Royds; I A N Irvine.*

Information available Full accounts were on file at the Charity Commission.

General Unfortunately we have been unable to update the following information since the last edition of this guide.

The Saints & Sinners Club has 100 members, who raise funds by holding golf tournaments and other events. Members nominate causes/organisations to support and grants generally range from £1,000 to £5,000.

In 1997/98 assets totalled £126,000 and the income only £12,000, although a balance of £67,000 had been carried forward from the previous year. Grants totalled £80,000. In 1996/97 the income was larger when the trust received £61,000 from a golf tournament.

Larger grants were £6,000 each to South Buckinghamshire Riding for the Disabled and The White Ensign Association and £5,000 to The Wooden Spoon Society. Other grants ranged from £1,000 to £3,000, with the exception of £500 to St John Ambulance. Beneficiaries included AJET, Diving Diseases Research Trust, Help the Aged – Berkshire, Marine Conservation Society, Reform Foundation Trust and The Actors' Charitable Trust.

Applications Applications are not considered unless nominated by members of the club.

The Salamander Charitable Trust

Christian, general

£75,000 (1999/2000)

Beneficial area Worldwide

Threave, 2 Brudenell Avenue, Canford Cliffs, Poole, Dorset BH13 7NW

Correspondent John R T Douglas, Trustee

Trustees *John R T Douglas; Mrs Sheila M Douglas.*

Information available Full accounts were on file at the Charity Commission.

General Founded in 1977, the principal objects of the trust are the:

* relief and assistance of poor and needy persons of all classes, irrespective of colour, race or creed

* advancement of education and religion

* relief of sickness and other exclusively charitable purposes beneficial to the community.

In 1999/2000 the trust's assets were valued at £1.8 million, which generated an income of just over £77,000. It gave £75,000 in the year, mainly in a large number of small grants. The accounts listed the top 14 grants made over £1,000 (no amounts were provided). Recipients included Birmingham Bible Institute, Christian Aid, FEBA Radio, London Bible College, Middle East Media, St James's PCC Poole, SAMS, SIM and Trinity College. Smaller grants were made to 239 institutions totalling £61,000, which is an average of £255 each.

Exclusions No grants to individuals. Only registered charities are supported.

Applications The trust's income is fully allocated each year, mainly to regular beneficiaries. The trustees will not respond to any further new requests.

Salters' Charities

General

£141,000 (1997/98)

Beneficial area Greater London or UK

The Salters' Company, Salters' Hall, 4 Fore Street, London EC2Y 5DE

Tel. 020 7588 5216

Correspondent The Charities Administrator

Trustees *The Salters' Company: Master, Upper Warden and Clerk.*

Information available Full accounts were filed at the Charity Commission up to 1999/2000, but up-to-date information was not yet available in the public files.

General Unfortunately we have been unable to update the information on this trust since the last edition of this guide.

The Salters' Company makes donations within the following criteria:

* 'as far as possible the charities selected should be nationwide in their application except for those connected with the City of London'

* 'smaller contributions to major charities will be discontinued and larger sums donated to a smaller number of charities within as wide a field as possible'

* the company should support those charities where Salters are involved.

Liverymen are encouraged to make personal enquiries regarding charities which they had initially nominated prior to a subsequent donation being considered. Visits should also be made to supported charities by liverymen and members of staff. Information from the Charity Commission database showed that in 1999/2000 the trust had an income of £150,000 and an expenditure of £154,000.

In 1997/98 the charities had an income of £151,000, of which £136,000 was a Gift Aid payment from the Salters' Company and £14,000 was a combination of a donation from another trust and the Corporate Fund of the company. Grants totalled £141,000, and were mostly for £1,000 to £2,000, though three were for considerably more and some for less. The trust broke down its giving as follows.

Children and youth
A total of £30,000, including one of two exceptionally large grants, £18,000 to Christ's Hospital. Other beneficiaries included Home-Start UK, Kidscape and Foundation for the Study of Infant Deaths. All the organisations in this category received grants the previous year.

Medical
A total of £37,000 in 26 donations, only three of which were to charities not supported the previous year. Recipients included Action on Addiction/Business Against Drugs, British Digestive Foundation, Fight for Sight, Home Farm

Trust and Westminster Pastoral Foundation.

Christian aid
£9,700 in seven donations, to charities such as: CARE, Church Urban Fund, Prison Fellowship and Stepping Stones Trust.

Environment/third world
£9,500 in three donations to World Conservation Monitoring Centre (£6,000), Tearfund (£2,500) and Marine Conservation Society (£1,000).

City
£31,000 including an exceptional £25,000 to the Lord Mayor's Appeal. The three other grants were to Lord Mayor Treloar Trust, St John Ambulance – City branch and Guildhall School of Music & Drama.

Armed forces
£6,000 in five donations (four recurrent) with recipients including District 5 Central London Sea Cadet Corps, Royal Star & Garter Home and SW London Army Cadet Force.

Other donations
£13,000 in 14 grants, over half of which were for under £1,000. These included Bryson House, Family Welfare Association, Oxfordshire Community Foundation and Police Convalescence and Rehabilitation Trust.

Many beneficiaries receive grants over a number of years.

Exclusions Grants are not normally made to charities working with people who are homeless unless there is some connection with a liveryman of the company.

Applications In writing to the correspondent.

The Sammermar Trust (formerly Adrian Swire Charitable Trust)

General

£55,000 (1998)

Beneficial area UK

Swire House, 59 Buckingham Gate, London SW1E 6AJ

Tel. 020 7834 7717

Correspondent Mrs D Omar

237

Trustees *Lady Judith; M Dunne; B N Swire; Sir Kerry St Johnson.*

Information available Accounts were on file at the Charity Commission, but without a list of grants.

General The trust, formerly known as Adrian Swire Charitable Trust, was established in 1988 with general charitable purposes. In 1999 the trust had an income of £274,000 and an expenditure of £234,000. Further information was not available for this year. In 1998 the trust had an income of £65,000 and grants totalled £55,000, but no grants list was available.

Applications In writing to the correspondent.

Coral Samuel Charitable Trust

General, health, the arts

£198,000 (1999/2000)

Beneficial area UK

Knighton House, 56 Mortimer Street, London W1N 8BD

Correspondent Mrs Coral Samuel, Trustee

Trustees *Mrs Coral Samuel; P Fineman.*

Information available Full accounts were provided by the trust.

General This trust was established in 1962 by Coral Samuel, wife of Basil Samuel. (There is an entry for the Basil Samuel Charitable Trust in *A Guide to the Major Trusts Volume 1.*) The trust makes grants of £10,000 or more to educational, cultural and social welfare charities plus a number of smaller donations to other charities.

In 1999/2000 the trust's assets totalled £3.2 million. The income of the trust was £203,000 and grants to charities totalled £198,000.

In total the trust made grants to 28 organisations, 12 of which were supported in the previous year. The four largest grants of £25,000 each went to British Museum Development Trust, Dulwich Picture Gallery, English National Opera and Sir John Soane's Museum Society. Grants of £10,000 or more included: Royal Opera House Trust (£20,000); National Maritime Museum (£15,000); and Royal National Institute

for the Blind and Natural History Museum (£10,000 each).

The remaining, smaller grants ranged from £500 to £5,000. A wide variety of organisations were supported including £5,000 each to Aylesbury Music Centre, Edinburgh & East of Scotland Deaf Society and Sail Training Association; Dauntsey's School (£3,600); Chicken Shed Theatre Company (£2,000); and British Wizo (£1,500).

Grants of £1,000 or under included £1,000 each to Ashmolean Museum, Ben Gurion University Foundation, National Autistic Society and Royal Free Hospital Breast Cancer Trust and £500 each went to Friends of MDA in Great Britain, Norwood Ravenswood and The Solti Foundation.

Exclusions Grants are only made to registered charities.

Applications In writing to the correspondent.

The Peter Samuel Charitable Trust

Health, welfare, conservation, Jewish care

£151,000 (1998/99)

Beneficial area UK, with a preference for local organisations in Berkshire

Farley Farms, Bridge Farm, Reading Road, Arborfield, Berkshire RG2 9HT

Tel. 0118 976 0412 **Fax** 0118 976 0147

Correspondent Miss Rachel Stafford, Secretary

Trustees *Rt Hon. Viscount Bearsted; Hon. Michael Samuel.*

Information available Accounts were on file at the Charity Commission.

General The trustees' report states: 'The trust seeks to perpetuate the family's interest in the medical sciences, the quality of life in the local areas, heritage and land/forestry restoration'. In 1998/99 the trust had assets of £3.8 million and an income of £93,000. A total of £151,000 was given in 60 grants ranging from £100 to £30,000.

The largest grants went to Pippin (£30,000), Pippin South West Development Project (£25,000) and Liberal Jewish Centre (£20,000). Other

grants ranged from £250 to £5,000 and beneficiaries included World Jewish Relief (£5,000), Jewish Memorial Council (£4,000), Cancer Research and Norwood Ravenwood (£3,000 each), Save the Children Fund (£2,000) and Royal National Institute for the Deaf (£1,000). Smaller grants included £500 each to Thames Valley Crimestoppers, Thames Valley Partnership and Winged Fellowship Trust and £250 each to Centre for Bilingual Educational in Israel and Cintra Playgroup. Woodland Trust received two grants totalling £600 and Ajex and Ajex Housing received £500 each.

Exclusions No grants to local charities outside Berkshire or to individuals.

Applications In writing to the correspondent. Trustees meet twice yearly.

The Sandra Charitable Trust

Health, social welfare, animal welfare

£301,000 to organisations (1998/99)

Beneficial area UK, with a preference for the South East

St Paul's House, Warwick Lane, London EC4P 4BN

Correspondent K Lawrence

Trustees *R Moore; M Macfayden.*

Information available Full accounts were provided by the trust.

General In 1998/99, the trust had assets of £12 million and an income of £362,000. Administration costs totalled £41,000. Grants for the year totalled £325,000 including £25,000 given in 63 grants to individuals. There were 50 grants to organisations listed in the accounts, totalling £253,000, with £47,000 given in smaller grants.

The trust's review of activities states that 'beneficiaries included nurses, charities involved in animal welfare and research, environmental protection and childcare.'

The largest grants went to SPARKS (£49,000), Barnardos (£25,000), Earls Court Homeless Families Project (£15,000), Florence Nightingale Foundation (£13,000) and NCH Action for Children (£11,000). Two organisations received £8,000 each, they were British Laser Appeal for Surgical Equipment & Research and Cancer Research Campaign.

The remainder of listed grants were mainly in the range of £2,000 and £3,000 but were for as much as £5,000. Recipients included The Civic Trust, Crisis at Christmas, Farming and Wildlife Advisory Group, Invalids at Home, Lloyds Officer Cadet Scholarship, Royal British Legion, Save the Children Fund and Wiseman Trust. Of the grants listed, 13 were recurrent from the previous year.

Applications In writing to the correspondent, although the trust's funds are largely committed. The trustees meet on a frequent basis to consider applications.

The Schapira Charitable Trust

Jewish

£121,000 (1999)

Beneficial area UK

c/o BDO Stoy Hayward, 85 Great North Road, Hatfield, Hertfordshire AL9 5BS

Tel. 01707 255888

Correspondent The Trustees

Trustees *Issac Y Schapira; Michael Neuberger; Suzanne L Schapira.*

Information available Accounts were on file at the Charity Commission, but without a narrative report.

General This trust appears to make grants exclusively to Jewish charities. In 1999 it received an income of £125,000 from Gift Aid donations. Grants totalled £121,000.

A total of 108 grants were made, although several organisations received more than one grant. The Society of Friends of the Torah, for example, received 13 grants amounting to £27,000. Other beneficiaries included Keren Association which received £9,000 in three grants and Gur Trust which received £6,000 in four grants. Smaller grants included those to New Rachmistrvke Synagogue (£3,800), Toldos Aharon (£2,000) and Gateshead Talmudical College (£1,000).

Applications In writing to the correspondent.

The Annie Schiff Charitable Trust

Orthodox Jewish education

£119,000 (1999/2000)

Beneficial area UK, overseas

8 Highfield Gardens, London NW11 9HB

Tel. 020 8458 9266

Correspondent J Pearlman, Trustee

Trustees *J Pearlman; Mrs R Pearlman.*

Information available Full accounts were on file at the Charity Commission.

General Grants are given exclusively to orthodox Jewish religious and educational institutions. In 1999/2000 the trust had assets of £260,000 and an income of £99,000. Grants ranging from £50 to £20,000 totalled £119,000.

The largest grants were £20,000 to Menorah Grammar School for running costs, £15,000 to Yerodei Torah School for running costs and £10,000 to Ben Zion Rakow Memorial Fund to perpetuate charitable work in memory of Rabbi Rakow.

In the previous year, smaller grants included London Jewish Girls High School (£5,000), Friends of Nachulat Osher Charitable Trust (£3,000), Hamayon (£2,000), Gateshead Talmudical College (£1,000) and Keren Hayesomin (£100).

Exclusions No support for individuals and non-recognised institutions.

Applications In writing to the correspondent, but grants are generally made only to registered charities. The trust states that presently all funds are committed.

The Schmidt-Bodner Charitable Trust

Jewish, general

£95,000 (1996/97)

Beneficial area Worldwide

36 St James's Close, Prince Albert Road, London NW8 7LQ

Correspondent Mr & Mrs B Schmidt-Bodner, Trustees

Trustees *B Schmidt-Bodner; Mrs E Schmidt-Bodner; M Diner; L Rosenblatt.*

Information available Full accounts were on file at the Charity Commission.

General In 1997/98 the trust had an income of £54,000 and an expenditure of £64,000. Unfortunately further information for this year was not available and the following information is repeated from the last edition of this guide.

This trust mainly supports Jewish organisations though it has also given a few small grants to medical and welfare charities. In 1996/97 it had assets of £917,000, an income of £53,000 and gave grants totalling £95,000. The largest were £21,000 to Jewish Care, £11,000 to Lubatvitch Foundation and £13,000 to St John's Wood Synagogue.

There were 14 other grants of £1,000 or more all to Jewish organisations. About 100 smaller grants were made, with a handful to well-known medical charities.

Applications In writing to the correspondent.

The Schreib Trust

Jewish, general

£302,000 (1996/97)

Beneficial area UK

147 Stamford Haill, London N16 5LG

Correspondent David Schreiber, Trustee

Trustees *Irene Schreiber; David Schreiber.*

Information available Accounts were on file at the Charity Commission, but without a list of grants or a full narrative report.

General Unfortunately we have been unable to update the following information since the last edition of this guide.

It is impossible to glean an enormous amount of information about this trust's grant-giving policies as only brief accounts were on file at the Charity Commission. Although the trust's objects are general, it lists its particular priorities as relief of poverty and advancement of religious education. In practice, the trust may only support Jewish organisations.

The trust's assets totalled £178,000 in 1996/97 and income for the year was £371,000 from donations, plus further income from rents. The trust made grants totalling £302,000, although it is not known who received the money or what size the grants were. There was a surplus of income over expenditure of £72,000.

Applications In writing to the correspondent.

The Schreiber Charitable Trust

Jewish

£174,000 (1998/99)

Beneficial area UK

9 West Heath Road, London NW3 7UX

Tel. 020 7433 3434

Correspondent G S Morris, Trustee

Trustees *Graham S Morris; David A Schreiber; Mrs Sara Schreiber.*

Information available Full accounts were on file at the Charity Commission.

General In 1974 the Schreiber family set up the trust with 20,000 £1 shares in Schreiber Securities Ltd. By 1990 a further 350,000 £1 shares were given to the trust along with £24,000. In 1997, the company (now called Sovent Limited) was placed into members' voluntary liquidation. The trust then received £850,000 and the annual report for 1997/98 stated that it was likely to receive more in following years.

In 1998/99 the trust's assets totalled £2 million and its income was £124,000 from investments and rents. The trust gave grants totalling £174,000. Larger grants were listed in the annual report and were made to 16 organisations, 6 of which had been supported in the previous year. Grants listed totalled £150,000 and ranged from £1,000 to £50,000.

By far the largest grant was £50,000 to British Friends of Yeshival Har Etzyon. Other recipients of larger donations were Yeshivas Shaare Torah (£25,000) and Friends of Rabbinical College Kol Torah (£16,000) with Aish Hatorah UK and British Friends of Har Etzyon receiving £12,000 each.

Other grants included those to Gateshead Talmudical College (£9,500), Finchley Road Synagogue (£6,600), Craven Walk

Charitable Trust (£3,700), Menorah Primary School (£1,500) and Yeshiva Horomo (£1,000).

Applications In writing to the correspondent. The trust states that all funds are currently committed.

The Scouloudi Foundation

Medicine and health, humanities, disabilities

£161,000 (1999/2000)

Beneficial area UK charities working domestically or abroad

c/o Hays Allan, Southampton House, 317 High Holborn, London WC1V 7NL

Tel. 020 7969 5500

Correspondent The Administrators

Trustees *Miss S E Stowell; M E Demetriadi; J D Marnham; J R Sewell.*

Information available Full accounts and a guide to its origins and procedures were provided by the trust.

General The foundation was established in 1962 by Irene Scouloudi, a historian and philanthropist, and to date has given £2.7 million in grants. In 1999/2000 the trust had an income of £250,000, assets of £5.6 million and made grants totalling £161,000 (£211,000 in 1998/99). The current policy of the trustees reflect the interests and intentions of the founder. The annual income is divided between three categories of grants (amount given in grants is shown in brackets):

Historical awards
An annual award is made to Institute of Historical Research at University of London to allow it to support research and publications in the field (£62,000).

Regular donations
These are made up of annual donations to a specified list of UK charities. It is the policy of the trustees to review the donees on a five-yearly cycle (£82,000). A total of 90 grants were awarded in this category, the highest of £5,000 went to Institute of Historical Research, University of London. Grants of around £1,000 each included those to Barnardos, Multiple Sclerosis Society, National Trust, Royal Commonwealth Society for the Blind and Save the Children Fund. The remaining grants were all for £850, most went to well-known UK organisations such as Age Concern England, Help the Hospices, National Trust, Raleigh International Trust, Salvation Army and Youth Clubs UK.

Special donations
These are made once a year in response to specific applications to fund capital projects and other extraordinary needs such as natural disasters (£17,000).

Five grants were awarded in this category, three of which went to British Red Cross projects in India (£3,000), Turkey (£2,000) and Venezuela (£3,000). Disasters Emergency Committee – Kosovo also received £4,000. Tate Gallery received a grant of £5,000. In previous years special donations have taken the form of smaller grants benefiting a wider range of organisations including more in the UK.

Distribution during the year can be broken down as shown in the table.

Exclusions Donations are not made to individuals, and are not normally made for welfare activities of a purely local

THE SCOULOUDI FOUNDATION – GRANT DISTRIBUTION 1999/2000

Category	Historical	Regular	Special	Total	%
Aged	–	£6,000	–	£6,000	4
Children & youth	–	£7,900	–	£7,900	5
Environment	–	£9,500	–	£9,500	6
Famine relief & overseas aid	–	£3,600	–	£3,600	2
Disability	–	£13,000	–	£13,000	8
Humanities	£62,000	£13,000	£5,000	£80,000	50
Medicine & health	–	£16,000	–	£16,000	10
Social welfare	–	£9,400	–	£9,400	6
Welfare of armed forces & sailors	–	£3,400	–	£3,400	2
Natural disasters	–	–	£12,000	£12,000	7
Total	£62,000	£82,000	£17,000	£161,000	100

nature. The trustees do not make loans or enter into deeds of covenant.

Applications Applications for special donations, giving full but concise details, should be sent to the administrators at the above address by 1 March for consideration in April.

Copies of the regulations and application forms for historical awards can be obtained from: The Secretary, The Scouloudi Foundation Historical Awards Committee, c/o Institute of Historical Research, University of London, Senate House, London WC1E 7HU.

The Searchlight Electric Charitable Trust

General
£70,000 (1998/99)
Beneficial area UK

Searchlight Electric Ltd, Water Street, Manchester M3 4JU
Tel. 0161 834 5452
Correspondent H E Hamburger, Trustee
Trustees *H E Hamburger; D M Hamburger; M E Hamburger; J S Fidler.*
Information available Full accounts were on file at the Charity Commission.

General The trust received a loan from Searchlight Electric Ltd to help set up the trust, this appears to have been mostly repaid.

In 1998/99 the trust had assets of £738,000 and an income of £100,000. Administration costs were low at just over £100 for the year and grants totalled £70,000. In total 25 organisations were supported with grants of over £250, half of which had received grants in the previous year. Grants under £250 totalled £6,300.

The largest grant was £38,000 to JJCT, also the major recipient in the previous year. Other larger grants were £5,000 to Heathlands Home for the Aged, £2,500 to Shaare Torah Yeshiva, £2,000 to Help for the Needy and £1,000 each to Young Israel Synagogue and Manchester Jewish Federation.

Other recipients included Community Care, Holy Law Synagogue, JNF, Manchester Grammar School and Yeshiva Etz Chaim.

In the past the trustees have stated that it is their policy to only support charities already on their existing list of beneficiaries or those already known to them.

Exclusions No grants for individuals.

Applications In writing to the correspondent, but note the above.

The Searle Charitable Trust

Sailing
About £60,000 but see below (1998/99)
Beneficial area UK

20 Kensington Church Street, London W8 4EP
Tel. 020 7761 7200
Correspondent Andrew D Searle, Trustee
Trustees *Andrew D Searle; Victoria C Searle.*
Information available Full accounts were on file at the Charity Commission.

General This trust was established in 1982 by Joan Wynne Searle. Following the death of the settlor in 1995 the trust was split into two. One half is administered by the son of the settlor (Searle Charitable Trust) and the other half by her daughter (Searle Memorial Trust).

The Searle Charitable Trust only supports projects/organisations for youth development within a nautical framework.

This trust's assets were valued at £2.9 million in 1998/99, and the income totalled £88,000. Grants included £51,000 to RONA Trust, also a major beneficiary in previous years. Unfortunately no further information on grants was available for this year. In the past grants have gone to organisations including Christopher James Memorial Trust, Joy to the World, Leg Up in Life Trust, Mark Pepy's Research Trust, NSPCC and Wooden Spoon Society.

Exclusions No grants for individuals or for appeals not related to sailing.

Applications In writing to the correspondent.

The Seedfield Trust

Christian, relief of poverty
£102,000 (1999)
Beneficial area Worldwide

Regent House, Heaton Lane, Stockport, Cheshire SK4 1BS
Correspondent David Ryan, Trustee
Trustees *J Atkins; K G Buckler; D Heap; D E Ryan; Mrs J Buckler; Revd L E Osborn.*
Information available Full accounts were provided by the trust.

General The trust's main objects are the furthering of Christian work and the relief of poverty.

In 1999 the trust had assets of £2.5 million and an income of £142,000, £23,000 of which came from donations. Grants totalling £102,000 were made in the year and administration costs of over £20,000 were recorded.

In 1999 the trust made 38 grants, 22 of the beneficiaries had been supported at the same or similar levels in the previous year. These included the three largest beneficiaries: European Christian Mission (£18,000); and Overseas Missionary Fellowship and Dorothea Trust (£10,000 each). Others which received ongoing support included Mission Aviation Fellowship (£7,500), Pentecostal Child Care Association (£3,000), Cosmo Club (£2,500) and Christian Action Research and Education and Wycliffe Bible Translators (£1,000 each).

There were 16 new organisations supported including Thana Trust (£5,000), SCORE (£1,300), Tearfund (£1,000), Prison Fellowship and Nandejara Children's Home – Paraguay (£500 each) and Bootle Evangelical Church (£250).

Applications In writing to the correspondent.

Leslie Sell Charitable Trust

Scout and guide groups

£110,000 (1999/2000)

Beneficial area UK

Ground Floor Offices, 52–56 London Road, St Albans, Hertfordshire AL1 1NG

Tel. 01727 843603   **Fax** 01727 843663

Correspondent J Byrnes

Trustees *Mrs M R Wiltshire; P S Sell; A H Sell.*

Information available Full accounts were on file at the Charity Commission.

General In 1999/2000 the trust had net assets of £1.9 million and an income of £168,000. Direct charitable expenditure totalled £110,000, leaving a surplus of £56,000.

Three grants were listed separately in the accounts, these were £7,000 to Cottlesloe School, £1,700 to Charlton Barn – a village hall and £700 to Ivinghoe Aston Village Hall, all of these were recurrent from the previous year. The other 161 grants totalling £96,000 went to scout and guide groups (including Rangers, brownies and sea scouts groups) throughout the UK from the Orkney Islands to Falmouth. Grants were mostly for £1,000 or less, however, a few larger grants were given to district or county scout/guide councils/associations.

Applications In writing to the correspondent.

Servite Sisters' Charitable Trust Fund

See below

£169,000 (1999)

Beneficial area UK and worldwide

Parkside, Coldharbour Lane, Dorking, Surrey RH4 3BN

Tel. 01306 875756   **Fax** 01306 889339
e-mail m@servite.demon.co.uk

Correspondent Michael J W Ward, Secretary

Trustees *Sister Joyce Mary Fryer OSM; Sister Ruth Campbell OSM;*

Sister Eugenia Geraghty OSM; Sister Catherine Ryan OSM.

Information available A grants list and information for applicants was provided by the trust but without up-to-date accounts.

General This trust is run by the English province of the international religious order of The Servants of Mary (known as Servites). The Province has 78 members, most of whom have given their working lives to the charitable activities of the order. When any of the members carry out any work independently of the charity, any earnings are covenanted to the charity.

The trust was set up in 1993 and makes grants principally to support:

- activities intended primarily to help women who are marginalised physically, spiritually or morally

- activities intended to alleviate the distress of refugees and other disadvantaged migrants.

The funds may also be used to help:

- the Servite family in the third world/ Eastern Europe

- students and youth groups the Servites are associated with.

Grants are one-off and average £2,500. In 1999 grants to 62 organisations totalled £169,000. UK grants included £7,200 to help an office in their work arranging bail for asylum seekers, £5,000 towards a coordinator's salary following an increased workload, £3,100 to renovate classrooms and install desks and equipment required to help educate women from deprived areas, £2,500 each towards the cost of a young mothers' support project and towards the salary of a project worker supporting prostitutes and £1,000 to help a women's development group with their revenue shortfall.

Overseas grants included £3,000 towards the cost of drug and outreach work with women with HIV/Aids in Cameroon, £2,700 towards equipment and furniture for a sewing group in India, £2,000 to pay a year's salary for teachers in Zambia and £850 to buy medical equipment to treat women and children in Nigeria.

Exclusions No grants towards building projects and no educational grants. No recurrent grants.

Applications In writing to the correspondent with brief details of your organisation, project and needs.

The Linley Shaw Foundation

Conservation

£60,000 (2000)

Beneficial area UK

National Westminster Bank plc, NatWest Private Banking, Kingston, 67 Maple Road, Surbiton, London KT6 4QT

Correspondent The Manager – Charities

Trustees *National Westminster Bank plc.*

Information available Non-financial information was provided by the trust.

General The trust supports charities working to conserve, preserve and restore the natural beauty of the UK countryside for the public benefit. The trust donated approximately £60,000 in 2000.

Generally the trust prefers to support a specific project, rather than give money for general use. In his will, Linley Shaw placed particular emphasis on those charities which organise voluntary workers to achieve the objects of the trust. This may be taken into account when considering applications. Grants can be given towards any aspect of a project. Previous examples include the cost of tools, management surveys and assistance with the cost of land purchase.

In 2000 grants totalled £60,000. The largest grants were to British Trust for Conservation Volunteers (£6,600) and £5,000 each to Carfare Winnowed, Trees for Life, Wildfowl and Wetlands Trust, West Country Rivers and Worcestershire Wildlife Trust.

Exclusions No grants to non-charitable organisations, or to organisations whose aims or objects do not include conservation, preservation or restoration of the natural beauty of the UK countryside, even if the purpose of the grant would be eligible.

Applications In writing to the correspondent. All material will be photocopied by the trust so please avoid sending 'bound' copies of reports etc. Evidence of aims and objectives are needed, usually in the form of accounts, annual reports or leaflets, which cannot be returned. Applications are considered in February/early March and should be received by December/early January.

The Sheepdrove Trust

Environment, educational

£426,000 approved to organisations and individuals (1999)

Beneficial area UK, but especially North Lambeth, London

2 Methley Street, London SE11 4AJ

Correspondent Mrs J E Kindersley, Trustee

Trustees *Mrs J E Kindersley; P D Kindersley; B G Kindersley; Mrs H R Treuillé.*

Information available Information was provided by the trust.

General The trust stated that it initiates its own projects. It also seeks to support projects in North Lambeth where appropriate. It also supports initiatives which increase sustainability, biodiversity and organic farming, such as research into organic seed production and nutrition. It funds work in educational research and spiritual care for the living and dying.

In 1999 the trust had assets of £20 million, an £8 million rise on the previous year due to a revaluation of investments. These assets generated an income of £620,000. After spending £53,000 on administration, the trust approved 37 grants totalling £426,000 to both organisations and individuals, 14 of these were recurrent.

The largest grants to organisations were £45,000 in total each to Elm Farm Research Centre and Forum for the Future, given in recurrent grants over three and four years respectively. Other recurrent grants included those to RIGPA International (£30,000), Institute for Education (£25,000), Mobile Creches (£20,000), Newbury Music Festival (£15,000), British Red Cross (£10,000), Invalids at Home (£6,000), Kennington Summer Projects (£3,000), Age Concern and Find Your Feet (£2,000 each) and Sustrans Route for People (£170).

One-off grants included those to Save Our World (£7,500) and Castle School (£280). Also a grant is paid each year to a specific concert at the Newbury Spring Festival, this year it was £20,000 to Zenith Ensemble.

The accounts included a donation of £31,000 to one individual, who is also living in accommodation owned by the trust.

Exclusions The trust stated: 'No grants to students or other individuals.'

Applications To the correspondent.

The Sheldon Trust

General

£208,000 (1999/2000)

Beneficial area UK, with priority to Warwickshire and Midlands

Box S, White Horse Court, 25c North Street, Bishop's Stortford, Hertfordshire CM23 2LD

Fax 01279 657626

e-mail charities@pothocary.co.uk

Correspondent The Trust Administrator

Trustees *Revd R S Bidnell; J K R England; R V Wiglesworth; J C Barratt; R M Bagshaw.*

Information available Full accounts were on file at the Charity Commission, with a very informative trustees' report, much of which is summarised below.

General The trustees concentrate their support on the Midlands. The main aims continue to be relieving poverty and distress in society, concentrating grants on community projects as well as those directed to special needs groups, especially in deprived areas. The trustees review their policy and criteria regularly. 'Although they have a central policy, a certain flexibility is ensured in reacting to changes in the environment and the community alike.'

In 1999/2000 the trust had assets of £3.4 million and an income of £165,000. Grants totalled £208,000, with the largest going to St Basil's Family Mediation for £10,000, most grants were between £1,000 and £5,000. Grants are divided into categories described below:

Individuals
To regionalise their interest in the Midlands, the trustees have continued to make an annual grant of £11,000 (increasing to £13,000 in 2000/2001) to

Birmingham – Money Advice & Grants (Personal Services), which make many small grants to individuals for clothing, furniture and travel expenses for visiting the sick as well as providing a debt counselling service.

Holiday projects
These receive an annual sum of about £5,000. In 1999/2000 these included the 3H Fund, Bethany Christian Fellowship, British Red Cross (Northamptonshire), CARP, Merseyside Children's Holiday, Peak (National Asthma Joint Holidays) and Winged Fellowship.

Special needs
Grants have been made to groups for equipment and general expenses to Breakthrough (West Midlands Area), Children's Heart Foundation, John Grooms Association for Disabled People, Nottingham Regional Society for Autistic Children and Adults, Rathbone Community Industry and Shaw Trust.

Community projects
Among those supported were Birmingham Settlement, Citizen Advocacy Solihull, Hillfields Youth and Activity, Midland Arts Centre, Nuneaton Boys Club, Withington Methodist Church and Youthwise.

Continuing grants
The following organisations have received recurrent grants: Amelia Methodist Trust, Asthma Training, Cascade, National Schizophrenia Fellowship (Dudley) and Rydal Youth Centre (Liverpool).

Exclusions 'The trustees will not consider appeals in respect of the cost of buildings, but will consider appeals where buildings have to be brought up-to-date to meet health, safety and fire regulations.'

Applications On a form available from the correspondent. The trustees met four times in 1999/2000, in April, July, November and February. The trust's report stated that they will 'for the present be committing a good proportion of their income to continuing grants which means that they will have less income for other charitable purposes'.

The Bassil Shippam & Alsford Charitable Trust

Older people, health, education, Christian

£209,000 (1998/99)

Beneficial area UK with a preference for West Sussex; international

Messrs Thomas Eggar Church Adams, 5 East Pallant, Chichester, West Sussex PO19 1TS

Tel. 01243 786111

Correspondent C W Doman, Trustee Administrator

Trustees *J H S Shippam; C W Doman; D S Olby; S W Young; Mrs M Hanwell; R Tayler; Mrs S Trayler.*

Information available Full accounts were on file at the Charity Commission.

General This is basically a Christian trust and the trustees mainly support charities active in the fields of care for older people, health, education and religion. Many of the organisations supported are in West Sussex.

In 1998/99 the trust had assets of £4.2 million and received investment income of £179,000 and donations totalling £76,000 from the late Mrs D L Alsford (£2.6 million in 1997/98).

Grants totalled £209,000, of which £12,000 was paid to five regular beneficiaries which receive several payments over the year by standing order. These were Outset Youth Action South West Sussex (£5,000 in total), West Sussex County Council Voluntary Fund (£2,200), Chichester District Council for the Elderly (£1,800), Shippams Retirement Association (£1,200) and West Sussex Probation Service and Social Skills Fund (£1,500 each).

A further 175 grants were made with at least 20 going to individuals. Most of the grants ranged from £100 to £500. By far the largest grant was £50,000 to Lodge Hill Residential Care. Other larger grants included £15,000 each to Christian Youth Enterprises Sailing Centre Ltd and British Luffce Parents and Friends Association and £10,000 to St Anthony's School.

Other grants were in the range of £50 to £5,000. A wide variety of organisations were supported with recipients including St Wilfred's Hospice, Chichester Eventide Housing Association, West Sussex Association for the Blind, Distressed Gentlefolk's Association, Sussex Autistic Society, Church Pastoral Aid Society, Raleigh International and Streatham Youth Centre.

Applications In writing to the correspondent. Applications are considered in May and November.

The Shipwrights Charitable Fund
(*incorporating* The Sir John Fisher Fund)

Maritime or waterborne connected charities

£76,000 (1998/99)

Beneficial area UK, with a preference for the London area

Worshipful Company of Shipwrights, Ironmongers' Hall, Barbican, London EC2Y 8AA

Tel. 020 7606 2376 **Fax** 020 7600 3519

Correspondent Capt. R F Channon

Trustees *The Wardens of the Shipwrights' Company.*

Information available Information for this entry was provided by the trust.

General Following a policy review in 1997/98, the trust guidelines were reconfirmed. The trust therefore continues to direct its funds towards:

- liverymen or their dependants in distress

- maritime or waterborne projects or activities

- City of London

- church work

- educational work (with the emphasis on support for young people).

The trust gave grants totalling £76,000 in 1998/99 broken down as follows:

Annual donations	£21,000
General donations	£33,000
Bursaries and berths	£22,000

Annual donations
20 grants with the largest being £4,000 to Royal Merchant Navy School Foundation for maintenance/education of seafarers'
orphans and dependants. Grants ranged from £24 to £2,000. Other recipients included British & International Sailors Society, City of London Outward Bound Association, Missions to Seamen, Sea Cadet Association Central Fund and Shaftesbury Homes & Arethusa (shore base and sail training for young people).

General donations
Larger grants included those to Discovery Dockland Trust for maintenance equipment (£2,500) and City of London School for a boat (£1,800). Another school received a grant of £1,700 towards library books, CD-ROMs etc. Various sea cadets and sea scouts around the country received grants of around £500 each.

Bursaries and berths
58 bursaries (awarded only to those sponsored by liverymen in response to an annual invitation) totalled £22,000 and were awarded for: voyages with Ocean Youth Club, Sail Training Association, Jubilee Sailing Trust and TS Royalist (Sea Cadet Corps); and for courses run by Outward Bound Trust.

Exclusions Any application without a clear maritime/water-borne connection. Outdoor activities bursaries are awarded only to young people sponsored by liverymen in response to an annual invitation. Marine biology activities are not supported.

Applications In writing to the correspondent. Applications are considered in February, June and November.

The Charles Shorto Charitable Trust

General

£118,000 (1998/99)

Beneficial area UK

Blackhams, King Edward House, 135a New Street, Birmingham B2 4NG

Tel. 0121 643 7070

Correspondent T J J Baxter

Trustees *Joseph A V Blackham; Brian M Dent.*

Information available Full accounts were on file at the Charity Commission.

General This trust was established under the will of Edward Herbert Charles

Shorto who died in 1997. Its 1998/99 annual report stated '… the trustees are not restricted as to the organisations to which they may contribute. As a result the trust has received a considerable number of applications for grants and donations from a wide range of charitable organisations'.

As well as supporting some of those organisations which applied, the trustees funded several major projects which they have investigated themselves:

- the installation of a new organ at Rugby School where Charles Shorto was a pupil
- works carried out in the church, hospital and medical centre in the community in which Charles Shorto lived.

In 1998/99 the trust approved further grants to the above two projects in excess of £430,000.

The trust anticipated that in 1999/2000 it would continue to develop and fund projects for the homeless and disadvantaged and consider joint venture projects providing these services, as well as making grants to other charities. In 1998/99 it had an assets of £4.9 million and an income of £180,000, 21 grants were made totalling £118,000. The largest donations were £13,000 to Cumnor PCC and £10,000 each to Age-2-Age, RNLI, St Loye's Foundation and Stephenson Locomotive Society.

Smaller grants were in the range of £1,000 to £7,700 and included £7,700 to East Budleigh PCC, £5,000 to Hearing Dogs, £2,000 to Crickhowell CRC and £1,000 to Morning Star Trust.

Applications In writing to the correspondent.

L H Silver Charitable Trust

Jewish, general

£98,000 (1997/98)

Wilson Braithwaite Scholey, 21–27 St Paul's Street, Leeds LS1 2ER

Tel. 0113 244 5451 Fax 0113 242 6308
e-mail mail@wilsonbraithwaite.com

Correspondent I J Fraser, Trustee

Trustees *Leslie H Silver; Mark S Silver; Ian J Fraser.*

Information available Full accounts were provided by the trust.

General This trust principally supports Jewish-based charities and appeal funds launched in the West Yorkshire area.

The trustees' report for 1998/99 stated that major donations have been made to educational institutions and Jewish charities. Most of the smaller donations were made to charities and appeal funds operating in the Leeds area. The income for the year was £52,000, it had assets of over £1 million. Grants totalled £98,000 (£210,000 1997/98). The trust is continuing to use assets to fund grants above their income, ending the year with a deficit of £47,000.

Altogether 22 grants were awarded. The three largest went to Joint Jewish Charitable Trust (£55,000) and JNF Charitable Trust and Variety Club of Great Britain (£10,000 each). One grant of £5,000, one of £2,500, two of £2,000, seven of £1,000, one of £600 and seven of £500 were also given.

Organisations to benefit included Leeds Girls High School – bursary appeal (£5,000), Community Security Trust (£2,500), Holocaust Educational Trust, National Heart Research and Wheatfields Hospice (£1,000 each), Leeds Jewish Welfare (£600), 'More than a Roof' and The Salvation Army (£500 each).

Applications The trustees state that 'the recipients of donations are restricted almost exclusively to the concerns in which the trustees take a personal interest and that unsolicited requests from other sources, although considered by the trustees, are rejected almost invariably'.

The Simpson Education and Conservation Trust

Environmental conservation, with a preference for the neotropics

£96,000 (1999/2000)

Beneficial area UK and overseas, with a preference for the neotropics (South America)

Honeysuckle Cottage, Tidenham Chase, Chepstow, Gwent NP16 7JW

Tel. 01291 689423 Fax 01291 689803
Correspondent N Simpson, Acting Chair

Trustees *Dr R N F Simpson, Chair; Prof. D M Broom; Dr J M Lock; Prof. S Chang; Dr K A Simpson.*

Information available Full and detailed accounts were on file at the Charity Commission.

General Established in 1998, the trust produced a detailed annual report for 1998/99 giving a full description of its activities. Its main objectives were listed as follows:

- the advancement of education in the UK and overseas, including medical and scientific research
- the conservation and protection of the natural environment and endangered species of plants and animals with special emphasis on the protection of forests and endangered avifauna in the neotropics (South America).

The trust receives its income from Gift Aid donations, which totalled £91,000 in 1998/99. Its priority for that year was 'to facilitate the formation and government approval of the Fundacion Jocotoco (FJ) conservation charity in Ecuador'. The charity is set up to begin work in the conservation of endangered special birds through the acquisition of forest habitat. The chair of this trust, an expert in ornithology and conservation, is also on the board of trustees for FJ.

In 1998/99 FJ received a grant of $77,000 (about £46,000) from the trust, making the trust its main supporter in that year.

The trust made further grants totalling £14,000 in 1998/99, as follows:

- Commonwealth Institute for the Deaf – £6,000 to cover half the cost of training a citizen of Guyana as a medical audio technician at Manchester University
- Gonville and Caius College, Cambridge 650th Anniversary Appeal – £6,000, to support environmental conservation related programmes
- RSPB – £1,000 towards their emergency appeal for funds to buy Kirkconnel Merse, Solway, Scotland
- Gloucestershire Wildlife Trust – £250
- Lord Treloar College – £250.

The trust informed us that in 1999/2000 it made grants totalling £96,000, of which 89% was given to FJ, accounting for 75% of FJ's total funding for that year. The programme in 2000/01 is following similar lines, with its grants comprising 30% of FJ's income.

Applications In writing to the correspondent. The day-to-day activities of this trust are carried out by e-mail, telephone and circulation of documents, as the trustees do not all live in the UK.

The Sinclair Charitable Trust

Jewish learning, welfare

£143,000 (1997/98)

Beneficial area UK

4th Floor, 38 Wigmore Street, London W1H 0BX

Tel. 020 7563 1000 **Fax** 020 7563 1001

Correspondent Dr M J Sinclair, Trustee

Trustees *Dr M J Sinclair; Mrs P K Sinclair; E J Gold.*

Information available Accounts were on file at the Charity Commission, but without a grants list and only a brief narrative report.

General This trust makes grants to Jewish organisations and usually just one or two charities each year that the Sinclair family has a personal interest in.

In 1997/98 it had assets of £19,000 and an income of £206,000. The trust receives substantial donations via a company controlled by Dr and Mrs Sinclair. Its administration costs totalled £52,000 in 1997/98 and grants were made totalling £143,000. Unfortunately a grants list was not included in the accounts on file at the Charity Commission.

Applications In writing to the correspondent.

The Huntly & Margery Sinclair Charitable Trust

Medical, general

£134,000 (1997/98)

Beneficial area UK

c/o Trowers & Hamlins, Trustees' Solicitor, Sceptre Court, 40 Tower Hill, London EC3N 4DX

Tel. 020 7423 8000 **Fax** 020 7423 8001

Correspondent Eric Payne

Trustees *Mrs A M H Gibbs; Mrs M A H Windsor; Mrs J Floyd.*

Information available Full accounts were on file at the Charity Commission.

General In 1997/98 the trust had assets of £1.5 million and an income of £56,000. Grants totalled £134,000 and went to 27 organisations. About half of these were recurrent from the previous year.

Rendcomb College has been the major beneficiary in recent years and received three grants totalling £109,000. The next largest grants were £5,000 to St Peter Farmington Church Restoration Appeal Fund, £3,000 to Injured Jockeys' Fund and £1,500 to Erskine Hospital 2000 Appeal. Eight grants of £1,000 were awarded, among those to benefit were Arthritis Care, Eating Disorders Association, St Swithin's Pyeworthy PCC and RNLI Edinburgh.

The 13 remaining grants ranged from £500 to £750 and included those to Dumfries & Galloway Action, National Trust for Scotland, Cloud Nine Fund, Children Nationwide, World Wildlife Fund, Syde Church PCC and SWT Red Squirrel Appeal.

The grants list showed some preference for animal charities and for health/welfare charities.

Applications In writing to the correspondent.

The John Slater Foundation

Medical, animal welfare, general

£158,000 (1998/99)

Beneficial area UK, with a preference for the north west of England especially West Lancashire

HSBC Trust Company (UK) Limited, Cumberland House, 15–17 Cumberland Place, Southampton SO15 2UY

Tel. 023 8053 1348

Correspondent The Secretary to the Trustees

Trustees *HSBC Trust Co. Ltd.*

Information available Full accounts were on file at the Charity Commission.

General In 1998/99 the trust had assets of £4.2 million and an income of £158,000. The trust gave 48 grants totalling £158,000, with at least half of the beneficiaries having received a similar sized grant the year before. The two largest grants went to Blackpool Ladies Sick & Poor and Trinity Hospital – Bispham. Other larger grants included Sup. G Richardson Memorial Youth Trust (£8,000), Mission to Deep Sea Fishermen (£6,500), Bury Grammar School for Girls (£6,000) and RSPB Leighton Moss (£5,000).

Grants for £1,000 to £4,000 were given to a range of organisations, particularly those working in the fields of medicine or animal welfare. Beneficiaries included Duchess of York Hospital for Babies and Wildlife Hospital Trust (£4,000 each), Blue Cross Hospital and Battersea Dogs Home (£3,000 each), Liverpool School of Tropical Medicine and Blackpool and Flyde Society for the Blind (£2,000 each) and Cats' Protection and Welfare Service (£1,800).

Other recipients included Bispham Parish Church, Guide Dogs for the Blind, Samaritans and West Lancashire Scouts.

Applications Applications are considered twice a year on 1 May and 1 November.

The SMB Trust

Christian, general

£131,000 (1998/99)

Beneficial area UK and overseas

15 Wilman Road, Tunbridge Wells, Kent TN4 9AJ

Tel. 01892 537301

Correspondent Mrs B M O'Driscoll, Trustee

Trustees *E D Anstead; P J Stanford; Mrs B O'Driscoll; J A Anstead.*

Information available Full accounts were on file at the Charity Commission.

General In 1998/99 the trust had assets of £5.2 million and an income of £169,000. The chair's report for this trust states: 'The trustees have continued to give regular support to a number of core charities covering a wide spectrum of needs'. One-off appeals are also considered.

During the year the trust gave 120 grants totalling £131,000, of which 51 were recurrent. Grants ranged from £200 to £4,000, but were mainly of £1,000. The London City Mission, as it appears to do every year, received one of the largest grants (£4,000). Other larger grants were to Pilgrims Homes (£4,000) and Salvation Army (£3,000).

Grants were also to Christian causes and to health and social welfare organisations. Recipients of £1,000 or more included British Red Cross, Church Army, Dentaid, Gideons International, International Integrated Health, National Schizophrenia Foundation, Peter Pan Playgroup and Refugees Arrivals Project. Some local organisations also received grants, for example: Christ Church, Little Heath; Liverpool City Mission; Salvation Army, Cirencester; and Walton Community Church.

Applications In writing to the correspondent.

The Albert & Florence Smith Memorial Trust

Social welfare

£187,000 (1998/99)

Beneficial area UK, with an emphasis on Essex

Tolhurst Fisher, Greenwood House, New London Road, Chelmsford, Essex CM2 0PP

Tel. 01245 495111 **Fax** 01245 494771

Correspondent The Secretary

Trustees W J Tolhurst, Chair; P J Tolhurst.

Information available Accounts were provided by the trust.

General The trust supports nominated charities on an annual basis, with the balance given to local charities in Essex. It has now been decided to concentrate its giving as follows:

- charities nominated by the original benefactors
- overseas projects jointly with CAFOD and Raleigh International
- Essex-based (only) church projects
- other Essex-related projects.

In 1998/99 the trust had assets of £3 million. The income was £372,000 and grants totalled £187,000, down from

£308,000 in the previous year. The report stated that the charity reduced grants in the year to ensure its stable financial position. This decrease has resulted in a net increase in funds. It is anticipated that as income levels improve in forthcoming years, the level of grants will increase.

Grants of £1,000 or more went to 31 organisations and these were listed in the accounts. Of these, 15 had received a grant in the previous year. The largest grant of £53,000 went to Essex Community Foundation, other recipients of large grants were Raleigh International (£25,000) and Southend Association of Voluntary Services (£10,000). There were 10 grants of £5,000 including those to Halstead Day Centre, NSPCC and Scope. Other grants went to UK health and welfare charities, and local causes in Essex, including several churches.

Applications In writing to the correspondent.

The Leslie Smith Foundation

General

£85,000 (1999/2000)

Beneficial area UK

The Old Coach House, Sunnyside, Bergh Apton, Norwich NR15 1DD

Correspondent M D Willcox, Trustee

Trustees M D Willcox; E A Rose.

Information available Full accounts were provided by the trust.

General In 1999/2000 the trust had assets of £2.7 million and an income of £187,000. Grants totalled £85,000.

The foundation, which regularly reviews its grant-making policy, is currently focussing on:

- children's hospices and bereavement counselling for children
- educational counselling
- matrimonial counselling
- children who are disabled
- welfare of retired clergy.

The foundation receives over 1,000 applications each year. In 1998/99, 18 grants were given, 13 of the recipients having received a grant in the previous year. The largest grants were to: Wessex Children's Hospice Trust, College of

St Barnabas, FWA Limited and Paul Strickland Scanner Appeal; Theatre Royal, Norwich (£8,000); and Relate and BAFECT (£6,000 each). Other grants included: Joseph Weld Hospice and Brettenham Dyslexia Foundation (£5,000 each); Royal British Legion (£3,000); and Norfolk Accident Rescue and St Peter & Paul, Berg Apton (£1,000 each).

Exclusions Registered charities only; no grants are available to individuals.

Applications In writing to the correspondent. Only successful appeals are acknowledged.

The N Smith Charitable Trust

General

£115,000 (1998/99)

Beneficial area Worldwide

Bullock Worthington & Jackson, 1 Booth Street, Manchester M2 2HA

Tel. 0161 833 9771

Correspondent The Trustees

Trustees J S Cochrane; T R Kendal; P R Green; J H Williams-Rigby.

Information available Full accounts were on file at the Charity Commission.

General In 1998/99 the assets had risen to £3.6 million, held in shares in a wide range of companies and it had an income of £111,000. After expenses of £20,000 (£18,000 of which was in legal costs), it gave £115,000 in donations. In the accounts grants were broken down into six categories. Examples of grants given within the different categories were as follows:

Poverty & social work
Grants totalling £41,000 went to 71 organisations. Most grants were for £1,000 each with one for £250 and another for £700. Beneficiaries included Acorns Children's Hospice Trust, Acrefund, Ipswich Housing Action Group, Manchester Diocesan Board for Church and Society and Willow Trust.

Education
A total of £13,000 was given in 21 grants. Half the grants were for £500 each, with the other half for £700. Beneficiaries included British Dyslexics, Cumbria Association of Clubs for Young People, Pestalozzi – Children for a Better World and Shaftesbury Society.

Overseas aid

18 grants were given totalling £16,000. They were either for £1,500 or £750 except one of £1,500. Recipients included ActionAid, Homeopathic Trust, Kosovo Appeal, Oxfam and Traidcraft Exchange.

Health & medical research

A total of £35,000 was given in 41 grants. Two thirds of the grants were for £500 with the remainder for £1,500. Beneficiaries included Action Research, British Lung Foundation, Leukaemia Research Fund, National Back Pain Association and War on Cancer.

Arts

Grants of £6,000 went to 10 organisations. All grants were for £500 and included those to Boilerhouse Theatre Company Ltd, Girls Choirs of Great Britain, Musicworks and York Early Music Foundation.

Environmental work & animals

Grants of £5,000 were given in 10 grants. Most grants were of £600 except two for £500 and two for £250. Recipients included Acorn Environmental Trust, Animals in Need, Devon Wildlife Trust, National Trust (Lake District), Soil Association and Woodland Trust.

Exclusions Grants are only made to registered charities and not to individuals.

Applications In writing to the correspondent. The trustees met in October and March.

The Stanley Smith UK Horticultural Trust

Horticulture

£84,000 to organisations (1998/99)

Beneficial area UK and, so far as it is charitable, outside the UK

Cory Lodge, PO Box 365, Cambridge CB2 1HR

Tel. 01223 336299 **Fax** 01223 336278

Correspondent James Cullen, Director

Trustees *John Norton; Christopher Brickell; John Dilger; Lady Renfrew; J B E Simmons.*

Information available Full report and financial statements provided by the trustees along with a copy of Guidelines to Applicants, April 2000.

General Established by deed in 1970 the trust's objects are the advancement of horticulture. In particular the trustees have power to make grants for the following purposes:

- horticultural research
- the creation, development, preservation and maintenance of public gardens
- the promotion of the cultivation and wide distribution of plants of horticultural or other value to mankind
- the promotion of the cultivation of new plants
- publishing books and work related to horticultural sciences.

In 1998/99 the trust's assets totalled £3.2 million and it had an income of £143,000. The director considered over 180 applications and 32 grants totalling £84,000 were made to organisations. Five scholarships totalling £39,000 were also awarded. A full grants list was provided in the trust's annual report.

Out of the general fund the largest grant of £10,000 went to Conifer Conservation Programme operated from Royal Botanic Garden, Edinburgh. Recipients of smaller grants included Curators of the University Parks – Oxford (£5,000), Flora for Fauna (£3,500), The Pukeiti Rhododendron Trust – New Zealand (£3,000), The Association of Garden Trusts (£2,000), The Marcher Apple Network (£1,200) and The Landscape Design Trust (£1,000). Six grants totalling £20,000 were given out from the approved grants fund. Beneficiaries included University of York (£5,700), Chelsea Physic Garden (£4,500) and University of Bangalore – India (£2,000). All of these grants were awarded over three years.

The director continues to provide advice to actual and potential applicants and to established projects which have already received grants. Any grant provided by the trust bears the condition that the recipient should provide within six months, or some other agreed period, a report on the use of the grant.

Exclusions No grants for projects in commercial horticulture (crop production) or agriculture, nor to support students taking academic or diploma courses of any kind, although educational institutions are supported.

Applications In writing to the correspondent. A detailed Guidelines for Applicants is available from the trust. The director is willing to give advice on how applications should be presented.

Grants are awarded twice a year, in spring and autumn. To be considered in the spring allocation, applications should reach the director before 15 February of each year; for the autumn allocation the equivalent date is 15 August. Potential recipients are advised to get their applications in early.

Solev Co Ltd

Jewish charities

£313,000 (1996/97)

Beneficial area UK

963 Finchley Road, London NW11 7PE

Correspondent R Tager, Trustee

Trustees *M Grosskopf; A E Perelman; R Tager.*

Information available Accounts were on file at the Charity Commission, but without a grants list.

General In 1997/98 the trust had an income of £381,000 and an expenditure of £479,000. This information was obtained from the Charity Commission database. Unfortunately further information for this year was not available for view in the public files.

In 1996/97 the trust had assets of £1.6 million which generated an income of £489,000. Grant giving was £313,000 and management and administrative costs were £10,000.

Only two donations are mentioned in the annual report: '£100,000 to the Dina Perelmam Trust Ltd, a charitable company of which Mr Perelman and Mr Grosskopf are governors; and £40,000 to Songdale Ltd, a charity of which Mr M Grosskopf is a governor.'

No grants list has been included in the accounts since 1972/73 when £14,000 was given to 52 Jewish charities. Examples then included Society of Friends of the Torah (£3,900); Finchley Road Synagogue (£2,300); NW London Talmudical College (£1,500); Yesodey Hatorah School (£700); and Gateshead Talmudical College (£400).

Applications In writing to the correspondent.

The Solo Charitable Settlement

Jewish, general

£71,000 (1997/98)

Beneficial area UK and Israel

Deloitte & Touche, Hill House, 1 Little New Street, London EC4A 3TR

Tel. 020 7303 3003

Correspondent Brian Ellison

Trustees *P D Goldstein; Edna Goldstein; R Goldstein; H Goldstein.*

Information available Full accounts were on file at the Charity Commission.

General The trust was established in 1983, by Peter David Goldstein. The trustees can hold the capital and income for 21 years to increase the trust's assets.

The assets have been steadily rising and by 1997/98 were valued at £4.9 million. These assets generated an income of £149,000. It gave 31 grants totalling £71,000, administration costs were high at £31,000 for the year. The trust supported a mix of previously supported and new organisations, almost all the grants were given to Jewish causes. The main beneficiaries were Joint Jewish Charitable Trust (£39,000), Ravenswood Foundation (£12,000), Ashten Trust (£5,500), JNF Charitable Trust (£5,300), Community Security Trust (£1,300) and Israel Music Foundation and Spiro Institute (£1,000 each).

Other grants were in the range of £65 to £800, but were mainly for smaller amounts under £250. Beneficiaries included South Bank Foundation (£800), World Jewish Relief (£500), Jewish Aid Committee (£200) and Anne Frank Exhibition (£100).

A small number of grants were made to non-Jewish charities including British Heart Foundation, Dementia Relief Foundation and NSPCC.

Applications In writing to the correspondent.

Songdale Ltd

Jewish

£91,000 (1992/93)

Beneficial area UK

81–82 Roman Way, London N7 8UP

Correspondent M Grosskopf, Governor

Trustees *M Grosskopf; Mrs M Grosskopf; Y Grosskopf.*

Information available Accounts were on file at the Charity Commission, but without a list of grants.

General In 1998/99 the trust had an income of £287,000 and an expenditure of £71,000. Unfortunately further information for this year was not available and the following information is repeated from the last edition of this guide.

This trust has regularly had a large surplus, with the assets increasing from £208,000 in 1988/89 to £676,000 in 1992/93. The income for this latest year was £173,000 and grants totalled £91,000.

The trust supports Jewish organisations, but no further information was available on the type or size of grants.

Applications In writing to the correspondent.

This entry was not confirmed by the trust but was correct according to information on file at the Charity Commission.

The South Square Trust

See below

£388,000 (1998/99)

Beneficial area UK

PO Box 67, Heathfield, East Sussex TN21 9ZR

Tel. & Fax 01435 830778

Correspondent Mrs Nicola Chrimes, Clerk to the Trustees

Trustees *C R Ponter; A E Woodall; W P Harriman; C P Grimwade; D B Inglis.*

Information available Condensed accounts were on file at the Charity Commission.

General The trust was established in 1979 with shares in Christie's International. The trust now has a wide range of investments and in 1998/99 its assets totalled £4.1 million generating an income of £190,000. Grants totalled £388,000.

General donations are made to registered charities working in the fields of the arts, culture and recreation, health, social welfare, medical, disability and conservation and environment. Community facilities and services will also be considered. Grants are made to individuals undertaking under or postgraduate courses in the fine and applied arts within the UK.

Grants were categorised by the trust as follows:

Annual donations to charities	£26,000
General donations to charities	£107,000
Students and single payment grants	£43,000
Bursaries and scholarships to schools/colleges	£212,000
Total	**£388,000**

Major grants over £1,000 in the annual and general categories were made to St Paul's School – Library Extension (£48,000), Kosovo Crisis Appeal (£5,000), RSPB – Dingle Marshes (£2,500) with £1,500 each to Disability Aid Fund, CHATA and Leuka 2000 Appeal. Other grants in these categories were not listed by the trust and no further information was available about the types of grants awarded.

The trust also gives grants to students for postgraduate or undergraduate courses connected with the fine and applied arts including drama, dance, music, but particularly related to gold and silver work. Students should be over 18 years old. Courses have to be of a practical nature. Help is given to various colleges in the form of bursary awards. A full list is available from the correspondent. Also see entry in *The Educational Grants Directory 2000/2001.*

Exclusions No grants given to individuals under 18 or those seeking funding for expeditions, travel, courses outside UK, short courses or courses not connected with fine and applied arts.

Applications

Registered charities
In writing to the correspondent with details about your charity, the reason for requesting funding, and enclosing a copy of your accounts. Applications are considered three times a year, in spring, summer and winter.

Individuals
Standard application forms are available from the correspondent. Forms are sent

out between January and April only, to be returned by the end of April for consideration in the following academic year.

The W F Southall Trust

Quaker, general

£271,000 (1998/99)

Beneficial area UK, with an interest in Birmingham

c/o Rutters Solicitors, 2 Bimport, Shaftesbury, Dorset SP7 8AY

Tel. 01747 852377 **Fax** 01747 851989

Correspondent S Rutter, Secretary

Trustees *Mrs D Maw; C M Southall; D H D Southall; Mrs A Wallis; M Holtom; Ms J Engelkamp; C Greaves.*

Information available Full accounts were on file at the Charity Commission.

General 'The trustees endeavour to support smaller charities where their help is more meaningful and especially when a trustee has detailed knowledge of the charity concerned.'

In 1998/99 the trust had assets of £4.9 million and an income of £234,000. Management expenses came to £26,000 for the year, and grants totalling £271,000 were made. They were divided into the following categories:

Category	Total	No. of grants
Central Committees of the Society of Friends	£52,000	3
Birmingham district charities	£7,200	3
Meeting House appeals	£4,000	3
Other Quaker charities	£27,000	22
Other charities	£181,000	117

The Central Committees of the Society of Friends category received the largest grant of £40,000 for Britain Yearly Meeting.

The three grants to Birmingham charities ranged from £1,000 to £3,000 and went to Birmingham Settlement, City of Birmingham YMCA and Fairbridge – West Midlands.

Meeting houses in Ambleside, Bedford and Sibford benefited from grants in that category.

The grants in the 'other charities' categories were given to a vast array of local and UK organisations working variously for human rights, ecology and conservation, overseas aid and development work, health, social welfare and a number of other innovative projects which Quakers have traditionally been associated with.

Grants of £5,000 or more went to Quaker Housing Trust (£10,000), Friends World Committee for Consultation (£7,000), Oxfam and Oxford Community Meditation (£6,000 each) with £5,000 each to Alternative Technology Centre, Money for Madagascar, Salt of the Earth, War on Want and Woodbroke.

Other smaller grants went to International Voluntary Service (£4,500), National Trust (£3,000), Amnesty International UK Human Rights Centre Appeal (£2,500), Forum for the Future (£2,000), VSO (£1,000) Coventry Cathedral Development Trust (£600) and Woodspring Association for the Blind (£500).

Exclusions No grants to individuals.

Applications In writing to the correspondent. Applications are considered in February/March and November. Applications received between meetings are considered at the next meeting.

Spar Charitable Fund

Children

About £200,000 (2000)

Beneficial area UK

Spar Landmark Ltd, 32–40 Headstone Drive, Harrow, Middlesex HA3 5QT

Tel. 020 8863 5511

Correspondent P W Marchant, Trustee

Trustees *The National Guild of Spar Ltd; R Harvey; P Marchant.*

Information available Accounts were on file at the Charity Commission, but without a narrative report or a grants list.

General In 2000 the trust had £200,000 income from donations which was available to be donated to a children's

hospice or hospital. In January 2000 the trust informed us that the beneficiary had already been chosen for that year. In 1999 the beneficiary was ChildLine. The trust informed us that it favours children's charities.

Applications In writing to the correspondent.

The Spear Charitable Trust

General

£200,000 (1999)

Beneficial area UK

Roughground House, Old Hall Green, Ware, Hertfordshire SG11 1HB

Tel. 01920 823071 **Fax** 01920 823071

e-mail franzel@farmersweekly.net

Correspondent Hazel E Spear, Secretary

Trustees *P N Harris; K B Stuart Crowhurst; F A Spear; H E Spear.*

Information available Full accounts were on file at the Charity Commission.

General This trust was established in 1994 with general charitable purposes and for the welfare of employees and former employees of J W Spear & Sons plc, their families and dependants.

In 1999 the assets of the trust stood at £5.3 million and the income was £199,000. Grants totalled £200,000 including £19,000 given in welfare grants and £73,000 listed as 'sundry donations' (less than £5,000 each).

Grants of £5,000 or more were listed in the accounts and were made to 11 organisations. These included £35,000 to Judisches Museum Franken, £14,000 to Spielzeug Museum – Nuremberg and £10,000 each to Purcell School and Yehudi Menuhin School.

Smaller grants included Hanover Band Trust (£9,200) and £5,000 each to Botton Village Appeal Fund, Children of Mukuru, Farm Africa, Grace Tricia Wang Lee Na Trust, Pesticide Trust and Woodland Trust.

Applications In writing to the correspondent.

The Jessie Spencer Trust

General

£90,000 (1998/99)

Beneficial area UK, with a preference for Nottinghamshire

1 Royal Standard Place,
Nottingham NG1 6FZ

Tel. 0115 950 7000

Correspondent Barbara Samba

Trustees *V W Semmens;
Mrs E K M Brackenbury; R S Hursthouse.*

Information available Full accounts were on file at the Charity Commission.

General In 1998/99 the trust had assets of £3.1 million and it had an income of £119,000. A total of £90,000 was given in 78 grants.

Grants were broken down by the trust into the following categories:

Category	No. of grants	Total
Accommodation	2	£800
Arts	5	£7,700
Churches	5	£17,000
Education	4	£2,600
Environment	2	£600
Groups/clubs	9	£12,000
Individuals	4	£1,100
Medical/disability	25	£27,000
Welfare	22	£21,000

Grants went to a wide range of organisations including some medical and welfare charities and a number concerned with music, there was a preference for charities based in Nottinghamshire. The largest grants were £10,000 each to Southwell Minister Choir and Monty Hind Club and £7,500 to Sybil Levin Centre. A further 11 grants were made over £1,000 with the remainder in the range of £100 to £600.

Local organisations to benefit included Nottingham Historic Churches Trust, Nottingham Regional Society for Autistic Children and Adults, Nottingham Music Society and local branches of Mencap, NSPCC and Salvation Army.

Other recipients included Marie Stopes International, Opera Restor'd, Raleigh International, Sense and Winged Fellowship Trust.

Applications In writing to the correspondent including the latest set of audited accounts. Unsuccessful applications will not be acknowledged.

W W Spooner Charitable Trust

General

£61,000 (1998/99)

Beneficial area UK, with a preference for Yorkshire especially West Yorkshire

Sovereign Street, PO Box 8,
Leeds LS1 1HQ

Correspondent Addleshaw Booth & Co.

Trustees *M H Broughton, Chair;
Sir J Hill; T Ramsden; R Ibbotson;
Mrs J M McKiddie; J H Wright.*

Information available Accounts were on file at the Charity Commission.

General The trust will support charities working in the following areas:

- young people – for example: groups focusing on young people's welfare, sport and education including school appeals, youth clubs, uniformed groups and adventure training organisations, and individuals for voluntary work overseas or expeditions

- community – for example: churches, associations, welfare and support groups

- health and welfare – the following causes may be supported: care of people who are sick, disabled or disadvantaged. Organisations that would be considered are victim support, hospitals, hospices, welfare organisations and selected medical and medical research charities

- the countryside – causes such as the protection and preservation of the environment and rescue services

- the arts – for example: museums, music and literary festivals etc. There is some support for the purchase of works of art for public benefit.

In 1998/99 the trust had assets of £2 million and an income of £55,000. A total of £61,000 was given in 138 grants. The trust supports a wide range of charities as the categories above suggest. The majority of the charities supported are in Yorkshire, in particular West Yorkshire – in 1998/99 around 50% of the charities supported were based in West Yorkshire. Many of the grants were recurrent and at least 10 were made to individuals. The largest grants were to New College, Oxford (£3,500), National Arts Collection Fund and New Hall, Cambridge (£2,000 each), Guide Dogs for the Blind (£1,700) with £1,500 each to Courtaulds Institute of Art and St Margaret's Parochial Church Council, Ilkley and £1,000 each to Leith School of Art and Yorkshire Ballet.

The remainder of grants were in the range of £150 and £850. Recipients included North of England Christian Healing Trust (£850), St Gemma's Hospice – Leeds (£750), Opera North and Leeds Housing Concern (£500 each), Bradford Relate Centre and Ilkley Talking Newspaper (£350 each), All Saints – Keighley (£250), ChildLine and Lake District Mountain Accident Association (£300 each), British Trust for Conservation Volunteers (£250), Green Meadow School – Guiseley (£200) and Yorkshire Dales Millennium Trust (£150).

Applications In writing to the correspondent.

The Stanley Foundation Ltd

Older people, medical, education, social welfare

£110,000 (1996/97)

Beneficial area UK

Flat 3, 19 Holland Park,
London W11 3TD

Tel. 020 7792 3854

Correspondent The Secretary

Trustees *Nicholas Stanley, Chair;
D J Aries; S R Stanley; Mrs E Stanley;
C Shale.*

Information available Full accounts were on file at the Charity Commission.

General In 1998/99 the trust had an income of £106,000 and an expenditure of £252,000. This information was taken from the Charity Commission database. Unfortunately the accounts for this year were not on file at the time of going to print. The following information is repeated from the last edition of this guide.

For many years, the trust has been supporting charities helping older people and medical, educational and social welfare charities. According to the correspondent, the trust may now change its areas of giving every one or two years.

Grants totalled £110,000 in 1996/97, but no further information was available for this year.

In 1994/95 the trust had an income of £148,000 from assets of £3.1 million and gave 62 grants totalling £170,000. The trust also made a commitment for a large grant (£500,000) to King's College, Cambridge which was to be paid in autumn 1995.

During the year the larger grants were £30,000 to St Mary's Hampstead Appeal, £15,000 each to King's College Cambridge and Wynn Institute and £11,000 each to NSPCC and Discovery Factory. Donations of £5,000 each went to Cancer Research, Cheek by Jowl, Crisis at Christmas and MacIntyre Charitable Trust.

The other grants were all for £250 to £4,000. Most were to medical causes, but other organisations to benefit included BTCV, Pavilion Opera, Percy Thrower Gardening Club and Young Champions Tennis Trust.

Applications In writing to the correspondent.

The Starfish Trust

Sickness, medical

£14,000 to organisations (1998/99) **but see below**

Beneficial area UK

PO Box 213, Patchway, Bristol BS32 4YY

Correspondent Robert N Woodward, Chief Executive

Trustees *Charles E Dobson; Mary Dobson.*

Information available Full accounts were on file at the Charity Commission.

General Priority is given to appeals from individuals and charitable organisations living or based within a 25-mile radius of central Bristol in the following areas:

• direct assistance to people who are disabled

• direct assistance to people for relief of illness or disease

• medical research and welfare in the above areas.

In 1998/99 the trust had assets of £4.8 million and an income of £4.3 million. This was due to a donation of £4 million from Dobson Family Settlement, which produced an income of £226,000 interest. Grants paid to organisations and individuals totalled just £30,000 (£108,000 in the previous year).

No grants list was included for the year, just a note stating donations totalled £30,000 including £16,000 in six grants to individuals. However, the report contained details of grants committed by the trust. The Jack and Jill Appeal, of which the correspondent is the campaign director, was given £1 million from the Dobson Family Settlement donated to build a new childrens' unit in the ground of Frenchay Hopital to cater for children of all ages including teenagers, with £500,000 to be paid in 1999/2000. Other commitments for that year were to Spencer Dayman Meningitis Research laboratories (£88,000 from a promised £140,000) and Changing Faces Charity (£20,000 from a promised £40,000). Commitments for future years were to Burton Hill School for the Disabled toward specialist accommodation (£500,000), Claremont School for a hydrotherapy pool (£50,000) and Colston School Challenge as matched funding for dogs for people who are disabled (£10,000). These commitments total £1.8 million, it is not know whether the surplus for the year will be transfered to assets.

Administration fees were very low at just £5,400, although salaries totalled £42,000 (£14,000 in the previous year). The accounts also noted under charitable expenditure depreciation of £93,000, which was calculated at 15% of the cost of office furniture and 25% of the cost of motor vehicles.

The trust has grown dramatically since the previous year, when the assets totalled £656,000 and the income was £101,000 including £90,000 in donations. Grants totalled £109,000. The largest grants were to St Peter's Hospice (£70,000) and Avon Youth Association (£2,00). Smaller grants were also made and totalled £16,000.

Applications In writing to the correspondent.

The Cyril & Betty Stein Charitable Trust

Jewish causes

£158,000 (1998/99)

Beneficial area UK and Israel

94 Wigmore Street, London W1U 3RF
Tel. 020 7493 1205
Correspondent D Clayton, Trustee
Trustees *Cyril Stein; Mrs Betty Stein; David Clayton.*

Information available Report and accounts were on file at the Charity Commission.

General The trust makes a small number of substantial grants each year, primarily for the advancement of the Jewish religion and the welfare of Jewish people.

In 1998/99 the trust had assets of £337,000 and an income of £182,000, including £159,000 in donations. Grants were given to 49 organisations totalling £158,000.

The top seven grants were listed in the accounts, including those to Institute for the Advancement of Education in Jaffa (£38,000), Friends of Maalot Educational Centre and L'Chaim Independent Charitable Trust (£11,000 each) and Project SEED and British Friends of Machon Meir (£5,000 each).

Applications In writing to the correspondent.

The Sir Sigmund Sternberg Charitable Foundation

Jewish, inter-faith causes, general

£226,000 (1998/99)

Beneficial area Worldwide

Clayton Stark, 5th Floor, Charles House, 108–110 Finchley Road, London NW3 5JJ

Correspondent D Clayton

Trustees *Sir S Sternberg; Lady H Sternberg; V M Sternberg.*

Information available Full accounts were on file at the Charity Commission.

General In 1998/99 the trust had assets of £2.9 million and an income of £771,000, of which £461,000 was from donations. Management and adminstration costs were high at £156,000 for the year. A total of £226,000 was given in 191 grants.

Ten grants were listed in the accounts, seven of which were recurrent from the previous year, with a further £73,000 given in unlisted smaller donations. By far the largest grant of the year was for £57,000 to Manor House Trust. Further grants over £10,000 went to Friends of the Hebrew University of Jerusalem (£33,000), Institute Of Archaeo-Metallurgical Studies (£20,000) and £11,000 each to One World Action and the Inter-religious Co-ordination Council in Israel. Other recipients were Holocaust Education Action, International Council for Christians and Jews and One World Action.

Applications The foundation has stated in the past that its funds are fully committed.

Stervon Ltd

Jewish

£209,000 (1998)

Beneficial area UK

c/o Stervon House, 1 Seaford Road, Salford, Greater Manchester M6 6AS

Tel. 0161 737 5000

Correspondent A Reich, Secretary

Trustees *A Reich; G Rothbart.*

Information available Full accounts were on file at the Charity Commission.

General 'The principal objective of the company is the distribution of funds to Jewish, religious, educational and similar charities.'

In 1998 the trust had assets of £146,000 and an income of £237,000, £158,000 of which came from donations. Grants totalled £209,000, the accounts listed 36 made over £500. They went to both previously supported and new organisations. Other donations totalled £15,000. The largest grants over £10,000 went to Chasdei Yoel (£45,000), Bnos Yisorel (£32,000) and UTA (£12,000).

Other smaller grants went to Machzikei Hadrass (£9,700), Shaarei Torah (£6,100), Friends of Masse Tsedoko (£5,500), Kesser Charities (£5,000), Jewish High School (£4,800), Agudas Yisroel Housing Association (£2,500), Beis Aharon Trust (£1,200), Friends of Mir (£750) and Manchester Yeshiva (£600).

Applications In writing to the correspondent.

The Stoller Charitable Trust

Medical, children, general

£518,000 (1999/2000)

Beneficial area UK, with a preference for the Greater Manchester area

c/o SSL International plc, Tubiton House, Oldham, Lancashire OL1 3HS

Tel. 0161 621 2003 **Fax** 0161 627 0932

Correspondent Alison M Ford, Secretary

Trustees *Norman K Stoller, Chair; Roger Gould; Jan Fidler.*

Information available Accounts were on file at the Charity Commission.

General The trust supports a wide variety of charitable causes, but with particular emphasis on those which are local, medically-related or supportive of children. There is a bias towards charities in Greater Manchester where the trust is based. It also endeavours to maintain a balance between regular and occasional donations and between making a few large grants and many smaller ones.

In 1999/2000 over 250 grants were made totalling £518,000. Most were for under £1,000, but donations of £10,000 or over went to Big Issue, Bolton Lads and Girls Club, Bridgewater Hall, Christie Hospital, Community Foundation for Greater Manchester, Emmaus – Greater Manchester, HALT, Hulme Grammar School, Make a Difference Appeal, Manchester High School, Manchester Grammar School, NSPCC and New Heart New Start.

Applications In writing to the correspondent. Applications need to be received by February, May, August or November. Trustees meet in March, June, September and December.

The Stone Foundation

Research into addiction, medical research, welfare

£155,000 (1998/99)

Beneficial area UK

20 Wilton Row, London SW1X 7NS

Correspondent Lady Gosling, Chair of the Trustees

Trustees *Lady Shauna Gosling; M J Kirkwood; T Millington-Drake.*

Information available Full accounts were on file at the Charity Commission.

General The foundation continues to fund the field of addiction, directing resources to the area of research, education and treatment of addiction to alcohol and drugs as well as focusing on the alleviation of other compulsive disorders.

In 1998/99 the assets of the foundation stood at £3.6 million, it had an income of £1.1 million of which £975,000 came from a donation from Harborn Co Limited. Grants totalled £155,000.

In 1998/99 the foundation made 12 grants, 6 of which were recurrent from the previous year. The largest grant was for £25,000 and went to the Chemical Dependency Centre. This was to help fund a quality assurance programme in alignment with European Association for the Treatment of Addiction UK standards. Other larger grants included £20,000 to Life Education Centres to fund mobile drug prevention classrooms for a schools education programme; £15,000 to Clouds House for the 'Families Plus' integrated family recovery programme; and £10,000 to British Liver Trust towards funding research into a help centre.

Other recipients of smaller grants were £8,000 to ADAS (Alcohol Drug Abstinence Service), £7,500 each to RAPT and National Association of Children of Alcoholics and £3,000 to Spires Centre.

Applications In writing to the correspondent. Trustees meet in January, April, June, September and November.

253

The M J C Stone Charitable Trust

General

£148,000 (1998)

Beneficial area UK

Estate Office, Ozleworth Park, Wotton under Edge, Gloucestershire GL12 7QA

Tel. 01453 845591

Correspondent M J C Stone, Trustee

Trustees *M J C Stone; Mrs L Stone; C R H Stone; A J Stone; N J Farquhar.*

Information available Full accounts were on file at the Charity Commission.

General While the trust has general charitable objects, giving to a range of causes, it has stated that its main area of interest is the advancement of education. Grants are given to establishments only, not individuals.

In 1998 it had assets of £380,000 and an income of £102,000, including £75,000 from Gift Aid donations. Grants totalled £148,000. While some of these were recurrent from the previous year, it was mostly new organisations that were supported.

Starting in 1998, the trust pledged to donate £100,000 to the Bradfield Foundation Music Centre, to be paid in four equal, annual instalments. This commitment accounted for the major grant of the year of £35,000. Other grants of £10,000 or more included: National Hospital Development Foundation (£29,000), United World College Atlantic (£13,000), Countryside Foundation for Education (£12,000) and £10,000 each to Magdelene College and University of Gloucestershire.

The remaining grants ranged from £1,000 to £5,000, with most for £1,000. They included those to Barnardos, Beckford Ball, Cotswold Care Hospice, Home-Start UK, Mentor Foundation, Regain and SeeAbility.

Grants under £1,000 were made to 25 organisations. They ranged from £250 to £750, but were mainly for smaller amounts. Organisations to benefit included Arthritis and Rheumatism Council, Greyhounds in Need, Museum of Hunting Trust, Sussex Young Cricketers and Teens in Crisis.

Applications 'Unsolicited applications will not be replied to.'

The Janatha Stubbs Foundation

General

£65,000 (1997/98)

Beneficial area Worldwide

Messrs Roberts Legge & Co, PO Box 4, Liverpool L37 1YJ

Correspondent J H Roberts, Trustee

Trustees *Mrs J L Laing; D W Stubbs; J H Roberts.*

Information available Full accounts were on file at the Charity Commission.

General In 1998/99 the trust had an income of £263,000 and expenditure of £248,000. Unfortunately we were unable to obtain further up-to-date information on this trust. This entry was included in the last edition of this guide.

The trust prefers to support the:

- raising of the artistic taste of the public whether in relation to music, drama, opera, painting, sculpture or otherwise in connection with the fine arts

- promotion of education in the fine arts

- promotion of academic education

- promotion of the Christian religion

- provision of facilities for recreation or other leisure time occupation.

The major development undertaken by the trust began in 1989 with the foundation of Ir Razzett tal Hbiberija, a leisure park in the fishing port of Marsascala in Malta. The park is especially designed for the needs and relaxation of people who are disabled.

The income of the trust in 1997/98 was £59,000 including £18,000 from the Moores Family Charity Foundation and £20,000 from the Fairway Trust. Grants totalled £65,000, of which £40,000 went to Razzett Tal Hbiberija. The Royal College of Music received £18,000 with smaller grants (£2,000 and less) to several music education establishments such as the Royal Northern College of Music. The only exception was a grant of £2,000 to the Winged Fellowship Trust (Southport).

Applications Unsolicited applications are not considered or responded to.

The Sutasoma Trust

Education, general

£58,000 (1996/97)

Beneficial area Worldwide

Eversheds, Daedalus House, Station Road, Cambridge CB1 2RE

Tel. 01223 355933

Correspondent Miss Lynn Wicks, Trust Administrator

Trustees *M K Hobart; Dr A R Hobart; M A Burgauer; J M Lichtenstein.*

Information available Full accounts were on file at the Charity Commission up until 1996/97.

General Unfortunately we have been unable to update the following information since the last edition of this guide.

The trust's objects are 'to advance education in particular by providing grants to graduate students in the social sciences and humanities' and general charitable purposes.

In 1996/97 the trust had assets of £2 million and an income of £84,000. Grants totalled £58,000, including £12,500 to Lucy Cavendish College (part for a fellowship now expired and part for a new fellowship). Other grants in the research fellowships and scholarships category ranged from £1,000 to £5,000, with organisations supported including Goldsmith College, Haverford College (USA), Universita Udayana and University College London.

Grants under 'general donations' were given to Merhamet (£3,000), Cambodia Trust (£2,000), Health Unlimited (£1,000) and The Women's Council (£500).

The trustees were also morally committed to providing up to £7,000 per annum to applicants under the 'Sutasoma Small Projects Award Fund'. This provides assistance by way of small single payments (to a maximum of £400) to full-time students for one-off projects related to their studies. These grants totalled £11,000 in 1997/98.

Future commitments totalled £47,000, including £38,000 for the Lucy Cavendish College Fellowship until March 2000.

Applications In writing to the correspondent.

The Swire Charitable Trust

General

£378,000 (1999)

Beneficial area Worldwide

John Swire & Sons Ltd, Swire House, 59 Buckingham Gate, London SW1E 6AJ

Tel. 020 7834 7717

Correspondent B N Swire, Trustee

Trustees *Sir J Swire; Sir Adrian Swire; B N Swire; M J B Todhunter; E J R Scott.*

Information available Full accounts were on file at the Charity Commission.

General In 1999 the trust had assets of £232,000 and an income of £201,000 which came mainly from donations from John Swire & Sons Ltd. Grants totalled £378,000. The two largest donations were to related charitable institutions, see below. There were 25 grants made of £1,000 and more. The largest grants were of £116,000 each going to the related John Swire 1989 Charitable Trust and the Sammermar Trust (*see separate entries*). Other larger grants went to St George's Hospital Medical School (£38,000), Air League Educational Trust (£15,000), VSO (£8,100), Cystic Fibrosis Trust – Young Artists' Exhibition (£6,000) and Prince's Trust (£5,000).

Other recipients included Duke of Edinburgh's Award (£3,500), Memorial Gates Trust (£3,000), Haven Trust (£2,000) and Multiple Births Foundation (£1,500). Seven grants of £1,000 were made including those to Cancer Research Campaign, Family Welfare Association, Mencap – Blue Sky Appeal and Ramsbury PCC.

About half of the grants were recurrent from the previous year.

Applications In writing to the correspondent. Applications are considered throughout the year.

The John Swire (1989) Charitable Trust

General

£252,000 (1999)

Beneficial area Worldwide

John Swire & Sons Ltd, Swire House, 59 Buckingham Gate, London SW1E 6AJ

Tel. 020 7834 7717

Correspondent B N Swire, Trustee

Trustees *Sir John Swire; J S Swire; B N Swire; M C Robinson; Lady Swire.*

Information available Full accounts were on file at the Charity Commission.

General The trust was established in 1989 by Sir John Swire. In 1999 it had assets of £6.2 million. The income was £371,000, of which £116,000 was from donations. Grants totalled £252,000 (£146,000 in 1998). A wide range of organisations were supported including some in the areas of arts, welfare, education, medicine and research. Many new organisations were supported by the trust, as well as some which received help in 1998.

By far the largest grant went to University College Oxford (£80,000). Other larger donations went to Countryside Alliance and Textile Conservation Centre (£10,000 each), Strode Park Foundation (£5,300) with £5,000 each to British Dyslexia Association, Faversham Society, RSPB – Elmley Marshes and Toynbee Hall and £4,000 to Canterbury Festival. The trust made 10 further grants between £1,300 and £2,500 and 15 grants of £1,000. Beneficiaries included Action for ME, British Red Cross, Down's Syndrome Association, Glyndebourne Festival, National Meningitis Trust, NSPCC and Royal Horticultural Society.

Applications In writing to the correspondent.

The Charles and Elsie Sykes Trust

General

£406,000 (1999)

Beneficial area UK and overseas, with preference for the northern part of the UK, in particular Yorkshire

6 North Park Road, Harrogate, North Yorkshire HG1 5PA

Correspondent David J Reah, Secretary

Trustees *John Ward, Chair; Anne E Brownlie; Martin P Coultas; Mrs G Mary Dance; Michael G H Garnett; John Horrocks; R Barry Kay; Michael W McEvoy; Dr Michael D Moore.*

Information available Full accounts with a detailed grants list were on file at the Charity Commission, but with only a limited narrative report.

General Grants are made to a broad variety of causes which the annual report broke down into 17 areas. Those receiving the largest proportion of funds in 1999 were:

Category	%
Social and moral welfare	19
Cultural and environmental heritage	12
Children and youth	10
Medical research	10
Physical disability	7
Medical health and mental disability	7

Other categories included animals and birds, overseas aid, people who are blind and partially sighted, education, older people, hospices and hospitals, services and ex-services and trades and professions.

In 1999 the trust had an income of £410,000 and assets of £11 million. Management and administration of the charity totalled £27,000. It gave 261 grants totalling £406,000 in two categories, annual and special donations.

Annual donations

There were 125 grants totalling £128,000. The largest grant went to Yorkshire Cancer for £5,000. Other recipients of larger grants included: St Michael's Hospice (£3,500), York Minister (£3,000); Barnardos, National Children's Homes and Royal National Institute for Deaf People (£2,000 each); Motor Neurone Disease (£1,500); and £1,000 each to Historic Churches Preservation Trust, Christian Aid and Bath Institute of Medical Engineering. Recipients of grants under £1,000 included Pestalozzi Village Trust (£900); Population Concern

(£800); Browning House – Leeds (£700); Prison Reform Trust (£600); One Parent Families – Scotland, Apex Trust and Relate – Harrogate (£400 each); and Whizz-Kidz (£300). About half the grants are repeated annually; many of these are to well known, UK organisations.

Special 'one-off' donations

A total of £278,000 was given in 136 grants. The largest grants were £25,000 to Royal Northern College of Music and £10,000 each to British Red Cross Turkey, Yorkshire Dales Millennium Trust, St George's Crypt More than a Roof Appeal and William Henry Smith School – Brighouse. Other large grants went to National Autistic Society – London and Selby Abbey Trust (£5,000 each); Royal National College for the Blind, Hereford (£4,000); The Royal College of Surgeons England (£3,000); Hartlepool Women's Refuge – Stockton and Deafblind UK (£1,500 each); and £1,000 each to Northumbria Daybreak – Corbridge, St Peter's – Leeds and Youth Action – Hull.

Recipients of smaller one-off grants included, North Yorkshire Venture Scouts – York (£750); Skipton Citizens Advice Bureau and Jonas Trust – Leyburn (£500 each) and Springwell Centres – Gateshead (£250). The trustees noted that applications to the trust for special grants exceeded 1,000, of which only 136 were successful. Many applications did not fit in with the trust's preferences (see exclusions below) or did not contain copies of their latest accounts examined or audited. A reduction in the 'quality' of applications from the previous year was also noted. The trust maintains a reserve approximate to an average year's income to enable a steady income for themselves and, therefore, their annual charities, while retaining the ability to give 'very large donations at what could be disadvantageous times'.

Exclusions The following applicants are likely to be unsuccessful: individuals; local organisations in the south of England; and recently established charities. Non-registered charities are not considered.

Applications Applications from registered charities may be made with full details and an sae to the above address. Applications without up-to-date audited or examined accounts will not be considered. The trust regrets that it cannot conduct correspondence with applicants.

The Hugh & Ruby Sykes Charitable Trust

General, medical, education, employment

£175,000 (1999/2000)

Beneficial area Principally South Yorkshire

Bamford Hall Holdings Ltd,
Bamford Hall, The Hollow, Bamford,
Hope Valley S33 0AU

Tel. 01433 651190

Correspondent Sir Hugh Sykes, Trustee

Trustees *Sir Hugh Sykes; Lady Sykes.*

Information available Accounts for 1996/97 were on file at the Charity Commission, but without a list of grants.

General This trust was set up in 1987 for general charitable purposes by Sir Hugh Sykes and his wife Lady Sykes. It supports local charities in South Yorkshire and Derbyshire, some major UK charities and a few medical charities. The trust had assets of £2.1 million by 1999/2000, comprised largely of capital and revenue donated by the founders. 'It is the policy of the trust to distribute income and preserve capital.' Existing commitments are expected to absorb income until 2003 when the trustees plan to review their grant-making policy.

The trust gave £175,000 in grants during 1999/2000. Recent commitments include support for a number of medical charities including Mencap, St Luke's Hospice and Westcare. The Prince's Youth Business Trust had been supported for a number of years.

Exclusions The trust does not normally support a charity unless it is known to the trustees. Grants are not made to individuals.

Applications Applications can only be accepted from registered charities and should be in writing to the correspondent. In order to save administration costs, replies are not sent to unsuccessful applicants. If the trustees are able to consider a request for support, they aim to express interest within one month.

The Sylvanus Charitable Trust

Animal welfare, Roman Catholic

£146,000 (1998)

Beneficial area Worldwide

Vernon Miles & Noble,
5 Raymond Buildings, Gray's Inn,
London WC1R 5DD

Tel. 020 7242 8688

Correspondent J C Vernor Miles, Trustee

Trustees *J C Vernor Miles; A D Gemmill; W E Vernor Miles.*

Information available Full accounts were on file at the Charity Commission.

General The trust was founded by Claude, Countess of Kinnoull, of California, USA, who was primarily interested in animal welfare and causes connected to the Roman Catholic religion as taught to and accepted by Catholics before the second Vatican Council (the trust places an emphasis on traditional teachings and practices). Most of the trust's money goes to animal welfare causes.

The trust makes mainly annual donations, a number of which are to organisations which the founder supported in her lifetime. Not many new causes or unsolicited applications are supported.

The trust has divided the accounts into two sections, the sterling section and the dollar section.

Sterling section

In 1998 this section had assets of £2 million, its income was £75,000 and 13 grants were made totalling £80,000, 9 of which were recurrent from the previous year.

By far the largest grant was £30,000 to Fraternity of St Pius X – Switzerland, also the major beneficiary in the previous year. Other grants over £5,000 were: £10,000 to Worth School Appeal, £8,000 to Mauritian Wildlife Foundation and £5,000 each to FRAME and Oeuvre d'Assitance aux Betes d'Abattoirs. Other grants ranged between £1,000 and £4,000 including those to the following animal organisations: Lynx Educational Trust, Liga Olhanense dos Amigos dos Animais Abandonods and RSPCA.

Dollar section

In 1997 this section had assets of $1.5 million (about £1 million), its income was $38,000 (about £25,000) and donations totalled $99,000 (about £66,000). In its annual report the trust again noted that more than the net income was donated in grants, which reflected the increase in the capital value of trust investments.

In total, 11 grants were made (10 were recurrent from the previous year). The largest grant went to Monterey Institute of International Studies in California ($30,000), also the major beneficiary in the previous year. Four grants of $10,000 each were awarded, all going to animal organisations including: Redwings Horse Sanctuary, Ventana Wilderness Sanctuary and Wildlife Conservation Society. The only non-animal beneficiaries in this section were Georgetown University ($5,000) and Oratorian Community ($3,000).

Applications In writing to the correspondent. Please note, the trust is not seeking applications as the income is usually fully committed.

The Stella Symons Charitable Trust

General

£59,000 (1997/98)

Beneficial area UK, with a possible preference for Warwickshire

20 Mill Street, Shipston on Stour, Warwickshire CV36 4AW

Correspondent J S S Bosley, Trustee

Trustees *Mrs M E Mitchell; J S S Bosley; Mrs K A Willis.*

Information available Full accounts were on file at the Charity Commission.

General In 1998/99 the trust had an income of £50,000 and an expenditure of £60,000. In 1997/98 the trust had assets of £829,000 and an income of £50,000. It gave over 200 grants totalling £59,000, only three of which were not for £200: £10,000 to Shakespeare Hospice, £100 to British Red Cross and £10 to King George's Fund for Sailors.

A wide range of causes were supported especially health, welfare, children and youth. While both UK and local charities were supported, the trust has shown some preference for the Midlands, particularly Warwickshire. Beneficiaries included Centrepoint, Frontline Project, Hackney Quest, Neuromuscular Society,

Nuneaton Boys Club, Peter Pan Playgroup, West Midlands Autistic Society, York Minster Fund and Youth Clubs Scotland.

Exclusions No grants to individuals.

Applications In writing to the correspondent.

The T.U.U.T. Charitable Trust

General, but with a bias towards trade union favoured causes

£108,000 (1998/99)

Beneficial area Worldwide

Congress House, Great Russell Street, London WC1B 3LQ

Tel. 020 7637 7116   **Fax** 020 7637 7087

Correspondent J L Wallace, Secretary

Trustees *Lord Christopher; J Knapp; J Monks; A Tuffin; M Walsh.*

Information available Accounts were provided by the trust but without a grants list.

General The trust was set up by the Trade Union movement in 1969 for the sole purpose of owning the unit trust management company. It was the intention that profits distributed by the company should go to good causes rather than individual shareholders. It is a requirement of the trust deed that all trustees must be trade unionists, the intention being to ensure that causes benefiting should broadly be those that would be supported by the movement.

During 1998/99 the trust had an income of £119,000 and assets of £1.7 million. Charitable donations of £108,000 were made (£94,000 1997/98). After taking into account expenses, £152,000 was transferred to the assets. Although the trust does not publish a specific list of grants, their newsletter gives details of the causes they support. Those to benefit included: Hope and Homes for Children, providing a small family home for ten children in Mozambique; Basement Project, helping to provide a range of services for excluded young people; Special Care Baby Unit at St. Peter's Hospital in Chertsey providing an urgently needed piece of life saving equipment; The GAP Foundation in The Gambia helping in their Crop Planting

project; Dogs for the Disabled for training dogs to help with a range of tasks; and Contact the Elderly to help recruit volunteer drivers.

The trustees aim to continue their policy of providing funds for a wide range of potential beneficiaries.

Applications In writing to the correspondent.

The Tajtelbaum Charitable Trust

Jewish, welfare

£282,000 (1996/97)

Beneficial area Generally UK and Israel

17 Western Avenue, London NW11 9EH

Tel. 020 8455 8516

Correspondent Mrs I Tajtelbaum, Trustee

Trustees *Mrs I Tajtelbaum; I Tajtelbaum; M Tajtelbaum; E Tajtelbaum; E Jaswon; H Frydenson.*

Information available Full accounts were on file at the Charity Commission up until 1996/97.

General Unfortunately we have been unable to update the following information since the last edition of this guide.

The trust makes grants to orthodox synagogues and Jewish educational establishments, and to homes for older people and hospitals, generally in the UK and Israel.

In 1996/97 the trust's assets totalled £1.4 million and it had an income of £427,000, mainly derived from rental income and Gift Aid donations. Grants totalled £282,000, of which 24 over £1,000 were listed in the accounts. These ranged up to £112,000.

The principal grant of £112,000 was given to Friends of Arad. Other larger grants were £28,000 to Gur Trust, £25,000 to Friends of Horim and £18,000 to Huntingdon Foundation.

Applications In writing to the correspondent.

Talteg Ltd

Jewish, welfare

£109,000 (1999)

Beneficial area UK, with a preference for Scotland

90 Mitchell Street, Glasgow G1 3NA

Correspondent F S Berkeley, Secretary

Trustees *F S Berkeley; M Berkeley; A Berkeley; A N Berkeley; M Berkeley; Miss D L Berkeley.*

Information available Accounts were on file at the Charity Commission, but without a grants list or a narrative report.

General In 1999 the trust had assets of £2.4 million and an income of £262,000, including £169,000 in donations. Grants totalled £109,000. Unfortunately, no grants list was included with the accounts.

No grants list has been available since 1993 when the trust had an income of £175,000 (£134,000 from donations) and gave £92,000 in grants. Of the 48 grants made in the year 34, including the larger grants, were to Jewish organisations. British Friends of Laniado Hospital received £30,000 and £20,000 each was given to Centre for Jewish Studies and Society of Friends of the Torah. The other grants over £1,000 were to JPAIME (£6,000), Glasgow Jewish Community Trust (£5,000), National Trust for Scotland (£2,300) and Friends of Hebrew University of Jerusalem (£1,000).

The remaining grants were all for less than £1,000 with several to Scottish charities including Ayrshire Hospice (£500), Earl Haig Fund – Scotland (£200) and RSSPCC (£150). Other small grants went to welfare organisations, with an unusual grant of £800 to Golf Fanatics International.

Applications In writing to the correspondent.

The Tanner Trust

General

£178,000 (1998/99)

Beneficial area UK and overseas

PO Box 4207, Worthing, West Sussex BN11 1PW

Tel. 01903 709229

Correspondent Mrs L Whitcomb

Trustees *Lucie Nottingham; Alice Williams; Peter Youatt.*

Information available Full accounts were on file at the Charity Commission.

General This trust was established by Margaret Daphne Tanner. In 1998/99 it had an income of £513,000, mainly Gift Aid donations; this excludes a legacy of £4.3 million from the settlor. In the year 126 grants totalling £178,000 were made.

Grants were given to UK and international causes, including a number of local organisations, particularly in the south of England. A wide range of organisations received grants, many of which were supported in the previous year.

The largest grant of £50,000 went to Farms for City Children. Grants of £5,000 each were made to Sudan Crisis Appeal and British Retinitis Pigmentosa Society.

The trust awarded 2 grants of £3,000, 2 of £2,500, 11 of £2,000 and 58 of £1,000. Organisations receiving grants included Friends of Saffron Walden Library (£3,000); Second Chance (£2,500); £2,000 each to Birkenhead Youth Club, Cornwall Country Playingfields Association, West Kirby Residential School, St Christopher's Fellowship and British Trust for Conservation Volunteers; and £1,000 each to Action Water, Earthwatch Europe, YMCA, Woodland Trust and Welfare Community Project.

The remainder of grants were all for under £1,000. Beneficiaries included Salvation Army, Snowdrop Trust, Arthritis Care, Sense, Shelter, Truro Christmas Toy Appeal and Whizz Kidz.

Exclusions No grants to individuals.

Applications The trust states that unsolicited applications are, without exception, not considered. Support is only given to charities that have previously been supported by the trust or those already known to the trustees.

The Tay Charitable Trust

General

£130,000 (1999/2000)

Beneficial area UK, with a preference for Scotland

6 Douglas Terrace, Broughty Ferry, Dundee DD5 1EA

Correspondent Mrs Elizabeth A Mussen, Trustee

Trustees *Mrs E A Mussen; G C Bonar; Miss Z Mussen.*

Information available Financial information was provided by the trust.

General In 1999/2000 the trust had assets of £3 million and an income of £166,000. Grants totalled £130,000, and management and administration costs were a low £1,300. All types of charity are considered by the trust. Four grants, those over 2% of the income, were listed in the accounts. They were Ninewells Cancer Campaign (£10,000) and £5,000 each to Byre Theatre, Ninewells Neurosurgery Unit and RNLI.

Exclusions No grants to individuals.

Applications No standard form, applications in writing to the correspondent, including a financial statement. An sae is appreciated.

C B & H H Taylor 1984 Trust

Quaker, general (see below)

£136,000 (1998/99)

Beneficial area West Midlands, Ireland and overseas

c/o Home Farm, Abberton, Pershore, Worcestershire WR10 2NR

Correspondent W J B Taylor, Trustee

Trustees *Mrs E J Birmingham; J A Taylor; W J B Taylor; Mrs C H Norton; Mrs C M Penny; T W Penny; R J Birmingham.*

Information available Full accounts and guidelines were provided by the trust.

General The trust's geographical areas of benefit are:

- organisations serving the West Midlands
- organisations outside the West Midlands where the trust has well-established links
- organisations in Ireland
- UK-based charities working overseas.

The general areas of benefit are:

- the Religious Society of Friends (Quakers) and other religious denominations
- healthcare projects
- social welfare: community groups; children and young people; older people; people who are disadvantaged and disabled; people who are homeless; housing initiatives; counselling and mediation agencies
- education: adult literacy schemes; employment training; youth work
- penal affairs: work with offenders and ex-offenders; police projects
- the environment and conservation work
- the arts: museums and art galleries; music and drama
- Ireland: cross-community health and social welfare projects
- UK charities working overseas on long-term development projects.

The work and concerns of the Religious Society of Friends receive 75% of grants. The trust favours specific applications. It does not usually award grants on an annual basis for revenue costs. Applications are encouraged from minority groups and woman-led initiatives. Grants, which are made only to or through registered charities, range from £500 to £3,000. Larger grants are seldom awarded.

In 1998/99 the trust had assets of £5.7 million and an income of £132,000. Management and administration totalled only £850. Grants were awarded to 105 organisations in the year totalling £136,000. The largest grant was £32,000 to Warwickshire Monthly Meeting, which also received the largest grant in the previous year. No other grant was for over £5,000. There were 52 grants awarded between £1,000 to £3,000 including those to Cape Town Quaker Peace Centre, Birmingham Settlement, Birmingham Association of Youth Clubs, Relate, Prisoners of Conscience, Oxfam Mozambique, Edith Cadbury Nursery School and Bible Lands Society.

Beneficiaries of smaller grants under £1,000 included Midland Spastic Association, Terrence Higgins Trust, Citizens Advocacy South Birmingham, BYV Adventure Camps, National Missing Persons Helpline and Urban Wildlife Trust.

Exclusions The trust does not fund: individuals (whether for research, expeditions, educational purposes, etc.); local projects or groups outside the West Midlands; or projects concerned with travel or adventure.

Applications There is no formal application form. Applicants should write to the correspondent giving the charity's registration number, a brief description of the charity's activities, and details of the specific project for which the grant is being sought. Applicants should also include a budget of the proposed work, together with a copy of the charity's most recent accounts. Trustees will also wish to know what funds have already been raised for the project and how the shortfall will be met.

The trust states that it receives more applications than it can support. Therefore, even if work falls within their policy they may not be able to help, particularly if the project is outside the West Midlands.

Trustees meet twice-yearly in May and November.

Applications will be acknowledged if an sae is provided.

Rosanna Taylor's 1987 Charity Trust

General

£67,000 (1999/2000)

Beneficial area UK

Pollen House, 10–12 Cork Street, London W1S 3LW

Tel. 020 7439 9061 **Fax** 020 7437 2680

Correspondent A J Winborn, Assistant Secretary

Trustees *The Cowdray Trust Limited.*

Information available Accounts were on file at the Charity Commission.

General In 1999/2000 the trust had assets totalling £1.7 million and an income of £29,000. Five grants were

made totalling £67,000, three of the recipients had been supported in the previous year.

During the year £33,000 was given to British Red Cross Society (£30,000), Burford Parochial Church Council (£20,000), Charities Aid Foundation (£16,000), World Villages for Children (£600) and Pearson Taylor Trust (£500).

The trust makes grants for general charitable purposes and past beneficiaries have included Cancer and Leukaemia in Childhood, Tree House Trust and Dhaka Ahsania Mission.

Exclusions No grants to individuals or non-registered charities.

Applications In writing to the correspondent. Acknowledgements are not sent to unsuccessful applicants.

The Ten Charitable Trust

Jewish

£66,000 (1996/97)

Beneficial area UK

27 Waterpark Road, Salford M7 4FT

Tel. 0161 834 7195

Correspondent M Halpern, Trustee

Trustees *M Halpern; J Halpern.*

Information available Accounts were available at the Charity Commission up until 1996/97, but without a grants list or a narrative report.

General Unfortunately we have been unable to update the following information since the last edition of this guide.

In 1996/97 the trust's assets totalled £194,000 and the income was £47,000, mainly from donations. Grants totalled £66,000. Further information was unavailable for that year.

The most recent grants list on file at the Charity Commission was for 1990/91 when grants totalled £111,000 and appeared to be given to Jewish charities. The largest grants were to Gur Trust (£15,000), Mishmeres Stam (£13,000) and Chasdei Yoel (£10,000).

Applications In writing to the correspondent.

The Loke Wan Tho Memorial Foundation

Environment, medical

£54,000 (1998/89)

Beneficial area Worldwide

PricewaterhouseCoopers,
9 Greyfriars Road, Reading RG1 1JG

Tel. 0118 959 7111

Correspondent Keith Westram

Trustees *Lady Y P McNeice; Mrs T S Tonkyn; A P Tonkyn.*

Information available Full accounts are on file at the Charity Commission.

General In 1998/99 the trust had assets of £1.6 million and an income of £62,000 from investments. Grants totalled £54,000. Most beneficiaries appear to receive one-off donations. The trust supports, environment/conservation organisations, medical causes and overseas aid organisations.

In total 17 grants were made, with the two largest going to Bird Life International for £13,000 (also the major beneficiary in previous years) and Flora and Fauna International for £12,000. Others grants were in the range of £1,000 to £5,000. Beneficiaries included World Wildlife Fund (£5,000), Global Cancer Concern (£4,000), Liverpool School of Tropical Medicine (£3,000), Scottish Seabird Centre (£1,500) and DEBRA (£1,000).

Applications In writing to the correspondent.

The Thompson Family Charitable Trust

Medical, veterinary, educational, general

£102,000 (1998/99), but see below

Beneficial area UK

Hillsdown Court, 15 Totteridge Common, London N20 8LR

Tel. 020 8445 4343

Correspondent Roy Copus

Trustees *D B Thompson; P Thompson; K P Thompson.*

Information available Accounts were on file at the Charity Commission.

General The trustees will consider applications from all types of charities but are particularly interested in the following sectors:

- medical
- veterinary
- educational.

The largest single grant made by the trust to date was for about £1.5 million for the construction of a school building. The report states that the bulk of its income is currently being accumulated with a view to funding other large capital projects in the future.

The trustees would like to note that they have a preference for making donations to charities with low administration costs i.e. charities staffed largely by volunteers.

The trust had assets of £23 million, £21 million of this was invested in short-term bank deposits. The income for 1998/99 was £1.9 million. It made 98 grants totalling £102,000. The grants list was made up of 17 grants over £1,000, 11 of £500 to £750, 69 of £100 to £200 and 1 of £50.

Larger grants went to Totteridge Manor Association (£15,000), Queen Elizabeth Hospital Children's Fund and Racing Welfare Charities (£10,000 each) and Grendley Charitable Trust (£9,000). Grants of £5,000 went to Chaucer – St Bernard's Hospital, Great Ormond Street Children's Charity, King Edward VI Aston School, One to One Project and TBA Equine Fertility.

Other recipients included Royal Veterinary College Animal Care Trust (£4,000); Arthritis and Rheumatism Council for Research and John Durkan Leukaemia Trust (£1,000 each); Stable Lads Welfare Trust (£600); Babes in Arms and Hope Nursery (£500 each); £200 to Peter Pan Playgroup, Samaritans and Shaftsbury Homes; and £100 each to Exhall Grange Project, Hope UK and White Lodge Children's Centre.

Applications In writing to the trustees.

The Thompson Fund

Medical, welfare, education, general

£54,000 (1998/99)

Beneficial area UK, with a preference for Sussex

83 Church Road, Hove, East Sussex BN3 2BB

Tel. 01273 772200

Correspondent The Trustees

Trustees *P G Thompson; P J Thompson; M H de Silva.*

Information available Full accounts are on file at the Charity Commission.

General In 1998/99 the trust had assets of £879,000, an income of £59,000 and gave grants totalling £54,000. Grants ranged from £250 to £5,000 and were made to 37 organisations, many of these were recurrent.

Two grants of £5,000 were made to Kemp Town Crypt Community Association and Institute of Neurology (University College London). South Downs Council for Voluntary Service received £4,500 and Motor Neurone Disease Association received £3,000. Other large grants went to The Chichester Cathedral Trust (£1,750), Martlet's Hospice, Live Music Now!, Canine Partners for Independence (all £1,500), Sense (£1,300) and Cot Death Society (£1,200).

Among those receiving grants of under £1,000 were Alzheimer's Disease Society and Calibre (both £750), Land & City Families Trust (£600), Disability Aid Fund, The Dystonia Society and Lupus UK (all £500).

The trust showed a preference for locally-based organisations, among those supported were Carers for Brighton and Hove (£1,600) and Cruse, Brighton and Hove (£300).

Exclusions No personal applications; grants only to other charitable and similar organisations.

Applications In writing to the correspondent.

The Thornton Foundation

General

£98,000 to organisations (1999/2000)

Beneficial area UK

Stephenson Harwood, 1 St Paul's Churchyard, London EC4M 8SH

Tel. 020 7329 4422

Correspondent Richard Thornton, Chair

Trustees *R C Thornton, Chair; Mrs S J Thornton; A H Isaacs; H D C Thornton; J G Powell.*

Information available Full accounts were provided by the trust.

General The object of the foundation is to make grants to charities selected by the trustees. The principal guideline of the trust is to use the funds to further charitable causes where their money will, as far as possible, act as 'high powered money', in other words be of significant use to the cause. Only causes which are known personally to the trustees and/or which they are able to investigate thoroughly are supported. The trust states it is proactive rather than reactive in seeking applicants.

In 1999/2000 the trust had assets of £4.7 million, the income for the year was £95,000. After administration expenses of £8,300 grants totalling £104,000 were made, including £5,800 in educational grants to individuals.

Grants ranged from £1,000 to £20,000, although only five grants were of £10,000 or more. Beneficiaries included Mary Rose Trust (£20,000), Peper Harow Foundation (£13,000), Hope House (£10,000), Prisoners of Conscience (£5,000), Children Action Rocket Enterprise (£1,500) and £1,000 each to Alone in London, BREAK – Parents of Handicapped Children, The Matthew Trust, Scope and Wolfson College, Cambridge. Out of the 24 grants made to organisations, 6 were supported in the previous year.

Applications The trust strongly emphasises that it does not accept unsolicited applications, and, as it states above, only organisations that are known to one of the trustees should consider seeking support.

The Thornton Trust

Evangelical Christianity, education, relief of sickness and poverty

£92,000 (1998/99)

Beneficial area UK and overseas

Hunters Cottage, Hunters Yard, Saffron Walden, Essex CB11 4AA

Tel. 01799 526712

Correspondent D H Thornton, Trustee

Trustees *D H Thornton; Mrs B Y Thornton; J D Thornton.*

Information available Full accounts were on file at the Charity Commission.

General Unfortunately we have been unable to update the information for this trust since the last edition of this guide.

The principal activities of the trust are the 'promotion of and the furtherance of education and the evangelical Christian faith and assisting in the relief of sickness, suffering and poverty'. The trust mainly supports churches, missionary societies and colleges/bible schools, but also gives to some non-Christian causes. In 1998/99 the trust had assets of £1.8 million and an income of £95,000, £35,000 of which came from Gift Aid. Grants to 74 organisations totalled £92,000, over half of these had been supported in 1997/98.

The three largest grants went to Keswick Convention (£25,000), Africa Inland Mission (£22,000) and Tearfund (£13,000). Other recipients of grants of £5,000 and over included Scripture Union (£7,500); St Andrew's Church, Hertford (£7,100); Youth with a Mission (£6,500); and £5,000 each to Meadow's Community Church, Over Baptist Church and Radcliffe Missionary College.

Beneficiaries of £1,000 to £4,000 included Tyndale House (£4,000), Universities and Colleges Christian Fellowship (£3,000), Bible Society (£2,500), Society for International Ministries (£1,500) and Barnabas Trust (£1,000). About 20 grants were made for under £1,000, recipients included Hospice in the Weald, Kingdom Trust, Log Wheel Trust, Relationship Foundation and Sizewell Hall Christian Centre.

Applications The trust states: 'Our funds are fully committed to charities which the trustees have supported for many years and we regret that we are unable to respond to the many calls for assistance we are now receiving.'

The Three Oaks Trust

Welfare (see below)

£186,000 to organisations (1998/99) but see below

Beneficial area Overseas, UK, with a preference for West Sussex

PO Box 243, Crawley, West Sussex RH10 6YB

Trustees *The Three Oaks Family Trust Co. Ltd.*

Information available Full and detailed accounts were on file at the Charity Commission.

General In 1998/99 this trust's assets totalled £6.4 million and it had an income of £234,000. Grants were approved totalling £378,000, of which £186,000 was paid to organisations and £15,000 to individuals. The remainder was reserved for future commitments; £33,000 to be paid in 2000 and £124,000 to be given during 2001–2005.

Of the grants to organisations donated during the year, £165,000 was given in grants of over £1,000 to 22 charities, most of which were registered charities. Some beneficiaries received more than one grant. Overseas projects received a total of £48,000. In its annual report, the trust listed the following categories shown with some examples of beneficiaries:

Projects which aid people with psychological or emotional difficulties
* Horsham Counselling Service (£10,000)
* The Information Shop for Young People (£4,000)
* Coventry Day Centre which supports individuals with psychological problems, for example, alcohol or drug abusers (£8,000)
* Relate (£5,000)

Educational projects where there is a special needs element
* The Fellowship of St Nicholas, a day care centre and support group for parents and children (£20,000)
* The Helen Arkell Centre for Dyslexia, which gives support to individuals and families living in the community – towards families staying together (£5,000)
* West Sussex County Council towards a psychotherapeutic service for children (£4,000)

Physical disability

- Disability Aid Fund (£11,000)
- Medical Foundation for the Victims of Torture (£5,000)

Welfare – illness

- The Raynauds and Scleroderma Association towards the salary of a welfare worker (£15,000)

Medical research

- The Royal Free Hospital (£5,000)

Environmental issues

- SUSTRANS – promoting the use of cycle paths (£5,000)

Overseas aid

- Help the Aged – ICARE towards a sight saving project in India
- Sightsavers for sight saving projects overseas.

Applications The trust states in its annual report that it intends to continue supporting the organisations it has supported in the past and is not planning to fund any new projects in the near future. To save administrative costs, it does not respond to requests unless it is considering making a donation.

The Thriplow Charitable Trust

Higher education and research

£71,000 (1998/99)

Beneficial area Preference for British institutions

PO Box 243, Cambridge CB3 9PQ

Correspondent Mrs E Mackintosh, Secretary

Trustees *Sir Peter Swinnerton-Dyer; Dr Harriet Crawford; Dr Karen Sparck Jones; Prof. Christopher Bayly.*

Information available Full accounts and guidance to applicants were provided by the trust.

General The charity was established by a trust deed in 1983. Its main aims are the furtherance of higher and further education and research, with preference given to British institutions. Projects which have generally been supported in the past include contributions to research study funds, research fellowships, academic training schemes, computer facilities and building projects. Specific projects are preferred rather than contributions to general running costs. Typically, the value of grants have been in the range of £3,000 to £15,000.

In 1998/99 the trust had assets of £3.4 million and an income of £83,000. Grants totalling £71,000 were given to 19 organisations (£110,000 in 1997/98).

The largest grants of £10,000 each went to Breakthrough Breast Cancer and Cambridge Foundation. Other recipients included West Dean College (£6,500), University of Sheffield and Marine Biological Association (£6,000 each), WellBeing and M Beaufort Institute of Theology (£5,000 each), Sidney Sussex College and Bournemouth & Poole College (£3,000 each), Northern School of Contemporary Dance (£1,400) and Oxford Youth Works (£500).

Exclusions Grants can only be made to charitable bodies or component parts of charitable bodies. In no circumstances can grants be made to individuals.

Applications There is no application form. A letter of application should specify the purpose for which funds are sought and the costings of the project. It should be indicated whether other applications for funds are pending and, if the funds are to be channelled to an individual or a small group, what degree of supervision over the quality of the work would be exercised by the institution.

Trustee meetings are held twice a year – in spring and in autumn.

The Tisbury Telegraph Trust

Christian, overseas aid, general

£65,000 (1998/99)

Beneficial area UK and overseas

35 Kitto Road, Telegraph Hill, London SE14 5TW

e-mail rogero@howzatt.demon.co.uk

Correspondent Mrs E Orr, Trustee

Trustees *John Davidson; Alison Davidson; Eleanor Orr; Roger Orr; Sonia Phippard.*

Information available Full accounts were provided by the trust.

General In 1998/99 the trust's assets totalled £80,000 and its income was almost entirely comprised of Gift Aid donations of £77,000. Grants totalling £65,000 were made to 60 organisations. Over half of these were made to either Christian or overseas aid related charities, although a wide range of organisations were supported.

The largest donation was £10,000 to Mid Hertfordshire Churches – Romania. Other larger grants were St Mary's PCC (£5,800), St Paul's PCC (£5,000) and Community of Celebration (£4,000). A total of 15 grants were made in the range of £1,000 to £3,500, recipients included Help the Aged (£3,500), Ethiopiaid (£3,000), World Vision (£2,500), Tearfund (£2,000), Christian Aid (£1,200) with £1,000 each to Crosslinks, Scope and Southwark Habitat for Humanity.

The remainder of grants were for under £1,000 and were mostly for amounts less than £500. Those to benefit included: Bible Society (£900); NSPCC (£600); Oasis Trust (£400); £300 each to Leprosy Mission, Samaritans and Traidcraft Exchange; Autistic Society and BibleLands (£250 each); Missionary Aviation Fellowship (£200); Ramblers' Association (£100); and RNLI (£50).

The grants list was made up of a mix of new and previously supported organisations.

Exclusions No grants for individuals towards sponsoring expeditions or courses.

Applications In writing to the correspondent. However, it is extremely rare that unsolicited applications are successful and the trust does not respond to applicants unless an sae is included.

The Tolkien Trust

Christian – especially Catholic, welfare and general

£60,000 (1998/99)

Beneficial area UK, with a preference for Oxfordshire

3 Worcester Street, Oxford OX1 2PZ

Tel. 01865 722106

Correspondent Mrs Cathleen Blackburn

Trustees *John Tolkien; Christopher Tolkien; Priscilla Tolkien.*

Information available Full accounts were on file at the Charity Commission.

General The trust's main assets are the copyright in certain works of J R R Tolkien. This provides the trust with its income, and although there is no permanent endowment, there should always be an income from book royalties. There appears to be a preference for Christian organisations, especially Catholic, then welfare and organisations in Oxfordshire.

In 1998/99 the income was £94,000, of which over £90,000 was from royalties. The trust gave 33 grants totalling £60,000.

Many of the beneficiaries, both UK and local had received grants in previous years. The largest were £13,000 to Find Your Feet Ltd, and £4,000 each to St Anthony's RC Church – Littlemore and Catholic Housing Aid Society. Five grants of £3,000, two of £2,500, two of £2,000 and five of £1,000 were awarded. Recipients included Bodleian Library – Oxford, Centre of St Martin's-in-the-Field, CAFOD, North Staffordshire Marriage Care, Oxford Marriage Care, Samaritans, St Barnabas Society, Shelter, Tabley Trust and Wrexham Concern Trust.

The remainder of grants were in the range of £150 and £800, but were generally for smaller amounts, including those to Council for the Amnesty International (£700), Protection of Rural England (£500), Christian Psychotherapy Foundation (£350), Safer World (£400) and Inter Faith Network (£150).

Exclusions No support for non-registered charities.

Applications In writing to the correspondent.

Tomchei Torah Charitable Trust

Jewish educational institutions

£70,000 (1998/99)

Beneficial area UK

Harold Everett Wreford, Harford House, 101–103 Great Portland Street, London W1N 6BH

Tel. 020 7637 8891 **Fax** 020 7580 8485
e-mail hew@dial.pipex.com

Correspondent A Frei, Trustee

Trustees *I J Kohn; S M Kohn; A Frei.*

Information available Full accounts were on file at the Charity Commission.

General This trust gives grants to Jewish educational institutions. Grants usually average about £5,000.

In 1998/99 the trust's assets were £58,000 and it had an income of £81,000 from Gift Aid donations. Grants totalled £70,000 and were made to 60 Jewish organisations, about two thirds of these were recurrent from the previous year.

By far the largest grant was £22,000 to Merkaz Hatorah. Other larger grants were £5,300 each to Chested Charity Trust and Parsha Limited, £3,500 to Woodstock Sinclair Trust and £2,500 to Notzer Chested.

Over 70% of grants were for amounts under £1,000, ranging from £40 to £900. Beneficiaries included Menorah Grammar School (£900) United Talmudical Academy (£430), Talmud Torah Education (£250) Friends of Bobov Foundation (£200), Jewish Learning Exchange (£150) and Holmleigh Trust (£40).

Applications In writing to the correspondent at any time.

The Tory Family Foundation

Education, Christian and medical

£80,000 (1998/99)

Beneficial area International and Kent, principally in the locality of Folkestone

The Estate Office, Etchinghill Golf, Folkestone, Kent CT18 8FA

Tel. 01303 862280

Correspondent P N Tory, Trustee

Trustees *P N Tory; J N Tory; Mrs S A Rice.*

Information available Full accounts were on file at the Charity Commission.

General The trust stated that grants are given predominantly to organisations local to Kent, particularly Folkestone, to benefit the community i.e. church halls, schools etc. Grants are also given to UK organisations if their work would benefit local people. A small number of grants are also given to overseas organisations.

The trust was established in 1984. By 1998/99 it had assets of £2.2 million and an income of £135,000. After expenses of £25,000 the trust gave 71 grants totalling £80,000, including a number to individuals. Many donations were recurrent from the previous year. The trust classified its grants as follows:

Local
Grants totalling £33,000 were given to 40 organisations and ranged from £100 and £5,000. Beneficiaries included Elam Village Hall (£3,000), Kent Wildlife Trust (£3,000), Metropole Arts Centre (£2,500) and Wye Rural Museum Trust (£2,000).

Health
Four grants were given totalling £13,000 and ranging from £100 to £10,000. Examples included East Kent Pilgrims' Hospice (£10,000), Countess Mountbatten (£500) and Lymphona Association (£200).

Education
Nine grants were given totalling £12,000 and were in the range of £250 to £2,000. Grants included Berenden School (£5,000), Population Concern (£2,000) and Electronic Aids for the Blind (£500).

Churches
One grant of £2,500 went to St Leonard's, Hyther .

Other
Three grants totalling £8,000 were given, ranging from £500 to £2,000. Examples included Woodland Trust (£2,000) and National Missing Persons Helpline (£500).

Overseas
Grants totalling £12,000 went to 14 organisations, ranging from £200 to £2,000. Grants of £2,000 each went to Apt Enterprise Development, Churches Commission, Marie Stopes International and Prisoners Abroad. Smaller grants included Sight Savers International (£1,000), UNICEF (£500) and humanitarian educational and long term projects (£100).

Exclusions Grants are given to registered charities only. Applications outside Kent are unlikely to be considered. No grants are given for further education.

Applications In writing to the correspondent. Applications are considered throughout the year.

The Towry Law Charitable Trust

Education, medical research

£319,000 (1998/99)

Beneficial area UK

Towry Law House, Western Road, Bracknell, Berkshire RG12 1RW

Tel. 01344 828009 **Fax** 01344 828205 **e-mail** dainslie@towrylaw.com

Correspondent D G Ainslie, Trustee

Trustees Hon. C T H Law; K H Holmes; D G Ainslie.

Information available Full accounts were on file at the Charity Commission.

General The trust makes grants for educational purposes for the benefit of people under 21, principally for children who are disabled, but also for medical research.

In 1998/99 the assets stood at over £2.9 million. It had an income of £375,000 of which £263,000 was covenanted income from a wholly owned subsidiary, Castle School Fees Ltd. Grants totalled £319,000 and ranged from £4,000 to £11,000. The trustees' report states that about 42% of grants were made to charities which specialise in helping or caring for children, or assisting children and young people with their education. Over 46% went to charitable bodies specialising in medical research or assisting people who are disabled or elderly.

In all 66 grants were made, all but 9 were recurrent. Eton College received two grants: £11,000 for bursaries and £10,000 for leadership awards. Other recipients of £10,000 were Berkshire Community Trust, Bristol Business School (University of the West of England), John Lister Postgraduate Medical Centre, Sargent Cancer Care for Children and University of Exeter. Other grants for the benefit of children included Barnardos, Children's Society, Children's World, NSPCC and Windsor and Maidenhead Adventure Playground.

Further grants in the area of medical research or helping people who are elderly or disabled included: Association for Spina Bifida and Hydrocephalus, Bristol Heart Foundation, National Star Centre for Disabled Youth, RNIB Sunshine School for Blind Children (Hydrotherapy Pool Appeal), SANE and Vitiligo Society.

Exclusions No grants to individuals, bodies which are not UK-registered charities, local branches or associates of UK charities.

Applications In October 2000 the trust stated that its grant-making policy was under review and new applications were not being considered.

The Toy Trust

Children

£250,000 (1998)

Beneficial area UK

British Toy & Hobby Association, 80 Camberwell Road, London SE5 0EG

Tel. 020 7701 7271

Correspondent Mrs Karen Baxter

Trustees The British Toy and Hobby Association; I H Scott; A Munn; N Austin; J Hunter.

Information available Full accounts were on file at the Charity Commission, without a full list of grants.

General This trust is administered by the British Toy and Hobby Association (BTHA) and all the trustees are also officers of the association. It makes grants to children's charities, including charities working in crisis situations which are connected with children.

In 1998 the trust had assets of £184,000, its income of £178,000 was derived mainly from fundraising events such as the Family Fun Day and a dinner dance. The BTHA also donated £38,000. Grants to 63 organisations totalled £250,000. The trust gave a list of the top seven donations. By far the largest grant went to Pre-school Learning Alliance for £80,000 (also the major beneficiary in the previous year). Other grants went to National Association of Toy & Leisure Libraries (£20,000), Toy Box (£15,000), Shelter (£6,700), Wirral Autistic Society and National Asthma Campaign (£6,500 each) and Africa Now (£6,000).

Applications In writing to the correspondent.

The Constance Travis Charitable Trust

General

£94,000 (1999/2000)

Beneficial area UK, with a preference for Northamptonshire

Quinton Rising, Quinton, Northamptonshire NN7 2EF

Tel. 01604 752424

Correspondent E R A Travis, Trustee

Trustees Mrs C M Travis; E R A Travis.

Information available Accounts were on file at the Charity Commission, but without a full list of grants.

General The trust was established in 1984 and by 1999/2000 had assets of £7.7 million. The income of the trust was £197,000 and grants were made totalling £94,000 (£117,000 in 1998/99). Although the trust has general charitable objects, there seems to be a preference for medical, welfare and educational causes and those based in Northamptonshire. Only larger grants over £4,000 were listed in the accounts. Beneficiaries were Macmillan Cancer Relief (£25,000), with £5,000 each to Harrow Development Trust, Northhamptonshire Association of Youth Clubs and Scope.

In recent years other recipients have included Age Concern – Northampton, Northampton High School, British Red Cross, NSPCC and Roy Castle Lung Cancer Foundation.

Exclusions No grants to individuals or non-registered charities.

Applications In writing to the correspondent.

Truedene Co. Ltd

Jewish

£184,000 (1996/97)

Beneficial area UK and overseas

Cohen Arnold & Co., 13–17 New Burlington Place, London W1X 2HL

Trustees H Laufer; M Gross; S Berger; S Laufer; S Berger; Mrs Sarah Klein; Mrs Z Sternlicht.

Information available Accounts were on file at the Charity Commission up until 1996/97, but without a grants list.

General Unfortunately we have been unable to update the following information since the last edition of this guide.

This trust's assets totalled £5 million in 1996/97. It had an income of £5,500, which was staggeringly different from the year before when it was £425,000. Donations totalled £184,000 (£7.8 million in 1995/96). Unfortunately a grants list was not included with the accounts at the Charity Commission since those for 1985/86, when grants were given to Jewish educational and religious organisations.

Applications In writing to the correspondent.

The Truemark Trust

General

£188,000 (1998/99)

Beneficial area UK only

PO Box 2, Liss, Hampshire GU33 6YP

Correspondent Mrs Judy Hayward

Trustees *Alan Thompson; Michael Collishaw; Michael Meakin; Richard Wolfe; Sir Thomas Lucas; Mrs W Collett.*

Information available Full accounts were on file at the Charity Commission.

General The trust supports small, local organisations and innovatory projects, with preference for neighbourhood-based community projects and innovatory work with less popular groups. The trust supported a wide range of organisations, its main areas of interest included groups working in the fields of community support, education, Christianity and those concerned with people who are young, elderly or disabled. Charities with locations ranging from Belfast to Leeds and Edinburgh to Brighton received grants.

Grants are usually one-off for a specific project or part of a project. Core funding and/or salaries are rarely considered.

In 1998/99 the trust had assets of £2.8 million and an income of £289,000.

It made 150 grants totalling £188,000 and ranging from £500 to £5,000. Administration costs were low at £2,100. Nearly 40% of grants were for £1,000 or more. Larger grants included £5,000 to Marlpool United Reformed Church – Ilkeston, £4,000 to Trail Blazers – at Feltham Young Offenders' Institution and £3,000 each to Tara Counselling & Personal Development Centre, University of Westminister and Age Concern – Teeside. The 20 recipients of £2,000 included Caerphilly YMCA, Norwich Youth for Christ, Peterborough Dial-A-Ride and Scouts – Truro & District Council.

Grants of £1,000 each included: 27a Access Art Space, Leicester; Bristol Shopmobility, Avon; Playspace, Bradford; Relate Keighley and Craven; Vauxhall Housing Co-operative, Liverpool; and YMCA, Wolverhampton.

Exclusions No grants to individuals, for scientific or medical research or for church buildings. General appeals from large UK organisations are not supported.

Applications In writing to the correspondent, including the most recent set of accounts, clear details of the need the project is designed to meet and an outline budget. Trustees meet four times a year (in March, June, September and December). Only successful applicants receive a reply.

Trumros Limited

Jewish

£212,000 (1999)

Beneficial area UK

14 Mayfield Garden, London NW4 2QA

Correspondent Mrs H Hofbauer, Trustee

Trustees *R S Hofbauer; Mrs H Hofbauer.*

Information available Full accounts were on file at the Charity Commission.

General This trust appears to support Jewish organisations only. In 1999 it had assets of £2.3 million and an income of £648,000, of which £418,000 came from rental income, £112,000 from donations and Gift Aid and £94,000 from a covenant from Emdastates Ltd. A total of

£212,000 was given in 128 grants, up from £80,000 in the previous year.

Over 40% of donations were for £1,000 or more, with the remainder being mainly for £500 or less. The three largest grants were: £20,000 each to Menorah Primary School, Centre for Torah Education Zichron Yaacov and Beis Yoseph Zvi Institutions. Other larger grants went to SOFOT (£11,000), General Cherra Kadish Jerusalem (£5,800), Oldos Aharon (£4,800), Jewish Learning Exchange (£2,000) and Gateshead Jewish Academy for Girls (£1,000).

Smaller grants included Beis Avrohom Synagogue (£600), London Jerusalem Academy, Friends of Ohr Someach and YMER (£500 each), Achiezer Assia (£200) and Israel Settlement Fund (£100).

Applications In writing to the correspondent, but note that the trust states it is already inundated with applications.

Tudor Rose Ltd

Jewish

£87,000 (1996/97)

Beneficial area UK

Martin and Heller, Accountants, 5 North End Road, London NW11 7RJ

Tel. 020 8455 6789

Correspondent The Secretary

Trustees *S Feldman; H F Feldman.*

Information available Accounts were on file at the Charity Commission, but without a grants list.

General The sparse accounts on file at the Charity Commission provide us with little information about this trust. It supports Jewish organisations and its grant-making has been growing steadily over the years it has been in existence; from £5,100 in 1993/94 to £87,000 in 1996/97.

In 1998/99 the trust had an income of £220,000 and an expenditure of £124,000. Further information was unavailable.

Applications In writing to the correspondent.

The Tufton Charitable Trust

Christian

£62,000 (1999)

Beneficial area UK

7 St James Square, London SW1Y 7JU

Trustees *Sir Christopher Wates; Lady Wates; J R F Lulham.*

Information available Full accounts were provided by the trust.

General The trust was registered in May 1989, as The Wates Charitable Trust, having since changed its name. The trustees have leased and adapted premises (at a cost of £587,000) for religious groups to hold retreats.

By 1999 the trust had assets of £739,000 and an income of £130,000. Grants totalled £62,000 and included six grants of £1,000 or more to organisations, four of which had also benefited the year before. Donations of less than 1,000 each totalled £1,800.

Grants listed in the accounts were to The Church of England (£29,000), Dartmoor Prison Chapel (£14,000), On the Move and Prison Fellowship (£5,000 each), London Goodenough Trust (£3,500) and Institute of Contemporary Christianity (£3,000).

Applications In writing to the correspondent including an sae.

The Douglas Turner Trust

General

£428,000 (1998/99)

Beneficial area West Midlands, particularly Birmingham; UK

1 The Yew Trees, High Street, Henley-in-Arden, Solihull B95 5BN

Tel. 01564 793085

Correspondent J E Dyke, Trust Administrator

Trustees *Sir Christopher Stuart-White; W S Ellis; D P Pearson; T J Lunt.*

Information available Full accounts were on file at the Charity Commission.

General The trust makes grants and loans to registered charities, mostly in the West Midlands. Most of the income is used to support charities on an annual basis, providing they can prove their need for continuing support. Grants are made to a variety of charities, most of which are local social welfare organisations. Awards are typically in the range of £1,000 to £5,000 but go as high as £40,000.

In 1998/99 the trust had assets of £13 million and an income of £438,000. Grants totalling £428,000 were made to 89 organisations. Management and administration fees were high at £57,000.

The largest grants were to Age Concern Birmingham TV Fund (£36,000), Worcester Cathedral Appeal Trust (£25,000) and £18,000 each to British Red Cross, Christian Aid, Oxfam and St Mary's Hospice. Other large grants were given to Orbit Housing Charitable Trust (£15,000), Birmingham Council for Old People (£12,000), Historic Churches Preservation Trust and Royal Academy of Arts (£10,000 each) and Acorn's Children's Hospice (£8,000).

Smaller grants went to Birmingham Settlement (£5,000), St Basil's Centre (£4,000), Birmingham Association of Youth Clubs and Birmingham Institute for the Deaf (£2,500 each), St Augustine's Church (£1,000), Dodford Children's Holiday Farm and Sutton Coldfield Sea Cadets (£750 each) and Charities Information Bureau (£200).

Exclusions No grants to individuals or non-registered charities.

Applications Telephone enquiries before formal applications are welcomed. Applications must include the latest annual report and accounts. There are no application forms.

The Florence Turner Trust

General

£145,000 (1998/99)

Beneficial area UK, but with a strong preference for Leicestershire

c/o Harvey Ingram Owston, 20 New Walk, Leicester LE1 6TX

Tel. 0116 254 5454 **Fax** 0116 255 4559

Correspondent The Clerk

Trustees *Roger Bowder; Allan A Veasey; Caroline A Macpherson.*

Information available Full accounts were provided by the trust.

General The trust supports a wide range of charities, particularly in the city and county of Leicester.

In 1998/99 it had assets of £4.6 million and an income of £175,000. Grants to 131 organisations totalled £145,000.

Grants of £1,000 and above were listed in the accounts and went to 40 organisations. The three largest donations went to Leicester Grammar School for bursaries, the library and prizes (£20,000), Leicester Charity Organisation Society (£11,000) and Heart of the National Forest Foundation – Visitor Centre (£10,000).

The remainder of listed grants were in the range of £1,000 to £5,000. Recipients included: University of Leicester – Children's Asthma Centre (£5,000); Willowbrook Primary School (£4,000); YMCA Leicester (£3,800); £2,000 each to Age Concern – Leicester, Leicestershire Guild of the Disabled and Tommy's Campaign – Leicester Royal Infirmary; Marie Curie Cancer Care (£1,600); Salvation Army – Leicester (£1,200); and £1,000 each to Charnwood Shelter Project, MacIntyre Housing Association and Woodland Trust. A further 91 grants below £1,000 were given totalling £37,000.

Exclusions The trust does not support individuals for educational purposes.

Applications In writing to the correspondent. Trustees meet every eight or nine weeks.

The R D Turner Charitable Trust

General

£63,000 (1998/99)

Beneficial area UK and overseas, with a preference for the Midlands

1 The Yew Trees, High Street, Henley-in-Arden, Solihull, West Midlands B95 5BN

Tel. 01564 793085

Correspondent J E Dyke, Administrator

Trustees *W S Ellis; D P Pearson; T J Lunt; Sir Christopher Stuart-White.*

Information available Full accounts were on file at the Charity Commission.

General The trust makes grants to the same beneficiaries each year, providing they satisfy the trustees of the need for continuing support.

In 1998/99 the trust's assets totalled £1.5 million, it had an income of £54,000 and made grants to 22 organisations totalling £63,000.

Beneficiaries of larger grants were Ironbridge Gorge Museum Development Trust and British Red Cross Disabled Club - Kidderminster (£10,000 each), Far Forest Youth Centre and St Giles' Cathedral – Edinburgh (£5,000 each) and £4,000 each to National Trust and National Trust for Scotland.

Other grants were mainly between £1,000 and £2,000. A number of organisations in the Midlands benefited, for example, League of Friends of The Kidderminster Hospitals, St John Ambulance – Kidderminster and St Peter's Church – Upper Arley. The remaining grants were to a variety of organisations, for example, Country Landowners Association Charitable Trust, Pattaya Orphanage – Thailand, Sail Training Association and Wildfowl and Wetlands Trust.

Exclusions No grants to non-registered charities or to individuals.

Applications In writing to the correspondent with a copy of your latest annual report and accounts. There are no application forms. The trustees meet in May, August, October and December to consider applications, which should be submitted in the month prior to each meeting. Please note, the trust states that its funds are at present fully committed. Telephone enquiries may be made before submitting an appeal.

The Ulting Overseas Trust

Training of Christian workers

£124,000 (1998/99)

Beneficial area Overseas only

62 The Drive, Rickmansworth, Hertfordshire WD3 4EB

Correspondent Nigel Sylvester, Director/Secretary

Trustees *Dr J B A Kessler; J S Payne; A J Bale; C Harland; Dr D G Osborne; Mrs M Brinkley; D Ford; T B Warren.*

Information available Full accounts were provided by the trust.

General The objects of the trust are to support those training for Christian ministry, teachers in theological education, theological institutions in developing countries and those seeking to assist in developing countries.

In 1998/99 it had assets of £2.8 million and an income of £88,000. Charitable donations were made to 30 organisations totalling £124,000, with the largest going to Scripture Union International and IFES (£16,000 each) and Langham Trust (£13,000). These organisations are regularly the major beneficiaries.

Other grants went to Interserve and Nairobi Evangelical Graduate School of Theology – Oxford Centre for Mission Studies (£8,000 each), Pan African Christian College (£6,000), Asian Theology Seminary (£5,000), Central University College – Accra (£2,000) and All Nations Christian College (£1,000). All the beneficiaries were Christian causes including a number of Bible colleges throughout the world.

Applications The funds of the trust are already committed. Unsolicited applications cannot be supported.

The Ulverscroft Foundation

People who are sick and visually impaired, ophthalmic research

£178,000 to organisations (1998/99)

Beneficial area UK, with a special interest in the Leicester area; other English speaking countries, particularly Australia, New Zealand, Canada and the USA

No. 1 The Green, Bradgate Road, Anstey, Leicester LE7 7FU

Tel. 0116 236 4325   **Fax** 0116 234 0205

Correspondent Joyce Sumner, Secretary and Administrator

Trustees *P H Carr; Michael Down; Allan Leach; A W Price.*

Information available Report and accounts were provided by the trust.

General Formed in 1973, the foundation's aim is to help improve the quality of life for people who are blind and partially sighted (visually impaired). The foundation finances:

• eye operating machines

• specialised medical ophthalmic equipment

• research into eye diseases

• library services for people who are visually impaired or the housebound e.g. mobile libraries

• computerised reading & other equipment for the visually impaired. All financial help given by the foundation is made through channels such as NHS Trusts, hospitals, schools, libraries and groups for the visually impaired.

In 1998/99 the trust had assets of £6.8 million and an income of £806,000, including £80,000 in donations and legacies and £692,000 from the sale of Ulverscroft Large Print Books. Grants to 29 organisations totalled £178,000, 7 of which were recurrent ophthalmological research grants.

Twelve grants over £1,000 were listed in the accounts. The largest grants went to Great Ormond Street Children's Hospital Ophthalmology Unit (£73,000), St Mary's Chair of Ophthalmology – Imperial College (£43,000), Institute of Child Health (£23,000) and University of New South Wales (£15,000). Other grants included £5,000 to HMP Lindholme Braille Project, £2,000 to Electronic Aids for the Blind, £1,500 to Buckinghamshire Libraries and £1,000 each to Hampshire Libraries and Soundaround.

Two grants totalling £1,300 were paid to individuals.

Exclusions Applications from individuals are not encouraged. Generally, assistance towards salaries and general running costs are not given.

Applications In writing to the correspondent. Applicants are advised to make their proposal as detailed as possible, to include details of the current service to people who are visually impaired, if any, and how the proposed project will be integrated or enhanced. If possible the trust asks for an estimate of how many people who are visually impaired use/will use the service, the amount of funding obtained to date, if any, and the names of other organisations to whom they have applied.

The success of any appeal is dependent on the level of funding at the time of consideration.

The trustees meet four times a year to consider applications.

United Trusts

General

£503,000 (1999/2000)

Beneficial area UK, but at present mainly north west England

PO Box 14, 8 Nelson Road, Nelson Road, Liverpool L69 7AA

Tel. 0151 709 8252 **Fax** 0151 708 5621
e-mail information@unitedtrusts.org
website www.unitedtrusts.org
Correspondent John Hugh Pritchard
Trustees *Up to 20 people elected by members.*

Information available Literature was available from United Trusts.

General The trusts promote tax-free charitable giving (mainly but not exclusively payroll giving) through the formation and development of workplace controlled charitable funds (called workplace trusts), and local citizen controlled charitable funds (called local trust funds) for distribution through United Trusts within the donor-designated local areas.

Grants are given to benefit charities serving within the local communities concerned. Potentially all charities are eligible, including in some areas grants are for the relief of individual cases of poverty and hardship (these are routed through 'umbrella charities'). United Trusts is not in itself a payroll-giving agency charity. Services are supplied in association with United Way, Charities Aid Foundation and all payroll-giving agency charities.

In 1999/2000 the trust had an income of £422,000 and an expenditure of £411,000. Grants totalled £503,000. No further information for this year was available.

The distributions by local United Trust Funds for 1995/96 (and 1994/95) were as follows:

Merseyside	£51,000	(£79,000)
Greater Manchester	£3,500	(£3,000)
Cheshire	£400	(£100)
Cumbria	£2,400	(£900)
Lancashire	£3,000	(£6,000)
Other	£700	(-)
Total	£61,000	(£89,000)

The breakdown of distributions by United Trusts Workplace Trusts in 1995/96 (and 1994/95) was:

Merseyside	£139,000	(£145,000)
Cumbria	£30,000	(£35,000)
Cheshire	£13,000	(£4,000)
Lancashire	£5,000	(£6,000)
Greater Manchester	£400	(£1,000)
Total	£187,000	(£191,000)

Exclusions 'Grants to individuals, called 'top-up funds', are made through 'umbrella charities' in cases where the government does not feel it has a responsibility.'

Applications It is requested that applications should be made to the secretary of the local United Trust Fund or Workforce Trust concerned if the address is known. Otherwise applications may be made to the correspondent at the above address.

The Van Neste Foundation

Third world, disabled and older people, religion, community and Christian family life, respect for the sanctity and dignity of life

£217,000 (1999/2000)

Beneficial area UK, especially the Bristol area, and overseas

15 Alexandra Road, Bristol BS8 2DD
Tel. 0117 973 5167
Correspondent Fergus Lyons, Secretary
Trustees *M T M Appleby, Chair; F J F Lyons; G J Walker.*

Information available Full accounts were on file at the Charity Commission.

General The trustees currently give priority to the following:

1. Third world
2. Disabled and older people
3. Advancement of religion
4. Community and Christian family life
5. Respect for the sanctity and dignity of life.

These objectives are reviewed by the trustees from time to time but applications falling outside are unlikely to be considered.

In 1999/2000 the trust had assets of £5.2 million and an income of £264,000.

After administration expenses of £18,000 (of which £13,000 went towards secretary's fees), 29 grants totalling £217,000 were given to 41 organisations.

The grants distributed can be broken down as follows:

Category	No. of grants	£
Third world	4	20,000
Disabled and older people	9	25,000
Advancement of religion	6	3,000
Community and Christian family life	5	65,000
Respect for the sanctity and dignity of life	5	104,000

The full list of grants with the accounts included the purpose of each grant made. The largest grants went to: Bristol University for a Chair in Ethics in Medicine (£72,000) and the housing estate health project (£50,000); and Family Education Trust for a grant for research into sex education (£20,000). The remainder of grants were between £250 and £6,000. Grants of £5,000 or more went to Franciscan Sisters of the Divine Motherhood for training African sisters (£6,000) and £5,000 each to Familia Trust for secure homes for orphan children in India, RW Bailey Memorial Trust for a training project for people who are disabled and Bristol Family Mediation Service towards running costs. Smaller grants went to Scope Bristol for an evening club for people who are disabled (£3,000), The Towersey Foundation for music therapy for palliative care patients (£1,000), Wesleyan Reform Church for a youth and child care project (£500) and £250 each to Grateful Society for older people and St Mary's Church Bath for an orphanage in Tanzania.

The trustees have approved grants to be made in the coming year amounting to £194,000. These will be met out of the income from the general fund. The foundation is connected with another charity, the Amazon Trust. While there are no financial relations between the charities, they share a majority of trustees.

Exclusions No grants to individuals or to large, well-known charities. Applications are only considered from registered charities.

Applications Applications should be in the form of a concise letter setting out the clear objectives to be obtained which must be charitable. Information must be supplied concerning agreed funding from other sources together with a timetable for achieving the objectives of the appeal and a copy of the latest accounts.

The foundation does not normally make grants on a continuing basis. To keep overheads to a minimum, only successful applications are acknowledged. Even then it may be a matter of months before any decision can be expected, depending on the dates of trustees' meetings.

The Vardy Foundation

Christian, education in the North East, general

£2.2 million (1997/98)

Beneficial area UK

c/o Reg Vardy plc, Houghton House, Wessington Way, Sunderland, Tyne & Wear SR5 3RJ

Tel. 0191 516 3636

Correspondent P Vardy, Trustee

Trustees *P Vardy; Mrs M B Vardy; R Dickinson.*

Information available Full accounts were on file at the Charity Commission.

General The trust was set up in 1989 with general charitable objectives. In 1997/98 it had an income of £356,000, from donations of £154,000 and investment income of £171,000. The trust's grant-making capacity of £2.2 million, way in excess of its income, appears to have come from funds transferred from the assets which decreased by £2.2 million in the year to £5.2 million.

Grants over £1,000 were given to 44 organisations and were listed in the accounts, 16 of these had been supported in the previous year. Grants were in the range of £1,000 to £50,000, but were mainly for smaller amounts. At least 15 were made to individuals. By far the largest donations were £1.3 million to Bethany Church and £542,000 to Emmanuel College in Gateshead, a regular beneficiary.

Other larger grants included Crusaders in the North (£50,000), Christian Action Research and Education Trust and County Durham Foundation (£25,000 each), Kepplewray Project (£18,000) with £10,000 each to Christian Institute and Youth for Christ.

Other smaller grants, ranging from £2,000 to £5,000, included those to Bible

Mission International, Caring for Life, NSPCC, Project SEED, The Red Cross and Save the Children Fund.

Unlisted grants to other charitable causes totalled £8,500, with 'other' individuals receiving £7,000.

Applications In writing to the correspondent.

The Vincent Wildlife Trust

Wildlife, environmental conservation

£301,000 (1998)

Beneficial area UK

3–4 Bronsil Courtyard, Eastnor, Ledbury, Herefordshire EHR8 1EP

Correspondent Dr Johnny Birks, Secretary

Trustees *Hon. Vincent Weir, Chair; Ronald Yarham; Michael Macfadyen.*

Information available Full accounts were on file at the Charity Commission.

General The trust continues to 'promote the study of, and research and education in relation to wildlife conservation and the establishment, control, development and maintenance of nature reserves'. The trust carries out mammal research and conservation, publishes survey reports and species leaflets and, where possible, seeks to purchase nature reserves when suitable sites become available. It also supports other wildlife charities.

In 1998 the trust's assets totalled £20 million. The income was £1.7 million, mainly from investments, but also from donations. Most of the income was used to fund the trust's own projects. Grants totalled £301,000.

Only four grants were given, these were to Herpetological Conservation Trust (£178,000), British Butterfly Conservation Trust (£100,000), Plantlife (£15,000) and Nottingham University (£9,000). Three of the donations were recurrent from the previous year.

The trust stated in October 2000 that their income is used mainly to fund their own conservation work, and any donations in future will be limited to just three named organisations.

Applications See above.

The William and Ellen Vinten Trust

Industrial education, training and welfare

£76,000 (1999/2000)

Beneficial area UK with a preference for Suffolk

Greene & Greene Solicitors, 80 Guildhall Street, Bury St Edmunds, Suffolk IP33 1QB

Tel. 01284 762211

Correspondent *Mrs K Callender, Secretary to the Trustees*

Trustees *D J Medcalf, Chair; W P Vinten; Major R C Bracewell; J V Crosher; M Shallow; A C Leacy.*

Information available Accounts were on file at the Charity Commission, but without a list of grants.

General The objects of the trust are the:

- furtherance of education and the welfare of people who are employees of industrial firms
- advancement of industrial training of beneficiaries by promoting research and development as part of education
- recreation and improvement of the public environment.

'A number of jointly funded projects, improving the teaching environment and politics, have come to fruition. Reports from schools showing that the proportion of students taking science and technology subjects in the sixth form, and their attainment, has improved since the initiative started about five years ago.'

In 1999/2000 this trust has assets of almost £2 million and an income of £75,000. Grants totalling nearly £76,000 were distributed between the following categories: education – £74,000 and welfare – £1,500. The trust had commitments for the next year of £64,000.

Applications This trust states that it is a pro-active charity which does not seek unsolicited applications.

The Viznitz Foundation

Not known

£14,000 (1991/92)

23 Overlea Road, London E5 9BG

Tel. 020 8557 9557

Correspondent H Feldman, Trustee

Trustees *H Feldman; E Kahan; E S Margulies.*

Information available Accounts were on file at the Charity Commission, but without a grants list or narrative report and only up to 1991/92.

General In 1991/92, the trust's assets totalled £776,000, it had an income of £163,000 and its total expenditure was only £17,000. Grants totalled £14,000.

Further or up-to-date information was unavailable on this trust, this entry was included in the last edition of this guide.

Applications In writing to the correspondent.

The Scurrah Wainwright Charity

Social reform, root causes of poverty and injustice

£165,000 to organisations (1998/99)

Beneficial area Preference for Yorkshire and South Africa

5 Tower Place, York YO1 9RZ

Tel. 01904 641971

e-mail joreilly@lifebyte.com

Correspondent J Reilly

Trustees *R S Wainwright; J M Wainwright; H A Wainwright; M S Wainwright; T M Wainwright; P Wainwright; H Scott; R Bhaskar.*

Information available Full accounts were on file at the Charity Commission, with a detailed review of their work.

General The trust supports a wide range of charitable projects with an emphasis on social reform and tackling the root causes of poverty and injustice. Applications from the north of England,

particularly Leeds and Yorkshire, generally will be given strong priority; the trustees also have an interest in Zimbabwe. In exceptional cases, the trust may make a personal award to an individual in recognition of some outstanding personal commitment relevant to the trust's interests.

Grants have ranged from less than £100 to over £25,000, but there is no minimum or maximum. Support may be given in stages, for example a £30,000 grant over three years via three annual payments of £10,000. Trustees prefer to receive a progress report within a year of making a grant, but this is not a condition of support.

In 1998/99 the trust had assets of £1.9 million and an income of £95,000. A total of £169,000 was given in 23 grants. Oxfam receives the largest grant each year, £39,000 in 1998/99, for its work in South Africa. An annual grant is also given to Zimbabwe Educational Foundation (based in Leeds), which received £10,000 this year. Other larger grants included those to FunderFinder (£7,800), Public Concern at Work (£6,000) and Caring for Life (£5,000).

Other recipients included AVSED (£4,000), Mount School (£3,000), University of Ulster (£2,800), Burley & Hyde Park Community Safety Project and Institute of Race Relations (£2,500 each), Baby Milk Action and Bridgeside (£2,000 each), University of York (£1,500) and Huddersfield Haranbee Association and Community Self-Build Agency (£1,000 each).

Four grants were made to individuals totalling £4,100.

Exclusions No grants for buildings, medical research or the welfare of animals.

Applications In writing to the correspondent. Applicants are expected to provide background information about themselves and/or their organisation, the work they wish to pursue and their plans for its practical implementation, which will involve an outline budget and details of any other sources of finance. The most recent income and expenditure and balance sheets should be included.

Trustees meet in March, July and November. Applications should be received by the first day of the preceding month.

The F J Wallis Charitable Settlement

General

£60,000 (1998/99)

Beneficial area UK, with some interest in Hampshire and Surrey

25 Chargate Close, Burwood Park, Walton-on-Thames, Surrey KT12 5DW

Correspondent F H Hughes, Trustee

Trustees *Mrs D I Wallis; F H Hughes; A J Hills.*

Information available Full accounts were on file at the Charity Commission.

General In 1998/99 the trust had assets of £1.3 million and an income of £88,000, administration costs were £8,700 for the year. The trust gave grants totalling £60,000. Only those grants made over £100 were listed in the accounts and were made to 110 organisations. About half of the grants were recurrent from the previous year.

The three largest grants went to British Red Cross Kosovo Appeal (£5,000) with £1,000 each to Care International UK – Sudan Crisis Appeal and Koestler Award Trust. About 90% of grants were for £500.

The majority of grants went to UK medical and welfare organisations with recipients including Association for Post Natal Illness, Barnardos, Children's Head Injury Trust, Defeating Deafness, Elimination of Leukaemia Fund, Invalids at Home, Prison Reform Trust, Research into Ageing, Salvation Army, WellBeing and Whizz-Kidz.

A small number of grants went to organisations working internationally and some in the fields of relief and the environment. Among those to benefit were Sight Savers International, OXFAM, VSO, WWF – UK, World Society for the Protection of Animals and Young People's Trust for the Environment.

Exclusions No grants to individuals or to local charities except those in Surrey or in Hampshire.

Applications In writing to the correspondent. No telephone calls. Applications are not acknowledged. Trustees meet in March, June, September and December and applications need to be received the month prior to the trustees' meeting.

Warbeck Fund Ltd

Jewish, the arts, general

£134,000 (1998/99)

Beneficial area UK and overseas

2nd Floor, Pump House, 10 Chapel Place, Rivington Street, London EC2A 3DQ

Tel. 020 7739 2224 **Fax** 020 7739 5544

Correspondent The Secretary

Trustees *Michael Brian David; Jonathon Gestetner; Neil Sinclair.*

Information available Full accounts were on file at the Charity Commission.

General Unfortunately we have been unable to update the following information since the last edition of this guide.

In 1998/99 the trust had assets of £156,000, which have been steadily decreasing over a number of years (£279,000 in 1997/98). The income was only £18,000. It gave over 120 grants totalling £134,000 ranging from £10 to Samaritans to over £26,000 to Chichester Festival Theatre Trust.

There were only 29 grants of £1,000 or more, at least half of which were to Jewish organisations and synagogues. Beneficiaries included Joint Jewish Charitable Trust (£11,000), British ORT (£10,000), World Jewish Relief (£6,000) and West London Synagogue (£3,700), London Symphony Orchestra (£2,600), Hope Charity (£2,500), Regain Trust for Sports Tetraplegics (£1,400) and London Ripieno Society (£1,000).

Almost all the remaining grants were for under £500 and were to similar types of organisations to those listed above: mainly Jewish and arts though there were a few for medical and welfare.

The funds are fully committed. The trust expects to distribute all its income and assets over the next few years.

Exclusions No grants to individuals or non-UK registered charities.

Applications According to the correspondent, it may not be worth writing to the trust.

The Ward Blenkinsop Trust

Medicine, social welfare, general

£204,000 to organisation (1998/99)

Beneficial area UK, with a special interest in the Merseyside area

Broxbury, Broomers Hill Lane, Codmore Hill, Pulborough, West Sussex RH20 2HY

Correspondent J H Awdry, Trustee

Trustees *A M Blenkinsop; J H Awdry; S J Blenkinsop; C A Blenkinsop; A F Stormer; H E Millin.*

Information available Full accounts were on file at the Charity Commission.

General The trust currently supports charities in the Merseyside area and charities of a medical nature, but all requests for funds are considered.

In 1998/99 the trust had an income of £279,000 and gave grants to: 60 charities totalling £204,000; 16 ex-employees totalling £8,100; and £4,600 in Christmas boxes for people of pensionable age.

Two-thirds of all grants are given to organisations in the Merseyside area for general charitable purposes, including Clatterbridge Cancer Research Trust (£20,000), National Museums and Galleries on Merseyside (£3,000), Wirral Inroads (£2,000) and £1,000 each to Birkenhead CAB and Mersey Park Playgroup. Grants were given to other organisations in north west England including Cheshire County Council which received £25,000 for its Youth Art Initiative and £15,000 for its South Africa Initiative, and Manchester Youth Theatre received £7,000.

UK groups were supported with a preference for medical charities, especially those connected with cancer. Beneficiaries included Royal Academy of Dancing Special Needs Programme (£17,000), International Spine Research Trust (£5,000), St John Ambulance (£4,000), National Asthma Campaign (£3,000), Roy Castle Lung Cancer Foundation (£1,500), Age Concern and British Polio Fellowship (£750 each) and Cancer Research Campaign (£50).

Exclusions No grants to individuals.

Applications In writing to the correspondent.

Mrs Waterhouse Charitable Trust

Medical, health, welfare, environment, wildlife, churches, heritage

£294,000 (1998/99)

Beneficial area UK, with an interest in Lancashire

25 Clitheroe Road, Whalley, Clitheroe BB7 9AD

Correspondent D H Dunn, Trustee

Trustees *D H Dunn; E Dunn.*

Information available Full accounts were on file at the Charity Commission.

General The trust mainly makes small recurrent grants towards core costs to charities in the Lancashire area. The trust's main object is to provide funds on a regular basis to augment the income of the charities so they can maintain and improve their services. A limited number of more substantial awards are also given, usually for capital projects. Grants range from £1,000 to £50,000.

In 1998/99 the trust had assets of £6.5 million and grants totalling £294,000 were given as follows: £132,000 was given to organisations in Lancashire; £65,000 to Lancashire branches of UK charities; and £97,000 was given to UK organisations for projects outside Lancashire.

Grants were broken down as shown below:

	No. of grants	Total
Medical and health		
general	17	£115,000
research	5	£24,000
children	8	£25,000
Welfare in the community		
older people	4	£8,000
children	10	£29,000
people who are deaf or blind	4	£14,000
general	7	£16,000
Environment and wildlife	6	£44,000
Church and heritage	5	£19,000

The largest grants were to BHRV Health Care NHS Trust (£50,000), National Trust Lake District Appeal (£25,000), Christie Hospital NHS Trust and Royal Society for the Protection of Birds (£10,000 each), St Peters Church – Salesbury (£7,000) and 16 grants of £5,000 each included those to Marie Curie Cancer Care, Diabetics Association, East Lancashire Hospice Fund, Multiple Sclerosis Society and National Kidney Research.

Other grants included £3,000 each to Fight for Sight, Parkinson's Disease Society and Winged Fellowship Trust and £2,000 each to Council for the Protection of Rural England, Friends of the Lake District, Salvation Army – Blackburn Citadel and Vincentian Volunteers.

Exclusions No grants to individuals

Applications In writing to the correspondent. There is no set time for consideration of applications, but donations are normally made in March each year.

The Weavers' Company Benevolent Fund

Young people at risk from criminal involvement, young offenders and prisoners' organisations

£184,000 (1999)

Beneficial area UK

Saddlers' House, Gutter Lane, London EC2V 6BR

Tel. 020 7606 1155 **Fax** 020 7606 1119
e-mail charity@weaversco.co.uk

Correspondent Freda Newcombe, Clerk

Trustees *The Worshipful Company of Weavers.*

Information available Full accounts and a detailed report and grants list were made available by the trust, along with a copy of their Guidelines for Applicants.

General In 1999 the trust had assets of £7 million and an income of £627,000 (£303,000 came from a grant of shares from the Weavers' Company General Fund). Management and administration of the fund totalled £40,000. Grants for the year totalled £184,000.

The trust supports projects helping:

* young people who for any reason are at risk from criminal involvement

* young offenders

* prisoners and ex-prisoners.

Applications may be considered from projects anywhere in the UK. The company only considers applications for specific projects, where any grant made can be applied for an identifiable purpose. It prefers to support small or new, community-based organisations rather than long-established, large, national or UK organisations. It is particularly interested in innovative projects. It is willing to consider applications for grants for equipment and capital projects, as well as salaries and running costs. Grants are usually in the range of £5,000 to £15,000, although applications for smaller amounts from small or new organisations are welcomed. Grants were listed under two categories, major grants (including renewals) and casual donations.

In 1999 26 major grants totalling £160,000 were awarded. The largest was for £20,000 to the Centre for Adolescent Rehabilitation. Other recipients were Safe Ground and Sutton Pastoral Foundation (£10,000 each), Centre 63 and Mansfield Settlement (£9,000 each), East London Schools Fund and Norfolk ACRO, (£7,000 each), City Road Youth Counselling Service (£5,000) and Warehouse Christian Trust (£1,000).

There were 43 'Casual donations' made totalling £15,000, these were mainly for £250. Beneficiaries included Barnswood Campsite, Cheshire Crimebeat, Heritage of London Trust, Homeless Action in Barnet, St Paul's Cathedral, Ting-a-Ling Youth Club and Whaddon Lynworth & Priors Neighbourhood Project. Two grants over £1,000 were included in this category going to Lord Mayor's Appeal and Prison Phoenix Trust.

Exclusions No grants to individuals, or to non-registered charities – unless they are intending to apply for charitable status. Grants are not normally made in response to general appeals from large, well-established charities whose work does not fall within one of the above categories.

The company does not provide long-term funding to any one organisation, and it would wish to be assured that all other possible sources of finance had been explored and that efforts were being made to obtain long-term funding from statutory and voluntary sources.

It does not often support central or umbrella bodies, but prefers assisting projects directly working in its chosen fields.

It is not the company's policy to provide for running costs or deficit funding for established projects, nor to provide grants to replace start-up funding provided by other statutory or charitable funds.

Applications A detailed Guidelines for Applicants is available from the trust.

Applicants should write in the first instance to the correspondent with details of their requirements and include a set of their most recent accounts. If an application is accepted for further consideration, an application form will be issued. The trustees meet three times a year in February, June and October. Applications may be submitted at any time and will be put to the next appropriate committee. 'Applicants should take into account the time it takes to process an application, raise queries and organise an assessment visit.'

Successful applicants are required to provide regular reports on progress.

The Mary Webb Trust

General

£289,000 (1998/99)

Beneficial area UK and overseas

Cherry Cottage, Hudnall Common, Little Gaddesden, Berkhamsted, Hertfordshire HP4 1QN

Correspondent Mrs C M Nash, Trustee

Trustees *Martin Ware; Mrs Jacqueline Fancett; Mrs Cherry Nash.*

Information available Full accounts were on file at the Charity Commission.

General The trust has continued its policy of generally supporting smaller charities. In 1998/99 the trust had assets of £1.1 million generating an income of £69,000. Grants, which appear to have been paid from the income and the assets, were given to 135 organisations and totalled £289,000.

The trust broke down its grant giving as follows :

	1998/99	(1997/97)
Social services	£94,000	(£98,000)
Health	£85,000	(£71,000)
Environment	£36,000	(£59,000)
International	£29,000	(£43,000)
Culture and recreation	£23,000	(£28,400)
Education and research	£14,000	(£15,000)
Philanthropic	£5,300	(£16,000)
Religion	£2,800	(£200)
Development/housing	nil	(£11,000)

Grants ranged from £500 to £20,000. The largest grants were to RNLI (£20,000), Gurkha Welfare Trust (£15,000), Little Gaddesden School Governers and The National History Museum (£10,000 each), Soil Association (£7,500), Peter

Pan Playgroup (£5,500) with £5,000 each to 15 charities including The Apage Trust, Berkshire Multiple Sclerosis Therapy Centre, Devoran Key Preservation Society, Eaton Bishop Church Spire and Bells Appeal, Elimination of Leukaemia Fund, Fenland Archaeological Trust, Hockley Church, Rupert Fund, Waveney Area Community Transport and ZSL Adopt an Animal.

Other beneficiaries included RAF Benevolent Fund (£3,000), £2,000 each to Deafblind UK, Listening Books and Riders for Health, £1,000 each to Berwick Swan and Wildlife Trust, Cambridge Victim Support, Chesham High School, Hope for Children, Queen Victoria Seamen's Rest, SSAFA, Swansea YMCA, Tools for Self Reliance and Well Women Centre and £500 each to Motability and Warrington Rape Crisis and Counselling Service.

Exclusions No grants to individuals or non-registered charities.

Applications The trust has previously stated that they are 'concerned by the large number of appeals received during the year. They prefer to make their own enquiries and find it difficult to handle the large volume of documents and unsolicited accounts sent to them'.

Trustees meet quarterly in March, May, August and December; applications need to be received by the month prior to the trustees' meeting.

The Weinstein Foundation

Jewish, medical, welfare

£85,000 (1997/98)

Beneficial area Worldwide

32 Fairholme Gardens, Finchley, London N3 3EB

Tel. 020 8346 1257

Correspondent M L Weinstein, Trustee

Trustees *E Weinstein; Mrs S R Weinstein; M L Weinstein; P D Weinstein; Mrs L A F Newman.*

Information available Full accounts were on file at the Charity Commission.

General In 1998/99 the trust had assets of £1.6 million and an income of £54,000. It gave over 80 grants totalling £85,000, over half of which were recurrent. Management and administration costs

were high at £17,000. Donations ranged from £30 to £15,000, 17 grants were for over £1,000 with the vast majority being for less than £500. Most beneficiaries were Jewish organisations. The three largest grants were £15,000 to British Friends of Caniado Hospital and £10,000 each to Jewish Marriage Council and SAGE.

Other larger grants included those to Woodstock Sinclair Charitable Trust (£5,900), Norwood Child Care – Ravenswood (£5,200), Chevras Ezras Nitzrochim Trust (£2,300), Kupas Tzedaka Vochested (£2,000), National Chaplaincy Board (£1,500) and London Jewish Academy (£1,000).

Grants under £1,000 included those to World Jewish Relief (£800), British Council of the Sha'are Zedek (£600), Jewish Children's Holiday Fund (£400), Friends of Mercaz Beth Jacob (£300), Church Housing Trust (£250) and British Friends of Boys Town Jerusalem (£150).

A few non-Jewish charities were supported including Project SEED and Scope.

Applications In writing to the correspondent.

This entry was not confirmed by the trust but was correct according to information on file at the Charity Commission.

The Stella & Ernest Weinstein Charitable Trust

Jewish

£94,000 (1997/98)

Beneficial area UK

Landau Morley, Lanmor House, 370–386 High Road, Wembley, Middlesex HA9 6AX

Tel. 020 8903 5122

Correspondent M G Freedman, Trustee

Trustees *E Weinstein; Mrs S W Weinstein; M G Freedman; Mrs L A F Newman.*

Information available Full accounts were on file at the Charity Commission.

General Unfortunately we have been unable to update the information for this entry since 1997/98.

In that year the trust's assets totalled £237,000 and it had an income of

£153,000, mainly from Gift Aid donations. Grants totalled £94,000.

In total there were 22 beneficiaries during the year and the main ones were as follows: North West London Jewish Day School (£34,000), Torah Chesed and Jewish Care (both £10,000), Jewish Marriage Council (£8,600) and Emunal College (£5,500). The remaining beneficiaries were also Jewish and received grants ranging between £360 and £5,000.

Applications In writing to the correspondent. Applications are considered at any time.

The James Weir Foundation

Health, social welfare, heritage, research

£162,000 (1998)

Beneficial area UK, with a preference for Scotland

84 Cicada Road, London SW18 2NZ

Tel. 020 8870 6233 **Fax** 020 8870 6233

Correspondent The Trustees

Trustees *Dr George Weir; Simon Bonham; William Ducas.*

Information available Full accounts were on file at the Charity Commission.

General In 1998 the trust had assets of £5.7 million and an income of £188,000. Management and administration costs were high at £44,000. About 150 grants were made totalling £162,000.

Most of the grants were for £1,000; only 9 were for £2,000. Recipients of £2,000 included British Association for the Advancement of Science, Care Connect, Royal Air Force Benevolent Fund, Tommy's Campaign and Wiltshire Community Foundation.

There is a preference for charities in Scotland with a number of grants being recurrent from the previous year. Grants of £1,000 were given to a variety of organisations particularly in the fields of health, social welfare and research. Organisations to benefit included Alzheimer's Disease Society, British Institute for Brain-Injured Children, Brittle Bones Society, NSPCC, Prison Reform Trust, Roy Castle Lung Cancer Foundation, St Mungos, Scottish Association for Mental Health, University of Edinburgh Development Trust and Weston Spirit.

Other organisations to benefit included Edinburgh Book Festival, High School of Glasgow and Scottish Wildlife Trust.

Exclusions Recognised charities only. No grants to individuals.

Applications In writing to the correspondent. Distributions are made twice yearly in June and November. Applications should be received by May or October.

The Weldon UK Charitable Trust

Major arts-related projects

£54,000 (1998/99)

Beneficial area UK

4 Grosvenor Place, London SW1X 7HJ
Tel. 020 7235 6146 **Fax** 020 7235 3081
Correspondent J M St J Harris, Trustee
Trustees J M St J Harris; H J Fritze.
Information available Full accounts were on file at the Charity Commission.

General In 1998/99 the trust had assets of £367,000 and an income of £25,000. Two grants totalled £54,000. This trust appears to be regularly making grants from both its income and its capital.

During the year grants were given to Royal Opera House Theatre (£50,000) and Yehudi Menuhin School (£3,900), both of which were also supported in the previous year. In 1997/98 other beneficiaries were National Portrait Gallery, Royal College of Music Development Fund, B'nac B'rith Leo Baeck (London) Lodge Trust Funds and Great Ormond Street Children's Hospital.

Exclusions No grants to individuals.

Applications In writing to the correspondent, but the trust has stated that it is fully committed with existing projects until at least 2003.

Wessex Cancer Trust

Cancer prevention, early detection, care and research in Dorset, Hampshire, Wiltshire, the Isle of Wight and the Channel Islands

£542,000 to organisations and individuals (1998/99)

Beneficial area Dorset, Hampshire, Wiltshire, the Isle of Wight and the Channel Islands

Bellis House, 11 Westwood Road, Southampton SO17 1DL
Tel. 023 8067 2200 **Fax** 023 8067 2266
e-mail wct@wct.k-web.co.uk
Correspondent Chris Beagley, Chief Executive
Trustees Hon. Mrs C M Villiers, Chair; M H Le Bas; Dr C A Baughan; Mrs J E Beschi; Dr P M S Gillam; D A Hoare; Mrs M J Kernick; Dr B Moran; Dr J R Murray; P M Perry; Dr G Sharp; R Starr; Dr J Stutley; T Titheridge; Dr J E White; N L Woodford.
Information available Full accounts were provided by the trust.

General This trust 'is a regional cancer charity, committed to raising funds to improve cancer care by promoting cancer prevention; supporting patients, familes and carers; providing education and information for patients, families and professionals; and funding early detection and research throughout Dorset, Hampshire, Wiltshire, the Isle of Wight and the Channel Islands'.

In 1998/99 the trust's assets totalled £883,000, it had an income of £709,000 which included £541,000 raised through donations and other fundraising and its total expenditure was £857,000. Grants totalled £542,000 and are described below.

General fund

Family grants (£250 and under)	£44,000
Conference/training contributions	£4,700
Small equipment purchases	£6,900
General grants for early detection of and research into cancer	£146,000

Children's fund

Family grants (£250 and under)	£5,200
Annual children's weekend away & Christmas outing	£4,500
Equipment	£4,300
General grants for early detection of and research into cancer	£72,000

Radiotherapy fund

Dorset Cancer Centre Patient Facilities Refurbishment	£100,000
St Mary's Hospital Portsmouth Oncology Day Unit	£150,000
Wessex R/T Centre Patient Facilities Completion	£4,800

Grants given for the early detection of, and research into, cancer (from both the General Fund and the Childrens Fund) ranged between £3,100 and £33,000. Larger grants included £33,000 towards 'shared care/ENB Nurse Training Support have a personal connection', £28,000 for the development of methods for diagnosing malignant disease through tissue identification, £15,000 towards a colorectal cancer population screening survey leading to the establishment of a weekly secreening clinic (Winchester) and £14,000 towards a lecturer/practioner post in Paediatric Oncology Nursing which is shared between Southhampton University Hospitals (NHS) Trust and University of Southampton.

Applications On a form available from the correspondent. Applications are considered twice a year. The next trustees' meeting at the time of going to print, was set for May 2001, applications should be sent in the previous month. The previous meeting had been in November.

The Earl & Countess of Wessex Charitable Trust (*formerly* The Bagshot Park Charity)

General – but see below

£82,000 (1999/2000)

Beneficial area UK

Farrer & Co., 66 Lincoln's Inn Fields, London WC2A 3LH

Tel. 020 7242 2022

Correspondent Jenny Cannon

Trustees *Mark Foster-Brown; Abel Hadden; Denise Poulton; Henry Boyd-Carpenter; Malcolm Cockren.*

Information available Accounts were on file at the Charity Commission.

General This trust was established by Prince Edward and Sophie Rhys-Jones shortly after their marriage last year and was initially named after their Surrey home. It is now named after themselves, and is up and running. It received its initial income from proceeds of the sale of the BBC's video of the royal wedding.

Beneficiaries have so far been 'registered charities with which the Earl and Countess have a personal connection'. The trust provided a schedule of donations made, organisations supported included Belfast Activity Centre, Classworks Theatre, Crimestoppers, Gifts in Kind UK, Haddo Arts Trust, Tuberous Sclerosis Association and Wessex Children's Hospice Trust. The grant-making seems to show some preference for arts, medical and community projects, however, it is still in its early days and any strong patterns have not yet fully emerged.

Applications On a form available from the correspondent. Applications are considered twice a year. At the time of going to print meeting were to be held every six months, in mid-May and mid-November with the closing dates for applications being 1 May and 1 November respectively.

West London Synagogue Charitable Fund

Jewish, general

£57,000 (2000)

Beneficial area UK

33 Seymour Place, London W1H 6AT

Tel. 020 7723 4404

Correspondent Mrs Kay Colton, Co-ordinator

Information available Information was provided by the trust.

General The trust stated that it makes grants to both Jewish and non-Jewish organisations. In 1999 the trust's assets totalled £68,000. It had an income of £61,000, comprised of proceeds from a bazaar and donations. In the following year, 57 grants were distributed totalling £57,000.

The largest grants were £100,000 each to two main charities, RNIB Sunshine House School and Juvenile Diabetes Foundation. This represented 34% of the total distribution. The remaining grants ranged between £250 and £5,000 and were given to Jewish, welfare, medical and interfaith orgainisations.

In the previous year beneficiaries included West London Synagogue, Berkeley Street Club, Norwood Ravenswood, Friends of Progressive Judaism in the UK and Rabbi Winer's Welfare Fund.

Applications In writing to the correspondent.

The Westcroft Trust

International understanding, overseas aid, Quaker, Shropshire

£94,000 (1998/99)

Beneficial area Unrestricted, but with a special interest in Shropshire – causes of local interest outside Shropshire are rarely supported

32 Hampton Road, Oswestry, Shropshire SY11 1SJ

Correspondent Mary Cadbury

Trustees *Mary C Cadbury; Richard G Cadbury; James E Cadbury; Erica R Cadbury.*

Information available Full accounts were provided by the trust.

General Currently the trustees have five main areas of interest:

- international understanding, including conflict resolution and the material needs of the third world
- religious causes, particularly for social outreach, usually for the Society of Friends (Quakers) but also of those originating in Shropshire
- development of the voluntary sector in Shropshire
- special needs of those with disabilities, primarily in Shropshire
- development of community groups and reconciliation between different cultures in Northern Ireland.

The trustees favour charities with low administrative overheads and those which pursue clear policies of equal opportunity in meeting need. Printed letters signed by the great and good are wasted on them, as is glossy literature. Few grants are given for capital or endowment. The only support for medical education is for expeditions abroad for pre-clinical students. Medical aid, education and relief work in developing countries is supported, but only through UK agencies. International disasters may be helped in response to public appeals. The core of the trust's programme is regular support for a wide variety of work towards international peace and understanding, social welfare and those with disabilities.

In 1998/99 the trust had assets of £2.2 million and an income of £90,000. After expenses of £6,000, it gave grants totalling £94,000.

As in previous years, the categories which received the largest allocations from the trust were international understanding and overseas aid, accounting for 37% (£35,000) of the trust's donations.

Social services, health and education in Shropshire received 21% of donations (£20,000) and elsewhere in the UK – 16% (£15,000). Quaker activities around the country received 25% of donations (£23,000). Other donations totalling £1,200 were made during the year to conservation and unclassified causes. The grants were listed in the following categories by the trust:

Category	No. of grants	Total
Religious Society of Friends Central committees	3	£5,300
Meeting houses	4	£1,500
Other funds, institutions and appeals	13	£17,000
Shropshire social service	23	£14,000
Education in the county	5	£3,100
Disabilities, health and special needs	4	£2,800
Medical and surgical research	6	£2,900
National Health	1	£450
Disabilities and special needs	9	£4,000
Social service – England, Wales, Scotland	11	£5,800
Social service – Northern Ireland	4	£1,700
Overseas medical aid	18	£9,700
Education	15	£8,500
Relief work	14	£10,600
International understanding	7	£6,400
Conservation	2	£600
Unclassified	1	£600

Most grants were for less than £1,000, with only 22 for £1,000 or more. The two largest grants were for £9,900 (in three payments) to Woodbrooke College and £4,000 to Bradford University Department of Peace Studies. Other recipients over £1,000 included Quaker Peace and Service (£3,600), D E C Hurricane Appeal (£2,000), British Epilepsy Association (£1,700) and Pant Memorial Institute (£1,000).

Those receiving grants under £1,000 included Quaker Home Services (£850), REMEDI (£700), Macmillan Cancer Relief and Women's Royal Voluntary Service (£500 each), Shropshire Youth Association (£350), Friends World Committee for Consultation (£250), Liverpool One Parent Families Trust (£180) and Shrewsbury Prison Chaplaincy Fund (£120).

Exclusions Grants to charities only. No grants to individuals or for medical electives, sport, the arts (unless specifically for people with disabilities in Shropshire), repairs to church buildings or armed forces charities. Requests for sponsorship are not supported. Annual grants are withheld if recent accounts are not available or do not satisfy the trustees as to continuing need.

Applications In writing to the correspondent. There is no application form or set format but applications should be restricted to a maximum of three sheets of paper, stating purpose, overall financial needs and resources together with previous years accounts if

appropriate. No acknowledgement will be given. Replies to relevant but unsuccessful applicants will be sent only if a self-addressed envelope is enclosed. As some annual grants are made by Bank Giro, details of bank name, branch, sort code, and account name and number should be sent in order to save time and correspondence.

Applications are dealt with about every two months.

The Whitaker Charitable Trust

Music education, prison, farming & woodland education, countryside conservation and alternative spirituality

£217,000 (1998/99)

Beneficial area Preference for charities in Nottinghamshire, Northern Ireland and Scotland

21 Buckingham Gate, London SW1E 6LS
Tel. 020 7828 4091/8 **Fax** 020 7828 5049
Correspondent E R H Perks, Trustee
Trustees E R H Perks; D W J Price; Lady E J R Whitaker.
Information available Full accounts were provided by the trust.

General In recent years the main beneficiaries of this trust have been United World College of the Atlantic and the Kopple Goodman Project, they are also currently interested in the following fields:

- local charities in Nottinghamshire and East Midlands
- music education
- agricultural and silvicultural education
- countryside conservation
- Scottish and Northern Irish charities
- spiritual matters
- prison-related charities.

In 1998/99 the assets stood at £6 million and the income was £250,000. Grants totalling £217,000 were given to 74 organsiations. Over half the total went to Atlantic College which received £100,000. Other large grants included Koppel Goodman Family Housing Ltd (£20,000), Marlborough College (two grants totalling £17,000) and Bristol Cancer

Help Centre (£10,000). There were 37 other grants of £1,000 or more, recipients included Opera North (£5,000), Bassetlaw Hospice (£4,000), Leith School of Art (£3,000), Lincoln Cathedral Fabric Fund, Marlborough College (£2,000 each), and £1,000 each to Dyslexia Institute, Mencap Lincolnshire, Sail Training Association, DARE, Self-Help and Willow Trust.

Recipients of smaller grants under £500 included Countrywide Workshops, Game Conservancy Trust – Upland Research Group, Goal Line Youth Trust, Safety Zone, Scottish Chamber Orchestra and Weston Initiative for Conductive Education.

Exclusions Support is given to registered charities only. No grants are given to individuals or for the repair or maintenance of individual churches.

Applications In writing to the correspondent.

Humphrey Whitbread's First Charitable Trust

Churches, the arts, elderly, disability, AIDS, general, but see below

£84,000 (1998/99)

Beneficial area UK, with a possible preference for Bedfordshire and adjoining counties

Howards House, Church Lane, Cardington, Bedfordshire MK44 3SR
Tel. 01234 838251
Correspondent Mrs Shirley Morrell
Trustees H Whitbread; S C Whitbread; C R Skottowe.
Information available Full accounts were on file at the Charity Commission.

General In autumn 2000 we were informed that this trust was reviewing its policy. However, at the time of going to print no decisions had been made on this.

In 1998/99 the trust made grants totalling £84,000, which was larger than usual (previously around £60,000 each year). The average grant size was between £200 and £1,000, although larger grants were made. The trust had a preference for making grants in Bedfordshire and adjoining counties. Further information was not available.

In 1994/95 grants totalled £60,000. The larger grants went to Cambridge Arts Trust and Cardington PCC (£3,000 each), Albany Trust (£2,700), HAWKS Outdoor Venture (£2,000), and Employment Development Unit, Family Welfare Association, Lincoln Cathedral, New to London Project, NSPCC, St Margaret's Fire & Restoration Appeal and Water Well (all £1,000). No other grants were over £1,000.

A wide range of charities were supported in the fields of welfare, medical, disability, animal welfare, heritage, arts and churches.

Exclusions No grants to non-registered charities or individuals.

Applications In writing to the correspondent, for consideration throughout the year. Please note it is likely that the contact information for this trust will be changing.

The Simon Whitbread Charitable Trust

Education, family welfare, medicine, preservation

£125,000 (1997/98)

Beneficial area UK, with a preference for Bedfordshire

Dawson & Co., 2 New Square, Lincoln's Inn, London WC2A 3RZ

Correspondent E C A Martineau, Administrator

Trustees *Mrs H Whitbread; S C Whitbread; E C A Martineau.*

Information available Full accounts were on file at the Charity Commission.

General Unfortunately we were unable to update the information for this trust since the last edition of this guide.

Set up by Major Simon Whitbread in 1961, in 1997/98 the trust had assets valued at £4.4 million. The income was £126,000 and grants were made totalling £125,000. Most grants were for £1,000 or less.

In total 88 grants were made during the year, and about half were for medical or disability charities. The largest grants were £10,000 each to RNLI and Kings Medical Research. Grants of £5,000 went to six organisations, including Wildfowl and Wetlands Trust, Canine Partners for Independence and Telephones for the Blind.

Education organisations which benefited included John Bunyan Upper School and Community College (£1,500) and Alameda Middle School Technology Fund (£500). Three individuals also received educational grants.

Local organisations in Bedfordshire to benefit included: Age Concern – a local branch (£2,500 in two grants); and £1,000 each to Bedford Music Club and Bedfordshire and Northamptonshire MS Therapy Centre.

Exclusions Generally no support for local projects outside Bedfordshire.

Applications In writing to the correspondent. Acknowledgements are not given. Please do **not** telephone.

The Colonel W H Whitbread Charitable Trust

Health, welfare, general

£207,000 (1998)

Beneficial area UK, with an interest in Gloucestershire

Winckworth Sherwood, 35 Great Peter Street, London SW1P 3LR

Tel. 020 7593 5000 **Fax** 020 7593 5099

Correspondent R H A MacDougald

Trustees *M W Whitbread; J J Russell; R H J Steel.*

Information available Full accounts, with a detailed trustees' report were provided by the trust.

General In 1998 the trust had assets totalling £5.7 million and an income of £207,000. A total of £207,000 was given in 80 grants. They were given to a range of UK organisations, as well as local organisations particularly in Gloucestershire. The largest grant was £6,000 to Royal Green Jackets Museum. The four recipients of £5,000 each were Aldenham School General Charitable Trust, Leonard Cheshire Homes, St John

Ambulance – Gloucester and St John Ambulance – Gloucestershire.

Eight grants were given ranging from £2,000 to £4,000. The majority (67) were for £500 or £1,000. Examples of beneficiaries include Acorns Children's Hospice Trust, Battersea Dogs Home, Chipping Norton Theatre, East Gloucestershire NHS Trust, Gloucester Historic Churches, Holburne Museum, Mencap, Red Cross Gloucestershire and Save the Children Fund.

A total of £100,000 was transferred from the grant fund for distribution to a new charity, but no further details were given about this.

Applications In writing to the correspondent. Trustees meet quarterly. Please note, successful applicants must cash their cheques within three months of receipt or, unless there are special circumstances, it is the trust's policy to cancel the cheque.

A H and B C Whiteley Charitable Trust

Art, environment, general

£172,000 (1998 /99)

Beneficial area England, Scotland and Wales, with a special interest in Nottinghamshire

Marchant and Co., Regent Chambers, Regent Street, Mansfield, Nottinghamshire NG18 1SW

Tel. 01623 655111

Correspondent Edward Aspley

Trustees *E G Aspley; K E B Clayton.*

Information available Accounts were on file at the Charity Commission.

General The trust was established in 1990 and derives most of its income from continuing donations. The trust deed requires the trustees to make donations to registered charities in England, Scotland, and Wales but with particular emphasis on charities based in Nottinghamshire. Beneficiaries are varied, but the largest grant (which typically accounts for around 50% of the funds) usually, perhaps always, goes to the Victoria and Albert Museum.

In the year ending March 1999 the trust's income totalled £62,000; £3,700 came from donations and £58,000 was generated from its assets of £1.6 million. In the previous year it had an income of £449,000, most of which came from donations.

A total of 14 grants were made in the year ranging from £600 to £35,000. The largest seven grants accounted for a large proportion of grant expenditure, these were: Terry Marsh Bird Rescue (£35,000), National Trust (£30,000), King's School (£25,000), Mansfield Cat Protection League (£20,000) and £10,000 each to Cancer Research, Heart Foundation and a scout group.

The remainder of grants included those to Stepping Stones (£7,000), Mansfield Home Start (£6,000) and Jerry Green Foundation and Southwell 2000 (each £5,000).

When the above rather brief entry was sent in draft to the trust so that it could, if it wished, check its accuracy, the reply, from Marchants solicitors firm of which trustee E G Apsley is a partner, asked first 'for written confirmation that you will pay for the costs of providing you with the information that you have required'. Caution about such open-ended legal charges means that the entry remains unchecked.

Applications None are invited. The trust does not seek applications.

The Norman Whiteley Trust

Evangelical Christianity, welfare, education

£171,000 to organisations and individuals (1998/99)

Beneficial area Cumbria and worldwide

Fallbarrow, Rayrigg Road, Windermere, Cumbria LA23 3DL

Correspondent D Foster, Secretary

Trustees B M Whiteley; P Whiteley; D H Dickson; J J R Ratcliff.

Information available Full accounts were on file at the Charity Commission.

General The trust supports Christian charities in Cumbria. In 1998/99 the trust had assets of £2.3 million and an income of £179,000. Administration costs were high at £23,000, 13% of the income.

Grants were made totalling £171,000 (£131,000 in 1997/98).

The trust gives both to organisations and individuals. The largest grant of £43,000 went to the Bethsham Sheltered Housing Association. There were 23 grants given over £500 which were listed in the accounts, 12 of these were recurrent and at least 5 went to individuals. Grants under £500 totalled £4,000, information was not available on the beneficiaries.

Other larger grants went to Kindersingkrien (£22,000), Baptistenge (£14,000), Holy Trinity (£12,000) and £10,000 each to Lakes Christian Centre and Potteries Trust.

Smaller grants included those to Bibellesbund (£7,800), St Thomas' Church (£5,000), Sports Reach (£2,500), NISCU – Furness (£2,400) and Victor Training (£750).

Exclusions Whilst certain overseas organisations are supported, applications from outside of Cumbria are not accepted.

Applications In writing to the correspondent. Trustees meet to consider applications two or three times a year.

The Whitley Animal Protection Trust

Animal care and protection, conservation

£246,000 (1999)

Beneficial area UK and overseas

Edgbaston House, Walker Street, Wellington, Telford, Shropshire TF1 1HF

Tel. 01952 641651 **Fax** 01952 247441 **e-mail** info@gwynnes.com

Correspondent Paul Rhodes, Secretary

Trustees E Whitley, Chair; Mrs P A Whitley; E J Whitley; J Whitley.

Information available Full accounts were on file at the Charity Commission.

General The objects of the trust are to support organisations concerned with the prevention of cruelty to animals or the promotion of the welfare of animals. Grants are also made to conservation charities.

In 1999 the assets were £10 million and the income was low at £333,000. It had

expenses of £67,000 (£31,000 of which was investment managers fees and £23,000 was legal fees). Grants totalling £246,000 were made to 18 organisations, a number of these had been supported in the previous years.

Six organisations received £10,000 to £65,000, including Fauna & Flora International (£65,000), Royal Geographical Society – Whitley Award Scheme (£43,000), Shropshire Wildlife Trust (£36,000), Tweed Foundation – Riparian Habitats Project (£25,000), WILDCRU – University of Oxford (£15,000) and London Zoological Society – Sea Horse Project (£10,000).

The remainder of grants were for £5,000 or £6,000 including Atlantic Salmon Conservation Trust – Lamberton Shiel Nets and World Wildlife Fund – Jordan Hill Project (£6,000 each) and £5,000 each to Royal Zoological Society of Scotland – Edinburgh Zoo, Forum for the Future, Awe Fisheries Trust, Spey Research Trust – Findhorn Habitat Survey, West Galloway Fisheries Trust and Hawk & Owl Trust.

Exclusions No grants to non-registered charities.

Applications In writing to the correspondent.

The Felicity Wilde Charitable Trust

Children, medical research

£80,000 (1999)

Beneficial area UK

Barclays Bank Trust Company Ltd, Executorship & Trustee Service, PO Box 15, Northwich, Cheshire CW9 7UR

Tel. 01606 313173

Correspondent Miss M Y Bertenshaw

Trustees Barclays Bank Trust Co Ltd.

Information available Accounts were on file at the Charity Commission.

General The trust has a preference for UK-registered charities which benefit children and those concerned with medical research, especially into the cause and cure of asthma. In 1999 it had assets of £2.1 million and an income of £80,000. Grants totalled £80,000 and were made to 37 organisations.

The two major beneficiaries of the year which both received £20,000 were Allergy and Inflammation Research Trust and National Asthma Campaign. Other larger grants were £10,000 to British Lung Foundation and £5,000 to Sick Children's Trust.

The remaining grants were in the range of £250 to £1,500, with almost half being for £500. Beneficiaries included £1,500 each to Anthony Nolan Bone Marrow Trust, Life Education Centres – Cheshire and Cornwall Children's Hospital Appeal and £1,000 each to Breast Cancer Campaign, REACH, Waverley Care Trust and Welsh Initiative for Conductive Education.

Among the organisations receiving £500 were Action for Kids Charitable Trust, Brainwave, Dermatrust, Different Strokes, Dystonia Society, Tommy's Campaign and WellBeing.

Exclusions No grants to individuals or non-registered charities.

Applications In writing to the correspondent at any time. Applications are considered quarterly.

The Wilkinson Charitable Foundation

Scientific research, education

£65,000 (1999/2000)

Beneficial area UK

Lawrence Graham, 190 Strand, London WC2R 1JN

Tel. 020 7379 0000 **Fax** 020 7379 6854

Correspondent B D S Lock, Trustee

Trustees *B D S Lock; Dr Anne M Hardy.*

Information available Full accounts were on file at the Charity Commission.

General The trust was set up for the advancement of scientific knowledge and education at Imperial College, University of London and for general purposes. Grants are only given to academic institutions.

The trustees have continued their policy of supporting research and initiatives commenced in the founder's lifetime and encouraging work in similar fields to those he was interested in.

In 1999/2000 the trust gave £65,000 in two major grants and about six smaller ones. Recipients included Imperial College; University College, London; and Wolfston College, Oxford. Accounts for this year were not available at time of publication.

In 1997/98 the trust had assets of £609,000 and an income of £122,000. It gave only eight grants, all for the advancement of scientific and medical knowledge and education, totalling £110,000.

The two largest grants went to Wolfson College, Oxford (£40,000) and University of Oxford, Inorganic Chemistry Department (£30,000). Other grants went to University College, London (£18,000); Imperial College of Science, Technology & Medicine, London (£16,000); University of Wales, Chemistry Department (£3,000); and Imperial College, Prostate Cancer Fund (£1,000). There were also two smaller donations of £500 each to Blond McIndoe Centre and Dystonia Society.

Exclusions No grants to individuals.

Applications In writing to the correspondent. Applications from individuals will not be considered.

The Williams Family Charitable Trust

Jewish, medical

£230,000 (1998/99)

Beneficial area Worldwide

8 Holne Chase, London N2 0QN

Tel. 020 8455 3051

Correspondent The Trustees

Trustees *Shimon Benison; Arnon Levy.*

Information available Accounts were on file at the Charity Commission, but without a narrative report.

General In 1998/99 the trust had assets of £1.6 million and an income of £114,000. After modest management charges of £2,400, grants to 115 organisations totalled £230,000. Only a quarter of these grants were of more than £1,000.

The largest grants were £65,000 to HaGemach Al-Shem Nahiem Zeev

Williams, £20,000 to Amutat El-Ad - Jerusalem and £18,000 to Yeshivat Hahesder Kiryat Arba. Other beneficiaries included Child Resettlement Fund (£10,000), Joint Jewish Charitable Trust (£5,000), Ariel Mifalei Torah (£4,000), Seeing Eyes for the Blind (£2,000), Beit Haggai Youth Village (£1,000), Cambridge University (£500), Victims of Arab Terror (£400), Jewish Aid Trust (£250), Elz Hayim (£200), Operation Wheelchairs (£100) and Israel Society for the Deaf (£50).

Applications In writing to the correspondent.

Dame Violet Wills Charitable Trust

Evangelical Christianity

£136,000 (1999)

Beneficial area UK and overseas, but there may be a preference for Gloucestershire

Ricketts Cooper & Co., Thornton House, Richmond Hill, Bristol BS8 1AT

Tel. 0117 973 8441

Correspondent H E Cooper, Secretary and Treasurer

Trustees *Dr D M Cunningham, Chair; H E Cooper; S Burton; A J G Cooper; Miss J R Guy; G J T Landreth; Prof. A H Linton; Revd J A Motyer; R D Spear; D G Cleave; Mrs M Lewis; J Dean; Revd Dr E C Lucas; Mrs R E Peskell.*

Information available Full accounts were on file at the Charity Commission.

General The trust supports evangelical Christian activities both in the UK and overseas. The trust's current areas of interest are:

- buildings
- missions UK
- missions other countries
- literature
- radio broadcasts
- sundries.

No long-term support is given. The trust states 'the grants are usually small but tailored to provide encouragement to the organisations concerned'.

In 1999 the trust had assets of £1.7 million and an income of £111,000. A total of £136,000 was given in 115 grants.

The largest beneficiary was Bristol Christian Youth Trust which received £10,000 for its Annex Fund and £5,000 for its Roof Repair Fund. Other groups supported included Echoes of Service – Bristol Missionaries (£6,600), Bethesda Church – Alma Road and Bradley Stoke Evangelistical Church – Bristol (£5,000 each), Evangelistic Literature Trust (£3,000), Living Waters Radio Ministry (£2,500), FEBA Radio and Universities and Colleges Christian Fellowship (£2,000 each), Eurovangelism (£1,000), Crossroads (£800), Kendal Road Baptist Church – Gloucester (£500), United Christian Broadcasters (£400) and St Andrews Parish Church – Clock (£100).

Exclusions Grants are not given to individuals.

Applications In writing to the correspondent. The trust states 'whilst a vast number of appeals are received each year, grants are more likely to be made to those which are personally known to one or more of the trustees'. Trustees meet in March and in September; applications need to be received by January or June.

The Harold Hyam Wingate Foundation

Jewish, medical, research, education, the arts, general

£242,000 to organisations (1998/99)

Beneficial area Mainly UK

20–22 Stukeley Street, London WC2B 5LR

Correspondent Karen Marshall, Administrator

Trustees R C Wingate; A J Wingate; R Cassen; D Wingate.

Information available Full accounts were provided by the trust.

General The principal objective of the charity is to support Jewish organisations and general charitable purposes. In particular, the trust aims to:

1. contribute towards the expenses of established charitable institutions
2. establish projects of study and research
3. initiate and sponsor new projects of study and research
4. establish and endow scholarships, fellowships, professional chairs, prizes and awards.

In 1998/99 the trust had assets of £18 million and an income of £785,000. It gave donations of £242,000 to organisations with a further £366,000 going on expenditure for the Wingate Scholarship Fund.

In addition to their traditional support for Jewish charitable work, the trustees support the performing arts, medical research, healthcare and education, in the latter case particularly where relevant to problems associated with social exclusion. The trustees are willing to consider capital projects on a highly selective basis.

The largest grant of £35,000 went to the National Film & Television School and £15,000 each went to English Touring Opera and Oxford Centre for Hebrew & Jewish Studies. Grants of £10,000 each went to Donmar Warehouse Productions, English National Opera, English Touring Opera, Jerusalem Foundation, London Academy of Music and Dramatic Art and Theatre Royal Bath (which also received a grant of £5,000).

Recipients of smaller grants within the trust's particular areas of interest include:

Education
Guildhall School of Music & Drama Foundation (£8,000), Courtauld Institute of Art (£2,500) and Advancement of Education in Jaffa (£1,000).

Jewish charities
Jewish Quarterly (£4,600), New London Synagogue (three grants totalling £3,000), Israel Museum (£1,800) and Jewish Blind & Disabled (£1,000).

Performing arts
British Youth Opera (two grants totalling £5,500), National Theatre (£2,500) and Young Vic Theatre (£500).

Medical research/healthcare
Imperial Cancer Research Fund (£6,500), Alzheimer's Disease Society (£5,000) and Medical Foundation (£1,000).

Several of the grants were recurrent from the previous year.

Exclusions No grants to individuals. The Wingate Scholarship Fund, for students over the age of 24, is separately administered by Faith Clark at the above address. Obtain details direct from her or from *The Educational Grants Directory*.

The trustees will not normally consider donations to the general funds of large charitable bodies, wishing instead to focus support on specific projects. In addition, the trustees will favour activities and projects that are, in the opinion of the trustees, unlikely to attract sponsorship from commercial sources.

Applications In writing to the correspondent. Applications are considered about every three months.

The Francis Winham Foundation

Welfare of older people

£439,000 (1998/99)

Beneficial area England

35 Pembroke Gardens, London W8 6HU

Tel. 020 7602 1261

Correspondent Mrs J Winham, Secretary

Trustees Francine Winham; Dr John Norcliffe Roberts; Gwendoline Winham, Josephine Winham.

Information available Full accounts were on file at the Charity Commission.

General Grants are given to both UK organisations (including their local branches) and local charities.

In 1998/99 the trust had assets of £3.7 million generating an income of £325,000. Grants to 110 organisations totalled £439,000 and ranged from £450 to £51,000.

Large grants to UK organisations included those to Age Concern (£51,000), SSAFA (£43,000), Universal Benevolent Society (£30,000), Charity Search (£23,000), Invalids at Home (£15,000) and Help the Hospice (£10,000). Other UK grants included IMPACT and Queen Elizabeth's Foundation for Disabled People (£5,000), RUKBA (£4,500), Disability Aid Fund (£2,000) and Iris Fund (£1,000).

Grants to local charities included Camden Housebound Link Service (£23,000), Countess of Brecknock Hospice Trust (£10,000), Victim Support Lambeth (£2,000), North Yorkshire County Council (£1,500), Norfolk &

Norwich Association for the Blind (£1,000), Balham Pensioners Centre (£750) and Hammersmith & Fulham Partnership Against Crime (£450).

Applications In writing to the correspondent. The trust regrets that it cannot send replies to applications outside its specific field of help for older people. Applications should be made through registered charities or social services departments only.

The Maurice Wohl Charitable Foundation

Jewish, health, welfare
£281,000 (1998/99)
Beneficial area UK and overseas

1st Floor, 7–8 Conduit Street, London W1R 9TG
Tel. 020 7493 3777
Correspondent J Houri
Trustees *Maurice Wohl; Mrs Vivienne Wohl; Mrs Ella Latchman; Prof. David Latchman; Martin Paisner; David Davis.*
Information available Full accounts were on file at the Charity Commission.

General The 1998/99 accounts state: 'the trustees receive applications from a wide range of charitable institutions including those engaged in medical and ancilliary services (including medical research), education, helping the disabled and the aged, providing sheltered accommodation, relieving poverty, developing the arts etc. The trustees consider all requests which they receive and make such donations as they feel appropriate.' In practice, grants are given to Jewish or medical organisations. This trust shares many of its trustees with The Maurice Wohl Charitable Trust, with which it works closely.

In 1998/99 the trust had assets of £17 million generating an income of £943,000. After high administration and management charges of £95,000, grants totalled £281,000, leaving a large surplus for the year.

The largest grant was £100,000 to University College London – Wohl Viron Centre. Other grants ranged from £50 to £10,000, although most grants were of £1,000 or less. Medical beneficiaries included Medical Aid Trust (£10,000),

Hospital Marie-Lannelongue – Paris (£3,100), £100 each to Alzheimer's Disease Society, Dystonia Society, Elimination of Leukaemia Fund, Mental Health Foundation, National Eczema Society, National Society for Epilepsy and St John Ambulance and £50 to National Centre for Cued Speech.

Jewish groups receiving support included Gateshead Jewish Boarding School and Jewish Care (£10,000 each), Friends of Ohel Torah Trust (£6,100), Yad Elizer (£3,700), Federation of Jewish Relief (£2,000), Institute for Jewish Policy Research (£1,000) and Fifth Avenue Synagogue – New York (£300). A grant of £100 was given to Chicken Shed Theatre Company.

Applications In writing to the correspondent.

The Maurice Wohl Charitable Trust

Jewish, general
£40,000 (1996/97)
Beneficial area Worldwide

1st Floor, 7–8 Conduit Street, London W1R 9TA
Tel. 020 7493 3777
Correspondent J Houri
Trustees *D Davis; Mrs E Latchman; M Wohl; Mrs V Wohl; Prof. D Latchman; M Paisner.*
Information available Full accounts were on file at the Charity Commission.

General The trust was established in 1965/66, by Maurice Wohl to support Jewish organisations and general charities in the UK and overseas. The activities of the trust have been cut back sharply since the late 1980s when it was giving grants totalling over £350,000 a year. In 1996/97, income was £188,000, similar to previous years, but grants totalled only £40,000 (£102,000 in 1995/96). The trust has regularly had a surplus of income over expenditure (£121,000 in 1996/97). This has been used to build up its assets, which now stand at £2.2 million.

In 1996/97, the trust gave 84 grants mainly to Jewish organisations. The main beneficiaries were Communaute Israelite de Geneve – Switzerland (£11,000), Society of Friends of the Torah – London

(£2,400) and Re'uth Friends of Israel (£1,200). Five grants of £1,000 were made, all to Jewish organisations.

The non-Jewish grants were mainly to national medical or welfare charities and were generally for around £100. Non-Jewish grants included those to Help the Aged, British Polio Fellowship, Greater London Fund for the Blind, Midland Sports Centre and MIND.

Exclusions No grants to individuals.

Applications To the correspondent in writing.

The Woo Charitable Foundation

Education in the arts
£300,000 (1998/99)
Beneficial area UK

277 Green Lanes, London N13 4XS
Correspondent John Dowling, Administrator
Trustees *Nelson Woo; Countess Benckendorff; Nigel Kingsley; Michael Trask; Jackson Woo.*
Information available Accounts were on file at the Charity Commission with a brief report.

General 'The Woo Charitable Foundation was established for the advancement of education through supporting, organising, promoting or assisting the development of the arts in England, together with the specific aim of helping children, young people and those less able to help themselves.' The trust informed us that it was endowed by property in the Far East and its income continues to come from those property investments.

The trust largely funds small projects in primary schools which aim to restore arts education (particularly drama and music) where it has been cut out of the National Curriculum. Grants range between £5,000 and £15,000. The trust stated that their aim is to create greater awareness of the foundation by promoting a successful education programme. It also aims to provide funding in the community, particularly in deprived areas, rural as well as urban.

In autumn 2000 the trust was in the process of introducing a bursary scheme. This would provide 20 grants per year of £5,000 each to artists who have finished formal education but are yet to establish 'meaningful careers'. These will be awarded twice a year – in spring and autumn.

Grants to organisations have included Serpentine Gallery Education (£12,000), Chance to Dance School (£10,000), Leicester School (£7,500), Ledbury Poetry Festival (£4,000) and Stagecoach Youth Theatre (£1,000).

Exclusions No grants for travel, building work and fundraising activities, especially abroad. Support is very rarely given to individuals, but note the above.

Applications In writing to the correspondent.

Woodlands Green Ltd

Jewish

£203,000 (1996/97)

Beneficial area Worldwide

Flat 27, Yew Tree Court, Bridge Lane, London NW11 0RA

Tel. 020 8209 1458

Correspondent D J A Ost, Trustee

Trustees A Ost; E Ost; D J A Ost; J A Ost.

Information available Accounts were on file at the Charity Commission, but without a list of grants.

General In 1997/98 the trust had an income of £274,000 and an expenditure of £185,000. Unfortunately further information for this year was not available and the following information is repeated from the last edition of this guide.

In 1996/97 the trust had assets of £622,000 and an income of £191,000, comprised of Gift Aid donations, income from investments and rent. Grants totalled £203,000, but unfortunately, no information was available on the size or number of beneficiaries.

The most recent grants list on file at the Charity Commission was for 1983/84, when all the beneficiaries were Jewish charities.

Applications In writing to the correspondent.

The Woodroffe Benton Foundation

General

£209,000 approved (1998/99)

Beneficial area UK

16 Fernleigh Court, Harrow, London HA2 6NA

Tel. 020 8421 4120

Correspondent Alan King

Trustees *James Hope, Chair; Kenneth Stoneley; Colin Russell; Miss Celia Clout; Peter Foster; Tony Shadrack.*

Information available Full accounts were on file at the Charity Commission. Accounts, but without a full grants list, were provided by the trust.

General The trust's objects are to support:

* people in need, primary care of people who are sick or elderly or those effected by the results of a local or national disaster

* promotion of education, in particular support to Queen Elizabeth Grammar School, Ashbourne and other schools in Derbyshire

* conservation, preservation, protection and improvement for public benefit of natural resources and amenity land in the UK.

The trust has three strands of grant-making: ongoing support to a core list of organisations; 'ad hoc' one-off grants to unsolicited applications; and grants of up to £5,000 each to charities selected by an individual trustee.

The trust, in partnership with Ifield Housing Society of Crawley, is funding the building of a nursing home, Woodroffe Benson House. A grant of £17,000 was given to Ifield Housing Society in 1998/99.

In 1998/99 the trust had assets of £5.7 million generating an income of £193,000. After high administration and management fees of £42,000, a total of £209,000 was approved to be given in 109 grants. The grant total was divided into: £113,000 paid during the year; £30,000 approved to be paid within a year; and £66,000 approved to be paid after more than one year.

The trust committed substantial ongoing grants to the following 15 organisations: Queen Elizabeth's Grammar School –

Ashbourne (£19,000), Ifield Park Housing Society (£17,000), Young Peoples Trust for the Environment (£16,000), Community Links and Victim Support (£10,000 each), Homeless Network (£5,000), St Jude's Community Association (£4,500) and nine other Derbyshire Schools (£4,500 in total).

A further 12 charities received ongoing support, mostly of smaller amounts. They included Winston Churchill Memorial Trust (£6,000), Royal Air Forces Association and RNLI (£3,000 each), Cystic Fibrosis Trust (£2,000) with £1,500 each to Royal National Mission to Fishermen, Royal Naval Benevolent Trust and Royal Star and Garter Home.

One-off grants were given to 53 of the 490 unsolicited applications received. The largest was £2,000 to Understanding Industry, the only one over £1,000. In addition, a total of £15,000 was given by individual trustees to 28 organisations, all grants were under £1,000.

Although there was a detailed breakdown of grant-making policy in the narrative report, including some examples of grants made as shown above, a full grants list was not included in the accounts.

Exclusions Grants are not made outside the UK and are only made to registered charities. No grants to individuals. Branches of UK charities should not apply as grants – if made – would go to the charity's headquarters.

Applications In writing to the correspondent. Trustees meet quarterly. The main grants are made at the end of the financial year in December. If applications have to be hand written (type written is preferred), then black ink should be used as applications are photocopied for the trustees. Audited accounts are invariably required. Applications are only acknowledged if an sae is included, and notification of the outcome is only sent to successful applicants.

World in Need

Christian objects

£278,000 (1997/98)

Beneficial area Worldwide

103 High Street, Oxford OX1 4EW

Tel. 01865 249111 **Fax** 0870 734 8246

website www.world-in-need.org.uk

Correspondent Rob John, Director

WORSHIPFUL COMPANY •

Trustees *M O Feilden, Chair; R Benson; J A Bridgland; J C Cole; A Radford; M Robson; D Saint; R Stanley; N K Wright; S Webster; R Young; A Greetham.*

Information available Full accounts were provided by the trust.

General In 1998/99 the trust had an income of £734,000 and an expenditure of £212,000. This information was taken from the Charity Commission database. Unfortunately the accounts were not on file for public viewing at the time of publication. The following information is repeated from the last edition of this guide.

This trust was established in 1965 and was previously known as Phyllis Trust. The objects of the trust are:

* the advancement of the Christian religion including the declaration of eternal life
* the relief of sickness, poverty and distress in any part of the world as an expression of Christian love.

The trust helps set-up trusts and charities and only funds these organisations. These projects are usually seed-corn projects, compatible with Christian objectives, which are seen to be initiating innovative work or developing the scale of an existing charity's activities. The trust aims to support projects which are potentially self-financing and self-managing after WIN's support has expired (usually after two or three years).

World in Need annually derives income from Andrews and Partners Limited (residential estate agency). In 1997/98 the trust received £385,000, including £218,000 from the Partners and further income from the Shops. The trust had assets of £3 million. Grants made during the year totalled £278,000.

The trustees in the annual report state that 'support is for projects that it has identified for itself in those areas of work identified by the trustees as important and significant. These projects are identified and developed through our own pro-active research. Thus, we do not set out to be a general grant-making trust, our resources are usually fully committed two to three years into the future and our response to general, unsolicited applicants in all cases must be a polite no'.

The focus activities of the trust in 1997/98 were the same as 1996/97, with grants made to the following main beneficiaries: Opportunity Trust (£108,000); The Catch Up Project (£89,000); and The Spire Trust (£66,000).

Opportunity Trust has since become self sufficient. The other two organisations will continue to be supported. The Catch Up Project is a teaching programme for children aged seven to nine years who find reading difficult. The Spire Trust works in the field of religious education, and in particular runs school assemblies. A grant was also paid to Burrswood Christian Centre for Healthcare and Ministry to support their registration as a non-surgical hospital and medical counselling facility (£15,000). This was probably an exceptional one-off grant, and was made due to a connection with the trust's founder.

Exclusions No grants to individuals or for the construction, restoration or alteration of buildings nor for the general subsidy of ongoing work.

Applications In writing to the correspondent, but see above. Trustees meet quarterly in March, June, September and December.

The Fred & Della Worms Charitable Trust

Jewish, education, arts
£117,000 (1998/99)
Beneficial area UK

Frederick House, 58a Crewyf Road, London NW2 2AD
Tel. 020 8458 1181
Correspondent F S Worms, Trustee
Trustees *Mrs D Worms; M Paisner; F S Worms.*
Information available Full accounts were on file at the Charity Commission.

General The trust was established in 1961, to support general charitable objects, but in practice, almost all the money is given to Jewish organisations. In 1998/99 it had an income of £115,000 and gave 19 grants totalling £117,000. The main grants were all to Jewish organisations. The largest of £22,000 went to British Friends of the Hebrew University of Jerusalem, with £20,000 each to Joint Jewish Charitable Trust and Jewish Educational Development Trust.

Other recipients of substantial grants included Child Resettlement Fund and B'nai B'rith District 15 (£8,000 each),

B'nai B'rith Hillel Foundation (£5,400), Jewish Care (£5,100), United Synagogue (£2,000) and British Friends of the Arts Museums of Israel (£1,300).

Eight grants of £1,000 were awarded, non-Jewish organisations to benefit included English National Opera, Duke of Edinburgh Award Scheme and English Heritage.

Applications In writing to the correspondent.

Worshipful Company of Chartered Accountants General Charitable Trust

General, education
£68,000 (1998/99)
Beneficial area UK

5 Cliffe House, Radnor Cliff, Folkestone, Kent CT20 2TY
Tel. 01303 248477
Correspondent J E Maxwell, Clerk
Trustees *J M Renshall; W K Gardener; Sir Jeremy Hanley; M N Peterson; D P J Ross; M A Yale; D T Young.*
Information available Full accounts were on file at the Charity Commission and were provided by the trust.

General The trust was started in 1988, in 1998/99 it had an income of £91,000 and assets of almost £1 million. In the early years the trustees concentrated on building up the fund's resources, but their aim now is to distribute. Grants totalled £68,000. The trustees' policy of giving, within their broad objectives has been to:

* give preference to at least one theme which has some direct or indirect relevance to the work of the profession
* focus on one or two major themes each year, where the trust's contribution will have an identifiable beneficial effect, enabling the recipients to achieve results not otherwise within their reach
* base major grants on recommendations and proposals put to them by members of the Livery.

283

Recent projects include:

1998 Master's Project

This involved the education of academically-able young people from non-privileged backgrounds. The trustees received 12 applications. On the recommendation of a selection panel the trustees agreed grants for three people totalling £26,000. This was made up of two annual bursaries of £4,000 per year for three years and £1,700 to buy an oboe to loan to a music student.

1998 Primary Schools Project

This involved promoting literacy and numeracy projects which were blocked by lack of finance. A selection panel considered 41 applications, 17 grants were made to schools in England and Wales totalling £25,000.

The remainder of the grants were of between £1,500 and £4,000 and went to a variety of prizes and projects including Chartered Accountants in the Community, Lord Mayor's Appeal and Voluntary Services Overseas.

Applications Applications must be sponsored by a liveryman of the company.

The Matthews Wrightson Charity Trust

Caring and Christian charities

£87,000 to organisations (1999)

Beneficial area UK and some overseas

The Farm, Northington, Alresford, Hampshire SO24 9TH

Correspondent Adam Lee, Secretary and Administrator

Trustees *Priscilla Wrightson; Anthony Isaacs; Guy Wrightson; Isabelle White.*

Information available Full accounts were provided by the trust.

General The trustees favour smaller charities or projects e.g. those seeking to raise under £25,000. They do not usually support large UK charities and those seeking to raise in excess of £250,000. However, support may be given to charities with a turnover greater than £250,000 if they are a previous recipient. There is a bias towards innovation,

Christian work and organisations helping disadvantaged people reintegrate into the community. The standard grant size in 2000 was £400. Grants are generally made from income rather than assets.

The assets in 1999 stood at £2 million and the income for the year was £83,000. The trust gave 193 grants totalling £96,000, of which £9,100 went to individuals. About a quarter of beneficiaries had received grants in the previous year. The grants were categorised as follows:

Category	Total	%
Arts causes	£14,000	14
Christian	£9,500	10
Disability	£13,000	13
Individuals	£9,100	10
Medical	£6,800	7
Older people	£3,800	4
Rehabilitation	£8,300	9
Worldwide	£5,800	6
Youth	£22,000	23
Miscellaneous	£4,000	4

The largest grant of £11,000 went to the Royal College of Art to support students who were finding their grants and other income inadequate and for awards to students to further ideas for UK industrial production. The next nine largest grants were for £1,000 or £1,200, recipients included DEMAND – Design and Manufacture for Disabilities, CARE – Christian Action Research and Education, Genesis Arts Trust, Keston Institute, Mongolia Project for Street Children, Peper Harow Foundation, Prison Fellowship and Rifleman's Aid Society.

Most of the other grants were for £400, beneficiaries included 3-2-6 Afterschool Club, Burnbake Trust, Turntable Furniture Project, Teddington Old People's Welfare Committee, Christians Against Poverty, Victim Support – Southwark and White Memorial Baptist Church.

Exclusions No support for individuals (other than visitors from abroad) seeking education or adventure for personal character improvement. No support for unconnected local churches, village halls, schools and animal charities.

Applications In writing to the correspondent. No special forms are used, although latest financial accounts are desirable. One or two sheets (usually the covering letter) are circulated monthly to the trustees, who meet every six months only for policy and administrative decisions. Replies are only sent to successful applicants; allow up to three months for an answer. Please

include an sae if an answer is required if unsuccessful.

The trust receives over 1,000 applications a year; 'winners have to make the covering letter more attractive than the 90 others received each month'.

Wychdale Ltd

Jewish

£158,000 (1998/99)

Beneficial area UK

89 Darenth Road, London N16 6EB

Correspondent The Secretary

Trustees *C D Schlaff; J Schlaff; Mrs Z Schlaff.*

Information available Accounts were on file at the Charity Commission, but without a grants list.

General This trust supports Jewish educational institutions. In 1998/99 it had assets of £264,000 and an income of £95,000 including donations of £73,000. After low management and administration costs of £2,000, grants totalled £158,000. Further information was not available.

Applications In writing to the correspondent.

This entry was not confirmed by the trust but was correct according to information on file at the Charity Commission.

The Wyseliot Charitable Trust

Medical, welfare, general

£94,000 (1998/99)

Beneficial area UK

17 Chelsea Square, London SW3 6LF

Correspondent J H Rose, Trustee

Trustees *E A D Rose; J H Rose; A E G Raphael.*

Information available Full accounts were on file at the Charity Commission.

General The trust states that the same charities are supported each year, with perhaps one or two changes. It is unlikely that new charties sending circular appeals will be supported and large UK charities are generally not supported.

In 1998/99 the trust had assets of £2.4 million and an income of £70,000, administration costs were exceptionally low at £500. Grants totalling £94,000 were made to 29 organisations, many of which were supported in the previous year. Donations were in the range of £500 to £3,000 and mostly went to organisations working in the fields of medicine and welfare with a few arts and youth organisations benefiting.

The largest grants were of £3,000 each and went to Centrepoint Soho, Enham Trust, Friends of the Royal Brompton Hospital, Macmillan Cancer Relief, Marie Curie Cancer Care, Notting Hill Churches Homeless Concern and Winged Fellowship Trust. Other grants included £2,000 each to BACUP, Leo Baeck College, Runnymead Trust and St Mungo's, £1,000 each to RUKBA, Vitiligo Society and Woodlarks Workshop Trust and £500 to Fleet School Music Fund.

Exclusions Local charities are not supported. No support for individuals.

Applications In writing to the correspondent, but note the comments above.

The Yamanouchi European Foundation

Medical

US$142,000 (1998/99)

Beneficial area Worldwide

Yamanouchi House, Pyrford Road, West Byfleet, Surrey KT14 6RA

Tel. 01932 345535/342291
Fax 01932 342404

Correspondent Dudley Ferguson, Trustee

Trustees *Masayoshi Onoda; Shigekazu Takahashi; Dudley Ferguson; John Lackie; Joseph Harford; Dr Toichi Takenaka; Jiro Ichinaka; Philippe Ballero; Prof. Peter van Brummeley; Yoshio Katogi.*

Information available Full accounts were on file at the Charity Commission.

General Unfortunately we have been unable to update the following information since the last edition of this guide.

The trust was established with four aims, they are to:

• provide long-term support to basic medical and related scientific programmes through organisations such as the Societe Internationale D'Urologie

• support selected short, medium and long-term projects, aimed at integrating basic science and clinical research through interdisciplinary projects

• provide facilities, promote or sponsor the exchange of ideas and views through lectures and discussions of an educational or cultural nature

• promote, assist or otherwise support charities.

The trust states that this is 'best accomplished by providing funding for basic scientific research, for the examination of public health and environmental policy issues, and for the support of educational and cultural exchange programmes'.

The foundation has established the 'Yamanouchi Award' and 'Lectureship' for medical research with US$30,000 every three years for each. These are being administered by Societe Internationale D'Urologie until 2000; and has established the Yamanouchi Fellowship – a scholarship to people in medical disciplines worth US$150,000 covering a two year support programme.

In 1998/99 grants to organisations totalled $142,000 (about £90,000), including a grant of US$75,000 which went to Institute Neurologicka Klinika. Three grants of £15,000, two grants of US$7,500 and a grant of £6,800 were made, including a grant to Sheffield Hallam University. The assets of the trust stood at US$11 million and the income for the year was US$606,000.

Applications In writing to the correspondent.

The Yapp Charitable Trust

Social welfare

£321,000 (1999/2000)

Beneficial area UK

28 Holly Grove, Lindley, Huddersfield, West Yorkshire HD3 3NS

Tel. 01484 513750 **Fax** 01484 513750
e-mail yapp.trust@care4free.net
Correspondent
Mrs Margaret Thompson, Trust Secretary and Administrator

Trustees *Revd Timothy C Brooke; Peter G Murray; Miss Alison J Norman; Peter R Davies; Peter M Williams.*

Information available Information was provided by the trust. The first year's accounts were not available at time of publication.

General The Yapp Charitable Trust was formed in 1999 from the Yapp Welfare Trust (two thirds share) and Yapp Education and Research Trust (one third share). However, rather than combining the criteria for the two trusts, the trustees decided to focus on small charities, usually local rather than UK charities. The trust now accepts applications only from organisations with a turnover of under £100,000 in the year of application, meaning many previous applicants are no longer eligible. The objects are restricted to registered charities in the UK and cover five categories as follows:

1. Care and housing of older people.

2. Welfare of children and young people (including youth clubs, youth hostels and students' hostels and similar institutions).

3. Care and special education of people who have learning disabilities, physical disabilities or mental health problems.

4. Advancement of moral welfare (e.g. treatment of alcohol dependency or drug abuse, rehabilitation of ex-offenders, marriage guidance counselling, etc.).

5. Advancement of education and learning (including 'lifelong learning') and of scientific and medical research.

Applications from outside these five areas cannot be considered.

The trust uses the CVS network to make contact with small charities and monitors applications and grants geographically.

Grants are available for capital or revenue. Applications for revenue funding can be for up to three years. Although more than half of the applications are for these grants, in practice priority is given to projects in 'less popular' fields where raising funds from the general public is difficult. Grants are usually of up to £3,000 each year for both one-off and recurrent grants.

In 1999 the trust had assets of £5.5 million, income in the first year was £420,000, of which about £321,000 was allocated in grants. The trust gave 123 grants, 19 of which were recurrent.

Grants included £5,000 over two years to Age Concern Coalville and District towards the running costs of a day centre for older people with learning difficulties; £10,000 over three years to Robin Hood Gardens Education and Training Trust towards running costs of ESOL classes to enable ethnic minority residents in Tower Hamlets to move on into education or employment; £9,100 over two years to Hope Glasgow to fund a part-time support worker to work with women offenders; £9,000 over three years to Social Care at Holy Cross towards the development of a volunteer visiting service for people who are elderly or disabled in an area of Plymouth; and £3,800 over three years to Rape and Sexual Abuse Counselling Centre, Darlington for rent of premises.

Exclusions Grants are only made to organisations which have charitable status. The following are not supported:

- applications made by, or on behalf of, individuals
- non-charities in the name, or under the umbrella, of a third party which is a charity
- educational expeditions
- school building or development funds, including playground developments and purchase of IT equipment
- projects with a shortfall greater than £10,000 in the year funding is sought
- charities which have received a grant from the fund within the last three years.

Applications On a form available from the administrator. Applicants may request a form by e-mail in Word 97 format if preferred, although all applications must be sent by post. All sections of the form must be completed, the correspondent is happy to advise applicants on how to complete the form. Applicants are advised to contact the

correspondent to see if the proposal is eligible for consideration.

Applications must include most recent acounts, and annual reports and newsletters are also appreciated, although the trust does not like bulky reports or specialist or technical documents.

Closing dates for applications are 31 January, 31 May and 30 September for consideration about six weeks later, and notification around two weeks after this. Applications are only confirmed as received if an sae is provided, although all applicants hear the outcome after the trustees' meeting. Late applications will be considered at the following meeting.

The Yorkshire & General Trust

Christian, welfare

£69,000 (1998/99)

Beneficial area Preference for North Yorkshire

1 High Street, Tadcaster, North Yorkshire LS24 9SB

Tel. 01937 832225

Correspondent Tina Harrison, Trustee

Trustees O G W Smith; P M E Smith; Mrs C M Harrison; N P Scarr.

Information available Full accounts were on file at the Charity Commission.

General The trust distributes income from its assets and donations received from Samuel Smith Old Brewery. In 1998/99 the trust had an income of £81,000 of which £78,000 came from a donation. A total of £69,000 was given in 33 grants, of these 13 were recurrent.

This trust mainly supports welfare organisations and has a preference for charities based in North Yorkshire. The largest grants were to Titus Trust (£14,000), Prison Fellowship (£13,000) and Gipton Outreach (£8,000). A further 12 grants were made over £1,000, including Seven Springs Play and Support Centre (£4,500), UCB (£3,000), Yo Yo Trust (£2,000), Agape and Faith in Leeds (£1,500 each), HCPT (£1,200) and North of England Healing Trust (£1,000).

Smaller grants in the range of £100 to £750 included Gateway to Mobility (£750), Leeds and Selby Alcoholic Advisory Services and Leeds Base 10 Turning Point (£600 each), Martin

House and St Leonard's Hospice (£250 each) and Tyneside Challenge (£100).

Exclusions No grants to animal charities.

Applications In writing to the correspondent. Trustees meet five times a year.

The William Allen Young Charitable Trust

General

£94,000 (1998/99)

Beneficial area UK, with a preference for south east England, especially London

The Ram Brewery, Wandsworth, London SW18 4JD

Tel. 020 8875 7000

Correspondent J A Young, Trustee

Trustees J A Young; T F B Young; J G A Young.

Information available Full accounts were on file at the Charity Commission.

General The trust was established in 1966, with shares in Young & Co.'s Brewery plc. In 1998/99 the trust had assets of £3.8 million (up by £2.1 million from the previous year) generating an income of £106,000. After expenses of only £7 it gave 61 donations totalling £94,000, only 13 grants were recurrent from the previous year.

Grants were given to a range of UK health and social welfare charities, but support was also given to a number of churches and education-related organisations. There was a slight preference for organisations based in south London. The two largest grants of £11,000 were given to Friends of King Edward VII Hospital and National Hospital Development Foundation. Other larger grants included West Hatch PCC (£8,000); £5,000 each to Children's Hospice South West, Anti-Slavery International and Kings College, Taunton; British Disabled Water Ski Association (£4,000); Ocular Diagnostic Centre, Ohio (£3,000); Merton Medical Centre (£2,000); and Ladies Samaritans (£1,500).

Grants of £1,000 were made to 17 recipients including Actors' Church

Union, Age Endeavour, British Cemetery Trust, Jubilee Sailing Trust, RNLI (Taunton), Lord Mayor's Appeal Leuka 2000, Rotary Club – Battersea, St Andrew's Parish Church – West Hatch and Trinity Hospice.

The remaining 29 grants were mainly for £500 or less. Recipients included Get Kids Going (£600), with £500 each to Abbeyfield House Appeal - Reading, Bryanston School, Mark Davies Injured Riders' Fund and Macmillan Cancer Relief, £200 to National Youth Music Theatre, and £100 each to Pathfinder NHS Trust and Scope.

Applications In writing to the correspondent.

The Elizabeth and Prince Zaiger Trust

Welfare, health, general

£142,000 (1998/99)

Beneficial area UK

6 Alleyn Road, Dulwich,
London SE21 8AL

Tel. 020 8670 3992

Correspondent D W Parry, Trustee

Trustees *D W Parry; P J Harvey; D G Long.*

Information available Full accounts were on file at the Charity Commission.

General As well as supporting general charitable causes, the trust has the following objects:

- relief of older people
- relief of people who are mentally and physically disabled
- advancement of education of children and young people
- provision of care and protection for animals.

In 1998/99 the trust's assets rose from £2.9 million to £8.6 million as a result of revaluation. The trust's income was £162,000, including £15,000 in donations. Administration fees were almost a third of the income at £53,000 and were mostly made up of one-off professional, legal and financial services. Grants totalling £142,000 were made to 73 organisations. Grants ranged from £100 to £5,000.

Organisations for older people which were supported included Cheshire Home – Isle of Wight (£3,500), Yeovil Day Care Centre (£2,500) and Queen Alexander Hospital Home (£2,000).

Grants to disability organisations included: £3,000 each to Association for Spina Bifida and Hydrocephalus, British Institute for Brain-injured Children, Down's Syndrome Association and Parkinson's Disease Society; Listening Books (£2,000); Association of Wheelchair Children (£1,000); Disability Now (£500); and East Somerset NHS Trust (£1,000). A grant of £2,500 was given to NSPCC and £500 to its Wells & City branch.

Educational grants included those to Preston School (£5,000), Grass Royal Junior School (£2,000), Avalon School (£500), Streatham Youth Centre (£250) and Pen Mill County Infants School (£200).

Animal causes supported included National Animal Welfare Trust (£3,500) and People's Dispensary of Sick Animals (£2,000).

Other grants included: £3,000 each to British Heart Foundation, Marie Curie Cancer Care and RNLI; King George's Fund for Sailors (£2,000); Samaritans (£1,500); and Salvation Army (£1,000).

Applications The trust does not respond to unsolicited applications, stating: 'we have an ongoing programme of support for our chosen charities.'

The I A Ziff Charitable Foundation

General, education, Jewish, arts, youth, elderly, medicine

£147,000 (1997/98)

Beneficial area UK, with a preference for Yorkshire, especially Leeds and Harrogate

Town Centre House,
The Merrion Centre, Leeds LS2 8LY

Tel. 0113 222 1234

Correspondent B Rouse, Secretary

Trustees *I Arnold Ziff; Marjorie E Ziff; Michael A Ziff; Edward M Ziff; Ann L Manning.*

Information available Full accounts were on file at the Charity Commission.

General In 1997/98 the foundation had assets of £2.2 million and an income of £274,000. About 90 grants were given totalling £147,000. Grants were made in the range of £12 to £50,000. Over half the grants made went to Jewish organisations. However education was the main area to benefit taking 60% of the total distributed. About a quarter of recipients had been supported in the previous year.

The largest grant of £50,000 was given to University of Leeds for the western campus business school building refurbishment programme. The Foundation for Education received £15,000 with Leeds University (Leeds Room in the LAM Institute in Hong Kong) and Clifton College receiving £10,000 each. All of these have received major grants in the past.

Other larger grants went to Leeds Jewish Welfare Board (£7,900), JJCT (£6,300), Harrogate International Festival and Royal Opera House (£5,000 each), Beth Hamedrash Hagadol Synagogue (£2,500) and the Israel Music Foundation (£1,500).

Grants of £1,000 and under included: £1,000 each to British Diabetic Association, Macmillan Cancer Fund and Hope Charity; £750 to British Israel Arts Foundation; £600 each to Western Marble Arch Synagogue and JNF; £500 to McGill University, Montreal; £250 each to B'nai Brith Hillel Committee and British ORT; £200 to Norwood Ravenswood; £100 to Jewish Museum; and £50 to British Heart Foundation. Beneficiaries local to the Yorkshire area included Leeds Grammar School Charitable Foundation, Harrogate Hebrew Congregation, Leeds Jewish Blind, Leeds Jewish Welfare Board, Harrogate Housing and ChildLine in Leeds. The trust has stated that a large proportion of its funds are earmarked for special projects requiring a large amount of funding for several years. The trustees also prefer to support charities with which they have some connection or which are known to them. Consequently unsolicited applications are unlikely to be successful.

Exclusions No grants to individuals.

Applications In writing to the correspondent, an sae ensures a reply. Initial telephone calls are welcome, but please note the above comments.

Subject index

The following subject index begins with a list of the categories used. These are fairly wide-ranging in order to keep the index as simple as possible. *The Grant-making Trusts CD-ROM* has a much more detailed search facility on the categories. There may be considerable overlap between some of these categories, particularly children, older people and young people with, for example, social/moral welfare or medicine and health.

The list of categories is followed by the index itself. Before using the index, please note the following:

How the index was compiled

1. The index aims to reflect the most recently recorded grant-making practice. It is therefore based on our interpretation of what each trust has actually given to, rather than what its policy statement says or its charitable objects allow it to do in principle. For example, where a trust states it has general charitable purposes, but its grants list shows a strong preference for welfare, we have indexed it as such.

2. We have tried to ensure that each trust has given significantly in the areas mentioned above (usually at least £15,000), therefore small, apparently untypical grants have been ignored for this classification.

3. The index has been compiled from the latest information available to us.

Limitations

1. It has not been possible to contact all 700 trusts specifically in regard to this index so policies may have changed.

2. Sometimes there will be a geographical restriction on the trust's grant giving which is not shown up in this index, or the trust may not give for the specific purposes you require under that heading. It is important to read the entry carefully, you will need to check:

(a) The trust gives in your geographical area of operation.

(b) The trust gives for the specific purposes you require.

(c) There is no other reason to prevent you making an application to this trust.

3. We have omitted the General category as the number of trusts included would make it unusable.

Under no circumstances should the index be used as a simple mailing list. Remember that each trust is different and that often the policies or interest of a particular trust do not fit easily into the given categories. Each entry must be read individually and carefully before you send off an application. Indiscriminate applications are usually unsuccessful. They waste time and money and greatly annoy trusts.

The categories are as follows:

Agriculture *page 290*

Arts, culture *page 290*

A very wide category including performing, written and visual arts, theatres, museums and galleries.

Children *page 291*

Mainly for welfare and welfare-related activities. (See below for young people.)

Disadvantaged people *page 291*

This includes people who are:

- socially-excluded
- socially and economically disadvantaged
- unemployed
- homeless
- offenders
- educationally disadvantaged
- victims of social/natural occcurences, including refugees and asylum seekers.

Economics, commerce, business *page 291*

Education/training *page 291*

Environment and animals *page 292*

This includes:

- education and research
- natural resources and ecology
- regeneration and development
- access to the countryside
- preservation of the environment, including buildings
- heritage.

Geography and foreign links *page 293*

This includes:

- travel expeditions and exploration,
- life/language of other countries
- industrial/economic links with other countries.

History *page 293*

Ill or disabled people *page 293*

This includes people who are ill, physically or mentally disabled, people with learning difficulties and people who have mental health problems.

Manufacturing industry and services *page 294*

Medicine and health *page 294*

This excludes medical research, which is listed separately.

Medical research page 296

Older people *page 296*

Philosophy *page 296*

This includes concern about values and attitudes, spiritual/personal growth and philosphies of particular individuals.

Political issues *page 296*

This includes:

• government and policy issues
• world policy issues, including third world development
• conflict resolution
• rights, justice and equity
• legal matters.

Religion general *page 297*

Mainly ecumenical or inter-faith work and where the trust gives grants to more than one faith.

Christianity *page 297*

This includes grants to churches, for Christian work and causes and for missionary work in the UK and overseas.

Judaism *page 297*

Science *page 298*

Social/moral welfare *page 298*

This is a very broad category, including:

• counselling and advice
• community organisations and development
• community care
• accommodation
• human relationships
• crime and punishment

Sport and recreation *page 299*

Voluntary sector management and development *page 300*

Young people *page 300*

Agriculture

Country Landowners Charitable Trust (CLACT)
Kulika Charitable Trust
John Oldacre Foundation
Frank Parkinson Agricultural Trust
Märit and Hans Rausing Charitable Foundation
Peter Samuel Charitable Trust
Stanley Smith UK Horticultural Trust
Whitaker Charitable Trust

Arts

Victor Adda Foundation
Richard Attenborough Charitable Trust
Benham Charitable Settlement
Bowerman Charitable Trust
British Record Industry Trust
Britten-Pears Foundation
Bulldog Trust
R M Burton Charitable Trust
Edward & Dorothy Cadbury Trust (1928)
Chapman Charitable Trust
Chase Charity
J A Clark Charitable Trust
John Coates Charitable Trust
Coppings Trust
Sidney & Elizabeth Corob Charitable Trust
Daiwa Anglo-Japanese Foundation
Leopold De Rothschild Charitable Trust
Dyers' Company Charitable Trust
Gilbert & Eileen Edgar Foundation
Elmgrant Trust
Equity Trust Fund
Follett Trust
Timothy Franey Charitable Foundation
Gordon Fraser Charitable Trust
Charles S French Charitable Trust
Garrick Club Charitable Trust
Gibbs Charitable Trusts
Simon Gibson Charitable Trust
Golden Charitable Trust
Jack Goldhill Charitable Trust
Grimmitt Trust
Grocers' Charity
R J Harris Charitable Settlement
Hinrichsen Foundation
Hobson Charity Ltd
Holst Foundation
P H Holt Charitable Trust
Idlewild Trust
Inverforth Charitable Trust

Ireland Fund of Great Britain
John Jarrold Trust
Jungels–Winkler Charitable Foundation
Kleinwort Benson Charitable Trust
Kobler Trust
Kohn Charitable Trust
David Laing Foundation
Lambert Charitable Trust
R J Larg Family Charitable Trust
Leche Trust
Sir Jack Lyons Charitable Trust
Michael Marks Charitable Trust
Marsh Christian Trust
Mayfield Valley Arts Trust
Nigel Moores Family Charitable Trust
National Manuscripts Conservation Trust
Normanby Charitable Trust
Odin Charitable Trust
Ofenheim & Cinderford Charitable Trusts
Old Broad Street Charity Trust
Old Possum's Practical Trust
Orpheus Trust
Ouseley Trust
Austin & Hope Pilkington Trust
John Porter Charitable Trust
Prince of Wales's Charitable Foundation
Quercus Trust
R V W Trust
Radcliffe Trust
Rainford Trust
Peggy Ramsay Foundation
Märit and Hans Rausing Charitable Foundation
Rowlands Trust
Audrey Sacher Charitable Trust
Dr Mortimer and Theresa Sackler Foundation
Coral Samuel Charitable Trust
N Smith Charitable Trust
Stanley Smith UK Horticultural Trust
South Square Trust
W W Spooner Charitable Trust
Janatha Stubbs Foundation
C B & H H Taylor 1984 Trust
Warbeck Fund Ltd
Mary Webb Trust
Weldon UK Charitable Trust
Humphrey Whitbread's First Charitable Trust
A H and B C Whiteley Charitable Trust
Harold Hyam Wingate Foundation
Fred & Della Worms Charitable Trust
Matthews Wrightson Charity Trust
I A Ziff Charitable Foundation

Children

Disadvantaged people

Economics, commerce, business

Education/ training

Neville & Elaine Blond Charitable Trust
Harry Bottom Charitable Trust
Bowerman Charitable Trust
Bowland Charitable Trust
British Record Industry Trust
Broadfield Trust
Palgrave Brown Foundation
Bulldog Trust
Burden Trust
Hon. Dorothy Rose Burns Will Trust
Arnold James Burton 1956 Charitable Settlement
R M Burton Charitable Trust
George Cadbury Trust
Edward & Dorothy Cadbury Trust (1928)
Carpenters' Company Charitable Trust
Chapman Charitable Trust
Chownes Foundation
J A Clark Charitable Trust
Coates Charitable Settlement
Vivienne & Samuel Cohen Charitable Trust
John & Freda Coleman Charitable Trust
Comino Foundation
Gordon Cook Foundation
Coppings Trust
Duke of Cornwall's Benevolent Fund
Sidney & Elizabeth Corob Charitable Trust
Dennis Curry Charitable Trust
Daiwa Anglo-Japanese Foundation
George Drexler Foundation
Dyers' Company Charitable Trust
Gilbert & Eileen Edgar Foundation
Edinburgh Trust, No 2 Account
Elmgrant Trust
Fairway Trust
Farthing Trust
Florence's Charitable Trust
Follett Trust
Four Acre Trust
Timothy Franey Charitable Foundation
Joseph Strong Frazer Trust
Charles S French Charitable Trust
Reginald Graham Charitable Trust
Grocers' Charity
Haberdashers' Eleemosynary Charity
Haramead Trust
Harbour Charitable Trust
Harbour Foundation
R J Harris Charitable Settlement
Charles Harris Charitable Trust
Martin Harris Charitable Trust
Peter Harris Charitable Trust
Haymills Charitable Trust
May Hearnshaw's Charity

Michael & Morven Heller Charitable Foundation
Simon Heller Charitable Settlement
Hobson Charity Ltd
Hockerill Educational Foundation
Holly Hill Charitable Trust
P H Holt Charitable Trust
Humanitarian Trust
Miss Agnes H Hunter's Trust
Ireland Fund of Great Britain
Irish Youth Foundation (UK) Ltd
Ironmongers' Quincentenary Charitable Fund
J A R Charitable Trust
Ruth & Lionel Jacobson Trust (Second Fund) No 2
Kurt and Olga Koerner Charitable Trust
Kohn Charitable Trust
Lawlor Foundation
Leche Trust
Ralph Levy Charitable Company Ltd
Localtrent Ltd
C L Loyd Charitable Trust
Sir Jack Lyons Charitable Trust
Jack & Pat Mallabar Charitable Foundation
Marsh Christian Trust
Maxwell Family Foundation
Robert McAlpine Foundation
Morris Charitable Trust
G M Morrison Charitable Trust
Moss Charitable Trust
Mutual Trust Group
Elani Nakou Foundation
Newby Trust Limited
Richard Newitt Fund
Gerald Palmer Trust
Rudolph Palumbo Charitable Foundation
John Porter Charitable Trust
Prince of Wales's Charitable Foundation
Radcliffe Trust
Rainford Trust
Ratcliff Foundation
Rhodes Trust Public Purposes Fund
Muriel Edith Rickman Trust
Ridgesave Limited
Riverside Charitable Trust Limited
Sir James Roll Charitable Trust
St James's Place Foundation
Rowlands Trust
Saddlers' Company Charitable Fund
Sheepdrove Trust
Bassil Shippam and Alsford Charitable Trust
Shipwrights Charitable Fund
Simpson Education and Conservation Trust

N Smith Charitable Trust
Leslie Smith Foundation
South Square Trust
St Gabriel's Trust
St James' Trust Settlement
Stanley Foundation Ltd
M J C Stone Charitable Trust
Janatha Stubbs Foundation
Sutasoma Trust
Hugh & Ruby Sykes Charitable Trust
C B & H H Taylor 1984 Trust
Thompson Family Charitable Trust
Thompson Fund
Thornton Trust
Three Oaks Trust
Thriplow Charitable Trust
Tory Family Foundation
Towry Law Charitable Trust
Constance Travis Charitable Trust
Truemark Trust
Vardy Foundation
Mary Webb Trust
Whitaker Charitable Trust
Simon Whitbread Charitable Trust
Norman Whiteley Trust
Wilkinson Charitable Foundation
Harold Hyam Wingate Foundation
Woo Charitable Foundation
Woodroffe Benton Foundation
Fred & Della Worms Charitable Trust
Worshipful Company of Chartered Accountants General Charitable Trust
Yapp Charitable Trust
Elizabeth and Prince Zaiger Trust
I A Ziff Charitable Foundation

Environment and animals

Viscount Amory's Charitable Trust
Animal Defence Trust
Ove Arup Foundation
Astor Foundation
Balcombe Charitable Trust
Lord Barnby's Foundation
Benham Charitable Settlement
Blair Foundation
Charlotte Bonham-Carter Charitable Trust
Harry Bottom Charitable Trust
A H & E Boulton Trust
Bromley Trust
Christopher Cadbury Charitable Trust
George W Cadbury Charitable Trust
George Cadbury Trust
Leslie Mary Carter Charitable Trust
Wilfrid & Constance Cave Foundation

Geography and foreign links

History

Ill or disabled people

Manufacturing industry and services

Medicine and health

Yorkshire & General Trust
William Allen Young Charitable Trust
Elizabeth and Prince Zaiger Trust
I A Ziff Charitable Foundation

Medical research

Adint Charitable Trust
Sylvia Aitken Charitable Trust
Astor Foundation
Balcombe Charitable Trust
Misses Barrie Charitable Trust
Benham Charitable Settlement
Birmingham Hospital Saturday Fund
    Medical Charity & Welfare Trust
Burden Trust
Arnold James Burton 1956 Charitable
    Settlement
Children's Research Fund
Colt Foundation
Dinwoodie (1968) Settlement
George Drexler Foundation
Gilbert & Eileen Edgar Foundation
Emmandjay Charitable Trust
Joseph Strong Frazer Trust
Frognal Trust
Gibbins Trust
Sydney & Phyllis Goldberg Memorial
    Charitable Trust
Mike Gooley Trailfinders Charity
Hamamelis Trust
Harbour Charitable Trust
Haymills Charitable Trust
Michael & Morven Heller Charitable
    Foundation
Simon Heller Charitable Settlement
Homelands Charitable Trust
John Jarrold Trust
Kohn Charitable Trust
Heinz & Anna Kroch Foundation
Edgar E Lawley Foundation
London Law Trust
Robert Luff Foundation Ltd
Lyons Charitable Trust
Madeline Mabey Trust
Robert McAlpine Foundation
G M Morrison Charitable Trust
Oakdale Trust
Odin Charitable Trust
Raymond Oppenheimer Foundation
Late Barbara May Paul Charitable
    Trust
Reginald M Phillips Charitable
    Foundation
Cecil Pilkington Charitable Trust
Märit and Hans Rausing Charitable
    Foundation
REMEDI
Muriel Edith Rickman Trust

Teresa Rosenbaum Golden Charitable
    Trust
Rowlands Trust
Peter Samuel Charitable Trust
Simpson Education and Conservation
    Trust
N Smith Charitable Trust
Starfish Trust
Stone Foundation
Charles and Elsie Sykes Trust
Three Oaks Trust
Towry Law Charitable Trust
James Weir Foundation
Wessex Cancer Trust
Felicity Wilde Charitable Trust
Harold Hyam Wingate Foundation
Yamanouchi European Foundation
Yapp Charitable Trust

Older people

Viscount Amory's Charitable Trust
Lord Austin Trust
Benham Charitable Settlement
Miss Jeanne Bisgood's Charitable Trust
Bill Butlin Charity Trust
D W T Cargill Fund
Joseph & Annie Cattle Trust
Charities Fund
Chase Charity
Chownes Foundation
Manny Cussins Foundation
George Drexler Foundation
Dumbreck Charity
Gilbert & Eileen Edgar Foundation
W G Edwards Charitable Foundation
Samuel William Farmer's Trust
Joseph Strong Frazer Trust
Charles S French Charitable Trust
Friarsgate Trust
Frognal Trust
Gibbins Trust
Grocers' Charity
Alfred Haines Charitable Trust
Helen Hamlyn 1989 Foundation
Christina Mary Hendrie Trust for
    Scottish & Canadian Charities
Cuthbert Horn Trust
Hudson Foundation
Miss Agnes H Hunter's Trust
Inman Charity
Inverforth Charitable Trust
J P Jacobs Charitable Trust
Dorothy Jacobs Charity
Edgar E Lawley Foundation
Marsh Christian Trust
Robert McAlpine Foundation
George A Moore Foundation
Morris Charitable Trust

Late Barbara May Paul Charitable
    Trust
Austin & Hope Pilkington Trust
Riverside Charitable Trust Limited
Cecil Rosen Foundation
Rowlands Trust
Bassil Shippam and Alsford Charitable
    Trust
Stanley Foundation Ltd
Towry Law Charitable Trust
Truemark Trust
Van Neste Foundation
Humphrey Whitbread's First
    Charitable Trust
Francis Winham Foundation
Woodroffe Benton Foundation
Matthews Wrightson Charity Trust
Yapp Charitable Trust
Elizabeth and Prince Zaiger Trust
I A Ziff Charitable Foundation

Philosophy

Polden-Puckham Charitable
    Foundation
Cliff Richard Charitable Trust
Sheepdrove Trust
Van Neste Foundation
Whitaker Charitable Trust

Political issues

A B Charitable Trust
Ajahma Charitable Trust
AS Charitable Trust
Richard Attenborough Charitable
    Trust
Miss Jeanne Bisgood's Charitable Trust
Bromley Trust
J A Clark Charitable Trust
Coppings Trust
Dinam Charity
Ireland Fund of Great Britain
J R S S T Charitable Trust
Lawlor Foundation
Leigh Trust
Lyndhurst Settlement
Marr-Munning Trust
Elani Nakou Foundation
Onaway Trust
Paget Charitable Trust
Philanthropic Trust
Polden-Puckham Charitable
    Foundation
Prince of Wales's Charitable
    Foundation
Eleanor Rathbone Charitable Trust
Servite Sisters' Charitable Trust Fund

W F Southall Trust
St James' Trust Settlement
C B & H H Taylor 1984 Trust
Tisbury Telegraph Trust
Tory Family Foundation
Van Neste Foundation
Scurrah Wainwright Charity
Westcroft Trust

Religion general

Chapman Charitable Trust
Duke of Cornwall's Benevolent Fund
Joseph Strong Frazer Trust
Inlight Trust
C L Loyd Charitable Trust
Mutual Trust Group
Gerald Palmer Trust
Austin & Hope Pilkington Trust
Sir James Roll Charitable Trust
Mrs Waterhouse Charitable Trust
Mary Webb Trust

Christianity

Almond Trust
Viscount Amory's Charitable Trust
Andrew Anderson Trust
Archbishop of Canterbury's Charitable Trust
AS Charitable Trust
Ashburnham Thanksgiving Trust
Barnabas Trust
Beacon Trust
Miss Jeanne Bisgood's Charitable Trust
Michael Bishop Foundation
Black Charitable Trusts
A H & E Boulton Trust
P G & N J Boulton Trust
Bowerman Charitable Trust
Bowland Charitable Trust
Britland Charitable Trust
Buckingham Trust
Burden Trust
D W T Cargill Fund
Joseph & Annie Cattle Trust
Childs Charitable Trust
Roger & Sarah Bancroft Clark Charitable Trust
John Coldman Charitable Trust
Mansfield Cooke Trust
Augustine Courtauld Trust
Cross Trust
Daily Prayer Union Charitable Trust Ltd
Dyers' Company Charitable Trust
Euroclydon Trust
Fairway Trust
Farthing Trust

Horace & Marjorie Gale Charitable Trust
Gibbs Charitable Trusts
Golden Charitable Trust
Grace Charitable Trust
Alfred Haines Charitable Trust
Kathleen Hannay Memorial Charity
Harnish Trust
May Hearnshaw's Charity
Hesed Trust
Stuart Hine Trust
Homelands Charitable Trust
Sir Harold Hood's Charitable Trust
Hope Trust
J A R Charitable Trust
H F Johnson Trust
Langdale Trust
Langley Charitable Trust
Lindale Educational Foundation
Maranatha Christian Trust
Marsh Christian Trust
Charlotte Marshall Charitable Trust
Marshall's Charity
Mason Porter Charitable Trust
Millfield Trust
Millhouses Charitable Trust
Minos Trust
Morgan Williams Charitable Trust
Oliver Morland Charitable Trust
Moss Charitable Trust
M N R Charitable Trust
National Catholic Fund
National Committee of The Women's World Day of Prayer for England, Wales, and Northern Ireland
Norwood & Newton Settlement
Ogle Christian Trust
Paget Charitable Trust
Panahpur Charitable Trust
Princess Anne's Charities
Cliff Richard Charitable Trust
River Trust
Saint Sarkis Charity Trust
Salamander Charitable Trust
Seedfield Trust
Bassil Shippam and Alsford Charitable Trust
Shipwrights Charitable Fund
SMB Trust
Albert & Florence Smith Memorial Trust
W F Southall Trust
Janatha Stubbs Foundation
Sylvanus Charitable Trust
C B & H H Taylor 1984 Trust
Thornton Trust
Tisbury Telegraph Trust
Tolkien Trust
Tory Family Foundation
Truemark Trust

Tufton Charitable Trust
Ulting Overseas Trust
Van Neste Foundation
Vardy Foundation
Westcroft Trust
Humphrey Whitbread's First Charitable Trust
Norman Whiteley Trust
Dame Violet Wills Charitable Trust
World in Need
Matthews Wrightson Charity Trust
Yorkshire & General Trust

Judaism

Henry & Grete Abrahams Second Charitable Foundation
Brian & Eric Abrams Charitable Trusts
Acacia Charitable Trust
Achiezer Association Ltd
Adenfirst Ltd
Alliance Family Foundation
Altamont Ltd
Amberstone Trust
ATP Charitable Trust
Bear Mordechai Ltd
Beauland Ltd
Belljoe Tzedoko Ltd
Bertie Black Foundation
Blair Foundation
Neville & Elaine Blond Charitable Trust
Bluston Charitable Settlement
A Bornstein Charitable Settlement
Brushmill Ltd
Arnold James Burton 1956 Charitable Settlement
R M Burton Charitable Trust
Carlee Ltd
Clydpride Ltd
Andrew Cohen Charitable Trust
Vivienne & Samuel Cohen Charitable Trust
Cooper Charitable Trust
Sidney & Elizabeth Corob Charitable Trust
Craps Charitable Trust
Manny Cussins Foundation
Leopold De Rothschild Charitable Trust
Debmar Benevolent Trust
Dellal Foundation
Dent Charitable Trust
Dwek Family Charitable Trust
George Elias Charitable Trust
Ellinson Foundation Ltd
Elman Charitable Trust
Elshore Ltd
Finnart House School Trust
Rose Flatau Charitable Trust
Gerald Fogel Charitable Trust

Fordeve Ltd
Gableholt Limited
Garvan Limited
Gertner Charitable Trust
Golden Charitable Trust
Jack Goldhill Charitable Trust
Grahame Charitable Foundation
Green Foundation
GRP Charitable Trust
Harbour Foundation
Haydan Charitable Trust
Bernhard Heuberger Charitable Trust
Humanitarian Trust
Hurdale Charity Limited
Dorothy Jacobs Charity
Ruth & Lionel Jacobson Trust (Second Fund) No 2
Jewish Child's Day
J E Joseph Charitable Fund
Bernard Kahn Charitable Trust
Stanley Kalms Foundation
Kasner Charitable Trust
Michael & Ilse Katz Foundation
C S Kaufman Charitable Trust
Mendel Kaufman Charitable Trust
Kobler Trust
Kohn Charitable Trust
Neil Kreitman Foundation
Lambert Charitable Trust
Largsmount Ltd
Rachel & Jack Lass Charities Ltd
Lauffer Family Charitable Foundation
Carole & Geoffrey Lawson Foundation
Lawson-Beckman Charitable Trust
Arnold Lee Charitable Trust
Jack Livingstone Charitable Trust
Harry Livingstone Charitable Trust
Localtrent Ltd
Locker Foundation
Loftus Charitable Trust
Luck-Hille Foundation
Sir Jack Lyons Charitable Trust
M & C Trust
 M D & S Charitable Trust
Marbeh Torah Trust
Stella and Alexander Margulies Charitable Trust
Hilda & Samuel Marks Foundation
Erich Markus Charitable Foundation
Melodor Ltd
Melow Charitable Trust
Menuchar Ltd
Laurence Misener Charitable Trust
Victor Mishcon Charitable Trust
Mitchell Charitable Trust
Mole Charitable Trust
Ruth and Conrad Morris Charitable Trust
Morris Family Israel Trust

MYA Charitable Trust
Willie Nagel Charitable Trust
Naggar Charitable Trust
Nemoral Ltd
Newpier Charity Ltd
Chevras Ezras Nitzrochim
Ruth & Michael Phillips Charitable Trust
George & Esme Pollitzer Charitable Settlement
Edith and Ferdinand Porjes Charitable Trust
John Porter Charitable Trust
J E Posnansky Charitable Trust
Premierquote Ltd
Premishlaner Charitable Trust
Mark Radiven Charitable Trust
Joseph & Lena Randall Charitable Trust
Rayne Trust
Rokach Family Charitable Trust
Rowanville Ltd
Michael Sacher Charitable Trust
Ruzin Sadagora Trust
Peter Samuel Charitable Trust
Schapira Charitable Trust
Annie Schiff Charitable Trust
Schmidt-Bodner Charitable Trust
Schreib Trust
Schreiber Charitable Trust
Searchlight Electric Charitable Trust
L H Silver Charitable Trust
Sinclair Charitable Trust
Solev Co Ltd
Solo Charitable Settlement
Songdale Ltd
Spear Charitable Trust
Cyril & Betty Stein Charitable Trust
Sir Sigmund Sternberg Charitable Foundation
Stervon Ltd
Tajtelbaum Charitable Trust
Talteg Ltd
Ten Charitable Trust
Tomchei Torah Charitable Trust
Truedene Co. Ltd
Trumros Limited
Tudor Rose Ltd
Warbeck Fund Ltd
Stella & Ernest Weinstein Charitable Trust
Weinstein Foundation
West London Synagogue Charitable Fund
Williams Family Charitable Trust
Harold Hyam Wingate Foundation
Maurice Wohl Charitable Foundation
Maurice Wohl Charitable Trust
Woodlands Green Ltd
Fred & Della Worms Charitable Trust

Wychdale Ltd
I A Ziff Charitable Foundation

Science

Armourers and Brasiers' Gauntlet Trust
Elmgrant Trust
Michael & Morven Heller Charitable Foundation
Simon Heller Charitable Settlement
Kohn Charitable Trust
Old Possum's Practical Trust
Märit and Hans Rausing Charitable Foundation
Rowlands Trust
Dr Mortimer and Theresa Sackler Foundation
Simpson Education and Conservation Trust
Thompson Family Charitable Trust
Wilkinson Charitable Foundation

Social/moral welfare

1989 Willan Charitable Trust
A B Charitable Trust
Access 4 Trust
Sylvia Adams Charitable Trust
Adint Charitable Trust
Ajahma Charitable Trust
Mrs M H Allen Trust
Andrew Anderson Trust
Armourers and Brasiers' Gauntlet Trust
Arnopa Trust
AS Charitable Trust
Ashworth Charitable Trust
Atlantic Foundation
Lord Austin Trust
Batchworth Trust
Peter Birse Charitable Trust
Miss Jeanne Bisgood's Charitable Trust
Bill Brown's Charitable Settlement
Burden Trust
Arnold James Burton 1956 Charitable Settlement
R M Burton Charitable Trust
George W Cadbury Charitable Trust
George Cadbury Trust
Leslie Mary Carter Charitable Trust
Thomas Sivewright Catto Charitable Settlement
Wilfrid & Constance Cave Foundation
Chapman Charitable Trust
Chase Charity

Coates Charitable Settlement

Vivienne & Samuel Cohen Charitable Trust

Augustine Courtauld Trust

Lord Cozens-Hardy Trust

Dyers' Company Charitable Trust

Edinburgh Trust, No 2 Account

Emerton-Christie Charity

Emmandjay Charitable Trust

Epigoni Trust

Fairway Trust

Fitton Trust

Rose Flatau Charitable Trust

Florence's Charitable Trust

Oliver Ford Charitable Trust

Four Acre Trust

Jill Franklin Trust

Joseph Strong Frazer Trust

Charles S French Charitable Trust

Simon Gibson Charitable Trust

Sydney & Phyllis Goldberg Memorial Charitable Trust

Jack Goldhill Charitable Trust

Green Foundation

Grimmitt Trust

Gunter Charitable Trust

Alfred Haines Charitable Trust

Lennox Hannay Charitable Trust

Kathleen Hannay Memorial Charity

Haramead Trust

Harbour Charitable Trust

R J Harris Charitable Settlement

M A Hawe Settlement

Hawthorne Charitable Trust

Haymills Charitable Trust

Hobson Charity Ltd

J G Hogg Charitable Trust

P H Holt Charitable Trust

Humanitarian Trust

Miss Agnes H Hunter's Trust

Ireland Fund of Great Britain

J A R Charitable Trust

J P Jacobs Charitable Trust

John Jarrold Trust

Jephcott Charitable Trust

Anton Jurgens Charitable Trust

Kleinwort Benson Charitable Trust

Kulika Charitable Trust

David Laing Foundation

Lambert Charitable Trust

Langdale Trust

Mrs F B Laurence 1976 Charitable Settlement

Kathleen Laurence Trust

Lawlor Foundation

Raymond & Blanche Lawson Charitable Trust

Leigh Trust

Lloyd's Charities Trust

Localtrent Ltd

London Law Trust

William & Katherine Longman Trust

C L Loyd Charitable Trust

Lyndhurst Settlement

M & C Trust

Erich Markus Charitable Foundation

Marsh Christian Trust

Leonard Matchan Fund Ltd

Maxwell Family Foundation

Robert McAlpine Foundation

Victor Mishcon Charitable Trust

Mitchell Charitable Trust

D C Moncrieff Charitable Trust

George A Moore Foundation

Morgan Williams Charitable Trust

Morris Charitable Trust

G M Morrison Charitable Trust

Moss Charitable Trust

Noel Buxton Trust

Normanby Charitable Trust

Oakdale Trust

Ofenheim & Cinderford Charitable Trusts

Onaway Trust

Paget Charitable Trust

Philanthropic Trust

Pilkington General Charity Fund

Austin & Hope Pilkington Trust

George & Esme Pollitzer Charitable Settlement

John Porter Charitable Trust

J E Posnansky Charitable Trust

Prince of Wales's Charitable Foundation

Princess Anne's Charities

Priory Foundation

Puebla Charitable Trust

Rainford Trust

Ratcliff Foundation

Eleanor Rathbone Charitable Trust

C A Redfern Charitable Foundation

Cliff Richard Charitable Trust

Riverside Charitable Trust Limited

Sir James Roll Charitable Trust

Cecil Rosen Foundation

Rowlands Trust

Audrey Sacher Charitable Trust

Saint Sarkis Charity Trust

Saints & Sinners Trust

Peter Samuel Charitable Trust

Sandra Charitable Trust

Scouloudi Foundation

Leslie Sell Charitable Trust

Servite Sisters' Charitable Trust Fund

Sheldon Trust

Shipwrights Charitable Fund

Sinclair Charitable Trust

N Smith Charitable Trust

Leslie Smith Foundation

Albert & Florence Smith Memorial Trust

South Square Trust

W F Southall Trust

W W Spooner Charitable Trust

St James' Trust Settlement

Stanley Foundation Ltd

Stone Foundation

Charles and Elsie Sykes Trust

Stella Symons Charitable Trust

Tajtelbaum Charitable Trust

Talteg Ltd

C B & H H Taylor 1984 Trust

Thompson Fund

Thornton Foundation

Three Oaks Trust

Tisbury Telegraph Trust

Tolkien Trust

Constance Travis Charitable Trust

Truemark Trust

Douglas Turner Trust

T.U.U.T. Charitable Trust

F J Wallis Charitable Settlement

Ward Blenkinsop Trust

Mrs Waterhouse Charitable Trust

Weavers' Company Benevolent Fund

Mary Webb Trust

Weinstein Foundation

James Weir Foundation

Whitaker Charitable Trust

Humphrey Whitbread's First Charitable Trust

Simon Whitbread Charitable Trust

Colonel W H Whitbread Charitable Trust

Norman Whiteley Trust

Harold Hyam Wingate Foundation

Maurice Wohl Charitable Foundation

World in Need

Matthews Wrightson Charity Trust

Wyseliot Charitable Trust

Yapp Charitable Trust

Yorkshire & General Trust

William Allen Young Charitable Trust

Sport

Chapman Charitable Trust

Gilbert & Eileen Edgar Foundation

Edinburgh Trust, No 2 Account

Football Association National Sports Centre Trust

Football Association Youth Trust

Joseph Strong Frazer Trust

Charles S French Charitable Trust

Richard Langhorn Trust

Lister Charitable Trust

Saddlers' Company Charitable Fund

Searle Charitable Trust

Geographical index

The following geographical index aims to highlight when a trust gives preference to, or has a special interest in, a particular area: county, region, city, town or London Borough. Please note the following:

1. Before using this index please read the following and the introduction to the subject index on page 289. We must emphasise that this index:

   (a) should not be used as a simple mailing list, and

   (b) is not a substitute for detailed research.

   When you have identified trusts, using this index, please read each entry carefully before making an application. Simply because a trust gives in your geographical area does not mean that it gives to your type of work.

2. Most trusts in this list are not restricted to one area; usually the geographical index indicates that the trust gives some priority for the area(s).

3. Trusts which give throughout England have been excluded, as have those which give throughout the UK, unless they have a particular interest in one or more localities.

   Trusts which give throughout Northern Ireland, Scotland and Wales have been included as they are far fewer in number.

4. Each section is ordered alphabetically according to the name of the trust.

The categories for the overseas and UK indices are as follows:

England

We have divided England into the following six categories:

North East *page 302*
North West *page 302*
Midlands *page 302*
South West *page 303*
South East *page 303*
London *page 304*

The trusts are listed as follows:

(a) Trusts giving throughout a whole region or at least two counties in it (or throughout London).

(b) Trusts giving in a particular county (or a particular borough in London).

(c) Trusts giving to a particular town or city within that county.

Channel Islands *page 304*

Wales *page 304*

The trusts are listed as follows:

(a) Trusts giving throughout the whole of Wales or a substantial part of it.

(b) Trusts giving in a particular region.

Scotland *page 304*

The trusts listed as follows:

(a) Trusts giving throughout the whole of Scotland or a substantial part of it.

(b) Trusts giving in a particular region.

Northern Ireland *page 304*

Overseas categories

Trusts giving overseas are listed in the following order:

Overseas general *page 304*

Trusts which give (a) to at least two continents in the world and (b) do not limit their giving to the third world.

Third world/developing world *page 305*

This includes trusts which support missionary organisations when they are also interested in social and economic development.

Individual continents *page 305*

These are listed in alphabetical order of continent. Trusts giving in that continent are ordered as follows:

(a) Trusts giving throughout the whole continent or a substantial part of it.

(b) Trusts giving in a particular region, the region being more than one country (e.g. East Africa).

(c) Trusts giving to a particular country within that region.

The Middle East has been listed separately. Please note that most of the trusts listed are primarily for the benefit of Jewish people and the advancement of the Jewish religion.

North East

1989 Willan Charitable Trust
Eventhall Family Charitable Trust
Ruth & Lionel Jacobson Trust
Mendel Kaufman Charitable Trust
Normanby Charitable Trust
Vardy Foundation

Yorkshire general

Harry Bottom Charitable Trust
Arnold James Burton Charitable Trust
R M Burton Charitable Trust
Manny Cussins Foundation
Earl Fitzwilliam Charitable Trust
Barry Green Memorial Fund
George A Moore Foundation
W W Spooner Charitable Trust
Charles & Elsie Sykes Trust
Scurrah Wainwright Charity
I A Ziff Charitable Foundation

East Yorkshire

Peter Birse Charitable Trust
Joseph & Annie Cattle Trust

North Yorkshire

Yorkshire & General Trust

Harrogate

Charles & Elsie Sykes Trust

South Yorkshire

Mayfield Valley Arts Trust
Hugh & Ruby Sykes Charitable Trust

West Yorkshire

Emmandjay Charitable Trust
L H Silver Charitable Trust

Leeds

I A Ziff Charitable Foundation

North West

Bowland Charitable Trust
Eventhall Family Charitabel Trust
Penny in the Pound Fund Charitable
  Trust
Pilkington General Charity Fund
John Slater Foundation
United Trusts

Cheshire

Pennycress Trust

Cumbria

Harold & Alice Bridges' Charitable
  Foundation
Sir John Fisher Foundation
Norman Whiteley Trust

Greater Manchester

Stoller Charitable Trust

Manchester

Alliance Family Foundation
Beauland Ltd
Dwek Family Charitable Trust
George Elias Charitable Trust
Jack Livingstone Charitable Trust
Localtrent Ltd
Mole Charitable Trust
Mark Radiven Charitable Trust

Isle of Man

George A Moore Trust

Lancashire

Harold & Alice Bridges' Charitable
  Trust
Florence's Charitable Trust
Barry Green Memorial Fund
M A Hawe Settlement
Riverside Charitable Trust Ltd
John Slater Foundation
Mrs Waterhouse Charitable Trust

Merseyside

Lord Cozens-Hardy Trust
P H Holt Charitable Trust
J P Jacobs Charitable Trust
Mason Porter Charitable Trust
Duncan Norman Trust Fund
Cecil Pilkington Charitable Trust
Pilkington General Charity Fund
Sir Harry Pilkington Trust
Rainford Trust
Eleanor Rathbone Charitable Trust
Ward Blenkinsop Trust

St Helens

Rainford Trust

Midlands

Michael Bishop Foundation
Christopher Cadbury Charitable Trust
Dumbreck Charity
Patrick Charitable Trust
Ratcliffe Foundation
Rowlands Trust
Sheldon Trust
R D Turner Trust

Derbyshire

Harry Bottom Charitable Trust
Hugh & Ruby Sykes Charitable Trust

Herefordshire

Hawthorne Charitable Trust

Leicestershire

Coates Charitable Settlement
Haramead Trust
Florence Turner Trust
Ulverscroft Foundation

Northamptonshire

Benham Charitable Settlement
Francis Coales Charitable Settlement
Earl Fitzwilliam Charitable Trust
Constance Travis Charitable Trust

Nottinghamshire

Charles Littlewood Hill Trust
Lady Hind Trust
Jessie Spencer Trust
Whitaker Charitable Trust
A H & B C Whiteley Charitable Trust

Shropshire

Millichope Foundation
Westcroft Trust

Warwickshire

Janet Nash Charitable Trust
Stella Symons Charitable Trust

West Midlands

Lord Austin Trust
Edward & Dorothy Cadbury Charitable
  Trust
George Cadbury Trust
Alfred Haines Charitable Trust
Lillie C Johnson Charitable Trust
Langley Charitable Trust
Edgar E Lawley Foundation
Millichope Foundation
Janet Nash Charitable Trust
Roughley Charitable Trust
Rowlands Trust
Saintbury Trust
C B & H H Taylor Trust
Douglas Turner Trust

Birmingham

Birmingham Hospital Saturday Fund
  Medical Charity & Welfare Trust
Langdale Trust
W F Southall Trust
Douglas Turner Trust

Worcestershire

Hawthorne Charitable Trust
Saintbury Trust

South West

J A Clark Charitable Trust
Leach Fourteenth Trust
Norman Family Charitable Trust
Tanner Trust

Avon

Higgs Charitable Trust
A M McGreevy No 5 Charitable
   Settlement
Van Neste Foundation

Bath

R J Harris Charitable Settlement

Bristol

Good Neighbours Trust
Mount 'A' & Mount 'B' Charitable
   Trusts

Cornwall

Elmgrant Trust
Devon
Viscount Amory's Charitable Trust
Ashworth Charitable Trust
Elmgrant Trust

Dorset

Mrs Jeanne Bisgood's Charitable Trust
Clover Trust
Alice Ellen Cooper-Dean Charitable
   Trust
Moss Charitable Trust
Wessex Cancer Trust

Gloucestershire

George Cadbury Trust
Good Neighbours Trust
Susanna Peake Charitable Trust
Mrs C S Heber Percy Charitable Trust
Ratcliff Foundation
Rowlands Trust
Saintbury Trust
Colonel W H Whitbread Charitable
   Trust
Dame Violet Wills Charitable Trust

Somerset

Roger & Sarah Bancroft Clark
   Charitable Trust
Good Neighbours Trust
Elizabeth & Prince Zaiger Trust

Wiltshire

Samuel Farmer's Trust
Walter Guinness Charitable Trust
R J Harris Charitable Settlement
Wessex Cancer Trust

South East

Francis Coales Charitable Trust
Hockerill Educational Foundation
Lawlor Foundation
Leach Fourteenth Trust
Sandra Charitable Trust
Tanner Trust
Humprey Whitbread's First Charitable
   Trust
William Allen Young Charitable Trust

Bedfordshire

Horace & Majorie Gale Charitable
   Trust
Simon Whitbread Charitable Trust

Berkshire

Englefield Charitable Trust
C L Loyd Charitable Trust
Gerald Palmer Trust
Peter Samuel Charitable Trust

Buckinghamshire

Bellinger Donnay Trust

Cambridgeshire

Earl Fitzwilliam Charitable Trust
Hudson Foundation

East Anglia

Britten-Pears Foundation
Simon Gibson Charitable Trust
D C Moncrieff Charitable Trust
Late Barbara May Paul Charitable
   Trust

East Sussex

Friarsgate Trust
Raymond & Blanche Lawson
   Charitable Trust

Essex

Augustine Courtauld Trust
Charles S French Charitable Trust
Hockerill Education Foundation
Albert & Florence Smith Memorial
   Trust

Hampshire

Charlotte Bonham-Carter Charitable
   Trust
George Cadbury Trust

John & Freda Coleman Charitable
   Trust
Sir Jeremiah Colman Gift Trust
Walter Guinness Charitable Trust
Moss Charitable Trust
F J Wallis Charitable Settlement

Basingstoke

Sir Jeremiah Colman Gift Trust

Hertfordshire

Hockerill Educational Foundation

Isle of Wight

Wessex Cancer Trust

Kent

John Coldman Charitable Trust
Raymond & Blanche Lawson
   Charitable Trust
Tory Family Foundation

Norfolk

Leslie Mary Carter Charitable Trust
Lord Cozens-Hardy Trust
Charles Littlewood Hill Trust
Lady Hind Trust
John Jarrold Trust
Pennycress Trust

Oxfordshire

Charkes Boot Trust
Sir Felix Brunner's Sons' Charitable
   Trust
Doris Field Charitable Trust
C L Loyd Charitable Trust
Tolkein Trust

Suffolk

Leslie Mary Carter Charitable Trust
Haymills Charitable Trust
William & Ellen Vinten Trust

Surrey

Billmeir Charitable Trust
John & Freda Coleman Charitable
   Trust
Sir Edward Lewis Foundation
F J Wallis Charitable Trust

Godalming

Hamamelis Trust

Sussex

Blatchington Court Trust
Gibbs Charitable Trust
Golden Charitable Trust
Kurt & Olga Koerner Charitable Trust
Moss Charitable Trust
River Trust

West Sussex

Barber Charitable Trust
Bowerman Charitable Trust
Fawcett Charitable Trust
Friarsgate Trust
Bassil Shippam & Alsford Charitable
    Trust
Three Oaks Trust

London

Henry & Grete Abrahams Second
    Charitable Foundation
Armourers and Brasier's Gauntlet
    Trust
Thomas Arno Bequest
Britland Charitable Trust
Cadogan Charity
Sir William Coxen Trust Fund
Timothy Franey Charitable
    Foundation
Charles S French Charitable Trust
Simon Gibson Charitable Trust
Harbour Foundation
Haymills Charitable Trust
Mrs E G Hornby's Charitable
    Settlement
J E Joseph Charitable Fund
Kleinwort Benson Charitable
    Settlement
Lawlor Foundation
Lloyd's Charities Trust
Mitchell Charitable Trust
Mulberry Trust
Chevras Ezras Nitzrochim
St Gabriel's Trust
Salters' Charities
William Allen Young Charitable Trust

Barnet

Sylvia Adams Charitable Trust

City of London

Cooks Charity
Haberdashers' Eleemosynary Charity

Islington

Morris Charitable Trust

Lambeth

Sheepdrove Trust

Merton

Vernon N Ely Charitable Trust

Channel Islands

Mount 'A' & Mount 'B' Charitable
    Trusts
Wessex Cancer Trust

Wales

Laura Ashley Foundation
Atlantic Foundation
Country Landowners Association
    Charitable Trust
Joseph Strong Frazer Trust
Gibbins Trust
Huggard Charitable Trust
Jenour Foundation
Marshall's Charity
Nigel Moores Family Charitable Trust
Oakdale Trust

North Wales

Penny in the Pound Fund Charitable
    Trust
Ratcliffe Foundation

South Wales

Simon Gibson Charitable Trust

Scotland

Sylvia Adams Charitable Trust
Cattanach Charitable Trust
Gordon Farser Charitable Trust
Christina Mary Hendrie Trust for
    Scottish & Canadian Charities
Hope Trust
Miss Agnes H Hunter's Trust
R J Larg Family Charitable Trust
Miller Foundation
Kurt & Olga Koerner Charitable Trust
Penny in the Pund Fund Charitable
    Trust
A M Pilkington's Charitable Trust
Russell Trust
Talteg Ltd
Tay Charitable Trust
James Wier Foundation
Whitaker Charitable Trust

West of Scotland

D W T Cargill Fund

Tayside

R J Larg Family Charitable Trust

Northern Ireland

Lawlor Foundation
Whitaker Charitable Trust
Westcroft Trust

Overseas general

Ajahma Charitable Trust
Almond Trust
Andrew Anderson Trust
Archbishop of Canterbury's Charitable
    Trust
Ashburnham Thanksgiving Trust
Ashworth Charitable Trust
Atlantic Foundation
Richard Attenborough's Charitable
    Trust
Barber Charitable Trust
Barnabas Trust
Batchworth Trust
Beacon Trust
Peter Birse Charitable Trust
Charles Boot Trust
A H & E Boulton Trust
P G & N J Boulton Trust
Britland Charitable Trust
Bromley Trust
Buckingham Trust
Burden Trust
Clara E Burgess Charity
Arnold James Burton 1956 Charitable
    Settlement
Thomas Sivewright Catto Charitable
    Trust
Childs Charitable Trust
Mansfield Cooke Trust
Marjorie Coote Animal Charity Fund
Cotton Trust
Criffel Charitable Trust
Cross Trust
Richard Desmond Charitable Trust
Dinam Charity
Dumbreck Charity
Earth Love Fund
Ebenezer Trust
Ecological Foundation
Edinburgh Trust, No 2 Account
Eighty Eight Charitable Trust
Vernon N Ely Charitable Trust
Euroclydon Trust
Famos Foundation Trust
Farthing Trust
Four Acre Trust

Timothy Franey Charitable
    Foundation
Gertner Charitable Trust
Graff Foundation
Grahame Charitable Foundation
Harnish Trust
Philip Henman Foundation
Hesed Trust
Bernhard Heuberger Charitable Trust
Stuart Hine Charitable Trust
J G Hogg Charitable Trust
Sir Harold Hood's Charitable Trust
Hope Trust
Hurdale Charity Limited
J P Jacobs Charitable Trust
JAR Charitable Trust
Jewish Child's day
H F Johnson Trust
David Laing Foundation
Martin Laing Foundation
Richard Langhorn Trust
Largsmount Ltd
Lauffer Family Charitable foundation
Mrs F B Laurence 1976 Charitable
    Settlement
Leach Fourteenth Trust
Leigh Trust
Lindale Educational Foundation
Loftus Charitable Trust
Lyndhurst Settlement
Sir Jack Lyons Charitable Trust
Maranatha Christian Trust
Michael Marks Charitable Trust
Melow Charitable Trust
Mercury Phoenix Trust
Millfield Trust
Millhouses Charitable Trust
Minos Trust
Morris Charitable Trust
Moss Charitable Trust
Edwina Mountbatten Trust
National Committee of the Women's
    World Day of Prayer
Oakdale Trust
Ogle Christian Trust
Old Braod Street Charity Trust
Onaway Trust
Paget Trust
Panahpur Charitable Trust
Austin & Hope Pilkington Trust
Polden-Puckham Charitable
    Foundation
J E Posnansky Charitable Trust
Puebla Charitable Trust
Eleanor Rathbone Charitable Trust
Marit & Hans Rausing Charitable
    Foundation
Saint Sarkis Charitable Trust
Salamander Charitable Trust

Scouloudi Foundation
Seedfield Trust
SMB Trust
N Smith Charitable Trust
Stanley Smith UK Horticultural Trust
Janatha Stubbs Foundation
Sutasoma Trust
Sylvanus Charitable Trust
Tanner Trust
C B & H H Taylor 1984 Trust
Loke Wan Tho Memorial Foundation
Thornton Trust
Three Oaks Trust
Tisbury Telegraph Trust
Tory Family Foundation
TUUT Charitable Trust
Mary Webb Trust
Norman Whiteley Trust
Whitley Animal Protection Trust
Dame Violet Wills Charitable Trust
Maurice Wohl Charitable Foundation
Maurice Wohl Charitable Trust
World in Need
Matthews Wrightson Charitable Trust
Yamanouchi European Foundation

Third world/ developing world

A B Charitable Trust
Access 4 Trust
Ajahma Charitable Trust
A S Charitable Trust
British Council for Prevention of
    Blindness
Jill Franklin Trust
John Jarrold Trust
Jephcott Charitable Trust
Marr-Munning Trust
Ogle Trust
Paget Charitable Trust
Scouloudi Foundation
Servite Sisters' Charitable Trust Fund
SMB Trust
N Smith Trust
Ulting Overseas Trust
Van Neste Foundation
Westcroft Trust

Africa

Noel Buxton Trust
Philanthropic Trust
Rhodes Trust Public Purposes Fund

East Africa
Kulika Charitable Trust

Tanzania
Miriam K Dean Refugee Trust Fund

South Africa
Scurrah Wainwright Charity
Zimbabwe
Scurrah Wainwright Charity

Americas

Central America
Caribbean
Rhodes Trust Public Purposes Fund

North America
George W Cadbury Charitable Trust
Catholic Charitable Trust
Col-Reno Ltd
Onaway Trust
St James' Trust Settlement
Sylvanus Charitable Trust
Ulverscroft Foundation

South America
Sylvia Adams Charitable Trust
Simpson Education & Conservation
    Trust

Asia

Sylvia Adams Charitable Trust
Philanthropic Trust

Far East
J E Joseph Charitable Fund

India
Miriam K Dean Refugee Trust Fund

Japan
Daiwa Anglo-Japanese Foundation

Australasia

Ulverscroft Foundation

Europe

Catholic Charitable Trust
Fidelity UK Foundation

Elani Nakou Foundation
Sylvanus Trust

Eastern Europe

Servite Sisters' Charitable Trust Fund

Ireland

Ireland Fund of Great Britain
Irish Youth Foundation (UK) Ltd
Lawlor Foundation
Ouseley Trust
C B & H H Taylor Trust

Italy

Mount 'A' & Mount 'B' Charitable
Trusts

Middle East

J E Joseph Charitable Fund

Israel

Brian & Eric Abrams Charitable Trusts
Acacia Charitable Trust
Adenfirst Ltd
ATP Charitable Trust
Bertie Black Foundation
Salo Bordon Charitable Trust
A Bornstein Charitable Settlement
R M Burton Charitable Trust
Vivienne & Samuel Cohen Charitable
Trust
Col-Reno Ltd
Craps Charitable Trust
Dent Charitable Trust
George Elias Charitable Trust

Ellinson Foundation Ltd
Elman Charitable Trust
Elshore Ltd
Finnart House School Trust
Grahame Charitable Foundation
Humanitarian Trust
Jewish Child's Day
Bernard Kahn Charitable Trust
Stanley Kalms Foundation
Kasner Charitable Trust
Neil Kreitmnan Foundation
Lambert Charitable Trust
Lauffer Family Charitable Trust
Locker Foundation
Luck-Hille Foundation
Marbeh Torah Trust
Melodor Ltd
Ruth & Conrad Morris Charitable
Trust
Morris Family Israel Trust
Naggar Charitable Trust
Nemoral Ltd
John Porter Charitable Trust
Premishlaner Charitable Trust
Mark Radiven Charitable Trust
Rowanville Ltd
Michael Sacher Charitable Trust
Ruzin Sadagora Trust
Annie Schiff Charitable Trust
Solo Charitable Settlement
Cyril & Betty Stein Charitable Trust
Sir Sigmund Sternberg Charitable
Foundation
Tajtelbaum Charitable Trust
Weinstein Foundation
Williams Family Charitable Trust
Maurice Wohl Charitable Foundation

Index